THE INFORMATION JUNGLE

A Quasi-Novel Approach
to Managing
Corporate Knowledge

THE INFORMATION JUNGLE

A Quasi-Novel Approach to Managing Corporate Knowledge

Clyde W. Holsapple
Professor of Decision Science and Information Systems
University of Kentucky

Andrew B. Whinston
Professor of Management, Economics, and Computer Science
Purdue University

Illustrations by Jon Kerry

DOW JONES-IRWIN
Homewood, Illinois   60430

This publication is designed to provide accurate and authoritative information in regard to the subject matter covered. It is sold with the understanding that the publisher is not engaged in rendering legal, accounting, or other professional service. If legal advice or other expert assistance is required, the services of a competent professional person should be sought.

From a Declaration of Principles jointly adopted by a Committee of the American Bar Association and a Committee of Publishers.

Project editor: Susan Trentacosti
Production manager: Stephen K. Emry
Jacket design: Reneé Klyczek Nordstrom
Compositor: Arcata Graphics/Kingsport
Typeface: 10/12 Palatino
Printer: The Maple-Vail Manufacturing Group

Library of Congress Cataloging-in-Publication Data

Holsapple, C. W.
   The information jungle: a quasi-novel approach to managing corporate knowledge/Clyde W. Holsapple, Andrew B. Whinston; illustrations by Jon Kerry.
      p.   cm.
   Includes index.
   ISBN 0-87094-977-2: $34.95
   1. Industrial management—Data processing.   2. Industrial management—Decision making.   I. Whinston, Andrew B.   II. Title.
HD30.2.H65   1988
658'.05—dc19   87–36780

Printed in the United States of America

1 2 3 4 5 6 7 8 9 0 MP 5 4 3 2 1 0 9 8

Dedicated with deepest gratitude and greatest affection to our parents

Jeanne and Van
Florence and Ed

Preface

Opportunity and Challenge

Social commentators often remark that we are in the early stages of an information revolution or that computers have ushered in an information age. The quantity and complexity of information existing today dwarfs that of yesterday. This state of affairs presents both an opportunity and a challenge to the modern manager. All else being equal, the more informed a manager is, the greater the likelihood that he or she will make more effective decisions. Also, the manager's efficiency in making those decisions is likely to be greater. Improved decision making is the opportunity, but there is a very big challenge to be met in the course of seizing this opportunity. That challenge is *the information jungle.*

Cognitive psychologists point out that there are definite limits to a normal human being's ability to mentally absorb, retain, and process information. Yet the growth of information is relentless, expanding day after day and year after year. Obviously, all information is not relevant to every manager. In attempting to become and remain well-informed, the manager needs to search out, recognize, capture, and cultivate that which is pertinent to his or her decision activities. In doing so, the manager carves paths through tangles of available information, wades through bogs of irrelevancies, vigilantly avoids lurking pitfalls of inaccuracy and inconsistency, and may even journey to inaccessible places. Because the task of discovering and capturing relevant information may be arduous and costly, it is crucial that information be diligently cultivated once it has been acquired. Otherwise, the captured information becomes just an extension of the greater jungle whence it came. This can happen all too easily as the volume and intricacies of the manager's information increase. Ideally, the manager's own acquired information should be more like a well-tended garden than a jungle.

One way for a manager to avoid the information jungle challenge is to be minimally informed, to ignore large amounts of relevant information because of an inability to carefully tend it. Of course, such a strategy also foregoes the opportunities that accrue from additional relevant information. Another strategy is to find a means for personally coping with large amounts of information. Today's desktop computers can be very helpful in this regard, but they are not the whole answer. Even with a computer and a popular software package such as 1-2-3® from Lotus®, personally coping with large volumes of information can become difficult. In general, only a small portion of the full potential of today's desktop computers has been tapped by those who use them. All too often there are small clearings in a computerized jungle rather than an expansive computerized garden.

A major reason for this is the lack of clear perspective about what it is that is being attempted. To the extent that a manager presides over a computerized jungle or tiny clearing, it is a reflection of a confused or very limited way of thinking. Energy follows thought. When a manager's thinking about the management of knowledge does not flow from a unified view or clear understanding of what is possible, it is no wonder that the resultant activity is arduous, error-prone, or limited in scope. *Knowledge,* not information, is the operative word here. A first step in seeing the big picture is to grasp the fact that what is commonly called information is but one type of knowledge. While it is certainly an important kind of knowledge, information is best understood as being part of a much greater corporate resource.

Knowledge is an essential corporate resource, for it is the lifeblood of decision making. Good decisions depend on the ability to deal effectively with knowledge of many kinds. Thus a manager's value to an organization is very much influenced by his or her knowledge management skills. Yet, how many managers have had formal training in the subject of knowledge management? How many can distinguish between information and other important kinds of knowledge? Does the typical manager appreciate why such distinctions are significant? Does he or she understand what computerized techniques are most appropriate for managing each type of knowledge? How can multiple types of knowledge be most effectively wielded in the course of a decision process? Experience is of course invaluable, but where can today's manager turn to intentionally acquire an understanding of this important subject?

Coverage

There are many books and business school courses that formally teach the concepts, principles, and techniques of managing human, financial, and material resources. But there are all too few that adequately cover the management of an organization's vital knowledge resource. This book breaks new ground by aiming to help fill the gap. It does so in several ways. A *unified framework* is presented for understanding the various types of knowledge. Numerous *real-life examples* demonstrate that solving a decision problem often involves the coordinated use of several types of knowledge. We provide a *highly practical coverage of the major computer-based techniques that managers can personally use* to represent and process the various types of knowledge. Special attention is given to the *integrated use of these techniques in managerial problem solving*.

The book is written for managers who are interested in enhancing their own knowledge management skills and those of their subordinates. It is for people who prefer to know the joy of managing knowledge rather than the drudgery of toil in an information jungle. It presents both traditional and novel concepts in an integrated environment for desktop computing. No prior exposure to computers is assumed. Nevertheless, the book also can substantially broaden the horizons of even the most veteran computer users. We believe all readers, from the novice to the experienced, can benefit by way of fresh insights, coherent perspectives, and a practical appreciation of the fundamentals of modern computer-based knowledge management techniques.

This is not a book about mainframe computers, information systems, data processing departments, how to become a computer professional, or how to use this or that software package. It is a book about *how to become a more productive and effective manager* by seeing the big picture of what knowledge management is all about and by personally exploiting multiple computer-based knowledge management techniques in an integrated fashion. The coverage of do-it-yourself computing is far-reaching: from simple calculations and text management to techniques of programming and artificial intelligence. Though the coverage is broad, it is by no means superficial. It provides a solid foundation for further learning and for readily becoming acclimated to an entire host of popular software packages.

Our coverage of knowledge management is organized into six major parts:

    I.   Knowledge and Computers

   II.   Getting Acquainted with Software

  III.   Managing Descriptive Knowledge

  IV.   Managing Presentation Knowledge

V.   Managing Procedural Knowledge

VI. Beyond the Limits

Part I examines the significance and nature of knowledge. It also covers the essentials of machines (i.e., computer hardware and its software) that can help manage knowledge. Part II introduces the four basic approaches for issuing requests to a software package and gives examples of some simple kinds of requests. Part III concentrates on problems involving the management of descriptive knowledge. Text management, data base management, and ad hoc inquiry techniques are introduced for representing and processing descriptive knowledge. Part IV is concerned with the management of presentation knowledge. Pertinent techniques of forms management, customized report generation, and graphics are applied. The management of procedural knowledge is dealt with in Part V, which shows that spreadsheet analysis and programming are two particularly valuable techniques for handling procedural knowledge. Part VI tells how to go beyond the limits of ordinary knowledge management software. It introduces rule management as an emerging technique for managing reasoning knowledge. It also explores the traits of an open architecture (including remote communications) and approaches for integrating multiple knowledge management techniques into a single architecture.

Orientation

Stylistically, we have taken a *novel* approach to presenting the subject matter. The story deals with the life and loves of Jack Vander, a regional sales manager in a book publishing company.[1] As the book unfolds, you will become increasingly acquainted with the activities of Jack and other managers in the company, particularly as they relate to knowledge management. Their interactions convey a vivid, concrete, realistic appreciation of the kinds of knowledge management problems that managers face in modern organizations.

As each problem is introduced, computer-based techniques that can be used to solve the problem are introduced. That is, we have adopted a *problem-solving orientation*. Techniques for managing knowledge are the means to the ends. They are not ends, in and of themselves. Unnecessary abstractions and technicalities are avoided in the discussions of these techniques. Instead, the *themes of analysis, design, and*

---

[1] The company and its employees are hypothetical. While its operations and needs are both typical and realistic, it is unrelated to any actual company.

implementation are interwoven throughout the book's fabric. Analysis is concerned with clearly understanding the nature of a problem. Design is concerned with formulating a plan for using one or more of the knowledge management techniques. Implementation is concerned with actually following a knowledge management plan to solve the identified problem.

As each technique is introduced in the context of solving problems, it is illustrated with the actual commands the managers use when interacting with real computer software. Results produced by the software are displayed in numerous figures and color screens, making it easy to follow the flow of processing. This illustration is crucial for conveying a practical understanding of computer-based knowledge management.

In considering what software to adopt for illustrative purposes, we used several criteria. First, it should provide an English-like command language for making knowledge management requests. It should also provide menu-guided and natural language approaches to making requests. Second, it should be a *single* piece of software capable of supporting all the major knowledge management techniques relevant to do-it-yourself computing. Each technique should be supported in depth, rather than superficially. Third, it should be possible to use multiple techniques in an integrated manner when working on a decision problem. Fourth, the software should be available on standard desktop computers, allowing readers to follow the examples on a hands-on basis if desired. Fifth, the software should have a proven track record of use in many organizations.

In light of these criteria, we have opted for a software package called KnowledgeMan® as the *instructional vehicle.*[2] This software is available for IBM® XT™ and AT™ (and compatible) microcomputers as well as VAX™ minicomputers. It supports the following knowledge management techniques in a highly integrated fashion: calculator, text management, data base management (both relational and postrelational), ad hoc inquiry, forms management, report generation, business graphics, spreadsheet analysis, programming, and remote communications. All computer screen photos and printouts appearing in this book were generated by version 2.01 of KnowledgeMan running on IBM XT or AT computers under the PC-DOS™ operating system.

We must emphasize that this is not a book about life as a sales manager, about using the KnowledgeMan software, about IBM microcomputers, or about the PC-DOS operating system. These four elements are woven into the story to make the central topic of knowledge management as clear and

---

[2] KnowledgeMan is a registered trademark of MDBS, Inc.

interesting as possible. Readers should have no difficulty in applying what is learned here to other managerial settings, to other computers, or to other software. Specific computers and software tools come and go in the marketplace. They tend to change over time. Nevertheless, the major knowledge management ideas conveyed in this book are lasting. The important computer-based techniques for managing knowledge are here to stay. The principle of synergistic knowledge integration, which we emphasize and illustrate in many ways, will have an increasingly significant impact on the shape of tomorrow's software tools. The book's central concept of a *knowledge management environment* in which managers can analyze, design, and implement solutions to their own knowledge-handling problems will continue to grow in importance.

We believe the book provides a solid platform for exploring other software implementations of the major knowledge management techniques and for readily mastering new software that will inevitably appear. Indeed, this book's state of the art treatment of the important topic of *knowledge management integration* should help stimulate the creation of new software tools that are even more powerful and more accessible than what is available today.

The Information Jungle also provides an excellent platform for venturing into more advanced knowledge management issues. For instance, this book has a sequel entitled *Manager's Guide to Expert Systems Using Guru*, published by Dow Jones-Irwin.[3] In the sequel, Jack delves into the detailed issues of developing and using business expert systems. It turns out that every technique presented in *The Information Jungle* can also be employed inside of modern business expert systems. The sequel uses an artificial intelligence environment named Guru® for illustrative purposes.[4] Because the Guru software is behaviorally a superset of KnowledgeMan, practically every example appearing in *The Information Jungle* could be carried out in an identical way with the Guru software package. Thus, *The Information Jungle* furnishes a valuable starting point for beginning to appreciate the emerging technology of business expert systems.

Acknowledgments

In closing, we express our thanks to the many practicing managers and management school students whose participation in our course-

---

[3] Clyde W. Holsapple and Andrew B. Whinston, *Manager's Guide to Expert Systems Using Guru* (Homewood, Ill.: Dow Jones-Irwin, 1986).

[4] Guru is a registered trademark of MDBS, Inc.

work and seminars has played an important role in the evolution of this book. The knowledge management problems are based, in part, on the very useful suggestions offered by Kristina Ferguson. The book's content has also benefited from comments of those who reviewed the manuscript, including Raymond Ballard, Ai-Mei Chang, and Kim Holsapple. We are highly appreciative of the tireless efforts of Kathey Freeman in typing the manuscript and taking the photos. In addition, Kathy O'Neal was instrumental in cheerfully helping us coordinate the entire production process.

The general atmosphere of our Management Information Research Center (MIRC) in Purdue University's Krannert Graduate School of Management was conducive to development of insights and perspectives presented in this book. MIRC has received generous corporate support from IBM, General Electric, Air Products, NEC Corporation, and others. Mr. Francis G. (Buck) Rodgers, Vice President of Marketing (now retired), and Mr. Charles Bowen, Director of Plans and Program Administration, both at IBM, have supported our MIRC program in many ways, and we wish to thank them.

Clyde W. Holsapple
Andrew B. Whinston

Contents

Function Keys. Control Switches: *Decimal Digit Switch. Printer Switches. Presentation Switches.* Environment Sensors. Context: *Saving and Loading. Selective Saving and Loading. Releasing.* Basic Ideas.

Setup. Line Access. Local Area Networks. Integrated Architectures: *Nested Integration. Confederation of Software Tools. Synergistic Integration.* Basic Ideas.

Part I

KNOWLEDGE AND COMPUTERS

Maybe the knowledge we need is out there . . . . somewhere.
I just hope I can find it in time.

Chapter One

The Significance of Knowledge

A sense of anticipation filled the banquet room as H. J. Rickert approached the podium. In his mid-fifties, Mr. Rickert had a distinguished look befitting the president of a large corporation. He was about to announce who had been selected as the company's outstanding regional sales manager. This annual award involves much more than an engraved plaque and a handshake. It means a hefty five-figure check.

Mr. Rickert's company, KC, Incorporated, is a book publisher headquartered in the midwest. KC has a national sales staff that covers 12 geographic regions. For each region there is a sales manager who is responsible for the sales representatives working within that region. Each rep services a prescribed territory within the region. This service includes visiting each retail book outlet in the territory on a regular basis to promote existing books, introduce new books, take orders, and inquire about bookstore needs that KC may be able to fulfill. A sales rep is also able to solicit and take book orders via the telephone.

Through the reps working in a region, each sales manager strives to provide the best possible service to customers. Over the years, Mr. Rickert has maintained the keynote of "delivering value" at the center of corporate consciousness [27]. This theme permeates all areas of KC's management, from the procurement of manuscripts, to the production of books, to the support of retail book outlets. Even so, Mr. Rickert never missed an opportunity to reinforce his view and the award ceremony was no exception.

"Our success as a company depends on the successes of our customers, the nation's retail book outlets. It never hurts to remember that our primary goal is to make them successful on a continuing basis. Our sales are a measure of the extent to which we succeed in meeting this goal. This year's record sales should be gratifying to us all." Rickert paused and surveyed the sales managers with a smile.

"Delivering value to our customers is the touchstone of all our efforts. It is the reason KC exists. This begins with our acquisition group, which procures titles that fill customer needs. It is made manifest through our production department, which creates quality products that can be supplied at attractive prices. You, as members of our sales group, are on the front lines of delivering value, making customers aware of what we can do for them and then seeing that it gets done.

"As you know, there is a cost for delivering value. Thus the sales you generate are not the only factor used in determining who will be named sales manager of the year. All else being equal it is better to achieve a certain sales level with low rather than high expenditures. Our continued existence and ongoing improvements depend on profitability. So the amount that your region contributes to corporate profit is the basis for this award.

"In comparing your respective contributions, we have taken regional differences into account. The winner is the sales manager whose region's contribution most exceeds the contribution we expected for that region." With special emphasis, he continued, "Tonight we are recognizing the one who has most effectively and efficiently managed available resources in the interest of delivering value to our customers—with the result of delivering value to our shareholders."

THE FOUR RESOURCES

Before continuing with the award ceremony, it is worthwhile to ponder the meaning and underlying implications of Mr. Rickert's last statement. Management is the art and science of using available resources to achieve some objective [23]. There are four basic kinds of resources available to each manager as he or she works to maximize a region's contribution to KC's profits: people, money, material, and knowledge. Each day, a manager controls and coordinates the use of these essential resources (see Figure 1–1). A manager's skill and productivity in dealing with the resources is directly reflected in the region's performance.

Human

On the human resource front, each manager works with from 7 to 12 sales reps, depending on the geographic peculiarities of the region. Aside from hiring and firing decisions, the manager is responsible for seeing that each rep is adequately trained. A rep needs to be well versed in both sales techniques and the company's 14 product lines. Keeping

FIGURE 1–1   Four resources to be managed when meeting an objective

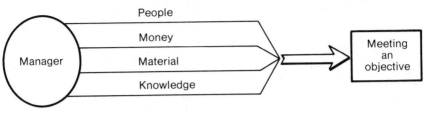

the reps up-to-date and fresh in both areas can be a time-consuming endeavor. It often involves considerable one-on-one contact aimed at strengthening individual weaknesses. Furthermore, this training is an ongoing process due to continuing changes in KC's product lines and their positioning relative to competitor's products.

Beyond the training aspect, managing human resources involves both motivation and evaluation [3]. There are, of course, numerous techniques for motivating sales representatives. Some of them may work well for one rep, but may be ineffective for others. One technique applied to all KC reps is commission-oriented compensation. In addition to a base salary, each rep receives a commission based on actual sales. Commission rates vary from one product line to another. For instance, photography books presently have a commission rate of .020 (a $2 commission on every $100 sold) while science fiction books have a .028 rate (a $2.80 commission for every $100 worth of science fiction books sold). The relative incentives for different product lines are determined by KC's corporate management and are uniform across all sales regions.

Another technique, used for both motivation and evaluation, involves quarterly quotas. At the beginning of a year, a regional manager assigns a sales quota for each product line to each rep. Unlike commission rates, a rep's quota levels are determined by his or her regional manager. A rep's quota for a product line normally varies from one quarter to the next. One rep's quotas for a particular product line typically differ from another rep's quotas for the same product line.

Setting quotas is a delicate matter. On the one hand, they should be sufficiently challenging to appeal to the sales rep's sense of achievement. On the other hand, they must be sufficiently realistic to avoid the discouragement that accompanies seemingly impossible goals. Furthermore, a quota must be perceived by both the manager and sales rep as being a fair basis for assessing the rep's performance (see Figure 1–2).

FIGURE 1–2   Comparison of a sales rep's actual sales versus quotas for selected product lines

	Quarter 1		Quarter 2	
Product line	Sales	Quota	Sales	Quota
Reference	7,024	6,040	4,005	3,997
Sports	6,240	5,400	6,903	8,488
Psychology	3,296	3,290	4,321	3,214
Science fiction	8,824	10,813	5,944	9,328
Romance	10,050	9,003	13,121	12,090

Not only is quota setting a delicate task, it is a complicated one as well. Each quota could possibly be influenced by a wide variety of factors including product line characteristics, seasonal trends, territory demographics, past performance of the salesperson, sales training programs, the expected number of new titles in a product line, advertising expenditures, general economic conditions in the territory, and much more. Overall, the quotas a manager sets within a region should be consistent with the region's sales targets for each product line. These product line sales targets for a given region are provided to the regional manager by KC's national sales manager.

Interestingly, the regional sales managers are human resources available to the national sales manager who, in turn, is a human resource managed by KC's vice president of marketing. At the ultimate level of management, this vice president is one of the human resources that H. J. Rickert himself deals with to achieve the organization's objective of delivering value to both customers and shareholders.

Financial

Each year, KC allocates a certain amount of money to each region for discretionary use. The regional manager has control over how a region's allocation will be employed to cover direct expenses incurred by both the manager and the sales reps. This includes expenses for transporation (e.g., maintenance and operation of KC company autos), hotels, meals, entertainment, telephone, postage, and local advertising. To manage available financial resources, a manager makes use of budgeting techniques [18].

As illustrated in Figure 1–3, a budget is constructed showing the month-by-month breakdown of proposed expenditures within the re-

FIGURE 1–3 Example of a regional expense budget

1986 Budget of Direct Selling Expenses for Region 7

	Jan.	Feb.	Mar.	Apr.	. . .	Total
Transportation						
Mileage	5,600	5,200	7,000	6,800	. . .	73,800
Maintenance	2,000	1,600	1,800	1,400	. . .	20,400
Hotel	1,500	1,300	1,900	1,800	. . .	19,500
Meals	2,800	2,500	3,020	2,820	. . .	33,420
Entertainment	680	640	750	700	. . .	8,310
Telephone	2,400	2,020	1,850	1,800	. . .	24,210
Postage	1,400	1,300	1,100	1,100	. . .	14,700
Miscellaneous	750	700	750	2,820	. . .	15,060
Total	17,130	15,260	18,170	19,240	. . .	209,400

gion. The total of all proposed expenditures appearing in the region's budget cannot exceed the annual level of financial resources given to that region. A regional manager uses this budget as a basis for preparing individual expense budgets for each person working within the region. As illustrated in Figure 1–4, an individual expense budget shows the amounts that a person (the manager or a sales rep) can spend for each type of expense in each of the months. A manager must construct individual expense budgets such that they are collectively consistent with the region's budget. For instance, the total of January telephone expenses across all individual budgets cannot reasonably exceed the January telephone expense shown in the region's budget.

FIGURE 1–4 Example of an individual expense budget

Budget of Direct Selling Expenses   Territory: 8
                                                      Sales Rep: Jackie

	Jan.	Feb.	Mar.	Apr.	. . .	Total
Transportation						
Mileage	661	640	693	687	. . .	8,043
Maintenance	100	80	90	70	. . .	1,020
Hotel	219	210	271	265	. . .	2,895
Meals	232	215	308	290	. . .	3,135
Entertainment	65	60	77	75	. . .	831
Telephone	240	210	155	155	. . .	2,280
Postage	125	105	113	113	. . .	1,368
Miscellaneous	76	76	76	76	. . .	912
Total	1,718	1,596	1,783	1,731	. . .	20,484

Budgeting is a technique for managing the region's financial re-sources. The manager plans how those resources are to be apportioned among different types of expenses and among different reps in various time periods. Once the plans are made, they guide the use of funds, give a basis for controlling expenditures, and furnish an additional way of assessing rep performance.

The individual budget furnished to a rep serves as a guideline for that rep's expenditures. At the end of each month, a sales rep submits an expense report to the manager for approval and reimbursement. The manager watches for any large variances between budgeted and actual expenses. If such variances are detected, they indicate that the use of available financial resources may be getting out of control. Monitor-ing expenditures in this way alerts the manager to situations where corrective actions may need to be taken to keep expenditures under control. It also gives a way of tracking rep performance. All else being equal, a rep who consistently comes in with underbudget expenditures is performing more effectively than one who does not. A rep's sales-to-expenditure ratio is also of interest for assessing performance.

Just as it may be advantageous for a sales rep to keep expenses beneath budgeted levels, it may also be worthwhile for the region as a whole to hold its discretionary spending below the amount allocated by KC. It is important for a manager to use the financial resources as efficiently as possible. The lower the level of expenditure needed to achieve a given sales level, the greater the region's contribution to corpo-rate profit. Each additional dollar spent in direct selling expenses should be compensated by sufficient additional sales to more than offset not only that dollar, but also the cost of the additional goods sold plus indirect selling and administrative costs attributed to those goods.

Material

KC, Incorporated possesses many physical, tangible assets ranging from its office buildings and factories to its printing and binding machinery, to raw materials such as paper and ink. These are KC's material resources. As with people and money, it is important to manage such resources in an efficient, effective manner [21]. The regional sales managers are less preoccupied with managing material resources than are managers in charge of book production, shipping, or building maintenance.

Some of the material resources available to a regional sales manager are furnished by KC. These include sample books, brochures, promo-tional posters, some office furniture, and company automobiles. An automobile is provided for the manager and for each sales rep. It is up to the manager to deploy these resources as desired. In addition,

FIGURE 1–5   **Typical microcomputer hardware configuration**

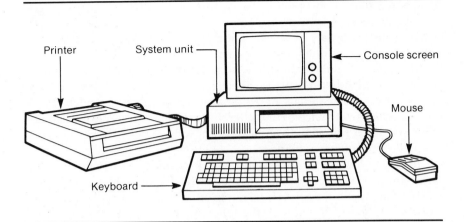

there are material resources acquired with the region's discretionary funds. These include such mundane objects as office supplies and equipment (e.g., a typewriter). A few regional managers have recently purchased desktop microcomputers for use in their home offices. One manager, Jack Vander, has actually been using a microcomputer for more than two years.

Sometimes called a "personal" computer, a microcomputer is a piece of hardware offering raw computing power comparable to what could be provided only by a large computer a few years ago [9], [11], [28]. This power is offered at only a small fraction of the cost of the larger machines and in only a small fraction of the space. Some of these micros do not even require a desktop, but weigh less than a dozen pounds and can rest comfortably in a person's lap.

A typical desktop microcomputer and its peripheral equipment are shown in Figure 1–5. The microcomputer's circuitry for processing instructions, along with its memory for storing knowledge, resides in the system unit. The keyboard and the mouse are devices that allow a computer's user to initiate some desired computer processing, respond to requests made by the computer, or transfer knowledge (from the user's mind) into the computer's memory. They are input devices. The console screen and the printer are devices that allow a computer to present the results of its processing to the user. The console screen is also the place where the computer can display requests, requiring a user response before processing continues. Machines such as this have the potential to be extremely valuable material resources to all of KC's regional sales managers.

Knowledge

A resource that is absolutely essential to any manager is knowledge. A manager may have enormous human, financial, and material resources at his or her disposal. However, without adequate knowledge the full potential of these other resources will not be exploited. Conversely, the manager with substantial knowledge can do a great deal with modest amounts of the other resources. Effective, efficient management of people, money, and materials depends very much on the availability of knowledge. As with each of the other three resources, simple availability of knowledge is not enough. Available knowledge needs to be managed in an efficient, effective manner.

It is worthwhile to understand that knowledge is not monolithic. There are distinct types of knowledge, each of which plays a particular role in a manager's activities [16], [17]. In effect, a manager is a knowledge worker who is concerned with the following basic types of knowledge:

- Descriptive knowledge.
- Presentation knowledge.
- Linguistic knowledge.
- Assimilative knowledge.
- Procedural knowledge.
- Reasoning knowledge.

As Figure 1–6 suggests, each action taken by a manager is based on the use of one or more of these types of knowledge.

In the case of a regional manager, there is knowledge about each sales rep, each product line, the sales performance for each product in each territory, the expenses incurred in each territory, the economic and market conditions within the region, and so forth. All of this is *descriptive* knowledge about the manager's current working environment. It characterizes the current state of the world in which the manager exists. This is the type of knowledge that is often simply referred to as "data" or "information."

Regional sales managers often need to make presentations to sales reps and to superiors. A manager therefore has knowledge about making presentations via forms, reports, graphs, and so on. He or she may want to generate a formal report of year-to-date sales rep performance broken down by product line. Or perhaps the manager wants to present a bar graph contrasting product sales and quotas to a particular rep. *Presentation* knowledge allows the desired appearance to be produced and is therefore quite different in purpose than descriptive knowledge, which allows the current state of affairs to be known. Appearances do make a difference when it comes to facilitating an understanding of

FIGURE 1–6   Managerial actions based on multiple types of knowledge

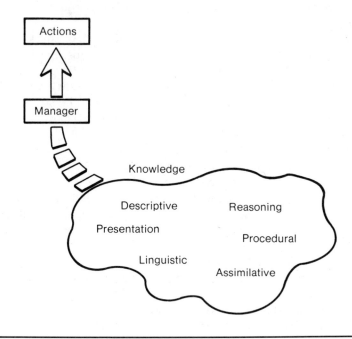

what is presented. A disorganized, incomplete presentation obscures, whereas a thorough, well-organized presentation enlightens. Presentation knowledge avoids the former and supports the latter.

Each regional manager also has knowledge about accepting the presentations of others. This involves *linguistic* knowledge that allows a manager to correctly interpret what is presented and *assimilative* knowledge that enables him or her to effectively filter what he or she sees and hears, separating the reasonable from the unreasonable. Linguistically, a manager knows what the term *gross margin rate* means. The manager also knows that a one-night hotel expense of $1,000 is unreasonable and should be rejected or questioned. Clearly, these two types of knowledge are fundamentally different from descriptive and presentation knowledge. Linguistic knowledge allows the presentations of others to be understood, while assimilative knowledge determines whether an incoming presentation will be accepted as a valid new piece of knowledge.

Another kind of knowledge is *procedural* in nature. This is simply knowledge about the sequence of steps (i.e., the procedure) needed to accomplish some task. It might involve the procedure used to hire a new sales rep, the series of steps a manager carries out to arrive at an economic forecast for a particular territory, or a sequence of calculations involved in deriving a budget.

Sales managers also work with *reasoning* knowledge. This knowledge consists of rules about what to do in certain situations. For instance, if a manager encounters a situation where the outlook for growth is high and unemployment is low, then his or her reasoning knowledge indicates that the territory's economy should be considered to be strong. Unlike procedural knowledge, which is concerned with *how to* do something, reasoning knowledge is concerned with *what to* do (e.g., what conclusions to draw if a specific situation exists).

A manager can acquire knowledge in a variety of ways. Course work in business schools imparts a great deal of knowledge. In particular, it tends to concentrate on the procedural and reasoning knowledge concerned with techniques for managing materials (e.g., inventory control, plant and facilities management, purchasing), people (e.g., organizational behavior, human resources administration, interpersonal communications), and money (e.g., finance, economics, accounting). In addition to formal training, knowledge of various types is also acquired by experience, observation, and outright purchase.

A major challenge facing KC's regional sales managers, and all modern knowledge workers for that matter, is the sheer magnitude of knowledge that can be acquired. The collective body of human knowledge is not only enormous, but continues to expand at an accelerating rate. The amount of knowledge a manager needs to acquire and use to achieve even a satisfactory level of performance is formidable. By further increasing the available knowledge resources, a manager will be able to raise the level of performance, provided the added knowledge is relevant. However, there is a danger lurking here: knowledge overload.

Like anyone else, a regional sales manager has cognitive limits for the amount of knowledge that can be absorbed and used in a given time period. Being overloaded with knowledge can be almost as counterproductive as having too little knowledge. Overload occurs when the volume of knowledge reaches a point where it either exceeds the knowledge worker's capacity to grasp and retain it or begins to detract from the effective use of individual pieces of knowledge.

Just as there are techniques for managing human, financial, and material resources, so too are there techniques for managing knowledge. A particular technique may be useful for handling several different types of knowledge. Conversely, several techniques might be usefully employed for a particular type of knowledge. Skillful knowledge management can help raise the threshold at which an overload begins to occur.

Even when there is no overload, skilled and clever use of *knowledge management techniques* results in much greater productivity. More can be accomplished more effectively, with less effort, in a shorter time.

Knowledge management skills can significantly enhance a manager's ability to get the most out of the other three kinds of resources. This is because the ability to work with knowledge underlies a manager's ability to work with people, money, and materials. It is also due to the fact that efficient management of knowledge leaves the manager with more time than he or she would otherwise have. This additional time lets the manager accomplish things that would otherwise remain undone; for example, giving greater attention to individual training needs of the reps or acquiring greater knowledge. The ultimate effect of improved knowledge management is improved performance by the manager, by the manager's region, and by the company as a whole.

A SECRET ALLIANCE

Back at the banquet room, H. J. Rickert was ready to announce the top-performing sales manager over the past year. As the preceding discussion indicates, a regional sales manager's job is not at all trivial. Furthermore, successful fulfillment of this job is important to the company's success. So when Rickert says he is recognizing the sales manager who best managed available resources, it is not an idle compliment. And it is backed up not only by a substantial monetary award, but by an increased potential for promotion due to the award's high visibility.

Rickert was aware of a sense of tension, as if everyone had inhaled deeply. Pausing, he looked slowly around at the regional managers. "I'm pleased to announce that the sales manager of the year is . . . Jack Vander."

Near the front of the room a man rose to the polite applause. He had an unassuming manner and appeared to be in his late 30s or early 40s. His measured, deliberate movements as he approached the podium suggested a person who was not inclined to do things by halves. The applause subsided as Jack stepped to the podium . . . just as he had done the prior year. But Mr. Rickert was not quite ready to relinquish the microphone.

With a firm handshake he said, "Congratulations, Jack, and here is your check." Turning to the audience, he continued, "As many of you know, Jack has been with us for more than a dozen years now and has always put in a solid performance. But last year was the first time he had won this award, and now he has turned in an even more impressive performance."

Looking to Jack, he said, "Perhaps you can let us in on the secret of your success. Over the years, the company has furnished all regional managers with comparable support, and yet you are suddenly able to excel. Have you found some secret ally?"

This made Jack smile. In soft-spoken tones that concealed his excitement, he replied, "My region's performance wouldn't have been possible without the creators of our outstanding product lines, coupled with my talented, hardworking sales representatives. But you are right. A bit more than two years ago, I did discover what has turned out to be a 'secret ally' for me. As our relationship has grown, this ally's value to me has steadily increased, to the point of being indispensable."

Jack was amused by the puzzled looks his remarks evoked. "The ally is a desktop computer. Its principal value is that it permits me to accomplish more in a shorter period of time. I find that it is a good means for more effective, productive record-keeping. It's extremely useful in helping me spot trends, recognize problem areas, carry out calculations, and analyze alternatives in a fast, accurate way. All of this is a tremendous aid in supporting my day-to-day decision-making activities. It even helps with routine clerical tasks such as preparing memos, letters, reports, and mailings.

"By helping me be more productive in managing the many kinds of knowledge that we all work with, the computer gives me more time to work with my sales reps. By giving them more help, their performance has increased dramatically over the past two years and this is reflected in the region's bottom line.

"Now you may well be wondering how I, someone without any formal computer training, could on my own master this technology. Well, I've not fully mastered it. But I do know enough about it to realize that there's plenty left to learn. I started out by using it for simple tasks and, mastering these, progressed to more ambitious uses. I must admit that having overcome my original apprehensions, I've often found the journey along this growth path to be downright entertaining and enjoyable. Bit by bit," Jack concluded with a wink, "I'm continuing to learn, and expect that this will result in further improvements in my region's performance for the upcoming year."

Jack's disclosures gave H. J. Rickert the seed of an idea. Why not begin to bring the other regional managers up to Jack's level of computer literacy? If all regions' performances could progress in the same way as Jack's, the impact for KC would be very positive indeed. He was aware that a couple of other regional managers had acquired microcomputers during the last year. However, their regions did not show the dramatic gains that Jack had achieved. As far as Mr. Rickert knew, the other regional sales managers had little, if any, direct exposure to computer usage.

Rickert rightly reasoned that if his idea was to work out successfully, he could not merely give each manager a desktop computer and a wish of good luck. He did not want to wait two years in hopes that the other managers could perhaps approximate Jack's present computer proficiency. He wanted quick, certain results. In chatting with Jack after the ceremony, Rickert was encouraged by Jack's assertion that an initial week's worth of intensive training would have saved him a great deal of learning time and would have allowed the computer to be immediately useful. It was clear that some practical initial training would be essential to ensure that everyone got off on the right track.

In subsequent discussions with the national sales manager and vice president of marketing, it was decided to put Mr. Rickert's idea into action. A one-week training session for all regional managers would take place at the company's main office in Kansas City, with shorter semiannual follow-up sessions. These sessions would introduce managers to practical computer-based techniques for managing knowledge. They agreed that Jack would be the ideal trainer for the initial session. Not only did he have an intimate understanding of the diverse knowledge management tasks facing regional managers, Jack knew how to accomplish these tasks with a computer. Being one of their own, he would have an immediate rapport with the regional managers and be able to appreciate their attitudes toward computer usage. Jack could speak with the authoritative voice of experience.

Securing Jack's cooperation in this project was the marketing vice president's responsibility. This involved enticing him with a sufficiently attractive package of incentives. In addition to Jack, a person from KC's corporate *information center* would attend to assist in the instruction. Like many companies, KC's main office has an information center composed of people who support the use of computers at that site. When someone untrained in computer science issues wants to make use of computers, the information center can provide advisory, guidance, educational, and consulting services to the potential user. Jack's assistant would be able to offer additional observations on what Jack presented and field any questions that Jack might be unable to answer.

COMPUTER–BASED KNOWLEDGE MANAGEMENT

Knowledge management is something that is done by nearly all workers in modern organizations [16]. Obviously much of the work done with knowledge is mental in nature. Typical knowledge management activities consist of:

Collecting	Creating
Storing	Deriving
Organizing	Presenting
Maintaining	Distributing
Recalling	Evaluating
Analyzing	Applying

the various pieces of knowledge. Over the centuries many devices have been invented to supplement the mind's capacity and ability to carry out these knowledge management activities. These range from such ancient aids as paper and the abacus to the printing press milestone [8]. More recent inventions include the familiar filing cabinets, Rolodex files, typewriters, visual and audio recording devices, tabulators, and hand-held calculators.

In the 1950s computers began to appear in business organizations as knowledge management aids. Since that time they have revolutionized the nature of organizations and management, affecting all types of business—manufacturing, agriculture, commerce, banking, construction, services, government, and so on. The degree of their impact has been comparable to that of the printing press in its era. As computers have continued to become simultaneously more powerful, smaller, and less expensive over the last 30 years, their impact has become ever more pervasive [7], [25].

What KC is planning for its regional managers would not have been possible in the 1950s, 1960s, or even the 1970s. But with the advent of powerful yet inexpensive desktop microcomputers in the 1980s, KC's plans are symptomatic of a trend in many businesses: making computers an integral part of knowledge management activities for all workers in the organization. Today's microcomputers can be instrumental in eliminating the tedious, cumbersome, and time-consuming aspects of knowledge management. They can therefore produce significant increases in knowledge worker productivity.

In the chapters that follow we shall see how each regional manager can increase his or her productivity with the aid of a microcomputer. But first, it is worthwhile to understand some of the major developments that have shaped the business-computing field over the past 30 years. These include the automation of record-keeping, the rise of decision support systems, the trend toward do-it-yourself computing, the appearance of environments for knowledge management, and the business use of artificial intelligence.

Record-Keeping

The importance of keeping accurate, up-to-date records is obvious. A business cannot survive for long without keeping adequate records about its customers, employees, sales, expenses, inventories, activities, and so forth. Before the computer era, record-keeping was primarily a manual endeavor. By automating the task of record-keeping, computers have had a significant impact on organizations and society. They have fostered new ways of operating companies, encouraged the birth and dramatic growth of certain industries, and affected the ways in which organizations interact with each other [7], [20], [25].

The tremendous growth in airline passenger travel, the multitude of banking services, the explosion in financial market trading volumes, and so forth would have been impossible without automated record-keeping. Computerized record-keeping has enabled an organization to store, maintain, and retrieve *masses* of descriptive knowledge about itself and its environment, as a basis for ongoing operations. This approach to record-keeping is generally faster, less costly, less error-prone, and able to handle larger volumes than earlier manual methods.

A computer-based system for record-keeping is commonly called a *management information system* (MIS) [20], [22], [29]. If used exclusively for accounting, an MIS might be called an accounting information system. If used only for marketing, an MIS might be called a marketing information system, and so forth. It provides information (i.e., descriptive knowledge) that management uses in controlling the operations of an organization. MIS departments that build and administer management information systems are pervasive throughout medium and large organizations. MIS departments are sometimes called data processing (DP) departments. Twenty years ago automated record-keeping was viewed as a breakthrough in organizational productivity. Today it is taken for granted as an absolute essential.

For instance, KC has an MIS department at its headquarters. Staffed by computer science professionals, this department creates management information systems that operate in the company's large ("mainframe") and medium-sized ("mini") computers. Such systems are designed so they can be used by persons who are not computer scientists. One of these is an order entry system that clerks use to record the orders that are placed for books. This system automatically checks customer records for credit worthiness, generates shipping lists for the shipping department, updates inventory records appropriately, and so on. The national sales manager also uses this system to track order levels for various product lines.

Even the smallest of organizations are now automating their record-keeping with inexpensive microcomputers. Lacking their own internal data processing staffs, they frequently use either generic or custom-built management information systems purchased from external sources. A generic MIS is one built to handle an ordinary set of record-keeping tasks such as those typically involved in handling employee payroll. Many companies are able to use this same generic "off-the-shelf" MIS because they all have the same record-keeping needs with respect to payroll. In contrast, an MIS may be custom-built to handle records in a specialized way, suited only to the needs of a particular company. In the former case, the company must conform to the generic MIS's record-keeping abilities. In the latter case, a custom-built MIS is tailored to conform to certain specialized record-keeping needs of the company.

Advances in record-keeping abilities have resulted from the evolution of tools for building management information systems, as well as the relentless onslaught of increasingly powerful computer hardware. The earliest record-keeping tools made use of *file management* techniques. File management techniques are still used today, especially in record-keeping applications where only a few types of records exist. By the mid-1960s, various inadequacies of file management had become widely recognized. In response to these shortcomings a new kind of record-keeping tool appeared, involving *data base management* techniques. These techniques continued to evolve through the 1970s and are widely used by MIS departments to develop large-scale management information systems [6].

By automating record-keeping activities for large volumes of descriptive knowledge, management information systems play an important role in modern organizations. However, beyond supplying management with timely standardized reports describing an organization and its environment, these systems make little direct contribution to actual decision-making activities. To increase the value of computers to management, a new kind of computer system began to emerge in the 1970s: decision support systems.

Decision Support

The essence of management is decision making for the purpose of determining what course of action will be taken. Up-to-date knowledge describing the environment in which a decision will be made is a necessary ingredient for good decision making. In addition, when a manager works at making a decision, he or she must be able to analyze and reason with this descriptive knowledge in appropriate ways. Whereas an MIS is a system for reporting, a *decision support system* (DSS) is a system for analyzing [4], [5], [19], [30]. A DSS allows a computer to support managers' decision processes through automated analysis.

Researchers in the various disciplines of management (e.g., operations research, finance, applied economics, etc.) have devised quantitative techniques and algorithms to assist decision makers. These techniques and algorithms are commonly referred to as models. They can be used to analyze knowledge about the environment. This analysis generates new facts, expectations, or beliefs as a basis for decision making. A *model* is procedural knowledge—a sequence of one or more steps that specify how to generate new knowledge from existing knowledge about the environment. Examples of common models include linear regression, optimization algorithms, inventory control procedures, rate of return computations, and so forth.

Like a management information system, a decision support system (DSS) has record-keeping capabilities. Though these capabilities are often more modest than those of an MIS, there is no reason why they must be so. Beyond record-keeping, a DSS has the following traits:

- It can carry out analyses by fitting descriptive knowledge with procedural knowledge to arrive at some expectations or beliefs.
- It furnishes users with powerful, convenient languages for making problem-solving requests.
- It can be used to support comparatively unstructured decision activities.

In a decision support system, models take the form of programs or functions that can be executed by the DSS. This execution occurs in response to a user's request. The language for stating the request should not require computer expertise on the part of a user. For instance, it may have an Englishlike appearance. It should support requests for ad hoc retrieval, as well as ad hoc "what if" analysis.

An *ad hoc request* is one that is made on the spur of the moment. It is often aimed at satisfying nonroutine, nonstandard, once in a lifetime needs. A computer's ability to handle ad hoc requests is important for supporting unstructured decision-making processes. Requests for *"what if" analysis* also provide important support for unstructured decision processes. These allow the manager to carry out analyses on descriptive knowledge that is hypothetical, anticipated, or proposed (rather than actual). A series of "what if" analyses can help a manager explore the effects of alternative decision options.

The classic structure of a decision support system [5] is shown in Figure 1–7. Notice that a DSS has three major parts or subsystems: a language system, a knowledge system, and a problem-processing sys-

FIGURE 1–7   **Generic structure of a DSS**

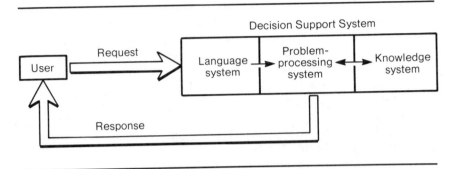

tem. A *language system* is the collection of all linguistic facilities provided by a DSS. These facilities allow a decision maker to issue requests to the DSS and to reply to any requests the DSS may make of the decision maker. The *knowledge system* of a DSS consists of descriptive knowledge about the decision maker's environment, perhaps some procedural knowledge, and some knowledge derived from analyzing the environment via models. The *problem-processing system* lies at the core of a DSS. It is able to understand a user's request as stated with the language system and process the knowledge system contents in order to satisfy a user's request for reports or analysis.

Within the DSS framework, file or data base management techniques can be used to handle descriptive knowledge. High-level query techniques are also valuable for ad hoc explorations of a data base of descriptive knowledge, allowing a manager to get at any piece of knowledge by means of a single Englishlike query. A decision support system's procedural knowledge can be handled by *programming* techniques. When a DSS is built, computer professionals in the MIS department devise programs that embody analytical models. Programs for standard kinds of analysis may already be available for immediate incorporation into the DSS. A more recent technique for handling procedural knowledge is the *spreadsheet* and it, too, may be used in a DSS.

By automating both record-keeping and analytical activities, decision support systems play an important role in modern organizations [1]. Because of their value and success, the demand for both decision support and management information systems has grown rapidly in many companies. By the end of the 1970s, this demand for both more and more extensive computer-based systems greatly exceeded the capacity of many companies' MIS departments to produce them. When such a situation occurred it was known as an "application backlog." Managers' requests for the MIS department to apply computer technology in the creation of systems for record-keeping and decision support accumulated into long waiting lines. There were lengthy delays before a requested application system came into existence. Some applications, which were potentially worthwhile in their own right, were rejected because they were not deemed to be as important as other record-keeping or decision support applications. A notable factor in helping to meet the demand for computer-based assistance has been the trend toward do-it-yourself business computing.

Do-It-Yourself Computing

A manager desiring an MIS or DSS has three basic alternatives. One is to have the computer professionals in the company's MIS department develop the desired system. This is subject to possible application backlogs and higher priorities being given to other MIS or DSS applications. Second, the manager might purchase the desired system from an external source. It may be off-the-shelf, or custom-built if there are no off-the-shelf systems that fit the manager's needs. Third, there is the do-it-yourself option in which the manager's own department directly handles its own computerized record-keeping and decision support needs.

Just 10 years ago, the third alternative would have been unthinkable for most managers. Neither the managers themselves nor the people who worked for them had the computer expertise or time necessary to personally develop management information or decision support systems. They did not have, nor could they be expected to have, skills comparable to those of the MIS department's computer professionals. They were the *end users* of record-keeping and decision support systems built by computer professionals, not the developers of those systems.

Although computer literacy among managers and graduates of business schools has increased noticeably over the past decade, these employees still do not have the skills of computer professionals [11]. They are still the users of systems built by the pros. Many of the tools developers use require skill levels that most managers have neither the time nor inclination to cultivate. But some of the computing techniques that these tools support have become increasingly accessible to persons who are not computer professionals, to the traditional end users of computers. The net effect is that end users can now directly satisfy many of their own record-keeping and decision support needs [24]. They are no longer constrained to simply using the MISs and DSSs that have been built for them.

How have computing techniques of the pros been made accessible to end users? Basically, by simplification. A wave of end-user tools for business computing has arisen. An end-user tool supports some useful subset of a technique that is more fully supported by the computer professional's tool. It is more accessible to the end user because it does not do as much. It therefore takes much less effort to learn and use. While an end-user tool does not allow a manager to replicate all of what can be achieved with a professional's tool, it does allow those who are not computer professionals to accomplish a great deal for themselves.

For example, data base management is a valuable technique for dealing with descriptive knowledge. Since the late 1960s computer professionals have made use of this technique (in its many variations) with tools called *data base management systems*. More recently, data base management tools designed especially for end users have appeared on the scene. These tools are generally less powerful, less versatile, and less flexible than their professional counterparts. They are also much less expensive and take much less time to master. With such a tool, a person does not need to be trained in the principles of MIS development and advanced data base management in order to use a computer to accomplish many small-scale and useful record-keeping tasks.

Today, there are many gradations of tools for data base management (and for other business-computing techniques), from those suitable only for computer novices to those suitable only for computer professionals. Between the two extremes are tools that can be appropriate for both seasoned end users and for the pros. A common attitude of novice end users is to choose a tool that is just good enough for present perceived needs. It is almost inevitable that an end user's needs will grow as experience and confidence in computer usage is gained. Thus, what was once just good enough can rapidly become a dead end, forcing the end user to begin again with a more capable tool. To avoid this, it is best to choose a tool that has a built-in growth path. It allows the computer novice to start out simply, to be productive quickly without having to master all aspects of the tool. It also allows the end user to incrementally progress to more advanced capabilities as the need arises.

Many companies have information centers that can help in choosing appropriate tools. A center is a sign of the commitment to encourage do-it-yourself end-user computing, helping to free the MIS department to concentrate on developing the more challenging, large-scale computer systems for end users [10], [24], [26]. Frequently affiliated with the MIS department, an information center promotes do-it-yourself business computing, educates end users about what is possible and how to achieve it, and provides ongoing assistance to end users. The information center is well versed in all the basic business-computing techniques, from data base management to spreadsheet analysis to graphics generation. For each of these techniques, it should be familiar with the many tools available for end users.

The trend toward do-it-yourself computing is well established in many organizations. At KC, for instance, the information center has been assisting end users in the home office for several years now. Jack's mission is to further this trend for the geographically scattered regional sales managers. However, his approach will be different than that taken in many organizations. He will not be discussing separate tools for each of the various business-computing techniques. Instead, Jack will be taking advantage of a comparatively recent development in the computer field: an integrated *knowledge management environment*.

A Knowledge Management Environment

A knowledge management environment (KME) is a single tool that supports a multitude of computer-based techniques for managing knowledge. Rather than a collection of tools, each devoted to a particular technique, a knowledge management environment integrates all techniques into one tool. Instead of one tool for doing data base management, another for programming procedural models, another for spreadsheet analysis, another for graphics generation, and so forth, all of these capabilities are available in a unified environment. Interestingly, a KME can be used for both record-keeping and decision support purposes without the necessity of formally developing a DSS or MIS.

The basic concept underlying this kind of tool is that it should allow a computer to serve as an environment for enhancing a human being's innate knowledge management capabilities. Regardless of whether a person is a novice end user, a computer professional, or somewhere in between, that person is a knowledge worker. He or she works with many kinds of knowledge in many ways in the course of carrying out daily activities. A bit of introspection makes it clear that the human mind has multiple kinds of knowledge management abilities that can be exercised independently or together. For instance, in arriving at a decision without computer support, the knowledge worker might access descriptive knowledge from memory or from a co-worker, analyze it with various mental models, sketch out graphs of the results, reanalyze the situation with altered assumptions, and write a report that presents a decision. The knowledge worker has a *mental* knowledge management tool that can be applied to diverse problems and whose integral capabilities can work separately or together. Similarly, a KME is a *computer-based* knowledge management tool that can be applied to diverse problems and whose integral capabilities can work separately or together [13].

With a KME, a knowledge worker's mental environment for managing knowledge is extended with a computer-based environment for managing knowledge. As Figure 1–8 suggests, a knowledge worker's mental capabilities can at any time make use of one or more of the KME's computer-based capabilities for knowledge management. A KME can be regarded as a world of *hyperknowledge*, supplementing and complementing a person's innate mental capabilities. The knowledge worker is poised at the center of the KME and can use any of its capabilities

FIGURE 1–8 Supplementing mental knowledge management capabilities with computer-based capabilities

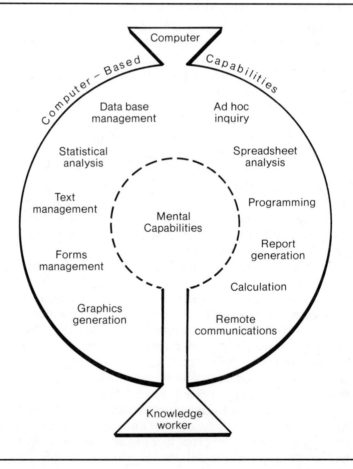

at any time to supplement his or her own mental capabilities in the course of dealing with a problem. From this center, the knowledge worker directs the computer's actions via one or more user interface mechanisms (denoted by the dashed line in Figure 1–8). In Chapter 2, several interface mechanisms are presented and the subsequent chapters show how the computer-based capabilities cited in Figure 1–8 can be employed by regional sales managers to increase their productivity.

In understanding the concept of a knowledge management environment, it is useful to recall the six types of knowledge identified earlier in this chapter. Each of these kinds of knowledge can be managed with a KME tool. There are two fundamental aspects to this computer-based knowledge management: representation and processing. Before a fragment of knowledge can be processed, it must be represented in some way. The way in which it is represented determines how it can be processed. For instance, how would Jack represent the knowledge that Kevin is a sales rep who works in territory number 2, was hired on September 30, 1981, and has a base salary of $2,500? As a sentence in a piece of text, as a record in a data base, as part of a spreadsheet, in a program's variables, or in some other manner? The choice depends largely on how Jack wants to process the knowledge.

Just as there are many possibilities for representing a piece of descriptive knowledge, so too may there be various ways for representing other types of knowledge. Each of the computer-based capabilities shown in Figure 1–8 involves a particular approach to *representing* knowledge and a particular technique for *processing* that knowledge. Each capability may be applicable to managing several kinds of knowledge, just as a given type of knowledge is susceptible to being handled by a mixture of one or more KME capabilities.

In the case of KC, each regional sales manager is a knowledge worker. Each will be learning how to operate within a knowledge management environment. The more that a manager is able to exploit a computer by means of the KME, the more productive he or she can be and the more valuable to KC. There are certain fundamental knowledge management skills that any manager should possess to be considered well rounded and competitive with other managers. For each type of knowledge it is important to understand the representation and processing techniques that are available. In the chapters that follow, you will see how KC's regional sales managers quickly acquire the basic skills for applying computer-based knowledge management techniques to their everyday activities. These fundamentals provide a solid foundation for continuing growth in the mastery of today's and tomorrow's computer power.

Artificial Intelligence

Although *artificial intelligence* (AI) has scarcely touched today's managers, it will begin to have dramatic and widespread impacts on their activities over the next few years. Looking further out, to the end of the century, practical fruits from the past 30 years of AI research will be commonplace. The application of artificial intelligence techniques will play a major role in reshaping traditional notions of what organizations are, of how they are managed, and of how decisions are made. All of this presents a major challenge and an important opportunity to today's managers and organizations. Though the transition will not be without growing pains, it will lead to tremendous increases in the productivity of managers and organizations. Those organizations in the forefront of applying AI methods to aid in management will have distinct competitive advantages over those that lag [15].

Artificial intelligence endeavors to make computers capable of displaying intelligent behavior [2]. This means behavior that would reasonably be regarded as intelligent if it were observed in humans. Two cornerstones of intelligence are the ability to understand natural language and the ability to reason. These in turn represent two principal areas of research in the AI field. This research has led to the discovery of practical methods for allowing computers to understand natural language and to solve problems by reasoning. The first involves a computerization of linguistic knowledge and the latter involves computer-based management of reasoning knowledge. It is important to understand that these methods do not pretend to employ the same internal mechanisms as a human in carrying out such activities. However, they do produce results that are more or less comparable to what would be expected of a human.

Perhaps the largest AI payoff will come in the realm of *expert systems* [14]. These are systems that employ AI reasoning techniques in order to offer expert advice about problems posed by their users. An expert system makes use of expertise that has been gathered from a human expert about how to solve a specific type of problem or class of related problems. The potential benefits of such systems range from the distribution and omnipresence of expertise to the formalization and preservation of an organization's reasoning knowledge. The commonly cited obstacles of long development times, high development costs, difficult development tools, and isolation from the mainstream of data processing are vanishing because of a new kind of tool for expert system development [12].

The impact of artificial intelligence has just begun to make itself felt in KC. In 1986 the MIS department formed a group to understand the technology of expert systems and begin developing small expert systems on an experimental basis. The group is especially interested in somehow integrating this technology into the business-computing mainstream. As Jack and the other regional managers will discover near the end of their conclave, expert system construction and consultation capabilities can be readily exercised along with the other knowledge management capabilities available in a KME. Jack has already become acquainted with *natural language* as one of the user interface mechanisms in a KME and will give the regional managers a taste of this AI fruit as the training session begins.

BASIC IDEAS

Knowledge is an essential resource. Without it, a company could not operate. But *knowledge in and of itself is insufficient. What good is knowledge without a mind trained to manage it?* It has significance only insofar as it can be used to meet objectives such as KC's goal of delivering value to customers. All else being equal, an organization will be more successful if it does a good job of knowledge management. This includes the management of all types of knowledge: descriptive (i.e., data, information), presentation, procedural, linguistic, assimilative, and reasoning knowledge. All too often, knowledge management skills are taken for granted rather than being actively and explicitly cultivated.

Managers and other knowledge workers are today faced with mountains and jungles of knowledge. There appear to be practical limits on the amount and variety of knowledge a mind can effectively deal with in a given period of time. However, computers can be a tremendous aid in pushing back such limits. Much of the knowledge management work that is or has been done mentally or mechanically can now be accomplished electronically. Automated record-keeping and decision support have been central advances in this direction. The continuing trend toward do-it-yourself computing means that managers and other end users can increasingly handle many of their own knowledge management needs without the intervention of computer professionals. This makes both the end users and computer professionals more productive at their respective jobs, and goes a long way toward unleashing the full potential of computers.

Historically, several distinct techniques have evolved for using computers, including data base management, programming, spreadsheet analysis, graphics generation, and text management. For each technique, many tools have been devised to allow that technique to be used on a computer. An alternative approach for delivering multiple techniques to a knowledge worker is a knowledge management environment. In a KME, each computer-based technique is viewed as a knowledge management capability and all of these capabilities are integrated into a single tool. Rather than a "tool box" equipped with separate tools, the computer becomes an environment where any or all knowledge management capabilities can be used individually or in tandem. The capabilities of traditionally separate tools are blended into a single "world" in which the knowledge worker lives and moves and has his or her being.

Along with KC's regional sales managers, you are about to explore this computer-based world of knowledge management, becoming acquainted with many useful approaches to representing and processing knowledge. All of today's major business-computing capabilities are examined in a unified KME. In addition, a flavor of some emerging AI capabilities is provided. It turns out that Jack's "secret" alliance is not as mysterious as it may appear at first glance. Do-it-yourself computing in a knowledge management environment is well within the reach of KC's regional sales managers. Because of the productivity gains that can result, it might well be regarded as a vital strategic alliance.

Using computers to manage knowledge in a more efficient, effective manner is strategically very significant for both the individual and the organization. For an organization, it presents the opportunity of gaining an edge over competitors or at least keeping pace with competitors. For an individual, it can mean much the same. All else being equal, an individual with good knowledge management skills is much more valuable to an organization than one with more limited skills. In the corporate world, H. J. Rickert is by no means alone in recognizing the significance of knowledge and its management.

References

1. Alter, S. *Decision Support Systems: Current Practice and Continuing Challenges.* Reading, Mass.: Addison-Wesley Publishing, 1980.

2. Barr, A., and E. A. Feigenbaum, eds. *The Handbook of Artificial Intelligence,* vols. 1–3. Los Altos, Calif.: William Kaufmann, 1982.

3. Beer, M. *Human Resource Management: A General Manager's Perspective.* New York: Free Press, 1985.

4. Bonczek, R. H.; C. W. Holsapple; and A. B. Whinston. "Developments in Decision Support Systems." In *Advances in Computers,* ed. M. Yovits. New York: Academic Press, 1984.

5. ———. *Foundations of Decision Support Systems.* New York: Academic Press, 1981.

6. ———. *Micro Database Management—Practical Techniques for Application Development.* New York: Academic Press, 1984.

7. Burke, J. *Connections.* Boston: Little, Brown, 1978.

8. ————. *The Day the Universe Changed.* Boston: Little, Brown, 1985.

9. DeVoney, C., and R. Summe. *IBM's Personal Computer.* Indianapolis: Que, 1982.

10. Head, R. V. "Information Resource Center: A New Force in End-User Computing." *Journal of Systems Management,* February 1985.

11. Hirsh, R. E. *Computer Literacy for Middle Management.* Englewood Cliffs, N.J.: Prentice-Hall, 1984.

12. Holsapple, C. W., and M. D. Gagle. "Expert System Development Tools." *Hardcopy* 7, no. 2 (1987).

13. Holsapple, C. W., and A. B. Whinston. "Aspects of Integrated Software." *Proceedings of the National Computer Conference,* Las Vegas, July 1984.

14. ————. *Business Expert Systems.* Homewood, Ill.: Richard D. Irwin, 1987.

15. ————. "Business Expert Systems—Gaining a Competitive Edge." Working paper, Krannert Graduate School of Management, Purdue University, West Lafayette, Indiana, 1986.

16. ————. "Knowledge-Based Organizations." *Information Society* 5, no. 2 (1987).

17. ————. "Software Tools for Knowledge Fusion." *Computerworld* 17, no. 15 (1983).

18. Johnson, R. W. *Financial Management.* Boston: Allyn & Bacon, 1971.

19. Keen, P. G. W., and M. S. Scott Morton. *Decision Support Systems: An Organizational Perspective.* Reading, Mass.: Addison-Wesley Publishing, 1978.

20. Lucas, H. C., Jr. *Introduction to Computers and Information Systems.* New York: Macmillan, 1986.

21. Marshall, P. W.; W. J. Abernathy; J. G. Miller; R. P. Olsen; R. S. Rosenbloom; and D. D. Wycoff. *Operations Management.* Homewood, Ill.: Richard D. Irwin, 1975.

22. McLeod R., Jr., *Management Information Systems.* Chicago: SRA, 1986.

23. Miner, J. B. *The Management Process.* New York: Macmillan, 1978.

24. Morse, J., and L. Chait. "In Info Centers, the User Always Comes First." *Data Management,* February 1984.

25. Naisbitt, J. *Megatrends.* New York: Warner Books, 1982.

26. Oglesby, J. N. "Seven Steps to a Successful Info Center." *Datamation* 33, no. 5 (1987).

27. Peters, T. J., and R. H. Waterman, Jr. *In Search of Excellence.* New York: Harper & Row, 1982.

28. Sanders, D. *Computers Today.* New York: McGraw-Hill, 1983.

29. Senn, J. A. *Information Systems in Management.* Belmont, Calif.: Wadsworth Publishing, 1987.

30. Sprague, R. H., Jr., and E. D. Carlson. *Building Effective Decision Support Systems.* Englewood Cliffs, N.J.: Prentice-Hall, 1982.

Aha, there it is!
Right, with plenty of time and effort to spare.

Chapter Two

The Environment

The sound of engines faded as Jack moved through the tunnel. His well-traveled briefcase held an assortment of notes, overhead transparencies, and computer diskettes. With these he felt prepared to share his computer experiences and insights with the other regional managers. As he ambled up a mild incline, Jack wondered idly what expectations they had going into tomorrow's opening session. He had previously met all of the regional managers, but was fairly well acquainted with only a couple of them. The next eight days were destined to open up new vistas for all concerned, even those who had already begun to dabble with computers on their own.

Emerging into the airport proper, Jack was greeted by Kansas City's autumn sunlight and a Monday afternoon drone of voices. He paused in momentary disorientation, typical of entering an unfamiliar environment for the first time. Quickly regaining his bearings, he scanned the crowd. His steel-blue eyes were drawn almost immediately to a young woman seated across the main hallway from where he stood. She appeared to be in her late 20s or early 30s and her attire was the epitomy of good taste. The black skirt and jacket were matched by a sea of small polka dots sprinkled generously on a red blouse. This combination was crowned with honey-blonde hair that flowed in a carefree fashion, almost reaching her shoulders.

Jack looked away. She couldn't be the one he was looking for . . . or could she? His gaze magnetically returned to her as if that were where his attention belonged. She was now looking at him while simultaneously rising. As Jack approached he was struck by her limpid blue eyes that conveyed an obvious intelligence, both perceptive and creative. An antique necklace of large gold beads hugged her neck and clinging to her ears were matching textured gold discs.

"You are Joy Toomey?" he asked hesitantly . . . and hopefully.

"That's right, and you must be Jack," she replied with a smile. Jack immediately recognized the same dulcet voice he had heard several times over the telephone. As they shook hands, he noticed an unusual bangle bracelet encircling her wrist. It was an even golder gold than the necklace and had a unique twisted braid design.

The information center had selected Joy to assist Jack during the training session. They had called each other during the preceding month to discuss the kinds of audiovisual equipment and computers that they should use during the session. Joy was selected because of her intimate familiarity with the knowledge management environment Jack had been using. A fairly large number of microcomputers at the home office were equipped with this KME and the MIS department used it to develop decision support systems on the company's VAX minicomputers.

On their stroll to the parking lot, Joy confirmed that the room reserved for training was ready to go. It was outfitted with five desktop computers, all of which had licensed copies of the KME. She explained that only one of the computers was the same make and model as Jack's own IBM XT machine. The others were compatible: two IBM Personal Computer AT computers and microcomputers manufactured by Compaq Computer Corporation and Digital Equipment Corporation. In a pinch, she could also borrow a Data General "laptop" computer that is compatible with the IBM XT computer, but much smaller in size. That machine also had a licensed copy of the KME.

Jack planned to use one of the desktop computers during his presentations. Joy had arranged to have a large screen television connected to this computer in such a way that the contents of the computer's console screen would simultaneously appear on the large TV screen. This would allow all the managers to easily follow Jack's examples, without trying to crowd around the computer's screen. During breaks and in the evenings the regional managers would be able to use the other computers for practice, gaining hands-on experience to reinforce what they were learning from Jack.

GETTING ACQUAINTED

Before long they reached her car. It was blue and European. As she drove to the hotel, Joy relayed the results of a preliminary survey she had taken. She had conducted the survey to get a feel for the kind of prior computer exposure the incoming managers had had. Of the two managers who had desktop computers, both had acquired their machines in the past 12 months. One, Stan Slaughter, was using a tool called

1–2–3 on his computer [4]. The other, Tracey McIntyre, had outfitted her computer with a text management tool.

"I've heard of 1–2–3. Isn't that a spreadsheet tool?" Jack asked.

"Right," nodded Joy. "It's the most widely used spreadsheet tool in the business world. It also has some graphing capabilities, though they're quite modest compared to what you're used to. Lotus, the company that produces 1–2–3, has been immensely successful and has contributed greatly to the popularity of do-it-yourself computing. Here at KC headquarters we have quite a few 1–2–3 users. Stan says that he's been using it to help make out expense budgets for his sales reps. But he's thinking about also trying to use it to keep performance records for his reps." She paused to see how Jack would react to Stan's plan.

"That strikes me as strange," Jack murmured. "I use data base management to keep track of performance records. Spreadsheets seem good for budgeting applications, but wouldn't they be pretty inconvenient for tracking performance data? It seems that he'd be going to a lot of unnecessary effort."

She was impressed by Jack's response. "That's for sure. But it's something we, in the information center, encounter over and over again: someone using the wrong tool for a job. Well, maybe the choice isn't exactly 'wrong,' but it's certainly not the most productive. I think the reason that people try to use a tool for tasks that could be much more easily accomplished in other ways is simply a lack of awareness. They learn how to use one tool, which supports a particular knowledge management technique such as spreadsheet analysis. They then make the, perhaps unconscious, mistake of trying to represent and process all pieces of knowledge of all types with that single technique. Even if they realize that there may be a better way, there may not be the time or inclination to learn (and then remember) how to use new tools that provide the additional techniques. When they recognize a new knowledge processing need and they know one technique, that's what they try to use regardless of whether it's appropriate or not."

"In a sense," mused Jack, "they become the slaves of a knowledge management technique instead of being the masters of it. I think I've pretty much avoided that predicament."

Realizing that she could not have said it better herself, Joy beamed with a Texas-sized smile. "The knowledge management environment you use is quite helpful in that regard. Whenever you encounter a new problem, you can choose the most appropriate technique or techniques for handling it. Because they're all available in a single tool, you don't have to learn and remember the peculiarities of separate tools. Nor do you have to switch back and forth among various tools when you want to use multiple knowledge management techniques for dealing with a single problem. I think the whole idea of using the right techniques for a given task is an important one to convey to the regional managers."

Jack nodded. "After I check in, I'd like to go over my notes with you. I've prepared them to guide the training sessions more or less along the same lines as my experiences. As regional managers, we all face the same diverse kinds of knowledge-handling problems. I plan to show how the computer can be effectively used in dealing with these problems. In my own experience, the problem has always preceded the technique. For a given problem, I've always looked for and learned about the best technique for solving it.

"But back to your survey, what did you discover about the regional managers who aren't using computers?"

"Well, the older managers generally have had no direct exposure to computer usage," she replied.

"So they're at the same point I was a couple of years ago," Jack noted.

"Without exception," she continued, "those under 30 used computers during their college days. Typically, each has taken an introductory computer science course that taught some programming language such as BASIC or FORTRAN [3], [13]. Just as typically, they seem to have the mistaken notion that programming is necessary for doing real work on a computer. I expect you'll be dispelling that myth."

Jack answered, "I don't plan to even mention the idea of programming until the session is nearly over. In my own case, I'd been using the computer for about a year before I began to write simple programs of my own. I knew the knowledge management environment furnished programming techniques, but didn't really see applications for them until I'd become more experienced with other techniques. I was able to accomplish a lot without knowing the first thing about programming. Only later did I recognize problems that could not be easily handled by other techniques furnished in the environment, problems that I eventually solved via a combination of programming and those other techniques."

Joy was relieved to hear that Jack had put programming in its proper place. She had seen too many unfortunate cases where people had become alienated from or intimidated by computers when their first exposure involved programming. In fact, from her survey she sensed that some of the managers suffered from this affliction. It would be interesting to see if Jack's instructional approach could overcome any residual negativism that might exist.

Pulling up to the hotel, she said, "When you've checked in, I'd like to check out the notes you mentioned. Let's meet in the courtyard."

After settling into his room, Jack entered the hotel's open-air courtyard, pulled a patio chair up to the round white table where Joy sat, and laid his notes before her. With a thoughtful expression, she slowly began to page through them. They had been arranged in outline form. Jack explained, "I've had overhead transparencies made for all the pages and will use them to guide the training. To illustrate various points made in the transparencies, I'll actually work out examples on the computer for projection on the large TV screen. I expect there will be a good deal of discussion to accompany the points and examples I've planned. And I hope you'll chime in whenever you think it's appropriate."

She looked up and smiled. "Don't worry about that." Her gaze returned to the pages. She liked what she saw. Following a brief but sufficient introduction to computer hardware and software basics, Jack launched into an examination of the main kinds of interfaces that a manager could use for communicating with a computer. He then proceeded to point out knowledge management problems that the managers faced. For each, he demonstrated that it could be handled using one or more of the environment's knowledge management capabilities, including:

Making calculations.	Forms management.
Text management.	Report management.
Data base management.	Graphics generation.
Ad hoc inquiry.	Spreadsheet analysis.
Generating statistics.	Programming.

Even though the training session was to be intensive, it would be impossible to cover all possible problems that confront a regional manager. She saw that Jack had chosen to cover representative problems, each of which could be solved by exercising one or a combination of these capabilities. These would serve as good patterns for the managers' own do-it-yourself computing.

Joy went through the notes in detail, offering several suggestions about points that deserved special emphasis and indicating a few places where she would beef up the presentation with her own descriptions. By dusk, they had stepped through the entire set of notes. Joy was impressed and was already thinking about adapting Jack's notes for training other managers in the company. Her apprehensions about Jack's ability had disappeared and as they dined she realized that he had a very soothing effect on her. For his part, Jack already felt a close rapport, even though they had not met before. It was reassuring to be working with someone on the same wavelength. As they parted in the night, he could not help but think that he saw the future in her eyes.

GETTING STARTED

It was 8 A.M. and there was an aroma of coffee in the air as Jack began to speak. His introductory comments were designed to set the regional sales managers at ease. He noticed that the national sales manager, whose office was just down the corridor, had slipped into the back of the meeting room. Joy had said that he planned to attend as much of the training session as his schedule would allow. Jack explained that the session would be divided into 16 modules of about three hours apiece. Each day, except Sunday, would have a morning and an afternoon module separated by a sizable break. During these breaks and in the evenings, the managers would reinforce what they had just learned with hands-on experience. Jack suggested that they carry out their computer practice in groups of two or three.

Concluding his preamble, Jack introduced Joy. She described the role of KC's information center and explained that its services would be available to each of the regional managers following the training session. She gave a number they could call for assistance on matters related to computer usage. "While you will be learning all the basics over the next few days, you may have additional questions in the future. If so, the center is ready to help you. We'll also consider the possibility of organizing future short courses on topics of general interest."

Her glance in Jack's direction signaled that she had finished. Motioning to the computer at his side, Jack said, "I understand that about half of you have previously used some kind of computer in one capacity or another. Bear with me while I cover the basic ideas of computer hardware and software for the uninitiated among us. The first point I want to make is an extremely important one that you should never lose sight of: *a computer is just a machine*. Like a typewriter, calculator, VCR, or automobile, it does what you 'tell' it to do. Working together, computer hardware and software are able to carry out specific tasks that you request.

"You need to understand a few basic things about a computer's hardware, its software, and the relationship between hardware and software. The *hardware* is what you see here." Jack waved his hand over the computer (Figure 1–5). "Notice that there are several distinct pieces of hardware connected by cables. In a moment we'll see exactly what these devices do. But what about the computer's software? If this is the hardware, then where is the software and more importantly what is the purpose of software?"

Stan, the spreadsheet man, volunteered, "The software is in the machine. The kind of software you have determines what you can do with the computer."

"That's right," chimed Joy, "*software* controls what kinds of requests you can make of the computer and what kinds of tasks the computer will be able to carry out. For instance, you can't request that a graph be drawn on the computer screen if the computer doesn't have software that knows how to cause the hardware to draw graphs. A computer like this one could be equipped with virtually thousands of different pieces of software. Each one allows you to make certain requests in a certain way for carrying out certain tasks. Each one allows the hardware to exhibit a certain behavior."

Jack joined in, "Without software, computer hardware is useless. Software is literally the know-how that allows hardware to exhibit the desired behavior prescribed by a user's request. When you get a computer, it needs to be furnished with the software (the know-how) that hardware can use in appropriately responding to whatever kinds of requests you may want to make. As we go through the week, you'll see there are many kinds of requests that a well-furnished computer can handle. But for now, let's take a closer look at the hardware devices you'll be using."

Hardware

Jack began his hardware discussion with the overview transparency shown in Figure 2–1. A user makes a request to the computer via some *input device*. The most common input device is a *keyboard*, which you can use to simply type in your request. Figure 2–2(a) shows the keyboard of the IBM XT computer that Jack is using for demonstration purposes. Keyboards of the other computers in the room vary somewhat, primarily in terms of the arrangement of keys (e.g., Figure 2–2(b)). In addition to a keyboard, a computer may have a mouse as an alternative input device (recall Figure 1–5). Jack focused on the keyboard.

The bulk of keys in the center of the Figure 2–2(a) keyboard are laid out like the keys on a common typewriter. This includes the space bar at the bottom, a row of number keys at the top, and Shift keys at the left and right. Each *Shift key* is designated by an arrow that points upward. Holding a Shift key down while pressing another key (e.g., the T key) has the same effect that would occur on a typewriter (e.g., the entry of an uppercase T). The *Caps Lock* key to the right of the space bar can be pressed once to cause all subsequent characters to be shifted into uppercase, without having to depress the Shift key for

FIGURE 2–1   Relationships of hardware devices

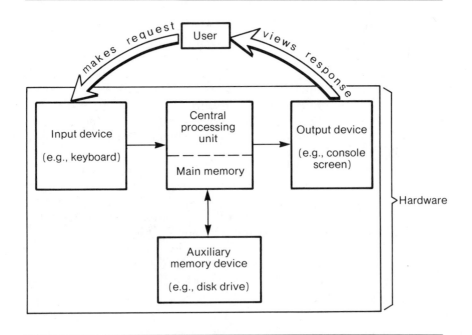

each one of them. By again pressing the Caps Lock key, the keyboard reverts to ordinary behavior.

Just to the right of the typewriter keys are two oversized keys with arrows pointing to the left. The top one is a *Backspace key*. Pressing this key causes the last character you typed in to be erased so you can enter a different character in its place. The Backspace key is very handy for immediately correcting typing errors. The crooked arrow (↵) key directly below the Backspace key is usually called the *Enter key*. On some keyboards it is labeled with the word "Enter" or "Return" rather than a crooked arrow. When you type in a request for the computer to do something, you need some way to indicate that the request is complete and you want the computer to carry out the requested actions. This is accomplished by simply pressing the Enter key.

On the left side of the keyboard there are two columns of *function keys*, labeled F1 through F10. Pressing a function key will cause the computer to carry out some operation. The exact nature of the operation corresponding to a particular function key depends on the software you are using. Some software will not do anything when you press a

FIGURE 2-2   The keyboard

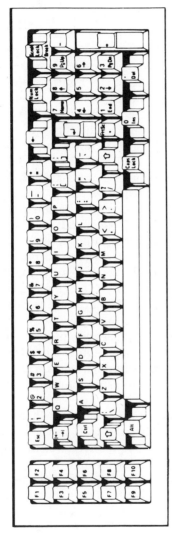

(a) Keyboard for an IBM XT

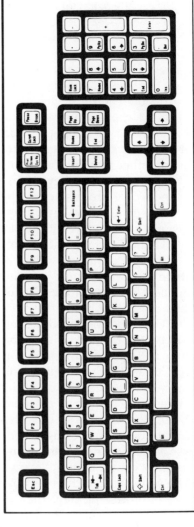

(b) Keyboard for an IBM AT

function key. Other software will carry out a commonly needed operation, thus allowing users to make the most frequently needed requests by pressing a single key rather than typing in a series of keystrokes. As will be discussed in Chapter 3, some software will even allow you to customize the behavior of function keys, so you can have any function key cause whatever operation you like whenever you press it.

On the right side of the keyboard there are some other special keys not usually found on typewriters. Collectively, these keys are sometimes called the "numeric keypad." Notice that the numbers are laid out like they would appear on an ordinary adding machine, calculator, or TV remote control device. Once you press the *Num Lock* key, you can use the numeric keypad as an alternative to the top row of the typewriter area for typing in numeric characters. If you again press the Num Lock key, the keys in the keypad will revert to their normal behavior rather than producing numeric input. What behavior is "normal" for one of these keys depends on the software you are using and the kind of processing in which you are engaged. Jack explained that the uses of these keys, the *Ctrl* (control) key, and *Esc* (escape) key would be introduced as needed during the ensuing week.

As Figure 2–1 suggests, the heart of a computer is its *central processing unit* or, as it is commonly called, the *CPU* [3], [9]. Physically, the CPU exists in the system unit box depicted in Figure 1–5. This hardware component consists of the electronic circuitry that actually carries out actions prescribed by the software held in its memory. The memory of a CPU is variously called the computer's *main memory*, primary memory, or central memory. If something is not in a computer's main memory, the CPU cannot process it; it must be transferred into main memory before it can be processed. As long as there is nothing in its main memory, a computer can do nothing.

When a computer is in operation, its main memory will contain software, the know-how or instructions that the CPU can look at in order to know what to do when a request is received via the input device. When you have finished making a request through the keyboard, the request is transferred to main memory where the CPU can examine it. The software, which is also in main memory, determines what sequence of processing steps the CPU circuitry will carry out in response to your request. These steps may involve such things as performing arithmetic operations, making comparisons, accepting additional input via the keyboard, changing the contents of main memory, or sending some contents of main memory to an output device that will display to you what it receives.

"As far as I'm concerned, understanding the details of how CPU circuitry does what it does is irrelevant." Jack looked to Joy for approval.

She nodded, "You're living proof of that, aren't you? Just as you can operate a car without being a mechanic, you can operate a computer without being an electrical engineer. Of course, it doesn't do any harm to know about the details of what's going on under the hood, but it's unnecessary. However, the general point about a computer being able to process something only when it is in main memory is an important one. In that connection, I'd also like to point out that software isn't the only thing that can be in main memory. In addition, there can be various kinds of knowledge that the software operates on as your requests are processed."

"For instance," Jack interjected, "if your request asks the computer to show a comparison of a sales rep's sales and quota figures across all product lines, those figures must somehow get into the main memory before they can be displayed on an output device. To handle such a request, the computer's main memory must contain software that causes the CPU to bring those figures into main memory. Once they are present, the software's next step is to have the CPU transfer them to the output device."

A hand shot up. It belonged to a fiftyish Brad Anderson. He had red hair, a determined chin, and a slightly puzzled look. "But where does it get the figures to bring into main memory? Why aren't they already there in main memory, along with the software that operates on them?"

"Those are good questions," replied Joy. "Let me answer the second one first. Ideally, it would be great if all the knowledge that software might need to operate on in responding to user requests were already present in main memory. But as it turns out main memory is not infinite, far from it. The machines we'll be using here have a main memory capacity of about 640,000 bytes. You can think of a byte as corresponding to a character. Thus, storing the name 'Brad' in the memory of one of these computers would consume 4 of its 640,000 bytes.

"Incidentally, in computer jargon you would say that this computer has 640 Kb of RAM." She went on to explain that the K is short for kilo and the b is short for bytes, so that 640 Kb refers to approximately 640 thousand bytes.[1] RAM is an abbreviation for *random access memory*, indicating that the CPU circuitry can randomly access any contents of main memory that it happens to need in responding to a user's request [3].

Brad persevered, "But isn't 640,000 characters more than enough

---

[1] K actually refers to 1,024 rather than 1,000, so 640 Kb means 655,360 bytes.

to accommodate both the software and a sales rep's quota and sales figures? Seems to me that it should be plenty."

"It probably is," answered Joy. "It's not uncommon for a fairly versatile piece of software to consume 400,000 to 500,000 bytes of a microcomputer's main memory. What's left over can be used to hold knowledge that the software can operate on, such as a rep's performance data. This memory space is sometimes called the data area, although other kinds of knowledge aside from data can be kept there. I prefer to think of it as the software's *work area*, because the software can work on any knowledge that is in this area of main memory. The performance figures for one or several reps could perhaps fit into the work area. But remember, you're probably interested in much more than performance data for a few reps."

"That's right," concurred Jack. "I use the computer to keep track of information about product lines, rep expenses, the reps themselves, and many other things. In addition to this descriptive knowledge, I also save budgeting formulas, templates for generating nice looking reports, memos, the meanings of new words I want the software to understand, and much more. Believe me, once you begin to appreciate the many ways in which a computer can make your life easier, you'll rapidly reach the point where you're using the software to manage many hundreds of thousands or even millions of bytes of knowledge."

"I see," nodded Brad. "Obviously, that can't all fit in main memory's work area at the same time. So the software must tell the CPU to bring into main memory whatever knowledge it needs to process a request, on an as-needed basis. I'll bet that's what the *auxiliary memory device* in your diagram refers to." He pointed to the lower portion of the projected transparency (see Figure 2–1).

"That's right." Jack was aware of a sense of relaxation, as if everyone had exhaled deeply. "Auxiliary memory devices are hardware components that can transfer knowledge to and from main memory at the behest of the software. This knowledge is stored on some auxiliary memory medium that can be mounted in the device. It's much the same idea as storing music on a disc or cassette tape that can be mounted in a device that accesses the encoded music. The computers we'll be using are equipped with two kinds of auxiliary memory devices: a hard disk drive and a floppy disk drive. Both are housed in the computer's system unit."

With Joy's help, Jack went on to describe these two kinds of auxiliary memory devices [3], [9], [12]. A *hard disk drive* is normally not visible to the user without removing the system unit's cover. Permanently mounted within this device is a small, rigid (i.e., "hard") disk that has a much larger capacity than main memory. Capacities on the order of 10 or 20 million bytes (Mb or megabytes) are commonplace for hard disks. Bytes are stored magnetically in concentric circles on the disk's surface. Each of these circles of bytes is called a track.

The disk drive has a motor that is able to spin the disk at very high speeds past the device's read/write head (an electromagnetic sensing and recording instrument). The drive can move the read/write head to any track and, as the disk spins by, the bytes in that track can be read by the head for transfer into main memory. Alternatively, bytes in main memory can be transferred to the disk drive where the head will write them as new bytes in the track. In either case, there is a drive light on the system unit that goes on whenever knowledge is being passed between central memory and auxiliary memory.

In principle, a *floppy disk drive* works in much the same way as a hard disk drive. But a major difference is that instead of a permanently resident hard disk, you can insert and remove floppy disks. A floppy disk, typically called a *diskette*, is a flexible disc of thin plastic enclosed in a square protective envelope. Sometimes, diskette envelopes are made of rigid plastic. This is common for small disks (e.g., three inches in diameter). For larger diskettes, such as the 5¼-inch size Jack uses, the envelope is typically made of cardboard. As shown in Figure 2–3(a), such an envelope has several holes. These allow the disk drive to get at the disk itself once you have inserted the diskette envelope into the drive. It is a good practice to store the diskette in a sleeve (Figure 2–3(b)) to protect those parts of the disk surface that are exposed through the envelope's holes.

The system unit has a slot for inserting and removing diskettes. As shown in Figure 2–4, there is a load lever that can be flipped up or down in front of the drive's slot. To insert a diskette into the drive, lift the load lever. If there is already a diskette in the drive, pull it out and put it in its sleeve. You can now slide the desired diskette into the drive. It must be inserted with the proper orientation. Jack demonstrated by showing that the diskette's label should be visible in the near-right corner as the diskette is pushed into the slot (see Figure 2–4). Once the diskette is in the drive, flip down the load lever and any knowledge stored on the diskette becomes available for transfer from the floppy disk drive to the work area in main memory. The reverse transfer is also possible, allowing new knowledge to be stored on the diskette.

As with a hard disk drive, this reading and writing of knowledge from and to auxiliary memory is accomplished by a read/write head positioned at the read/write opening (Figure 2–3(a)). The floppy disk drive grips the round disk at the drive hole (Figure 2–3(a)) and spins it within the square envelope. As this happens, a track on the disk's

FIGURE 2–3   A diskette

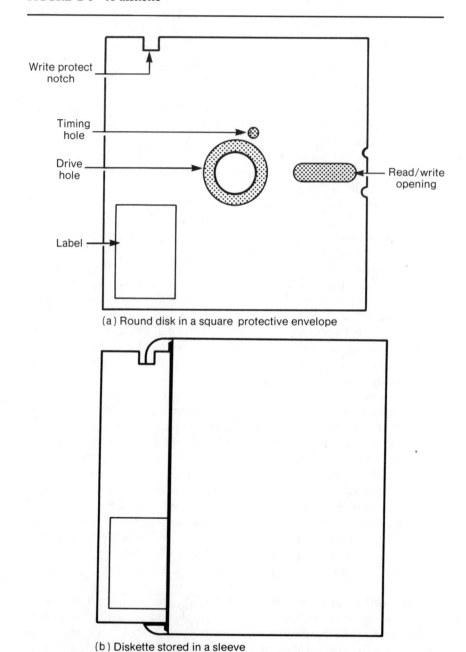

(a) Round disk in a square protective envelope

(b) Diskette stored in a sleeve

FIGURE 2–4   Inserting a diskette into a drive

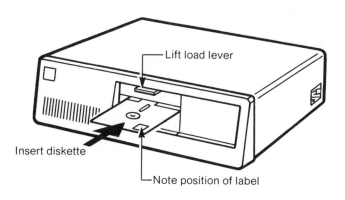

surface passes by the read/write head, which either senses the bytes that are there or electromagnetically records new bytes in the track. A timing hole (Figure 2–3(a)) allows the drive to detect the starting radius for the disk's tracks, so the reading or writing can be properly synchronized. The write protect notch (Figure 2–3(a)) can be covered with a sticker provided with the diskette. When this is done, the drive will be unable to write to (i.e., alter) the diskette. This can prevent accidental modification or erasure of knowledge on a diskette whose contents you don't want to change.

An earnest-faced Dan Scholz interrupted to ask, "I get the idea of how these auxiliary memory devices work, but what's the point of having two different kinds of disk drives?"

Joy responded, "For one thing, hard and floppy disks have very different capacities. This 5¼-inch floppy disk holds 360 Kb, which is a miniscule amount compared to a hard disk. Up to 180 K bytes can be stored on each side. Notice that each side of the diskette has a read/write opening." Turning the diskette to show its other side, she continued, "This is called a double-sided floppy. A single-sided diskette would have a read/write opening on one side only and would have only half the storage capacity. Most floppy disk drives these days are able to work with double-sided diskettes.

"Another important difference is that hard disk drives are much faster than floppies. When the software causes a transfer between the work area in main memory and the auxiliary memory, it will be significantly faster if a hard disk is used."

Dan interrupted again, "It seems that a hard disk is the best of all worlds . . . greater capacity, faster responses, and no need to shuffle diskettes in and out of a drive. Is a floppy drive really worthwhile for anything?"

"In my case," Jack acknowledged, "I tend to do most of my work with the hard disk. But floppies are good for a couple of things. For one, I don't want my hard disk cluttered with a lot of knowledge that I don't frequently use. For instance, I presently don't have much need to work with the sales rep performance figures of two years ago. So I keep this knowledge on a floppy disk. It's available on the rare occasions when I need it, without getting in the way the rest of the time.

"Second, I use the floppies to keep backup copies of knowledge stored on the hard disk. In case some piece of knowledge on the hard disk becomes damaged through a hardware malfunction, a system failure (such as a power outage), or an error that I myself might make, then I wouldn't have to reconstruct it from scratch. I could use the backup copy instead. Though I've rarely needed to use a backup, it can save a lot of time and work if some damage were to occur."

From his computer experience, Stan pointed out another role of diskettes. "As a practical matter, when you purchase a piece of software, it's provided on one or more diskettes. Compared to a hard disk, a diskette is very portable and inexpensive."

"That's right," Joy confirmed. "Diskettes are a very convenient way to carry large amounts of knowledge with you . . . whether you're buying it at a store to take home with you or making a trip across the country where you'll use it on a different machine. Some people here at company headquarters have their own computers at home. They can use diskettes to easily take the day's computer work home with them for additional processing over a weekend. On Monday morning, new results can then be brought back to the office on diskettes to continue the processing. Diskettes also give you an easy way to mail knowledge to each other or to the home office. And we at the home office could mail large amounts of computer-usable knowledge to you via diskettes."

Turning to another point in his outline, Jack said, "There is one other notion to understand about the difference between main memory and auxiliary memory. It's that main memory is volatile. When you turn off the computer, the contents of RAM go away." He snapped his fingers.

"In contrast, auxiliary memory—be it hard or floppy—is not volatile. When you turn off the computer, whatever is stored on a disk will still be there when you later turn it on again . . . provided you don't physically damage it, of course."

"Do you mean," asked Brad thoughtfully, "that main memory is sort of a short-term memory and auxiliary memory is more like a long-term memory? When I'm concentrating on a problem there are certain things in my mind that are there for a very short period of time and they're gone when I turn my attention to something else or solve the problem. If I think I may need one of these things later, then I write it down or make a special mental note of it (and hope that it's not forgotten when I later need it). Thus I save some things in longer term memory so I can later recall them. It seems that a computer does something quite similar, at least in principle."

"That's a very good analogy," nodded Joy. "It also highlights the importance of being sure that any knowledge in the short-term work area that you intend to use later is properly saved in long-term auxiliary memory before you switch to a different piece of software or turn off the computer."

Moving along, Jack pointed to the diagram of hardware devices (Figure 2–1). "There's one kind of hardware component that we haven't yet discussed, namely *output devices*. There are two different output devices attached to each computer we'll be using: a console screen and a printer."

Motioning to the *console screen* perched atop the system unit (Figure 1–5), Jack described the role of this device [3], [9], [12]. As each character is typed in via the keyboard it is normally echoed to the console screen. If a typing error is made it will be evident by looking at the console screen. One way to correct an error is by means of the Backspace key. Jack noted that the software they would be using supported other means of correcting typing errors.

Not only does the screen give visual feedback during keyboard usage, it also shows the effects that software produces in response to a request. For instance, when performance figures are requested, the software takes care of pulling them together (e.g., finding them on the disk and bringing them into the work area) and causing the CPU to send them to the screen for viewing. "Thus, the keyboard allows you to send messages to the computer and the console screen allows the computer to send messages to you," concluded Jack.

Typically, a screen can display up to 25 rows of output at a time, with each row showing up to 80 characters. Though some console screens are monochrome, all those used in the training session were color screens. These color screens allow characters to be displayed in any of seven different colors against a background of any of the seven colors. In addition, the computers were equipped with circuitry[2] enabling them

---

[2] On Jack's IBM XT this was in the form of a color graphics circuit board in the system unit.

FIGURE 2–5   A printer

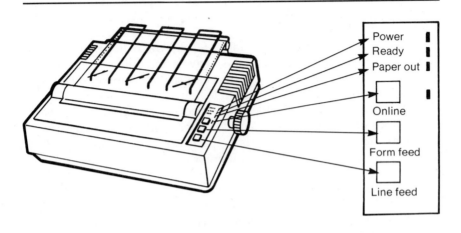

to produce graphical images on the screen (see Photos 30 and 33 in the color insert).

Pointing to the printer (Figure 2–5), Jack proceeded to describe the other output device they would use [3], [9], [12]. The *printer* can be used to get a printed copy of output shown on the console screen. This output is often referred to as *hard copy* or *printouts*. After demonstrating how to insert paper into the printer and turn the printer on, Jack described the printer's control panel. When the printer is turned on, the panel's power light will be on. In order to get a printout, the printer must be *online*. Whether the printer is online or not can be controlled by pressing the printer's *Online button*. The *Online light* next to the button will come on when the printer is online and able to accept output from the CPU.

If you press the Online button while its light is on, the light goes off and the printer is said to be *offline*. In this state it cannot accept output from the CPU. While the printer is offline, the other two control panel buttons can be used to advance the paper either a line at a time (the *Line Feed button*) or a page at a time (the *Form Feed button*). After adjusting the paper, the printer should be put back online again. Jack emphasized that one should never make a request for printed output when the printer is not online.

Joy polished off the printer introduction by explaining that they would all be using what are called dot matrix printers. This kind of printer forms each output character or symbol by a unique arrangement of dots, similar to what you commonly see on a bank's time/temperature signs. She explained that there are other, more expensive kinds of printers whose output looks as if it had been typed on a high-quality electric typewriter. These are called letter quality printers. Then there are laser printers that do not impact the paper as they print. They produce very high-quality printouts much faster than conventional impact printers. They also cost considerably more than impact printers.

Software

As already explained, software is a sequence of instructions. When these instructions are in main memory, they can be carried out by the CPU. The act of carrying out software instructions is referred to as *executing* or *running* the software. While a piece of software is executing, it can accept and process a user's requests. On receiving a request, it may prompt the user on the console screen to make new entries that clarify the request or provide new knowledge to be stored in memory. Conceptually, software is a kind of procedural knowledge specifying how the CPU should react to user entries. Like other kinds of knowledge, software can be stored on a long-term basis in auxiliary memory.

There are three major classes of software: hosts, application systems, and tools. One kind of host software is called an *operating system* [3], [5]. Jack explained that when a computer is turned on, operating system software is automatically read into the computer's main memory and it remains there while the computer is operating. This loading of the operating system into main memory is often referred to as *booting* the computer. As this happens, a disk drive light will come on and you will hear the drive in operation. When this is finished, execution of the operating system begins.

All operating systems do not exhibit the same behavior or accept the same commands. But most can carry out a common collection of basic tasks. In the case of the PC-DOS operating system Jack uses, the operating system's first actions involve asking you to enter the current date (e.g., type in 5/14/87 and press the Enter key) and time (e.g., type in 10:10 and press Enter for 10 past 10 A.M.) as shown in Figure 2–6. You will then see the operating system's prompt (e.g., C>) on the left margin of the screen. Whenever you see this kind of prompt, it means the operating system is ready to accept a request from you.

Joy added, "When you boot one of the computers here, either the PC-DOS™ or MS-DOS® operating system is read into main memory and begins executing. The IBM computers use PC-DOS. IBM-compatible computers from other manufacturers use MS-DOS, which behaves like PC-DOS. If you understand how to use PC-DOS, then you understand how to use MS-DOS, and vice versa."

FIGURE 2–6   Getting the operating system prompt

```
Current date is Tue 1-01-1980
Enter new date: 5/14/87

Current time is 0:01:05.58
Enter new time: 10:10

C>
```

Brad, quickly catching on, asked, "So you mean we can make the same kinds of requests to either PC-DOS or MS-DOS, but what kinds of requests can we make to these operating systems when we see the prompt?"

Jack replied, "Probably the most important kind of request is that you can tell the operating system to execute any other piece of software that presently exists in auxiliary memory. You make the request by simply typing in the software's name and then pressing the Enter key. A copy of that piece of software is automatically brought into main memory and, once its execution begins, the CPU obeys its instructions rather than the operating system. When processing finishes for this software, the operating system again takes control of the CPU's behavior. At that point, you might request the operating system to bring another piece of software into main memory for execution."

"I was wondering how you get a piece of software into main memory so you can ask it to do its thing," said Brad. "Now, I see. The operating system, which is always resident in main memory, allows me to execute any other software that I choose to use. Can the operating system accept any other kinds of requests?"

"Yes," responded Jack, "there are quite a few other requests you can make, but with one exception I don't need to use them frequently. The exception is the DIR command, which can be used to see a directory of things presently stored on a disk."

Joy chimed in, "From the operating system's viewpoint, knowledge residing on a disk is organized into files and each file has a name. For instance, each piece of software that you can execute is stored in a file. As Jack suggested earlier, you can execute a piece of software by typing in the name of the file that holds it. As you'll see later many other kinds of knowledge can be held in a disk's files for a variety of uses."

Jack continued, "The DIR command lets you see the names of files existing on a disk. Names begin with alphabetic characters and can be up to eight characters long. Optionally, there can be an extension of up to three characters for a file name. An extension usually indicates what a file can be used for. For instance, files containing software that can be executed by the operating system are traditionally given EXE extensions, indicating that they're executable. On the other hand, files containing textual passages might be given TXT extensions."

He proceeded to demonstrate the DIR command by simply typing

```
DIR
```

in response to the operating system prompt [5]. Figure 2–7 shows a partial list of what appeared on the console screen. Because the operating system prompt was C>, these are files that exist on drive C. By convention, the system unit's hard disk drive is referred to as drive C. Its floppy disk drive is called drive A. On machines such as the IBM AT having two floppy disk drives, the floppy drives are called A and B. By typing

```
DIR A:
```

in response to the operating system prompt, Jack could have produced a listing of files existing on the diskette in drive A.

Each row in the output from DIR refers to one file. The file's basic name is shown first, followed by its extension. Then there is a number indicating how many bytes of the disk are occupied by the file. Finally, the date and time at which the file came into existence are shown. "For the time being," Jack concluded, "don't worry about what knowledge is in these various files and don't worry about how they came into existence. We'll get to that later. Just remember that when you want to know what exists on a disk you can invoke the DIR command."

FIGURE 2–7   Partial results of a DIR request

```
USRMAN    EXE     52224    8-16-86    10:07a
IBMCOL    TRM       255    8-16-86    10:07a
KTAB      TRM      1595    8-16-86    10:07a
KMAN      EXE    251200    8-16-86    10:08a
KMHELP    HLP    203201    8-16-86    10:09a
KGUIDE    HLP    146719    8-16-86    10:09a
KPAINT    OVL      8784    8-16-86    10:11a
KCHAT     OVL     99056    8-20-86     3:33p
WORDMAN   EXE     56160    8-20-86     3:33p
WMAN      HLP      6016    8-20-86     3:34p
WORDLST   DIC      1024    8-20-86     3:34p
```

There are several variations of the DIR command beyond the simple usage Jack described. Explanations of these and other requests that can be made appear in the documentation for your operating system (e.g., [5]).

Now that all understood the basic role of operating system software as a host for executing other software, Joy briefly mentioned that there is another kind of host software: *windowing shells.* Though an understanding of such hosts was not necessary for the broad spectrum of knowledge management activities they would be exploring, she thought it would not hurt for the managers to be aware of these shells. Briefly, a windowing shell is a piece of software that allows the console screen to display one or more boxes, each of which is called a window. Some of the better known windowing shells include Microsoft's WINDOWS™, IBM's TopView™, and Quarterdeck's DesQ™ [14].

Like an operating system, a shell lets you request that some piece of software be executed. Your interaction with that software occurs through one of the windows on the screen. Unlike most ordinary operating systems, a shell allows you to start the execution of other software before the first one is finished. Each executing piece of software is assigned to a window through which you can make inputs to it and can view outputs from it. At any moment, you can actively interact with one piece of software through its window. A shell allows you to switch back and forth among the windows in order to interact with different pieces of software as desired.

"That's enough about host software," announced Jack. "Let's take a look at the other two classes of software: application systems and tools. These are the two basic kinds of software that you can tell an operating system to execute. An application system is software that performs special processing pertaining to a particular application area such as accounting, personnel administration, or inventory control."

Joy elaborated, "Application systems are created by computer professionals for use by people who may not be generally knowledgeable about computers. For instance, our company's MIS department could develop a rep performance application system for you. When you execute this software, it would allow you to store, modify, and view performance figures. And it would allow you to do so without really knowing much, if anything, about computers."

She paused and then said briskly, "But that's all this application system would do. It couldn't be used for other applications such as budgeting, accounting, personnel, inventory control, and so on. In contrast, a software tool is not tied to any particular application area. It could be used to handle problems in any of the areas I just mentioned. In fact, software tools are what computer professionals use to create application system software."

Tracey, who had been listening quietly, said, "Let's see if I understand the difference between these two classes of software." She had a warm, sunburnt complexion and very white even teeth to contrast with her auburn hair.

"Can we say that an application system is sort of like a bicycle, car, or dishwasher? It's like a consumer product that doesn't take much skill or training to use. And it's specifically designed to be applied in a certain way. In contrast it seems that software tools correspond to the machine tools that would exist in a factory where consumer products are built. They are used by skilled, trained workers. I presume that, like a machine tool, a software tool's capabilities are not restricted to a single application."

Jack looked at Joy, smiling, "That's a good analogy, don't you agree?" She nodded as Jack continued. "Now in this training session, each of you will learn how to use a software tool."

"But wait a minute," interrupted a baffled Brad, "I thought tools were for computer professionals with years of training in computer science. How do you expect me to become a pro within the next week?"

Smiling politely, Joy replied, "Have faith. As it turns out not all tools are strictly for the pros. Actually, there's a continuum ranging from strictly professional tools all the way down to strictly hobbyist tools. We'll be working in the middle of this continuum with a tool that is used by people without prior computer exposure. This same tool's advanced capabilities are exercised by the pros, but we'll not get into those."

"Elaborating on Tracey's analogy," Jack added, "there are some tools that can be used outside of the factory in your own workshop. Some of these tools for do-it-yourselfers are lightweight, hobbyist tools while others may be more heavy-duty and durable. I think you'll find that the software tool we'll be using will allow you to handle just about any knowledge management needs on your own."

When expressed in that way, it relieved Brad's apprehension. But he had one additional concern. "You said we would be learning to use one software tool. Can one tool really support a wide range of knowledge management activities?"

"That's right," jumped in Tracey, "the text management tool I've been using is OK for working with letters, memos, and some kinds of reports. But it's not much good for tracking a rep's performance figures."

Stan piled on, "I've been using a spreadsheet tool and it's great for budgeting, but it's no help for handling memos and letters. I can somewhat use it to keep performance figures, but it's a bit unwieldy for that."

"Whoa," said Jack, "time out. It may sound amazing, but I've been using a single tool to handle all the things you've mentioned . . . and much more. I've never considered or felt a need for using a collection of separate tools."

Joy elaborated, "Some software tools are called stand-alone tools. A stand-alone tool is oriented toward a single knowledge management technique. It gives you one way of representing knowledge stored on disk together with a way for processing that knowledge.

"Another, newer kind of software tool is an environment for knowledge management. It is a single piece of software that supports all the knowledge representation and processing capabilities typically found in a collection of separate tools. With an environment there is no need to switch back and forth among distinct tools. Nor do you need to learn and remember the idiosyncrasies of separate tools. The many knowledge-handling capabilities of an environment can be fused together in such a way that their total effect is much greater than the sum of their individual effects, allowing you to do things that are simply impossible with an assortment of stand-alone tools. When you work in such an environment this synergy can be quite valuable" [6], [7].

"It looks as if this is going to be an interesting adventure," commented Dan. There was a murmur of assent from the group. "I assume we'll get to use one of these knowledge management environments."

"Right," replied Jack, "we'll be using a particular knowledge management environment. The company will be supplying each of you with a licensed copy of this same software tool to use on your own computers back home. As you'll see, this tool furnishes a computer-based environment for representing and processing many types of knowledge in many different ways."

To this point, Debbie Bell had been sitting back, simply taking in the proceedings. Her unusually long straw-blonde hair cascaded well past the waist of her navy blue suit. Several years back, in her college days, she had taken a couple of computer science courses and she found the present discussion to be a useful refresher. "I'm curious, Jack," she said, speaking for the first time, "how did you happen to choose this particular software tool?"

"It was fate," he replied quickly and half-seriously. "When I made up my mind to take the computer plunge, I talked to a neighbor who worked at a local computer store. He gave me an important piece of advice. Always choose the software you want first and then choose the hardware. It would have been a colossal mistake to buy a computer and then discover that the software I'd like to use wouldn't work on that machine. Thankfully, he didn't push me hard toward a particular software product, but encouraged me to make up my own mind. He probably realized that we might be neighbors for a long time to come.

"To help me decide, he loaned me recent issues of popular computing publications such as *PC Magazine* and *Byte*. Though some of the articles were too technical for me, there were many that described the features of various software tools in terms I could understand [1], [15]. After reading through these, I settled on one that seemed to fit my philosophy."

"And what philosophy is that?" Debbie was now even more curious.

"Well, it may sound unorthodox and I realize there may be other approaches to choosing software," Jack hesitated, "but I view it like choosing a partner." He paused slightly to cast a furtive glance in Joy's direction. She was listening attentively. Jack continued, "Or you might even say that choosing your software is in many ways like choosing a mate.

"So, I was looking for something I could live with not only right away but also on an ongoing basis. I wanted to choose one that would accept me as I am, not demanding more skill than I possess at any moment in time. Yet, the software should allow me to grow, to become more and to do more. Even more than *allowing* me to grow it should *help* me to grow by being able to offer what I need when I progress to a point of sensing some new need. I'm not willing to settle for a series of encounters with the superficial or one-dimensional. Instead, I was looking for both depth and great variety in a single software package.

"Now all this may sound overly idealistic, but in retrospect I'm happy with the choice I made. My productivity with the computer has steadily grown. In a sense I'm a different person than I was before, in that I can now accomplish so much more in a given time frame. You might say that a bond has developed in which I view the capabilities of this software as an extension of myself. If it were to disappear, I believe I'd feel that a part of me was missing."

For a moment, no one spoke. Jack's words carried total conviction and Debbie found herself nodding in agreement with the rest. "I must say your approach has a certain appeal," commented Joy, "though I'd never heard it explained that way in any of the computer science courses I took in school. What you're saying is that the choice of software is not a decision to be taken lightly. You're looking for a compatible, long-term companion that you won't outgrow." She paused slightly to cast her own furtive glance in Jack's direction. He too was listening attentively. "It should be able to meet the variety of knowledge management needs that arise in the course of your decision-making activities, both today and tomorrow."

Jack continued, "So far, at least, the tool I happened to choose has filled that role for me. Its name is KnowledgeMan, which is short for Knowledge Manager." Jack was using Version 2 of this software tool [2], [8], [10], [11]. Although he did not realize it, almost all features of the KME could be used in an identical way within a more extensive KME called Guru [16].

"Any of us is, of course, free to purchase and use other software if we like. For my part, I haven't yet found any reason to do so. However, if you've plans in that direction, this training session will alert you to what sorts of things to consider when acquiring other software tools."

BASIC IDEAS

Glancing at his watch, Jack called for a break. He had a good feeling about how things had gone so far. Most of the managers were emerging into what was a new world for them. The initial apprehension and disorientation of some were to be expected and turned out to be momentary. He was pleased with how quickly they were gaining their bearings in this new realm. What's more, he had a definite impression that with Joy's help he had led them to see something very attractive and promising in their new surroundings. To be sure, they were still confronted with many mysteries, but these would gradually be penetrated in the days to come. In Jack's view this process of enlightenment would be uplifting and enjoyable for all concerned.

The managers now understood not only the difference between hardware and software, but also the way in which these two wares fit together. There are several devices that constitute a computer's hardware. A user enters requests and new knowledge into a computer via an input device such as a keyboard. The computer's CPU is a device that takes action to satisfy a user's request. The exact sequence of actions that a CPU's circuitry takes is determined by the software residing in its main memory. These actions can involve doing arithmetic, making comparisons, accepting further input from the keyboard, transferring knowledge between main and auxiliary memory, sending responses to an output device, and so forth.

In addition to software, main memory can contain various knowledge in a work area. Auxiliary memory, in the guise of hard and floppy disks, serves as the computer's large-scale, long-term memory. Many kinds of knowledge can be stored in a disk's files and transferred to and from the relatively small, volatile work area on an as-needed basis. As Joy reiterated to one of the managers during the break, hardware operates on software, which operates on knowledge. Or in other words, available knowledge determines what software does, which in turn determines what hardware does. It is worth remembering that software itself is a kind of procedural knowledge.

There are three basic classes of software. Just as hardware is an environment in which software is used, host software, such as an operating system, serves as an environment within which the other two types of software can be executed. As its name implies, application system software is designed to handle a particular application. In contrast, a tool is not application-specific. A stand-alone tool supports a particular knowledge representation and processing technique. It is possible for the capabilities normally found in multiple stand-alone tools to be available in a single tool. Such a tool is called a knowledge management environment. It provides a realm in which a user can apply any or all of the standard knowledge representation and processing techniques, separately or synergistically, as warranted by a particular knowledge management problem.

In the remainder of the training session, each manager will learn how to move about and accomplish things in a knowledge management environment. Each will explore and conquer previously unknown territory. By blending with and mastering this environment, each will extend his or her own innate knowledge management capabilities. Each will gain an appreciation of how everyday business needs can be handled with the main knowledge representation and processing techniques available for do-it-yourself computing. The first step in getting acclimated to a knowledge management environment is one of becoming acquainted with the available ways for interfacing with it.

References

1. Aarons, R. N. "Wising Up with KnowledgeMan." *PC* 3, no. 4 (1984).
2. Baker, J. *Mastering KnowledgeMan/2*. Lafayette, Ind: 1987.
3. Bohl, M. *Information Processing with BASIC*. Chicago: SRA, 1984.
4. Cain, N. W. *1-2-3 at Work*. Reston, Va.: Reston, 1984.
5. *Disk Operating System User's Guide*. Boca Raton, Fla.: IBM, 1983.
6. Holsapple, C. W. "Synergistic Software Integration for Microcomputers." *Systems and Software* 3, no. 2 (1984).
7. Holsapple, C. W., and A. B. Whinston. "Aspects of Integrated Software." *Proceedings of the National Computer Conference*, Las Vegas, July 1984.
8. *KnowledgeMan Reference Manual*, version 2. Lafayette, Ind.: MDBS, Inc., 1985.
9. Lucas, H. C., Jr. *Information Systems Concepts for Management*. New York: McGraw-Hill, 1986.
10. Roeder, G. *The Book of KnowledgeMan*, vol. 1. Chelmsford, Mass.: All-Hands-On Press, 1984.
11. _____. *The Book of KnowledgeMan*, vol. 2. Chelmsford, Mass.: All-Hands-On Press, 1985.
12. Sanders, D. *Computers Today*. New York: McGraw-Hill, 1983.
13. Schriber, T. J. *FORTRAN Case Studies for Business Applications*. New York: John Wiley & Sons, 1969.
14. Sullivan, K. B. "Windows Is Edging Out TopView as a Standard." *PC Week* 3, no. 16 (1986).
15. Walker, J. W. "KnowledgeMan." *Byte* 9, no. 2 (1984).
16. Williamson, M. "In Guru, the Business World Finally Has Its First, True AI-Based Micro Package," *PC Week* 3, nos. 11–14, 1986.

Part II

GETTING ACQUAINTED WITH SOFTWARE

We'll have that.

James, bring the things from the table.

What about their commissions?

It looks like a perfect fit.

Chapter Three

Interfaces

One of the first things you need to understand about any software tool is how to tell it what you want, that is, how to interface with it. This means much more than the physical act of pressing keys on a keyboard. It means understanding what requests are possible. Different software tools typically handle different requests. Even though two tools may functionally be able to do similar things, the way in which requests can be specified is likely to be different for one than it is for the other.

There are four major interface styles that might be encountered when dealing with various pieces of software: menus, natural languages, command languages, and customized interfaces. With a *menu interface* you make a request by selecting an option from a menu (list) of choices. When using a *natural language interface,* you make a request in your own conversational terms. With a *command language interface,* you make a request by specifying a command in some specially structured language. A *customized interface* is designed especially to fit some specific needs of a user.

Usually, a software tool will support one of these four interface styles. Sometimes, a single piece of software will support multiple interface styles, allowing you to use whichever style seems most comfortable at any moment in time. Each style has certain advantages and disadvantages. Each is appropriate for certain kinds of tasks and certain classes of users. Jack was about to demonstrate each of the four interface styles for making requests in the KnowledgeMan environment, though he personally tended to make requests most often through the command language interface.

No matter what kind of request is made and what style is used in making it, the software will make use of one or more kinds of knowledge in satisfying that request. Collectively, the universe of knowledge availa-

FIGURE 3–1 Generic structure of a knowledge management environment

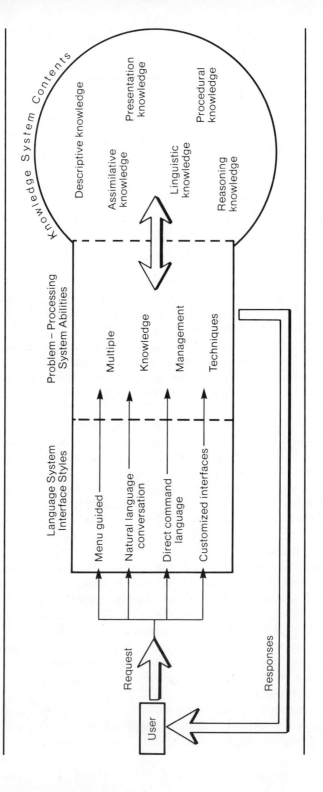

ble to the software is called its *knowledge system* (recall Figure 1–7). Physically, this knowledge is stored in a collection of disk files, with different types of knowledge being held in different kinds of files. The contents of main memory's work area can be regarded as an additional, short-term part of the knowledge system. KnowledgeMan itself is an example of a *problem-processing system*. It is able to solve user requests or problems by processing the contents of its knowledge system. Each of the four user interfaces is an example of a *language system*. Each interface furnishes some kind of language for making requests. Because KnowledgeMan fits the generic DSS structure portrayed in Figure 1–7 and is consistent with the view shown in Figure 1–8, it can be referred to as an environment for decision support [2], [3]. Figure 3–1 adapts the generic DSS structure to a knowledge management perspective.

ENTRY INTO THE KNOWLEDGE MANAGEMENT ENVIRONMENT

Seated in front of the demonstration computer, Jack pushed the system unit's power switch. The machine hummed softly and disk drive lights flickered on the front of the system unit. He felt a bit like one of the characters from a popular book in KC's science fiction product line. This character piloted a machine that could transport himself and others into new worlds of thought at the flick of a few switches. But there was nothing fictional about the knowledge management environment Jack and the others were about to enter through the small desktop machine.

In only a few moments they had been booted into the operating system. Jack entered the current date and time as the rest watched the console output on the large TV screen. The C> prompt appeared (recall Figure 2–6). Barely pausing in the operating system, Jack pushed onward to the knowledge management environment. The entrance was made with little effort or fanfare, by typing

```
KMAN
```

and then pressing the Enter key in response to the C> prompt [4]. Jack explained that the KnowledgeMan software existed in a file named KMAN.EXE on drive C. Thus, typing KMAN causes the operating system to bring this software into main memory and begin executing it.

The screen cleared momentarily and then a logo message appeared identifying the software and its vendor. The second thing they noticed on entering this environment was a prompt to type in a user name. Jack typed

PHOTO 1   First impressions of the knowledge management environment

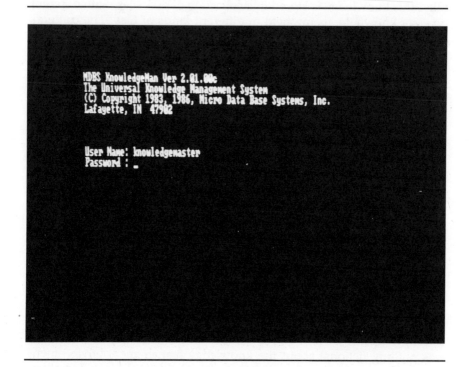

```
knowledgemaster
```

and pressed the Enter key. A new prompt for a password appeared.
Jack typed

```
MDBS
```

giving the screen the appearance shown in Photo 1. Notice that Jack's
response to the password prompt was not echoed to the screen.

"The first thing you do in this environment," explained Jack, "is
to identify yourself by furnishing a *user name*. The environment checks
the name you furnish against a list of valid user names existing in its
knowledge system. These are held in a disk file named KPASS.IGU.
Along with each user name, there is a corresponding *password*. Until
you can furnish the correct password for the user name you typed,
you won't be able to do anything in the environment. You'll get some
more chances to provide a valid name and password in case you made
a mistake."

"How does the knowledge describing valid names and passwords get into KPASS in the first place?" asked Debbie. "And how can you change that knowledge?"

"Good questions," noted Jack. "When you get the software, it comes with a ready-made KPASS file containing one user name and password, namely KNOWLEDGEMASTER and MDBS respectively. It also comes with a separate piece of utility software on a file named USRMAN.EXE. This is a tool for managing who the valid users are. When you execute it, its usage is so simple that I'll not bother to even demonstrate it here."

"So," continued Debbie, "I can make up a much shorter user name and password if I like. I don't have to type out KNOWLEDGEMASTER and MDBS every time I enter the environment."

"Yes," Jack nodded, "that's what I've done for my own knowledge system at home."

Stan, the spreadsheet man, frowned. "I don't see the point of all this user name and password business. Why can't I start making requests right away, as soon as I enter the environment? The 1-2-3 software tool that I use doesn't require me to introduce myself to it before I can begin making requests."

"The text management tool I use doesn't care who is using it either," added Tracey.

Jack shrugged. Coming to his rescue, Joy said, "As it turns out, you can easily set up the environment so the user name and password prompts won't appear. But when you do so, you leave your knowledge system completely open to anyone who knows how to execute the software. Anyone can look at or change any of the knowledge held there, with or without your permission or awareness. In many organizational settings, such as here at the home office, that's highly undesirable or even totally unacceptable.

"Furthermore, there are situations where multiple people need to share the same knowledge system. But we don't want all of them to be able to get at all of its knowledge. Each should be allowed to view or modify only a certain distinct subset of the knowledge. The USRMAN utility can be used to assign different *access privileges* to different users. When this is done the environment automatically thwarts any user's attempt to access something that he or she is not privileged to access. Access privileges are stated in terms of access codes. I only mention this because you may occasionally stumble across references to access codes in some places in the environment. You can ignore such references completely, because for the time being none of you will be sharing your knowledge system with anyone else. Another advanced aspect of security that you may run across in this environment is encryption.

Like access codes, it can be a good thing to have, but can be safely ignored by newcomers."

"To summarize," Jack said, "the most that a newcomer needs to know to successfully enter the environment is a user name and corresponding password." With that, he pressed the Enter key to conclude his MDBS password response. The "door" was now open for making knowledge management requests.

MENU-GUIDED REQUESTS

The environment's menu-guided interface begins with the prompt

```
New session name:
```

[5]. If desired, a name of your own choosing can be given to any session of menu-guided processing. When you exit from a session of menu-guided processing, you can have the environment save an entire description of the final state of that session in a file (having an ISF extension) in its knowledge system. That descriptive knowledge can be used as the starting point for resuming the same menu-guided session at some later time.

If one or more previously saved sessions had existed in the knowledge system, the new session name prompt would not have appeared. Instead, you would first be asked whether you want to resume a prior session. If you responded affirmatively, a list of saved sessions would appear so you could choose the one you wanted to resume. "By naming and saving sessions you can interrupt the work you are doing and later pick up right where you left off," Jack noted. Because he was just giving them a feel for what a menu-guided session was like, he explained that there was no need to bother giving the session a name or saving it for later resumption. He simply pressed the Enter key in response to the new session name prompt.

Picking an Option

A menu immediately appeared in the upper left corner of the screen (Photo 2). "A menu always tells you what your *options* are at any moment," Jack explained. "Looking at this menu, you can see that our current options are to set up (don't worry about what that means), to do some computations, to engage in data management activities, and so on. Using a menu interface is pretty much a matter of picking a desired option each time you see a menu. When you pick an option, what happens next depends on the option you selected. A new menu

PHOTO 2   Main menu for knowledge management

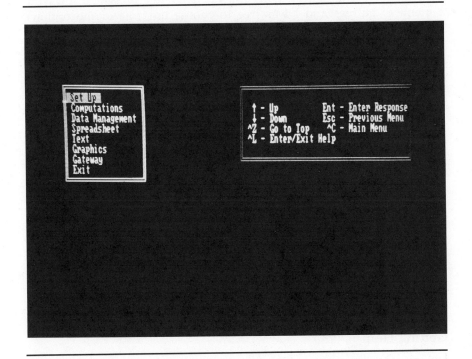

may appear, showing you a new set of options. You may be prompted to type in something or something might be displayed to you for viewing purposes."

"But how would I know which option to pick?" asked Dan. "For instance, if I wanted to look at some rep performance figures, what would I do?"

Motioning toward the screen, Jack replied. "Which option you pick from this main menu depends on what kind of knowledge management technique you want to use. If you're unfamiliar with a particular option, then you probably don't want to pick it. As it turns out, I've been using data base management techniques to represent and process my own rep's performance data, so I would pick the Data Management option. If someone else were using text management techniques to handle performance data, he or she would pick the main menu's Text option. A third person might try to use spreadsheet techniques for such data. In that case, the Spreadsheet option would be chosen."

Brad interrupted, "Before you go on, let's see if I understand the basic philosophy of this kind of interface. Last night, I had dinner at the La Scala restaurant near my hotel. The waiter presented me with a menu of entrees and I was free to choose any one of the options shown there. I steered clear of dishes I didn't recognize or wasn't interested in. Aren't we doing the same kind of thing here, only in a different environment?"

"Yes, it's quite similar, " responded Jack, relishing Brad's instructive comparison.

"But at the restaurant," Brad continued, "I could ask for an explanation of what I'd be getting if I were to choose some entree that I wasn't familiar with. Can we do the same thing here?"

"You sure can," answered Jack. Pointing to the box in the upper right corner of the screen (Photo 2), he explained that it showed what would happen if certain special keys were pressed. "Suppose you are unsure about the Data Management option. You need some help to understand what would happen if you were to choose it. You can get that help by using two of the special keys described in the box. Notice that the Set Up option is presently highlighted. I can use the down arrow key to get to the Data Management option and once it is highlighted I simply press Control-L to get some 'elp."

Getting Help

Jack pressed the numeric keypad's down arrow key once to move the highlighting cursor down to the Computations option. He pressed it again so that Data Management was now the highlighted option. He then depressed the Ctrl key on the left side of the keyboard and while holding it he also pressed the L key. A description of what would happen if he were to choose the Data Management option appeared to the right of the menu (see Photo 3). Such descriptions are usually called *help text*. Notice that the help text for Data Management says that if this option were picked, another menu would appear having eight options of its own for manipulating data represented in a tabular fashion.

Joy interjected for a moment to clarify the notion of *control keys*. Jack had referred to pressing "Control-L," and the box of special keys in Photo 2 had indicated the ^L could be used to get help text. She pointed out that Control-L and ^L are just two synonomous ways of saying the Ctrl key should be held down while pressing the L key. "In computer lingo, the little 'hat' symbol in front of a letter is a traditional, short-hand way of indicating that the control key should be pressed simultaneously with the letter key. As you'll see there are many

PHOTO 3   Help for the Data Management option

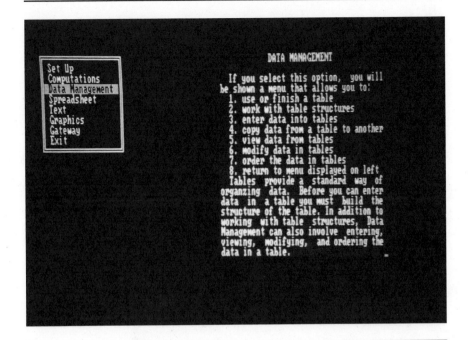

such control keys that can be quite handy, not only with a menu interface but with the other interface styles as well."

Jack pressed the space bar to clear the help text from the screen. It reverted to its former appearance (Photo 2). "Just to give you a taste of the menu style of making a request, let's see how we would solve Dan's desire to see some rep performance figures. Before we began this morning, I put some of the knowledge about my own region into the knowledge system on this machine." He had accomplished this by using an operating system command to transfer files from diskettes he had prepared on his own computer to the demonstration computer's hard disk. This included a *table* containing knowledge about rep performance through the first three quarters.

Data Selection: An Example

"To choose an option," Jack explained, "all you need to do is press the key corresponding to its first letter. It doesn't matter which option happens to be highlighted when you do this. Alternatively, you can

PHOTO 4   Data Management menu

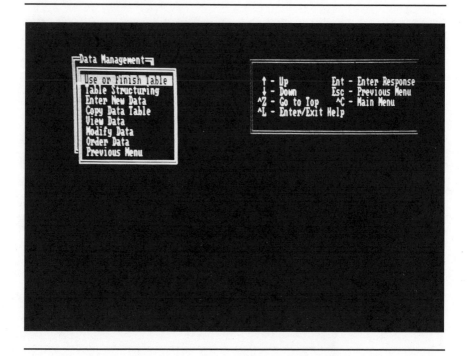

pick an option by using arrow keys to move the cursor so it highlights the desired option. Then press the Enter key to actually make the selection." Jack pressed the D key and, as expected, a new menu appeared as shown in Photo 4. Notice that this Data Management menu is positioned on top of the main menu, concealing all but its top and left borders. Also observe that the selected option is automatically displayed in the main menu's top border.

Jack pointed out that the eight options appearing in the Data Management menu were the same as those described in the help text for the main menu's Data Management option. He demonstrated that help text could be viewed for any of the options in this new menu by using the same ^L approach. Jack pressed the U key to select the Use or Finish Table option. This resulted in yet another menu as shown in Figure 3–2(a). He explained that the table holding performance data needed to be put in use before they could view its contents. Thus he picked the Use Table option by pressing the U key. As before, the selected option appears on the menu's top border, but in this case no new menu popped down on top of the others.

FIGURE 3–2   Putting a table in use

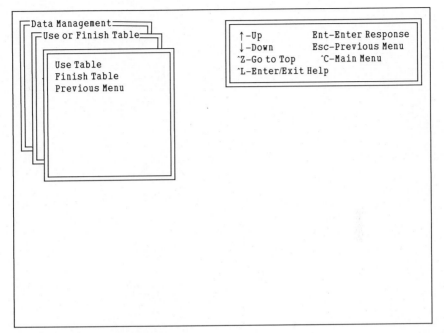

```
┌─Data Management════════╗
│ ┌─Use or Finish Table══╗ ║        ┌──────────────────────────────────────┐
│ │                      ║ ║        │ ↑–Up           Ent–Enter Response   │
│ │                      ║ ║        │ ↓–Down         Esc–Previous Menu    │
│ │   Use Table          │ ║        │ ^Z–Go to Top      ^C–Main Menu      │
│ │   Finish Table       │ ║        │ ^L–Enter/Exit Help                  │
│ │   Previous Menu      │ ║        └──────────────────────────────────────┘
│ │                      │ ║
│ │                      │ ║
│ │                      │ ║
│ │                      │ ║
│ └──────────────────────┘ ║
│                          ║
└──────────────────────────╝
```

(a) The Use or Finish Table menu

Instead, a menu of the knowledge system's tables that were available for use appeared in the lower right portion of the screen as shown in Figure 3–2(b). Explaining that PERF is the name he used for the table of performance data, Jack moved the cursor down to highlight the PERF option and pressed the Enter key. The PERF table was now in use and the screen took on the appearance of Figure 3–2(c). This is almost identical to Figure 3–2(a). The only difference is at the bottom of the screen where the request USE PERF appears.

Joy chimed in, "Whenever you've made enough menu selections to make it clear what you're requesting, the environment will automatically echo that request to the bottom of the screen. Think about what Jack has just done. From the point where we were looking at the main menu, he has pressed the five-key sequence D, U, U, ↓, and Enter, in order to request that the environment use the PERF table. As we'll see later this same request would be made with a different keystroke sequence if we were using a different interface style."

"Now that we have put the performance table in use, let's take Dan's suggestion and actually view some of the data it contains. To do this, I'll press P to get back to the previous menu, namely the Data

FIGURE 3–2   (continued)

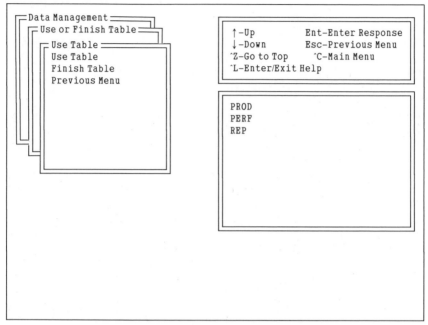

(b) A menu of tables available for use

Management menu that we'd seen earlier." The screen reverted to the appearance shown in Photo 4. Jack pressed the V key to select the View Data option. This resulted in the five-option View Data menu shown in Figure 3–3(a), indicating that there are several ways in which a table's data can be viewed. Because Dan was interested in seeing a listing of data from several of the table's performance *records* all at once, Jack pressed the L key. They were now confronted with the new menu shown in Figure 3–3(b). As always, help text can be examined for any of these to find out what will happen if it is picked.

Jack picked the Choose Table option first. Because there may be many tables simultaneously in use, he picked this option to indicate which of those tables he wanted to view. Of course, he chose the PERF table when asked for his choice and the screen once again returned to the appearance in Figure 3–3(b). Next he picked the Choose Fields option from this List menu. As shown in Photo 5, a new menu appeared in the lower right portion of the screen. This is a menu of *fields.*

"As you know," Jack reminded them, "there are several aspects of performance that we keep track of. On a quarter-by-quarter basis we need to know the actual sales and expected quota for a rep with

FIGURE 3–2 (concluded)

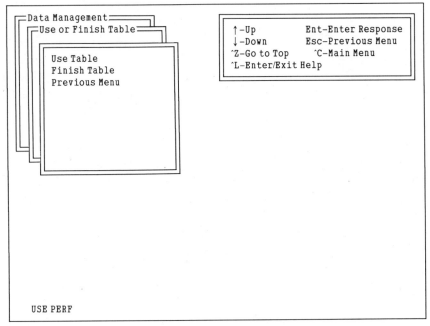

(c) Request generated by menu selections

respect to a product line. These basic categories of information are, by tradition, called fields. As you can see from the Field menu, there are several fields or categories of data in my performance table. Each is shown in capital letters, followed by a label describing what those letters stand for. Thus TID is the name of a field and indicates that a particular territory ID exists in each performance record. Similarly, each performance record also has the first name of that territory's rep, a product ID, quota figures for that product in that territory, and sales figures for that product in that territory. So, Dan, what kinds of performance data do you want to see?"

Dan replied, "Let's view the territory ID, rep's first name, product ID, first quarter sales, and first quarter quota. I guess that means you'll want to choose TID, FNAME, PID, S1, and Q1 from the menu."

"Right," said Jack. With the cursor highlighting the TID option, he pressed the Enter key. An asterisk appeared to the left of the field name. He selected the other four fields in a similar fashion, each being automatically marked with an asterisk. He mentioned that pressing the Enter key for a field already having an asterisk would cause it to be deselected. Jack also noted that the word "More" in the bottom

FIGURE 3–3   Menus for putting together a view request

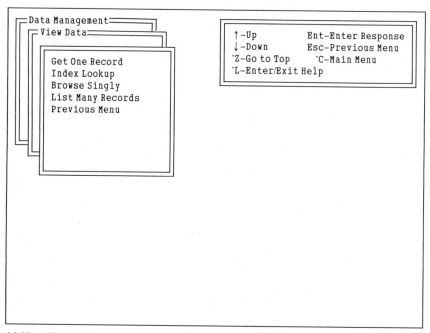

(a) View Data menu

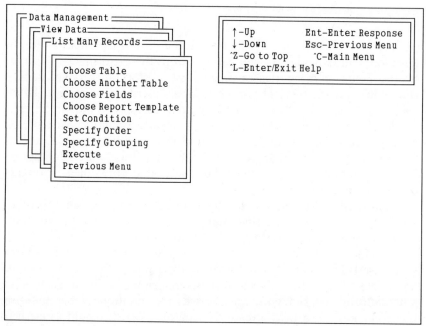

(b) List menu

FIGURE 3–3 (concluded)

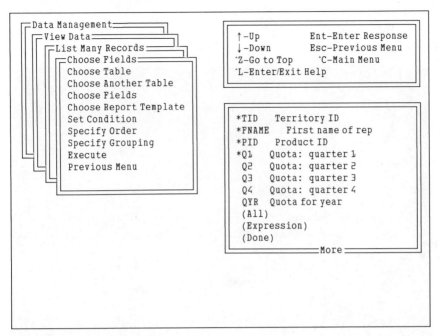

(c) Field selections

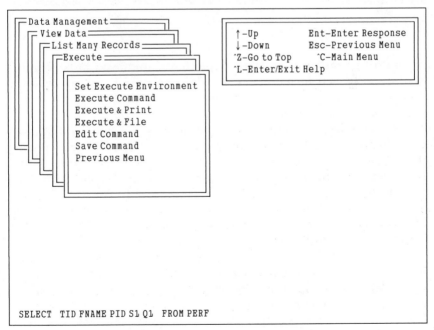

(d) Execute menu and request generated by menu selections

PHOTO 5   Choose Fields menu

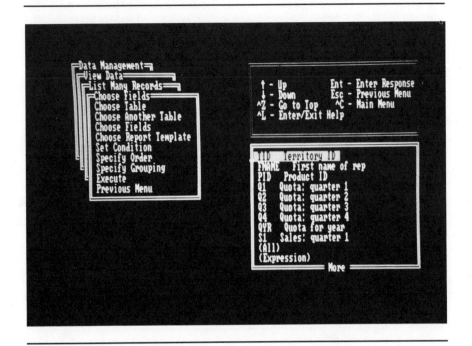

border of the menu meant there were too many fields to be simultaneously displayed in the menu. He demonstrated that they could be brought into view by pressing the down arrow while the cursor is already on the last visible option.

Having selected the five fields Dan desired, Jack moved the cursor to highlight the "(Done)" option as shown in Figure 3–3(c). Pressing the Enter key brought him back to the List menu of Figure 3–3(b). Being ready for the request to be executed, he pressed the E key. The Execute menu appeared as portrayed in Figure 3–3(d). The request generated by the foregoing menu choices was displayed along the bottom of the screen. It simply tells the environment what kinds of data to select from the PERF table for viewing purposes.

Notice that the Execute menu gives a user many interesting options for controlling exactly what will happen during execution. The first option lets you set up such things as a listing title, customized column headings, intercolumn output spacing, and so forth. The next three Execute options allow you to control where the output will be sent: to the screen, to a printer, or to a file on disk. You can even edit the generated SELECT command and save it as part of the session for subsequent execution. Keeping his example simple, Jack picked the Execute Command option. The screen quickly filled with the results shown in Figure 3–4(a). By pressing the space bar, the screen filled with the rest of the results including summary statistics (see Figure 3–4(b)). The asterisks for statistical variance indicate values that are too large to be displayed in the available space.

After pausing briefly for a discussion of the displayed results, Jack pressed the space bar. The Execute menu and generated request (Figure 3–3(d)) reappeared on the screen. At this point Jack could have reexecuted the generated command in some other fashion if desired. Instead, he pressed the P key to return to the List menu (Figure 3–3(b)), because Dan asked if he could see a shorter list showing only those cases where sales exceeded the quota. Jack moved the cursor to highlight the Set Condition option in this menu. Picking that option, he proceeded to demonstrate how Dan's condition could be specified to augment the original request by making yet other menu selections (from menus not illustrated here). This eventually yielded a screen identical to Figure 3–3(d), except that

FIGURE 3–4   Results of executing the viewing request

TID	FNAME	PID	S1	Q1
0	Kim	ref	7024	6040
0	Kim	bus	6854	7320
0	Kim	spo	6240	5400
1	Kris	rom	10050	9003
1	Kris	psy	7540	8090
1	Kris	bio	7604	7400
2	Kevin	pho	7604	7400
2	Kevin	sfi	10390	9439
2	Kevin	spo	7773	6509
2	Kevin	bus	4321	3009
2	Kevin	ref	4222	3214
3	Tina	psy	4222	3214
3	Tina	bus	5944	6903
3	Tina	com	5944	5388
3	Tina	rom	4590	5000
4	Toby	rom	5009	4982
4	Toby	psy	2607	5000
4	Toby	bus	5003	4842
5	Kerry	psy	5003	4842
5	Kerry	ref	5590	6030
5	Kerry	pho	12222	10700
6	Karen	bus	12222	10700

(a) First screenful of results

FIGURE 3–4   (concluded)

```
TID    FNAME    PID    S1        Q1

 6     Karen    rom     6090      6040
 6     Karen    com    13121     12090
 7     Kathy    pho     7884      8553
 7     Kathy    ref     5032      4679
 7     Kathy    sfi     4360      4339
 8     Jackie   bio     4360      4339
 8     Jackie   ref     4996      5004
 8     Jackie   spo     5345      5004
 9     Carol    rom     5345      5004
 9     Carol    bus     4005      3997
 9     Carol    com     8488      6903
                       217004    206377    Sum
                         6576      6254    Ave
                       ******    ******    Var
                         2580      2261    Sdv
 0     Carol    bio     2607      3009    Min
 9     Toby     spo    13121     12090    Max

Number of Observations: 33



Please press space bar to continue_
```

(b) Second screenful of results

SELECT TID FNAME PID S1 Q1 FROM PERF FOR Q1<S1

now appeared as the generated request. Jack explained that further
conditions could be added in the same way, different fields could be
selected, a different ordering of the output rows could be chosen, and
so forth.

Menu Pros and Cons

"Enough of menus," Jack exclaimed. "I think you now have a reasonable
understanding of this interface style. No matter what you want to do
through a menu-guided interface, the way in which you accomplish it
is always essentially the same. Once we cover the various knowledge
management techniques in the days ahead, you'll be able to exercise
any of them through this kind of interface. The most important point, "
he paused for added emphasis, "is that you do not have to understand
all the options before you can begin using some of them."

Thoughtfully, Brad remarked, "You've given us a good taste of
what it means to interface with software via menus. It all seems quite

straightforward to me. At any moment, all the available options are shown and it doesn't seem to take many keystrokes to accomplish a task. As Joy said, the keystrokes that are used to generate a request can be regarded as an expression in the menu language. However, you really don't have to think of what you're doing in terms of computer language expressions. Instead, everything is so visual, so there's really no language to learn or remember. Tell me, are there any disadvantages to this interface style?"

Jack thought for a moment. "I suppose the biggest disadvantage is that menus are relatively rigid and inflexible. Unlike some other interface styles, they don't give you a way to directly say what you want and if it's not on the menu you can't ask for it. That's not bad for a beginner or casual user. But it wasn't long before I found that menus often seemed to get in the way, so I opted for more direct interface styles where I could just say what I wanted. It's like being a regular at a restaurant where you are well acquainted with what you can order. It would seem constraining if you always were forced to look at menus and point out your selections instead of merely saying what you want, and this includes the ability to ask for things that may not be standard fare on the menu."

Stan added, "The menu-guided interface you showed us seems to have far more options than what I'm accustomed to and there are quite a few more levels of submenus."

"That points out another possible drawback of menus," remarked Joy. "If a piece of software has extensive capabilities, then the number of options that need to be presented to a user can naturally become quite large. Sometimes novice users tend to confuse extensiveness with complexity and feel overwhelmed if there are lots of options. But just because there are lots of options doesn't necessarily mean that something is complex to use. The degree of complexity depends on how well organized the flow of menus is. Of course, the less a piece of software can do, the smaller the number of options you'll see in its menu interface.

"As a practical matter, a tool with very extensive capabilities usually does not support the same degree of processing functionality in its menu-guided interface as it does in its command language interface. Even though the menu interface you've seen supports quite a few options, I can do much more with the environment's command language interface. The menu interface doesn't allow me to get at the full range of knowledge-processing power and flexibility."

Jack nodded in agreement. "On the positive side, keep in mind that menu interfaces are good at guiding a user's thought processes. When a user is unsure about how to think about some knowledge management problem, menus can impose a structure on the user. Re-

FIGURE 3–5   Exit menu

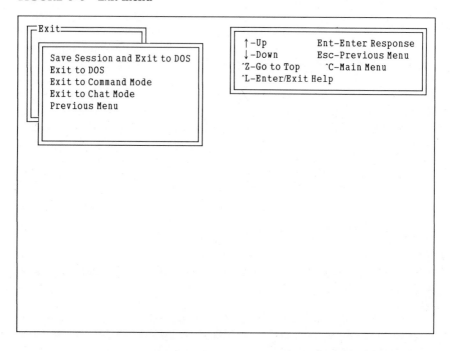

member how we addressed Dan's request. The menus forced us to make certain choices at certain stages in a reasonable way. In summary, menus are a good interface in cases where you want or need guidance and where extensive functionality or freedom are unnecessary."

Having concluded his demonstration of the menu-guided interface style, Jack selected Previous Menu options until he was back to the main menu shown in Photo 2. Once there, he pressed the E key to choose its Exit option. As depicted in Figure 3–5, the resultant Exit menu gave several choices for exiting from the menu interface. Jack picked the Exit to DOS option, causing the PC-DOS prompt of C> to appear.

NATURAL LANGUAGE INTERFACE

Whereas a menu-guided interface imposes a highly structured regimen on the way in which you make requests, a natural language interface tends to minimize the structure. With this kind of an interface, the environment does not tell you what moves you can make each step of the way. It simply waits for you to make a request using your everyday conversational mode of expression. What you would normally say to another person, you now just type in via the keyboard. This interface style aims to be free flowing and conversational. The main idea is that the environment follows your train of thought rather than guiding you to think along certain lines [1].

In a short preamble to Jack's demonstration, Joy pointed out that the topic of natural language interfaces is a major branch in the field of artificial intelligence. Researchers in that field are still working at methods to improve the computer's ability to comprehend our natural language utterances. Nevertheless, fairly potent natural language interfaces are now in everyday use in the business world [6].

Joy explained that certain things should be true of an interface in order for it to be considered a natural language interface. A true natural language interface can understand requests in a user's own natural language, which may not consist wholly of grammatically correct English statements. It can accept sentence fragments and ungrammatical expressions, just as a human listener can. It is not restricted to plain English. A natural language interface is conversational, which implies that it can understand new requests in the context of earlier requests. If it does not comprehend some term used in a request, then it will ask the user to define what the term means. From that point onward, it will know what that term means in later requests.

Chatting

Because Jack no longer wanted to use the menu-guided interface, he entered the knowledge management environment in a slightly different way than he had done earlier. He typed

KMAN –G

in response to the operating system prompt [4]. The -G is an indication that the menu-guided interface would not appear on gaining entry to the environment. As execution of KnowledgeMan began, Jack entered the same user name and password as before. Photo 1 shows what the group saw as Jack completed typing the password. When he pressed the Enter key, a small underscore appeared as shown in Figure 3–6. It is called the *command prompt*. Though not visible in the figure, a small blinking light appeared immediately following the underscore.

Jack explained, "Whenever you see this underscore symbol and the blinking light next to it, KnowledgeMan is ready to accept a direct command from you." He paused with a thoughtful look, then smiling he abruptly said, "Close your eyes." Instead, they responded with searching looks. "I'm going to type in a preparatory command that

FIGURE 3–6   The command prompt

```
MDBS KnowledgeMan Ver 2.01.00c
The Universal Knowledge Management System
(C) Copyright 1983, 1986, Micro Data Base Systems, Inc.
Lafayette, IN 47902


User Name: knowledgemaster
Password :

  —
```

will make our natural language excursion a bit more comfortable, but for the time being I don't want you to worry about what this command means. You'll see later."

Jack wanted to alter the settings of a couple of *environment controls,* to facilitate the group's viewing of outputs from the upcoming natural language requests. He typed

`E.PAUS=TRUE;E.DECI=0`

and pressed the Enter key. As they would learn later (Chapter 4) there are many environment controls that can be altered to tailor the environment's behavior to meet specific processing desires. Here, Jack was setting two controls. The first would cause console screen output to pause each time the screen became full and the second would cause zero decimal digits to be displayed for numeric data. He did not have to make these changes before making natural language requests, but they would make the viewing of results from those requests more convenient.

Again confronted by the command prompt, Jack announced, "Open your eyes. The command I'm going to use now is CHAT. We'll take a

FIGURE 3–7   Command to begin natural language interaction

```
MDBS KnowledgeMan Ver 2.01.00c
The Universal Knowledge Management System
(C) Copyright 1983, 1986, Micro Data Base Systems, Inc.
Lafayette, IN 47902


User Name: knowledgemaster
Password :

_E.PAUS=TRUE;E.DECI=0
_CHAT "A:MYWORD.DIC"
```

look at other commands later. The CHAT command causes the environment to begin accepting conversational natural language requests." Jack proceeded to type

```
CHAT "A:MYWORD.DIC"
```

and these characters appeared immediately following the command prompt (see Figure 3–7).

"All I've done here is tell KnowledgeMan that I want to chat in my own conversational style. Because I expect that we'll be teaching KnowledgeMan some new terms and phrases as we go along, I've specified the location and name of a file that will hold this new linguistic knowledge. The A: means that the file will physically reside on the diskette in drive A. The extension of DIC indicates that MYWORD will be used as a *dictionary* for holding the terms and phrases we define." Jack went on to explain that a user could construct lots of different dictionaries and designate any one of them for use in a given chat. These dictionaries provide a way of representing linguistic knowledge in the environment's knowledge system.

PHOTO 6   Environment asking for a natural language request

Data Selection Examples

Having typed in and described the CHAT command, Jack pressed the Enter key. The screen immediately took on the appearance portrayed in Photo 6. Jack continued, "Whenever the screen looks like this, you can type in a natural language request. Just for practice, let's use the same table of performance data that we used earlier with the menu interface. Instead of stepping through menus to see a list of tables and then choosing PERF, I simply type in what I want." He proceeded to type

```
use perf
```

and pressed the Enter key. The resultant screen appearance is shown in Figure 3–8. At this point the PERF table was now in use. Jack pressed the space bar causing the environment to ask for another request (i.e., Photo 6 reappeared).

"Question," said a voice from the back of the room. "What does

FIGURE 3–8   Requesting that the PERF table be used

```
┌─────────────────────────────────────────────────────────────────────┐
│ ┌──────────────────────Kman Natural Language──────────────────────┐ │
│ └─────────────────────────────────────────────────────────────────┘ │
│  Your request? use perf                                              │
│                                                                      │
│                                                                      │
│                                                                      │
│                                                                      │
│                                                                      │
│                                                                      │
│                                                                      │
│                                   i                                  │
│                                                                      │
│                                                                      │
│  Please press space bar to continue                                 │
│                                                                      │
└─────────────────────────────────────────────────────────────────────┘
```

the word 'Kman' at the top of the screen mean? Does it have something to do with the Cayman Islands, maybe a special dialect that we need to learn?"

"As far as I know," responded Jack, "it doesn't really mean anything. I'd just ignore it. The important thing at the top of the screen is the phrase 'Natural Language.' Whenever you see it, you know that the environment's natural language interface is being used. It's not oriented toward any particular dialect." Pausing, he peered to the back and said, "I'll bet it could even understand your natural language."

"Why don't we give each of you a chance to use your own natural language in making a request about the performance figures?" offered Joy. Jack nodded with a smile. "As you think about what you might like to request, keep in mind what the environment knows about performance figures. Because the PERF table is now in use, it knows that there are certain categories of data called PID, TID, FNAME, Q1, S1, Q2, S2, and so forth. It also knows about the values of PID, TID, FNAME and all the rest that exist in the table." In other words, the names of fields and the data contents of tables can be regarded not only as descriptive knowledge, but can also be used as linguistic knowledge.

"Just to give you the idea," Jack volunteered, "let's ask for the same data that we had viewed earlier by making menu selections. As before, I want the environment to show me TID, FNAME, PID, S1, and Q1 data. But now I can just say what I want instead of stepping through layers of menus." Jack proceeded to type

```
show me the tid,fname,pid,s1 and q1
```

as shown in Figure 3–9(a). When he pressed the Enter key, the screen filled just as it had under menu guidance (Figure 3–9(b)). After pausing to view the data Jack pressed the space bar to see the rest of it (Figure 3–9(c)). He noted that statistics were not displayed because the request had not asked for them.

Pressing the space bar, he brought Photo 6 back into view and waited for someone else to make a request. Tracey was first to react, "I'd like to know which of those have S1 below Q1." Jack obliged by typing in

```
which of those have S1 below Q1?
```

FIGURE 3–9(a)   Natural language request

```
┌─────────────────────────────────────────────────────────────┐
│  ┌──────────────────── Kman Natural Language ─────────────┐  │
│  └───────────────────────────────────────────────────────────┘  │
│   Your request? show me the tid,fname,pid,s1 and q1            │
│                                                               │
│                                                               │
│                                                               │
│                                                               │
│                                                               │
│                                                               │
│                                                               │
│                                                               │
│                                                               │
│                                                               │
│                                                               │
└─────────────────────────────────────────────────────────────┘
```

FIGURE 3–9(b) First screenful of results

TID	FNAME	PID	S1	Q1
0	Kim	ref	7024	6040
0	Kim	bus	6854	7320
0	Kim	spo	6240	5400
1	Kris	rom	10050	9003
1	Kris	psy	7540	8090
1	Kris	bio	7604	7400
2	Kevin	pho	7604	7400
2	Kevin	sfi	10390	9439
2	Kevin	spo	7773	6509
2	Kevin	bus	4321	3009
2	Kevin	ref	4222	3214
3	Tina	psy	4222	3214
3	Tina	bus	5944	6903
3	Tina	com	5944	5388
3	Tina	rom	4590	5000
4	Toby	rom	5009	4982
4	Toby	psy	2607	5000
4	Toby	bus	5003	4842
5	Kerry	psy	5003	4842
5	Kerry	ref	5590	6030
5	Kerry	pho	12222	10700
6	Karen	bus	12222	10700

FIGURE 3–9(c) Second screenful of results

TID	FNAME	PID	S1	Q1
6	Karen	rom	6090	6040
6	Karen	com	13121	12090
7	Kathy	pho	7884	8553
7	Kathy	ref	5032	4679
7	Kathy	sfi	4360	4339
8	Jackie	bio	4360	4339
8	Jackie	spo	5345	5004
9	Carol	rom	5345	5004
9	Carol	bus	4005	3997
9	Carol	com	8488	6903

Please press space bar to continue

and pressing the Enter key. Figure 3–10(a) shows those cases where first quarter sales were below corresponding quotas. This is a subset of the result produced for the prior request.

"Notice what has just happened," Joy reminded them. "You've made a request that is based on the result of the prior request. It illustrates an essential aspect of natural language processing. Like a conversation between two people, new requests can be understood in the light of former requests."

"Do you mean that I could now say something like 'let me see their S3 and Q3 too'?" asked Stan.

"Let's find out," said Jack as he typed in

```
let me see their S3 and Q3 too
```

as the new request. Upon pressing the Enter key they saw (Figure 3–10(b)) that once again the request was correctly understood in the context of former requests. To further drive home Joy's point, Jack typed

```
do any of these have S3 less than Q3?
```

FIGURE 3–10   Requests comprehended with respect to prior requests

TID	FNAME	PID	S1	Q1
0	Kim	bus	6854	7320
1	Kris	psy	7540	8090
3	Tina	bus	5944	6903
3	Tina	rom	4590	5000
4	Toby	psy	2607	5000
5	Kerry	ref	5590	6030
7	Kathy	pho	7884	8553
8	Jackie	ref	4996	5004

Please press space bar to continue

(a) Which of those have S1 below Q1?

FIGURE 3–10 (concluded)

S3	Q3	TID	FNAME	PID	S1	Q1
6908	6400	0	Kim	bus	6854	7320
8059	7765	1	Kris	psy	7540	8090
8004	8990	3	Tina	bus	5944	6903
5032	4213	3	Tina	rom	4590	5000
7050	6007	4	Toby	psy	2607	5000
6320	3001	5	Kerry	ref	5590	6030
6236	5678	7	Kathy	pho	7884	8553
3600	3998	8	Jackie	ref	4996	5004

Please press space bar to continue

(b) Let me see their S3 and Q3 too

S3	Q3	TID	FNAME	PID	S1	Q1
8004	8990	3	Tina	bus	5944	6903
3600	3998	8	Jackie	ref	4996	5004

Please press space bar to continue

(c) Do any of these have S3 less than Q3?

as the next request. As depicted in Figure 3–10(c), they could now see that there were two cases where a rep had failed to meet a product line's quota in both the first and third quarters.

New Words

Brad was frowning, "I get the idea of being able to base new requests on earlier requests to zero in on what I want to see, but there's something that troubles me. When I talk to a person I wouldn't naturally use terms like PID or Q1. Instead, I'd say product or quarter one quota. If this really follows my natural language, I shouldn't have to use those abbreviations."

"Well," smiled Jack, "let's see if it can understand you. What do you want to say?" Beginning from the usual starting point (Photo 6), Jack typed

```
give me the territory and product where sales is above 10000
```

verbatim as Brad spoke. Upon pressing the Enter key, the environment complained that "territory" was an unrecognized word. As shown in Photo 7 a small menu of choices was presented in the center of the display. Jack picked the Permanent Definition option because he wanted to include the meaning of "territory" as a permanent part of the MY-WORD dictionary.

A prompt appeared, asking for the new permanent definition of territory. Jack typed

```
TID
```

yielding the screen shown in Figure 3–11(a). By pressing the Enter key, territory became a part of the MYWORD dictionary. "As long as you are chatting with this dictionary lurking behind the scenes, you'll never again be asked for the meaning of 'territory.' As you can see, 'product' is also detected as an unrecognized word," Jack proceeded to handle it in exactly the same way (Figure 3–11(b)).

Only the word "sales" remained unrecognized. When the Unrecognized Word menu again appeared, Jack picked the Temporary Correction option, because it was likely that sales might mean something else in a later request. Brad explained that for the time being he was referring to sales in any of the first three quarters, so Jack typed in

```
S1,S2,S3
```

PHOTO 7   Unrecognized Word menu

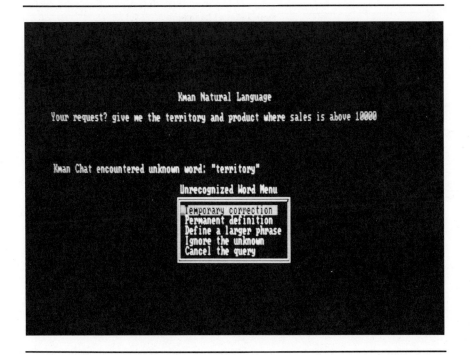

as shown in Figure 3–11(c). Pressing the Enter key caused the cases in Figure 3–12 to be displayed. Each had at least one sales figure in excess of 10,000. Jack pressed the space bar to return to Photo 6.

To demonstrate that the two permanent definitions were indeed known to the environment, Jack typed

```
show me the territory,fname,product,S1 and Q1
```

immediately yielding the results shown in Figures 3–9(b) and (c) without any interaction concerning unrecognized words. Brad and the others were convinced that, like a person, the environment could learn and use new terms. "Now I understand," he claimed, "and I see why, once you get the knack of it, you tend to use the abbreviated field names. They can save a lot of typing."

FIGURE 3–11   Defining unrecognized words

```
┌──────────────────────────────────────────────────────────────┐
│ ┌──────────────────── Kman Natural Language ────────────────┐ │
│ └                                                            ┘ │
│                                                                │
│ Your request? give me the territory and product where sales is above 10000│
│                                                                │
│                                                                │
│ Kman Chat encountered unknown word: "territory"                │
│                                                                │
│                     Unrecognized Word Menu                     │
│                   ┌──────────────────────────┐                 │
│                   │ Temporary correction     │                 │
│                   │ Permanent definition     │                 │
│                   │ Define a larger phrase    │                 │
│                   │ Ignore the unknown       │                 │
│                   │ Cancel the query         │                 │
│                   └──────────────────────────┘                 │
│                                                                │
│ Enter new permanent definition: TID                            │
│                                                                │
│                                                                │
│                                                                │
│                                                                │
└──────────────────────────────────────────────────────────────┘
```

(a) Letting territory be synonomous with TID

A Statistics Example

It was Debbie's turn to make a request. "I'd like something beyond just the presentation of stored data. How about some computations? For instance, can it show me the quota averages for romance?" Continuing again with Photo 6, Jack typed

```
show me the quota averages for romance
```

and pressed the Enter key. The environment encountered two unknown words: quota and romance. As shown in Figure 3–13(a), he gave quota a temporary meaning (i.e., "correction") of Q1, Q2, Q3, Q4. He then gave romance a permanent definition of rom (Figure 3–13(b)), which is the product ID already associated with the romance product line. Notice in Figure 3–13(c) that the response to the request shows the averages for each of the quarterly romance quotas.

"Whoops," Debbie remarked, "this doesn't tell me which rep goes with which row of quota figures. Ask what their first names are."

FIGURE 3–11 (concluded)

```
┌─────────────────────────────────────────────────────────────────────┐
│  ┌──────────────────────── Kman Natural Language ──────────────────┐ │
│  └──────────────────────────                    ─────────────────────┘
│                                                                       │
│  Your request? give me the territory and product where sales is above 10000
│                                                                       │
│                                                                       │
│  Kman Chat encountered unknown word: "product"                        │
│                                                                       │
│                          Unrecognized Word Menu                       │
│                          ┌──────────────────────┐                     │
│                          │ Temporary correction │                     │
│                          │ Permanent definition │                     │
│                          │ Define a larger phrase│                    │
│                          │ Ignore the unknown   │                     │
│                          │ Cancel the query     │                     │
│                          └──────────────────────┘                     │
│                                                                       │
│  Enter new permanent definition: PID                                  │
│                                                                       │
│                                                                       │
│                                                                       │
│                                                                       │
└───────────────────────────────────────────────────────────────────────┘
```

(b) Letting product mean PID

```
┌─────────────────────────────────────────────────────────────────────┐
│  ┌──────────────────────── Kman Natural Language ──────────────────┐ │
│  └──────────────────────────                    ─────────────────────┘
│                                                                       │
│  Your request? give me the territory and product where sales is above 10000
│                                                                       │
│                                                                       │
│  Kman Chat encountered unknown word: "sales"                          │
│                                                                       │
│                          Unrecognized Word Menu                       │
│                          ┌──────────────────────┐                     │
│                          │ Temporary correction │                     │
│                          │ Permanent definition │                     │
│                          │ Define a larger phrase│                    │
│                          │ Ignore the unknown   │                     │
│                          │ Cancel the query     │                     │
│                          └──────────────────────┘                     │
│                                                                       │
│  Enter correction: S1,S2,S3                                           │
│                                                                       │
│                                                                       │
│                                                                       │
│                                                                       │
└───────────────────────────────────────────────────────────────────────┘
```

(c) Temporary definition of sales to mean S1, S2, S3

FIGURE 3–12   Territory and product for S1, S2, or S3 over 10,000

TID	PID	S1	S2	S3
1	rom	10050	12453	8023
2	sfi	10390	8639	8765
3	bus	5944	10359	8004
5	pho	12222	11980	8332
6	bus	12222	11980	8332
6	com	13121	11590	10075

Please press space bar to continue

Continuing again from Photo 6, Jack typed

whta are their fnames?

and pressed the Enter key before he noticed that he had mistyped the first word. The environment immediately responded with the question

By "whta" do you mean "what"? <yes>

to which Jack responded affirmatively by pressing the Enter key. As shown in Figure 3–14, it is now clear which reps have which romance quotas.

A Graphics Example

Looking at the results, Dan asked, "Viewing numbers may be OK much of the time. But is there some way to see their proportions more visually, in a graph for instance? Can it give me a pie graph based on first quarter quotas labeled with the first name of reps and showing the percentage of each slice in the pie?" Jack typed in the new request

FIGURE 3–13 Getting averages

```
┌─────────────────────────────────────────────────────────┐
│ ┌──────────────── Kman Natural Language ───────────────┐ │
│ └──────────────────────────────────────────────────────┘ │
│                                                           │
│  Your request? show me the quota averages for romance     │
│                                                           │
│                                                           │
│  Kman Chat encountered unknown word: "quota"              │
│                                                           │
│                          Unrecognized Word Menu           │
│                       ┌─────────────────────────┐         │
│                       │ Temporary correction    │         │
│                       │ Permanent definition    │         │
│                       │ Define a larger phrase   │         │
│                       │ Ignore the unknown       │         │
│                       │ Cancel the query         │         │
│                       └─────────────────────────┘         │
│                                                           │
│  Enter correction: Q1,Q2,Q3,Q4                            │
│                                                           │
│                                                           │
└─────────────────────────────────────────────────────────┘
```

(a) Temporary quota definition

```
┌─────────────────────────────────────────────────────────┐
│ ┌──────────────── Kman Natural Language ───────────────┐ │
│ └──────────────────────────────────────────────────────┘ │
│                                                           │
│  Your request? show me the quota averages for romance     │
│                                                           │
│                                                           │
│  Kman Chat encountered unknown word: "romance"            │
│                                                           │
│                          Unrecognized Word Menu           │
│                       ┌─────────────────────────┐         │
│                       │ Temporary correction    │         │
│                       │ Permanent definition    │         │
│                       │ Define a larger phrase   │         │
│                       │ Ignore the unknown       │         │
│                       │ Cancel the query         │         │
│                       └─────────────────────────┘         │
│                                                           │
│  Enter new permanent definition: rom                      │
│                                                           │
│                                                           │
└─────────────────────────────────────────────────────────┘
```

(b) Permanent romance definition

FIGURE 3–13   (concluded)

Q1	Q2	Q3	Q4	PID	
9003	10229	8340	11340	rom	
5000	4678	4213	3998	rom	
4982	4678	8744	7432	rom	
6040	5020	5555	6666	rom	
5004	4468	5830	7223	rom	
6006	5815	6536	7332		Ave

Please press space bar to continue

(c) Average romance quotas

show the fnames and q1 in pie graph for romance with percentages

and paused to let everyone look at it (Figure 3–15). Though it was not grammatically the prettiest of requests, Dan indicated it was what he had in mind. When Jack pressed the Enter key to finalize the request, a pie graph appeared as shown in Photo 8. By pressing the space bar the familiar sight of Photo 6 reappeared.

Natural Language Pros and Cons

Jack sensed that the managers were intrigued by this interface style. But now that they were fairly conversant in its traits, it was about time to examine another interface style. Jack summarized, "As you've seen, with a natural language interface there is no new language to learn or remember. You just use your own natural language. If the environment doesn't comprehend a term you use it tells you so and is willing to learn its meaning from you. There is considerable flexibility of expression, allowing the same need to be expressed in many different

FIGURE 3–14 Incorporating first names

FNAME	Q1	Q2	Q3	Q4	PID
Kris	9003	10229	8340	11340	rom
Tina	5000	4678	4213	3998	rom
Toby	4982	4678	8744	7432	rom
Karen	6040	5020	5555	6666	rom
Carol	5004	4468	5830	7223	rom
	6006	5815	6536	7332	

Ave

Please press space bar to continue

FIGURE 3–15 Requesting a percentage pie graph

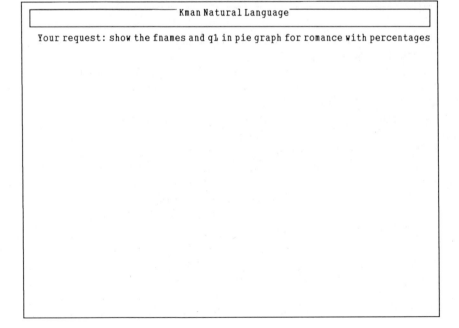

Kman Natural Language

Your request: show the fnames and q1 in pie graph for romance with percentages

PHOTO 8   Pie graph showing first quarter quotas

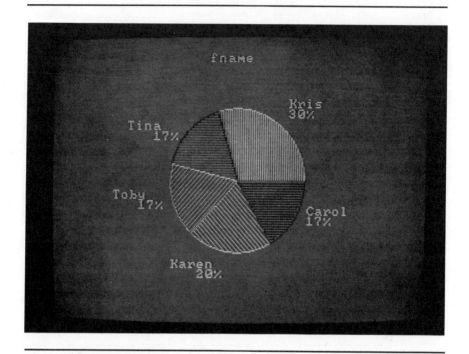

ways. You can be terse and use many abbreviations or you can be wordy if you like."

"Let me add a few words of caution," Joy added somewhat mysteriously. "Using a natural language interface can become almost too enjoyable. It's easy to get hooked as you explore the limits of its ability to understand you. Obviously, it can't understand to the same degree as a person. You can certainly make requests that today's natural language interfaces don't handle. But it's an adventure to see how far they can go in approaching the ideal of understanding as well as a person. Even after you've become a seasoned user of a good natural language interface, you'll still find yourself amazed from time to time by what it can understand. On the other hand there is also the possibility of misunderstanding, just as there is between two people."

Her blue eyes drifted in Jack's direction as she continued, "For instance, suppose I made the request: 'give me romance.' It might be interpreted meaning sales for the romance product line, or quotas for the romance product line, or maybe something else. The listener, be it human or machine, will interpret the request in one way and take actions based on that interpretation. If that interpretation didn't match my own and I discovered that fact, I'd be disappointed. Even worse, if they didn't match and I didn't discover it, the resultant actions may be unwittingly inadequate for my needs. This could lead to erroneous responses or decisions on my part. So natural language interfaces can be great, especially for first-time or casual computer users, but it's worth remembering that they do have limitations."

COMMAND LANGUAGE INTERFACE

A third kind of interface style available in the knowledge management environment is a command language. In terms of what it allows a knowledge worker to accomplish, it is by far the most versatile and flexible interface. But unlike the menu and natural language interfaces, it requires you to learn a "new" language. This language consists of a collection of commands. Each command has a fixed syntactic structure and will cause a particular processing action to occur [4]. Ideally, a command's syntactic structure should be Englishlike in appearance and should convey some notion of the processing action that will occur when a user enters that command. These features facilitate the user's learning and remembering of commands.

Menu-Generated Commands

"Actually," Jack explained, "you've already seen several examples of commands. Remember our practice with the menu interface. When I had made enough menu choices for the environment to discern what I wanted, it displayed a generated request at the bottom of the screen. Each of those generated requests was actually a valid command in the environment's command language." These included commands such as

`USE PERF`   (Figure 3–2(c))

and

`SELECT TID FNAME PID S1 Q1 FROM PERF`   (Figure 3–3(d))

"As an alternative to making menu selections," he continued, "I could directly enter any such command to achieve exactly the same effect as the corresponding menu choices. Any command that can be produced by the menu interface can be directly executed by typing it in through the command interface. The only prerequisite is that you know how to correctly state the desired command."

"It seems to me," commented Debbie, "that the menu interface's ability to display generated commands could be a good way to become acquainted with the command language. Can the natural language interface help familiarize us with the command language in a similar way?"

Natural Language-Generated Commands

"It sure can," replied Jack. "Let me show you." The screen looked like Photo 6 at this point. He typed in the one-word request

```
preview
```

and pressed the Enter key. The screen reverted to its usual expectant appearance (i.e., Photo 6). From this point onward, the natural language interface would display the command language equivalent for each natural language request before actually carrying out the requested actions. As an example, Jack typed the natural language request

```
who has romance?
```

and pressed the Enter key. The screen immediately assumed the appearance portrayed in Figure 3–16(a).

Notice the command generated by Jack's three-word natural language request

```
SELECT fname pid FROM perf WHERE pid EQ "rom"
```

This command tells the environment to select FNAME and PID data from the PERF table for every record having "rom" as the product ID. It is one of over a hundred distinct kinds of commands available in this environment. The natural language interface is versatile enough to generate over a dozen of these kinds of commands in response to natural language requests.

"What you're seeing here," explained Joy, "is the result of behind the scenes interpretation of a natural language request. Whenever a request is made, the natural language interface works at translating it into the environment's command language, just as the menu interface translates keystrokes involved in menu selections into a command statement. In either case it is the generated command that is executed in order to produce the result displayed on the screen."

Jack pressed the space bar to execute the generated command. Figure

FIGURE 3–16 Commands generated by natural language request

```
┌─────────────────────────── Kman Natural Language ───────────────────────────┐
│ ┌──────────────────────────────────────────────────────────────────────┐    │
│ └──────────────────────────────────────────────────────────────────────┘    │
│                                                                              │
│   Your request? who has romance?                                             │
│                                                                              │
│                                                                              │
│   Generated Command: LET E.STAT = FALSE                                      │
│                      SELECT fname pid FROM perf WHERE pid EQ "rom"           │
│                                                                              │
│                                                                              │
│                                                                              │
│                                                                              │
│                                                                              │
│                                                                              │
│                                                                              │
│                                                                              │
│                                                                              │
│                                                                              │
│                                                                              │
│   Please press space bar to continue                                         │
└──────────────────────────────────────────────────────────────────────────────┘
```

(a) Asking for reps with data for the romance product line

```
┌──────────────────────────────────────────────────────────────────────────────┐
│   FNAME    PID                                                                 │
│                                                                                │
│   Kris     rom                                                                 │
│   Tina     rom                                                                 │
│   Toby     rom                                                                 │
│   Karen    rom                                                                 │
│   Carol    rom                                                                 │
│                                                                                │
│                                                                                │
│                                                                                │
│                                                                                │
│                                                                                │
│                                                                                │
│                                                                                │
│                                                                                │
│                                                                                │
│   Please press space bar to continue                                           │
└──────────────────────────────────────────────────────────────────────────────┘
```

(b) Reps for which there are data about romance

FIGURE 3–16 (concluded)

```
┌──────────────────────────────────────────────────────────────────┐
│┌───────────────────── Kman Natural Language ─────────────────────┐│
│└──────────────────────────────────────────────────────────────────┘│
│                                                                    │
│  Your request? please show me their Q1, Q2 and Q3 data too         │
│                                                                    │
│                                                                    │
│  Generated Command: SELECT q1 q2 q3 fname pid FROM perf WHERE pid EQ "rom" │
│                                                                    │
│                                                                    │
│                                                                    │
│                                                                    │
│                                                                    │
│                                                                    │
│                                                                    │
│                                                                    │
│                                                                    │
│                                                                    │
│                                                                    │
│                                                                    │
└──────────────────────────────────────────────────────────────────┘
```

(c) Asking for more detailed data

```
┌──────────────────────────────────────────────────────────────────┐
│  Q1      Q2      Q3      FNAME    PID                               │
│                                                                    │
│  9003    10229   8340    Kris     rom                              │
│  5000    4678    4213    Tina     rom                              │
│  4982    4678    8744    Toby     rom                              │
│  6040    5020    5555    Karen    rom                              │
│  5004    4468    5830    Carol    rom                              │
│                                                                    │
│                                                                    │
│                                                                    │
│                                                                    │
│                                                                    │
│                                                                    │
│                                                                    │
│  Please press space bar to continue                                │
└──────────────────────────────────────────────────────────────────┘
```

(d) Display of the SELECT command results

3–16(b) shows the result. "Let's see some more details for these," he said. Pressing the space bar again to return to the Photo 6 appearance Jack typed

```
please show me their Q1, Q2 and Q3 data too
```

and pressed the Enter key. Figure 3–16(c) shows the generated command. Notice that it is the same SELECT command seen before, except data for the Q1, Q2, and Q3 fields are now being selected too. Pressing the space bar, Jack allowed the environment to go ahead and process this SELECT command, yielding the screen shown in Figure 3–16(d).

After viewing the results, he pressed the space bar to again revert to Photo 6. "If you use this preview feature much, you'll see situations where a single natural language request (e.g., to get a graph) can generate an entire sequence of commands. You'll also discover that many different natural language requests can generate exactly the same command. This is just reflective of the fact that there may be many ways to say the same thing. As you become increasingly familiar with the command language, the preview facility can be helpful in checking that your natural language requests are interpreted in the ways you expect.

"Let's quit chatting and go on to take a look at how you would enter a command directly, without having it generated by the menu-guided or natural language interfaces." With that, Jack simply typed

```
quit
```

and pressed the Enter key. The screen went blank, except for an underscore *command prompt* in the upper left corner. "What would you do now?" he asked and waited for a reply.

There were several shrugs and then to fill the silence someone exclaimed, "Help!"

Direct Entry of Commands

"That's exactly right," Jack said quickly. "As it turns out, HELP is a command that you can use to get helpful information about the environment's command interface. This includes descriptions of what commands are available to you, what those commands do, and what their correct syntax is. It also includes examples of command usage. Watch." He typed

```
HELP
```

PHOTO 9   Getting help

KnowledgeMan Help   214

MAIN HELP MENU

_KnowledgeMan's Operating Environment   Spreadsheet

Syntax   Line-at-a-Time I/O Management

Data Management   Form I/O Management

Ad Hoc Inquiry/Statistics/Conversion   Procedures

Calculator (Functions)   Optional KnowledgeMan Components

FNEXT (ctrl-F) select next option   FENTER (return) choose option
FSUP (ctrl-U) return to prior screen FABORT (escape) terminate help

and pressed the Enter key. The screen was immediately transformed from near emptiness to the appearance of Photo 9. Here, they saw a Help menu. Rather than a menu for making processing requests, this kind of menu gives you a structured way for choosing what you want to receive help about. There are literally hundreds of screens of help available. To make a choice you merely move the small blinking cursor to the topic of interest (e.g., via arrow keys in the numeric keypad) and press the Enter key.

Jack quickly stepped through a couple levels of Help menus to get a description of the SELECT command.[1] The command's syntax was highlighted in a red box beginning in the upper left corner of the screen, and a description appeared below it. Jack pressed the Esc key to escape from the help display and get a command prompt at the bottom of the screen. With the help display still in view, he directly typed

_____

[1] Alternatively, he could have simply typed HELP SELECT instead of HELP in order to get to the SELECT description right away.

PHOTO 10 Help about the SELECT command

```
SELECT expressions FROM table FOR conditions scope

    Generate a report with a column for each expression and a row for each
    table record retrieved. LIST can be used instead of SELECT.

    The table must be in use. If <FROM table> is omitted, the default table is
    assumed. If <FOR conditions> is omitted, each record within the scope is
    retrieved. If <scope> is omitted, the entire table is considered.

    Automatic grouping and/or dynamic sorting is possible:
SELECT expressions FROM table FOR conditions scope GROUP BY breaks ORDER BY key

More help?
    expressions: specify simple (field) or more complex expressions
    conditions: specify criteria which is used as basis for record retrieval
    scope: restrict processing to a desired portion of the table
    breaks: indicate basis for grouping of rows in a report
    key: indicate basis for dynamic sorting of rows; UNIQUE qualifier
    utility/environment variables: control report appearance, routing
    examples: selecting records from a table

    FNEXT (ctrl-F) select next option     FENTER (return) choose option
    FSUP (ctrl-U) return to prior screen  FABORT (escape) terminate help
_SELECT Q1,Q2,Q3,FNAME,PID FROM PERF WHERE PID="rom"_
```

```
SELECT Q1,Q2,Q3,FNAME,PID FROM PERF WHERE PID="rom"
```

which was the same command generated earlier via the natural language
interface. The resultant appearance is shown in Photo 10.

As soon as Jack pressed the Enter key, the command was executed
and the selected data appeared as shown in Figure 3–17. The command
interface was immediately ready to accept another command alongside
the underscore prompt. Jack now demonstrated the OUTPUT command
by typing

```
output 9003+10229+8340
```

and pressing the Enter key. The resultant sum of the first three romance
quotas for Kris was output immediately to the screen as shown in Figure
3–18. Jack commented that, as with natural language requests, direct
commands can be typed in either upper- or lowercase letters.

"So," noted Tracey, "you don't have to get help each time you
use a command."

FIGURE 3–17   Results of Photo 10 SELECT command

Q1	Q2	Q3	FNAME	PID
9003	10229	8340	Kris	rom
5000	4678	4213	Tina	rom
4982	4678	8744	Toby	rom
6040	5020	5555	Karen	rom
5004	4468	5830	Carol	rom
—				

"That's correct," he replied. "Help is there if you want it. But if you're already familiar with the command you want to use, you can simply type it in when you see the command prompt. Notice that the environment is already waiting for our next command. As we move along in the training session, you'll be learning about many other commands available through this interface style. But for now there is only one other command to show you." He typed in

```
bye
```

and pressed the Enter key. As Figure 3–19 illustrates, BYE is the command to use when you want to leave the knowledge management environment and return to the operating system.

"Suppose," said Stan, "I wanted to make some more natural langauge requests instead of leaving to the operating system. Instead of using the BYE command could we have used the CHAT command again, just as we had done earlier?" Stan was thinking of how they had begun chatting in the first place (recall Figure 3–7).

"Yes," nodded Jack. "Just as SELECT, OUTPUT, and BYE are commands, so too is CHAT a command. Its effect is to initiate a natural

FIGURE 3–18 An OUTPUT command and its result

```
Q1      Q2      Q3      FNAME   PID

9003    10229   8340    Kris    rom
5000    4678    4213    Tina    rom
4982    4678    8744    Toby    rom
6040    5020    5555    Karen   rom
5004    4468    5830    Carol   rom
_output 9003+10229+8340
        27572
_
```

FIGURE 3–19 Saying BYE to the environment

```
Q1      Q2      Q3      FNAME   PID

9003    10229   8340    Kris    rom
5000    4678    4213    Tina    rom
4982    4678    8744    Toby    rom
6040    5020    5555    Karen   rom
5004    4468    5830    Carol   rom
_output 9003+10229+8340
        27572
_bye



C>
```

language conversation rather than retrieving data, outputting the value of an expression, or exiting to the operating system."

Command Language Pros and Cons

"Thus far," said Joy, "you've seen examples of only a few commands, but as we progress you'll begin to see that the command language interface offers greater functionality and flexibility of actions than the other two interface methods. It also turns out to yield faster processing because the environment doesn't have to transform your inputs into a command. You directly specify the command you want.

"Sometimes people shy away from this interface style because they need to learn and remember pertinent parts of the command language. There is a price to be paid for flexibility, functionality, and freedom to do what you want when you want it. But as you'll see, it's really a fairly small price in terms of your effort. You can begin with a few commands and be productive right away. Command languages are especially well suited for frequent, heavy-duty users."

CUSTOMIZED INTERFACES

At its simplest, a customized interface is a modified version of one of the other three interfaces. For instance, instead of the black background and white foreground of the command interface, the colors might be modified to black on green. The next chapter describes some of the ways you can tailor the built-in interfaces to suit your own tastes.

Jack explained that beyond the tailoring of existing interfaces, the environment can accommodate entirely new interfaces. For instance, its command language can be used to develop entirely new interfaces. He pointed out that a person who develops a customized interface has considerable latitude in designing it to conform with the needs of a particular user or the requirements of a particular application. "As we go along," he said, "we'll dabble a bit in making some custom interfaces for our own use, but will concentrate primarily on the built-in interfaces."

A customized interface normally involves at least three kinds of knowledge: linguistic, presentation, and procedural. All of this knowledge relating to an interface is stored in the knowledge system, where it can be accessed by the environment on an as-needed basis. The developer must design a language through which users will make their requests. There are several possibilities. Requests might be made by keystroke responses to custom-built menus, by filling in blank slots in electronic forms presented on the screen (e.g., Photo 14 in the color

PHOTO 14   The sales representative form with data

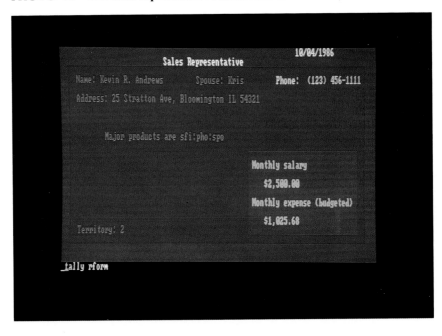

PHOTO 17   Browsing with PRODFORM

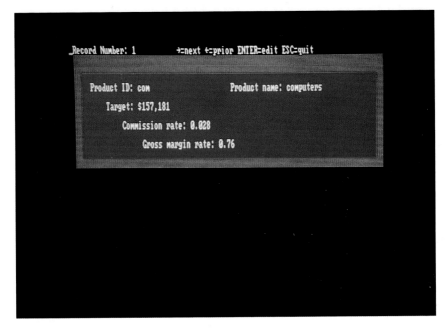

PHOTO 18 Browsing with PERFFORM

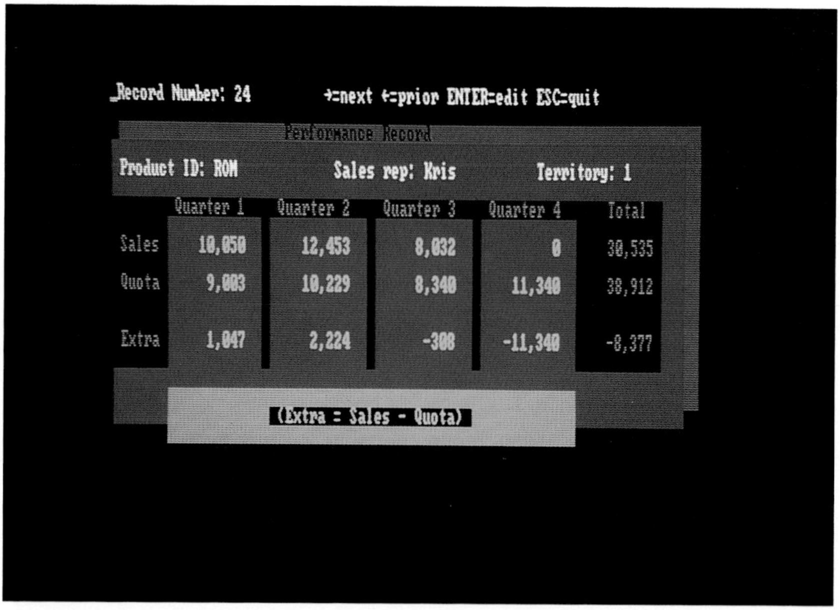

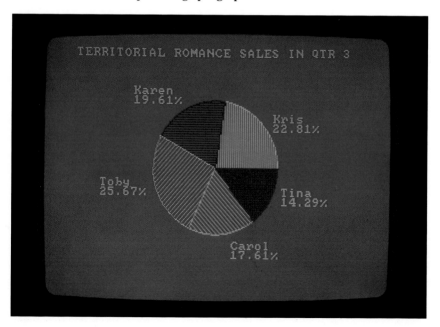

PHOTO 30 A labeled percentage pie graph

PHOTO 33   Karen's sales and quotas for three product lines

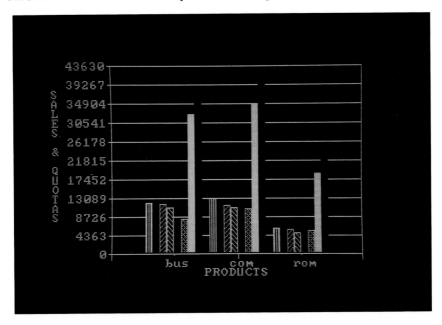

PHOTO 37   Graphing with a user-specified axis range

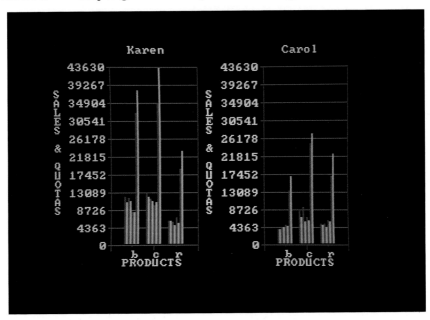

PHOTO 39   Activating cell for stylized presentation

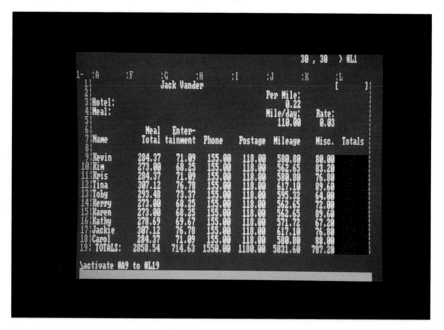

PHOTO 40   Automatic highlighting of expense totals that exceed 60 percent
of corresponding salaries

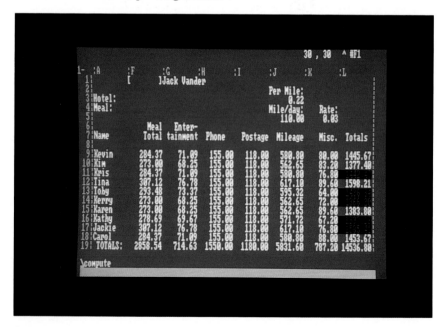

insert), by responding to customized prompts, or by entering statements in a newly designed, specialized command language. Some combination of these is possible in a single, tailor-made interface. Similarly, the developer has many possibilities for designing the presentations that a user will see on the screen (e.g., their colors, positions, arrangements). The developer must also specify how the environment is to respond to a request submitted through the customized interface. To the extent that this specification involves a sequence of steps or operations (i.e., a procedure), the developer must also represent procedural knowledge in the knowledge system.

The primary advantage of a customized interface over the other interfaces is that it is designed to fit the particular needs of some user (or class of users). The drawback of this approach is that it takes time and effort to design and build. In-depth treatments of how to build elaborate customized interfaces for this environment can be found in [7], [8].

BASIC IDEAS

Any piece of software provides at least one interface mechanism that allows a user to make requests. Some software offers a menu-guided interface style that shows the user available options each step of the way. A request is made by stepping through various levels of menus and making desired choices. In contrast, a natural language interface does not present the user with options. Instead, a user simply types in a request in conversational terms. If the software does not understand a request, then it interacts with the user for clarification. This may involve the correction of a user's typographical errors and misspellings. It may also involve learning about new terms and incorporating them into a dictionary. A natural language interface is also conversational in the sense that it can understand a new request in the context of preceding requests.

A third interface style consists of a command language. With this interface, a user makes a request by entering one of the language's structured commands in response to a command prompt. It is not permissible to deviate from a command's predefined syntax. Unlike a natural language interface, there is generally only one way of saying something via a command interface. What a command language may lack in terms of variety of expression can be offset by the variety of actions that can be requested. Joy put it nicely when she said, "Instead of focusing on many different ways to say the same thing, a command language focuses on many different things each of which is said in one particular way."

Sometimes, software will allow its built-in interfaces to be customized in various ways. In other cases, it may allow entirely new interfaces to be developed to suit the special needs of a user. As a user becomes more experienced, he or she may want to do some of this development work. Alternatively, it could be done by a computer professional who is trained and skilled in such matters.

No one interface style is best for all persons and all types of knowledge management tasks. Furthermore, the same person may desire to use different interface styles at different times. With this in mind some pieces of software are designed to support multiple interface styles, allowing a user to adopt whatever style seems most appropriate at a given time. Of the four interface styles available in the knowledge management environment, Jack has chosen to concentrate mainly on the command language because it allows the greatest number of knowledge management capabilities to be exercised. As the regional sales managers will see, the Englishlike nature of the commands make them fairly easy to learn.

References

1. Harris, L. R. "Natural Language Simplifies Computer Access." *Systems and Software* 3, no. 1 (1984).
2. Holsapple, C. W., and A. B. Whinston. "Integrated DSS Development Tools for Microcomputers." *DataPro Research Report MC51–050*, 1984.
3. _____. "Toward an Environment Theory of Decision Support." *Conference on Integrated Modeling Systems*. Austin, Tex., October, 1987.
4. *KnowledgeMan Reference Manual*, version 2. Lafayette, Ind.: MDBS, Inc., 1985.
5. *KnowledgeMan User's Guide*, version 2. Lafayette, Ind.: MDBS, Ind., 1985.
6. Rauch-Hindin, W. B. *Artificial Intelligence in Business, Science and Industry*, vol. 1. Englewood Cliffs, N.J.: Prentice-Hall, 1986.
7. Roeder, G. *The Book of KnowledgeMan*, vol. 1. Chelmsford, Mass.: All-Hands-On Press, 1984.
8. _____. *The Book of KnowledgeMan*, vol. 2. Chelmsford, Mass.: All-Hands-On Press, 1985.

At the helm.

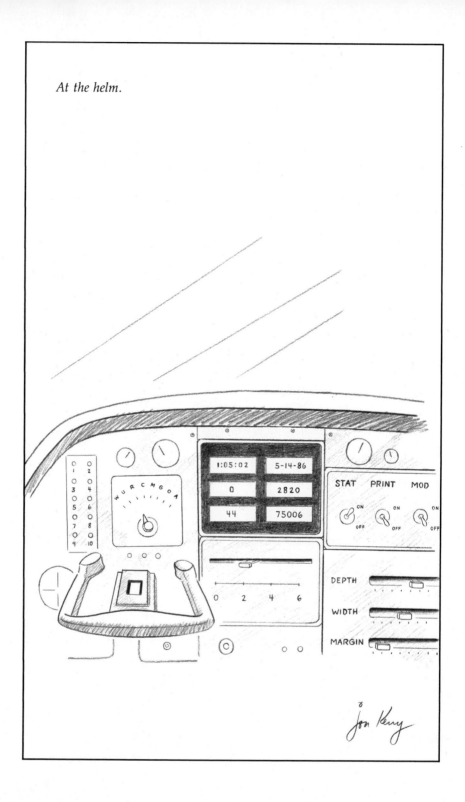

Chapter Four

Calculations and Trappings

The training session resumed, with Jack taking stock of where they were. "Now that you know about the various styles available for making requests, we can begin to take a look at what kinds of requests you can make. What kinds of knowledge management activities can you instigate in this environment? Exactly what commands are available for causing various kinds of knowledge to be represented and processed by the computer? We'll answer these questions gradually, in the context of dealing with a variety of everyday knowledge management problems that we all face.

"One everyday problem or task we're all familiar with is the need to carry out various *calculations*. Let's see how you can solve such needs by issuing commands within the environment. It's not all that different than using a hand-held calculator." Jack had decided to begin with simple calculation problems, not because they were particularly exciting, but because they represented familiar territory. As such, commands for calculating would make an ideal first excursion into the knowledge management environment. It would also give him a chance to introduce some of the basic trappings that could be carried along on any of their future journeys in the environment.

There is a useful perspective that should always be kept in mind, namely that a knowledge management environment is an extension of one's own mental environment (recall Figure 1–8). There are many different routes of activity you can take in a knowledge management environment. The commands available to you serve as the steering mechanism that allows you to determine where you want to go or what you want to do in the environment. You stand at the helm and decide what commands to invoke. The helm is equipped with various *trappings* such as storage compartments, control switches, sensors, and definable "pushbuttons." In computer jargon, these are respectively called working variables, environment variables, utility variables, and macros. All four are introduced in this chapter as Jack demonstrates some of the environment's calculation capabilities.

CALCULATIONS

Jack entered the environment in the customary way, by typing KMAN and then -G in response to the operating system's prompt. As he provided the user name and password, he explained that calculations involved *expressions* just like those used in high school math class. Expressions can be composed of constants, variables, and operators [1]. "When you type in an expression, the environment will automatically compute a *value* for it. If you want to see that value, you would type it in as part of an OUTPUT command as we saw earlier.

"Suppose you have eight sales reps. What would be the added monthly cost of giving each a $41.57 increase in the entertainment allowance?" In response to the underscore command prompt, Jack typed

    output 8*41.57

and pressed the Enter key.[1] The result of 332.56000 appeared immediately beneath the command. A new command prompt appeared on the line beneath the result.

"But wait a minute," Brad frowned, "where's the dollar sign and why are all those zeros showing?"

"Aha," said Jack, "so you'd like to see the result pictured differently? Watch closely what happens when I press the Control-Z key." He pressed ^Z and the character sequence

    output 8*41.57

instantly appeared alongside the underscore. He smiled at the surprised looks. Saying nothing, he continued typing on the same line so that

    output 8*41.57 using "$ddd.dd"

was the new command's final appearance. As shown in Figure 4–1, the result was now pictured the way Brad wanted it to be.

---

[1] Unless otherwise noted, it is henceforth assumed that the Enter key is pressed at the conclusion of an entry.

FIGURE 4-1   Outputting the result of a calculation

```
MDBS KnowledgeMan Ver 2.01.00c
The Universal Knowledge Management System
(C) Copyright 1983, 1986, Micro Data Base Systems, Inc.
Lafayette, IN  47902


User Name: knowledgemaster
Password :

_output 8*41.57
     332.56000
_output 8*41.57 using "$ddd.dd"
$332.56
_
```

Command Recall and Editing

Jack explained about ^Z: "Whenever you are faced with the command prompt, you can use Control-Z to immediately bring your entire last command into view as the start of your new command. In this case, I just tacked a new clause onto the end of it to get rid of the extra zeros and slapped a dollar sign on the front of the calculated value. As we'll see later you can make other kinds of changes to a *recalled command* before pressing the Enter key to have it executed. As we move along remember that Control-Z can be used to recall any kind of command, not just an OUTPUT command."

"That's pretty nifty," said Stan, "and I can see where it would save a lot of keystrokes. But tell us more about the new clause you tacked on the end."

Jack explained that the USING clause tells the software what conventions to use when portraying a value on the screen. The series of characters enclosed in quotes is called a *picture*. This picture of $ddd.dd says that the result should be displayed with a dollar sign in front, followed by up to three digits (d stands for digit), then a decimal point, and finally two more digits. "We'll take a closer look at pictures a little later."

There was another question. "If I'm doing many calculations, I'd really find it very cumbersome to have to type the word OUTPUT every time. Isn't there some shorter way of making such requests?"

"Yes," replied Jack, "and it's the approach that I take in my own work. You simply type a question mark instead of the word OUTPUT. Let me show you by revising our last command. I'll use Control-Z to recall it, only this time I won't be tacking anything onto the end. Instead, I'll eliminate the word OUTPUT from the recalled characters and insert a question mark in its place. Watch."

He pressed the ^Z key, instantly bringing the characters

```
output 8*41.57 using "$ddd.dd"
```

into view on the command line. A little blinking cursor was positioned after the last character. While a command is being entered, this cursor indicates where the next typed-in character will appear. If the destructive Backspace key (recall the keyboard discussion in Chapter 2) is pressed, the character to the left of the blinking cursor disappears and the cursor, along with all other characters to the right of it, moves left one position.

To eliminate the word OUTPUT and its trailing blank, Jack first needed to position the cursor on the digit 8. He did this by pressing ^S to move the cursor leftward to that position. Notice that ^S just moves the cursor; it does not alter any characters in the command. In a similar manner ^D will move the cursor rightward to a desired position. With the cursor blinking on the 8, Jack pressed the Backspace key and held it down until the word OUTPUT and its trailing space had vanished. All the while the cursor moved leftward as if "gobbling up" the vanishing characters, leaving

```
_8*41.57 using "$ddd.dd"
```

on the command line with the cursor still blinking on 8.

To insert a question mark in the cursor's position, Jack merely typed in a question mark. It appeared at the start of the command entry, giving

```
_?8*41.57 using "$ddd.dd"
```

with all existing characters automatically shifting to the right to make room for it. Because this was the shorthand version of the OUTPUT

FIGURE 4–2   **Shorthand version of the OUTPUT command**

```
MDBS KnowledgeMan Ver 2.01.00c
The Universal Knowledge Management System
(C) Copyright 1983, 1986, Micro Data Base Systems, Inc.
Lafayette, IN  47902


User Name: knowledgemaster
Password :

_output 8*41.57
     332.56000
_output 8*41.57 using "$ddd.dd"
$332.56
_?8*41.57 using "$ddd.dd"
$332.56
_
```

command he desired, he pressed the Enter key to execute it. The resultant screen appearance is shown in Figure 4–2.

"Of course," remarked Jack, "if you wanted you could have typed in this command line from scratch, without recalling and editing the former command. The result would be the same. As it turns out there are other control keys you could use for editing a recalled command. We'll not digress into those now. One more point: All of these *editing operations* can be used when entering a command from scratch as well as when you begin with a recalled command. In either case, pressing the Enter key tells the environment that you are satisfied with the command and it should be executed."

Constants

Constants are oftentimes involved in calculations. Jack's examples made use of two constants: 8 and 41.57. A *constant* is simply an unchanging, literal value. Sometimes, constants are called "literals" in computer jargon. Not all constants are numeric. Jack explained that they would be using three basic kinds of constants: numeric, string, and logical. Each is subject to certain kinds of calculations.

A *numeric constant* is simply a number. It may consist of an integer (a number with no decimal point) or it may be a decimal number. On the whiteboard Jack wrote out examples of several numeric constants:

2800

.018

−1.15

The first is an integer, while the second and third are decimal numbers. A numeric constant cannot include any symbols other than digits, a decimal point, and a sign (+ or −). For instance, $332.56 is not a legitimate numeric constant because of the dollar sign. It is a fancy portrayal of the numeric value 332.56.

A *string constant* consists of a string of text enclosed in a matching pair of double quotes. This text can involve practically any characters that have corresponding keys on the keyboard. Jack gave a few examples of string constants:

"Jack Vander"

"11/12/1979"

"The sales are:"

All the characters that make up each of these string constants are to be interpreted as a whole, literally and verbatim. Joy explained that string constants are enclosed in quotes to differentiate them from individual words used in commands. Unlike the words in commands, which can be interchangeably typed in upper- or lowercase, the case of a letter in a string is normally significant. Whereas the command word OUTPUT is equivalent to the word Output (or output, outPUT, etc.), the string "Jack Vander" is different from the "jack vander" string.

A *logical constant* consists of either the word TRUE or the word FALSE. Because it is not enclosed in quotes (i.e., it is not a string constant), any mixture of upper- and lowercase letters is acceptable. Thus, TRUE is the same as true and False is the same as FALSE. "As we'll see shortly," Jack concluded, "logical and string constants can be just as valuable as the more familiar numeric constants."

Variables

A constant value is fixed. It cannot vary: 2820 is always 2820, "Jack" is always "Jack", and TRUE is always TRUE. In contrast, the value of a *variable* can vary. Jack explained that a variable has a name, a type, and a value. He wrote several examples on the whiteboard:

SALARY	int	2800
COMMIS	num	.018
REPNAME	str	"Kevin"
NEW	logic	false

"These are examples of working variables, which means you have complete control over them, how and when they'll be used, and even their very existence. As we'll see later, there are other kinds of variables that can be used in an environment. At any time, you can bring a new working variable into existence by simply stating its name and giving it a value. The value you assign to a variable determines the type."

In this environment, the command for assigning a value to a variable is LET. Each variable name can be a combination of up to eight alphabetic or numeric characters, but must start with a letter. Jack demonstrated by entering the four LET commands shown in Figure 4–3. "You can think of each working variable as being a little storage compartment where we can place a value for later use. Whenever we want to use a variable's value we simply type its name. For instance, let's output the values of REPNAME, SALARY, and COMMIS." He typed

```
?repname,salary,commis
```

and the response is shown in Figure 4–4.

At any time a variable's value can be changed with another LET command. The new value determines the variable's type. For instance, the command

```
let salary=2905.73
```

would not only give SALARY a new value but would make its type numeric (i.e., allowing decimal numbers) rather than its former type of integer. Jack noted that it is all right to assign the value of one variable to another variable. To demonstrate this he typed the two commands

FIGURE 4–3   Assigning values to variables

```
MDBS KnowledgeMan Ver 2.01.00c
The Universal Knowledge Management System
(C) Copyright 1983, 1986, Micro Data Base Systems, Inc.
Lafayette, IN  47902


User Name: knowledgemaster
Password :

_output 8*41.57
     332.56000
_output 8*41.57 using "$ddd.dd"
$332.56
_?8*41.57 using "$ddd.dd"
$332.56
_let salary=2500
_let commis=.018
_let repname="Kevin"
_let new=false
_
```

```
let c=commis
?c
```

producing the result shown in Figure 4–5.

"In deference to Brad, its time to point out that the word LET in a LET command is optional. Usually, I omit it myself. Even though that's not as Englishlike, it saves some keystrokes. In future examples, I'll leave out the LET when issuing assignment commands." Jack paused, "Earlier we saw that constants could be involved in calculating the value of expressions. Well, you can also use variables in a calculation."

Expressions

Variables and constants of the same type can be combined into an expression. An expression's type is determined by the types of its variables and constants. Expressions can contain *operators* that indicate how the expression is to be evaluated. The operators that can be used in an expression depend on the expression's type.

Jack explained that a *numeric expression* consists of one or more numeric constants or numeric variables connected by numeric operators

FIGURE 4-4 Outputting variables' values

```
MDBS KnowledgeMan Ver 2.01.00c
The Universal Knowledge Management System
(C) Copyright 1983, 1986, Micro Data Base Systems, Inc.
Lafayette, IN 47902


User Name: knowledgemaster
Password :

_output 8*41.57
     332.56000
_output 8*41.57 using "$ddd.dd"
$332.56
_?8*41.57 using "$ddd.dd"
$332.56
_let salary=2500
_let commis=.018
_let repname="Kevin"
_let new=false
_?repname,salary,commis
Kevin    2500.00000      0.01800

-
```

such as +, −, /, *, and ** (exponentiation). He wrote out several examples of numeric expressions on the whiteboard:

SALARY

2800

SALARY+COMMIS*10000

2800+.018*10000

(2800+.018)*10000

The first two have no operators because they involve only one term apiece. The third is an expression involving two variables, a constant, and two operators. The last two expressions are alike, except for the parentheses. When calculated, their values will be different.

Joy elaborated, "Things inside of parentheses are always evaluated first. The exponentiation operator (if present) gets the next highest precedence, followed by division and multiplication, and finally addition and subtraction. The expression 2800+.018*10000 means that .018 should be multiplied by 10,000 before adding 2,800 to the result. In contrast, the expression (2800+.018)*10000 means that the parenthesized 2,800

FIGURE 4–5   Assigning one variable's value to another

```
The Universal Knowledge Management System
(C) Copyright 1983, 1986, Micro Data Base Systems, Inc.
Lafayette, IN  47902


User Name: knowledgemaster
Password :

_output 8*41.57
     332.56000
_output 8*41.57 using "$ddd.dd"
$332.56
_?8*41.57 using "$ddd.dd"
$332.56
_let salary=2500
_let commis=.018
_let repname="Kevin"
_let new=false
_?repname,salary,commis
Kevin    2500.00000      0.01800
_let c=commis
_?c
      0.01800

_
```

and .018 should be added together before multiplying the result by 10,000. Thus, these two expressions will have different calculated values."

Jack turned to *string expressions,* which are composed of one or more string constants or string variables. If there is more than one constant or variable, they are connected by a string operator such as + (concatenation). He wrote three examples of string expressions on the whiteboard:

"2820 Elm Street"

STREET+CITY

"The rep's name is "+REPNAME

The first is just a single string constant and involves no operator. The second concatenates the values of the two string variables STREET and CITY. The third example concatenates the value of REPNAME to the end of a four-word string constant.

Just as numeric expressions have numeric values and string expressions have string values, a *logical expression* will always have a logical value. When calculated, its value will be either TRUE or FALSE. The simplest kind of logical expression is a single logical constant or variable. More interesting logical expressions involve comparisons of the "is this greater than that" variety. A comparison, formally called a *relational expression*, is concerned with the relationship between two things of like type. Common relationships include greater than, greater than or equal to, less than, less than or equal to, equal, and not equal. In a logical expression these relationships take the form of the *relational operators:*

GT   GE   LT   LE   EQ   NE

or equivalently:

>   >=   <   <=   =   <>

To illustrate, Jack wrote several logical expressions on the whiteboard. Each was a comparison involving one of the relational operators:

SALARY GE 2000

COMMIS∗10000<185.2

"Kris" GT "Kevin"

COMMIS EQ .023

The first expression compares the value of the SALARY variable to the numeric constant 2000. When this expression's value is calculated, the result will be either TRUE or FALSE. It will be TRUE if the present value of SALARY is greater than or equal to 2,000; otherwise it will be FALSE. Similarly, the second expression evaluates to TRUE if 10,000 times the COMMIS value is less than 185.2; otherwise it is FALSE. The third expression shows that you can compare strings as well as numbers. Its value calculates to TRUE because Kr is greater than Ke in alphabetic sequence. The fourth example would be calculated to be TRUE only if .023 is the value of the COMMIS variable.

Given the group's understanding of simple logical expressions, Jack now gave an example of a *compound logical expression* involving more than just one comparison:

REPNAME GE "Kevin" AND SALARY<=2900

This logical expression will evaluate to TRUE if and only if both of the comparisons are TRUE. In general, relational expressions can be connected into a single logical expression by logical operators such as AND (or equivalently &) and OR. If OR had been used in the above example, the evaluation would yield TRUE if either or both of the comparisons were TRUE.

"Notice," Jack said, "we are dealing with calculations that you can't do on a hand-held calculator where you can key in only numeric expressions for evaluation. Here, you can work with string and logical expressions as well."

"That's nice, but I'm wondering," Dan said hesitantly, "why we should care about calculating strings and things. Isn't numeric calculation enough?"

Jack rubbed his chin and thought for a moment. "String and logical calculations are important. In fact, they are so pervasive in our own mental endeavors that we tend to take them for granted. Think about how many times during a day you put together strings of text and store away or present the result. Think about how often you compare one thing to another, where the result of the comparison (either TRUE or FALSE) influences what you will do next or what conclusion you will draw about some situation."

Joy added, "All three kinds of calculations are elementary facets of knowledge management. So we should expect any knowledge management environment to furnish a multifaceted calculation capability."

Calculation is one technique of knowledge management. With it, knowledge is represented in the guise of expressions: numeric, string, and logical expressions. Recall that a knowledge management technique involves not only representation, but processing as well. In the case of calculation, the processing consists of evaluating expressions. Results of expression evaluations can be used in many ways in a knowledge management environment. For the present, Jack pointed out two of these: outputting the result and storing the result as the value of a variable. Figure 4–6 portrays some of the examples he typed in for the group.

In general, any type of expression can be specified in an OUTPUT or LET command. The first example in Figure 4–6 merely outputs the result of a numeric expression. The second uses the LET command to adjust the value of the SALARY variable. The value of the expression SALARY*1.1 becomes the new value of SALARY. Jack confirmed this by outputting the value of SALARY. The fourth and fifth examples output the values of logical and string expressions, respectively. As the sixth example shows, it is possible to output different kinds of values in a single OUTPUT command by simply separating the expressions with a comma. In this case, the value of a string expression (constant) is appended with the value of a numeric expression (variable) and the number is presented according to a picture.

It is sometimes useful to store the results of a calculation by assigning it to a variable. That result can later be used by simply referring to the variable. There is no need to later retype the same expression or to remember an expression's result once that result has been assigned to

FIGURE 4–6   Outputting and assigning evaluation results

```
_?salary+commis*10000
     2680.00000
_let salary=salary*1.1
_?salary
     2750.00000
_?salary+commis*12000>5000
FALSE
_?"Name is "+repname
Name is Kevin
_?"The salary is: ",salary using "$dddd.dd"
The salary is: $2750.00
_let pay=salary+commis*12000
_let who="Pay for "+repname+" : "
_?pay>5000
FALSE
_?who,pay using "$d,ddd.dd"
Pay for Kevin: $2,966.00
_
```

a variable. The seventh and eighth examples in Figure 4–6 assign the results of numeric and string calculations to the PAY and WHO variables respectively. With the final two examples, Jack illustrated that the results had been successfully stored and could be easily referenced by simply mentioning the variable names in subsequent commands.

Functions

In addition to constants, variables, and operators, an expression can also contain functions. A *function* carries out a specific kind of operation to produce a value. The operation is one that is not easily expressed in terms of operators like +, −, **, /, or *. However, it can be easily expressed by referring to the function by name. Software that supports functions typically gives each function a name that is suggestive of the kind of operation it carries out. For instance, in the KnowledgeMan environment, SQRT is the name of a function that calculates square roots. The value produced by a function may depend on *arguments* specified with the function. Arguments are traditionally enclosed in a matching pair of parentheses following the function's name.

"Let's look at the notion of functions with an example that's familiar to you all," Jack said. "Remember in high school math class you learned a complex method for computing the square root of a number. This method involved the usual numeric operators and if you were able to remember the method I dare say you could now use this computer to calculate the square root of any number. But you would need to go through several calculations. Alternatively, you could simply refer to the SQRT function that's available in this environment.

"Suppose you want to see the square root of 25. You would simply type in an OUTPUT command like this." Jack entered the command

```
?sqrt(25)
```

and the result of 5 immediately appeared on the screen. He explained that SQRT is the function and 25 is its argument.

"So," interjected Dan, "if I wanted the square root of 257.89, I would use it as the argument instead of 25."

"Right," replied Jack. "A function's argument simply tells what you want the function to operate on in producing its result or value."

"Am I correct in assuming that a function can be used anywhere in an expression, regardless of whether that expression appears in an OUTPUT command or a LET command?" asked Tracey.

"Yes," Jack responded. "Anywhere that you could use a constant or variable in an expression that's being evaluated, it's OK to use a function. It doesn't make any difference what kind of command is involved or where the expression is used. What's more, a function's arguments don't have to be constants as in the example we just saw. Arguments can be variables or expressions involving operators and even other functions."

"It is worth noting," chimed Joy, "that functions are traditionally classified according to the kinds of values they can produce. Thus, SQRT is an example of a *numeric function* because it always produces a numeric result. There are many other numeric functions available to you in this environment. Similarly, there is a group of *string functions*, each of which produces strings of text as values. *Logical functions* are those that yield either TRUE or FALSE as a value. Of course the type of a function must match the type of the expression in which it appears. It doesn't make sense to use the SQRT function in a string expression, for instance."

Jack proceeded to step the group through examples of function usage. Figure 4-7 shows how several of these appeared on the screen. The first two examples shown there are left over from his explanation of the SQRT function. The third and fourth OUTPUT commands illustrate the MAX and MIN functions, respectively. Each of these functions has

FIGURE 4–7   Function examples

```
_?sqrt(25)
      5.00000
_?sqrt(257.89)
     16.05895
_?max(pay,commis*175000)
   3150.00000
_?min(pay,commis*175000)
   2966.00000
_?tojul("5/14/1987")
 147769.00000
_?tojul("11/1/87")-tojul("5/14/87")
    171.00000
_?time()
13:23:08
_?trim(who),pay using "$d,ddd.dd"
Pay for Kevin:$2,966.00
_?repname,upcase(repname),locase(repname)
KevinKEVINkevin
_let target=44+tojul("5-14-87");?target
 147813.00000
_?todate(target,"/",4)
06/27/1987
_?todate(44+tojul("5-14-87")," ",4)
06 27 1987

_
```

two arguments. The MAX function's value is always the maximum of its two arguments. The MIN function returns the minimum of its two arguments' values.

"Another numeric function is TOJUL. Unlike the other numeric functions we've seen thus far," explained Jack, "TOJUL takes a string expression as its argument. Nevertheless, it still produces a numeric result. This number is the Julian equivalent of the calendar date that appears as TOJUL's argument. This function is especially useful when you need to calculate the number of days between two dates. For instance, as you can see there are 171 days between May 14 and November 1.

"The TIME function is an example of a string function. The value of this function will always be the current time. As you can see it is now 23 minutes and 8 seconds past 3 in the afternoon."

"Wait a minute," interrupted Brad, "that looks like a number to me. I thought you said that TIME is a string function."

"It is," Jack replied. "Remember, it's perfectly alright for a string of text to contain numbers as well as other symbols, but a number cannot contain colons."

"I see," nodded Brad, "and TIME has no arguments?"

"Right," said Jack, "we don't need to give the TIME function anything to operate on. It simply looks at the computer's internal clock. There are a few other functions that don't need any arguments, but most need at least one. The arguments that a particular function needs are usually self-evident and make common sense. In time you'll become well acquainted with them. If you happen to forget what arguments a function needs or the order in which they need to be stated, you can look up the function in the reference manual or just use the HELP command to get an on-screen description.

"A very handy string function is TRIM. It trims off all trailing blanks from the string value of its argument and returns the result. Remember that the WHO variable has a trailing blank. We can get rid of it by trimming WHO." Compare Jack's TRIM example in Figure 4–7 to the last example in Figure 4–6. The results are identical except for the trimmed value of WHO.

Jack spent little time on the UPCASE and LOCASE functions. They are very simple. UPCASE produces a string that is just like the value of its argument, except all alphabetic characters are in uppercase. The LOCASE function yields an entirely lowercase value. This is illustrated by the OUTPUT command in Figure 4–7 that outputs the value of REPNAME, its uppercase rendition, and its lowercase rendition.

"Let me show you one more string function for now," Jack continued. "It is the TODATE function. Suppose we have a target date that is 44 days away from May 14, 1987. What calendar date is it? It's easy enough to find the Julian number for that date." He illustrated by adding 44 to the Julian number for May 14, 1987, and assigning the result to the TARGET variable. Outputting the value of TARGET showed its value was 147813. Notice that multiple commands can be entered on the same line if they are separated by semicolons. The Enter key is not pressed until the last of a line's commands has been typed.

"But we want the actual date, not just a Julian number. The TODATE function will calculate a calendar date for the Julian number. This function has three arguments. The first is for the number. The second is for the symbol we want TODATE to use for separating month from day and day from year in the result. Here, I'll use a slash. The third argument indicates how many year digits should appear in the resultant text string. In this case, let's use 4." The result is illustrated in the second to last example in Figure 4–7. In the final example, Jack showed that it was not necessary to invent or use the TARGET variable. One function can be part of the expression that is the argument of another function.

In closing this introduction to functions, Jack noted that other functions (including various logical functions) would be discussed later when their uses to the managers would be more evident. Tables 4–1 and

TABLE 4-1 Some common numeric functions

Function and arguments	Result	Example
ABS(arg)	Absolute value of the numeric arg	ABS(37–85) is 48
EXP(arg)	Mathematical constant e (2.71828 . . .) raised to power indicated by the numeric arg	EXP(1) is 2.71828
LEN(arg)	Length (in characters) of the string arg	LEN("Jack & Joy") is 10
LN(arg)	Natural logarithm of the numeric arg	LN(.018) is −4.01738
LOG(arg)	Base 10 logarithm of the numeric arg	LOG(44) is 1.64345
MATCH(arg1,arg2)	Position of the first character of the first substring in the string arg1 that matches the string arg2	MATCH("sales representative", "re") is 7
MAX(arg1,arg2)	Larger of the values of the numeric arg1 and arg2	MAX(12*3,72/2.1) is 36
MIN(arg1,arg2)	Smaller of the values of the numeric arg1 and arg2	MIN(12*3,72/1.9) is 36
RAND(arg)	Random number using the numeric arg as the generator's seed	RAND(0) is a number in the range 0 to 1
SIN(arg)	Sine for arg number of radians	SIN(.5) is 0.47943
SQRT(arg)	Square root of numeric arg	SQRT(6.25) is 2.5
TOJUL(arg)	Julian number for calendar date of string arg	TOJUL("5 14 52") is 134986
TONUM(arg)	Numeric correspondence to digits in string arg	TONUM("123") is 123
TRUNC(arg)	Truncated version of the numeric arg	TRUNC(28.20) is 28.00

4–2 provide a summary of a few of the functions that can be used when making calculations in this environment. A complete list appears in the reference manual [1]. Different users typically use different subsets of available functions depending on their calculation needs. There is no need for a user to be concerned about available functions that are not pertinent to his or her needs.

PICTURES

A *picture* is one way of controlling the appearance of a data value. Jack had already given some examples of how the appearance of a value could be altered by using a picture (recall Figures 4–1, 4–6, and 4–7). A picture is sometimes called a mask or a format. In the Knowledge-Man environment a picture is a sequence of characters within a matching pair of double quotes. These characters control, on a character-by-character basis, the presentation of a data value.

Each character in a picture is either a *literal* or a *placeholder*. In the picture "$d,ddd.dd" that Jack used earlier (Figure 4–6), the dollar sign, comma, and period are literals. They literally appear at the indicated positions no matter what numeric value is being presented using this picture. Some lowercase letters (such as d) have a special meaning when used in a picture. Rather than being presented literally, they serve as placeholders for characters that make up the value being presented. The d placeholder means that a digit can be substituted in its place when a value is presented.

Thus, the picture "$dd,ddd.dd" means that up to two digits can be presented between the dollar sign and comma, up to three digits can be presented between the comma and period, and two digits will follow the period. This is true no matter what number is presented through the picture. However if the number exceeds 99,999.99, asterisks will appear in place of digits (i.e., $**,***.**) indicating that the value is too large to be displayed through this picture. Also if the number has more than two decimal digits (e.g., 4,321.123), then only the first two will be presented ($ 4,321.12) when using the picture.

"Let's take a closer look at pictures," Jack remarked. "There are other useful placeholders aside from d. Each placeholder is a lowercase letter. In general, you can use any characters that do not behave as placeholders as literals in a picture." He went on to describe the placeholders shown in Table 4–3.

"Any alphabetic character can be presented in the picture position occupied by an a placeholder. The c placeholder is similar, except digits can also be presented in positions that it occupies. Any character at all can be presented in the position occupied by the r placeholder.

TABLE 4–2 Some common string functions

Function and arguments	Result	Example
CHSTR(arg1,arg2,arg3)	Same as the string arg1 except that the first occurrence of the string arg2 in arg1 is changed to the string arg3	CHSTR("5/14/1987","19"," ") is "5/14/87"
LOCASE(arg)	Lowercase version of the string arg	LOCASE("ROMANCE") is "romance"
STRPAD(arg1,arg2,arg3)	Same as string arg1 except it is padded with repetitions of the string arg3 until its length achieves the number indicated by the numeric arg2	STRPAD("good",7,"*") is "good***"
TIME()	Current time	TIME() is the current time
TODATE(arg1,arg2,arg3)	String date for the Julian numeric arg1, delimited by the string arg2 and having the numeric arg3 digits	TODATE(134986,"*",4) is "05*14*1952"
TRIM(arg)	Same as string arg, except trailing blanks are trimmed	TRIM("Kevin ") is "Kevin"
UPCASE(arg)	Uppercase version of the string arg	UPCASE("Romance") is "ROMANCE"

TABLE 4–3   Common picture placeholders

Placeholder	Displayed as
a	Any alphabetic character
c	Any alphanumeric character
r	Any character
u	Uppercase version of alphabetic character
l	Lowercase version of alphabetic character
d	Any digit (sign or decimal point)
f	Any digit except left-side literals float rightward

The u and l placeholders cause the alphabetic characters presented at their positions to be converted to upper- and lowercase, respectively. These placeholders are useful in pictures intended for use with text string values.

"We've already seen how the d placeholder works. The f placeholder is like d, with an important exception. If the value being presented has fewer digits than there are placeholders in the picture, then blank

FIGURE 4–8   Sample picture usage

```
_?salary
      2750.00000
_?salary using "d,ddd"
2,750
_?123.4 using "ddd.dd"
123.40
_?1.234 using "dd.dd"
 1.23
_?salary using "dd.dd"
**.**
_?salary using "$ddd,ddd.ddd"
$  2,750.000
_?123.4 using "$ddd,ddd.ddd"
$    ,123.400
_?salary using "$fff,fff.dd"
  $2,750.00
_?123.4 using "$fff,fff.ff"
    $123.40
_?repname using "laaaaa"
kevin
_?repname using "Rep: ulllll"
Rep: Kevin
_let tele="3174475987";?tele using "(ddd)ddd-dddd"
(317)447-5987
_
```

spaces replace the extra leftmost d placeholders. In contrast, extra f placeholders essentially disappear and any literals on the left end of the picture 'float' rightward to meet the leftmost digit."

"I can see where that's useful," said Stan, "but what happens if there is a comma between two f placeholders that disappear? Does the comma float too?"

"No," Jack explained, "the comma would also disappear. Only the leftmost literals in a picture will float to the right, which is exactly the kind of behavior you would like to have. In general, any literal between a pair of vanishing f placeholders disappears as well. Let's try out a few examples to get a clearer picture of how the various placeholders work. They're pretty simple once you do a few examples to get the knack of it." Figure 4–8 shows a screenful of the examples Jack presented.

"It's worth mentioning," added Joy, "that later you'll see how pictures can be used to automatically check the validity of values that are being stored in the knowledge system. They can do more than control the presentation of values. You'll also see that pictures can be used in commands other than the OUTPUT command that Jack has just shown."

DEFINABLE PUSHBUTTONS

"You may have noticed," reflected Jack, "that I tend to use the question mark symbol rather than the word *output* when entering an OUTPUT command. It saves a lot of keystrokes. Similarly, I can save keystroke effort when invoking the LET command by simply omitting the word *let*. These are built-in features for saving keystroke effort. But you can also invent your own terms for saving keystroke effort.

"It's much the same idea as defining the behavior of a radio pushbutton in your car. You can set the pushbutton to designate a frequently desired station. Once the button is defined to be a particular station, you can simply push it to get that station whenever you want. Similar effort-saving trappings are available in this environment: macros and function keys."

Macros

In reassuring tones Joy broke in, "Don't be concerned about the word *macro*. It's just a bit of standard computer science jargon. A macro is nothing more than a name that you give to an entire series of keystrokes, so that when you need to enter those keystrokes you can merely enter the macro name instead of all the keystrokes it represents. In a way, a macro is a 'pushbutton' you can use to get the entire series of keystrokes you've defined for it."

"Actually," smiled Jack, "a macro is no big deal once you understand it and that won't take us long."

He went on to explain that, like a variable name, a macro name can be from one to eight alphanumeric characters beginning with a letter. When a macro name is a single letter it literally is a pushbutton, for pushing that single key will be interpreted by the environment in an identical way to entering the entire series of keystrokes it represents. When you invent a new macro its name should be chosen so as not to conflict with words already in the command language or existing variable names.

"All you are saying," inquired Debbie, "is that inventing a macro is like defining a new word or term in the command language, right?"

"It's really that simple," nodded Jack. "As you enter a command you can type in macros for part or all of it, provided you've previously defined their meanings. Let's see how you define a macro.

"First, identify some keystroke sequence that you expect to type over and over again in various commands. For instance, there's the sequence SALARY+COMMIS that we used in several calculations. Instead of typing it out every time, we could use a macro. Let's call the macro SC."

Jack showed how SC could be defined with the MACRO command by typing

```
macro sc salary+commis
```

In a MACRO command, the new macro's name (SC) is followed by its meaning or definition (SALARY+COMMIS). To illustrate how SC could be used, Jack typed the commands

```
?sc*12000
?sc*13500 using "$ff,fff.dd"
```

The results appeared on the screen as shown in Figure 4-9. Jack proceeded to define another macro named PIC for a frequently used picture. As shown, he referred to PIC in two subsequent OUTPUT commands.

"Whenever you want to see the names of all the macros presently defined in the environment, you can use the SHOW command." He illustrated by typing

```
show macro
```

to get the expected results shown in Figure 4-9. He then proceeded to point out that SHOW can also be used to show the text of either of these macros by entering the commands

FIGURE 4–9 Macro examples

```
_macro sc salary+commis
_?sc*12000
    2966.00000
_?sc*13500 using "$ff,fff.dd"
 $2,993.00
_macro pic using "$ff,fff.dd"
_?sc*13500 pic
 $2,993.00
_?salary pic
 $2,750.00
_show macro
PIC
SC
_show pic
   Macro : USING "$ff,fff.dd"

_show sc
   Macro : SALARY + COMMIS

_
```

```
show pic
show sc
```

as depicted in Figure 4–9. Like variables, macros exist in the environment's working memory.

"Let's see," Dan said cautiously, "if I understand the difference between a macro and a variable. Whenever I want, I can invent a new variable or a new macro. A variable is like a small storage compartment where I can keep a value, perhaps a value that I've calculated, and then get at that value again by mentioning the variable's name. On the other hand, a macro is a user-defined term—a pushbutton as you call it—that is essentially a synonym for some series of keystrokes. In effect, this feature allows me to add new words to the command language. Whenever I use one of these words, the environment will know what I mean."

"That's a good explanation," said Jack. He added, "Because a variable can have a value, we can classify variables according to the types of values they have: numeric, string, and logical variables. In contrast, macros do not have values and therefore there is no notion of different types of macros." In knowledge management terms, a variable is a way of representing descriptive knowledge whereas a macro is a way of representing linguistic knowledge.

Function Keys

Most keyboards are equipped with function keys labeled F1, F2, . . . F10. In the keyboard of Figure 2–2(a), these special keys are positioned on the left side of the keyboard. In Figure 2–2(b), there are twelve function keys along the top of the keyboard. The behavior that results from pressing one of these keys depends on what software happens to be executing. With some software packages, each function key has a predetermined effect that the user cannot alter. Other software packages give users varying degrees of freedom in defining the behavior that results from pressing a function key. In such cases, the function keys are literally user-definable pushbuttons.

"If you like," Jack announced, "you can use function keys to achieve results similar to what we got with macros. Instead of defining a new term and its associated keystroke sequence, you can define a keystroke sequence for an existing function key. Whenever you later press that key, its entire sequence of associated keystrokes automatically appears on the screen beginning at the present cursor position. It's just as if you typed them all yourself, except you merely pushed a single button!"

To illustrate, Jack decided to let the F2 key be redefined as SALARY +COMMIS. He accomplished this by using the REDEFINE FUNCTION command, as follows

```
redefine function 2 "salary+commis"
```

From this point onward, pressing F2 would cause SALARY+COMMIS to appear at the cursor position. When the underscore prompt reappeared, he very slowly and deliberately pressed the ? key and then F2. After pressing the question mark key, the command line looked like

```
_?
```

When he pressed F2, its associated string of characters instantly appeared so the line now looked like

```
_?salary+commis
```

Thus 14 characters now appeared on the screen as the result of only two keystrokes. He finished off this OUTPUT command as shown in Figure 4–10.

FIGURE 4–10 Defining function key behavior

```
_redefine function 2 "salary+commis"
_?salary+commis*10000
    2930.00000
_redefine function 3 " using \"$fff,fff.ff\""
_?salary using "$fff,fff.ff"
   $2,750.00
_redefine function 1 "help\13"
_help
```

"I notice that you enclose the function key's definition in a matching pair of quotes," commented Stan. "What happens if I want the definition itself to contain some quote marks? For instance, if I want F3 to be USING "$fff,fff.ff" won't those extra quotes confuse the software?"

"They certainly will," Joy answered, "unless you preface every quote mark that's part of the definition with a backslash symbol. In general, whenever you want to use quotes within quotes, just include backslashes in this way."

Jack illustrated by typing

```
redefine function 3 " using\"$fff,fff.ff\""
```

Notice that each of the two embedded quotes is prefaced by a backslash (\). If the backslashes had not been used, the second rather than fourth quote mark would have signaled the end of the definition. To demonstrate that F3 was now defined according to Stan's specifications, Jack typed

```
?salary
```

and paused. He then pressed F3. The command line immediately took
on the appearance

```
_?salary using "$fff,fff.ff"
```

which is what Stan desired.

"I presume," resumed Stan, "that I could use the same approach
to make a quote mark appear literally in a picture, so it's not interpreted
as indicating the end of a picture."

"That's right," Joy responded. "As a matter of fact, you would
also use the backslash approach to make a placeholder letter appear
literally with a picture. For example, if you want a lowercase c to be
treated as a literal rather than a placeholder in a picture—"

"—You put a backslash in front of it," interrupted Stan. She nodded
in assent.

"While we are talking about backslashes, let me show you one
other thing," remarked Jack. "Sometimes I want a function key to cause
the execution of an entire command. For instance, if you frequently
need help, you might want to define F1 as being equivalent to the
HELP command."

"Wouldn't you just invoke the REDEFINE command to give function
1 a meaning of help?" asked Tracey.

"Almost," replied Jack, "but not quite. Let's see what would happen." He proceeded to execute

```
redefine function 1 "help"
```

and when the underscore prompt reappeared, he pressed F1. Sure
enough, the HELP command appeared so the line looked like

```
_help
```

with a blinking cursor following the word.

"Now I could press the Enter key to execute this command," Jack
said, "but I won't. What I really wanted was to avoid that." He pressed
the destructive Backspace key to get rid of the word help.

"I see," nodded Tracey. "What you want is to include the Enter
keystroke as part of the definition of F1. But how can you do that? If
you were to press the Enter key after typing help, that would be a
signal that you were finished with the REDEFINE command when you
really weren't. The quote terminating the definition would be missing."

"Exactly," smiled Jack. "What we need is a way to specify the

Enter key as part of the definition without actually entering it. Here is another place where the backslash can come to our rescue. Watch."

He typed the command

```
redefine function 1 "help\13"
```

and pressed the Enter key to execute it. He explained that 13 is a standard internal computer code for the Enter key. It is called the Enter key's ASCII (pronounced "ask ee") code. ASCII stands for American Standard Code for Information Interchange. For each possible keystroke (including those that don't produce characters on the screen) there is a unique ASCII code number. When a backslash appears in a function key definition and is immediately followed by a number in the range 0 through 255, the environment assumes that you mean the key corresponding to the ASCII code number. Many software packages allow you to refer to a key by its ASCII number as an alternative to actually pressing the key. Each has its own way (such as a leading backslash) of allowing you to indicate that a number should be interpreted as an ASCII code rather than an ordinary number.

To demonstrate that the new definition of F1 worked, Jack pressed F1. The screen momentarily took on the appearance shown in Figure 4–10, but as the Enter key was now automatically issued, this screen was almost immediately replaced by the familiar help screen shown in Photo 9. In general, this environment permits you to redefine any function key whenever you like, making it easy to change the behavior of a function key on the fly. Even though the keyboard appears to have only 10 function keys, there are really 40. The 30 extras are attained by simultaneously pressing a function key and either the Shift, Alt, or Ctrl (Control). These too can be defined by the REDEFINE FUNCTION command, using function numbers 11 (shift F1) through 40 (Alt F10).

CONTROL SWITCHES

A control switch gives a user a way of controlling some aspect of the software's behavior. Some pieces of software have no control switches. Others have many switches, allowing users to tailor the software's behavior to suit their respective tastes and needs. As with the user-definable pushbuttons, you do not need to know about control switches in order to operate in a knowledge management environment. Their existence can be entirely ignored if desired. But as you become a regular traveler in the environment, you will find that these gadgets can make the journey more comfortable and convenient.

In the KnowledgeMan environment, control switches take the form of *environment variables* [1]. An environment variable differs in a couple of ways from the working variables like SALARY and WHO that Jack introduced earlier. Unlike a working variable, an environment variable automatically exists when you enter the environment. Secondly, an environment variable serves a different purpose than the working variables invented by a user. Rather than being primarily a storage compartment for storing some piece of descriptive knowledge, an environment variable is a switch whose setting is changed by merely changing its value.

For the most part, the settings of environment variables are a way of representing certain linguistic (e.g., whether macros should be ignored or not) and presentation (e.g., the console screen's background color) knowledge. The environment uses this knowledge in understanding user requests and in presenting responses to the user. The environment variable settings exert a powerful influence over the command language interface.

Decimal Digit Switch

"You may have wondered," suggested Jack, "why the results of calculations always showed five digits to the right of the decimal point unless we used a picture."

"I was wondering when you would come to that," confirmed Brad. "I'd like a way to get just two decimal digits without having to use a .dd picture every time I do an OUTPUT command."

"Well," Jack responded, "the environment has a switch that allows you to set the number of decimal digits to two. It's named E.DECI. This is an example of a special kind of variable that's called an environment variable. Every environment variable name begins with E dot, so they're easy to recognize. By simply changing the value of an environment variable you are in effect setting a control switch to cause the environment to behave in a certain way."

He explained that there are many dozens of environment variables in this environment. As with working variables, some of these are numeric (e.g., E.DECI), others can have string values, and still others are logical in type. For the present, he decided to introduce only a few of these control switches. He planned to discuss others later, on an as-needed basis. To look at E.DECI's current setting, Jack issued the command

```
?e.deci
```

FIGURE 4–11   **Environment variable examples**

```
_?e.deci
        5.00000
_let e.deci=2;?salary
        2750.00
_?e.deci
        2.00
_?e.oprn
FALSE
_let e.oprn=true
_?salary using "$f,fff"
$2,750
_?e.oprn
TRUE
_let e.echo=true
_?salary*12
        33000.00
_?repname+" was the top rep in January."
Kevin was the t
_let e.lstr=50
_?repname+" was the top rep in January."
Kevin was the top rep in January.
_let e.oprn=false
_?e.bacg
UUUUA
_let e.bacg="uuuug"
```

with the response shown in Figure 4–11. Every environment variable has an initial setting that is traditionally called its *default* value. To change E.DECI from its default to 2, Jack used a LET command

```
let e.deci=2
```

and proceeded to illustrate the effect of this new setting by outputting the values of SALARY and E.DECI itself. As shown in Figure 4–11, the environment now presented numeric values with two rather than five decimal digits.

Printer Switches

"There are a few other environment variables that I tend to use often. One of these is E.OPRN, which controls whether or not the output from commands will be sent to a printer. So far, we haven't used a printer, but let's see what you would do if you needed to have the environment's responses output on a piece of paper. First be sure that paper has been inserted into your printer so it's ready to start printing at the top of a page. Be sure the printer's power switch is turned on and that the printer is online."

With that he turned on the printer's power switch and pressed the Online button. The Power, Ready, and Online lights (recall Figure 2–5) were now on. Now, if Jack were to issue a new command, its result would still appear only on the console screen. This is because E.OPRN is a logical environment variable whose default is FALSE, meaning output is not to be sent to the printer. Once it is set to TRUE, all subsequent responses to commands will appear not only on the screen but on the printer paper as well. To illustrate, Jack issued the commands

```
?e.oprn
let e.oprn=true
?salary using "$f,fff"
?e.oprn
```

with the results shown on the console screen in Figure 4–11. In addition, the results of the last two commands were printed on paper. There they appeared on two consecutive lines as

```
$2,750
TRUE
```

Jack stressed that the *printer must be online* when E.OPRN is TRUE.

"So," inquired Debbie, "only the results of commands go to the printer and not the commands themselves?"

"Correct," Jack replied, "for as long as E.OPRN remains set to TRUE. If you were to let it be FALSE again, the printer would once again be unused. Now there is a way to have your commands echoed to the printer along with their results."

"Let me guess," she said quickly. "I'll bet there's another control switch for that and it's probably called something like E.ECHO."

"That's exactly what it's called," Jack responded in a satisfied tone. "Like E.OPRN, E.ECHO is a logical environment variable. Obviously, its default setting is FALSE. Watch what happens when I let it be TRUE."

He issued the command

```
let e.echo=true
```

which appeared on the screen but not on the printer. From this point onward, every command issued would be echoed to the printer, until either E.OPRN or E.ECHO was set to FALSE. To demonstrate, he invoked the commands

FIGURE 4–12   Sample printout

```
$2,750
TRUE
?salary*12
       33000.00
?repname+" was the top rep in January."
Kevin was the t
```

```
?salary*12
?repname+" was the top rep in January."
```

and in both cases the command was echoed to the printer along with its result. Figure 4–12 shows the printout that Jack had produced thus far.

Presentation Switches

"What happened to the result of your last OUTPUT command?" asked Stan. "Part of it is missing."

"Lester did it," he said briskly. Amused by the puzzled looks, he continued, "There's an environment variable named E.LSTR that controls the maximum length of string values that will be output when a picture is not used. It's default value is 15, which is why only the first 15 characters of the calculated string were output by the last command. You can go to great lengths to see the full value of a string by enlarging E.LSTR to, say, 50."

Jack issued the commands

```
let e.lstr=50
?repname+" was the top rep in January."
```

with the on-screen results as shown in Figure 4–11. From this point onward strings of up to 50 characters could be output in their entirety. Jack set E.OPRN back to FALSE to discontinue the printed output.

"Let me show you an example of a string environment variable," Jack said. "It's named E.BACG and is used to control the screen's background color. Suppose you get tired of looking at the black default background while entering commands. You can set E.BACG to get any of six other colors. Let's go to a green background."

As shown in Figure 4–11, E.BACG's default value is a string of five characters (UUUUA). Jack explained that each of these five stood for the background color to be used in a particular kind of processing.

The fifth is for the screen background while entering interactive commands. He noted that they should not be concerned with the first four for the time being. The A stands for black. With three exceptions, each color is denoted by its first letter. The exceptions are black, blue, and brown, all of which start with the same letter. To differentiate among them, they are denoted by A, U, and O, respectively.

Thus, to switch the screen's background color for command entry to green, Jack issued the command

```
let e.bacg="uuuug"
```

From that point onward all commands and their responses would be presented against a green background, until E.BACG's fifth color code is changed to some other color. He mentioned that foreground colors could be governed in a similar fashion with the E.FORG environment variable.

Table 4–4 summarizes several of the available environment variables that might be of interest to beginners. Others will be introduced from time to time in the chapters that follow. As the table suggests, the important factors to understand about an environment variable are its name, type, default value, permissible values, and the behavior it controls.

ENVIRONMENT SENSORS

Some software packages provide built-in sensors that allow a user to examine the present state of affairs during execution. A sensor is a monitoring mechanism built into the software. In case of a knowledge management environment, it is continually monitoring some aspect of the environment; for example, what is the most recent error, what is the present date, what are the most recently computed statistics, or what is the current position in a spreadsheet. At any time, a user can look at a sensor to get a current "reading." The reading seen may well be different from the reading that is seen later for the same sensor.

"Aside from environment variables," Jack announced, "there is one other class of built-in variables that you can use in the environment. These are called *utility variables*. They're easy to spot, because instead of beginning with E dot, they begin with a crosshatch. Unlike any of the variables we've seen so far, the values of utility variables can be automatically changed by the environment itself to reflect some happening. I find them particularly useful when doing statistical analyses, but let's not get into that now.

"For the time being, I'll show you a simple example. It makes use

TABLE 4–4 Summary of some environment variables

Environment variable name	Type	Default value	Permissible values	Controls
E.DECI	numeric	5	0–14	Number of decimal digits presented when a picture is not used
E.LSTR	numeric	15	0–255	Number of string characters presented when a picture is not used
E.OPRN	logical	FALSE	FALSE or TRUE	Whether responses are sent to printer
E.ECHO	logical	FALSE	FALSE or TRUE	Whether commands are echoed to the printer when E.OPRN is TRUE
E.BACG	string	UUUUA	A (blAck) O (brOwn) U (blUe) R (Red) M (Magenta) G (Green) W (White)	Background screen color to be presented for various kinds of processing
E.FORG	string	WWWWW	A (blAck) O (brOwn) U (blUe) R (Red) M (Magenta) G (Green) W (White)	Foreground screen color to be presented for various kinds of processing

of a utility variable named #DATE, whose value will always be set to the current date by the software. Remember that I told the operating system what today's date is. Well, it should now also be the present value of #DATE. Let's see."

He issued the command

```
?#date
```

and the response of

```
09:30:86
```

appeared on the screen. To add a slight flourish he invoked the command

```
?"The current date is "+#date
```

with the result of

```
The current date is 09:30:86
```

being output to the screen.

"Now," Jack continued with a twinkle in his eyes, "I want you to tell me how to define a macro—call it D180—that will always output the date 180 days in the future, regardless of what the current date happens to be."

The room was silent except for the soft hum of the computer. If the group was really comprehending what he had been saying since the last break, they would be able to answer.

Debbie was the first to break the silence. "I think I know. The macro's text will be a string expression involving the #DATE utility variable with the TOJUL and TODATE functions."

"Show us," replied Jack, sweeping his hand toward the machine. She took the helm and entered the command

```
macro d180 ?todate(tojul(#date)+180,"/",4)+"is 180 days from now."
```

Jack and Joy smiled in unison. Debbie was right on the mark. Notice that she used the ? as part of the macro's text, in effect defining a completely new command named d180. Its result will always be a date that is 180 days past whatever date happens to be sensed in the environment. Just to check, Debbie typed

```
d180
```

following the underscore prompt and pressed the Enter key. The result of

```
03/29/1987 is 180 days from now.
```

flashed onto the screen.

"That's certainly a lot faster than manually calculating the result by looking at a calendar," remarked Dan as several heads nodded. "I understand that utility variables work like sensors, but can you also treat them like normal variables in the sense of assigning new values to them yourself?"

"Sure," replied Joy, "just issue a LET command as usual. In fact, there are some utility variables that don't behave as sensors at all. By assigning desired values to them you can influence such things as the column headings that will appear for query results or the legend messages that will appear on graphics screens. But don't worry about them for now. I'm sure Jack will fill you in on these when we get to the query and graphics techniques of knowledge management."

CONTEXT

Glancing at his watch, Jack announced, "It's about time to take a break and give you a chance to try some calculations on your own and get some firsthand experience with the various kinds of trappings we've discussed. But before I turn you loose on the computers in the back of the room, there's an important topic we haven't yet covered. What would happen to all our variables, macros, new environment settings, and current utility variable values if we were to turn off this computer while you take your break?"

"It would all go away," Stan answered alertly, "even if you're just leaving the environment and going back to the operating system."

"Right," Dan agreed, "because it's all remembered in the computer's main memory and as you told us earlier that's the short-term volatile memory."

"Of course," continued Jack, "it's no problem if we don't care about losing the knowledge we have entered into the knowledge system, if we don't need to pick up again later as if we had never left the environment."

"But," interrupted Brad, "what happens if you want to use some of the same macros or working variables or environment settings? Should we just leave the computer turned on and stay in the environment until we're ready to continue?"

"That would work, especially if you'll only be away for a short time and you don't need to exit back to the operating system in the interim," answered Jack.

"What we need," Tracey declared thoughtfully, "is a way to save all or some of the things from our present processing *context* in the environment's long-term memory on disk, and then a way to load it back into the environment's short-term working memory when we later want to resume. That would allow us to do whatever we like in the interim. Are there commands for doing this?"

Saving and Loading

"There sure are," replied Jack. "They are the SAVE and LOAD commands. With SAVE, you can preserve working variables, macros, environment variables, utility variables, and other kinds of knowledge we haven't yet discussed in a disk file. Because its contents describe the present processing context, such a file is called a context file. Hours, days, or months later, you can invoke the LOAD command to have the saved portion of the earlier context reinstated into your present context."

"We might say," chimed Joy with a smile, "SAVE lets you take something out of context, while LOAD lets you put things into context."

In describing the SAVE command, Jack explained that you need to furnish a name for the file that will be created. By convention, a context file has an extension of ICF. Deciding to call the context file SEP30.ICF and to store it on the diskette in drive B, he issued the command

```
save to "b:sep30.icf"
```

and the drive light for drive B came on as the context was saved. On completion, a new underscore prompt appeared on the screen as the environment was ready to accept his next command

```
bye
```

This returned control of the computer to the operating system. They were now out of the knowledge management environment. Incidentally, it is normally a good idea to return to the operating system before turning off the computer's power.

To show everyone that there was now indeed a file named SEP30.ICF on the drive B diskette, Jack issued the command

```
DIR SEP30
```

to the operating system. It responded by showing this file name, its size, and creation date. Then Jack reentered the environment in the usual manner. He invoked the SHOW MACRO and various OUTPUT commands to demonstrate that no vestige of the former processing existed in the present context.

To load the saved knowledge from the context file into the present processing context, Jack issued the command

```
load from "b:sep30.icf"
```

and again the drive B light went on, as the knowledge about macros and the various kinds of variables was transferred to the environment's working area in main memory. Jack invoked SHOW MACRO and various OUTPUT commands to confirm that all the former macros and working variables were now available. He also used OUTPUT commands to confirm that the changed environment variable settings (e.g., E.DECI of 2) had been restored.

Selective Saving and Loading

"What if I wanted to get back only the macros and didn't care about the other things?" someone asked.

Jack replied that the LOAD command would look like

```
load from "b:sep30.icf" with "m"
```

where the M stood for macros. He elaborated that loading could occur with any combination of macros (M), working variables (W), environment variables (E), and utility variables (U). Thus, the command

```
load from "b:sep30.icf" with "me"
```

would load all the saved macros and environment variable settings, but not the working variables' or utility variables' values.

Similarly, when SAVE is invoked, it is permissible to save only a selected portion of the context. For instance, the command

```
save to "b:s30.icf" with "wm"
```

saves only the working variables and macros in the S30 context file on drive B. Subsequent loads from this file can, of course, load no more than what was saved.

"I notice," said Debbie, "that you have not mentioned function key definitions as being a savable part of the context. It seems everything can be saved, what about them?"

Joy took this question. "In this environment, for whatever reason, SAVE and LOAD ignore the function key definitions. But there's a simple trick you can use to avoid retyping your favorite function key definitions every time you enter the environment."

Even before Joy had finished, a solution dawned on Debbie, "All I need to do is declare macros for my REDEFINE FUNCTION commands. These macros can be saved and loaded just like any others, and once loaded I can quickly execute them."

That was the trick Joy had in mind. It turns out that there are other ways to save and execute a whole batch of REDEFINE FUNCTION commands, but she deemed it premature to discuss them now. These alternatives will become clear in Chapter 13.

Releasing

"One last note," she added, "before we break. Sometimes you may want to get rid of a macro or variable that you don't intend to reference again. Doing so releases the main memory that it occupies for other uses. At some point you could have so many macros, variables, and other things in the environment's work area that it is too full or clogged up to handle your subsequent processing needs. So it's not a bad idea to release things you don't need any more."

Joy went on to explain that this is accomplished with the RELEASE command. Jack demonstrated that the command

```
release sc
```

made the SC macro vanish. His subsequent

```
show macro
```

command showed the existing macro names and SC was no longer among them. Similarly, to release the variable REPNAME from the present context, the command would be

```
release repname
```

If desired, utility variables can be released from a context in the same manner. However, it is neither possible nor desirable to release environment variables.

BASIC IDEAS

Calculation is a worthwhile knowledge management technique. It involves representing knowledge in the guise of an expression and processing such knowledge to establish a value for the expression. Numeric calculations, string calculations, and logical calculations are all useful and important. Through various examples, follow up, and hands-on practice, the group of sales managers now appreciated the difference between numeric, string, and logical expressions. They understood that expressions could contain constants, variables, and functions, plus operators to connect them if more than one was involved. Calculations can be routinely requested in commands such as LET and OUTPUT. Pictures can be used to determine the appearance of calculated values when they are output. The use of expressions for calculation will recur over and over again in the chapters that follow.

Many commercially available software packages provide varying subsets of the kinds of trappings discussed here: small storage compartments, definable pushbuttons, control switches, and sensors. What these are called and what they look like to a user differ from one package to another. In the knowledge management environment used by KC, they are called working variables, macros (and function keys), environment variables, and utility variables. *Trappings facilitate a knowledge worker's ability to move about and interact with the environment.* Commands such as HELP, OUTPUT (?), LET, MACRO, SHOW, REDEFINE FUNCTION, SAVE, LOAD, RELEASE, and BYE are used to steer the direction of processing within the environment. Collectively, the various trappings resemble a dashboard or control panel of conveniences for the knowledge worker. Though Jack used calculations as a vehicle for introducing the basic kinds of trappings, they are also applicable to the other knowledge management techniques described in the remaining chapters. Where appropriate, he will introduce new environment or utility variables, define new macros or function keys, and make use of additional working variables.

Reference

1. *KnowledgeMan Reference Manual*, version 2. Lafayette, Ind.: MDBS, Inc., 1985.

Part III

MANAGING DESCRIPTIVE KNOWLEDGE

How long a time lies in one little word.
(*Shakespeare*, King Richard II)

You certainly have a way with words.

Chapter Five

Text Management

Every sales manager deals with large amounts of descriptive knowledge. While the working variables used in calculations are good for handling small or isolated items of descriptive knowledge, they are not so well-suited for managing large amounts of descriptive knowledge or situations where there are many items that are tightly interrelated. As Tracey correctly pointed out during the break, a string variable is fine for storing a single string of text, but what if you need to prepare a document describing a rep's performance for the vice president of sales? Trying to do so by assigning strings (e.g., sentences) to variables and then concatenating them (i.e., with the + operator) in OUTPUT commands would be extremely cumbersome. In this chapter you will see how Tracey's concerns are addressed by text management: a technique for representing knowledge as large, free-flowing pieces of text and for processing this text in various ways [2].

Reconvening the session, Jack declared, "Now that you've seen how the computer can be used as a glorified calculator, let's see how it can also be used as a super typewriter. As you know, in our day-to-day activities we often have occasion to prepare memos, letters, narrative descriptions, policy documents, directives, specifications, and notes on various topics. All of these contain knowledge, or at least we hope they do."

His last statement evoked a few chuckles. He continued, "All of these things that you could do on a typewriter are candidates for the next technique we'll be discussing: text management. Just as we would expect an environment to support calculations, we'd also expect it to support text management. Both are very basic knowledge management techniques. Of course, you'll be able to do a lot more with the automated approach to text management than you could do with an ordinary typewriter.

"You all are already familiar with textual representation of knowledge, since it is the entire basis of reading and writing. As you'll see we can process chunks of text in various ways in this environment. We can create text, make electronic modifications to text while it appears on the console screen, and we can view it."

"If I might interject," Tracey said, "I've not previously done text management in an environment, but I have been using a text management package for a while. Though it can't do calculations and the many other things that Jack has hinted at as possible in this environment, I can confirm that automated text management is much faster than conventional typing. It's so much more convenient for composing and editing text, because you're working with an electronic image of the text rather than a paper version. You only commit it to paper once you're satisfied with its content. And when you want to simply examine the text, it's so much faster to scan a single electronic image than shuffling through multiple pieces of paper."

Both Jack and Joy smiled at this unanticipated testimonial. Joy added, "In addition to the speed and convenience advantages, there's another benefit that people often notice. It's the greater accuracy and thoroughness that automated text processing permits when editing or searching through a piece of text."

Software dedicated to text management may range from modest text editors to sophisticated, heavy-duty word processors as Figure 5–1 suggests. Between the two extremes is a middle ground of text processors. All three are concerned with text management and the dividing lines between the three categories are not always clear. But in general, as one progresses from the text editor extreme there are more features and conveniences available to the user. Software in the word processing category affords the most elaborate and extensive text management facilities. In some cases, the term *word processor* is used to refer not just to software but an entire hardware-software configuration specially designed to handle very advanced text management tasks.

Word processors are typically used by knowledge workers whose whole job revolves around the manipulation of pieces of text [1], [5]. For them, heavy-duty text management software is preferable. They are likely to deal with very large documents, very many pieces of text, very elaborate formatting, or complex mixtures of font types and sizes. At the other extreme, text editors tend to be used by those for whom line-at-a-time management of text is sufficient (e.g., programmers) [7]. They do not need to format the text in special ways or prepare elaborate documents.

A manager's text-handling needs normally fall somewhere between the two extremes. On the one hand, text editors are too rudimentary

FIGURE 5–1   Text management spectrum

Text editors	Text processors	Word processors
• Manage text line-by-line	• Full-screen text management	• Full-screen text management
• Few control keys	• More control keys	• Many control keys
• No block processing	• Block processing	• Elaborate block processing
• No format controls	• Many format controls	• Elaborate format controls
• No word wrap	• Word wrap	• Word wrap
• No on-screen help	• On-screen help	• On-screen help
• Used by programmers	• Middle ground	• Used for clerical tasks
		• Spelling checker
		• Thesaurus

to be very useful for preparing nice-looking notes, memos, correspondence, and narratives. On the other hand, full-blown word processors may well be overkill. A manager's forte is decision making. While it is important to support decision processes and convey the results textually where appropriate, a manager's activities do not concentrate on elaborate text management. When a very fancy or large-scale document is required, it is normally more effectively handled by a knowledge worker who specializes in text management techniques, rather than personally by the manager.

Unlike text editor, text processor, and word processor software packages, the text management capability presented in this chapter is not some isolated tool. It is an integral component of a larger environment [4]. As will be shown in this and succeeding chapters, the effect of this integration is that other techniques (e.g., calculation) can be freely exercised in the midst of text management. If the synergy effect is disregarded, then the strictly text management aspects that Jack will cover are at the level of a text processor or perhaps a low-end word processor. They address the major general-purpose text management needs of KC's sales managers.

THE TEXT COMMAND

Having shed his coat and rolled up his sleeves, Jack said, "Let's get to work on a piece of text. Regardless of whether you want to work on a new piece of text or some text that you created previously, you invoke the TEXT command."

In response to the usual underscore prompt, Jack typed

```
text "a:gmrnote.txt"
```

but did not press the Enter key. He paused to interpret this command, explaining that it indicated a desire to process the text held in a file named GMRNOTE.TXT on the diskette in drive A. If no such file existed (which was the case here), the environment would assume a new piece of text was to be created and it would be stored in a new file named GMRNOTE.TXT on the drive A diskette. Jack named it GMRNOTE because he planned to create a note describing *gross margin rates*.

Though text processing uses a portion of the environment's working memory, the text itself is not considered to be part of the context for saving and loading purposes. Instead, each piece of text is preserved in a file on disk. Such files are normally called *text files* and commonly have an extension of TXT. They can exist alongside context files in a knowledge system. Just as the SAVE and LOAD commands operate exclusively on context files, the TEXT command operates exclusively on text files.

Jack pressed the Enter key to execute his TEXT command. The environment's blue text screen immediately appeared with the contents shown in Figure 5–2. He explained, "Whenever you see such a screen you can work on the electronic image of a piece of text. The top line of the text screen, called the *status line,* is reserved for tracking the present status of your text processing and for issuing commands. The remaining 24 lines of 80 columns each is the *text area* where the image of your text will appear. Of course, since we haven't yet created any text, this area is now empty except for the blinking cursor in its top-left corner. If there had already been some text in the GMRNOTE file, that text would have been displayed in the text area."

Brad interrupted, "But what if I need to work on a piece of text that's more than 24 lines long?"

"You're free to do so," Jack replied quickly. "In this environment each piece of text can have thousands of lines and each line can be up to about 250 characters long. The only restriction is that you can't view all of a big chunk of text at the same time. The text area is like a window allowing you to look at a 24 by 80 part of the text at any one time. As we'll see later, it's easy to 'move' any desired part of the text into this window whenever you want."

Seeing that Brad was satisfied, Jack explained the status line contents in more detail. The line and column indicators show the cursor's present position in the text. At this moment the cursor was blinking at line 1 and column 1. He emphasized that this is the cursor's position in the text, as opposed to its position on the screen. For instance, if lines 101 through 124 of a piece of text were presently visible in the text area and the cursor was at the same physical screen location shown in Figure

FIGURE 5–2 The text screen

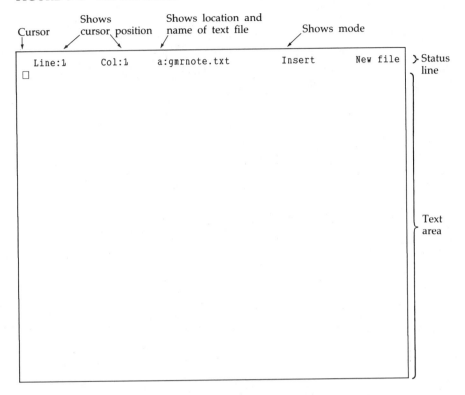

Cursor   Shows cursor position   Shows location and name of text file   Shows mode

5–2, the line indicator would show 101 rather than 1. This lets you easily know what part of a large piece of text is being displayed at any moment.

The status line also shows the name of the text file, prefaced by its drive location. The word "Insert" shows the current mode of text entry that is in effect. *Insert mode* means that as each new character of text is typed, the cursor and any characters at or to the right of it move right one column to make room for the insertion of the new character. The alternative *replacement mode* of entry causes the character presently at the cursor (if any) to be replaced by the newly typed character. When this entry mode is in effect the word "Replace" appears on the status line instead of "Insert."

"To begin creating new text I simply begin typing just as if I were using a typewriter," said Jack. He matched his words with actions by typing a few sentences until the screen appeared as shown in Figure 5–3. As he pressed each key the column indicator automatically increased by one to reflect the cursor's new position until it reached 66. At that

FIGURE 5-3   Creating some new text

```
 Line:b      Col:52     a:gmrnote.txt  Insert              Press 'L for help
For each product line, a region is given an annual sales target
by the KC vice president of sales. The vice president also
determines the commission rate for each product line. In
addition, each product line has a particular gmr (gross margin
rate)which indicates the percentage of its sales that constitutes
the gross profit before deducting selling expenses.
```

point it automatically jumped to the start of the next line, the line indicator increased by one, and the column indicator was reset to 1. At no point did Jack need to think about a carriage return as he would with a typewriter. He just kept on typing.

For instance, as he neared the end of the first line the word "target" was momentarily followed by a space and the letter b in the 66th column

```
For each product line, a region is given an annual sales target b
```

When he pressed the letter y, the cursor not only jumped to the second line, it carried the unfinished word (i.e., the letter b) with it

```
For each product line, a region is given an annual sales target
by
```

This same kind of behavior occurred at the end of each line Jack typed. He explained that this is known as *word wrap*. If there is not enough room for a word to fit entirely on a line before hitting the right margin (e.g., column 66 in this example), the entire word automatically wraps around to the start of the next line.

"As you are typing in new text you may realize that you've made an error. If so, you can correct it immediately in the same way that you can correct errors made when typing in a command. The same control keys we saw earlier work in the same way here." Jack was referring to ^S (move the cursor left) and ^D (move the cursor right), as well as the destructive Backspace key. As it turns out, there are many other control keys that can be useful during text creation or editing.

CONTROL KEYS FOR EDITING TEXT

Anytime there is text appearing in the text area, that text can be *edited* by inserting, deleting, and changing characters, words, lines, or blocks of lines. Control keys can be used to accomplish many of these editing operations. As the status line in Figure 5–3 shows, you can press ^L to get help about what control keys are available for text editing. Jack pressed ^L, bringing a control key summary into view as shown in Figure 5–4.

Cursor Movement

"Notice," explained Jack, "that the first line of help tells us we can use Control-E and Control-X to move the cursor up and down a line from its present position. The second tells us, as we've previously seen, that Control-S and Control-D move the cursor left and right by one character. In the third line, you can see that Control-F and Control-A will make word-at-a-time moves to the left and right. When you want to edit something, you need to move the cursor to it and that's what some of the control keys are for."

"What's the meaning of words such as FUP and FDOWN in front of the control keys?" asked Tracey.

Joy replied, "This environment can run on a variety of machines and under different operating systems. Some of those machines or operating systems don't allow the same control keys that we are using in the IBM PC-DOS world to have the same effects in those other worlds. Regardless of what the host is, the environment's functionality is the same. The words that start with F describe a basic functionality—such as moving the cursor up or down—that exists across different hosts. For instance, FDOWN is accomplished here by the Control-X key. But with a different operating system it might be accomplished by some other key as designated by the help information you would see there."

"What you're saying," Tracey responded, "is that we don't have to be concerned about words like FUP and FDOWN since we're not going to be switching between incompatible operating systems or com-

FIGURE 5–4   Control key help

```
 Line:6      Col:52    a:qmrnote.txt  Insert                    Press ^L for help
---------------------------------------------------------------------------------
FUP       ^e line up              | FDOWN     ^x line down
FLEFT     ^s character left       | FRIGHT    ^d character right
FNEXT     ^f next word            | FPRIOR    ^a prior word
FSTART    ^v beginning of line    | FEND      ^b end of line
FSUP      ^u screen up            | FSDOWN    ^n screen down
FABORT    ^[ command mode toggle  | FEXIT     ^c exit system
FDELETE   ^r delete cursor character | FINSERT  ^w toggle insert/replace
FZAP      ^h destructive backspace | PRESTART  ^z restart input
FDLINE    ^t delete cursor line   | FILINE    ^q insert line
FSPLIT    ^p split line at cursor | FJOIN     ^o join line with next
FENTER    ^m end current line     | FHELP     ^l display help text
FSLEFT    ^g screen left          | FSRIGHT   ^k screen right
------------------------- press any key to continue -------------------------
```

puters. They're just little general-purpose reminders of the functionality achieved by some corresponding control key."

Motioning to the screen, Brad joined in, "That seems like an awful lot of control keys to keep track of."

"Not really," rejoined Tracey. "I have keys for the same functionalities with my text management package."

"The important point," offered Jack, "is that you don't have to keep them all in mind all the time. When you want to do a particular editing operation, you either know what control keys to use or you don't. If you don't, simply press Control-L and scan the summary until you spot the desired functionality and corresponding key. Actually the keys are fairly easy to remember even without the help because they are arranged in logical patterns on the keyboard. Let me show you what I mean."

Jack placed a transparency that looked like Figure 5–5 on the overhead projector. He pointed out the central diamond shape formed by the four keys that move the cursor one space in any direction. At the top is ^E (up one line), at the bottom is ^X (down one line), at the right is ^D (right one column), and at the left is ^S (left one column). On either side of ^D and ^S are the keys to make larger leaps to the

FIGURE 5–5   Control key patterns for cursor movement

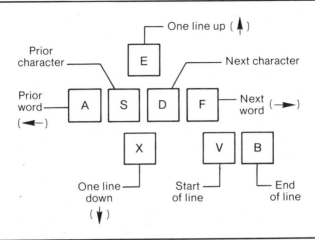

right (^F) or left (^A). In passing, Jack mentioned that the four arrow keys on the numeric keypad could also be used for moving the cursor in either horizontal or vertical directions.

Insertion, Deletion, and Restoration

Jack placed another transparency on the projector as depicted in Figure 5–6. The shaded key is one that had already been discussed. To its left are keys that deal with insertion and to its right are keys that deal with deletion and restoration. The ^W key is used to switch back and forth (i.e., "toggle") between the two modes of text entry discussed earlier. Jack explained, "If you are presently in Insert mode, Control-W will put you into Replace mode, and vice versa. Which mode you want to be in depends on the kind of processing you want to do. On the opposite side of the E key is Control-R, which deals with the opposite of character insertion. When you press it, the character at the cursor is deleted.

"The Control-Q and Control-T keys form another insertion-deletion pairing further out from the E key. Whenever you want to insert an entire new line prior to the cursor line, just press Control-Q. On the other hand when you want to delete the present cursor line, just press Control-T and it goes away. If you decide that you didn't really want to delete it after all, you can restore the last deleted line prior to the present cursor line by just pressing Control-Y. Let me demonstrate some of these keys by editing the text we've created."

FIGURE 5–6 Control key patterns for insertion, deletion, and restoration

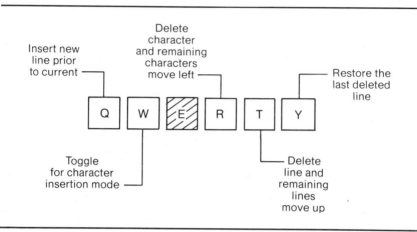

He pressed the space bar to remove the control key help from the screen, reverting to the appearance in Figure 5–3. The first change he made was to insert a space before the word "which" in the second to last line. This was accomplished by using control keys to move the cursor to the "w" in "which" and then pressing the space bar to insert a blank space. In the bottom line he wanted to insert the word "direct" prior to "selling." Jack moved the cursor to the "s" in "selling" and typed in the word "direct" followed by a space. The screen now had the appearance shown in Figure 5–7. He explained that it is permissible to insert multiple words in the same place if desired.

"How would you capitalize the gross margin rate abbreviation?" asked Dan.

"Now that's a case where we want to replace something that already exists rather than inserting something new, so we want to be in Replace mode rather than Insert mode. Remember, that's what Control-W is for." With this remark he pressed ^W and the word "Replace" replaced "Insert" in the status line. He moved the cursor to the "g" in "gmr" and typed GMR. As each of these three capital letters was entered, it replaced the corresponding lowercase letter, yielding the screen appearance shown in Figure 5–8.

"I think the text would look better if you indented the first line a few spaces," Stan said. "I guess that's another example of insertion."

Jack nodded and pressed Control-W. The word "Insert" reappeared in the status line. He moved the cursor to the "F" in the word "For" and pressed the space bar three times. As each space was inserted the

FIGURE 5–7   Inserting a space and a word

```
  Line:6      Col:42    a:gmrnote.txt  Insert            Press ˆL for help
For each product line, a region is given an annual sales target
by the KC vice president of sales. The vice president also
determines the commission rate for each product line. In
addition, each product line has a particular gmr (gross margin
rate) which indicates the percentage of its sales that constitutes
the gross profit before deducting direct selling expenses.
```

entire line moved a position to the right. The text screen now appeared as shown in Figure 5–9.

"I'm beginning to get the knack of this," Brad declared. "It's sure more powerful and flexible than a typewriter. Suppose we wanted to add some new text describing the region's sales target, GMR, and commission rate for various product lines. Would you just move the cursor down a way and begin typing these new things?"

Jack answered by moving the cursor down to line 8 and typing in the line

```
ID   Name     Target   Commission   GMR
```

and pressing the Enter key to signal that he was done with that line. The cursor jumped to the start of line 9. He proceeded to type in a line describing each of several products until the text screen appeared as shown in Figure 5–10. At the end of each of the new lines he pressed the Enter key because he did not want the lines to wrap together.

After a brief survey of the screen, Jack said, "Let's insert a gentler lead in for the product descriptions. All I need to do is move the cursor

FIGURE 5–8 **Character replacement**

```
   Line:4        Col:49      a:gmrnote.txt  Replace                 Press ˊL for help
For each product line, a region is given an annual sales target
by the KC vice president of sales. The vice president also
determines the commission rate for each product line. In
addition, each product line has a particular GMR (gross margin
rate) which indicates the percentage of its sales that constitutes
the gross profit before deducting direct selling expenses.
```

FIGURE 5–9 **Indenting a line**

```
   Line:1        Col:4       a:gmrnote.txt  Insert                  Press ˊL for help
   For each product line, a region is given an annual sales target
by the KC vice president of sales. The vice president also
determines the commission rate for each product line. In
addition, each product line has a particular GMR (gross margin
rate) which indicates the percentage of its sales that constitutes
the gross profit before deducting direct selling expenses.
```

FIGURE 5–10   Adding product descriptions

```
Line :14      Col:1      a:gmrnote.txt Insert              Press ^L for help
   For each product line, a region is given an annual sales target
by the KC vice president of sales. The vice president also
determines the commission rate for each product line. In
addition, each product line has a particular GMR (gross margin
rate) which indicates the percentage of its sales that constitutes
the gross profit before deducting direct selling expenses.

ID    Name         Target    Commission    GMR
BUS   business     173000          .022    .34
PSY   psychology   102000          .018    .36
ROM   romance      235000          .024    .64
REF   reference    224000          .019    .38
PHO   photography   86000          .020    .28
```

up to the blank line and press Control-Q to insert a new blank line. Then, I just type." He began a new paragraph and entered the new text as shown in Figure 5–11. The new text did not fit completely on the new line, so as Jack kept typing word wrap occurred to another new line that was inserted automatically."

"It would look better if you could separate the column headings from the actual data," Stan suggested. "I guess you would use Control-Q to insert a blank line beneath the heading and then type in some dashes on that line."

Jack moved the cursor to the BUS line and pressed ^Q. The lines of data were pushed down to make room for the new blank line beneath the heading line. He typed in dashes on that line to get the effect Stan desired. For good measure, Jack moved the cursor to the start of the heading line and held the space bar down until the heading was approximately centered under the preceding text. He repeated this for each line below the heading until it was visually aligned. The result is portrayed in Figure 5–12.

Brad had a more challenging task, "Let's see you put romance before business."

Jack thought for a moment that maybe he should have Joy show

FIGURE 5–11 Line insertion

```
 Line:16      Col:1     a:gmrnote.txt   Insert                Press ^L for help
   For each product line, a region is given an annual sales target
by the KC vice president of sales. The vice president also
determines the commission rate for each product line. In
addition, each product line has a particular GMR (gross margin
rate) which indicates the percentage of its sales that constitutes
the gross profit before deducting direct selling expenses.
   In our region the product targets, commissions, and GMRs are
as follows:

ID      Name          Target    Commission    GMR
BUS     business      173000          .022    .34
PSY     psychology    102000          .018    .36
ROM     romance       235000          .024    .64
REF     reference     224000          .019    .38
PHO     photography    86000          .020    .28
```

FIGURE 5–12 Moving the data

```
 Line:17      Col:1     a:gmrnote.txt   Insert                Press ^L for help
   For each product line, a region is given an annual sales target
by the KC vice president of sales. The vice president also
determines the commission rate for each product line. In
addition, each product line has a particular GMR (gross margin
rate) which indicates the percentage of its sales that constitutes
the gross profit before deducting direct selling expenses.
   In our region the product targets, commissions, and GMRs are
as follows:

        ID      Name          Target    Commission    GMR
        ---     -----------   ------    -----------    ---
        BUS     business      173000          .022    .34
        PSY     psychology    102000          .018    .36
        ROM     romance       235000          .024    .64
        REF     reference     224000          .019    .38
        PHO     photography    86000          .020    .28
```

PHOTO 11   Managing a piece of text

how this could be done, then he saw the light. "First, I'll delete the romance line," which he did by moving the cursor to it and pressing ^T. That line vanished with the other lines automatically moving upward to occupy its former space.

"Hold on," said Brad, "I wanted you to move it, not get rid of romance. Who wants to type in that whole line again in a different position?"

"Nobody," replied Jack with a sly look, "especially not me. All I do is move the cursor to the business line and press Control-Y to bring the romance back into our lives." In doing so, he used ^Y to restore the most recently deleted line in a new position, as shown in Photo 11.

Splitting and Joining Lines

There were two other control keys that Jack briefly described and demonstrated. The ^P key splits the line containing the cursor. All of the characters at and to the right of the cursor are split away from the current line to be inserted as a new line directly beneath it. The ^O key has the reverse effect by joining the line that is below the cursor to the end of the cursor line. These two keys are complementary in the sense that the two-key sequence of either ^P^Q or ^Q^P leaves the text unaltered.

Jack moved the cursor to the 'a' in 'are' on line 8 (see Photo 11). He proceeded to type

```
(gross margin rates)
```

followed by a space. The word wrap forced this parenthetical expression to a new line so the paragraph now consisted of the three lines

```
In our region the product targets, commissions, and GMRs
(gross margin rates) are
as follows:
```

with the cursor blinking after 'are' in the second line. To join the two short lines together, Jack simply pressed ^O. He showed that the result of

```
In our region the product targets, commissions, and GMRs
(gross margin rates) are as follows:
```

could be split again by pressing ^P and then joined once more by again pressing ^O. This kind of functionality is very handy for working with large pieces of lines.

TEXT EDITING WITH COMMANDS

"I think you can now more fully see the value of working with an electronic image of text as opposed to a paper image." Jack's remark evoked a murmur of assent. "The control keys for text editing are pretty powerful. Going a step further, you can also use commands for editing text."

Obviously, there is a limit on the number of control keys available and this places a limit on the number of distinct functionalities that can be accomplished with a single control key. To furnish even greater functionality to a user, some text management software has a user press a sequence of two (or more) control keys to designate a particular task. Other software may offer menu selections (e.g., in a status line) for designating additional tasks beyond those accomplished via a single keystroke. Yet another approach is to support commands for the addi-

FIGURE 5–13   Command entry while processing text

```
 Line:12    Col:1     a:gmrnote.txt  Command:           Press 'L for help
   For each product line, a region is given an annual sales target
by the KC vice president of sales. The vice president also
determines the commission rate for each product line. In
addition, each product line has a particular GMR (gross margin
rate) which indicates the percentage of its sales that constitutes
the gross profit before deducting direct selling expenses.
   In our region the product targets, commissions, and GMRs are
as follows:


     ID    Name           Target   Commission   GMR
     ---   -----------    ------   ----------    ---
     ROM   romance        235000       .024      .64
     BUS   business       173000       .022      .34
     PSY   psychology     102000       .018      .36
     REF   reference      224000       .019      .38
     PHO   photography     86000       .020      .28
```

tional functionalities. The environment examined here uses this latter
approach.

"But where do you type in a command on the text screen?" asked
Debbie. "How can the environment understand that what you're typing
is a command rather than part of the text?"

"Simple," Jack replied. "Whenever you want to issue a command,
just press the Escape key. This lets the cursor escape from the text
area and jump to the status line where you are prompted to enter a
command. Watch."

Starting with the text screen shown in Photo 11, he pressed the
Escape key. The word "Insert" in the status line was immediately replaced by the "Command:" prompt as shown in Figure 5–13. The blinking cursor was now positioned immediately following this prompt, awaiting Jack's command.

"But how would I know what commands are available?" Brad asked.

"In the same way you could see what control keys are available,"
Jack replied.

"By pressing the Control-L key?"

"Right. Because the command prompt is showing in the status line,
the environment assumes that you want help with the commands avail-

FIGURE 5–14   Help on the text-processing commands

```
Line:12      Col:1      a:gmrnote.txt    Command:              Press ^L for help
--------------------------------------------------------------------------------
READ     read a file to be edited    |  WRITE    save text to a file
BEGIN    set the start of a block    |  END      set the end of a block
COPY     copy a block of text        |  MOVE     move a block of text
UNBLOCK  remove block markers         |  NUMBER   toggle line numbers
SEARCH   search for a text pattern    |  MODIFY   change a text pattern
INSERT   insert a file at cursor      |  DELETE   delete portion of text
STOP     save work and exit editor    |  BYE      return to KNOWLEDGE MAN
PRINT    print file on list device    |  FORMAT   set word wrap
CANCEL   cancel current file edit     |  GOTO     position at line
TOP      position at top of file      |  BOTTOM   position at end of file
QUIT     quit text processing         |
--------------------------------------------------------------------------------
         PSY    psychology     102000      .018    .36
         REF    reference      224000      .019    .38
         PHO    photography     86000      .020    .28
```

able for processing text, rather than help about control keys." With that, Jack pressed ^L and the screen took on the appearance shown in Figure 5–14. The commands are highlighted in uppercase. The help will remain on the screen until either a command has been entered in the status line or the Escape key is pressed to bring the cursor back into the text area.

"Though some of these help explanations may seem a bit cryptic," commented Joy, "the text command help can be a useful reminder of what's available. Jack will illustrate what some of these commands actually do. Once you get the knack of a few of the most commonly used ones, you can readily pick up the others on your own."

Numbering and Cursor Movement

"Let's start with a very simple command that lets you see line numbers in front of each line of text," suggested Jack. "It is the NUMBER command. The line numbers that will appear aren't actually part of the text. They just appear on the screen to help keep track of the lines." Jack typed in this command so that

FIGURE 5–15   Numbered text

```
  Line:12     Col:1      a:gmrnote.txt   Insert              Press 'L for help
1          For each product line, a region is given an annual sales target
2          by the KC vice president of sales. The vice president also
3          determines the commission rate for each product line. In
4          addition, each product line has a particular GMR (gross margin
5          rate) which indicates the percentage of its sales that constitutes
6          the gross profit before deducting selling expenses.
7             In our region the product targets, commissions, and GMRs are
8          as follows:
9
10                   ID   Name          Target   Commission    GMR
11                   ---  -----------   ------   ----------    ---
12                   ROM  romance       235000      .024       .64
13                   BUS  business      173000      .022       .34
14                   PSY  psychology    102000      .018       .36
15                   REF  reference     224000      .019       .38
16                   PHO  photography    86000      .020       .28
17
18
```

```
Command: number
```

now appeared on the status line. When he pressed the Enter key to
signal the end of the command, the text screen took on the appearance
shown in Figure 5–15. The cursor resumed its former position in the
text.

"As it turns out," Jack continued, "you don't have to type out the
full name of text commands like NUMBER. For instance, simply typing
NUM is sufficient." To illustrate, he pressed the Escape key, once again
bringing the cursor into the status line for command entry. He typed
in

```
num
```

and when he pressed the Enter key the numbers disappeared, reverting
to Photo 11.

Line numbering is most useful when working with a very long
piece of text. Other commands that are especially useful for handling
large pieces of text are TOP, BOTTOM, and GOTO. By entering the
command

```
top
```

the first 24 lines of text will appear in the text area and the cursor will be positioned in the top line. Similarly, the BOTTOM command causes the last lines of text to be brought into view and positions the cursor in the bottom line. By entering the command

```
goto 137
```

the 137th line will come into view and the cursor will go to that line. The number for any existing line of text can be specified with the GOTO command.

Searching for a Pattern

"Suppose we want to scan a long piece of text for all instances of some word or pattern of characters," said Jack. "One way would be to visually examine each line of text for the pattern. There's another, much faster, way to search for the pattern. It's the SEARCH command. Let's say you want to quickly find all occurrences of GMR in the text, to see if that term is properly used everywhere."

Jack escaped to the status line and issued the command

```
search
```

there. The environment responded with the question

```
Search pattern?
```

in the status line. Jack answered by typing

```
GMR
```

resulting in the screen appearance shown in Figure 5–16. When he pressed the Enter key, indicating the end of the pattern, the blinking cursor immediately moved to the first instance of GMR in the text and another question

```
Continue (y/n)?
```

appeared in the status line. Jack responded by pressing the y key and the cursor immediately moved to the next occurrence of GMR in the text. If he had responded by pressing the n key, the search would

FIGURE 5–16   Specifying a search pattern

```
  Line:12     Col:1     a:gmrnote.txt   Search pattern? GMR
    For each product line, a region is given an annual sales target
  by the KC vice president of sales. The vice president also
  determines the commission rate for each product line. In
  addition, each product line has a particular GMR (gross margin
  rate) which indicates the percentage of its sales that constitutes
  the gross profit before deducting selling expenses.
    In our region the product targets, commissions, and GMRs are
  as follows:


        ID     Name         Target   Commission   GMR
        ---    -----------  ------   ----------    ---
        ROM    romance      235000      .024       .64
        BUS    business     173000      .022       .34
        PSY    psychology   102000      .018       .36
        REF    reference    224000      .019       .38
        PHO    photography   86000      .020       .28
```

have terminated with the most recently found GMR. As long as the y
key is pressed, the search proceeds to successive instances of GMR
until all have been found.

Modifying a Search Pattern

Drawing on her text management experience, Tracey asked, "How could
you have the environment search for each abbreviation 'GMR' and replace it with the phrase 'gross margin rate'?"

"That's a very useful operation," answered Jack, "and it's accomplished with the MODIFY command. With this command you can do
everything you can do with SEARCH, plus you get the chance to have
the found GMRs replaced by the full phrase."

He demonstrated by escaping to the status line and issuing the
command

```
modify
```

there. As with SEARCH, he was asked to furnish a search pattern
and, as before, he responded with GMR. A new question

FIGURE 5–17   Specifying a replacement pattern

```
Line:10    Col:54    a:gmrnote.txt   Replacement pattern? gross margin rate
  For each product line, a region is given an annual sales target
by the KC vice president of sales. The vice president also
determines the commission rate for each product line. In
addition, each product line has a particular GMR (gross margin
rate) which indicates the percentage of its sales that constitutes
the gross profit before deducting selling expenses.
  In our region the product targets, commissions, and GMRs are
as follows:


        ID    Name          Target   Commission   GMR
        ---   -----------   ------   ----------   ---
        ROM   romance       235000        .024    .64
        BUS   business      173000        .022    .34
        PSY   psychology    102000        .018    .36
        REF   reference     224000        .019    .38
        PHO   photography    86000        .020    .28
```

```
Replacement pattern?
```

appeared in the status line. Jack answered by typing

```
gross margin rate
```

resulting in the screen appearance shown in Figure 5–17.
    On pressing the Enter key, the question

```
Automatic change (y/n/q)?
```

appeared in the status line. Jack explained that pressing the y key would
cause the replacement pattern to automatically replace every instance
of the search pattern. Pressing the q key would cause the MODIFY
command to immediately quit. Jack pressed the n key because he wanted
to step through instances of the search pattern one at a time.
    Each time the cursor moved to an instance of the search pattern,
the question

```
Modify (y/n/q)?
```

FIGURE 5–18   MODIFY's replacement results

```
  Line:10      Col:54    a:gmrnote.txt  Insert            No more found
   For each product line, a region is given an annual sales target
 by the KC vice president of sales. The vice president also
 determines the commission rate for each product line. In
 addition, each product line has a particular GMR (gross margin
 rate) which indicates the percentage of its sales that constitutes
 the gross profit before deducting selling expenses.
   In our region the product targets, commissions, and gross margin rates are
 as follows:


         ID    Name          Target  Commission   GMR
         ---   -----------   ------  ----------   ---
         ROM   romance       235000     .024      .64
         BUS   business      173000     .022      .34
         PSY   psychology    102000     .018      .36
         REF   reference     224000     .019      .38
         PHO   photography    86000     .020      .28
```

appeared in the status area. Pressing the y key would cause that instance of the search pattern to be modified according to the replacement pattern. Pressing the n key would make no modification to it. As long as the q key is not pressed, the cursor continues to find occurrences of the search pattern until all have been examined. Jack chose not to modify the first GMR, but when the cursor moved to the second one he pressed the y key. The modification was made immediately and the cursor went on to the third GMR, which Jack did not modify. The text screen now had the appearance shown in Figure 5–18.

Block Processing

"Earlier you showed that it's easy to move individual lines about in the text, but what if I need to move a whole block of lines?" asked Dan. "Let's say I want the first paragraph to appear after the product descriptions."

"First, you use the BEGIN and END commands to indicate where the block begins and ends. Then you would move the cursor to the new location desired for that block. The MOVE command will then move the block to that location." Jack then proceeded to demonstrate.

FIGURE 5–19 Moving a block of text

```
  Line:18      Col:1      a;gmrnote.txt  Insert              Press ^L for help
     In our region the product targets, commissions, and gross margin rates are
  as follows:


          ID    Name          Target    Commission   GMR
          ---   -----------   ------    ----------   ---
          ROM   romance       235000          .024   .64
          BUS   business      173000          .022   .34
          PSY   psychology    102000          .018   .36
          REF   reference     224000          .019   .38
          PHO   photography    86000          .020   .28


  \B    For each product line, a region is given an annual sales target
  by the KC vice president of sales. The vice president also
  determines the commission rate for each product line. In
  addition, each product line has a particular GMR (gross margin
  rate) which indicates the percentage of its sales that constitutes
  the gross profit before deducting selling expenses.\E
```

He moved the cursor to the start of line 1, escaped to the status line, and typed the command

```
begin
```

there. The symbols \B instantly appeared at the start of line 1 to mark the beginning of the block. He moved the cursor to the end of the paragraph (line 6, column 52), escaped to the status line, and typed the command

```
end
```

there. The symbols \E instantly appeared at the end of the paragraph to mark the end of the block and the entire block was now displayed in low (muted) intensity to contrast it from the rest of the text.

Jack positioned the cursor at the start of line 18 beneath the product descriptions. He escaped to the status line and typed in

```
move
```

there. As soon as he pressed the Enter key the text screen changed as shown in Figure 5–19. Jack explained that to get rid of the block markers and restore the block's text to normal intensity, the UNBLOCK command could be used. Instead, he moved the cursor to the start of line 1 and reissued the MOVE command. The paragraph jumped back to its former position. He then escaped to the status line and typed

```
unblock
```

there to bring the screen back to its Figure 5–18 appearance.

"With my text management package," Tracey noted, "I can not only move a block, but I can also copy a block. Can we do the same thing in this environment?"

Jack answered affirmatively. "It works exactly like the MOVE command, except the command's name is COPY and instead of moving the block, a new copy of the block is inserted at the cursor's most recent position in the text area."

Other Text-Processing Commands

There were two other text commands that Jack touched on briefly. They were the FORMAT and BYE commands. He explained that when the FORMAT command is entered in the status line, the environment gives you a chance to turn the automatic word wrap feature on or off as desired. If word wrap is in force, you are also given a chance to specify how long a line can be before the wrapping begins.

The BYE command lets you temporarily suspend work on a piece of text. When this command is issued the text screen vanishes and the underscore prompt appears. Nontext commands like LET and OUTPUT can then be executed. To resume the text processing simply enter

```
text
```

at an underscore prompt. This brings the text screen back into view, allowing text processing to resume. The text screen will look the same as it did before issuing the BYE command.

"But I thought BYE took us out of the environment and back to the operating system," said Brad with a concerned look.

"It does," replied Jack, "if you enter it in response to the underscore prompt. Here we were just saying bye to the text processing, in order to get back to the underscore prompt. When you invoke BYE while processing text, it just means that you want to get out of text management, for the moment at least."

"So if I'm working on text and want to get clear out to the operating system, I'd need to do BYE BYE," Brad chuckled.

"I can see where the ability to temporarily suspend text processing could be very useful," remarked Tracey. "Sometimes when you're working on a piece of text, you might need to pause to do some calculations or other processing and then reflect the results in the text without the inconvenience of switching from one software tool to another. But I'd like to see this integrated environment idea carried a step further. Sometimes it would be useful to issue a nontext command right in the middle of text processing and have the result automatically incorporated into the text."

EXTENDED TEXT COMMANDS

Jack smiled, for Tracey had anticipated the next topic he planned to present. Traditional text management packages have no concept of nontext commands. However, in a truly integrated knowledge management environment, commands not traditionally regarded as being for text processing can be invoked right in the midst of text management. Because these commands (e.g., OUTPUT, LET) can be used independent of text management they may be called "nontext" commands. On the other hand, they may also be called "extended text" commands. They can be regarded as innate text management facilities because they can be invoked like ordinary text-specific commands (e.g., SEARCH, UNBLOCK). They effectively extend an environment's text management capability well beyond what is possible with a traditional text management package [3].

"Let's take an example to see what Tracey has in mind," offered Jack. "In our note we may want to refer to the total target." Beginning with Photo 11 he moved the cursor to line 17 and began to type in a new sentence

```
The region's total target for these five products is
```

and then stopped. "Here's a point where we'd like to use our calculation skills to fill in the missing part of the sentence. So that's exactly what we'll do. As always, we escape to the status line when we want to issue a command."

He pressed the Escape key and proceeded to type

```
\?(235+173+102+224+86)*1000 using " $fff,fff."
```

FIGURE 5–20 Calculation result embedded in text

```
Line:17     Col:53    a:gmrnote.txt  Insert              Press ^L for help
  For each product line, a region is given an annual sales target
by the KC vice president of sales. The vice president also
determines the commission rate for each product line. In
addition, each product line has a particular GMR (gross margin
rate) which indicates the percentage of its sales that constitutes
the gross profit before deducting selling expenses.
  In our region the product targets, commissions, and gross margin rates are
as follows:
          ID    Name         Target   Commission   GMR
          ---   -----------  ------   ----------   ---
          ROM   romance      235000        .024    .64
          BUS   business     173000        .022    .34
          PSY   psychology   102000        .018    .36
          REF   reference    224000        .019    .38
          PHO   photography   86000        .020    .28
The region's total target for these five products is $820,000.
```

in the status line. This is exactly like a normal OUTPUT command except that it is prefaced with a backslash. In general when a command that is not text specific is invoked, it needs to be prefaced in this way.

Pressing the Enter key to execute the command, he remarked, "That's all there is to it. It's just as if you calculated and typed in the result yourself."

As shown in Figure 5–20, the calculation result was output to the cursor's most recent position in the text (as indicated by the status line's line and column numbers.)

"Can you use any of the nontext-specific commands in this way?" asked Tracey.

"Almost," answered Jack. "Though I've not personally tried them all, as far as I know you can use most of them. As you'll see later today and in the days ahead there are many new commands for which this is particularly valuable. The main thing to keep in mind is that whatever visual result the command would normally produce outside the text management confines is automatically embedded in the text at the most recent cursor position. You can then edit it just like other text that has been typed in the conventional way. If you don't want the result of a command to appear in the text, you just BYE out of text management, issue the command, and then get back in by typing the word TEXT."

"What about commands like LET that have no visual result?" inquired Stan.

"They still have their usual effects," Jack responded. "They just aren't reflected in the text image. For instance, you are perfectly free to let E.DECI have a different value right in the midst of text processing. Because the LET command has no visual result, the text is unaffected. Nevertheless the value of E.DECI is indeed changed."

TEXT PRESERVATION AND RECALL

As you create or edit a piece of text, your creations and changes are not committed to the text file. It remains unaffected until you issue a command to the environment requesting that all changes made to the text's electronic image be preserved in the text file. Not only does this allow generally faster processing, it also insulates an original version of text from an edited version until you are satisfied that the edited version should be preserved in the text file, either replacing the original version or being written into a new text file.

To preserve text in a text file, the WRITE command is issued. To later recall preserved text for processing via the text screen there are two possibilities. If not currently working on a piece of text, the TEXT command is invoked as described earlier. Alternatively, if you are already working through the text screen, then the READ command can be used.

Preservation

"Now that you know how to work on a piece of text, you need to know how to preserve the fruits of your labors," Jack declared. "If we were to leave the environment and go back to the operating system right now, the GMR note we've prepared would perish. It would not become a part of the knowledge system and would be inaccessible when we reenter the environment.

"When you reach a point where you are satisfied with the text you are working on, you should issue a command to have it written to a text file. This can be done at any time by pressing the Escape key to bring the cursor into the status line and then issuing the WRITE command."

Jack demonstrated by escaping to the status line and typing the command

```
write
```

there. When he pressed the Enter key the light for drive A came on as the present electronic image of the text was written to the GMRNOTE.TXT file. When this operation concluded the cursor returned to its former position in the text. In this case, the text file did not previously exist, so the environment created it. If GMRNOTE.TXT had already existed, its former contents would have been replaced by the current electronic image of the text.

"There's a variation of the WRITE command that I've often found useful," Jack continued. "Sometimes, when working on a piece of text that has previously been preserved, I want to write the newly edited version to a text file. But I don't want it to replace the present version already in the GMRNOTE.TXT file. All I need to do is issue the WRITE command again, but this time it would be appended with the name of a new file where the new version of the text is to be stored. Suppose we made some further changes in the text screen and we wanted to store this new version in a file named NEWGMR.TXT."

He explained that this would be accomplished by escaping to the status line and issuing the command

```
write "a:newmgr.txt"
```

there. As a result there would now be an alternative version of the GMR notes stored in the knowledge system along with the original.

"So we can use this approach to make as many variations of a piece of text as we like," observed Dan. "You can later recall any of these whenever you want. But exactly how do you recall a particular piece of text?"

Recall

Jack reminded them that one way to recall a piece of text is with the TEXT command. "If you're not presently working on a piece of text, just invoke the TEXT command along with the desired text file name when you see the underscore prompt. The file's content will immediately appear in a text screen where you can process it as desired."

"That's clear enough, but what if I'm already working on a piece of text and decide that I want to work on another?" asked Tracey.

"Well, first of all remember to write what you're working on if there are changes you want to preserve," Jack responded. "Then escape to the status line and use the READ command. Suppose, for instance, that while working on GMRNOTE.TXT you decide to work on the NEWGMR.TXT."

He explained that this would be accomplished by escaping to the status line (after doing a WRITE, if desired) and issuing the command

```
read "a:newgmr.txt"
```

there. As a result, this file's text would be read into the text area, replacing the text that had previously been displayed there. In addition, the status line's file name would become NEWGMR.TXT instead of GMRNOTE.TXT.

TEXT PRINTOUTS

Aside from creating, searching, editing, preserving, and recalling text, there is another aspect of text processing. It is text printing. A good text management capability will support two basic kinds of text printing. One allows you to get a verbatim printout of the electronic image of text you are presently processing through the text screen. Such printouts can be requested at any time while the text is being created or edited. The second kind of text printing lets you get a printout of any piece of text in the knowledge system, even though you may not be working on it when requesting the printout. In a full environment, this means that a command to print text can be invoked even when there is no text screen in view (i.e., in response to the underscore prompt).

Before examining the two kinds of text printing, Joy explained how to prepare a printer for printing text (or anything else for that matter). Her explanation and Jack's subsequent examples pertained to the IBM Graphics Printers (Figure 2–5) and the standard-sized perforated printer paper they would all be using. Some variations might have been necessary if they had been using different printers and paper sizes. As she started, the BYE command had been used to temporarily suspend the processing of GMRNOTE.TXT and the underscore prompt was visible on the screen.

Preliminaries

"First of all," she began, "while the printer is not online or is turned off, turn the paper feed knob so that the printer's print head is at the top of a page. Notice that I've positioned the paper so the print head is just beneath the perforation, with the top of the ribbon even with the perforation. This can be done before or after entering the environment, but should be done before beginning to use the printer.

"There is one other thing to do before you begin using the printer. You need to tell the environment what *page depth* to use. Obviously, the environment has no way of knowing how many lines can be accommodated on each page of the paper feeding into the printer. If you don't tell it otherwise, it will assume a page depth of 60 lines. The paper we'll be using allows 65 lines per page. So how do we convey this to the environment?"

"Could it be done by setting some control switch to the desired number?" Stan asked thoughtfully. "Maybe there's an environment variable for the page depth setting."

"Exactly," answered a pleased Joy. "It is named E.PDEP and its default value is 60. So all you need to do is let it be 65." With that she executed the command

```
let e.pdep=65
```

and explained, "The environment keeps a count of how many lines have been sent to the printer. When the 65th line is reached, the environment sends a message to the printer, telling it to eject to the top of the next page before printing the next line. As it starts this new page, the environment begins counting from 1 again. When it again hits 65 another *page eject* happens, and so on."

Jack interjected, "There's a third bit of preparation before you begin printing. It's simply to be sure the printer is online. From this point onward do *not* manually adjust the paper with either the paper feed knob or the line feed button."

Joy paused to let Jack's admonition sink in and then she added, "If you fail to follow this rule, you'll put the actual position of the paper in the printer out of sync with the environment's internal line counting. The result will be undesired page ejection behavior."

"I see the importance of keeping things in sync," remarked Stan, "but what if I've printed several lines on a page and want the next thing I print to begin a new page. If I shouldn't manually adjust the paper to the top of a new page, then how can I get to the beginning of a new page?"

"That's a very good question," responded Jack, "and there's a very good answer. You just tell the environment that you want to eject to the top of a new page. This is done with the EJECT command." He demonstrated by typing

```
eject
```

alongside the underscore prompt. When he pressed the Enter key to execute this command, the paper in the printer ejected to the beginning of the next page. "By telling the environment to begin a new page, it is aware that the internal line counter should be adjusted accordingly."

Joy added, "If things do get out of sync, EJECT will not leave the paper positioned at the top of a page. In such a case, put the printer offline and manually adjust the paper to the start of a new page. This should bring things back into sync. Be sure to put the printer back online before trying to print."

Simple preparatory steps like those described by Joy and Jack are common for software packages capable of producing printouts. In the case of KnowledgeMan there are three steps to consider when entering the environment:

1. Manually adjust the printer's paper to the top of a page.

2. Set E.PDEP to a suitable page depth.

3. Be sure the printer is online.

These are recommended regardless of what is being printed: calculation results, text, or other knowledge discussed in later chapters.

Printing a Text Image

Jack invoked the TEXT command to get the text screen shown in Figure 5–20 and pressed ^Q to insert a blank line before the final sentence. To get a printout of this electronic text image he escaped to the status line and issued the command

```
print
```

there. The printer sprang into action, printing out each line just as it appeared on the screen. If there had been more lines of text than could fit in the text area, all of the lines would have been printed. If the number of lines had exceeded the E.PDEP limit, an automatic page eject would have occurred and printing would continue at the top of the next page, and so forth.

"I notice," commented Tracey, "that there is no space in the left margin of the printout. How would I get, say, two spaces in the printout's left margin, without having to put them into the text image?"

Jack replied that the printer's margin size is controlled by an environment variable named E.PMAR whose default value is 0. He escaped to the status line and issued the command

```
\let e.pmar=2
```

FIGURE 5–21   Two printings of an electronic text image

```
    For each product line, a region is given an annual sales target
by the KC vice president of sales. The vice president also
determines the commission rate for each product line. In
addition, each product line has a particular GMR (gross margin
rate) which indicates the percentage of its sales that constitutes
the gross profit before deducting selling expenses.
    In our region the product targets, commissions, and gross margin rates are
as follows:

         ID    Name          Target   Commission   GMR
         ---   -----------   ------   ----------   ---
         ROM   romance       235000      .024      .64
         BUS   business      173000      .022      .34
         PSY   psychology    102000      .018      .36
         REF   reference     224000      .019      .38
         PHO   photography    86000      .020      .28

The region's total target for these five products is $820,000.

    For each product line, a region is given an annual sales target
by the KC vice president of sales. The vice president also
determines the commission rate for each product line. In
addition, each product line has a particular GMR (gross margin
rate) which indicates the percentage of its sales that constitutes
the gross profit before deducting selling expenses.
    In our region the product targets, commissions, and gross margin rates are
as follows:

         ID    Name          Target   Commission   GMR
         ---   -----------   ------   ----------   ---
         ROM   romance       235000      .024      .64
         BUS   business      173000      .022      .34
         PSY   psychology    102000      .018      .36
         REF   reference     224000      .019      .38
         PHO   photography    86000      .020      .28

The region's total target for these five products is $820,000.
```

there. This did not affect the text area contents in any way. Jack then escaped to the status line once more where he issued the PRINT command just as before. The same text was printed out further on down on the same page. As Figure 5–21 shows, the only difference was that a two-space left margin was used for the second printing.

"Now sometimes I don't want to print out the entire text image, but only a part of it," observed Jack. "To do this, I would again use the PRINT command but would also specify the range of lines I'm interested in. Let me show you, but this time let's have our printout begin a new page."

With Jack looking in his direction, Stan volunteered, "You'll have to ask for an eject first. And because the EJECT command can be used outside of text processing, you should preface it with a backslash when you enter it in the status line."

Jack did exactly as Stan recommended, entering

\eject

FIGURE 5–22   Selective printing of a partial text image

ID	Name	Target	Commission	GMR
---	-----------	------	----------	---
ROM	romance	235000	.024	.64
BUS	business	173000	.022	.34
PSY	psychology	102000	.018	.36
REF	reference	224000	.019	.38
PHO	photography	86000	.020	.28

in the status line. The printer responded by ejecting the paper to the top of a new page. Jack then escaped to the status line and issued the command

```
print range 9,17
```

there. This caused text lines in the range 9 through 17 to be printed. He ejected, giving the printout page shown in Figure 5–22.

Printing a Text File

"Even though we're no longer working in the text screen, we can still get a text printout. But instead of printing the electronic image for which we just suspended processing, we can print the content of any text file." Jack paused, "If there were a hundred text files preserved in our knowledge system we could right now choose to get a printout for any of them with the PRINT TEXT command."

Jack explained that there is another very important difference between the PRINT and PRINT TEXT commands. "The PRINT command is a 'what you see is what you get' command. In contrast, the PRINT TEXT command *formats* the text as it's being printed. There are literally dozens of formatting possibilities open to us, so we somehow need to convey to the environment what format conventions it should employ as it prints the text. This is done by embedding format codes into the text itself. Let me show you what I mean."

He proceeded to modify the text by inserting four new lines until the screen appeared as shown in Figure 5–23. Each was an example of a *format code*. When a format code is put into a piece of text, it occupies a line all its own. That line begins with the period (.) symbol to distinguish it from normal text lines. Jack explained that the ll 60 code indicates that PRINT TEXT should format the text in such a way that the *l*ine *l*ength of subsequent printed lines is no more than 60 characters. The ad code indicates that the spacing of words in subsequent printed text

FIGURE 5–23   Embedded format control codes

```
  Line:21     Col:1     a:gmrnote.txt  Insert         Press ^L for help
.11 60
.ad
    For each product line, a region is given an annual sales target
by the KC vice president of sales. The vice president also
determines the commission rate for each product line. In
addition, each product line has a particular GMR (gross margin
rate) which indicates the percentage of its sales that constitutes
the gross profit before deducting selling expenses.
    In our region the product targets, commissions, and gross margin rates are
as follows:
.nf
            ID    Name         Target   Commission   GMR
            ---   ----------   ------   ----------   ---
            ROM   romance      235000       .024     .64
            BUS   business     173000       .022     .34
            PSY   psychology   102000       .018     .36
            REF   reference    224000       .019     .38
            PHO   photography   86000       .020     .28
.fi

The region's total target for these five products is $820,000.
```

lines should be *ad*justed to produce an even right margin. The nf code
means that subsequent printed lines should *n*ot be *f*illed with as much
text as they can hold, but should terminate as shown in the preserved
text. Finally, the fi code indicates that subsequent printed lines should
be *f*illed with as much text as possible, up to the ll limit.

Jack used the WRITE command to preserve these changes in the
GMRNOTE.TXT file on drive A. He then escaped to the status line
and issued the command

```
print
```

there and then ejected, producing the printout page shown in Figure
5–24. He emphasized that, as always, the PRINT command yielded a
verbatim printout of the electronic text image, control codes included.
As he was about to demonstrate, the PRINT TEXT command yielded
a very different printout.

"Before invoking the PRINT TEXT command you may need to throw
a couple of control switches. The E.OPRN environment variable should
be TRUE, otherwise the text won't be 'printed' on paper. Also you

FIGURE 5–24   Verbatim printout produced by PRINT

```
.ll 60
.ad
     For each product line, a region is given an annual sales target
by the KC vice president of sales. The vice president also
determines the commission rate for each product line. In
addition, each product line has a particular GMR (gross margin
rate) which indicates the percentage of its sales that constitutes
the gross profit before deducting selling expenses.
     In our region the product targets, commissions, and gross margin rates are
as follows:
.nf

          ID    Name          Target    Commission    GMR
          ---   -----------   ------    ----------    ---
          ROM   romance       235000        .024      .64
          BUS   business      173000        .022      .34
          PSY   psychology    102000        .018      .36
          REF   reference     224000        .019      .38
          PHO   photography    86000        .020      .28
.fi

The region's total target for these five products is $820,000.
```

should let E.PDEP be 66 instead of the usual 65." He BYEd out of text processing and suited his words with actions by invoking the commands

```
e.oprn=true
e.pdep=66
e.pmar=8
```

where the optional LET was omitted from the start of each. For good measure he set the printer margin to 8 spaces.

"Now let's use the PRINT TEXT command to get a formatted printout of the text in GMRNOTE.TXT," he continued. At the underscore prompt Jack typed

```
print text "a:gmrnote.txt"
```

and the printer began to chatter. As it printed each line on paper, that same line was also displayed (i.e., "printed") on the console screen. When there were no lines left to be printed, an automatic eject occurred, leaving the printer ready to begin a new page. The resultant printout is shown in Figure 5–25.

Additional Format Codes

The group was obviously impressed by the neatness of the result and by the fact that so little effort was required to get a desirable format.

FIGURE 5–25   Formatted printout produced by PRINT TEXT

```
            For each product line, a region is given an annual  sales
        target by the KC vice president of sales. The vice president
        also  determines  the commission rate for  each product line.
        In addition, each product line has a particular  GMR  (gross
        margin  rate)  which  indicates  the percentage of its sales
        that constitutes the gross profit before  deducting  selling
        expenses.
            In our region the product targets, commissions, and gross
        margin rates are as follows:

             ID    Name          Target    Commission    GMR
             ---   -----------   ------    ----------    ---
             ROM   romance       235000       .024       .64
             BUS   business      173000       .022       .34
             PSY   psychology    102000       .018       .36
             REF   reference     224000       .019       .38
             PHO   photography    86000       .020       .28

        The  region's  total  target  for  these  five  products  is
        $820,000.
```

"As you can see," observed Jack, "PRINT TEXT interprets the format codes and takes appropriate actions, rather than printing them verbatim as PRINT does. There are several dozen such codes that allow you to do some very fancy formatting, but I've found that the four used in this example are sufficient for most of my needs. For now, I'll just mention a few others that I occasionally use."

Jack pointed out that PRINT TEXT skipped four lines at the top of the page and, though it could not be seen in this example, four lines are also skipped at the bottom of a page. He explained that this could be avoided by putting the four control code lines

```
.m1 0
.m2 0
.m3 0
.m4 0
```

at the start of a text file. The total of the numbers following m1 and m2 control how many lines are skipped in each page's top margin. Similarly, m3 and m4 control each page's bottom margin.

The ss and ds format codes control spacing between lines of printed text. If the format control line

```
.ds
```

appears then all succeeding lines are double spaced. Similarly when
the format control line

```
.ss
```

appears, all succeeding lines are single spaced. Jack also mentioned
the na control code. If you do not want the interword spacing to be
adjusted to make even right margins for succeeding lines, then

```
.na
```

can be included as a line in the text.

"For now," Jack concluded, "let me tell you about just one more
control code that is very useful for combining the contents of multiple text files in the course of a single PRINT TEXT operation. Suppose that we wanted some additional text existing in some other
file, say A:EXTRA.TXT, to be included after the first paragraph of
GMRNOTE.TXT is printed." He explained that this is easily accomplished by inserting the line

```
.it "a:extra.txt"
```

after the first paragraph preserved in the GMRNOTE.TXT file. The code
'it' stands for "include text."

"I'd suggest," chimed Joy, "that you focus on the format codes
Jack has presented. As you become more experienced, you may want
to look at the documentation to acquaint yourself with other format
control codes." Details of this presentation knowledge that can be represented and processed in text files can be found in [4].

Nonprinter Printing

Referring to some notes he had made, Brad commented, "I can see
where just a handful of format control codes gives a quite powerful
and versatile way of formatting the text that we print. I understand
the difference between a verbatim PRINT of text that's being worked
on and the formatted PRINT TEXT of a text file's content. But I still
have three questions.

"First, why do we need to let E.PDEP be 66 when using PRINT
TEXT, whereas you said it could be 65 whenever we're doing any other
kind of printing?"

Jack shrugged and looked to Joy for support. She responded, "Because it works if you do and may not work if you don't. With a different

printer and paper size, something else might work. Just accept it as a fact of life in this environment."

"Second," continued Brad, "is it necessary to suspend your present text processing with BYE in order to use the PRINT TEXT command? I understand the appeal of being able to directly print a text file's contents without looking at a text screen, but it seems that sometimes I might want to print a formatted rendition of a text file while using a text screen. Is that possible?"

"It certainly is," Jack answered. "Remember, commands such as PRINT TEXT, which can be invoked outside of the text status line, can also be invoked on the status line if you prefer. All you need to do is preface your PRINT TEXT command with a backslash."

Nodding, Brad posed his third question, "It's easy enough to print a formatted rendition of text, but what if I want to edit a formatted version of a piece of text? It's all well and good that formatted text appears on the console screen as it's being printed. But it seems to me that I might want to preview and perhaps make alterations to a formatted version of the text before I send it to the printer."

"That's a very good observation," said Jack in a congratulatory tone. "Recall that PRINT TEXT requires E.OPRN to be TRUE in order to have the printer print the text. If you leave E.OPRN set to FALSE while invoking PRINT TEXT, the formatted text will be 'printed' only to the console screen. This is one way to preview the formatted text before committing it to paper. But it flashes by fairly quickly and you don't get a chance to edit it.

"What you would really like is to have the formatted text 'printed' to a text file, which you can then scan and edit in the usual ways. Take GMRNOTE.TXT for instance. How could we get a formatted version of it 'printed' to a disk file called, say, PREVIEW.TXT on drive A? Well, it turns out to be very straightforward when you know about E.ODSK and #DSKOUT."

Jack explained that #DSKOUT is a string utility variable whose value can be set to a file name (qualified by a drive indicator if desired). When the E.ODSK environment variable is changed from its default value of FALSE to TRUE, the environment will store all subsequent environment responses in the #DSKOUT file. Thus E.ODSK plays a role similar to that of E.OPRN, except it causes results to go to a disk file instead of the printer.

He proceeded to demonstrate how E.ODSK and #DSKOUT could address Brad's concern, by executing the commands

```
e.oprn=false
#dskout="a:preview.txt"
e.odsk=true
```

PHOTO 12   Working with formatted text

```
Line:1     Col:1    a:preview.txt  Insert              Press ^L for help
```

For each product line, a region is given an annual sales
target by the KC vice president of sales. The vice president
also determines the commission rate for each product line.
In addition, each product line has a particular CMR (gross
margin rate) which indicates the percentage of its sales
that constitutes the gross profit before deducting selling
expenses.

In our region the product targets, commissions, and gross
margin rates are as follows:

ID	Name	Target	Commission	CMR
ROM	romance	235000	.024	.44
BUS	business	173000	.022	.34
PSY	psychology	102000	.018	.36
REF	reference	224000	.019	.38
PHO	photography	86000	.020	.28

The region's total target for these five products is
$820,000.

Then he issued the very same PRINT TEXT command that had produced
the formatted text printout shown in Figure 5–25

```
print text "a:gmrnote.txt"
```

This time the printer was silent because E.OPRN had been set to FALSE.
However, the light for drive A came on as the formatted text was
"printed" into the PREVIEW.TXT file and onto the console screen. At
the conclusion of this operation, the familiar underscore prompt appeared on the screen awaiting Jack's next command.

He set E.ODSK back to FALSE because he was finished sending
results to the text file on disk. Jack then executed

```
text "a:preview.txt"
```

which produced Photo 12. As all could see this was the formatted version
of the GMRNOTE.TXT file's contents. It could be viewed and modified
just like any other piece of text. Jack demonstrated that the PRINT

command could be used to produce a verbatim printout of this text image. He escaped to the status line and issued the commands

```
\e.pmar=0;e.pdep=65
```

there. This returned the page margin to its default of 0 and the page depth to the value Joy had recommended. Escaping again to the status line, he typed

```
print
```

and on pressing the Enter key, the same printout shown earlier in Figure 5–25 was generated.

"It's interesting," Tracey noted, "that this ability of formatted printing to produce a new text file also gives a way to merge text from separate files into a single new file. All you have to do is use the 'it' format control code wherever you want to grab the text from another file and PRINT TEXT does the rest."

DESKTOP PUBLISHING

During the ensuing break, the sales managers gained some first-hand text management experience by practicing what they had learned from Jack and Joy. At the same time, Jack himself was learning about a comparatively new aspect of text management called *desktop publishing* [6].

"Lately," he said, "I've begun to hear a good deal about desktop publishing, but I don't really know what it is. Can you explain it to me?"

"I'm not sure there's a universally accepted meaning," Joy replied, "but I can give you my impressions of what is involved in desktop publishing. I could even show you what's involved if you were to give me a KISS™[1] and the right software."

"Who knows," he speculated, "maybe that can be arranged sometime."

Joy explained that desktop publishing typically requires the use of a laser printer rather than the dot matrix printers the sales managers were using. The KISS that she mentioned is a brand of laser printer that is quite powerful in spite of its small size and relatively low cost (under $2,000). The software she referred to can take pieces of text, such as those the managers were now producing, together with various

---

[1] KISS is a trademark of QMS, Incorporated.

kinds of graphics produced by graphics software packages and allow a user to arrange them into page layouts like those found in newspapers, magazines, and books. It then prints the resultant pages on a laser printer such as KISS.

"Desktop publishing software," she elaborated, "is sometimes called page composition software. It lets you design page layouts and formats in newspaper-style columns with graphics interspersed wherever you like. It lets you choose from among many different fonts, so that headlines may be in one style and size of type, subheads in another, paragraphs in still another, footnotes in yet another, and so on. Available fonts range from those popular in magazines and books to fancy script or Old English fonts.

"The text for filling in page layouts can come from text files prepared with a text processor. The graphics may include business graphics such as pie and bar plots, scanned photos or sketches, charts, diagrams, and various decorations. These visual images are prepared and stored in files by corresponding graphics software. The files can be accessed by the desktop publishing software as pages are being composed. A desktop publisher can usually show an on-screen display of a page—its content, layout, and fonts—before it is sent to the printer. It can allow what is seen to be adjusted and rearranged before printing the screen display."

"So desktop publishing can be very handy for preparing things like newsletters, elaborate documents, books, or just about anything that needs to have a 'published' look," Jack observed thoughtfully. "But it's really not the kind of facility that we managers would have much use for in our own activities."

"True," confirmed Joy, "but it is interesting that some desktop publishing features are beginning to creep into some word processing packages. I would expect this trend to continue."

BASIC IDEAS

Managers often need to work with pieces of text. *The purpose of text management software is to allow computers to ease tasks such as creating, storing, editing, scanning, recalling, and formatting text.* This software ranges from rudimentary line-at-a-time text editors to very extensive word processors that allow free cursor movement anywhere in the text area of a console screen. Desktop publishers can also be placed at the upper end of the text management spectrum.

As Jack showed the group, *text representation and processing is not limited to stand-alone software packages* that do text management but nothing else. It can also be provided as an *integral capability of a knowledge manage-*

ment environment. In such a setting, pieces of text are preserved as text files in the knowledge system. A user creates, edits, and scans a piece of text via a text screen (i.e., brought into view by the TEXT command). Such a screen has a status line and a text area that serves as a 24 × 80 window for viewing part of an electronic image of the text.

While the text screen is visible, the text can be processed with control keys and commands. Some control keys are used to move the cursor to desired locations in the text. There is a control key to toggle between the insertion and replacement modes of inserting new characters. There are others for inserting, deleting, restoring, splitting, and joining lines of text. To issue a command, the user escapes to the status line, types the command, and presses the Enter key. The environment furnishes a variety of commands (e.g., SEARCH, MODIFY, BEGIN, END, COPY, MOVE, UNBLOCK, READ, WRITE, PRINT) that are for exclusive use in the text screen's status line. Other commands (e.g., LET, OUTPUT) that are available when the text screen is not displayed can also be invoked in the status line by prefacing them with a backslash. Their visual responses (if any) are automatically deposited in the text area.

Processing an electronic image of text can be temporarily suspended at any time (by invoking BYE in the status line) and later resumed (by invoking TEXT). The present text image can be preserved at any time (WRITE) to update its text file or create a new text file. While the text screen is visible, a verbatim printout of the text image can be requested (PRINT). At any time, a formatted printout can be requested for any text file (PRINT TEXT). The formatting is controlled by embedding presentation knowledge in the guise of format codes within the text file.

As the managers exercised their newfound text management prowess, Dan expressed an important reservation about this technique. "Obviously, text management is a worthwhile technique for us to understand. It will help us out in dealing with notes, memos, letters, and some kinds of reports. But it seems to me that it's of little value in handling other things. For example, in the GMR note, we arranged part of the text to form a little table of product line descriptions and it was OK to look at, but we really can't do much else with it.

"Suppose I want to browse through only those products whose GMR exceeds a certain amount and whose target is below some specific level. I'd like to do this without having to look through all of the data. Text processing is no help in that regard and as the number of products increases, having some browsing help would be important. Or suppose I try to keep track of my reps' performance data over the course of a year in a text file. That's a lot of data. If I wanted to bump up everyone's third quarter romance quota by 5.2 percent, how would I do it? Or if I just wanted to see the first quarter comparison of quota to sales for a particular rep on a particular product line, I'd really like a more powerful processing mechanism than pattern searching through the text. And what if I wanted the performance records sorted in some way? Nice as text management is, it just seems to me that there are many everyday problems of data organization and processing that it cannot handle well and in some cases that it can't handle at all."

In unison, Jack and Joy acknowledged, "You're right." They smiled, realizing that Dan's concerns would soon be resolved by the exploration of a different knowledge management technique.

References

1. Ashley, R.; J. N. Fernandez; and R. Sansom. *WordStar without Tears: A Self-Teaching Guide.* New York: John Wiley & Sons, 1985.
2. Greenia, M. W. *Professional Word Processing in Business and Legal Environments.* Reston, Va.: Reston, 1985.
3. Holsapple, C. W. "Synergistic Software Integration for Microcomputers." *Systems and Software* 3, no. 2 (1984).
4. *K-Text Supplement,* version 2. Lafayette, Ind.: MDBS, Inc., 1985.
5. Lund, P. H., and B. A. Hayden. *Understanding and Using WordPerfect.* St. Paul, Minn.: West Publishing, 1987.
6. Simpson, D. "Desktop Publishing: Sifting Type from Hype." *Mini-Micro Systems* 20, no. 1 (1987).
7. Thiel, L. A. "WordMaster: More than a Replacement for ED." *Microsystems,* March 1983.

Just for the record, let's get this all out on the table.

Chapter Six

Data Management

Dan correctly noted that there are some kinds of descriptive knowledge that cannot be adequately processed with text management techniques. Text management methods are well suited for free-flowing text and perhaps small amounts of tabular text such as the product line descriptions in GMRNOTE.TXT. However, they are not well suited if the tabular arrangement involves many rows and columns, if some values are computed from others, if there is a need to do processing other than editing (e.g., selective viewing, sorting), and so on. For these reasons, a knowledge management environment provides other techniques for representing and processing descriptive knowledge. The most prevalent are various techniques that are collectively referred to as data management.

In contrast to text management, data management is a highly structured approach to record-keeping. Generally, a data management technique provides for the structured representation of data and the flexible processing of that data. There are several well-established data management techniques that go by such names as hierarchical, CODASYL-network, relational, and postrelational [7]. They are all very similar in allowing data to be organized into records: sales rep records, product line records, performance records, expense records, and so forth. They differ in terms of their provisions for representing relationships among the various types of records. For instance, a sales rep record may be related to many performance records and a performance record is related to a particular sales rep record. One data management technique may represent such a relationship differently than another technique (see Appendix A). Because their approaches to representing data relationships can differ, the data processing approaches provided by these techniques can also differ.

When studying a data management technique (also known as a data model) it is important to understand its provisions for representing data and their interrelationships. It is also important to understand the data management technique's provisions for processing those data and interrelationships. Jack would focus on *relational data management* since that is what he had been using in the environment. The postrelational data management technique is also available as an integral part of this environment [8], [10]. However, it is a very powerful technique used primarily by computer professionals for developing application systems that efficiently handle very large amounts of data with numerous or complex interrelationships [1], [4], [6], [9]. Relational data management is more suitable for the relatively modest, do-it-yourself needs of many knowledge workers.

Initially proposed in 1970, relational data management organizes descriptive knowledge in a tabular fashion [3]. A table consists of records of a particular type. Thus, records about the various sales reps could make up one table, records about sales performance could constitute another, and so forth. A collection of related tables, such as those just mentioned, is often called a *data base* and each individual table is called a *relation*. As Jack will illustrate, the relationships between records in a pair of tables are represented by redundancy when using the relational data management technique.

There are numerous software packages that support tabular or table-like data representation. Technically speaking, many of them do not qualify as relational data base management systems because they do not support either of the two standard relational languages for processing tables. Nevertheless, they are often loosely characterized as being "relational." One of the two standard languages involves commands (e.g., PROJECT and JOIN) that operate on existing tables to produce new tables. The other is a higher level language that avoids the production of intermediate tables in achieving a desired processing result. Both kinds of table-processing facilities can be found in the KnowledgeMan environment. In addition, Jack has found other worthwhile table-processing commands in this environment, commands that have no counterparts in the standard relational languages. As the session resumed, he was prepared to describe those table-processing commands that he most frequently used.

TABLES AND FIELDS

"Remember," Jack began, "when we put together the GMR note, part of the text was arranged in a tabular fashion. Each column denoted a particular kind or category of data. The ID column was for our standard three-letter product IDs, the commission column was for product commission rates, and so on. Each row in the tabular configuration consists of one data value for each column or category of data. Taken together, all of the values in a row are a record of information known about one or another product line.

"Now when we put this product line data in the text, we—not the environment—imposed the tabular appearance on the text. There is an alternative. Just as the environment knows about free-form pieces of text and is able to accept commands for processing such objects, so too does it know about tables as objects in their own right. It is able to accept commands designed specifically for processing tables. So when we want to structure and process data in a tabular way, we are free to do so without having to work on it as a piece of text. Just as the environment's knowledge system can hold pieces of text in text files, it can also hold tables of data in *table files*."

Structure

Jack explained that every table has a name and a structure. A table's name is usually chosen to be descriptive of the type of records it contains. A table's structure is defined in terms of the columns or categories of data that can exist in the table. Traditionally, a table's data categories are called *fields*. Each field is given a name that indicates the kind of data it holds.

"For instance," Jack explained, "we might define a table named PROD to hold records about the various product lines. This table's structure might involve fields named PID (product ID), PNAME (product name), TARGET (product's sales target), GMR (product's gross margin rate), and CRATE (commission rate for a product). This structure will allow each product record we create in the table to have five data values: an ID, name, target, gross margin rate, and commission rate. If there were other categories of data that we wanted to keep track of for each product, we would define additional fields in the PROD table's structure."

Figure 6–1 shows two conventional and equivalent ways of diagramming the PROD table's structure. Sketching diagrams of this kind can be a useful shorthand way of conveying table structures for purposes of discussion. In each case, a rectangle encloses the table's field names and the rectangle is labeled with the name of the table. As the number of fields per table becomes larger, the top style of diagram becomes increasingly unwieldy relative to the second kind of diagram.

FIGURE 6–1   Alternative diagrams of the PROD table's structure

PROD

PID	PNAME	TARGET	GMR	CRATE

PROD

PID
PNAME
TARGET
GMR
CRATE

Content

Jack continued, "Once you've decided on a table's structure and used a command to define that structure to the environment, you can begin creating records in the table. These records are the table's content. Each record conforms to the table's structure by having one value for each field. A table's records are stored in a disk file."

"Can you process a table's records with the TEXT command?" someone asked.

"Not with the TEXT command per se," answered Jack. "However, as you'll eventually see, table-processing commands can be used very effectively in the midst of text processing. What's more, you'll also see that text and table data can be used together in a single command."

Joy added, "Physically, the content of a table file is arranged very differently than the content of a text file. A table file's content is encrypted, which means that if you were to try to view it like a piece of text you would think it was gibberish. This is a security feature that helps prevent unauthorized persons from seeing a table's content. While this and other data security mechanisms are absolutely essential for some users, I don't think they'll be of much concern to us."

Jack continued, "Just as a context file has a different extension from a text file, a table file normally has yet another extension. It is ITB."

Field Characteristics

"Earlier," Jack recalled, "I said that a table's structure is specified in terms of its fields and that every field is given a name. Of course different fields should have different names. Well, a field has other characteristics aside from its name. Whenever you invent a field, you'll need to say what its type is. A field's stated type controls what kind of data values are permissible for it."

Jack explained that, just like a variable, a field can be either string, numeric, integer, or logical in type. Once a type has been stated, all values of that field throughout the table must adhere to that type. For example, the GMR field would be declared to be numeric. This means the environment will permit only numeric values to be stored for the GMR field.

"So," interjected Debbie, "unlike a variable's type, a field's type is not determined by the value it happens to have at any moment. Instead, we determine a field's type, and the field's value in each record is not allowed to deviate from that type. If we were to try to store a text string as the GMR value in some record, I presume the environment would prevent us from making such an error."

"That's right," Joy responded. "Whenever you create or alter a record's value for a field, the environment checks to be sure that the new value is of the correct type for that field. In computer jargon, this is called *type checking* and is helpful in preventing you from making inadvertent errors."

"Now as I see it," proceeded Debbie, "a field also differs from a working variable in that lots of values can simultaneously be stored for a field—one value per record. A working variable has but one value at a time. I suppose you'll be showing us how to access all of a field's values."

"Right again." This time Jack fielded her observations. "Because a field exists only as part of a table's structure, and there can be many records in a table, the table can store many values for a field with each value pertaining to a specific record. In a little while I'll be showing you how to create and subsequently get at a field's values. But first, there are some other characteristics of fields I want to cover."

He explained that when a field is designated as having string values, a size must also be stated. The size indicates the maximum number of characters allowed for any value of the field. For example, PID would be designated as a string field of size 3 because a product ID never exceeds three characters.

"The other field characteristics I'll mention are optional," Jack noted. "You can use them if you like. You can also ignore them if you like, but they can be mighty handy sometimes. Remember when we used pictures with output commands? Well, we can also use pictures with fields. If we use a picture in our specification of a field, that picture will control the appearance of any of that field's values when it is presented on the screen or printer. The picture also determines what values are valid for the field on a character-by-character basis. Thus if the third placeholder in a field's picture is a d, then the environment will prohibit a nondigit from appearing in that position in any of the field's values.

"When declaring a field, we can give it a label if we like. A label is just a description of the meaning of a field. For instance, a label of 'gross margin rate' might be given to the GMR field. I think labels are most useful when you give a field a short name whose meaning is not immediately obvious. It's a simple matter to look at the label for any field whenever you like.

Virtual Fields

"In my experience most fields tend to be actual. By that I mean, their values are actually stored in a table."

"Where else could they be stored if they're really part of the table?" interrupted Stan.

"Well, it's possible to have fields whose values are never stored," Jack replied mysteriously. "The values don't actually exist anywhere until the very moment you want to look at one of them. At that moment, the value materializes."

Tracey joined in, "You mean to say we can have a field whose values take up no storage space, but yet are always present when we need them?"

"Exactly," was Jack's terse response.

"But if a value is not stored, how can I update it when it needs to be changed?" asked a now mystified Stan. "I can't change what's not there!"

"That's true, but you don't have to," replied Jack. "The environment makes all updates for you—automatically and with 100 percent accuracy. You never have to even think about changing values for this kind of field."

Thoroughly mystified, Stan murmured, "It sounds like magic."

Giving in to the group's curiosity, Jack explained, "The kind of field I'm referring to is called a *virtual field*. Though its values are never stored, they are virtually available all the time. You define a virtual field just like an actual field, with one exception. You include an expression that tells the environment how to calculate the field's values whenever a value is needed.

"All five fields we've discussed for the PROD table are actual fields. We might include a sixth field in the table called CTARG, whose value in a particular record would be the product line's commission target. If this were an actual field what would we have to do?"

Along with the others, Stan saw the light. "As you create each record, you would need to type in the product of that record's CRATE and TARGET values as being the actual CTARG value. In addition, whenever a CRATE or TARGET value changes, you would have to make a corresponding change to the actual CTARG value. But if you let CTARG be a virtual field, you would just define its values as always being equal to CRATE*TARGET. Then you'd never have to actually enter or change a value for the CTARG field."

"And," added Tracey, "the environment would never actually store a CTARG value. It would just calculate CTARG values on an as-needed basis."

"That's right," confirmed Jack. "The calculation you specify for a virtual field can involve any of the kinds of expressions you learned about earlier. It can be a numeric, string, or logical calculation."

Security

There was one other field characteristic that Jack mentioned very briefly. Any field (or an entire table for that matter) can have *access codes*. This is another of the security mechanisms built into the environment. As Joy pointed out earlier, the sales managers probably would not need to use the environment's security features. However, from time to time they might see references to a field's read access codes and write access codes. Respectively, these can control who is able to view (i.e., read) the field's values and who will be allowed to alter (i.e., write) the field's values. Jack assured the group that they could safely ignore such references [1]. "Getting into a detailed discussion of data security would take us too far afield at this time."

DEFINING A TABLE

As discussed previously, once a table's structure has been envisioned (e.g., via a diagram), it needs to be defined. For example, the PROD table structure of Figure 6–1 must be defined to the environment before records can be created in it. The definition of a table includes the table name, the name of a disk file that will hold the table, and declarations of the table's fields along with their respective characteristics.

"Tables are defined with the DEFINE command," Jack announced. "With this command you can produce an empty table. It will have no records, but the particular structure of data values that can exist within a record is established. A little later I'll show you ways of creating records in a table once it's been defined. First, let's see how you would actually define the PROD table."

A Table for Product Data

With that he entered the command

```
define prod
```

at the underscore prompt. When he pressed the Enter key to execute the command, the environment presented him with the prompt

```
FILE?
```

asking for the name of the disk file that should hold the PROD table. Jack entered

```
"a:prod.itb"
```

explaining that he wanted the PROD table to be physically stored in a file named PROD.ITB on the diskette in drive A. If the drive qualifier (a:) had been omitted, the table's file would reside on the hard disk from which the system was booted.

As soon as Jack pressed the Enter key after the closing double quote, a different prompt appeared on the next line. This was the

```
FIELD?
```

prompt, asking for the name and characteristics of the table's first field. Jack answered by typing

```
pid str 3 using "aaa"
```

to indicate that PROD's first field would be PID, that this field can have string values of up to three characters apiece, and that each of those characters must be alphabetic. When Jack pressed the Enter key to conclude his reply, another FIELD? prompt appeared on the next line. He typed

```
pname str 17 using "%17r"
```

to define the PNAME field as being string in type with a size of 17 characters. He explained that the picture "%17r" is a shorthand equivalent of "rrrrrrrrrrrrrrrrr" where the r placeholder can stand for any character.

"You mean," interceded Brad, "that %17 are not treated as literals?"

"Correct," Jack nodded. "The % in a picture is a signal that a number

FIGURE 6-2   Defining the PROD table

```
_define prod
FILE? "a:prod.itb"
FIELD? pid str 3 using "aaa"
FIELD? pname str 17 using "%17r"
FIELD? target num using "fff,ffd"
FIELD? gmr num using "f.dd"
FIELD? crate num using "f.ddd"
FIELD?

_
```

and placeholder will follow. The number indicates how many repetitions of the placeholder are to be assumed beginning at the % position in the picture. So for PID we could have equivalently specified the picture as "%3a" but no typing effort would have been saved in that case."

"Speaking of typing effort," commented Stan, "what happens if you make a mistake when typing in a field definition?"

"If you haven't yet pressed the Enter key when you notice your error, you can just use the usual control keys, like Control-S and Control-D, to edit your entry." Jack paused, "But if you see the error of your ways after committing the definition with the Enter key, then you'll need to use the REDEFINE command that I'll talk about later."

Jack quickly plowed through the remaining fields in a similar way until the screen appeared as depicted in Figure 6-2. As shown, these fields were defined as being numeric in type and each had a different picture reflective of the magnitude of numeric values it could have. After defining the last field (CRATE), the FIELD? prompt again appeared. Because there were no more PROD fields to define, Jack pressed the Enter key to terminate the DEFINE command and the underscore prompt appeared indicating that another command could be entered. The record-less PROD.ITB file now existed on the drive A diskette. It was prepared to accept new records adhering to the just defined PROD structure.

"Defining the PROD table seems simple enough," Dan noted, "but what about things like labels and virtual fields?"

Tables for Sales Rep and Performance Data

Smiling, Jack handed an envelope to Joy. She opened it and began passing out its contents as Jack explained, "These are copies of printouts that I made when defining two other tables: REP and PERF. They already

FIGURE 6–3   Diagrams of REP and PERF table structures

REP	representative
FNAME	first name
MIDI	middle initial
LNAME	last name
NAME	full name
SPOUSE	spouse name
HDATE	hire date
PHONE	phone number
TID	territory ID
STREET	street
CITY	city
STATE	state
ZIP	zip
ADDR	full address
MOSAL	monthly salary
MOEXP	monthly budgeted expense
MAJORP	major products

PERF	performance
TID	territory ID
FNAME	first name
PID	product ID
Q1	quota for quarter 1
Q2	quota for quarter 2
Q3	quota for quarter 3
Q4	quota for quarter 4
QYR	quota for the year
S1	sales for quarter 1
S2	sales for quarter 2
S3	sales for quarter 3
S4	sales for quarter 4
SYTD	sales year to date
MAJOR	major product

exist on the diskette in drive A and I've even filled some records into them already. But don't worry about the records for the time being. Notice that the table definitions do show examples of labels, virtual fields, logical field types, and additional kinds of pictures."

The front page of Jack's handout portrayed the structures of the REP and PERF tables as shown in Figure 6–3. Alongside the field names he included a brief description of each. Names of virtual fields are indented. Figures 6–4 and 6–5 contain the printouts of the DEFINE command being used to define the REP and PERF tables respectively. To get these printouts, Jack had set both E.OPRN and E.ECHO to TRUE before invoking the DEFINE command.

Commenting on the REP definition in Figure 6–4, Jack drew the group's attention to the pictures used for the various fields. The FNAME picture's u placeholder will force the first character of each first name stored in the table to be in uppercase, even if a user forgets to press the shift key when typing in that character. Jack pointed out that the SPOUSE picture is identical in effect to FNAME picture. The only difference is that the former is expressed in a shorthand manner. The HDATE, PHONE, and TID pictures make use of several literals (slashes, parentheses, a dash, blanks, and digits). Having these literals saves typing effort. As hire dates and phone numbers are being typed, the literals automatically appear. Jack also mentioned that the presentation value of such literals would become more evident when they began viewing the table's data. The n placeholders in the pictures are similar to d placeholders, only more restrictive. A decimal point or sign $(+, -)$ cannot replace an n (i.e., numeral only) placeholder during the entry of a data

FIGURE 6–4   Defining the REP table

```
define rep
FILE? "a:rep.itb"
FIELD? fname str 8 using "uaaaaaaa"
FIELD? midi str 2 using "ur"
FIELD? lname str 10 using "u%9a"
FIELD? name str 22 =trim(fname)+" "+midi+" "+trim(lname)
FIELD? spouse str 8 using "u%7a"
FIELD? hdate str 10 using "nn/nn/19nn"
FIELD? phone str 14 using "(nnn) nnn-nnnn"
FIELD? tid str 3 using "n   "
FIELD? street str 15 using "%15r"
FIELD? city str 12 using "u%11a"
FIELD? state str 2 using "uu"
FIELD? zip str 5 using "nnnnn"
FIELD? addr str 38 =trim(street)+", "+trim(city)+" "+state+" "+zip using "%38r"
FIELD? mosal int using "nnnnn"
FIELD? moexp num using "fffff.ff"
FIELD? majorp str 11 using "aaa:aaa:aaa"
FIELD?
eject
```

FIGURE 6–5   Defining the PERF table

```
define perf
FILE? "a:perf.itb"
FIELD? tid str 3 using "n  " labeled "Territory ID"
FIELD? fname str 8 using "uaaaaaaa" labeled "First name of rep"
FIELD? pid str 3 using "aaa" labeled "Product ID"
FIELD? q1 num using "ffffff" labeled "Quota: quarter 1"
FIELD? q2 num using "ffffff" labeled "Quota: quarter 2"
FIELD? q3 num using "ffffff" labeled "Quota: quarter 3"
FIELD? q4 num using "ffffff" labeled "Quota: quarter 4"
FIELD? qyr num =q1+q2+q3+q4 using "nnnnnn"
FIELD? s1 num using "ffffff" labeled "Sales: quarter 1"
FIELD? s2 num using "ffffff" labeled "Sales: quarter 2"
FIELD? s3 num using "ffffff" labeled "Sales: quarter 3"
FIELD? s4 num using "ffffff" labeled "Sales: quarter 4"
FIELD? sytd num =s1+s2+s3+s4 using "nnnnnn" labeled "Sales year to date"
FIELD? major logic using "11111" labeled "Major prod for rep"
FIELD?
eject
```

value. Finally, he reminded them that an r placeholder can stand for anything, whereas the a placeholder can be replaced only by alphabetic characters.

"There are two virtual fields defined in the REP table," observed Jack. "Both are defined in terms of string calculations. The first, NAME, involves the concatenation of three fields defined earlier, with appropriate trimming and spacing. The value of NAME in any record will always be the string of text calculated by trimming trailing spaces from the record's FNAME value, adding a space, adding the record's MIDI value, another space, and the record's trimmed LNAME value. As you can see, the other virtual field—ADDR—has a similar calculation involving four of the record's other fields. Aside from including the expression that specifies the kind of calculation you want, defining a virtual field is like defining an ordinary actual field."

"Are there any limitations on the kinds of expressions we can use for a virtual field?" asked Stan. "Can the expressions include working variables in addition to fields? Can we use all of the functions provided for doing stand-alone calculations within this domain of data management?"

"Yes, yes, and yes," Jack replied. "As for variables, I believe you can even include utility or environment variables in a virtual field's calculation if you so desire. The calculations are not limited to string expressions like those shown in REP. You can also use logical or numeric calculations if you like. Notice that the PERF table definition has two numeric virtual fields: QYR and SYTD. The value of QYR for any record is always guaranteed to be the sum of the present Q1, Q2, Q3, and

Q4 values for that record. Similarly, a record's SYTD value is always calculated to be the sum of whatever its S1 through S4 values happen to be at the moment that the SYTD value is accessed.

"In this table there's a label for almost every field. Personally, I usually don't specify labels, but I've included some here to show you how to do it if you're so inclined. This table also has an example of a logical field. Because each PERF record will pertain to a particular rep's performance figures for a particular product line, that record either will or will not involve one of the rep's major product lines. So I've included the MAJOR field whose value will be TRUE for major performance records and FALSE for records that don't deal with a rep's major products. Notice that its five picture placeholders will always force MAJOR's values to appear entirely in lowercase, regardless of how they are initially entered."

"In looking at the PERF definition," remarked Tracey, "it's clear that you used the same type and picture over and over again. Is there some way to avoid retyping commonly used phrases such as the 'num using "fffff" labeled' phrase that appears for eight of your field definitions?"

"I know how," piped up Brad. "You would just use the REDEFINE FUNCTION command to let one of the function keys be equivalent to an entire phrase."

"That's right," agreed Jack. He elaborated that Tracey's desire could be satisfied by using the command

```
redefine function 10 "num using \"fffff\" labeled"
```

before beginning to define the PERF table. Whenever needed during the DEFINE command interaction, function key F10 would be pressed and the phrase

```
num using "ffffff" labeled
```

would appear at the cursor position. Jack reminded them that the two backslashes were included to indicate that the immediately following quotes were to be interpreted literally and not as an end of F10's new definition.

SHOWING A TABLE

"Earlier," Jack recalled, "we saw that the SHOW command could be invoked to show a list of macros or to show the meaning of any individual macro. Well, the SHOW command can also be invoked to show a list of the tables that are presently in use, to show the structure of any one of these tables, or to show the characteristics of any individual field. This can be quite handy if at some moment you happen to forget which tables are in use, what their fields are, or the characteristics of some field. Let me show you how it works."

Having just defined the PROD table, Jack decided to show its structure. He did so by invoking the command

```
show prod
```

The environment reacted by showing a list of the PROD fields and their respective characteristics on the console screen. In addition to the five fields Jack had defined, one other field (named #MARK) was shown. He commented that they would later examine the purpose of this special field that the environment installs in every table. The field list was prefaced by various general information about the table such as the date on which it was defined, the date of the most recent modification, the size of each record (in bytes), and the number of records it presently held (currently 0).

Because some tables have more fields than can be simultaneously displayed on the screen, Jack remarked that he tended to have E.PAUS set to TRUE before showing a table's structure. Otherwise, the display scrolled by so rapidly that it couldn't be absorbed. The default value of this environment variable is FALSE. When its value is TRUE, the display will pause as soon as the screen fills. Pressing the space bar will display the next screenful and so forth until all the table structure has been shown. "On the other hand," he added, "if I'm just interested in getting a printout of the SHOW results, then I let E.PAUS be FALSE and the results are printed without interruption. I don't have to keep pressing the space bar to allow the printing to continue.

"Sometimes you may be interested in the characteristics of only one particular field, say GMR, and not the others. You can invoke SHOW to examine that field's traits without having to step through all the other fields." He illustrated by entering the command

```
show prod.gmr
```

The environment reacted by showing the characteristics of the PROD table's GMR field. Any other PROD field's traits can be shown by substituting its name for GMR in the above command.

"As soon as we define a table, it is in use," Jack declared. "That simply means we are free to process it. If a table is not in use we can't process it. At any moment you can check on what tables happen to be in use by using a simple variant of the SHOW command. Watch."

FIGURE 6–6   Showing what tables are in use

```
_show
Tables Currently in Use:
Table name    File name
----------    ---------
 PROD         a:prod.itb  (default)
_dir   "a:"




   Volume in drive A has no label
   Directory of A:\

PERF      ITB      3635    9-28-86   11.34a
REP       ITB      2388    9-28-86   12:05p
GMRNOTE   TXT       945   10-01-86    9:39p
PREVIEW   TXT      1346   10-01-86   10:28a
PROD      ITB       347   10-01-86    2:23p
```

Jack entered the command

```
show
```

and the environment responded by showing that the PROD table was in use. It also displayed the fact that the PROD table exists in the file PROD.ITB on the drive A diskette. This SHOW command and the response are portrayed at the top of the console screen shown in Figure 6–6.

"Why is there only one table in use?" asked Dan. "I thought you had also defined the REP and PERF tables. Aren't they also on drive A?"

"You're right," Jack answered. "They're there, but they are not now in use. I defined them and put data in them about a month ago, but today I haven't done anything with them. So far we've only worked with the PROD table, in the sense of defining its structure and existence."

"I see," said Dan. "If we were to get out of the environment, back to the operating system, we could execute its DIR command to see that the PERF.ITB and REP.ITB files actually do exist along with PROD.ITB on the drive A diskette."

"Right, but you really don't need to leave the environment in order to see a directory of the files available on a drive. That's because the environment has its own DIR command. Let me show you how it works."

As shown in Figure 6–6, Jack executed the command

```
dir "a:"
```

to get a directory of all files on drive A. The figure shows a partial list of the DIR command results. Notice that the three table files Dan referred to are all there. Joy pointed out that any phrase that could legitimately follow the word DIR in the operating system command could also follow the word DIR in the environment's directory command. The only difference is that the phrase (e.g., "a:") must be enclosed in quotes in the environment's DIR command.

USING AND FINISHING TABLES

"Alright, but how do you put a table in use when it's not currently in use?" Dan persisted. "Surely you can have more than one table in use at a time."

"Yes," Jack replied, "you can have many tables in use simultaneously. This fact is extremely important, since you'll oftentimes want to work on several tables, perhaps in a single operation. To put a table in use, you use the USE command."

He proceeded to execute the USE command twice

```
use "a:rep.itb"
use "a:perf.itb"
```

to put the REP and PERF tables in use. Had these tables existed on the computer's hard disk, in the same directory as the environment software, Jack could have referred to the table names instead of the names of the files containing the tables. To show that there were now three tables in use, Jack again invoked the SHOW command with the results shown in the upper portion of the console screen in Figure 6–7.

"After you've been using a table for a while," Jack continued, "you may find that you no longer need it for the time being. In such a case, you can invoke the FINISH command to tell the environment you're finished processing it."

Joy chimed in, "Finishing a table frees up some of the environment's work area for other purposes. Whenever you put a table in use, a portion of the work area is allocated for managing the transfer of records between disk and main memory where they can actually be acted on

FIGURE 6–7   Using and finishing tables

```
_use "a:rep.itb"
_use "a:perf.itb"
_show
Tables Currently In Use:
Table name    File name
----------    ---------
 PERF         a:perf.itb
 REP          a:rep.itb
 PROD         a:prod.itb (default)
_finish rep
_show
Tables Currently In Use:
Table name    File name
----------    ---------
 PERF         a:perf.itb
 PROD         a:prod.itb (default)
_finish all
_show
No tables open
```

by the environment software. This portion of main memory is often called a *buffer*. It contains images of those records that are susceptible to immediate processing. If a record whose image isn't in the buffer is needed, the environment takes care of bringing it into the buffer where it can be processed. At the same time, it also takes care of sending images that were in the buffer back out to the disk file. Whenever something comes into the buffer, something that was already there has to go out to make room for the new images."

"Doesn't that mean," observed Debbie, "that we won't have to worry about explicitly telling the environment to bring individual records into the work area from disk or to save individual records from the work area to disk?"

"Exactly," Joy replied. "All of that's handled automatically for you—beneath the surface—as long as the table is in use. When you finish a table, the images in its buffer are flushed out to disk and you won't be able to process it until you again put it in use."

Jack demonstrated the FINISH command by invoking

```
finish rep
```

to finish the REP table. As depicted in Figure 6–7, he then executed the SHOW command, confirming that the REP table was no longer available for use. To finish all tables remaining in use, the word "ALL" is used in place of a specific table name.

"By the way," he added, "when you BYE out of the environment any unfinished tables are automatically finished for you. But if you leave the environment in any other way, the tables will not be finished, which means you may not be able to use them again; so you should always say BYE as you leave the environment."

"I notice that whenever you show a list of the tables in use," observed Stan, "one of them is designated as the 'default' table. What does that mean?"

"I think you can pretty much ignore it for now," Jack replied and looked to Joy.

"Keep in mind the fact that you can have multiple tables simultaneously in use," she suggested. "Many of the data management commands you are about to learn normally require you to specify which table you're talking about. However, if you don't specify a table in the command, the environment assumes that you want it to process the default table. For example, if instead of typing FINISH REP, Jack had just typed FINISH, the default table would have been finished instead of REP. The DEFAULT command can be used to make a different table the current default. To issue this command, you just type the word DEFAULT followed by the name of the in-use table that you want to be treated as the new default table."

CREATING RECORDS

Once a table has been defined, records can be created in it either immediately or at some later date. The only requirement is that the table must be in use. Generally speaking, there are two basic approaches to record creation: interactive and batch. *Interactive creation* means that a user types in a record's data values as the record is being created. Though it is not part of the standard relational data management languages, some software packages facilitate the interactive creation activity by prompting the user with field names. The record's data values can then be typed in alongside their corresponding field names. *Batch creation* means that a batch of records is created by taking data from some nontable source and attaching it to the table. The nontable source might be a text file, a context file, or a file produced by some external software package. Jack proceeded to illustrate both approaches to record creation in the knowledge management environment.

FIGURE 6–8   Ready to start creating the first PROD record

```
Record Number: 1        ENTER=start creating this record ESC=quit

PID:      __
PNAME:    _____
TARGET:   __ , __
GMR:      __ . __
CRATE:    __ . ___
```

Interactive Creation

In preparation for interactively creating some PROD records, Jack put the PROD table in use and he changed the E.LMOD environment variable from its default TRUE value to FALSE. "For now, don't worry about the purpose of this control switch," he said reassuringly. "We'll take a look at its role a little later. To create PROD records you use the CREATE command."

He demonstrated by invoking the command

```
create record for prod
```

This caused the screen to clear momentarily before taking on the appearance shown in Figure 6–8. "The top line indicates the current status of record creation for the table. In this case it tells us we are about to create record number 1. The status line also gives instructions about what we can do next. As you can see, if I press the Enter key creation of record 1 will begin. Alternatively, I could press the Escape key to quit the creation process.

FIGURE 6-9   Ready to enter the record's PID value

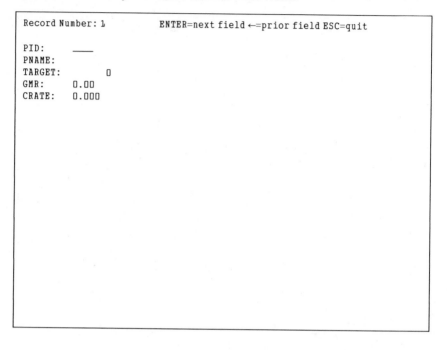

```
Record Number: 1          ENTER=next field ←=prior field ESC=quit

PID:        ____
PNAME:
TARGET:        0
GMR:        0.00
CRATE:      0.000
```

"Beneath the status line, you can see a prompt for each of the table's fields. Each is followed by an entry line whose length matches the field's picture. Notice that the literals we specified in field pictures appear automatically in the entry lines. Now watch what happens when I press the Enter key."

As he pressed it, the cursor jumped from the status line to the short entry line following the PID prompt. The instructions in the status line changed, initial values of zero were given to the three numeric fields, and an initial blank value was given to the PNAME field. The screen now appeared as depicted in Figure 6–9. Jack proceeded to type in the value

sfi

for the new record's PID field. As the status line instructions indicate, when he then pressed the Enter key, the cursor jumped to the next field's entry line. Figure 6–10 shows the resultant screen appearance. He typed

science fiction

FIGURE 6–10   Ready to enter the record's PNAME value

```
┌─────────────────────────────────────────────────────────────────────┐
│ Record Number: 1         Enter=next field ←=prior field ESC=quit      │
│                                                                       │
│ PID:      sfi                                                         │
│ PNAME:    ─────────────────                                          │
│ TARGET:          0                                                    │
│ GMR:      0.00                                                       │
│ CRATE:    0.000                                                      │
│                                                                       │
│                                                                       │
│                                                                       │
│                                                                       │
│                                                                       │
│                                                                       │
│                                                                       │
│                                                                       │
│                                                                       │
│                                                                       │
│                                                                       │
│                                                                       │
│                                                                       │
│                                                                       │
└─────────────────────────────────────────────────────────────────────┘
```

on the PNAME entry line and pressed the Enter key. The cursor jumped
to TARGET's entry line as shown in Figure 6–11. Jack typed

200100

as TARGET's value. He continued in this way to enter

.72

for GMR. He then paused after pressing the Enter key following this
last field's value. The screen now had the appearance shown in Figure
6–12 and the blinking cursor was positioned to enter the final field's
value.

"At this point," he advised, "it's a good idea to review all the
data values you've just typed in for the new record, because when
you press the Enter key while the cursor is in the last field, the record
is actually inserted in the table. If your review identifies an error you'll
want to fix it first. Suppose that we really want a science fiction target
of 200000 instead of 200100, then we can use an arrow key to move
the cursor to TARGET's value and edit it using the usual control keys."

Using the arrow key indicated in the status line, he moved the

FIGURE 6–11   Ready to enter the record's TARGET value

```
Record Number: 1          Enter=next field ←=prior field ESC=quit

PID:      sfi
PNAME:    science fiction
TARGET:   ___,__0
GMR:      0.00
CRATE:    0.000
```

cursor to the TARGET value. It was positioned on the 2. He used ^D
to move it to the 1. Because he wanted to replace this digit with a 0,
he pressed ^W to switch to the replacement mode of character entry
and typed 0 to replace the 1. Then he pressed the Enter key twice to
get back down to the CRATE field. There he typed in the value

.028

When he then pressed the Enter key for this last field, the screen momentarily cleared before presenting a fresh set of prompts for creating another
record. Its appearance was identical to the one they had seen earlier
(Figure 6–8) with one exception: The status line now showed a record
number of 2 instead of 1.

   Jack went on to create three more records in this same way. His
entries for the second, third, and fourth records were:

com	spo	bio
computers	sports	biography
278000	132000	108000
.76	.51	.48
.028	.023	.022

FIGURE 6-12   Ready to enter the record's CRATE value

```
Record Number: 1          Enter=next field ←=prior field ESC=quit

PID:      sfi
PNAME:    science fiction
TARGET:   200,100
GMR:        .72
CRATE:    _.__0
```

After creating the fourth record the status line's record number showed 5. He pressed the Escape key to terminate the CREATE command without entering a fifth record. The underscore prompt reappeared, awaiting his next command.

"One last point about interactively creating records is E.LMOD," Jack concluded. "If this environment variable's value is TRUE when you execute CREATE, then each new record is created by modifying a visual image of the last record. Instead of being presented with blanks and zeros when you start creating a new record, you would see the values of the last record you created plugged in as a starting point for the new record. You could then use the usual control keys for editing these values until they reflect the new record that you want."

"Why would you want to do that?" Brad inquired.

"It can save a great deal of typing effort in some cases," Jack replied. "If you are creating a whole series of records and successive records have the same values for certain fields, you won't have to type in a repeated value multiple times. You only need to type it once and it automatically appears as the starting value for subsequent records. Of course, you are free to edit it or type in an entirely new value of it as desired."

Batch Attachment

"I'm curious," said Debbie, "why you created only four PROD records. What about the other product lines?"

"I could have continued adding more records with the CREATE command," Jack answered. "Even now we could again execute the exact same CREATE command to add more records to the PROD table. But there may be an easier way. Remember, in our GMR note we've already typed in some of the product line data. Why type it in again?"

"You mean there's a way to transfer data from a text file into an actual table?" she asked.

"Yes," he nodded. "We can transfer a whole batch of data with a single command. This command attaches the data as new records at the end of the table. But it can't work on just any arbitrary arrangement of data. For instance, it needs to know where one string value leaves off and the next one begins. Obviously, it can interpret blanks between numbers as separating the numbers, but it can't do the same for string values. For this reason we need to do some quick editing of the data in GMRNOTE.TXT."

Jack invoked the TEXT command with GMRNOTE.TXT to bring that file's text into view. First, he used ^T to delete all lines other than the five lines of product data. He successively positioned the cursor on the first nonblank character in each of these lines and held down the destructive Backspace key until each line's leading blanks had vanished. He then inserted a comma after each sequence of characters that would become a string field's value. When used in this way, the comma is called a *delimiter*. It shows where a string value ends. Jack escaped to the status line, and issued the command

```
write "a:pdata.txt"
```

there, giving the screen the appearance shown in Figure 6–13. This saved the edited version of GMRNOTE.TXT in a file named PDATA.TXT without disturbing the original version. He again escaped to the status line and issued the BYE command. The underscore prompt reappeared.

"What we're now going to do," explained Jack, "is attach each line in the PDATA file as a new record in the PROD table. But before we do so we need to let the environment know that we're using a comma as our string delimiter. We just set the E.DELI environment variable accordingly."

He proceeded to enter the command

```
let e.deli=","
```

FIGURE 6–13   Delimited PDATA text for batch record creation

```
 Line:5        Col:1      a:gmrnote.txt  Command: write "a:pdata.txt"
ROM   ,romance     ,235000      .024   .64
BUS   ,business    ,173000      .022   .34
PSY   ,psychology  ,102000      .018   .36
REF   ,reference   ,224000      .019   .38
PHO   ,photography ,86000       .020   .28
```

and noted that the choice of a comma delimiter was somewhat arbitrary. If he had separated the string values in PDATA.TXT with a colon, then the value of E.DELI would have been set to a colon. Without further ado, he executed the command.

```
attach from "a:pdata.txt" to prod with pid,pname,target,crate,gmr
```

causing the A drive light to come on briefly as the PDATA text became new records attached to the end of the PROD table.

"Why did your ATTACH command give both the table and field names?" asked Dan. "It seems that if you give the table name, the environment should be able to figure out what its fields are."

"Oh, it can," Jack answered, "but it can't know that the values in PDATA are not in the same order as PROD's fields. If I had left off the sequence of field names, the GMR values would have become CRATE values, and vice versa. As it is, the first PDATA value becomes a PID, the second becomes a PNAME, the third a TARGET, the fourth a CRATE, and the fifth a GMR, which is just what we want."

"I might add," Joy added, "that you don't have to specify all of a table's fields with an ATTACH command. If the batch of data you're using doesn't have values for some fields, then you just omit those particular field names from the command. Also it's worth noting that many other arrangements of batch data, beyond the example Jack gave you, are susceptible to being attached into a table. For instance, Stan, you could use your 1–2–3 spreadsheet package to produce a file of data that could be attached into a table in this environment via a single ATTACH command."

BACKUP COPIES

"Before leaving the topic of record creation, I want to alert you to the importance of backups," Jack announced. "Once you've created some records in a table, you should think about backing up the table by making a replica of it. If the file containing your table were to become damaged in some way, you would have to define the table again and recreate all of its records again. That could take a lot of time for large tables even if you do have a printout of all the table's records. However, if you have a backup copy of the file this effort can be avoided. Our operating system has a command that allows you to copy an existing file to a new file. But you don't have to leave the environment in order to run this COPY command."

Jack demonstrated by invoking the environment's RUN command

```
run "copy a:prod.itb b:prodbak.itb"
```

What appears inside the quotes can be any valid operating system command. In this case, it is an operating system COPY command that makes a replica of the PROD.ITB file existing on the drive A diskette [5]. The replica file will be named PRODBAK.ITB and will be created on the diskette in drive B. This approach can be used to make a copy of any kind of knowledge system file at any time.

VIEWING RECORDS

In a skeptical tone someone said, "You've been telling us that you've created some records in the PROD table, but how do we know that they're really there? How do we know that the ATTACH command really attached the five new records to the table?"

"That's a good question," responded Jack. "I guess the rest of you have just been taking my word for it that the records now really exist in the PROD table. In this environment there are several commands that we can invoke for viewing records. Each is intended for a particular kind of viewing. Here, we'll look at two of the simplest viewing commands: OBTAIN and BROWSE. The OBTAIN command obtains a specific record from a table and displays its field values. The BROWSE command lets you browse through a table's records in either a forward or reverse direction. It also gives you a chance to edit the values of records as you are browsing."

Obtaining a Particular Record

"Suppose we want to obtain the first record from the PROD table," Jack began his description of the OBTAIN command. He typed

```
obtain first record from prod
```

and the environment immediately responded by displaying all the field values for that record. Each value was displayed to the right of its field name. Even the #MARK field was shown and Jack reminded the group to ignore it for the time being. To obtain the next record in the PROD table, he typed

```
obtain next from prod
```

and the values of its fields were displayed. He then pressed ˆZ and the Enter key to repeat the last command. This caused the table's third record to be obtained and displayed. The console screen now appeared as shown in Figure 6–14.

"You can obtain records in the opposite direction if you like, beginning with the last one and progressing through prior ones. Guess what the commands would be?" he said.

"Probably something like OBTAIN LAST and PRIOR records from PROD," offered Brad.

He was correct as Jack demonstrated by executing the three commands

```
obtain last from prod
obtain prior from prod
obtain prior from prod
```

Here again Jack avoided actually typing the third command. He just pressed ˆZ to recall the previous command and then pressed the Enter key to execute it. The resultant screen with the expected results appears in Figure 6–15.

"I take it you could keep going in the prior direction until you

FIGURE 6–14   Obtaining the first and next records

```
_obtain first record from prod
 Record Number: 1
 #MARK:      FALSE
 PID:        sfi
 PNAME:      science fiction
 TARGET:     200,100
 GMR:        0.72
 CRATE:      0.028
_obtain next from prod
 Record Number: 2
 #MARK:      FALSE
 PID:        com
 PNAME:      computers
 TARGET:     278,000
 GMR:        0.76
 CRATE:      0.028
_obtain next from prod
 Record Number: 3
 #MARK:      FALSE
 PID:        spo
 PNAME:      sports
 TARGET:     132,000
 GMR:        0.51
 CRATE:      0.023
 _
```

reach the first record," commented Stan. "But can you switch directions whenever you like?"

Jack answered by executing

```
obtain next from prod
```

which again brought the eighth record into view. He explained that the most recently accessed record in a table is called the table's *current record*. Whenever OBTAIN PRIOR or OBTAIN NEXT is requested, it is with respect to the current record and the newly obtained record becomes the new current record.

"Isn't there some way to get at a record more directly, without having to step through them in sequence?" asked Dan. "Suppose I want to directly obtain the fifth record."

Again Jack responded by executing a command

```
obtain 5 from prod
```

causing the data from PROD's fifth record to be displayed. This record was now the current record.

FIGURE 6–15   Obtaining the last and prior records

```
_obtain last from prod
 Record Number: 9
 #MARK:      FALSE
 PID:        PHO
 PNAME:      photography
 TARGET:     86,000
 GMR:        0.28
 CRATE:      0.020
_obtain prior from prod
 Record Number: 8
 #MARK:      FALSE
 PID:        REF
 PNAME:      reference
 TARGET:     224,000
 GMR:        0.38
 CRATE:      0.019
_obtain prior from prod
 Record Number: 7
 #MARK:      FALSE
 PID:        PSY
 PNAME:      psychology
 TARGET:     102,000
 GMR:        0.36
 CRATE:      0.018

 _
```

Obtaining Records that Satisfy Conditions

"Could it now obtain the next record whose TARGET value exceeds, say, 221,000?" Tracey asked.

"Sure," Jack replied as he typed the command

```
obtain next from prod where target > 221000
```

and executed it. The values of record number 8 were displayed, leaving the screen as shown in Figure 6–16. "You can include any kind of logical expression as the condition in an OBTAIN command. In this case the next record, after the current one, that yields a TRUE value for the calculation of TARGET>221000 is the one that is obtained. You're perfectly free to embed logical calculations in the OBTAIN command.

"Now suppose I want to obtain some romance information. I really don't care about that record's relative position with respect to the current record, so I won't qualify the command with the word PRIOR or NEXT. I just use the following." He executed the command

```
obtain record from prod for pid="ROM"
```

FIGURE 6–16   Obtaining records directly

```
_obtain next from prod
 Record Number: 8
 #MARK:     FALSE
 PID:       REF
 PNAME:     reference
 TARGET:    224,000
 GMR:       0.38
 CRATE:     0.019
_obtain 5 from prod
 Record Number: 5
 #MARK:     FALSE
 PID:       ROM
 PNAME:     romance
 TARGET:    235,000
 GMR:       0.64
 CRATE:     0.024
_obtain next from prod where target > 221000
 Record Number: 8
 #MARK:     FALSE
 PID:       REF
 PNAME:     reference
 TARGET:    224,000
 GMR:       0.38
 CRATE:     0.019

 —
```

and the romance record's data were immediately displayed. Jack pointed out that the words FOR and WHERE are interchangeable. Either one denotes the start of a *condition* that is being specified. Notice that the logical expression in this example involved a string field and a string constant, whereas the prior example's logical expression involved a numeric field and a numeric constant. Compound logical expressions (recall Chapter 4) can also be used as conditions.

"It's very interesting," Jack continued, "that the fields of a table's current record can be used just like working variables. Suppose we want to know what the total commission would be if the romance target were met. We simply multiply the TARGET field by the CRATE field." He illustrated by executing the OUTPUT command

```
?target*crate
```

to which the environment responded by calculating 5640. "You're entirely free to intermix calculations with data management commands and either can be issued in the midst of text processing," he added.

A condition is always a logical expression just like those introduced in Chapter 4. However, it usually involves one or more fields, though

FIGURE 6–17   Mixing calculations and record viewing

```
_obtain record from prod for pid="ROM"
 Record Number: 5
 #MARK:     FALSE
 PID:       ROM
 PNAME:     romance
 TARGET:    235,000
 GMR:       0.64
 CRATE:     0.024
_?target*crate
     5640.00000
_obtain first record from prod where target*crate > 5640
 Record Number: 2
 #MARK:     FALSE
 PID:       com
 PNAME:     computers
 TARGET:    278,000
 GMR:       0.76
 CRATE:     0.028
_?"If ",pid," target is met, ",target*crate using "$ff,fff","is commission"
If com target is met, $7,784 is commission

 —
```

it can also contain working variables if desired. As shown in Chapter 4, a logical expression can itself have numeric calculations on either side of a relational operator. Jack illustrated this by executing

```
obtain first record from prod where target*crate > 5640
```

to obtain the first PROD record whose total targeted commission exceeds the targeted commission for romance. It turned out to be the second record in PROD, the computer product line.

"But what is the targeted computer commission?" someone asked and Jack responded with an appropriate OUTPUT command, leaving the screen with the appearance shown in Figure 6–17.

Changing an Obtained Record

"OK, so I can now obtain any record I like," said Debbie thoughtfully. "And I see how I can use its values in calculations. But what if I want to change one of its values? For instance, suppose I obtain the sports record and in looking at the TARGET value decide to increase it by 4.5 percent."

FIGURE 6–18   Changing values in the current record

```
_obtain from prod for pname="sports"
 Record Number: 3
 #MARK:     FALSE
 PID:       spo
 PNAME:     sports
 TARGET:    132,000
 GMR:       0.51
 CRATE:     0.023
_let target=target*1.045
_obtain 3 from prod
 Record Number: 3
 #MARK:     FALSE
 PID:       spo
 PNAME:     sports
 TARGET:    137,940
 GMR:       0.51
 CRATE:     0.023
_target=target/1.045
_?target
132,000

_
```

"You could use the LET command, just as we did when calculating new values for working variables. Watch," commanded Jack. He executed several commands giving the screen the appearance shown in Figure 6–18. After obtaining the sports record, he used the LET command to set its new target be 4.5 percent greater than its current target. He again obtained the sports (i.e., third) record to convince them that TARGET's value had indeed changed. To set the sports target back to its original value Jack used another LET command, this time omitting the optional word LET. Finally, he output the current record's TARGET value to verify that it had reverted back to its original value.

"Just so you don't get the idea that we can obtain records from only the PROD table, I'm going to put the PERF and REP tables in use too. The REP table contains records for the reps in my region and the PERF table contains some of their performance records on various product lines through the first three quarters." Jack invoked the USE command twice to put the two tables in use.

"Let's take a look at the data for the rep who works in territory 6," he suggested and proceeded to execute the command

```
obtain record from rep for tid="6"
```

FIGURE 6–19   Obtaining a REP record

```
_use "a:perf.itb"
_use "a:rep.itb"
_obtain record from rep for tid="6"
 Record Number: 7
 #MARK:      FALSE
 FNAME:      Karen
 MIDI:       V.
 LNAME:      Bruckner
 NAME:       Karen V. Bruckner
 SPOUSE:
 HDATE:      05/14/1982
 PHONE:      (433) 422-8201
 TID:        6
 STREET:     44 Tan Ave.
 CITY:       Madison
 STATE:      WI
 ZIP:        66667
 ADDR:       44 Tan Ave., Madison WI 66667
 MOSAL:       2800
 MOEXP:       1335.00
 MAJORP:     com:bus:rom
 _
```

resulting in the screen depicted in Figure 6–19. Jack pointed out that all of the data values were displayed according to the pictures used for their respective fields. Recall the REP table definition that he had handed out earlier (Figure 6–4). Notice also that the calculated values for the two virtual fields (NAME and ADDR) are consistent with those fields' definitions.

Calculating with an Obtained Record

"All of the OBTAIN variations we did with the PROD table could also be done with the REP table. But I think you get the idea by now, so let's go on to obtain something from the PERF table. Notice from the last field in the REP record that one of this particular rep's major product lines is business books. Let's see how she has performed for that product thus far this year." Jack executed the command

```
obtain record from perf for fname="Karen" and pid="bus"
```

resulting in the display of the PERF table's 22nd record.

To see how much she needed to sell in the fourth quarter to meet her annual quota for this product line, he invoked the command

```
?perf.qyr - perf.sytd
```

giving the screen appearance portrayed in Figure 6–20. Because the calculation result of 5548 is less than Q4, it is clear that Karen is ahead of the pace needed to meet her quota for business books. Notice that the foregoing calculation involved the two virtual fields defined for the PERF table (recall Figure 6–5).

"I'm curious," Stan remarked, "about why you prefaced the field names with the table name in your OUTPUT calculation. Earlier you didn't do that when outputting the targeted romance commission."

"The reason I didn't do it before," Jack explained, "is because REP is presently our default table. To reference the fields of tables that are not the default in an OUTPUT or LET command you need to qualify them with their table names as I've just done. Otherwise, the environment is unable to recognize them as field names. Alternatively I could have used the DEFAULT command to make PERF the default table and then just typed '?QYR–SYTD' to get the same result. By the way, since PROD was the default table, the words FROM PROD could have been omitted from the OBTAIN commands involving that table."

Browsing through a Table's Records

"I can see where the OBTAIN command is worthwhile for getting at a particular record," Dan declared. "But if I wanted to view all of the REP records that have a monthly salary in excess of, say, $2,400, then I'd have to repeatedly execute OBTAIN commands. Isn't there some way to do things like that by executing a single command?"

"When you want to rummage about in a table, I'd suggest the BROWSE command," Jack advised. "It lets you browse in either direction through all the records that satisfy whatever condition you're interested in, without having to issue more than one command."

To satisfy Dan's request, Jack entered the command

```
browse rep for mosal > 2400
```

causing the screen to momentarily clear before the first REP record with a MOSAL in excess of 2400 appeared as shown in Figure 6–21. In addition to displaying the record's values, the environment provides a status line at the top of the screen. It indicates the number of the record presently in view, plus instructions about what can be done

FIGURE 6–20   Obtaining a PERF record

```
_obtain record from perf for fname="Karen" and pid="bus"
 Record Number: 22
 #MARK:    FALSE
 TID:      6
 FNAME:    Karen
 PID:      bus
 Q1:         10700
 Q2:         11009
 Q3:          8443
 Q4:          7930
 QYR:        38082
 S1:         12222
 S2:         11980
 S3:          8332
 S4:             0
 SYTD:       32534
 MAJOR:    true
_?perf.qyr - perf.sytd
    5548.00000
_
```

FIGURE 6–21   First record displayed by BROWSE REP FOR MOSAL > 2400

```
 Record Number: 1          →=next ←=prior ENTER=edit ESC=quit

 FNAME:    Kevin
 MIDI:     R.
 LNAME:    Andrews
 NAME:     Kevin R. Andrews
 SPOUSE:
 HDATE:    08/30/1981
 PHONE:    (123) 456-1111
 TID:      2
 STREET:   25 Stratton Ave
 CITY:     Bloomington
 STATE:    IL
 ZIP:      54321
 ADDR:     25 Stratton Ave, Bloomington IL 54321
 MOSAL:     2500
 MOEXP     1025.68
 MAJORP:   sfi:pho:spo
```

FIGURE 6–22   Second record displayed by
                BROWSE REP FOR MOSAL > 2400

```
┌─────────────────────────────────────────────────────────────────┐
│ Record Number: 2            →=next ←=prior ENTER=edit ESC=quit    │
│                                                                   │
│ FNAME:      Kim                                                   │
│ MIDI:       G.                                                    │
│ LNAME:      Anders                                                │
│ NAME:       Kim G. Anders                                         │
│ SPOUSE:                                                           │
│ HDATE:      04/06/1979                                            │
│ PHONE:      (312) 553-6754                                        │
│ TID:        0                                                     │
│ STREET:     8242 Wabash                                           │
│ CITY:       Chicago                                               │
│ STATE:      IL                                                    │
│ ZIP:        68909                                                 │
│ ADDR:       8242 Wabash, Chicago IL 68909                         │
│ MOSAL:         2600                                               │
│ MOEXP:          896.74                                            │
│ MAJORP:     ref:bus:spo                                           │
│                                                                   │
│                                                                   │
│                                                                   │
│                                                                   │
│                                                                   │
└─────────────────────────────────────────────────────────────────┘
```

next. Jack pressed the appropriate arrow key to get to the next rep having a monthly salary over $2,400. The result of that single keystroke is depicted in Figure 6–22. As the status line of this screen shows, record number 2 happened to be the next one satisfying BROWSE's condition. The status line instructions remained the same.

Jack pressed the same arrow key to browse to the next record with a sufficiently high monthly salary. The resultant screen appearance is shown in Figure 6–23. Notice that record number 3 was skipped, implying that its MOSAL value did not exceed 2400. In the same way Jack went ahead to the next record satisfying the condition. The screen now appeared as shown in Figure 6–24, with the seventh REP record being displayed.

Editing Values while Browsing

"Just a moment," Jack halted. "Kevin was recently married, but when we saw his record earlier I don't think his new wife's name was filled in. Let's go back and check."

As the status line shows, there is an arrow key that lets the browsing

FIGURE 6–23   Third record displayed by
                BROWSE REP FOR MOSAL > 2400

```
Record Number: 4            →=next ←=prior ENTER=edit ESC=quit

FNAME:      Tina
MIDI:       F.
LNAME:      Lee
NAME:       Tina F. Lee
SPOUSE:     Ben
HDATE:      12/13/1981
PHONE:      (317) 299-8393
TID:        3
STREET:     7892 Meridian
CITY:       Indianapolis
STATE:      IN
ZIP:        46662
ADDR:       7892 Meridian, Indianapolis IN 46662
MOSAL:        2800
MOEXP:         988.20
MAJORP:     bus:com:rom
```

go to prior records if desired. Jack pressed that key and the screen in
Figure 6–23 reappeared. He pressed it two more times to get to Kevin's
record (Figure 6–21) and sure enough this record had a blank value
for the SPOUSE field. Jack explained that whenever you want to edit
field values for the record currently displayed, you merely press the
Enter key as indicated by the status line instructions.

Because he wanted to edit the SPOUSE field now showing on the
screen (Figure 6–21), he pressed the Enter key. The cursor immediately
jumped from the status line down to the first field's value and the
status line instructions changed so that they were now viewing the
screen portrayed in Figure 6–25.

"That's interesting," commented Dan. "The status line looks just
like it does when we are creating records. Come to think of it, the
whole screen looks very similar, the main difference being that here
values are already filled in while in CREATE we fill in the values."

"Right," said Jack, smiling at Dan's perceptivity. "What's more,
CREATE and BROWSE work the same way when it comes to editing
a field's value. Remember that with CREATE we can go back and edit
a previously entered value in the record we're creating. Well, once we

FIGURE 6–24   Fourth record displayed by
BROWSE REP FOR MOSAL > 2400

```
Record Number: 7              →=next ←=prior ENTER=edit ESC=quit

FNAME:     Karen
MIDI:      V.
LNAME:     Bruckner
NAME:      Karen V. Bruckner
SPOUSE:
HDATE:     05/14/1982
PHONE:     (433) 442-8201
TID:       6
STREET:    44 Tan Ave.
CITY:      Madison
STATE:     WI
ZIP:       66667
ADDR:      44 Tan Ave., Madison WI 66667
MOSAL:       2800
MOEXP:      1335.00
MAJORP:    com:bus:rom
```

bring the cursor into the displayed values of a browsed record, we can edit any of those values in the same way. If you don't want to edit the value presently highlighted by the cursor, you just press the Enter key and the cursor goes to the next field's value. Once the cursor is at the value you want to edit, you just edit it in the normal way and then press the Enter key to go on to the next field."

Jack demonstrated by pressing the Enter key three times to bring the cursor to the SPOUSE field's blank value. Because the NAME field is a virtual field the cursor automatically skipped past its value (i.e., virtual values can't be edited since they do not actually exist). He typed in

```
Kris
```

and pressed the Enter key. The cursor moved to the HDATE value and the screen appearance was the same as Figure 6–25, except that Kris now appeared as the SPOUSE value. If desired, other values in this record could be edited in the same manner. Jack did not need to make any further changes, so he pressed the Enter key until it reached

FIGURE 6–25   Editing while browsing

```
Record Number: 1            ENTER=next field ←=prior field ESC=quit

FNAME:      Kevin
MIDI:       R.
LNAME:      Andrews
NAME:       Kevin R. Andrews
SPOUSE:
HDATE:      08/30/1981
PHONE:      (123) 456-1111
TID:        2
STREET:     25 Stratton Ave
CITY:       Bloomington
STATE:      IL
ZIP:        54321
ADDR:       25 Stratton Ave, Bloomington IL 54321
MOSAL:       2500
MOEXP:       1025.68
MAJORP:     sfi:pho:spo
```

the last (MAJORP) field. Pressing it once more exited from the editing of this record and brought the next one (Figure 6–22) into view.

Pressing the indicated arrow key twice brought him back to record number 7 (Figure 6–24). He pressed it again to continue the browsing forward to the next record with a MOSAL over 2400. It turned out to be record number 10. Pressing it again caused the cursor to jump out of the status line to an underscore prompt following the record's last field. As usual this meant the environment was ready to accept the next command. The BROWSE command had terminated because there were no more REP records satisfying its condition. The screen now appeared as shown in Figure 6–26.

Conditional Browsing

"Any kind of condition you could specify for an OBTAIN command could also be specified for a BROWSE command," Jack remarked. "The browsing behavior with the ability to edit values is always the same regardless of what condition, if any, you put on a BROWSE command. The condition just restricts which of a table's records will be accessible to you as you browse."

FIGURE 6–26   Last record displayed by BROWSE REP FOR MOSAL > 2400

```
Record Number: 10          →=Next ←=prior ENTER=edit ESC=quit

FNAME:     Carol
MIDI:      0.
LNAME:     Lynn
NAME:      Carol O. Lynn
SPOUSE:
HDATE:     11/01/1979
PHONE:     (412) 832-5643
TID:       9
STREET:    58 Cater Dr.
CITY:      Midland
STATE:     MI
ZIP:       40098
ADDR:      58 Cater Dr., Midland MI 40098
MOSAL:     2750
MOEXP:     1229.73
MAJORP:    com:rom:bus
_
```

Jack proceeded to present additional examples of conditional browsing to further familiarize the group with some of the possibilities. The examples included the following BROWSE commands

```
browse rep for lname="Smith"
```

which browsed through only those REP records with a last name of Smith,

```
browse perf for qyr*.75 < sytd
```

which browsed through the performance records for which year-to-date sales had not yet surpassed three fourths of the annual quota,

```
browse perf for qyr*.75 < sytd and major
```

which does the same as the previous command but with the further restriction that only those with MAJOR equal to TRUE are browsed.

He also gave some examples where the conditions' logical expressions involved a new kind of relational operator other than the usual >, <, =, and so on. This was the IN operator. For instance, the command

```
browse rep for tid in ["3","9","2"]
```

browses through REP records whose territory ID is 3 or 9 or 2. Jack explained that this command is logically equivalent to

```
browse rep for tid="3" or tid="9" or tid="2"
```

but is more compact. The square brackets enclosed a class of values. The logical expression

```
tid in ["3","9","2"]
```

will be calculated as being TRUE if the value of TID matches any value in the class.

"But what if the class is very large?" asked Tracey. "Suppose I want to browse through the reps who were hired in 1979. Would I have to enumerate all the possible dates for 1979 in a class for HDATE? That would be downright prohibitive."

"You're right," Jack answered. "There is a much easier way to specify such a class. It's done with a *wild card symbol* that the environment will interpret as matching any string of characters. That symbol is an asterisk."

He demonstrated by executing the command

```
browse rep for hdate in ["*79"]
```

which browsed through only those REP records whose HDATE values ended with the characters 79. The asterisk formed a match with any and all characters preceding the last two in each HDATE value.

"So the asterisk is sort of like a wild card in many card games," Tracey confirmed. "It can be thought of as standing for practically anything. Can you put it anywhere in a class string you're trying to match? I mean, could I use it to browse through the reps who were hired in April?"

"Sure," replied Jack. "Wherever you put it, it will match with anything." He invoked the command

```
browse rep for hdate in ["04*"]
```

to browse through the reps hired in April. For good measure, he executed

```
browse rep for fname in ["K*y"]
```

to demonstrate that the wild card string match character could be embedded among other characters. This resulted in a browse through those reps whose first names begin with K and end with y. Had there been a rep with Ky as a first name, it would have been included because * matches with anything (including nothing).

"Now, let me test you," said Jack. "How would we browse through all reps that have romance as a major product line?"

Tracey pondered for a moment. "Any REP record that has rom as part of its MAJORP field is one we want to view. But there are three product lines that make up each MAJORP value and if rom is there it could be first, last, or in the middle. So what we want to do is include an asterisk on both sides of rom. Is that allowed?"

Jack nodded and executed the command

```
browse rep for majorp in ["*rom*"]
```

to prove that Tracey had the right solution. He went on to demonstrate that the command

```
browse rep for majorp in ["*rom*","*sfi*"]
```

got all reps with romance, science fiction, or both as major products.

"Sometimes," Jack added, "I need a more restrictive kind of wild carding. Instead of matching just anything, I want to match one of a select class of characters. For instance, suppose I need to browse through the reps with hire dates in 1982, 84, or 85. I'd use the following command." He executed the command

```
browse rep for hdate in ["*8[245]"]
```

where the [245] will match with any of the digits 2, 4, and 5. This is equivalent to the command

```
browse rep for hdate in ["*82","*84","*85"]
```

which would require more typing effort.

Browsing for Selected Fields

"It's now clear to me that conditions provide a very flexible way of focusing on desired records in a table. But," observed Debbie, "I'd also like a way to focus on certain fields as I'm browsing. For instance, I might want to focus on third quarter performance while browsing

FIGURE 6–27   Browsing through PERF with selected fields

```
Record Number: 1          →=next ←=prior ENTER=edit ESC=quit

FNAME:    Kim
PID:      ref
S3:         8090
Q3:         7844
```

through performance records. I really don't want to visually wade through all the data. I'd like to see the rep's name, the product ID, the third quarter sales figure, followed by the third quarter quota. And that's all I want to see for each record as I browse."

"You've hit on a very good point," complimented Jack. "Browsing can be a lot more convenient when you're able to select only certain fields for display and editing. Let me show you how you can tell the environment what fields you want to browse with."

In keeping with Debbie's example, he executed the command

```
browse perf with fname,pid,s3,q3
```

resulting in the screen shown in Figure 6–27. As he browsed through successive PERF records, their values for these four fields were the only ones displayed. Notice that the fields were requested in a different order than the order in which they had been defined for the table. A condition can still be specified when browsing with selected fields. Jack illustrated with the command

```
browse perf for s3>2000 & sytd>.75*qyr with fname,pid,s3,q3
```

which had a compound condition. The condition can refer to fields that will not be viewed during browsing (e.g., sytd, qyr).

NEW TABLES FROM OLD

"Occasionally," Jack declared, "I find that it's worthwhile to be able to make new tables from existing tables, where the new table contains a subset of the data in an existing table. The subset may be formed by pulling out only those records that satisfy some condition, by pulling out the data values for selected fields, or by both."

"So it's just like browsing," chimed Joy, "except that instead of viewing and possibly editing some subset of a table's data, those data are converted into a new table that you can process just like any other table. To do this you use the CONVERT command. But before you use it to make new tables, you'll need to switch an environment variable from its default setting of 1 to the value 4. This is the E.CF variable. Its value controls what conversion format the environment will follow in arranging the converted data. Several formats are supported, but we'll only be interested in the tabular format for now. To have CONVERT produce tables rather than other things, you simply let E.CF be 4."

"You mean it gives us a way to come up with a new table without having to use the DEFINE, CREATE, or ATTACH command?" asked Dan.

Converting a Subset of Fields

"That's right," Jack resumed. "Let's say we want to make a new table consisting of the third quarter data from the PERF table. Let's call it PERF3 and keep it in a file named PERF3.ITB on the diskette in drive A. It would have the same number of records as PERF, but each PERF3 record would only have data for the PID, FNAME, TID, Q3, and S3 fields. We can do all this with a single CONVERT command."

To convert PERF data for the five fields into a new table named PERF3, Jack invoked the commands

```
e.cf=4
convert pid,fname,tid,q3,s3 from perf to "a:perf3.itb"
```

causing the disk drives to spring into action. As they slipped back into silence, the familiar underscore prompt appeared, awaiting the next command. The new table now resided in the disk file named PERF3.ITB on the drive A diskette. The contents of the PERF table were unaffected. PERF3 was now available for use and Jack browsed through its records to demonstrate that it could be processed just like any other table.

Converting a Subset of Records

"Could you now make a new table from PERF3 itself," asked Brad, "consisting of only those records for which sales are at least as great as the quota? We might call it TOPPERF3."

Jack felt good that Brad was keeping up with the spirit of the discussion. Nodding, he answered, "Yes, all we have to do is put a condition in the CONVERT command. Watch!"

Jack executed the command

```
convert * from perf3 for q3 ge s3 to "a:topperf3.itb"
```

resulting in the new table of top performances in the third quarter. He explained that the asterisk following CONVERT meant that all of the fields of the existing table were to be copied to the new table. Instead of the asterisk, he could have typed out the names of all PERF3 fields, but the simple asterisk was much more convenient. Jack browsed through the TOPPERF3 records to satisfy the group that the conversion had really taken place.

Dual Conversion

Stan frowned, "I don't see why we should have to use two CONVERT commands to produce the TOPPERF3 table from the PERF table. It seems things would go much faster if you could do it all at once."

"You're right and you can," Jack acknowledged. He went on to explain that, in practice, he would have employed the single command

```
convert pid,fname,tid,q3,s3 from perf for q3 ge s3 to "a:topperf3.itb"
```

to achieve the same effect, but much more quickly and without producing any intermediate tables.

Converting to an Existing Table

"Good," responded Stan as his face became thoughtful. "What happens if the target table already exists when you do a CONVERT? Would the converted data become new records in the target table, in addition to the records already there?"

"Right again," answered Jack.

"But you must be careful," Joy cautioned. "If the target table already exists, it must be structurally identical to the table that would have resulted if it had not already existed. For instance, you can't expect to convert product IDs into an existing monthly salary field. That wouldn't make sense."

"Let's take an example that would make sense," Jack said carefully. "Suppose I'd made a new table called MIDPERF3 having the same fields as TOPPERF3. This new table might have performance records that are not at the top level but have sales within, say, 10 percent of their quotas. I could add the MIDPERF3 records into the TOPPERF3 records with a single CONVERT command."

He wrote the command

```
convert * from midperf3 to "a:topperf3.itb"
```

on the whiteboard to show what would be done. Joy nodded in approval.

Converting from Multiple Tables

"Maybe it's asking for too much," Tracey said hesitantly, "but I can envision situations where I'd like to form a new table from related data in two existing tables. As an example, imagine that I have made a table called BRIEFREP whose records contain the TID, MOSAL, and MOEXP field values from REP. I'd like to produce a new, enlarged version of the PERF3 table. Each record in this new table should have the monthly salary and monthly budgeted expense for the rep whose performance has been recorded there. Can CONVERT take the related data from PERF3 and BRIEFREP to generate this new table?"

"I was wondering when someone would come to that," remarked Jack. "What you've so ably described is actually pretty straightforward with the CONVERT command. The main differences from what we've seen before are that we'll need to identify two source tables for the conversion and we'll have to indicate what basis to use for determining which record in BRIEFREP is related to which record in PERF3."

On the whiteboard he wrote out the command

```
convert * from perf3 from briefrep for perf3.tid=briefrep.tid to "a:mix3.itb"
```

and looked to Joy for approval. She concurred and went on to explain that the condition gave the environment a basis for relating each PERF3 record with a corresponding BRIEFREP record. As each PERF3 record is considered, its TID value is noted. The environment identifies the BRIEFREP record whose own TID value matches that of the PERF3 record. Together the data values of these two records form a new record in the MIX3 table whose structure involves all fields from both tables.

This process is repeated for every PERF3 record until each has been examined and mated with its matching BRIEFREP record.

Glancing at his watch, Jack saw that it was time for a break. "I've given you plenty to digest. I'd suggest you practice with the new data management commands you've learned, particularly the DEFINE, CREATE, USE, FINISH, SHOW, OBTAIN, and BROWSE commands. The ATTACH and CONVERT commands are sometimes useful and are worth knowing about, but in my experience they tend not to be used all that heavily. On the table in front are diskettes with copies of the REP, PERF, and PROD tables we've been using. You can practice with them if you like."

AFTER-HOURS RELATIONS

Meeting that evening, Joy and Jack put a table in use within an entirely different environment. She wore an intensely blue dress, horizontally wrapped with thin black stripes. In addition to the gold trappings he had already become accustomed to, Jack quickly noticed a new one encircling her waist. It was a golden chain of large linked ovals, whose color matched her other accoutrements. He found himself concentrating intently and felt that his thought processes were exceptionally clear. After so many years of fruitless browsing, perhaps he had found what he was looking for.

They ordered the same surf and turf entree with identical trimmings. She chose a virgin mary for starters and he began with cranberry juice. Their chitchat turned to business when the drinks arrived.

"You know," she said, reaching out to lightly touch his arm, "I think our 'children' are progressing nicely. It's very rewarding to see their growth and to think about what's to come in the next few days. They'll be well equipped for making it on their own."

"I feel the same way," confirmed Jack, still tingling from the unexpected touch. "And I must thank you for your help in making things a success. You've been a bigger boost to me than you may perhaps realize."

Joy's blue eyes smiled warmly in response. Basking in her acknowledgment, Jack wondered whether this would be a proper time to bring up a topic about which he had become quite curious. "If you don't mind," he paused with momentary apprehension, "I'd like to talk about relations with you."

She inhaled deeply and appeared to tense slightly. After all, it had been a long day and she was hoping to discuss other matters with him. "Oh, alright," she consented, "but just for a little while and you needn't be so formal with me. Even though a table is formally called a relation in the jargon, let's just call it a table—which is a much more descriptive term anyway."

Smiling, Jack thought for a moment, unsure what to say next. Then, following her lead, he observed, "As I understand it, tables must be processable with a certain standard language in order for data management software to qualify as a relational data base management system."

"That's right," confirmed Joy. "Actually, it could be either or both of two standard command languages: *relational algebra* and *relational calculus*. If data management software lets you define tabular files, but doesn't provide the commands from one of these two languages, then it's more correctly called a data file manager rather than a relational data base manager. A good tip-off for recognizing when you're dealing with a file manager is that its documentation equates the term *file* with the term *data base*. But to be sure, you really need to take a look at the commands provided for processing tables."

Relational Algebra

"I see," mused Jack. "Well, tell me about this relational algebra. Does the environment we're using support algebraic commands? The data management commands I've been using don't seem all that mathematical."

"Actually, it does support the basic relational algebra commands," she answered, "though you might not realize it at first glance. These commands are named PROJECT, SELECT, JOIN, and UNION. There are a few others but these are the main ones. Each of these commands has the effect of producing a new table from an existing table."

Joy went on to explain that PROJECT produces a new table by extracting a copy of certain columns (i.e., field values) from an existing table. The algebraic SELECT produces a new table by extracting a copy of certain rows (i.e., records) from a single existing table. Unlike these two commands, the JOIN command produces a new table from two existing tables. The new table's fields are the same as those defined for the two existing tables. The new table's records are formed by joining together matching rows from the two existing tables. Two rows match if they have the same value for some designated pair of fields, where one field is from one table and the other field is from the other table. The UNION command produces a new table by attaching the records of one existing table to those in another table. The two tables must be structurally the same.

"Very interesting," Jack declared. "All of those commands seem like bits and pieces of a single command that I'm familiar with: CONVERT. Doesn't relational algebra have a CONVERT command?"

"No," replied Joy [2]. "It gives only these more elementary operations. It's up to a user to put them together in a proper sequence in order to produce the desired table. That's why relational algebra is called a *procedural* language. You need to put together a series of commands—a procedure—to get the table you want. With relational algebra, you don't have the luxury of a CONVERT command that can do it all at once. Do you see how you could invent the algebraic commands in the knowledge management environment?"

"Sure," Jack answered, "I'd just declare some macros. There would be one for PROJECT, JOIN, and UNION. But I couldn't make a macro for SELECT because it's already the name of another command for making ad hoc queries into a data base composed of tables."

"Right," Joy nodded. "Interestingly, the multitable SELECT command to which you refer is the core command of the relational calculus language. I think our 'kids' will really light up when they see how powerful it is in stating ad hoc queries. But if you want to make a macro that has the same behavior as the lower level algebraic SELECT you'll need to pick a different name for it—maybe something like CHOOSE would be a good choice."

The macros that Jack and Joy discussed would, of course, be declared with the following four commands

```
macro project convert
macro join convert *
macro union convert *
macro choose convert *
```

Once this linguistic knowledge is present in the knowledge system, the earlier command

```
convert pid,fname,tid,q3,s3 from perf to "a:perf3.itb"
```

could be equivalently executed as

```
project pid,fname,tid,q3,s3 from perf to "a:per3.itb"
```

thereby supporting the algebraic PROJECT command. The previous

```
convert * from perf3 for q3 ge s3 to "a:topperf3.itb"
```

command could equivalently be expressed as

```
choose from perf3 for q3 ge s3 to "a:topperf3.itb"
```

thereby supporting the algebraic SELECT (i.e., CHOOSE) functionality. The former CONVERT command

```
convert * from midperf3 to "a:topperf3.itb"
```

could be equivalently executed as the algebraic UNION command by entering

```
union from midperf3 to "a:topperf3.itb"
```

Finally, the command

```
convert * from perf3 from briefrep for perf3.tid=briefrep.tid to "a:mix3.itb"
```

that Jack had described to the group could equivalently be expressed as the JOIN command

```
join from perf3 from briefrep for perf3.tid=briefrep.tid to "a:mix3.itb"
```

Jack continued, "Knowing about PROJECT, JOIN, and so forth is all well and good, but I think I'll stick to CONVERT, which can handle the processing of relational algebra without having to put together procedures and keep track of intermediate tables."

"I agree CONVERT is more convenient," Joy said, "but you wanted to know what the algebraic commands are. You might also like to know that tables in this environment can have certain structural features that are not innate features of standard relational data base management. Examples include virtual fields, pictures, and labels."

"Really?" asked a surprised Jack. "I find pictures and virtual fields to be very handy things. But tell me about the other language, the relational calculus."

Relational Calculus

"You already know a good deal about it," she said somewhat mysteriously.

"Oh?" he responded.

"Yes, the SELECT command that you'll be describing for the ad hoc query portion of the session forms the heart of the standard language for relational calculus. It's better known as SQL: Structured Query Language," she explained.

"Oh," he acknowledged. Jack would be presenting this command to the group a bit later (Chapter 8). "Joy, I sure am glad you were selected to join me in this project."

"The feeling is mutual," she purred, secretly wondering whether a lasting union might be forming.

BASIC IDEAS

Data management in its various guises is an extremely valuable way of structuring and processing descriptive knowledge. Broadly speaking, there are two main branches in the data management field. One is data file management, which often allows data to be structured in a more or less tabular fashion but which does not support either of the standard relational command languages. The other branch is data base management. Here there are classic, well-defined techniques (i.e., data models) for representing and processing a data base. These include the relational, hierarchical, CODASYL-network, and postrelational approaches.

A data base is not a file, but rather a collection of interrelated records of many different kinds (e.g., performance, rep, product, and expense records). *These records and their relationships are represented according to the structuring conventions of a data model and processed with the data model's commands.* Together, a data model's structuring conventions and processing language form a data management technique. Usually data base software packages are designed to support one or another of these techniques. A knowledge management environment may support multiple techniques.

Like many do-it-yourself computer users, Jack focused on the environment's relational technique of managing data. Its postrelational technique is of primary interest to professional application systems developers. *The relational technique organizes a data base's records into tables.* Relationships between tables' records are established by repeating one table's data in another table (e.g., the territory ID data in both PERF and REP). Defining each table's structure is straightforward (DEFINE). Each of its fields is specified. Standard relational field specifications can be usefully embellished with pictures and virtual fields.

Records can be created in a table either interactively (CREATE) or in batches (e.g., ATTACH from a text file). Once created, records can be viewed either by obtaining them one at a time (OBTAIN) or by browsing through those that meet desired conditions (BROWSE). Although a browsing command is not part of standard relational languages, it is nevertheless a valuable approach to both viewing and editing individual records. All of a relational data base's tables do not need to be actively in use at the same time. Any can be finished (FINISH) or put back in use (USE) whenever desired.

Of the two standard relational command languages, relational algebra is the more rudimentary. It provides a few commands (e.g., PROJ-ECT, JOIN, UNION, single table SELECT) for producing new tables from existing tables. Normally a specific sequence of such commands must be executed to arrive at a desired new table. The procedural nature of the algebra can be avoided, as can the proliferation of intermediate tables, with the use of the environment's CONVERT command. This allows the traditionally separate algebraic operations to be handled non-procedurally in a single command.

There are several interesting data management problems that cannot be easily addressed with the processing commands introduced thus far. Jack deals with these in Chapter 7. It should be remembered that within an environment *the tables constituting a data base embody but one kind of knowledge representation technique. Tables coexist in a knowledge system alongside knowledge represented in other ways* (e.g., as text or contexts). It is therefore permissible to freely interweave data management commands with calculation requests and text management.

References

1. Bonczek, R. H.; C. W. Holsapple; and A. B. Whinston. *Micro Database Management—Practical Techniques for Application Development.* New York: Academic Press, 1984.

2. Bradley, J. *File and Data Base Techniques.* New York: Holt, Rinehart & Winston, 1982.

3. Codd, E. F. "A Relational Model of Data for Large Shared Databanks." *Communications of the ACM* 13, no. 6 (1970).

4. Derfler, F. J., Jr. "MDBS the Third: If You Have to Ask the Price . . . ." *PC* 2, no. 1 (1983).

5. *Disk Operating System.* Boca Raton, Fla.: IBM, 1983.

6. Holsapple, C. W. "Micros Get Mainframe Data Scheme." *Systems and Software* 3, no. 5 (1984).

7. ————. "A Perspective on Data Models." *PC Tech Journal* 2, no. 1 (1984).

8. ————. "Uniting Relational and Postrelational Database Management Tools." *Systems and Software* 3, no. 11 (1984).

9. Johnson, J. "Big Push in Micro Software." *Datamation* 29, no. 1 (1983).

10. *KnowledgeMan Reference Manual,* version 2. Lafayette, Ind.: MDBS, Inc., 1985.

Kim's sales figure? . . . . It's outstanding in its field.

Chapter Seven

More Data Management

Jack expected that the initial hands-on encounter would whet their appetite for more. He was right. As the session resumed, the managers now had first-hand experience in defining tables, creating records, viewing records, editing records, and converting existing data into new tables. With this background, they could now easily appreciate the desirability of and outright need for grasping more, for delving more deeply into the potentials of this knowledge management technique. As they thought about how to apply what they had learned to various kinds of everyday problems, it became apparent that some additional table-processing commands would be most helpful.

There was a flurry of questions. OBTAIN and BROWSE were fine for viewing records one at a time, but how can you get a tabular listing of all of a table's records so you can see them all at once? BROWSE is great for spur-of-the-moment editing of a record's data, but is pretty laborious if you want to make the same kind of change to a field's values across many records. For instance, is there a way to reduce all the TARGET values by 45 percent without having to step through each record and edit its TARGET value? Is there some way to eliminate unwanted records from a table? Can a table's records be reordered once they have been created?

Someone wanted to have the PERF records sorted by product ID. Someone else had made an error while defining a table but did not notice the error until record creation began. Yet another manager wanted to add a new field to the PERF table's existing structure. How can you redefine a table's structure, even though it may already contain records? Can a table be renamed? And is there some way to destroy a table that is no longer needed, freeing its disk space for other uses?

These are exactly the kinds of questions Jack had anticipated. He had encountered them himself when first endeavoring to apply the tabular data management technique to sales management problems.

Fortunately, the environment provided straightforward ways for addressing all these needs, so Jack was well prepared to answer the questions that arose [7]. In addition, he planned to introduce the notion of table indexing as a way of speeding up the access to individual records in large tables. Finally, he intended to lead a discussion on data base design, identifying several issues worth considering when determining what tables to define in a data base, what fields to include in which tables, and what characteristics to specify for these fields.

LISTING A TABLE'S RECORDS

"Whenever you want to see a *listing* of all a table's records," Jack began, "you just issue a LIST command that tells the environment which table's records should be listed. They'll then appear on the console screen, one record per line. If there are too many records to fit on one screenful, they'll scroll by rapidly until all have been displayed, unless E.PAUS is switched to TRUE. Let me show you."

Jack put the PROD, REP, and PERF tables in use. As a shortcut, he omitted the ITB extensions, explaining that USE assumed an ITB extension unless explicitly told otherwise. He then executed the command

```
list
```

and the console screen took on the appearance shown in Figure 7–1.

Brad looked surprised, "I understand the list of records, but what's that stuff after the last record?"

"It looks like a statistical summary of the columns' data," Debbie offered. "Evidently the LIST command gives us more than what we bargained for."

"If you don't care about statistics, then you can just ignore them like I'm going to do for the time being. In fact, it's simple to get rid of them. You just switch the E.STAT environment variable to FALSE from its default setting of TRUE. From that point on, the environment won't do a statistical analysis of the data you list," explained Jack. He planned to reopen the issue of statistical analysis later (Chapter 8), but for now he set E.STAT to FALSE.

Role of a Default Table

"I'm curious about why the environment listed the PROD table's records rather than the contents of one of the other tables you put in use," said Tracey. "Your LIST command doesn't mention which table you want it to process."

FIGURE 7–1   Listing the default table's contents

```
_use "a:prod"; use "a:rep"; use "a:perf"
_list
PID        PNAME          TARGET    GMR   CRATE

sfi    science fiction   200,000   0.72  0.028
com    computers         278,000   0.76  0.028
spo    sports            132,000   0.51  0.023
bio    biography         108,000   0.48  0.022
ROM    romance           235,000   0.64  0.024
BUS    business          173,000   0.34  0.022
PSY    psychology        102,000   0.36  0.018
REF    reference         224,000   0.38  0.019
PHO    photography        86,000   0.28  0.020

                         ***,***   4.47  0.204   Sum
                         170,900   0.50  0.023   Ave
                         ***,***   0.03  0.000   Var
                          67,713   0.17  0.004   Sdv
BUS    biography          86,000   0.28  0.018   Min
spo    sports            278,000   0.76  0.028   Max

Number of Observations: 9
_
```

"I took a shortcut," Jack replied. "Because PROD was the first table I put in use, it serves as the default table. You can verify this with the SHOW command. If I don't tell the environment which table the command should process, then it processes the default table." He went on to explain that he could have entered

`list from prod`

to get the same listing shown in Figure 7–1. The command

`list from perf`

would yield a listing of the PERF table's records and so on. "By the way, once you list records from a specified table, that table automatically becomes your current default."

Controlling the Presentation of a Listing

"Now the PERF table has a lot more records than PROD does," observed Stan, "and I understand that a TRUE E.PAUS will make viewing of

FIGURE 7–2 Column wraparound

TID	FNAME	PID	Q1	Q2	Q3	Q4	QYR	S1	S2	S3
	S4	SYTD	MAJOR							
0	Kim	ref	6040	8309	7844	9402	31595	7024	7732	80
90	0	22846	true							
0	Kim	bus	7320	8050	6400	8503	30273	6854	8120	69
08	0	21882	true							
0	Kim	spo	5400	6300	7839	8390	27929	6240	5995	80
32	0	20267	true							
1	Kris	rom	9003	10229	8340	11340	38912	10050	12453	80
32	0	30535	true							
1	Kris	psy	8090	6209	7765	7590	29654	7540	7900	80
59	0	23499	true							

these manageable, a screenful at a time. But the PERF table also has many more fields than PROD. It seems the screen might not be wide enough to list all of the columns for PERF."

"Let's see what happens," Jack replied. He let E.PAUS be TRUE and then issued the command to list PERF's records. Stan was right; all of the PERF column headings did not fit on a single line. Headings for the S4, SYTD, and MAJOR fields wrapped around to the second line. Each record's values wrapped around onto two lines as well. Figure 7–2 illustrates this wrapping behavior for the listing's headings and its first few records.

Studying the screen, Stan thought for a moment and then said, "If there is some way we could reduce the amount of space between the listing's columns, then it might just fit. Maybe there's an environment variable that controls the amount of space displayed between columns?"

"There sure is," rejoined Jack. "Its name is E.SPAC and its default setting is 2. Let's set it to 0 and see what happens." He did so and again issued the command to list PERF's records. The first screenful of PERF records now appeared as shown in Figure 7–3(a). When Jack pressed the space bar the screen was transformed as shown in Figure 7–3(b).

FIGURE 7–3 Listing the PERF data

TID	FNAME	PID	Q1	Q2	Q3	Q4	QYR	S1	S2	S3	S4	SYTD	MAJOR
0	Kim	ref	6040	8309	7844	9402	31595	7024	7732	8090	0	22846	true
0	Kim	bus	7320	8050	6400	8503	30273	6854	8120	6908	0	21882	true
0	Kim	spo	5400	6300	7839	8390	27929	6240	5995	8032	0	20267	true
1	Kris	rom	9003	10229	8340	11340	38912	10050	12453	8032	0	30535	true
1	Kris	psy	8090	6209	7765	7590	29654	7540	7900	8059	0	23499	true
1	Kris	bio	7400	6290	7200	8005	28895	7604	6905	8349	0	22858	true
2	Kevin	pho	7400	6290	7200	8904	29794	7604	6905	8349	0	22858	true
2	Kevin	sfi	9439	8378	8050	9872	35739	10390	8639	8765	0	27794	true
2	Kevin	spo	6509	7734	6698	7590	28531	7773	8090	6879	0	22742	true
2	Kevin	bus	3009	4321	2789	3456	13575	4321	6500	2509	0	13330	false
2	Kevin	ref	3214	2345	3256	6112	14927	4222	2444	3459	0	10125	false
3	Tina	psy	3214	2345	3256	6112	14927	4222	2444	3459	0	10125	false
3	Tina	bus	6903	7538	8990	9311	32742	5944	10359	8004	0	24307	true
3	Tina	com	5388	4399	7900	7980	25667	5944	8888	9042	0	23874	true
3	Tina	rom	5000	4678	4213	3998	17889	4590	3997	5032	0	13619	true
4	Toby	rom	4982	4678	8744	7432	25836	5009	3997	9037	0	18043	true
4	Toby	psy	5000	4006	6007	6900	21913	2607	4839	7050	0	14496	true
4	Toby	bus	4842	4006	5302	4980	19130	5003	5903	4003	0	14909	true
5	Kerry	psy	4842	4006	5302	4980	19130	5003	5903	4003	0	14909	true
5	Kerry	ref	6030	4985	3001	5883	19899	5590	4880	6320	0	16790	true
5	Kerry	pho	10700	11009	8443	7930	38082	12222	11980	8332	0	32534	true
6	Karen	bus	10700	11009	8443	7930	38082	12222	11980	8332	0	32534	true

(a) First screenful

TID	FNAME	PID	Q1	Q2	Q3	Q4	QYR	S1	S2	S3	S4	SYTD	MAJOR
6	Karen	rom	6040	5020	5555	6666	23281	6090	5900	6904	0	18894	true
6	Karen	com	12090	11069	10806	9665	43630	13121	11590	10075	0	34786	true
7	Kathy	pho	8553	7543	5678	6779	28553	7884	7903	6236	0	22023	true
7	Kathy	ref	4679	5368	5002	3998	19047	5032	4002	4398	0	13432	true
7	Kathy	sfi	4339	4228	3989	4867	17423	4360	4271	3359	0	11990	true
8	Jackie	bio	4339	4228	3989	4867	17423	4360	4271	3359	0	11990	true
8	Jackie	ref	5004	4678	3998	6012	19692	4996	5400	3600	0	13996	true
8	Jackie	spo	5004	4468	5830	7223	22525	5345	5400	6200	0	16945	true
9	Carol	rom	5004	4468	5830	7223	22525	5345	5400	6200	0	16945	true
9	Carol	bus	3997	4378	4832	3901	17108	4005	4436	4998	0	13439	true
9	Carol	com	6903	5882	6031	8456	27272	8488	9321	7021	0	24830	true

—

(b) Second screen

Printed Listings

"I presume we can let E.OPRN be TRUE if we want a listing to appear on a printout," remarked Dan.

"Right," nodded Jack. "Remember, before you send results to the printer you may want to prepare by using the EJECT command to begin a new page. Also recall that E.PDEP will control how many lines will be printed before beginning a new page and E.PMAR determines the left margin. If E.PAUS is TRUE, the printing will pause as each printed page is completed. Pressing the space bar causes it to go ahead to the next printed page."

Jack set E.PDEP to the usual 65, ejected to begin a new page, let E.OPRN be TRUE, and then executed the command

```
list from perf
```

As each line of the listing appeared on the screen it was simultaneously printed yielding the Figure 7–4 printout. Unlike the screen listing, this

FIGURE 7–4   Printout of table listing

Page	1											
TID	FNAME	PID	Q1	Q2	Q3	Q4	QYR	S1	S2	S3	S4	SYTD MAJOR
0	Kim	ref	6040	8309	7844	9402	31595	7024	7732	8090	0	22846true
0	Kim	bus	7320	8050	6400	8503	30273	6854	8120	6908	0	21882true
0	Kim	spo	5400	6300	7839	8390	27929	6240	5995	8032	0	20267true
1	Kris	rom	9003	10229	8340	11340	38912	10050	12453	8032	0	30535true
1	Kris	psy	8090	6209	7765	7590	29654	7540	7900	8059	0	23499true
1	Kris	bio	7400	6290	7200	8005	28895	7604	6905	8349	0	22858true
2	Kevin	pho	7400	6290	7200	8904	29794	7604	6905	8349	0	22858true
2	Kevin	sfi	9439	8378	8050	9872	35739	10390	8639	8765	0	27794true
2	Kevin	spo	6509	7734	6698	7590	28531	7773	8090	6879	0	22742true
2	Kevin	bus	3009	4321	2789	3456	13575	4321	6500	2509	0	13330false
2	Kevin	ref	3214	2345	3256	6112	14927	4222	2444	3459	0	10125false
3	Tina	psy	3214	2345	3256	6112	14927	4222	2444	3459	0	10125false
3	Tina	bus	6903	7538	8990	9311	32742	5944	10359	8004	0	24307true
3	Tina	com	5388	4399	7900	7980	25667	5944	8888	9042	0	23874true
3	Tina	rom	5000	4678	4213	3998	17889	4590	3997	5032	0	13619true
4	Toby	rom	4982	4678	8744	7432	25836	5009	3997	7050	0	18043true
4	Toby	psy	5000	4006	6007	6900	21913	2607	4839	7050	0	14496true
4	Toby	bus	4842	4006	5302	4980	19130	5003	5903	4003	0	14909true
5	Kerry	psy	4842	4006	5302	4980	19130	5003	5903	4003	0	14909true
5	Kerry	ref	6030	4985	3001	5883	19899	5590	4880	6320	0	16790true
5	Kerry	pho	10700	11009	8443	7930	38082	12222	11980	8332	0	32534true
6	Karen	bus	10700	11009	8443	7930	38082	12222	11980	8332	0	32534true
6	Karen	rom	6040	5020	5555	6666	23281	6090	5900	6904	0	18894true
6	Karen	com	12090	11069	10806	9665	43630	13121	11590	10075	0	34786true
7	Kathy	pho	8553	7543	5678	6779	28553	7884	7903	6236	0	22023true
7	Kathy	ref	4679	5368	5002	3998	19047	5032	4002	4398	0	13432true
7	Kathy	sfi	4339	4228	3989	4867	17423	4360	4271	3359	0	11990true
8	Jackie	bio	4339	4228	3989	4867	17423	4360	4271	3359	0	11990true
8	Jackie	ref	5004	4678	3998	6012	19692	4996	5400	3600	0	13996true
8	Jackie	spo	5004	4468	5830	7223	22525	5345	5400	6200	0	16945true
9	Carol	rom	5004	4468	5830	7223	22525	5345	5400	6200	0	16945true
9	Carol	bus	3997	4378	4832	3901	17108	4005	4436	4998	0	13439true
9	Carol	com	6903	5882	6031	8456	27272	8488	9321	7021	0	24830true

printed listing had a page number at the top of the page. If a multipage listing had been generated, the pages would have been consecutively numbered. Jack noted that they could suppress this page numbering by switching the E.SPGN environment variable from its FALSE default to a TRUE value.

Before leaving the LIST command he had one more suggestion for getting compact listings. Many printers have the ability to produce print-outs with a compressed print, allowing more characters per line in printouts. To make a printer use this smaller-sized type, the CPU needs to send a special signal to the printer. Jack explained that for the IBM Graphics Printers they were using, this signal is a nonprintable character whose ASCII code is 15 [7]. To send this signal to the printer he entered the command

```
print chr(15)
```

where CHR is a KnowledgeMan function whose value is the character corresponding to its ASCII code argument. The printer would now print up to 132 compressed characters per line instead of normal-sized characters, of which no more than 80 could fit on a line.

He set E.SPAC back to 2 and set E.PWID to 132. The latter environment variable controls how wide a printed page can be. By upping its value from the 120 default, Jack was allowing the maximum possible compressed characters per line. Reexecuting the LIST command resulted in the more compact, tidier printout shown in Figure 7–5. He explained that the command

```
print chr(14)
```

would cause their printers to revert to normal-sized type [7].

"The ability to see a listing on the screen or printer is just dandy, but let's say I'm preparing a performance report with the TEXT command," said Tracey. "I've entered a good chunk of text when it occurs to me that here's a point where I'd like to put a listing of PERF records. That is, I want the listing right there in the text itself, as if I'd typed it all in myself. Could I do that?"

"Wouldn't you just escape to the status line and issue the LIST command prefaced by a backslash?" asked Brad. "The result would appear wherever your cursor was. Seems to me that it should work just like outputting a calculation result into your text."

"It does," confirmed Jack. "Thus you can quickly embed a table listing directly in your text without any chance of error. Once it's part of the text, you're free to edit it just like any other part of the text!"

FIGURE 7–5   Compressed print

Page	1												

TID	FNAME	PID	Q1	Q2	Q3	Q4	QYR	S1	S2	S3	S4	SYTD	MAJOR
0	Kim	ref	6040	8309	7844	9402	31595	7024	7732	8090	0	22846	true
0	Kim	bus	7320	8050	6400	8503	30273	6854	8120	6908	0	21882	true
0	Kim	spo	5400	6300	7839	8390	27929	6240	5995	8032	0	20267	true
1	Kris	rom	9003	10229	8340	11340	38912	10050	12453	8032	0	30535	true
1	Kris	psy	8090	6209	7765	7590	29654	7540	7900	8059	0	23499	true
1	Kris	bio	7400	6290	7200	8005	28895	7604	6905	8349	0	22858	true
2	Kevin	pho	7400	6290	7200	8904	29794	7604	6905	8349	0	22858	true
2	Kevin	sfi	9439	8378	8050	9872	35739	10390	8639	8765	0	27794	true
2	Kevin	spo	6509	7734	6698	7590	28531	7773	8090	6879	0	22742	true
2	Kevin	bus	3009	4321	2789	3456	13575	4321	6500	2509	0	13330	false
2	Kevin	ref	3214	2345	3256	6112	14927	4222	2444	3459	0	10125	false
3	Tina	psy	3214	2345	3256	6112	14927	4222	2444	3459	0	10125	false
3	Tina	bus	6903	7538	8990	9311	32742	5944	10359	8004	0	24307	true
3	Tina	com	5388	4399	7900	7980	25667	5944	8888	9042	0	23874	true
3	Tina	rom	5000	4678	4213	3998	17889	4590	3997	5032	0	13619	true
4	Toby	rom	4982	4678	8744	7432	25836	5009	3997	9037	0	18043	true
4	Toby	psy	5000	4006	6007	6900	21913	2607	4839	7050	0	14496	true
4	Toby	bus	4842	4006	5302	4980	19130	5003	5903	4003	0	14909	true
5	Kerry	psy	4842	4006	5302	4980	19130	5003	5903	4003	0	14909	true
5	Kerry	ref	6030	4985	3001	5883	19899	5590	4880	6320	0	16790	true
5	Kerry	pho	10700	11009	8443	7930	38082	12222	11980	8332	0	32534	true
6	Karen	bus	10700	11009	8443	7930	38082	12222	11980	8332	0	32534	true
6	Karen	rom	6040	5020	5555	6666	23281	6090	5900	6904	0	18894	true
6	Karen	com	12090	11069	10806	9665	43630	13121	11590	10075	0	34786	true
7	Kathy	pho	8553	7543	5678	6779	28553	7884	7903	6236	0	22023	true
7	Kathy	ref	4679	5368	5002	~ 3998	19047	5032	4002	4398	0	13432	true
7	Kathy	sfi	4339	4228	3989	4867	17423	4360	4271	3359	0	11990	true
8	Jackie	bio	4339	4228	3989	4867	17423	4360	4271	3359	0	11990	true
8	Jackie	ref	5004	4678	3998	6012	19692	4996	5400	3600	0	13996	true
8	Jackie	spo	5004	4468	5830	7223	22525	5345	5400	6200	0	16945	true
9	Carol	rom	5004	4468	5830	7223	22525	5345	5400	6200	0	16945	true
9	Carol	bus	3997	4378	4832	3901	17108	4005	4436	4998	0	13439	true
9	Carol	com	6903	5882	6031	8456	27272	8488	9321	7021	0	24830	true

TABLE MODIFICATION

There are two distinct kinds of modifications that can be made to tables: those that modify its structure and those that modify its content. The CREATE and BROWSE commands can be used to modify a table's content, but in no way do they affect its structure. Jack was about to introduce other commands for modifying table content. These are the CHANGE, MARK, COMPRESS, and SORT commands. Also on his agenda was the REDEFINE command for modifying a table's structure and the DE-STROY command for destroying a table (both its structure and content). Before making significant modifications to a table, it may be prudent to make a backup copy as discussed in Chapter 5. In the event that a problem arises during or because of the modification, the modification can be restarted with the backup copy of the table.

Changing Multiple Records at Once

"When you want to make the same kind of change to many values of a field, use the CHANGE command," Jack recommended. "This command is also a good way to make a change to a single field value based on some calculation. You can put calculations right in a CHANGE command."

He pointed out that some of PROD's records had lowercase PID values while others had uppercase values (see Figure 7–1). "What if we wanted to make them all lowercase for a uniform appearance?" he asked. "You could use BROWSE to step through the PROD records one by one and edit the five PID values that are in uppercase. But it would be much quicker to use a CHANGE command. Watch."

Jack executed the commands

```
change pid in prod to locase(pid); list from prod
```

reminding them that LOCASE is a built-in function whose value is always the lowercase rendition of its argument's value. Thus the CHANGE command changed each PID value in PROD to lowercase. The LIST command showed them that all the PID values were indeed now in lowercase.

"Someone earlier asked how the sales targets could be reduced by 45 percent. Well, we can do it very conveniently with a single CHANGE command." As he spoke, Jack issued the commands

```
change target in prod to target-.45*target;list
```

The changes were calculated and made very rapidly. As soon as CHANGE was finished, LIST showed the effect on the TARGET values, yielding the screen appearance shown in Figure 7–6.

"Can we base a change to one field on values of other fields in the same record?" Debbie perceptively asked. "Suppose we want to now increase each TARGET value by its corresponding commission rate, but only for those product lines having a gross margin rate of at least 60 percent."

Jack replied silently for a change, by simply executing the command

```
change target in prod to target*(1+crate) for gmr>=.6
```

Notice that each new TARGET value is calculated from the record's existing TARGET and CRATE values. The command's condition ensures that such a change is made to only those PROD records for which the

FIGURE 7–6   Changing the PID and TARGET values

```
_change pid in prod to locase(pid); list from prod
PID        PNAME          TARGET   GMR  CRATE

sfi   science fiction    200,000   0.72  0.028
com   computers          278,000   0.76  0.028
spo   sports             132,000   0.51  0.023
bio   biography          108,000   0.48  0.022
rom   romance            235,000   0.64  0.024
bus   business           173,000   0.34  0.022
psy   psychology         102,000   0.36  0.018
ref   reference          224,000   0.38  0.019
pho   photography         86,000   0.28  0.020
_change target in prod to target-.45*target; list
PID        PNAME          TARGET   GMR  CRATE

sfi   science fiction    110,000   0.72  0.028
com   computers          152,900   0.76  0.028
spo   sports              72,600   0.51  0.023
bio   biography           59,400   0.48  0.022
rom   romance            129,250   0.64  0.024
bus   business            95,150   0.34  0.022
psy   psychology          56,100   0.36  0.018
ref   reference          123,200   0.38  0.019
pho   photography         47,300   0.28  0.020
_
```

GMR value is greater than or equal to the .6 level. Figure 7–7 shows how the screen appeared after Jack listed the changed PROD. In comparing this to Figure 7–6, it can be seen that only those records with GMRs of at least .6 were changed.

"The conditions you specify for CHANGE commands can be just like the conditions you've used for OBTAIN and BROWSE," Joy emphasized. "And the expressions you specify for calculating changed values can be just like any of the expressions you've seen before. In addition to fields, it can contain working variables, functions, and even utility variables if you like."

Deleting Records

"From time to time," Jack remarked, "you'll want to not just change some records, but get rid of them altogether. I've found there are two main causes for this. On rare occasions I may discover that I've accidentally created a record that doesn't belong in the table. But more common is the situation where a record does belong until something changes in the outer world to render that record inappropriate."

"You mean a situation like I had last spring," interjected Debbie,

FIGURE 7–7   Conditional change based on multiple fields

```
_change target in prod to target*(1+crate) for gmr>= .6
_list
PID        PNAME           TARGET    GMR   CRATE

sfi   science fiction     113,080   0.72  0.028
com   computers           157,181   0.76  0.028
spo   sports               72,600   0.51  0.023
bio   biography            59,400   0.48  0.022
rom   romance             132,352   0.64  0.024
bus   business             95,150   0.34  0.022
psy   psychology           56,100   0.36  0.018
ref   reference           123,200   0.38  0.019
pho   photography          47,300   0.28  0.020
_
```

"where one of my territories was taken away and put into Pete's region. If I'd had a REP table, I would have needed to delete the rep who was no longer mine and from the PERF table I would have wanted to delete all performance records for my lost territory."

"That's a good example," Jack complimented her.

The normally taciturn Pete Garcia spoke. "What Debbie clears from her tables I'd want to create in mine."

"Right," nodded Jack. Looking at Debbie, he continued "and for Pete's sake you should make a copy or at least a listing of what you delete before actually deleting it. Probably the best thing would be to use the CONVERT command to make a new table having only those PERF records you intend to delete. You could send a diskette with that table to Pete, who could then use the CONVERT command to put its records into his own PERF table.

"In any event let's see how we'd delete certain records from a table. It's a two-step process. First we *mark* the records we want to delete. Second, we *compress* the table by eliminating all of its marked records."

"Does this have something to do with that #MARK field you told us to ignore before?" asked Stan. "Whenever I do an OBTAIN it always shows that #MARK has a FALSE value, no matter which record in which table I'm obtaining."

"You're right," Jack answered, "every table is automatically given a #MARK field. When you create a record in the table its value for #MARK is automatically set to be FALSE. As long as a record's #MARK value is FALSE, the record remains unmarked. But as soon as you make it TRUE, the record is said to be marked and is a candidate for deletion from the table."

Stan was getting the idea. "So if we needed to delete, say, territory 6 from the REP table, we would obtain that record and mark it by using the LET command to make its #MARK value TRUE."

"That's one way," agreed Jack, "but there's an easier way that involves only one rather than two commands. This new command is MARK. Watch how it works."

To mark the REP record for territory 6, he executed the command

```
mark record in rep for tid="6"
```

causing the disk drive light to briefly light up as the value of #MARK was made TRUE. To confirm that the record was now marked Jack obtained it, producing the screen appearance depicted in Figure 7–8. Whereas #MARK for this record formerly had been FALSE (recall Figure 6–19), it was now clearly TRUE.

"Notice," Jack continued, "the record is still there in the table. It's not yet gone. It is still subject to processing by other commands like BROWSE, CONVERT, LIST, and CHANGE as long as the E.IMRK environment variable remains at its default setting of FALSE. If it were switched to TRUE, these commands would ignore all marked records even though they still exist in the tables.

"To actually eliminate the marked REP record, we would use the COMPRESS command. But I'm not going to demonstrate it because I want to keep all the reps around for later examples. Besides, this particular rep is the last one in the world I'd want to lose."

He explained that the COMPRESS command would be invoked as follows

```
compress rep
```

to eliminate all marked records from the REP table. To compress some other table, its name would be used instead of REP. He also admonished them to remember that once a table is compressed, its marked records are gone. If there is any doubt about whether they should really be eliminated, a backup of the original table should be kept.

FIGURE 7–8 Marking a record

```
_mark record in rep for tid="b"
_obtain for tid="b"
 Record Number: 7
 #MARK:    TRUE
 FNAME:    Karen
 MIDI:     V.
 LNAME:    Bruckner
 NAME:     Karen V. Bruckner
 SPOUSE:
 HDATE:    05/14/1982
 PHONE:    (433) 442-8201
 TID:      b
 STREET:   44 Tan Ave.
 CITY:     Madison
 STATE:    WI
 ZIP:      bbbb7
 ADDR:     44 Tan Ave., Madison WI bbbb7
 MOSAL:    2800
 MOEXP:    1335.00
 MAJORP:   com:bus:rom
 _
```

"Why is it," asked Debbie, "that record deletion is a two-step process? Why not just have a single deletion command that eliminates records straightaway?"

Jack shrugged and looked to Joy for support. As usual, she gave it. "As you suggest, some data management software uses a one-step deletion approach. The philosophy of two-step deletion is that you have more of a chance to check exactly what it is you'll be deleting before committing yourself. After using the MARK command, you can browse through the table to see that those and only those records you intend to eliminate have been marked. Only then, when you're satisfied, will you do the actual table compression."

"I see." Debbie elaborated, "If I see that something has somehow become marked that shouldn't be or vice versa, I have a chance to change the mark. If the entire deletion were handled in one command and I happened to make an unnoticed error in the command's condition, I could end up losing a lot of records that I really didn't mean to delete."

"But wait a minute," frowned Brad. "The BROWSE command doesn't display #MARK's values."

"Unless you want it to," said Joy, completing his sentence. She gave an example. The command

```
mark records in perf for tid="6"
```

was used to mark all records in PERF for which the TID value was 6. To then browse through the PERF records to check their markings, the command

```
browse perf with tid,#mark
```

was used. It displayed only the TID and #MARK values of each record.

"But there's an even faster way to check on which records in a table are marked," Jack asserted, "without even having to look at #MARK values for individual records. Just use the LIST command like this."

He executed the command

```
list from perf for #mark
```

which resulted in a listing of three records as shown in Figure 7–9. "Even though #MARK values aren't listed, the condition guarantees that these are the only marked records. Only records with a #MARK

FIGURE 7–9   Listing of marked records

```
_list from perf for #mark
TID  FNAME PID  Q1    Q2     Q3     Q4    QYR   S1     S2    S3    S4   SYTD MAJOR

6   Karen bus 10700 11009  8443  7930 38082 12222 11980 8332     0 32534true
6   Karen rom  6040  5020  5555  6666 23281  6090  5900 6904     0 18894true
6   Karen com 12090 11069 10806  9665 43630 13121 11590 10075    0 34786true
—
```

of TRUE will make the condition TRUE. Thus they're the only ones that will be listed."

Because he did not want to actually eliminate any records, Jack unmarked the marked records in PERF and REP by executing two UN-MARK commands

```
unmark records in perf
unmark records in rep
```

remarking that like MARK, an UNMARK could have a condition to selectively unmark only certain records in a table.

Sorting Records

Relational data base management theory is very clear on the topic of ordering a table's records. No particular order is to be assumed and the standard relational processing commands make no provision for reordering the sequence of records in a table [3]. Nonetheless, having a table's records *sorted* in a particular order can be quite useful during browsing and for examining a listing. The knowledge managment environment allows any table's records to be sorted with the SORT command.

"If you're like me," Jack speculated, "you would usually like to browse through or list your PROD records alphabetically based on their respective IDs. It just makes it easier to find things when you know where to look. Let me show you how we can sort the product records based on the PID field."

He executed the commands

```
sort prod by pid;list from prod
```

When the sorting had ended, the table's contents were listed to show the new sorted order. The biography record was now first in the table and the sports record was last. Unless otherwise indicated in the SORT command, the environment assumes that the sorting should occur in an ascending, rather than descending, sequence.

"I think I would like to have the records sorted from highest to lowest sales targets," Pete said.

Jack responded with the commands

```
sort prod by descending target;list from prod
```

which left the screen with the appearance shown in Figure 7–10. Now the computers record was first in the table and the photography record

FIGURE 7–10   Sorting a table's records

```
_sort prod by pid; list from prod
PID         PNAME          TARGET    GMR   CRATE

bio   biography          59,400   0.48  0.022
bus   business           95,150   0.34  0.022
com   computers         157,181   0.76  0.028
pho   photography        47,300   0.28  0.020
psy   psychology         56,100   0.36  0.018
ref   reference         123,200   0.38  0.019
rom   romance           132,352   0.64  0.024
sfi   science fiction   113,080   0.72  0.028
spo   sports             72,600   0.51  0.023
_sort prod by descending target; list from prod
PID         PNAME          TARGET    GMR   CRATE

com   computers         157,181   0.76  0.028
rom   romance           132,352   0.64  0.024
ref   reference         123,200   0.38  0.019
sfi   science fiction   113,080   0.72  0.028
bus   business           95,150   0.34  0.022
spo   sports             72,600   0.51  0.023
bio   biography          59,400   0.48  0.022
psy   psychology         56,100   0.36  0.018
pho   photography        47,300   0.28  0.020
-
```

was last. Notice how the sorted table's listings differ from the listing in Figure 7–1.

"What if there is a tie?" asked Tracey. "If we sort the PERF table by PID, there will be several records for each product id. Could we sort the records that tie based on some other field such as descending SYTD?"

Jack nodded and executed the command

```
sort perf by pid,descending sytd
```

to have the PERF records sorted first by product ID and secondarily by descending year-to-date sales. Figure 7–11 depicts a printed listing of the rearranged PERF contents. Contrast them with the previous record ordering shown in Figure 7–5. Notice that for each PID value the records are now ordered from highest to lowest sales performance; for instance, the six business records are ordered by descending SYTD values.

In general, any number of fields can be specified as the sorting criteria in a SORT command and each can be prefaced by an ASCENDING or DESCENDING direction. Acceptable abbreviations for these two directions are AZ and ZA respectively. Furthermore, complex expressions

FIGURE 7–11   PERF sorted by PID and descending SYTD

Page   1

TID	FNAME	PID	Q1	Q2	Q3	Q4	QYR	S1	S2	S3	S4	SYTD	MAJOR
1	Kris	bio	7400	6290	7200	8005	28895	7604	6905	8349	0	22858	true
8	Jackie	bio	4339	4228	3989	4867	17423	4360	4271	3359	0	11990	true
6	Karen	bus	10700	11009	8443	7930	38082	12222	11980	8332	0	32534	true
3	Tina	bus	6903	7538	8990	9311	32742	5944	10359	8004	0	24307	true
0	Kim	bus	7320	8050	6400	8503	30273	6854	8120	6908	0	21882	true
4	Toby	bus	4842	4006	5302	4980	19130	5003	5903	4003	0	14909	true
9	Carol	bus	3997	4378	4832	3901	17108	4005	4436	4998	0	13439	true
2	Kevin	bus	3009	4321	2789	3456	13575	4321	6500	2509	0	13330	false
6	Karen	com	12090	11069	10806	9665	43630	13121	11590	10075	0	34786	true
9	Carol	com	6903	5882	6031	8456	27272	8488	9321	7021	0	24830	true
3	Tina	com	5388	4399	7900	7980	25667	5944	8888	9042	0	23874	true
5	Kerry	pho	10700	11009	8443	7930	38082	12222	11980	8332	0	32534	true
2	Kevin	pho	7400	6290	7200	8904	29794	7604	6905	8349	0	22858	true
7	Kathy	pho	8553	7543	5678	6779	28553	7884	7903	6236	0	22023	true
1	Kris	psy	8090	6209	7765	7590	29654	7540	7900	8059	0	23499	true
5	Kerry	psy	4842	4006	5302	4980	19130	5003	5903	4003	0	14909	true
4	Toby	psy	5000	4006	6007	6900	21913	2607	4839	7050	0	14496	true
3	Tina	psy	3214	2345	3256	6112	14927	4222	2444	3459	0	10125	false
0	Kim	ref	6040	8309	7844	9402	31595	7024	7732	8090	0	22846	true
5	Kerry	ref	6030	4985	3001	5883	19899	5590	4880	6320	0	16790	true
8	Jackie	ref	5004	4678	3998	6012	19692	4996	5400	3600	0	13996	true
7	Kathy	ref	4679	5368	5002	3998	19047	5032	4002	4398	0	13432	true
2	Kevin	ref	3214	2345	3256	6112	14927	4222	2444	3459	0	10125	false
1	Kris	rom	9003	10229	8340	11340	38912	10050	12453	8032	0	30535	true
6	Karen	rom	6040	5020	5555	6666	23281	6090	5900	6904	0	18894	true
4	Toby	rom	4982	4678	8744	7432	25836	5009	3997	9037	0	18043	true
9	Carol	rom	5004	4468	5830	7223	22525	5345	5400	6200	0	16945	true
3	Tina	rom	5000	4678	4213	3998	17889	4590	3997	5032	0	13619	true
2	Kevin	sfi	9439	8378	8050	9872	35739	10390	8639	8765	0	27794	true
7	Kathy	sfi	4339	4228	3989	4867	17423	4360	4271	3359	0	11990	true
2	Kevin	spo	6509	7734	6698	7590	28531	7773	8090	6879	0	22742	true
0	Kim	spo	5400	6300	7839	8390	27929	6240	5995	8032	0	20267	true
8	Jackie	spo	5004	4468	5830	7223	22525	5345	5400	6200	0	16945	true

involving multiple fields, working variables, and so on can be used as sort criteria. As an example, the command

```
sort perf by za tid,az(qyr-sytd)/q4
```

would sort the PERF records first by descending territory IDs. Among records with the same TID value there is a secondary sorting. It is based on how close, in percentage terms, the rep is to achieving the fourth quarter quota while also achieving the annual quota for a product line.

Structural Modification

"Now that we've discussed approaches to modifying a table's content, let's take a look at how we can modify its structure," Jack announced. "This is accomplished with the REDEFINE command. Because you're all well versed and rehearsed in the DEFINE command, there's not much new to say about REDEFINE. The two are very similar. The only .major difference is that REDEFINE operates on an existing table. Thus, in addition to allowing you to define new fields, REDEFINE lets you rename, delete, or alter the characteristics of existing fields."

Data management software packages vary widely in terms of their facilities for structural modification. Some allow only more limited kinds of structural modification. For some, structural modification can be a very time-consuming endeavor. Because structural modification can be a fairly drastic action, potentially affecting every record as well as the structure, it may be advisable to make a backup copy of a table before modifying its structure. This is particularly true for large tables with many thousands, or even hundreds, of records.

"REDEFINE is a command that I rarely use," Jack maintained, "yet it's been indispensable on those occasions when I have needed it. I believe that if you carefully think out the design of your tables before you define them, you too will rarely need to use REDEFINE."

"Jack's right about that," Joy confirmed. "I've seen all too many cases where novices, and even some application developers who should know better, begin defining the structure without any preparation. They don't analyze what it is that they are trying to do. Analysis is important to reach a good understanding of what categories of data will be needed, how they will be needed, and what their natural interrelationships are. They don't design the data base structure in advance based on a clear understanding of what they're trying to do. They just begin defining tables on the spur of the moment, in a haphazard fashion. It's no wonder that they then spend a lot of time redefining as bit by bit they discover what it is that they really want to do.

"True, they can define some tables and create some records in them in a few minutes. But, so what, if it's not what they really wanted. The fallacy of this instant gratification philosophy is that it usually ends up being more time-consuming in the long run. In my opinion, there's no substitute for investing some effort up front in careful analysis and design rather than taking the haphazard approach. Obviously, if you were going to build a house, you'd think out what you want in advance rather than plunging in without any forethought and improvising as you go along. Well, the same thing is true when building a data base."

"Amen," said Jack to her sermon, "and we'll chat about design issues before we break. Nonetheless, even with the best laid plans, you still might need to redefine a table once or twice in your life. So let's see how it's done. By the way, if you don't remember or have a printout of the table's current structure, you might want to use the SHOW command to refresh your memory, or get a printout."

He proceeded to execute the command

```
redefine prod
```

to which the system responded with the prompt

```
FILE?
```

Recall that this is the same prompt that results from the DEFINE command. Jack simply pressed the Enter key because he did not want to alter the name of the disk file holding the PROD table.

As with the DEFINE command, he was next presented with the

```
FIELD?
```

prompt. He responded by typing

```
+oldtitle int using "nnnn"
```

explaining that this would add a new integer field named OLDTITLE to the table's structure. It could be used to keep track of the number of titles in a product line that were carryovers from prior years. Whenever a plus is the first character typed after a field prompt, what follows will be understood to be a new field.

When Jack had examined what he had typed for OLDTITLE and was satisfied that he had made no errors, he pressed the Enter key and another

```
FIELD?
```

prompt appeared. He responded by typing

```
+newtitle int using "nnnn"
```

to add another field to PROD's structure. This NEWTITLE field could be used to hold a count of new titles introduced into a product line in the current year. He pressed the Enter key and another

```
FIELD?
```

prompt appeared. This time, Jack decided to add a virtual field whose value would be the commission target. He typed

```
+ctarget num =crate*target using "ffffff"
```

and pressed the Enter key to again get the usual prompt.

"I think you now get the idea of how we can add fields to a structure," Jack declared. "Now suppose we want to rename an existing field. Instead of beginning with a plus, we'd begin with an asterisk followed by the new name and the current name. Watch."

With that he entered

```
*gmrate,gmr
```

to change the GMR field name to GMRATE. Pressing the Enter key brought another

```
FIELD?
```

prompt. Jack responded by typing

```
target num using "$f,fff,fff"
```

and pressing the Enter key.

"Notice that this time I didn't begin with any special symbol like a plus or asterisk. Instead, I entered the name of an existing field, TARGET, followed by some field characteristics. These characteristics become the new characteristics of the TARGET field. If you recall the original definition of the TARGET field you'll see I've left its type unchanged but have given it a fancier picture. You can change any field's characteristics in this way, by just typing in what you ideally would have entered for that field when originally specifying it via the DEFINE command.

"Now let's stop the redefinition and take a look at the results of our handiwork. Just as with DEFINE, you quit by pressing the Enter key when you see the field prompt." When he did so, there was some disk activity before the familiar underscore prompt appeared. To prove that the table now had a new structure, Jack executed the command

```
obtain first from prod
```

and the screen took on the appearance shown in Figure 7–12. It showed that GMR was now named GMRATE, that TARGET now used the newly specified picture, and that there were three new fields. The OLDTITLE and NEWTITLE fields had 0 values for this and all other records in the table. Their values could now be set as desired in any of the usual

FIGURE 7–12   Adding, renaming, and altering fields

```
_redefine prod
FILE?
FIELD? +oldtitle int using "nnnn"
FIELD? +newtitle int using "nnnn"
FIELD? +ctarget num =crate*target using "fffff"
FIELD? *gmrate,gmr
FIELD? target num using "$f,fff,fff"
FIELD?
_obtain first from prod
 Record Number: 1
 #MARK:     FALSE
 PID:       com
 PNAME:     computers
 TARGET:    $157,181
 GMRATE:    0.76
 CRATE:     0.028
 OLDTITLE:    0
 NEWTITLE:    0
 CTARGET:   4401
```

ways (BROWSE, CHANGE, LET). As expected, CTARGET already had a value because it was a virtual field.

"What about subtracting fields from the table's structure?" Dan asked. "Would you just use a minus instead of a plus?"

"Exactly," Jack replied. "In fact, let me restore the table to its original structure, except for TARGET. I'll change its picture to permit one more digit and get rid of the literals."

He proceeded to again invoke the REDEFINE command and make the modifications. At the conclusion, he again obtained the first record. The screen appeared as shown in Figure 7–13. The three new fields were now gone, GMRATE was again GMR, and TARGET's values no longer had embedded literals.

Before leaving the topic of structural modification, Jack mentioned one other command: RENAME. It can be executed to give a different name to a table. For example, the command

```
rename prod to product
```

would rename the PROD table so that it would henceforth be called PRODUCT. Jack did not execute this command, as he felt no urgent need to rename this table.

FIGURE 7–13   Subtracting fields from the PROD structure

```
_redefine prod
FILE?
FIELD? -oldtitle
FIELD? -newtitle
FIELD? *gmr,gmrate
FIELD? target num using "fffffff"
FIELD? -ctarget
FIELD?
_obtain first from prod
 Record Number: 1
 #MARK:    FALSE
 PID:      com
 PNAME:    computers
 TARGET:    157181
 GMR:       0.76
 CRATE:     0.028

 _
```

Destroying a Table

"Usually, you'll not want to destroy a table." There were a few chuckles as Jack continued, "But occasionally the knowledge system's data base may contain a table that you have absolutely no use for. Remember that finishing a table merely puts it out of action for the time being. It doesn't destroy the table, thank goodness. But why have tables that you never intend to use again cluttering up your disk? Keeping track of the useful tables is all I want to do.

"Suppose you've executed the CONVERT command to produce a new table named TEMP and then you convert it into another table so that you no longer care about TEMP. That is, TEMP was just a temporary intermediate table in the overall scheme of things. You can destroy it with the DESTROY command."

He went on to explain that the command

```
destroy temp
```

would be executed. The environment would respond by asking for a confirmation of the name of the file holding the TEMP table

```
FILE?
```

to which a response such as

```
"a:temp.itb"
```

would be entered. Once the Enter key is pressed following the file name, the point of no return has been passed. All traces of the table's prior existence are destroyed. It is possible to get a reprieve from the destruction by entering no file name (just pressing Enter) or pressing the Escape key.

INDEXING A TABLE

"As you realize," Jack reminded them, "the PERF table we've been using is only a fraction of the size of a real PERF table, which would have many more records. As the number of records increases, you would naturally expect the environment to take longer to obtain a particular record based on some condition. On average, there are more records to look through in order to find the one you want. You can speed up the access to individual records in a table by making and using an *index*."

"I get it," acknowledged Dan. "Just like we'd use an index to quickly locate some desired topic in an encyclopedia, the environment can use an index to quickly locate some desired record in a table."

"That's the idea!" exclaimed Jack. "All we have to do is command the environment to make an index and then have it use the index when we want it to."

To clarify the connection between an index and a table, Joy sketched a diagram like the one in Figure 7–14. It shows a subset of the Figure 7–11 PERF records. "Imagine," she said, "that the PERF table contains only these 14 records. We know that each record can be uniquely identified by its territory ID and product ID. But neither a TID value nor a PID value by itself is sufficient to identify an individual PERF record. Many records can have the same TID value and many records can have the same PID value, but no more than one PERF record has a particular TID PID value pair.

"Because the joint value of these two fields uniquely identifies each record in the table, we might want to base an index on them. For each possible value pair, the index will contain location information that tells the environment where the corresponding PERF record is located. The fields on which an index is based are traditionally called the *index key*. The location information that accompanies each index

FIGURE 7–14   Visualization of an index for the PERF table

Index based on TID,PID

Key Location			PERF					
			TID	FNAME	PID	Q1	...	MAJOR
0 bus	●							
0 spo	●							
1 bio	●		1	Kris	bio	7400	...	true
2 bus	●		8	Jackie	bio	4339	...	true
2 spo	●		6	Karen	bus	10700	...	true
3 bus	●		3	Tina	bus	6903	...	true
3 com	●		0	Kim	bus	7320	...	true
4 bus	●		4	Toby	bus	4842	...	true
6 bus	●		9	Carol	bus	3947	...	true
6 com	●		2	Kevin	bus	3009	...	false
8 bio	●		6	Karen	com	12090	...	true
8 spo	●		9	Carol	com	6903	...	true
9 bus	●		3	Tina	com	5388	...	true
9 com	●		2	Kevin	spo	6509	...	true
			0	Kim	spo	5400	...	true
			8	Jackie	spo	5004	...	true

key value in the index is often called a *pointer*. It commonly consists of the physical address of the corresponding record in the disk file holding the table. Rather than write out physical disk addresses in this diagram, I've used arrows to show where the pointers lead.

"Now let's say we want to access the com record for territory 6. We would issue a command indicating an index key value of 6 and com. Once the environment knows the index key value we're interested in, it looks up that value in the index to see where the corresponding record is located. Knowing that location, it can then directly access the record without having to rummage through any other PERF records in search of the one with a TID of 6 and a PID of com."

Jack appreciated Joy's little dissertation on the internal workings of indexing, but for the managers' benefit added, "Let me assure you that you don't need to think about the internal makeup of an index or about pointers in order to make and use an index. You never look at or explicitly change the contents of an index. But I do have one more question for you, Joy. I've read where this environment uses B-tree indexes. What does that mean?"

"It means that access via an index will be faster than it would be if the environment weren't employing B-tree indexing," she answered [4]. "B-tree, and there are several variants of it, refers to a particular way of organizing and processing the entries in an index. It's quite different than my diagram showing a linear sequencing of entries in sorted order based on their key values. In keeping with your advice, it's not necessary to know about their insides in order to make good use of them."

Making an Index

"Well then," Jack continued, "let's see how we would make an index for PERF and let's let the table be indexed by TID and PID. We can do it with a single INDEX command. As Joy's diagram suggests, an index is stored in a separate file from the file holding the PERF table. Thus, in the index command we'll need to provide the name for the *index file* that the environment will be making. Since our index key will be made up of TID and PID, let's call this index file PERFTP and we'll use the customary IND extension."

Jack proceeded to execute the command

```
index "a:perftp.ind" for perf by tid,pid
```

After some disk drive activity, the underscore prompt reappeared and an index for PERF based on the two-field index key existed in the PERFTP.IND file on the drive A diskette. The index was immediately available for use with the table.

"Of course," Jack stated, "the more records a table has, the longer it takes to make an index because the index itself will need to be longer. Also, the more fields you designate for an index key, the more time it will take to make an index."

"I presume we could make an index for each of the other tables in a similar way," commented Debbie. "Could we make more than one index for the same table? Suppose I also wanted to be able to optimize my access to PERF records based on FNAME and PID. Could we now make another index having those two fields as its index key?"

He replied that any table could simultaneously have multiple indexes. To make the additional index Debbie suggested, a command such as

```
index "a:perffp.ind" for perf by fname,pid
```

could be executed. Indexes for the other tables could also be made with the INDEX command.

Retrieval via an Index

"Now that we have an index for PERF," Jack declared, "we can rapidly retrieve any PERF record by stating its index key value. Suppose we want to see the territory 6 performance for romance. The command for doing this is PLUCK. As I think you'll see, if we had a line of books about chickens, we could have some real fun with this command."

As the managers looked on in amusement, Jack plucked the desired record from PERF by executing the command

```
pluck "6","rom" from perf
```

leaving the screen with the appearance shown in Figure 7–15. Even for a small table like PERF, there was a noticeable pickup in the speed with which the record was displayed relative to an OBTAIN command. To stress the speed differential Jack executed

```
obtain from perf for tid="6" & pid="rom"
```

bringing the same record into view, but not quite as quickly.

"I can tell there's a speed difference," Brad agreed, "but we're talking about a fraction of a second for OBTAIN versus an even smaller fraction of a second for PLUCK. As a practical matter, I'd rather stick with OBTAIN than go to the extra effort of making an index."

"That's probably the best course for a table of this size," responded Jack. "But as tables become larger the difference becomes more pronounced."

"Right," chimed Joy. "Here at headquarters we have tables well in excess of 10,000 records and indexing makes a tremendous difference. The decision about whether to index or not to index is really fairly easy to make. If you are satisfied with the retrieval speed achieved without indexing, then don't bother to make an index. If you're not satisfied, then make an index."

"Going back to my earlier question about multiple indexes per table," said Debbie, shifting gears, "how does the environment know which one is pertinent for a particular PLUCK command?"

Jack recommended that in such situations her PLUCK command should indicate which index to use. For instance, the previous PLUCK command would have been stated as

```
pluck "6","rom" from perf using "a:perftp.ind"
```

and the next PLUCK command might be

```
pluck "Toby","bus" from perf using "a:perffp.ind"
```

FIGURE 7–15   Table indexing

```
_index "a:perftp.ind" for perf by tid,pid
_pluck "6","rom" from perf
Record Number: 25
#MARK:     FALSE
TID:       6
FNAME:     Karen
PID:       rom
Q1:           6040
Q2:           5020
Q3:           5555
Q4:           6666
QYR:         23281
S1:           6090
S2:           5900
S3:           6904
S4:              0
SYTD:        18894
MAJOR:     true
_
```

employing the other index. He further suggested that a frequently needed pair of table and index references in a PLUCK command could be macroized to save typing effort.

"There's another thing you should be aware of when a table is used with an index," Jack noted. "When you invoke commands like OBTAIN, BROWSE, and LIST, the records are retrieved according to the index order rather than their actual physical order in the table. It's as if they are virtually sorted based on the index key, though they are not actually sorted in the table itself."

Using a Table with an Index

As Jack had demonstrated, as soon as an index is generated it is in use with the table. He explained that when a table is finished, any indexes in use with it are also finished. When the table is later put back into use with the USE command, one or more of its indexes can be put into use with it. For example, the command

```
use "a:perf.itb" with "a:perftp.ind"
```

would allow the PERF table to be used with its PERFTP index. Similarly, the command

```
use "a:perf.itb" with "a:perftp.ind","a:perffp.ind"
```

would allow PERF to be used with either of the indexes. The first one specified in the USE command is called the primary index, while all others are referred to as secondary indexes.

"When plucking via a primary index," Jack noted, "you are not required to specify the index file name in your PLUCK command. You must do so for secondary indexes. Also, the primary index key is the basis for the virtual sorting of the table's records. Secondary index keys have no effect on this."

Modifying an Indexed Table

"I have one last question about indexed tables," Debbie said. "If I'm using a table with an index, what happens to the index when I modify the table? As I create new records or modify existing ones, is the index automatically updated to be consistent with the new table contents?"

"Yes," replied Jack. "As long as you have not switched the E.INUP environment variable from its default TRUE value, in-use indexes are automatically updated as tables are modified. But there are three exceptions: the REDEFINE, SORT, and COMPRESS commands. After invoking one of these commands for an indexed table, you will want to then invoke INDEX to make a new, up-to-date index."

"That makes sense," commented Debbie. "For such obviously drastic modifications, it would be faster to just regenerate the index rather than trying to update it as the modifications are occurring. I suppose that's also the purpose of E.INUP."

"Right," nodded Jack. "If you're going to be making extensive modifications to a table with, say, the BROWSE command, your editing will be slowed down if the index is updated piecemeal as you make each alteration. So you might want to switch E.INUP to FALSE, do your editing, and then make a new index all at once. At any rate, if when you modify a table E.INUP is FALSE or the table's indexes are not in use, then the indexes become obsolete."

DATA BASE DESIGN

A relational data base consists of all tables pertaining to a particular problem area such as sales management. A data base is one of the ways of representing knowledge in an environment's knowledge system. A data base is not a table or a file. Nor is a table a file. To qualify as a relational data base, the relational algebra or relational calculus commands must be provided for processing tables' records. For well over a decade computer scientists have studied the issue of what constitutes a "good" relational data base design. In the course of their studies, they have invented many special terms including domain, candidate key, functional dependency, full functional dependence, first normal form, second normal form, third normal form, Boyce-Codd normal form, and fourth normal form [1], [2], [6].

Though Joy was acquainted with such terms, Jack was not. He had successfully designed data base tables without being a computer scientist. He planned to pass his design insights along informally through a group discussion, focusing on tables for a sales manager's data base.

"As Joy stressed earlier," Jack began, "it's worth taking some time to design your tables before you actually begin to define and use them. Obviously, before you can begin to design something, you should get clear about what your needs are. You should analyze just what it is you want to do with your data base. What kinds of data do you want to store? What kinds of data do you want to see in printouts, on the console screen, or incorporated into future text that you might develop?

"Once you understand an application area such as sales management, you can begin to design the data base structure. What tables should it have? What data categories should be incorporated into which tables? What characteristics should each of these fields have? Are the relationships that exist among tables adequately represented?

"In our case, we all pretty much understand the sales management application, what basic categories of data—fields—are needed, and what we need to do with the data in those categories. Let's get right to the design issues and see why I designed REP, PERF, and PROD the way I did. I think it's pretty intuitive why I put fields like LNAME, FNAME, HDATE, MOSAL, and so on in the REP table. Collectively, those fields make up the major attributes of a rep that we're interested in."

Identifying the Smallest Common Denominators

There was a murmur of assent, but Brad did have a question. "Why do you have the three fields FNAME, LNAME, and MIDI instead of just a single actual field called NAME, whose values would be the full names of the reps?"

Jack answered briskly, "Mainly because I expected that I'd often want to access the first name separately from the last name, and vice versa. Sometimes I want only the first and last names, without the middle initial. Because I also frequently want the full name, I settled on a virtual field for it. I think it's a good idea to break a category of data into the smallest chunks you might need to access independently of each other and let each chunk become a field."

"That seems reasonable," Brad commented. "I see you played the same game with addresses and their component parts. On the other hand, a field like MOSAL really isn't capable of being usefully broken down into smaller categories of data."

Representing Relationships between Tables

Jack looked slowly around the room. Everyone seemed satisfied so far. "Now I have a question for you. Why do you suppose I designed TID into both the REP and PERF tables? Why not just have it in one or the other, but not in both?"

Dan was the first to answer, "If you left it out of REP, there would be no way for that table's records to keep track of which territories the reps work in. Similarly, if you left it out of PERF you couldn't tell which territory a particular performance occurred in and that is essential information."

"Well," Jack retorted, "why not put TID in the PROD table as well?"

"Because a product line is not exclusively related to one particular territory," answered Dan. "It wouldn't make sense to store a particular territory ID as part of a product line's data."

"Your reasons are very good ones," Jack smiled. "But there's yet another reason why TID is repeated in both tables."

Debbie offered another reason, "By having TID in both places, you are making a relationship between the PERF and REP tables. Each record in the PERF table will be related to a particular REP record by virtue of the fact that their TID values match. Conversely, each REP record will be related to every PERF record that has the same TID value. Remember, you made use of this fact when you demonstrated how CONVERT could be used to make new records in a new table by joining together records with matching TID values."

Jack smiled even more, for Debbie had identified the one and only way for representing interrecord relationships in a relational data base: *field redundancy.* Other data models furnish additional approaches for representing such relationships. These are summarized in an article Joy had given to Jack to help him understand relationship possibilities [5]. An adaptation of the article is in Appendix A.

Joy now chimed in, "The particular kind of relationship Debbie has just identified between PERF and REP is an example of what's often called a many-to-one relationship. There can be *many* PERF records with the same TID value possessed by at most *one* REP record. This is an extremely common kind of relationship between two tables in a relational data base. Does anyone see another many-to-one relationship between a pair of tables?"

"I do," responded Stan. "There's a many-to-one relationship from PERF to PROD based on the PID field that they both have. For many PERF records with the same PID value we can have one PROD record whose PID value matches. From another viewpoint each PROD record can be related to many PERF records by giving them all the same PID value."

"Right," Joy confirmed. "It's worthwhile being able to recognize such relationships as you design your data base. If you were to end up with the same field in two table structures, but this duplication did not represent a many-to-one or one-to-one relationship, then you should probably rethink the design of those two tables. In such a situation your design would not conform to what computer scientists call third normal form—3NF for short. If a data base design is in third normal form, they usually consider it to be a fairly 'good' design. A full explanation of 3NF really is quite complex, so let's not get bogged down in it here. It's enough to recognize that non-one-to-many is a clue that you would be well advised to reconsider your design."

Another Reason for Field Redundancy

"Whew," Jack sighed. "I've another question for you. Why include FNAME in PERF when we already have TID there to identify each performance territory and to form a relationship with the corresponding REP record? If we can use this relationship to get at the matching REP record, the first name will be available to use. Why store it again in the PERF table?"

"It seems that having it in both places would be more convenient," Tracey declared. "For instance, when you're retrieving PERF records you'll have the first name right there without having to be concerned about dealing with the other table and matching the REP record with the same TID value."

"Exactly. But you should avoid carrying this kind of field redundancy to extremes," Jack cautioned. "For instance, it may be OK to repeat REP's FNAME field in PERF, but you wouldn't want to repeat all the REP fields in PERF!"

"That would make PERF pretty unwieldy," Tracey acknowledged.

"Not only that," added Jack, "it would also consume considerable disk space and working memory unnecessarily. Worse still, every time you changed a value in the REP table, you would have to take the time to change that value in every record where it's repeated in the PERF table!

Designing a Table for Expense Data

"Now for practice, let's design the structure of a table that you've not yet seen but whose purpose is obvious. It's a table for holding the actual expenses that each rep incurs for each month. What fields should this EXPENSE table have?"

As various fields were identified, Jack wrote them on the whiteboard. His list eventually included:

HEXP	(hotel expense)	HNO	(hotel: nights out)
MEXP	(meal expense)	MNO	(meals, number of)
PHONE	(phone expense)	ENT	(entertainment
POSTAGE	(postage expense)		expense)
MISC	(miscellaneous expense)	TRANS	(transportation expense)
TOTAL	(total expense for month)	TID	(territory ID)

before there were no more suggestions. They had agreed that all of these would be actual fields with the exception of TOTAL, which would be designated as a virtual field.

"Something is missing," claimed Jack. All was quiet, so he hinted, "Each record will have the actual expense information for a certain territory in a certain month. The value of TID will tell us which territory it is and allow us to access the corresponding REP record. But what month do that record's expenses belong to?"

"We need a MONTH field," Stan offered. "Its value in each record will tell in what month the record's expenses were incurred. As a result we'll have 12 EXPENSE records for each territory by year's end. Thus, there would be a many-to-one relationship from EXPENSE to REP."

"That would work," Brad commented, "but what about playing the same game Jack did for the PERF table. Just as PERF has S1 through S4 and Q1 through Q4 for different time periods, we could have HEXP1 through HEXP12, PHONE1 through PHONE12, and so on for the EXPENSE table."

"In principle," Jack responded, "that would work, but we would end up with dozens of fields in the same table and that might well be clumsy to work with relative to Stan's solution."

"I see another option," Debbie said. "Don't invent any new fields beyond those we've listed. Instead, we could define 12 tables: EXP1 through EXP12. All would have the same structure. But they would contain data for different months. So the relationship between, say, EXP5 and REP is a special case of one-to-many. I suppose you would call it one-to-one, since there will be one REP record for each EXP5 record and vice versa."

"I see a couple of potential problems with Debbie's design," remarked Pete. "For one, if you want to do cross-month comparisons, you'll have to juggle several tables to do so. Second, it would be tiresome to type in the same field responses to the DEFINE command 12 times."

"Your second concern is easy to solve," rejoined Jack. "There's a command named IMPRESS that can define an entire new table by taking an impression of an existing table's structure. Your other concern is legitimate. The bottom line is that each of the three suggested solutions has certain advantages and disadvantages. It's up to you as the designer to choose the structure that you believe will best suit your anticipated processing needs. I just wanted to make you aware of some of the options you have."

BASIC IDEAS

When data is stored in a table, the ability to get a quick listing of its records is very important (LIST). Each line in the listing contains a record. Each column contains a field's values. A listing can be routed to the console screen, printer, or piece of text currently being edited. Chapter 8 introduces a much more powerful command for exploring tables' contents on an ad hoc basis. It is a command in the relational calculus language known as SQL (Structured Query Language).

There are two basic aspects of table modification. A table's content can be modified in several ways. There are record-at-a-time editing (BROWSE), multirecord conditional changes based on calculations (CHANGE), record marking (MARK) for eventual elimination (COMPRESS), and record sorting based on any of a variety of criteria (SORT). Secondly, a table's structure can be modified by adding, renaming, subtracting, or altering fields (REDEFINE). A table can also be renamed (RENAME) or completely destroyed (DESTROY) if desired.

Access to records in a large table can be significantly speeded by means of an index. When making an index for a table (INDEX) one or more of the table's fields are designated as the index key. Once a table has been indexed any of its records can be directly retrieved by furnishing the desired index key value (PLUCK). As an indexed table is modified, its indexes can be automatically updated to remain consistent with the table's new content.

Thoughtful analysis of data-handling needs coupled with careful data base design should precede the actual definition and population of tables. Haphazard design necessitates frequent table redefinition and is likely to be less productive in the long run than a reasonable degree of planning. Theorists have invented notions of a "good" relational data base design (e.g., at least third normal form). From a practical standpoint, restricting interrecord relationships to the many-to-one or one-to-one goes a long way toward meeting the ideal of a "good" design. In the final analysis, however, it is user convenience that dictates data base design.

References

1. Atre, S. *Data Base, Structured Techniques for Design, Performance, and Management.* New York: John Wiley & Sons, 1980.
2. Bonczek, R. H.; C. W. Holsapple; and A. B. Whinston. *Micro Database Management—Practical Techniques for Application Development.* New York: Academic Press, 1984.
3. Bradley, J. *File and Data Base Techniques.* New York: Holt, Rinehart & Winston, 1982.
4. Comer, D. "The Ubiquitous B-Tree." *ACM Computing Surveys* 11, no. 6 (1979).
5. Holsapple, C. W. "A Perspective on Data Models." *PC Tech Journal* 2, no. 1 (1984).
6. Kent, W. "A Simple Guide to Five Normal Forms in Relational Database Theory." *Communications of the ACM* 26, no. 2 (1983).
7. *KnowledgeMan Reference Manual*, version 2. Lafayette, Ind.: MDBS, Inc., 1985.

What is . . . ?
What if . . . ?

Chapter Eight

Ad Hoc Inquiry and Statistics

As the session reconvened, Jack was heartened by what he heard. The managers were engaged in lively discussions about their hands-on data management experiences in the just ending break. Tapping a pen on the overhead projector he gained their attention and said thoughtfully, "It's worth pausing for a moment to reflect on how far we've come in the past couple of days."

The room was silent as each person seemed to mentally review what had been accomplished. Jack looked at Joy and, as their eyes met, a quiet smile played around her lips. She understood quite well that his words were, in their own special way, intended just as much for her as for the sales managers. Breaking the reverie, he continued, "I think we can all see that there is much more to explore, much more that would be interesting and valuable to discover."

The room was filled with an air of agreement and reserved anticipation as he began introducing them to a new knowledge management technique. "You now are acquainted with an assortment of commands for manipulating data in tables. Aside from defining and redefining a table's structure, the data management technique lets you create, modify, and view a table's records. If you think about it, you can use data management commands to pack a lot of knowledge into tables.

"For instance, there are all kinds of facts buried in the PERF table. Beyond the raw numbers there is much more. There's the fact that Kim's second quarter quota for reference books is higher than her first quarter reference quota but less than her fourth quarter reference quota. There is the fact that she'll need fourth quarter reference sales of at least 8749 to meet her annual quota. There are the facts that reference performance data exist for five of the reps, one of these has a lower annual quota than the others, and some are above the annual average quota. With the data management commands, how would you discern such facts?"

"I'd use the LIST command," replied Tracey. "Then I'd look at the resultant listing to ferret out what it is I'm interested in at the moment, such as who has not met their quotas in quarter 1. If I wanted to know their respective shortfalls, I could then use values from the listing to calculate the shortfalls."

"Sure, that would work," added Brad, "but there ought to be a better way. I like the LIST command for quickly checking myself to see that modifications I was attempting to make were indeed made. But we need an easier way than the data management commands for quickly uncovering whatever facts might be buried in a table. Browsing through, obtaining, or plucking records one by one is OK for some things but these methods don't give you the big picture all at once. On the other hand, listing the entire contents of a table can give too big a picture."

"I agree," declared Dan. "With a listing you have to eyeball a lot of data that's not relevant to your needs at the moment. A moment later you may want to focus on some other subset of the listing. Each time you have to visually pick out what it is you happen to be interested in. And if you want to do some calculations, then they have to be done separately, one by one. Also, using Tracey's example, what if I wanted to see the shortfalls grouped by product line and within each group wanted to see them arranged by highest to lowest shortfall? Seeing what you're looking for, arranged in a convenient way, could be a big help in quickly studying it."

"So what you would like to have," summarized Jack, "is a way to tell the environment to do the eyeballing, calculating, grouping, and ordering for you. As you work on making a decision, you reach a point where you need to find out something from your data base of tables before you can move ahead. You would like to make a spur of the moment, *ad hoc inquiry* that would show you no more and no less than what it is you're trying to discover. This could well be a once in a lifetime query, something you've never thought of exploring before and you may never need to examine again.

"In any event when you see the query result, your decision process can continue. Of course, the result will probably influence the direction of your thinking and may well stimulate you to make another ad hoc inquiry, and so on until you've gathered what knowledge you need along your way to making a decision."

"Carrying this idea a step further," Joy chimed, "your inquiry may involve more than *what is* visible in the table. In supporting your decision process, you may want to make hypothetical queries. This is often referred to as *'what if'* analysis. For instance, what if all romance quotas were hiked by 8 percent? Who would now have romance shortfalls and how large would they be?"

"Well," smiled Jack, "our entire wish list for 'what is' and 'what if' explorations is satisfied with a single command called SELECT. Each SELECT command is an ad hoc query that can draw on data held in one or more tables to satisfy our spur of the moment information needs. The result of a SELECT command is a tabular display of desired data on the console screen or printer. We'll also be taking a look at a variant of SELECT. It is the STAT command, which allows us to get just a statistical summary of selected data values rather than a full display of those values."

The SELECT command that Jack was about to describe can be used by persons who are altogether unfamiliar with the data management commands discussed in Chapters 6 and 7. As such, ad hoc inquiry stands as a knowledge management technique in its own right. As the term *inquiry* suggests, this technique is concerned exclusively with the retrieval of knowledge. The SELECT command, as Jack intended to present it, is patterned along the lines of the comparable query command that forms the core of SQL, an Englishized rendition of the relational calculus access language [2], [3], [4].

USEFUL PRELIMINARIES

Before launching into the SELECT command, Jack reminded the group of a few notions with which they were already familiar. As with any command that will make use of table contents, SELECT requires that the table be in use. He entered the environment and executed the commands

```
use "a:rep.itb"
use "a:perf.itb" with "a:perftp.ind"
use "a:prod.itb"
```

to put the REP, PERF, and PROD tables in use. He further pointed out that if, say, the REP table's file were on the present hard disk directory rather than the drive A diskette, then the simpler command

```
use rep
```

would suffice.

Jack reminded them about the existence of environment variables. Just as they were applicable to earlier knowledge management techniques, they would be applicable for ad hoc inquiry as well. Thus, if

E.PAUS were set to TRUE, the display of a query's results would pause after each screenful and resume each time the space bar is pressed. As usual, E.OPRN would control whether a query's results would be sent to the printer. The E.PDEP, E.PMAR, and E.PWID environment variables would have their usual effects on printouts. Jack set the E.PDEP variable to its customary 65 value. He also switched E.STAT to FALSE, so that statistics would not be calculated automatically in response to each ad hoc inquiry.

Because SELECT results are displayed in a tabular fashion, the E.SPAC setting determines how many spaces will separate adjoining columns. Jack switched E.SPAC from its default value to a setting of 1. And just to add a little color to the proceedings he executed the LET commands

```
let e.forg="wwwwc"
let e.bacg="uuuuu"
```

to get a cyan foreground against a blue background on the console screen. Recall (Chapter 4) that the fifth color codes of these environment variables determine the colors seen when issuing commands for the underscore prompt. Jack noted that the third color codes controlled the text screen colors. The other codes control colors for other kinds of screens that had yet to be discussed.

FIELD SELECTION

"In its most basic form," Jack explained, "the SELECT command lets you identify which of a table's fields you're interested in seeing values for. You merely list the desired fields' names following the word SELECT and they become column headings for the command's result."

"We can pick any subset of the fields we want?" asked Tracey. "And can they be in any order?"

"Sure," Jack answered. "The columns will be arranged in the same order you use when designating the fields, regardless of the field sequence you used when defining the table's structure. Let's take an example."

Jack proceeded to execute the query command

```
select tid,city,name,phone,mosal from rep
```

with the environment's answer being immediately displayed as shown in Figure 8–1. He explained that the commas between field names were optional. Spaces could also be used to separate field names or a space could follow each comma if desired.

FIGURE 8–1　Designating query fields

```
_select tid,city,name,phone,mosal from rep
TID    CITY          NAME              PHONE        MOSAL

2    Bloomington   Kevin R. Andrews  (123) 456-1111  2500
0    Chicago       Kim G. Anders     (312) 553-6754  2600
1    Dayton        Kris H. Raber     (513) 333-9989  2400
3    Indianapolis  Tina F. Lee       (317) 299-8393  2800
4    Fort Wayne    Toby C. Terry     (345) 123-4567  2000
5    Grand Rapids  Kerry H. Jones    (632) 098-7654  2250
6    Madison       Karen V. Bruckner (433) 442-8201  2800
7    Milwaukee     Kathy F. Smith    (415) 567-8901  2100
8    Columbus      Jackie V. Smith   (322) 861-6543  2400
9    Midland       Carol O. Lynn     (412) 832-5643  2750
_
```

"When I use queries," Jack continued, "I often find that the results of one will stimulate me to think of another. Sometimes, the new query is very similar to the last one. For instance, I may want to include some additional fields, leave out some of the earlier fields, or both. When your new query is a modified version of your last query, you don't have to type it all in again from scratch. Just remember that pressing Control-Z brings the last command into view so you can edit it as desired."

He pressed the ˆZ key, causing the former query to reappear alongside the underscore prompt. With ˆS, he moved the cursor from the end of the line to the space in front of FROM and then typed

`,moexp`

followed by the Enter key. Executing this edited query left the screen with the appearance shown in Figure 8–2. Notice that the first three lines of Figure 8–1 are no longer available, having scrolled out of view to make room for the new query's results.

"Is there some way to clear the results of the former query from the screen before going on to a new query?" Stan inquired.

FIGURE 8–2   Executing an edited query

```
2   Bloomington  Kevin R. Andrews     (123)  456-1111  2500
0   Chicago      Kim G. Anders        (312)  553-6754  2600
1   Dayton       Kris H. Raber        (513)  333-9989  2400
3   Indianapolis Tina F. Lee          (317)  299-8393  2800
4   Fort Wayne   Toby C. Terry        (345)  123-4567  2000
5   Grand Rapids Kerry H. Jones       (632)  098-7654  2250
6   Madison      Karen V. Bruckner    (433)  442-8201  2800
7   Milwaukee    Kathy F. Smith       (415)  567-8901  2100
8   Columbus     Jackie V. Smith      (322)  861-6543  2400
9   Midland      Carol O. Lynn        (412)  832-5643  2750
_select tid,city,name,phone,mosal,moexp from rep
TID     CITY             NAME            PHONE     MOSAL    MOEXP

2   Bloomington  Kevin R. Andrews     (123)  456-1111  2500  1025.68
0   Chicago      Kim G. Anders        (312)  553-6754  2600   896.74
1   Dayton       Kris H. Raber        (513)  333-9989  2400  1132.61
3   Indianapolis Tina F. Lee          (317)  299-8393  2800   988.20
4   Fort Wayne   Toby C. Terry        (345)  123-4567  2000  1080.53
5   Grand Rapids Kerry H. Jones       (632)  098-7654  2250  1229.64
6   Madison      Karen V. Bruckner    (433)  442-8201  2800  1335.00
7   Milwaukee    Kathy F. Smith       (415)  567-8901  2100   882.74
8   Columbus     Jackie V. Smith      (322)  861-6543  2400  1006.45
9   Midland      Carol O. Lynn        (412)  832-5643  2750  1229.73
_
```

"For that," answered Jack, "you can invoke the CLEAR command." Suiting his actions to his words he executed the command

```
clear
```

causing the screen to become blank except for an underscore prompt in the top left corner.

"But wait," Stan commanded. "When you do that, Control-Z won't bring back your last SELECT command for editing."

"True," Jack responded. "It would bring back CLEAR which is our most recent command. If after a query you wanted to both clear the screen and then execute an edited rendition of that query what would you do?"

Quickly responding to his quiz, Debbie answered, "Instead of entering the CLEAR command right away, you'd press Control-Z to bring back the last query. You'd edit it as desired and then move the cursor to the start of the line where you would type the CLEAR command followed by a semicolon. As a result there would be two commands in the same line: CLEAR and then your query. Pressing the Enter key would execute them in succession."

"That makes sense," Stan affirmed. "Alternatively, after typing in my initial query, I could type a semicolon and CLEAR before pressing the Enter key for execution. That way, the screen would clear after query results are displayed and I'd still be able to use Control-Z to get that command line back for editing."

"You're right," Jack declared, "but there's a problem with your approach. As soon as the last line of query results is displayed, the screen would instantly be cleared. You wouldn't get much of a chance to see the results. What you'd like to do is have the environment wait before clearing, until you've had a sufficient chance to examine the results. You can tell it to wait by including the WAIT command after your query and before the CLEAR."

On the whiteboard, he showed that Stan would want to enter the three commands

```
select tid,city,name,phone,mosal from rep;wait;clear
```

on a single command line before pressing the Enter key. The query results would remain displayed until the space bar was pressed to terminate the wait. The screen would then clear.

"Is there an easy way to select all the fields without having to type in all their names?" Dan wanted to know.

"Yes," answered Jack. "Instead of typing in field names, you just type an asterisk. Used in this way, it has sort of a wild card meaning like we saw before. Only here, it matches all the table's field names."

Jack demonstrated the use of the asterisk by executing the command

```
select * from prod
```

producing the screen appearance shown in Figure 8–3. Notice that one field is not included. The exception is #MARK, which you have to explicitly request if you want it. Jack noted that E.IMRK has the same effect here that we saw earlier. If it is switched to TRUE, the environment will ignore marked records when answering your queries.

EXPRESSION SELECTION

"A very handy feature of queries is that you're not limited to just fields. Any of the kinds of calculation expressions you've worked with can be requested along with the fields. Let's say we want to examine the reps' weekly salaries. Well, the numbers we desire aren't explicitly stored in the REP table, but there is sufficient data there to determine what the weekly salary rates are. We can let SELECT dig it out for us by just including an appropriate numeric expression."

FIGURE 8–3   Selecting all fields

```
_select * from prod
PID        PNAME           TARGET   GMR CRATE

com computers             157181  0.76 0.028
rom romance               132352  0.64 0.024
ref reference             123200  0.38 0.019
sfi science fiction       113080  0.72 0.028
bus business               95150  0.34 0.022
spo sports                 72600  0.51 0.023
bio biography              59400  0.48 0.022
psy psychology             56100  0.36 0.018
pho photography            47300  0.28 0.020

_
```

Jack showed how this could be accomplished by executing the command

```
select tid name mosal*12/52 from rep
```

which left the screen as depicted in Figure 8–4. Notice that the proper calculation was performed for each row of the query result. Jack explained that the T01 heading for the third column serves as a title for the query's first calculated expression. Had the query included additional calculated expressions, their column titles would have been T02, T03, and so on.

Reminding them of the role of E.DECI, Jack provided another query example of distilling data that existed only implicitly in the REP table. He executed the commands

```
e.deci=2
select name majorp mosal+moexp (moexp+mosal)*12 from rep
```

to see the monthly and annual sums of budgeted expenditures for each of the sales reps. The resultant screen is portrayed in Figure 8–5. The final two columns contain data derived from the table's contents.

FIGURE 8–4   Integrating a calculation with a query

```
_select tid name mosal*12/52 from rep
TID           NAME                  TO1

 2    Kevin R. Andrews            576.92308
 0    Kim G. Anders               600.00000
 1    Kris H. Raber               553.84615
 3    Tina F. Lee                 646.15385
 4    Toby C. Terry               461.53846
 5    Kerry H. Jones              519.23077
 6    Karen V. Bruckner           646.15385
 7    Kathy F. Smith              484.61538
 8    Jackie V. Smith             553.84615
 9    Carol O. Lynn               634.61538
 _
```

FIGURE 8–5   Integrating multiple calculations with a query

```
_e.deci=2
_select name majorp mosal+moexp (moexp+mosal)*12 from rep
          NAME          MAJORP          TO1           TO2

Kevin R. Andrews     sfi:pho:spo      3525.68       42308.16
Kim G. Anders        ref:bus:spo      3496.74       41960.88
Kris H. Raber        rom:psy:bio      3532.61       42391.32
Tina F. Lee          bus:com:rom      3788.20       45458.40
Toby C. Terry        rom:psy:bus      3080.53       36966.36
Kerry H. Jones       pho:ref:psy      3479.64       41755.68
Karen V. Bruckner    com:bus:rom      4135.00       49620.00
Kathy F. Smith       pho:ref:sfi      2982.74       35792.88
Jackie V. Smith      spo:ref:bio      3406.45       40877.40
Carol O. Lynn        com:rom:bus      3979.73       47756.76
_
```

"Is there some way we can choose our own column headings for expressions?" asked Don, another of the more reserved sales managers.

Giving Jack a rest, Joy answered, "Yes and we'll get to that a bit later. Of course you could redefine REP to have virtual fields for each of the two expressions. The names of those fields would then appear as column headings when referenced in a query. But you probably don't want to make virtual fields for expressions that you're interested in only on an ad hoc basis. And you certainly would not want to make actual fields for storing the data in columns T01 and T02.

"By the way, you're perfectly free to use any of the built-in functions we discussed earlier. For instance, let's see how many days each rep has been employed."

As she gestured in Jack's direction, he took her cue by executing the commands

```
e.deci=0
select name, #date, hdate, tojul(#date)-tojul(hdate) from rep
```

producing the Figure 8–6 screen. Notice that variables (e.g., #DATE) other than fields can be incorporated into a query. Joy asked him to show an example of string and logical calculations in a query and he complied by executing the command

```
select upcase(pname), target, gmr*target>75000 from prod
```

leaving the screen as shown in Figure 8–7. The first expression employs the UPCASE function to transform product names from their stored lowercase values. The second expression is logical, resulting in either a value of TRUE or FALSE depending on whether a product's targeted gross contribution to profits is in excess of 75,000.

Retaking the lead, Jack stressed, "Expressions in queries can be very useful for 'what if' analysis in addition to 'what is' analysis. For instance, what if all salaries were increased by 6 or 7 percent? We could compare the effects of such increases against the current monthly salaries with a single query, *without* affecting the table's data in any way whatsoever!"

To drive home his point, Jack executed the command

```
select name, mosal, mosal*1.06, mosal*1.07 from rep
```

resulting in the screen shown in Figure 8–8. Although the table's records were unchanged, the group was now able to get a feel for the effects of making such salary adjustments.

FIGURE 8–6 A function and variable in a query

```
_e.deci=0
_select name, #date, hdate, tojul(#date)-tojul(hdate) from rep
         NAME                  #DATE        HDATE          TO1

Kevin R. Andrews            10/03/86     08/30/1981         1860
Kim G. Anders               10/03/86     04/06/1979         2737
Kris H. Raber               10/03/86     04/08/1982         1639
Tina F. Lee                 10/03/86     12/13/1981         1755
Toby C. Terry               10/03/86     02/25/1985          585
Kerry H. Jones              10/03/86     06/10/1983         1211
Karen V. Bruckner           10/03/86     05/14/1982         1603
Kathy F. Smith              10/03/86     07/03/1984          822
Jackie V. Smith             10/03/86     04/12/1980         2365
Carol O. Lynn               10/03/86     11/01/1979         2528
  _
```

FIGURE 8–7 String and logical calculations in a query

```
_select upcase(pname), target, gmr*target>75000 from prod
         TO1          TARGET    TO2

COMPUTERS            157181   TRUE
ROMANCE             132352   TRUE
REFERENCE           123200   FALSE
SCIENCE FICTION     113080   TRUE
BUSINESS             95150   FALSE
SPORTS               72600   FALSE
BIOGRAPHY            59400   FALSE
PSYCHOLOGY           56100   FALSE
PHOTOGRAPHY          47300   FALSE
  _
```

FIGURE 8–8   A "what if" query

```
_select name, mosal, mosal*1.06, mosal*1.07 from rep
         NAME             MOSAL        TO1            TO2

Kevin R. Andrews         2500        2650.00        2675.00
Kim G. Anders            2600        2756.00        2782.00
Kris H. Raber            2400        2544.00        2568.00
Tina F. Lee              2800        2968.00        2996.00
Toby C. Terry            2000        2120.00        2140.00
Kerry H. Jones           2250        2385.00        2407.50
Karen V. Bruckner        2800        2968.00        2996.00
Kathy F. Smith           2100        2226.00        2247.00
Jackie V. Smith          2400        2544.00        2568.00
Carol O. Lynn            2750        2915.00        2942.50
_
```

Jack went on to explain that a macro could be very convenient if they wanted to repeatedly test out different salary adjustment factors. He demonstrated by executing the three commands

```
macro saltest select tid name mosal mosal*fac from rep
fac=1.065
saltest
```

with the results shown in Figure 8–9. The first command defined the new query command SALTEST, which when executed would use the value of a working variable named FAC to calculate an adjusted salary for each rep. His second command let FAC have a value of 1.065. The third executed SALTEST, producing the displayed query results. Whenever a different factor is desired after some intervening queries, the value of FAC would be changed accordingly. SALTEST would then be executed without necessitating a retyping of the SELECT command.

"'What if' analyses can be extremely valuable in supporting decisions," claimed Jack. "In the next few days you'll see other techniques for 'what if' analyses, including forms management, spreadsheet management, and procedural modeling. Though they take more effort than ad hoc queries, they too can be valuable 'what if' facilities."

FIGURE 8–9 A new command for repeated "what ifs"

```
_macro saltest select tid name mosal mosal*fac from rep
_fac=1.065
_saltest
TID            NAME           MOSAL          T01

 2    Kevin R. Andrews        2500           2662.50
 0    Kim G. Anders           2600           2769.00
 1    Kris H. Raber           2400           2556.00
 3    Tina F. Lee             2800           2982.00
 4    Toby C. Terry           2000           2130.00
 5    Kerry H. Jones          2250           2396.25
 6    Karen V. Bruckner       2800           2982.00
 7    Kathy F. Smith          2100           2236.50
 8    Jackies V. Smith        2400           2556.00
 9    Carol O. Lynn           2750           2928.75
 _
```

COSMETICS

The group had already seen that the presentation of a query's results can be somewhat controlled. A field's picture determines the presentation of its values. Environment variables determine the presentations for expressions, working variables, and utility variables depending on the type of value being displayed. For string values, E.LSTR (default 15) controls how many characters are displayed. Similarly, there is an E.LNUM environment variable (default 14) that determines how wide a numeric column will be and E.DECI controls the number of decimal digits. Beyond these facilities, it turns out that pictures can be used directly in a query, column headings can be controlled, and a title can be specified for the result.

Pictures in a Query

"Remember how the OUTPUT command works," said Jack. "We can use a picture with any expression to cause its value to be presented in a certain way. Well, we can do exactly the same thing in a SELECT command."

FIGURE 8–10   Using pictures in a query

```
_select trim(fname)+" "+lname using "%20r", mosal*12 using "$ff,fff" from rep
         TO1                 TO2

Kevin Andrews       $30,000
Kim Anders          $31,200
Kris Raber          $28,800
Tina Lee            $33,600
Toby Terry          $24,000
Kerry Jones         $27,000
Karen Bruckner      $33,600
Kathy Smith         $25,200
Jackie Smith        $28,800
Carol Lynn          $33,000
–
```

He demonstrated by executing the command

```
select trim(fname)+" "+lname using "%20r", mosal*12 using "$ff,fff" from rep
```

producing the result shown in Figure 8–10. The picture for the string expression caused the first column to be 20 characters wide. If that picture had not been used, the E.LSTR setting would have controlled the column's width (resulting in a truncated display of any expression values exceeding that width). Jack used another familiar picture with the query's second expression. All of its numeric values were presented in an edited fashion within a column whose width was 7 (up to 5 digits, a dollar sign, and a comma).

"As a tip," Jack suggested, "if there is a picture that you intend to use repeatedly in one or more queries, you might want to define a macro for it to avoid retyping it every time you need it. I usually pick a short macro name that is descriptive of the picture. For instance, you might use R20 as the name for a picture of 20 r placeholders or F5 to name a picture of 5 f placeholders. This makes them easy to remember. Let me show you what I mean."

FIGURE 8–11   Macroized pictures in a query

```
_macro f7 using "$f,fff,fff"
_macro f7dd using "$f,fff,fff.dd"
_select pid using "ull", target f7, target/12 f7, gmr, target*gmr f7dd from prod

PID    TARGET        T01     GMR     T02

Com    $157,181     $13,098  0.76    $119,457.71
Rom    $132,352     $11,029  0.64     $84,705.28
Ref    $123,200     $10,267  0.38     $46,816.00
Sfi    $113,080      $9,423  0.72     $81,417.60
Bus     $95,150      $7,929  0.34     $32,351.00
Spo     $72,600      $6,050  0.51     $37,026.00
Bio     $59,400      $4,950  0.48     $28,512.00
Psy     $56,100      $4,675  0.36     $20,196.00
Pho     $47,300      $3,942  0.28     $13,244.00
_
```

He proceeded to add some linguistic knowledge to the knowledge system by executing the commands

```
macro f7 using "$f,fff,fff"
macro f7dd using "$f,fff,fff.dd"
```

which resulted in two new words (F7 and F7DD) that the environment could now comprehend. To show how these could be put in a query, he executed the command

```
select pid using "ull", target f7, target/12 f7, gmr, target*gmr f7dd from prod
```

leaving the screen appearance as shown in Figure 8–11. Notice that the query's first picture caused PID values to be edited so they are presented as beginning with uppercase letters. Jack explained that a picture can be used with a field that was defined with some other picture. The query picture temporarily overrides the field's normal picture. This trait is also illustrated by the query's picture (F7) for TARGET.

Query Column Headings

"I presume," commented Debbie, "that these macroized pictures could also be referenced in OUTPUT commands. But let's go back to the earlier question of column headings. Now that we know how to govern the presentation of data in the columns, how can we influence what the column headings are?"

Nodding, Jack replied, "Your presumption is on the mark. As for column headings, we can control them by means of #LEGEND. That is what's called a utility array. Unlike a variable, which is a compartment for storing one value, an *array* is a group of compartments. Each of these compartments is called an *array element* and has a value of its own. An array element is referenced by enclosing a subscript in parentheses after the array name. For example, #LEGEND(2) refers to the second element in the #LEGEND array.

"If E.LEGH is switched from its FALSE default to TRUE, the environment will use the values of #LEGEND's elements as column headings. The value of #LEGEND(1) will become the first column's heading, the second element's value will serve as the second column's heading, and so on. Suppose we want different headings for the T01 and T02 columns produced by our last query. Here's what we could do."

Jack executed the following four commands

```
dim #legend(5)
#legend(3)="TARGET(mo)"
#legend(5)="TARGET PROFIT"
e.legh=true
```

explaining that the third column's heading would now be TARGET(mo), the average monthly target. Similarly, the fifth column would now be headed by TARGET PROFIT, indicating that its contents referred to the targeted contributions to profit.

"The three LET commands are clear enough, but what does the DIM command do?" asked Brad. "Does it mean that the headings will be dimmed compared to the usual intensity of the rest of the screen?"

"No, not quite," Jack replied brightly. "DIM stands for dimension. When you intend to work with an array, this command tells the environment what dimensions you want. In this case, I've dimensioned #LEGEND to consist of five elements. If there were, say, seven columns to furnish headings for, I would have made its dimension 7."

"But you only gave values to two of the #LEGEND elements," Tracey noted. "What about the other three?"

"Their column headings will be the same as they would be if E.LEGH were still FALSE," Jack answered. "Only if a #LEGEND element has

FIGURE 8–12   #LEGEND elements as column headings

```
_dim #legend(5)
_#legend(3)="TARGET(mo)"
_#legend(5)="TARGET PROFIT"
_e.legh=true
_select pid using "ull", target f7, target/12 f7, gmr, target*gmr f7dd from prod

PID    TARGET    TARGET(mo)  GMR TARGET PROFIT

Com    $157,181   $13,098 0.76   $119,457.71
Rom    $132,352   $11,029 0.64    $84,705.28
Ref    $123,200   $10,267 0.38    $46,816.00
Sfi    $113,080    $9,423 0.72    $81,417.60
Bus     $95,150    $7,929 0.34    $32,351.00
Spo     $72,600    $6,050 0.51    $37,026.00
Bio     $59,400    $4,950 0.48    $28,512.00
Psy     $56,100    $4,675 0.36    $20,196.00
Pho     $47,300    $3,942 0.28    $13,244.00
—
```

a value will it override the normal heading for the corresponding column. Watch how it works."

Query Title

He executed the same query that he had used before, yielding the screen appearance shown in Figure 8–12. "Let's get a little fancier by spacing the columns farther apart and putting a title on the query result. There is a utility variable named #TITLE. If it has a value, that value serves as the query result's title. By default, #TITLE has no value, so let's give it one that is descriptive of our last query's purpose."

After switching E.SPAC to 4, he executed the LET command

```
#title="Target Analysis by Product Line (" + #date +")"
```

to establish a title for the query that would follow. Observe that the present date is incorporated into this title. Jack executed the same query again, with the result shown in Figure 8–13. He explained that this same title would appear on all subsequent query results, unless #TITLE were given a different value or no value (i.e., a null value). Similarly,

FIGURE 8–13   **Titled query results**

```
_e.spac=4
_#title="Target Analysis by Product Line (" + #date +")"
_select pid using "ull," target f?, target/12 f?, gmr, target*gmr f?dd from prod

Target Analysis by Product Line (10/03/86)

PID        TARGET        TARGET(mo)      GMR    TARGET PROFIT

Com      $157,181        $13,098        0.76    $119,457.71
Rom      $132,352        $11,029        0.64     $84,705.28
Ref      $123,200        $10,267        0.38     $46,816.00
Sfi      $113,080         $9,423        0.72     $81,417.60
Bus       $95,150         $7,929        0.34     $32,351.00
Spo       $72,600         $6,050        0.51     $37,026.00
Bio       $59,400         $4,950        0.48     $28,512.00
Psy       $56,100         $4,675        0.36     $20,196.00
Pho       $47,300         $3,942        0.28     $13,244.00
 —
```

as long as E.LEGH remained TRUE, columns 3 and 5 for all subsequent queries would have the same headings unless the corresponding #LEGEND elements were given different or null values. Jack executed the commands

```
#title=""
e.legh=false
```

to take away the #TITLE value and to turn off the use of #LEGEND for headings. He also switched E.SPAC back to a value of 1.

Cosmetic Pros and Cons

Reminiscing, Joy observed, "The use of pictures, legends, and titles for queries does not in any way affect the information content of query results. They just allow you to make cosmetic changes to the presentation of that content. For many ad hoc queries you probably won't want to bother with cosmetics, but just take the results as they naturally occur. On the other hand, there will be situations where you'll want a printout of query results, which you'll keep for future reference. In that case, you may well want to dress up the results so you won't have to recall what calculation T01 referred to and so you can readily tell one printout from another by looking at its title."

"I agree," Jack confirmed. "For queries to the console, I usually don't bother with cosmetics. But with a little extra effort, you can make query printouts more attractive, not only for your own use, but for presentation to others as well. It gives a way of generating quick, clean reports. But as good as this is, as we delve deeper into the environment we'll discover something far more attractive."

Joy looked at him and smiled, for she knew what he had in mind. Very fancy and elaborate reports could be custom-built with a knowledge management technique known as report generation. Compared to ad hoc queries, this technique gives extensive control over the layout of values and titles in a formal report. Formal report generation is discussed in Chapter 10.

CONDITIONAL QUERIES

To this point Jack had covered *unconditional queries*. These are queries whose results contain one line for each record existing in a table. In contrast, a *conditional query* usually will result in fewer lines than there are records in the table. This is because it has a condition that excludes undesired records from being processed. In this environment, any of the conditions that could be specified for data management commands (e.g., OBTAIN, BROWSE, CONVERT, CHANGE in Chapters 6 and 7) can also be specified in a query. As with data management commands, a query condition can begin with either the word WHERE or FOR and it consists of a logical expression.

"I think you can begin to appreciate the real power of ad hoc queries when you incorporate conditions into them," Jack asserted. "As a complement to everything you already know about queries you can add everything you already know about conditions. When you pose a conditional query for some table, a line will be displayed for each record whose field values make that condition TRUE. As you might expect, a query condition can include not only fields but also references to working variables, utility variables, functions, array elements, and other things we've not even discussed yet.

"Let's say we want to quickly identify all performance records that were below quota in both of the first two quarters in order to take corrective action. Clearly we don't want to have to eyeball all of the PERF records, so we let the environment do it for us with a conditional query. Watch."

FIGURE 8–14   Conditional queries

```
_select fname pid q1 s1 q2 s2 from perf where s1<q1 & s2<q2
 FNAME    PID   Q1   S1     Q2    S2

Tina      rom   5000  4590   4678  3997
Kerry     ref   6030  5590   4985  4880
_select fname pid q1 s1 q2 s2 from perf where s1<q1 or s2<q2
 FNAME    PID   Q1   S1     Q2    S2

Kim       bus   7320  6854   8050  8120
Kim       ref   6040  7024   8309  7732
Kim       spo   5400  6240   6300  5995
Kris      psy   8090  7540   6209  7900
Tina      bus   6903  5944   7538  10359
Tina      rom   5000  4590   4678  3997
Toby      psy   5000  2607   4006  4839
Toby      rom   4982  5009   4678  3997
Kerry     ref   6030  5590   4985  4880
Kathy     pho   8553  7864   7543  7903
Kathy     ref   4679  5032   5368  4002
Jackie    ref   5004  4996   4678  5400
 —
```

To demonstrate Jack executed the query

```
select fname pid q1 s1 q2 s2 from perf where s1 < q1 & s2 < q2
```

pointing out that it had a compound condition composed of the conjunction of two relational expressions. The immediate result was that the six selected field values were displayed for each of the two records satisfying the condition.

"How would you expand to get all those records that fell short of quota in either of the first two quarters?" Brad asked.

Jack pressed ^Z to bring back the last query and edited it so that the OR operator now appeared in place of the condition's AND (&) operator. He pressed the Enter key to execute this new query, leaving the screen with the appearance shown in Figure 8–14.

He then executed another query, intending to discover those performance records for which the improvement in second quarter sales over first quarter sales exceeded the improvement expected with respect to quotas. This query was

```
select fname pid q1 s1 q2 s2 q2-q1 s2-s1 from perf where s2-s1> q2-q1 & q2 > q1
```

FIGURE 8–15   Query conditions involving numeric calculations

```
_select fname pid q1 s1 q2 s2 q2-q1 s2-s1 from perf where s2-s1>q2-q1 & q2>q1
   FNAME    PID   Q1      S1      Q2      S2        TO1            TO2

Kim        bus   7320    6854    8050    8120      730.00         1266.00
Kris       rom   9003   10050   10229   12453     1226.00         2403.00
Kevin      bus   3009    4321    4321    6500     1312.00         2179.00
Tina       bus   6903    5944    7538   10359      635.00         4415.00
Carol      bus   3997    4005    4378    4436      381.00          431.00
_select fname pid q1 s1 (s1-q1)/q1  from perf where (s1-q1)/q1>= .13
   FNAME    PID   Q1      S1         TO1

Kim        ref   6040    7024       0.16
Kim        spo   5400    6240       0.16
Kevin      bus   3009    4321       0.44
Kevin      ref   3214    4222       0.31
Kevin      spo   6509    7773       0.19
Tina       psy   3214    4222       0.31
Kerry      pho  10700   12222       0.14
Karen      bus  10700   12222       0.14
Carol      com   6903    8488       0.23
  —
```

with the second part of the condition ensuring that only those records
for which there is an expected improvement would be considered. As
shown in Figure 8–15, the results show that business books tended to
be ahead of the expected pace. Also shown are the results of another
query that identifies those performance records whose sales in quarter
1 exceeded their corresponding quotas by at least 13 percent.

"How about an analysis of the business, romance, and computer
lines?" Dan asked. "I'd like to see how far along each rep is in meeting
the annual objectives for these products in terms of both the ratio of
sales to quota and a comparison of how much will have to be sold in
the fourth quarter (if any) versus the fourth quarter quota."

Jack responded by executing the query

```
select fname,pid,sytd,qyr,sytd/qyr,max(qyr-sytd,0) using "fffff",q4,q4>qyr-sytd
from perf where pid in ["bus","rom","com"]
```

producing the screen appearance shown in Figure 8–16. Notice that
the query was too long to fit on a single line. Nevertheless, Jack just
kept on typing without pressing the Enter key until he reached the

FIGURE 8–16   Analysis of year-to-date sales for certain products

```
_select fname,pid,sytd,qyr,sytd/qyr,max(qyr-sytd,0) using "fffff",q4,q4>qyr-sytd
 from perf where pid in ["bus","rom","com"]
   FNAME    PID   SYTD    QYR     T01     T02        Q4      T03

  Kim       bus   21882   30273   0.72    8391      8503    TRUE
  Kris      rom   30535   38912   0.78    8377     11340    TRUE
  Kevin     bus   13330   13575   0.98     245      3456    TRUE
  Tina      bus   24307   32742   0.74    8435      9311    TRUE
  Tina      com   23874   25667   0.93    1793      7980    TRUE
  Tina      rom   13619   17889   0.76    4270      3998    FALSE
  Toby      bus   14909   19130   0.78    4221      4980    TRUE
  Toby      rom   18043   25836   0.70    7793      7432    FALSE
  Karen     bus   32534   38082   0.85    5548      7930    TRUE
  Karen     com   34786   43630   0.80    8844      9665    TRUE
  Karen     rom   18894   23281   0.81    4387      6666    TRUE
  Carol     bus   13439   17108   0.79    3669      3901    TRUE
  Carol     com   24830   27272   0.91    2442      8456    TRUE
  Carol     rom   16945   22525   0.75    5580      7223    TRUE
  _
```

very end. In general, as a command of any kind is being entered, it will automatically wrap around to succeeding lines on the screen as needed. The results of this query show the raw SYTD and QYR values for the desired product lines. The T01 column displays the percentage of sales relative to quota. The next two columns compare the amount yet needed to meet the annual quota versus the fourth quarter quota. The last column flags as TRUE those lines where sales are ahead of the expected pace.

"As I think you can see," Jack declared, "your imagination is about the only real constraint on what queries you may want to ask about a table's content."

MULTITABLE INQUIRY

As Joy had explained to Jack, relational calculus allows data to be garnered from two or more tables in a single operation. It obviates the need to put together a proper procedure of PROJECT, JOIN, and algebraic SELECT commands in order to produce a table with the desired data. A SELECT query is a realization of the nonprocedural relational calculus approach to retrieval. One query can display results where each line is based on related data from multiple tables [3].

"In all of your query examples," observed Stan, "you've dealt with but· one table at a time. I can think of many situations where I'd like to see related data from more than one table all at once. For example, suppose I'd like to examine the performance data for products having a commission rate of at least 2.4 percent and included there I'd like to see the year-to-date commissions paid for each. Of course this involves related records stored in the PERF and PROD tables. Neither table by itself would have enough data to address my ad hoc needs. Obviously, I could use a CONVERT command to produce a new table having all the related data and then execute LIST or SELECT to take a look at it. But it sure would be nice if I didn't have to produce a new table just to get at the data I'm interested in. I mean for an ad hoc query process to be useful we shouldn't have to get bogged down in doing data management, right?"

"Right," affirmed Jack. "It turns out that you are free to specify multiple tables in a SELECT command, just as you learned how to do in a CONVERT command. But there's a big difference. Query results are displayed directly to you, whereas CONVERT results in a table. So to pose your query, you could type something like this."

Jack typed the query

```
select perf.tid, perf.pid, prod.pname, perf.sytd*prod.crate
from perf from prod where perf.pid =prod.pid & prod.crate ge .024
```

in which he prefaced each field name by its table name. Also unlike the earlier queries, he indicated two tables from which the data were to be retrieved and included a record-matching criterion in the query's condition. This criterion says that a PERF record is to be considered as being related to a PROD record if their PID values are equal. He pressed the Enter key to produce the results shown in the top portion of Figure 8–17.

"In the case of CONVERT, the order in which we specified the tables made a difference," recalled Debbie. "Do we use the same convention with a query?"

"Yes," confirmed Jack. "You just specify the table with the most detailed data first. PERF has more detailed data than PROD. Or, to use Joy's terminology, in a proper query a table will have a many-to-one relationship with the table that follows it. There can be many PERF records having the same PID value as one, but no more than one, PROD record."

"Right," chimed Joy. "For each PERF record, the environment will

FIGURE 8–17 Processing two tables with a single query

```
_select perf.tid, perf.pid, prod.pname, perf.sytd*prod.crate from perf from prod
 where perf.pid=prod.pid & prod.crate ge .024
 TID  PID       PNAME                 TO1

 1    rom   romance                 732.84
 2    sfi   science fiction         778.23
 3    com   computers               668.47
 3    rom   romance                 326.86
 4    rom   romance                 433.03
 6    com   computers               974.01
 6    rom   romance                 453.46
 7    sfi   science fiction         335.72
 9    com   computers               695.24
 9    rom   romance                 406.68
 _select tid, pid, prod.pname, sytd*prod.crate from perf from prod where pid=prod
 .pid & prod.crate gt .024
 TID  PID       PNAME                 TO1

 2    sfi   science fiction         778.23
 3    com   computers               668.47
 6    com   computers               974.01
 7    sfi   science fiction         335.72
 9    com   computers               695.24
 _
```

find the one PROD record with the same PID value. The values of these two records are used to produce a line in the result you see. For this query there were 10 such matches that also satisfied the desired commission rate level of at least 2.4 percent."

Shortening Long Queries

"I realize that we're asking for more in a multitable query, but isn't there some way to make such queries shorter?" inquired Brad.

"There are several ways," Jack answered. "For one, we really don't have to preface every field name by its table name. Fields from the first table you specify in a query can be unadorned."

To demonstrate, he pressed ^Z and edited the previous query by eliminating every PERF preface to a field. He also changed the second part of the condition, to restrict the query to only those PROD records having commission rates in excess of 2.4 percent. On executing this query, the screen appeared as shown in Figure 8–17.

"As you know," Jack continued, "macros or function keys can also be used to reduce typing effort. Suppose you frequently want to ask queries involving records in PERF and PROD that are related on the basis of the redundant PID field. Then it would make sense to define a macro, say PP, for that part of the queries that's always the same."

As he spoke, Joy wrote the corresponding MACRO command

```
macro pp from perf from prod where pid=prod.pid
```

on the whiteboard. Any query involving fields from the two tables could now make use of this macro. For instance, the just executed query could now be more compactly expressed as

```
select tid,pid,prod.pname,sytd*prod.crate pp & prod.crate gt .024
```

For even further compaction, Jack suggested that macros such as

```
macro pn prod.pname
macro pcr prod.crate
```

could be specified for PROD fields. The same query could then be expressed as

```
select tid,pid,pn,sytd*pcr pp & pcr gt .024
```

"How about using the natural language interface?" asked Debbie. "With it we could be very concise and not even have to indicate what tables contain the desired data."

"If you do so," Jack advised, "be sure to have the preview feature turned on so you can see the query generated by your request. Check it closely to be sure it's what you intended."

"That's good advice," Joy added. "Remember that there is always a possibility that a natural language request may not be interpreted as you intended. As the requests become more complex, it's only natural that this likelihood increases. In contrast, using the command interface to issue a SELECT query leaves little room for misinterpretation because it is a very structured language."

Querying More than Two Tables at Once

"It's pretty clear how we can use SELECT to query two tables at a time," Pete remarked. "But what about three tables? For example, we might want the query you just made expanded so that each line shows the related rep name."

"No matter how many tables are involved," Jack responded, "we use the same basic approach. Put the most detailed table first, preface fields from the other tables by their field names, and remember to include the desired intertable matching criteria for the second and each succeeding table."

He pressed ^Z to bring back the former query (i.e., the second query in Figure 8–17). As Pete desired, he edited it to include REP.NAME as the first column to be displayed. He inserted a picture for the calculation's results and added

```
from rep where tid=rep.tid
```

to the end of the query. He pressed the Enter key to execute this query. The result was the same as before, except each of the five lines now began with the appropriate rep name. To show them that the query could also be conditioned on the REP table's data, without even displaying that data, Jack pressed ^Z. He edited the query by eliminating the CRATE restriction from the PROD condition and adding

```
& rep.state="IN"
```

to the REP condition, explaining that he wanted to focus on the Indiana performances. When he executed this query, the screen appeared as shown in Figure 8–18.

Joy elaborated, "Notice that for each table after the first, you'll have a condition indicating what field in that table is to be mated with what field in a previously specified table. The PROD condition mates its PID with the PERF table's PID. The REP condition mates its TID with the PERF table's TID. It's interesting that in this single query, we've made use of the many-to-many relationship existing between products and reps. A rep can sell many products and a product can be sold by many reps. We utilized this relationship by means of two many-to-one relationships: PERF to PROD and PERF to REP."

"Would it make any difference if REP and its condition switched places with PROD and its condition?" Tracey inquired.

"No," replied Jack. "Since each is mated with PERF and not with each other, the only requirement is that they must follow PERF, which has the most detailed data."

"I take it we can have a condition for the PERF table if we so desire," Don speculated.

"Sure," Jack responded. "However, it should not involve fields from any table other than PERF. Similarly, the second table's condition should not involve fields in tables that have yet to be specified. It can reference PERF and PROD fields. In general, a condition can refer to fields of any tables that have been identified previously in the query."

FIGURE 8–18   Processing three tables with a single query

```
_select rep.name, tid, pid, prod.pname, sytd*prod.crate using "$ff,fff.dd" from
perf from prod where pid=prod.pid & prod.crate > .024 from rep where tid=rep.tid

         NAME          TID PID      PNAME           TO1

Kevin R. Andrews       2    sfi  science fiction    $778.23
Tina F. Lee            3    com  computers          $668.47
Karen V. Bruckner      6    com  computers          $974.01
Kathy F. Smith         7    sfi  science fiction    $335.72
Carol O. Lynn          9    com  computers          $695.24
_select rep.name, tid, pid, prod.pname, sytd*prod.crate using "$ff,fff.dd" from
perf from prod where pid=prod.pid from rep where tid=rep.tid & rep.state="IN"
         NAME          TID PID      PNAME           TO1

Tina F. Lee            3    bus  business           $534.75
Tina F. Lee            3    com  computers          $668.47
Tina F. Lee            3    psy  psychology         $182.25
Tina F. Lee            3    rom  romance            $326.86
Toby C. Terry          4    bus  business           $328.00
Toby C. Terry          4    psy  psychology         $260.93
Toby C. Terry          4    rom  romance            $433.03
 —
```

Motioning to the top of the Figure 8–18 screen, Don said, "So the restriction on commission rate could be included in the REP condition if we wanted."

"Right," nodded Joy, "but it's probably more efficient to include it in the PROD condition since it refers exclusively to data held in the PROD table. Speaking of efficiency, if the second or subsequent table in a query has an index, its condition can be replaced by a PLUCK command. Thus PLUCK PID could replace WHERE PID=PROD.PID if PROD had an index based on product ID in use. Had PROD been a large table, plucking would have been noticeably faster than the condition Jack used."

DYNAMIC SORTING

"Earlier," Jack reminded them, "you worked with a data management command named SORT. It actually changed the order of records in a table. Well, you can also do sorting within an ad hoc query. But this will not affect the order of records in the table or tables you are querying. It affects only the ordering of lines in the query's result. It is therefore referred to as *dynamic sorting*.

"Any of the queries we've looked at so far and, in fact, all that we will look at can be amended with an ORDER BY clause to cause the resulting lines to be dynamically sorted. Because you know how to specify an order in the SORT command, you also already know how to do the same thing in a query's ORDER BY clause. A few examples should sort of refresh your memories."

Jack executed the command

```
select tid name spouse addr from rep order by ascending lname fname
```

where the query results were to be sorted first on the basis of LNAME values and secondarily on the basis of FNAME values. Notice that it is permissible to order the query results based on fields that are not included in those results. As Figure 8–19 shows, this query does not produce LNAME or FNAME columns, yet the lines are ordered by those fields.

"I presume," noted Debbie, "we can leave out the ASCENDING if we want to, just as we could with the SORT and INDEX commands."

Nodding, Jack pressed ^Z to edit the former query. He eliminated the ASCENDING and inserted a condition prior to the ORDER BY clause. On executing this query, the screen took on the appearance portrayed in Figure 8–19. The condition restricted the resultant lines to those reps with spouses and these lines were ordered by ascending LNAME and FNAME values. As with all queries, neither command in Figure 8–19 affected the table contents.

Mixing Orders

"I also assume," Debbie continued, "we can have a mixture of ascending and descending orders, just as we did with data management commands."

"Sure," Jack responded. "In general, you can have as many fields as you like and any can be prefaced by ASCENDING or DESCENDING. Or you can use the AZ and ZA synonyms for these two words if you like. Your ORDER BY fields can actually come from different tables if that's what you want. Let's say we need to see the first quarter quotas for the reps where the commission rates are above 2.2 percent. We might want the results ordered by product ID and within each product ID the lines should be ordered by descending quota."

With that, Jack executed the command

```
select pid prod.name q1 fname from perf from prod
where prod.crate gt .022 & pid=prod.pid order by pid, descending q1
```

FIGURE 8–19   Dynamic sorting of a query's results

```
_select tid name spouse addr from rep order by ascending lname fname
TID          NAME            SPOUSE            ADDR

0    Kim G. Anders                     8242 Wabash, Chicago IL 68909
2    Kevin R. Andrews     Kris         25 Stratton Ave, Bloomington IL 54321
6    Karen V. Bruckner                 44 Tan Ave., Madison WI 66667
5    Kerry H. Jones       Kendra       128 Spiceland, Grand Rapids MI 35988
3    Tina F. Lee          Ben          7892 Meridian, Indianapolis IN 46662
9    Carol O. Lynn                     58 Cater Dr., Midland MI 40098
1    Kris H. Raber        Kevin        314 Miami, Dayton OH 46783
8    Jackie V. Smith      David        32 New Jersey, Columbus OH 33464
7    Kathy F. Smith       Tom          85 Griese Ln, Milwaukee WI 65543
4    Toby C. Terry                     2028 Prescott, Fort Wayne IN 45567
_select tid name spouse addr from rep where spouse ne " " order by lname fname
TID          NAME            SPOUSE            ADDR

2    Kevin R. Andrews     Kris         25 Stratton Ave, Bloomington IL 54321
5    Kerry H. Jones       Kendra       128 Spiceland, Grand Rapids MI 35988
3    Tina F. Lee          Ben          7892 Meridian, Indianapolis IN 46662
1    Kris H. Raber        Kevin        314 Miami, Dayton OH 46783
8    Jackie V. Smith      David        32 New Jersey, Columbus OH 33464
7    Kathy F. Smith       Tom          85 Griese Ln, Milwaukee WI 65543
_
```

yielding the screen appearance in Figure 8–20. As usual, a comma in the query is optional and could be omitted if desired. Motioning to the results, Jack commented that this ordering made it very easy to quickly see the progression from highest to lowest quota for each of the high-commission product lines. If the query results were not ordered, such patterns would not be as obvious.

Ordering by Calculations

"There's one other aspect of dynamic sorting that I'd like to mention," Jack announced. "It can sometimes be very useful to include full-blown expressions in an ORDER BY clause. You're not limited to ordering by existing field values, but can order by the values of calculations involving fields, variables, functions, and so forth. Let's take an example."

He proceeded to execute the command

```
select fname pid s1 q1 s1-q1 using "fffff" from perf
where pid in ["rom","bus","com","ref"] order by fname, descending s1-q1
```

FIGURE 8–20   Mixed ordering for a multitable query

```
_select pid prod.pname q1 fname from perf from prod where prod.crate gt .022 &
pid=prod.pid order by pid, descending q1
PID        PNAME          Q1      FNAME

com computers            12090   Karen
com computers             6903   Carol
com computers             5388   Tina
rom romance               9003   Kris
rom romance               6040   Karen
rom romance               5004   Carol
rom romance               5000   Tina
rom romance               4982   Toby
sfi science fiction       9439   Kevin
sfi science fiction       4339   Kathy
spo sports                6509   Kevin
spo sports                5400   Kim
spo sports                5004   Jackie
_
```

leaving the screen as depicted in Figure 8–21. Notice that the results
are ordered first by ascending FNAME values. Secondly, within each
group of repeated FNAME values, the lines are ordered from best performance to worst where the difference between sales and quota is taken
as a measure of goodness. Again, the ordering of query results gives
a convenient way for seeing certain patterns. Carol did best for computer
books and "worst" for business books. The same happened to be true
for Tina's performance, while Karen did very well for both of those
product lines. Such patterns would be more difficult to visualize if the
results had not been ordered. Jack mentioned that they would later
see more graphic ways to visualize data patterns (Chapter 11).

Dynamic versus Static Ordering

"I see the value of having query results sorted in certain orders," Brad
remarked. "But if you had already used SORT to put the table's records
in the desired order, you wouldn't need to bother with an ORDER BY
clause when making a query."

"That's true," Jack reacted. "If there's a particular order that you
tend to use repeatedly when querying a table, then it makes sense to

FIGURE 8–21 Query ordering based on calculations

```
_select fname pid s1 q1 s1-q1 using "fffff" from perf where pid in ["rom",bus",
"com","ref"] order by fname, descending s1-q1
  FNAME   PID   S1     Q1     T01

Carol    com   8488   6903   1585
Carol    rom   5345   5004    341
Carol    bus   4005   3997      8
Jackie   ref   4996   5004     -8
Karen    bus  12222  10700   1522
Karen    com  13121  12090   1031
Karen    rom   6090   6040     50
Kathy    ref   5032   4679    353
Kerry    ref   5590   6030   -440
Kevin    bus   4321   3009   1312
Kevin    ref   4222   3214   1008
Kim      ref   7024   6040    984
Kim      bus   6854   7320   -466
Kris     rom  10050   9003   1047
Tina     com   5944   5388    556
Tina     rom   4590   5000   -410
Tina     bus   5944   6903   -959
Toby     bus   5003   4842    161
Toby     rom   5009   4982     27
—
```

SORT the table into that order in advance. That would not only save you from repeatedly specifying the same ORDER BY clause, it would give faster query processing. The software wouldn't have to take time to sort query results in the same order over and over again for separate queries."

As he said this, Joy was reminded of Jack's keen interest in relations the prior evening. She made a mental note to later tell him that his suggestion would not be feasible for software that strictly confines itself to the relational data model. This is because the relational data model has no concept of an ordering for the records held in a table. Its access languages have no counterpart to the SORT command, relying exclusively on dynamic sorting. Nevertheless, his suggestion was useful for the knowledge management environment.

"But," Jack emphasized, "beyond your favorite sorted order, there will usually be lots of other orders you'll want to explore on an ad hoc basis. For these, dynamic sorting is best. Obviously, the dynamic sorting of a query's results will typically be faster than SORT. The query sorts only a selected subset of the table's data, whereas SORT has to sort all the records. Also, if the table is indexed, it will have to be reindexed after SORT, while queries don't affect indexes."

FIGURE 8–22   The UNIQUE qualifier in a query

```
_select unique fname pid s1 q1 s1-q1 using "fffff" from perf where pid in ["rom"
,"bus","com","ref"]order by fname, descending s1-q1
  FNAME  PID    S1     Q1     T01

Carol    com   8488   6903   1585
         rom   5345   5004    341
         bus   4005   3997      8
Jackie   ref   4996   5004     -8
Karen    bus  12222  10700   1522
         com  13121  12090   1031
         rom   6090   6040     50
Kathy    ref   5032   4679    353
Kerry    ref   5590   6030   -440
Kevin    bus   4321   3009   1312
         ref   4222   3214   1008
Kim      ref   7024   6040    984
         bus   6854   7320   -466
Kris     rom  10050   9003   1047
Tina     com   5944   5388    556
         rom   4590   5000   -410
         bus   5944   6903   -959
Toby     bus   5003   4842    161
         rom   5009   4982     27
  _
```

"That makes sense," said Brad, "and when I do have a frequently needed order that's different from the table's order, I can just define a one- or two-keystroke macro for the entire ORDER BY clause if I want."

"That's right. It seems that you have it all sorted out now," chuckled Jack.

THE UNIQUE QUALIFIER

Pointing at the results from the last query (Figure 8–21), Jack said, "There's one slight problem with this. As your eyes scan the first column, they tend to read the same names again and again. In my opinion it would be visually cleaner if, once a rep name appears, it wasn't repeated in successive lines. In other words, I'd like to see each name appear uniquely in the first column. Well, it turns out that this is very easy to do."

Jack pressed ^Z to bring back the former query. He edited it by simply inserting the word UNIQUE in front of FNAME. Execution of the resultant query produced the screen shown in Figure 8–22. Notice that the query result is the same as that of Figure 8–21, except successive values of the same first name are not repeated. For presentation pur-

FIGURE 8–23   Multiple UNIQUE qualifiers in a query

```
_select unique pid, fname, q1, q2, q3, q4, qyr, sytd, unique major from perf whe
re pid in ["r*","b*"] order by pid sytd
PID    FNAME     Q1      Q2      Q3      Q4      QYR     STYD   MAJOR

bio Jackie     4339    4228    3989    4867   17423   11990  true
    Kris       7400    6290    7200    8005   28895   22858
bus Kevin      3009    4321    2789    3456   13575   13330  false
    Carol      3997    4378    4832    3901   17108   13439  true
    Toby       4842    4006    5302    4980   19130   14909
    Kim        7320    8050    6400    8503   30273   21882
    Tina       6903    7538    8990    9311   32742   24307
    Karen     10700   11009    8443    7930   38082   32534
ref Kevin      3214    2345    3256    6112   14927   10125  false
    Kathy      4679    5368    5002    3998   19047   13432  true
    Jackie     5004    4678    3998    6012   19692   13996
    Kerry      6030    4985    3001    5883   19899   16790
    Kim        6040    8309    7844    9402   31595   22846
rom Tina       5000    4678    4213    3998   17889   13619
    Carol      5004    4468    5830    7223   22525   16945
    Toby       4982    4678    8744    7432   25836   18043
    Karen      6040    5020    5555    6666   23281   18894
    Kris       9003   10229    8340   11340   38912   30535
_
```

poses, many people would find this more palatable than the repetition that results when UNIQUE is not employed.

"Are there any restrictions on which field or calculation UNIQUE can be used with?" asked Dan.

"Not really," Jack replied. "If I had put it in front of PID instead of FNAME, no blank entries would appear in the FNAME column. However, there would have been three in the PID column: one each for Kerry's and Kim's ref lines, plus one for Toby's bus line. Sometimes, you may want to designate more than one column in the same query to be unique."

To demonstrate this, he executed the command

```
select unique pid, fname, q1, q2, q3, q4, qyr, sytd, unique major
from perf where pid in ["r*","b*"] order by pid sytd
```

producing the screen appearance shown in Figure 8–23. Interpreting the MAJOR column, Jack explained that biography is a major product for Kris, business books are major products for Toby through Karen, and all lines from Jackie's reference onward are for major products.

CONTROL BREAK GROUPING

"We can make the distinction between groups of lines even more pronounced," Jack claimed, "by having space left between groups in the displayed results of a query. This is done by including a GROUP BY clause before a query's ORDER BY clause. It indicates what field should be used as a basis for grouping lines in the query's display. The spacing between groups will be one blank line if we switch E.SECB from its FALSE default to a value of TRUE. Let me show you what I mean."

After letting E.SECB have a TRUE value, Jack executed the query

```
select unique tid, unique fname, pid, s1, q1, (s1/q1)*100 using "fff.dd%%"
from perf where tid>"4" group by tid order by tid, za s1/q1
```

resulting in the screen appearance portrayed in Figure 8–24. The lines are ordered by TID and, for each TID value, by the descending ratio of first quarter sales to quota. The lines are grouped by TID, with a visual break occurring between groups. Notice that both TID and FNAME have UNIQUE qualifiers that suppress the repetition of their values within a group.

"In computer jargon," Joy explained, "a *control break* is said to occur whenever the TID value in one line differs from that of the previous line. Whenever a control break happens, a line is skipped before displaying the next group. If Jack had left E.SECB at its FALSE setting, an automatic eject would have happened before displaying the next group. That is, only one group at a time would be displayed on the screen or, if E.OPRN were TRUE, only one group would be printed per page. By letting E.SECB be TRUE, we suppress the automatic eject at control breaks."

Motioning toward the query's results, Jack resumed, "Notice how easy it is to get an impression of first quarter performance for each rep. We can quickly see that Carol and Karen have beaten their quotas on every product line, while each of the others has fallen short for one product. Kerry is at only 92.7 percent of his reference quota, Kathy at only 92.18 percent of her photography quota, and Jackie barely missed her reference quota."

"How would you group the same records into just two groups: those that met their respective quotas and those that didn't?" Stan inquired.

Jack thought for a moment before responding, "That's a good question because it illustrates that we can group not only by individual fields but also by calculation results. In this case, we'll want the environment to calculate whether S1 exceeds Q1 for each line and group the lines on that basis."

FIGURE 8–24   Grouping of query results based on a field

```
_e.secb=true
_select unique tid, unique fname, pid, s1, q1, (s1/q1)*100 using "fff.dd%%" from
 perf where tid>"4" group by tid order by tid, za s1/q1
 TID   FNAME  PID   S1     Q1     TO1

 5    Kerry   pho   12222  10700  114.22%
             psy    5003   4842  103.33%
             ref    5590   6030   92.70%

 6    Karen   bus   12222  10700  114.22%
             com   13121  12090  108.53%
             rom    6090   6040  100.83%

 7    Kathy   ref    5032   4679  107.54%
             sfi    4360   4339  100.48%
             pho    7884   8553   92.18%

 8    Jackie  spo    5345   5004  106.81%
             bio    4360   4339  100.48%
             ref    4996   5004   99.84%

 9 .  Carol   com    8488   6903  122.96%
             rom    5345   5004  106.81%
             bus    4005   3997  100.20%
 _
```

To demonstrate, Jack pressed ˆZ and edited the former query's GROUP BY and ORDER BY clauses to get the command

```
select unique tid, unique fname, pid, s1, q1, (s1/q1)*100 using "fff.dd%%"
from perf where tid>"4" group by s1>q1 order by za s1/q1
```

which he executed by pressing the Enter key. The screen now appeared as shown in Figure 8–25. The results were ordered by descending S1 to Q1 ratios (i.e., descending levels of performance in percentage terms). They were grouped based on the logical calculation of S1>Q1. Lines in the first group all have TRUE values for this calculation, while those in the second group all have FALSE values for it.

"What about subgroups?" asked Debbie. "Let's say we need to see first quarter performance grouped first by product ID and then, within each product group, a further grouping into those that met their quotas and those that didn't."

Jack explained that they were free to identify multiple grouping criteria in a GROUP BY clause. He demonstrated by executing the command

```
select unique pid fname s1 q1 (s1/q1)*100 using "fff.dd%%" from perf
where pid in ["rom","ref","psy"] group by pid, q1>s1 order by pid, za s1/q1
```

FIGURE 8–25   Grouping of query results based on a calculation

```
_select unique tid, unique fname, pid, s1, q1, (s1/q1)*100 using "fff.dd%%" from
  perf where tid >"4" group by s1>q1 order by za s1/q1
TID   FNAME   PID   S1      Q1      TO1

9     Carol   com   8488    6903    122.96%
6     Karen   bus   12222   10700   114.22%
5     Kerry   pho   12222   10700   114.22%
6     Karen   com   13121   12090   108.53%
7     Kathy   ref   5032    4679    107.54%
9     Carol   rom   5345    5004    106.81%
8     Jackie  spo   5345    5004    106.81%
5     Kerry   psy   5003    4842    103.33%
6     Karen   rom   6090    6040    100.83%
8     Jackie  bio   4360    4339    100.48%
7     Kathy   sfi   4360    4339    100.48%
9     Carol   bus   4005    3997    100.20%

8     Jackie  ref   4996    5004    99.84%
5     Kerry   ref   5590    6030    92.70%
7     Kathy   pho   7884    8553    92.18%
—
```

to satisfy Debbie's query. This yielded results as shown in Figure 8–26. The lines are ordered by PID and secondarily by descending S1 to Q1 ratios. They are grouped first by PID and secondly by whether Q1 exceeded S1. Thus there are two subgroups for each product ID.

"Grouping can help when you're groping," Jack paused and smiled, "for knowledge that's in a table but not immediately obvious."

STATISTICS GENERATION

"As you know," Jack continued, "sometimes our decisions don't depend solely on seeing individual data values. They may also depend on various *statistics* such as counts, sums, averages, minimums, and maximums. The statisticians among you may also be interested in standard deviations and variances. In this environment there are a couple of ways to generate statistics. They can accompany individual data values in the results of ad hoc queries. Alternatively, you can get statistical summaries without seeing any individual data values if you like. In either case, generated statistics are automatically stored as values of elements in special utility arrays so you can later make use of them as desired."

FIGURE 8–26   Multiple grouping criteria

```
_select unique pid fname s1 q1 (s1/q1)*100 using "fff.dd%%" from perf where pid
in ["rom","ref","psy"] group by pid, q1>s1 order by pid, za s1/q1
PID   FNAME    S1     Q1     T02

psy Tina     4222   3214  131.36%
    Kerry    5003   4842  103.33%

psy Kris     7540   8090   93.20%
    Toby     2607   5000   52.14%

ref Kevin    4222   3214  131.36%
    Kim      7024   6040  116.29%
    Kathy    5032   4679  107.54%

ref Jackie   4996   5004   99.94%
    Kerry    5590   6030   92.70%

rom Kris    10050   9003  111.63%
    Carol    5345   5004  106.81%
    Karen    6090   6040  100.83%
    Toby     5009   4982  100.54%

rom Tina     4590   5000   91.80%
 —
```

Queries with Automatic Statistics

Jack reminded them that at the outset of their exploration of ad hoc queries, he had switched E.STAT to FALSE. He now let E.STAT be TRUE, explaining that customary ad hoc query results would now be augmented by a statistical summary for each displayed column. To illustrate, he executed the query

```
select * from prod
```

which left the screen appearance as shown in Figure 8–27. For each numeric column six statistics are generated: sum, average, variance, standard deviation, minimum, and maximum. If a statistic is too large to be displayed for its column's picture, asterisks appear (e.g., the TAR-GET variance). For string columns, only the minimum and maximum values are displayed. The count statistic is simply the number of observations (i.e., lines of data values) produced by the query.

Jack explained that there are seven environment variables that control which statistics are to be displayed. These are:

FIGURE 8–27   Full statistics for each query column

```
_e.stat=true
_select * from prod
PID        PNAME           TARGET  GMR CRATE

com computers             157181 0.76 0.028
rom romance               132352 0.64 0.024
ref reference             123200 0.38 0.019
sfi science fiction       113080 0.72 0.028
bus business               95150 0.34 0.022
spo sports                 72600 0.51 0.023
bio biography              59400 0.48 0.022
psy psychology             56100 0.36 0.018
pho photography            47300 0.28 0.020

                          856363 4.47 0.204 Sum
                           95151 0.50 0.023 Ave
                          ****** 0.03 0.000 Var
                           38635 0.17 0.004 Sdv
bio biography              47300 0.28 0.018 Min
spo sports                157181 0.76 0.028 Max

Number of Observations: 9
_
```

E.DSUM   E.DMIN
E.DAVE   E.DMAX
E.DVAR   E.DCNT
E.DSDV

Each is logical in type and has a default value of TRUE, meaning that its corresponding statistic will be displayed. "If you're not interested in displaying one or another statistic," Jack advised, "just switch its environment variable to FALSE. For instance, I'll suppress the variance, standard deviation, minimum, and count statistics for our next query. In that query, I want to explore how much of the fourth quarter quota needs to be made in order to meet the annual quota for business books."

After setting the four environment variables to FALSE, Jack executed the query

```
select tid,fname,sytd,qyr,qyr-sytd using "fffff",q4,((qyr-sytd)/q4)*100
using "fff.dd%%" from perf where pid ="bus" order by (qyr-sytd)/q4
```

producing the results shown in Figure 8–28. Notice that Kevin needs to achieve only 7.09 percent of his fourth quarter quota in order to meet his annual quota. At the other extreme, Kim will need to make

FIGURE 8–28   Query displaying statistics subsets for fields and calculations

```
_e.dvar=false
_e.dsdv=false
_e.dcnt=false
_e.dmin=false
_select tid,fname,sytd,qyr,qyr-sytd using "fffff",q4,((qyr-sytd)/q4)*100 using
"fff.dd%%" from perf where pid="bus" order by (qyr-sytd)/q4
TID   FNAME   STYD    QYR     TO1     Q4      TO2

2     Kevin   13330   13575   245     3456    7.09%
6     Karen   32534   38082   5548    7930    69.96%
4     Toby    14909   19130   4221    4980    84.76%
3     Tina    24307   32742   8435    9311    90.59%
9     Carol   13439   17108   3669    3901    94.05%
0     Kim     21882   30273   8391    8503    98.68%

              120401  150910  30509   38081   445.14% Sum
              20067   25152   5085    6347    74.19%  Ave
9     Toby    32534   38082   8435    9311    98.68%  Max
_
```

98.68 percent of her fourth quarter quota. Jack pointed out that several
interesting facts could be gleaned from the statistics. Year-to-date business book sales total 120,401 versus the total annual quota of 150,910.
This means a total of 30,509 in new sales need to be generated to meet
the annual quota. Because this is actually less than the total fourth
quarter quota of 38,081, the region is ahead of its expected pace.

"Statistical comparisons are sometimes helpful," asserted Jack. "You
might want to compare one rep's vital statistics to those of another
rep. Or, you may want to compare statistics for different product lines.
These things can be done in a single query by means of the GROUP
BY clause. Not only will a space appear at each control break, statistics
for the preceding group will also appear. Furthermore, statistics across
all groups will be displayed at the very end of the query results." Jack
demonstrated this with the query shown in Figure 8–29.

Statistics Only

It is not always desirable to display all the raw data observations that
go into generating statistics, particularly if large amounts of data are
involved. Nevertheless, statistics may need to be viewed on an ad hoc

FIGURE 8–29 Statistics at a query's control breaks

```
_e.dmax=false
-select unique pid,tid,fname,sytd,qyr,qyr-sytd using "fffff",q4,((qyr-sytd)/q4)*
100 using "fff.dd%%" from perf where pid in ["psy","bio"] group by pid order by
pid, (qyr-sytd)/ q4
PID TID   FNAME   STYD   QYR   TO1   Q4    TO2

bio 1   Kris    22858  28895  6037  8005  75.42%
    8   Jackie  11990  17423  5433  4867 111.63%

            34848  46318 11470 12872 187.04% Sum
            17424  23159  5735  6436  93.52% Ave

psy 3   Tina    10125  14927  4802  6112  78.57%
    1   Kris    23499  29654  6155  7590  81.09%
    5   Kerry   14909  19130  4221  4980  84.76%
    4   Toby    14496  21913  7417  6900 107.49%

            63029  85624 22595 25582 351.91% Sum
            15757  21406  5649  6396  87.98% Ave

            97877 131942 34065 38454 538.96% Sum
            16313  21990  5678  6409  89.83% Ave
_
```

basis. These may be statistics for certain fields and calculational expressions. They may be conditional statistics, pertaining only to data in
certain records. Jack explained that such processing can be accomplished
with the STAT command. "If you know how to state a SELECT command," he asserted, "then you already know how to state a STAT
command. STAT looks like SELECT with a few exceptions. The word
SELECT is replaced by the word STAT, no UNIQUE qualifiers are used,
and no ordering or grouping is specified. A STAT command generates
statistics regardless of the E.STAT setting."

After switching E.STAT to FALSE and E.DMAX to TRUE, he executed three STAT commands as shown in the screen of Figure 8–30.
The first illustrated that statistics could be generated for numeric calculations (e.g., S1−Q1) as well as fields. The second suggested that a condition could be specified to restrict the statistical analysis to data from
certain (e.g., bus) records. His third example showed that multiple tables
could be involved in a statistical analysis and a picture could be specified
for any of the resultant columns of statistics.

FIGURE 8–30 The statistics command

```
_e.stat=false;e.dmax=true
-stat s1 q1 s1-q1 from perf
  S1      Q1         T01

217004 206377      10627.00 Sum
  6576   6254        322.03 Ave
 13121  12090       1585.00 Max
_stat s1 q1 s1-q1 from perf for pid="bus"
  S1      Q1         T01

 38349  36771       1578.00 Sum
  6392   6129        263.00 Ave
 12222  10700       1522.00 Max
_stat s1 q1 s2 q2 s3 q3 prod.crate*(s1+s2+s3) using "$ff,fff.dd" from perf from
prod where prod.pid=pid
  S1      Q1     S2     Q2     S3     Q3       T01

217004 206377 224747 198444212395 204522  $14,748.37 Sum
  6576   6254   6811   6013   6436   6198     $446.92 Ave
 13121  12090  12453  11069  10075  10806     $974.01 Max
 _
```

Using Statistical Results

"It's clear," Dan observed, "that the capability to generate statistics on the fly can be useful in some decision processes. It also seems to me that there will be situations where I've generated statistics, then done some other processing only to discover that I'd like to use those same statistics again. But it's unlikely that I'll have remembered what those statistics were. Is there some way, short of writing them down or printing them out, that we can keep statistics around for later use?"

"I was just getting to that," Jack replied. "Remember that there are some utility variables, like #DATE, whose values are automatically set by the environment for our use. There are also some *statistical utility arrays* whose values are automatically set to hold the most recently computed statistics. For instance, #SUM is a built-in array whose elements' values are the sums generated by the last STAT or SELECT command. The value of #SUM(1) is the first column's sum, #SUM(2) is the second column's sum, and so on. Just like working variables, you can reference any of these elements in commands of your choosing."

FIGURE 8–31   Using statistical results in a query condition

```
_stat moexp mosal from rep
  MOEXP  MOSAL

10807.32 24600 Sum
 1080.73  2460 Ave
 1335.00  2800 Max
_select name mosal moexp from rep where mosal < #aver(2)
             NAME        MOSAL   MOEXP

Kris H. Raber          2400  1132.61
Toby C. Terry          2000  1080.53
Kerry H. Jones         2250  1229.64
Kathy F. Smith         2100   882.74
Jackie V. Smith        2400  1006.45
_select name mosal moexp from rep where mosal < #aver(2)-#stdv(2)
             NAME        MOSAL   MOEXP

Toby C. Terry          2000  1080.53
Kathy F. Smith         2100   882.74
 _
```

He went on to give them the names of all the statistical utility arrays:

#SUM	#STDV
#AVER	#MIN
#VAR	#MAX

There is also a utility variable named #CNT, whose value is always the number of observations (i.e., count) on which the other statistics are based. Jack pointed out that the values of these statistical sensors are always updated, regardless of whether the statistical values are displayed. In fact, E.DAVE, E.DSUM, and all the other statistical display switches could be FALSE, yet the statistical sensors will still be updated.

Jack gave a brief demonstration of how the preserved statistical results might be used. As shown in Figure 8–31, he generated statistics for the MOEXP and MOSAL fields. He then issued a query to see the reps whose monthly salaries were below average. Many other commands could have intervened between the STAT and SELECT commands. Then, to see which reps had monthly salaries more than one standard deviation below the mean (i.e., the average) he issued another query. Notice

FIGURE 8–32 Basing query calculations on statistical results

```
_select name mosal (mosal/#sum(2))*100 using "ff.dd%%" moexp (moexp/#sum(1))*100
using "ff.dd%%" from rep order by za mosal az moexp
        NAME            MOSAL  T01     MOEXP    T02

Tina F. Lee             2800  11.38%   988.20   9.14%
Karen V. Bruckner       2800  11.38%  1335.00  12.35%
Carol O. Lynn           2750  11.18%  1229.73  11.38%
Kim G. Anders           2600  10.57%   896.74   8.30%
Kevin R. Andrews        2500  10.16%  1025.68   9.49%
Jackie V. Smith         2400   9.76%  1006.45   9.31%
Kris H. Raber           2400   9.76%  1132.61  10.48%
Kerry H. Jones          2250   9.15%  1229.64  11.38%
Kathy F. Smith          2100   8.54%   882.74   8.17%
Toby C. Terry           2000   8.13%  1080.53  10.00%
_select name mosal moexp from rep where mosal>#aver(2) & mosal<#aver(1)
        NAME            MOSAL  MOEXP

Kevin R. Andrews        2500   1025.68
Kim G. Anders           2600    896.74
Tina F. Lee             2800    988.20
_?#aver(1),#aver(2)
        1080.73       2460.00

_
```

that it refers to a statistic (standard deviation of column 2) whose value was not displayed in the STAT results.

Clearing the screen, he said, "You can also use past statistical results to calculate query results. Suppose we want to see what percentages of the region's total salaries and expenses are apportioned to each rep. Even though there are no statistics now in view we can easily express such a query."

To demonstrate, he executed the query

```
select name mosal (mosal/#sum(2))*100 using "ff.dd%%" moexp
(moexp/#sum(1))*100 using "ff.dd%%" from rep order by za mosal az moexp
```

producing the results in the top portion of Figure 8–32. Notice that the lines are ordered primarily by descending MOSAL and then by ascending MOEXP.

"Could we now pick out the reps with above average salaries and below average expense budgets, if there are any?" Stan asked.

"Sure," Jack answered, "providing there are some."

As shown in Figure 8–32 he executed the query

```
select name mosal moexp from rep where mosal>#aver(2) & moexp<#aver(1)
```

and discovered there were three such reps. He then invoked the OUT-PUT command for the first two elements of #AVER to verify that the query was answered properly.

"I presume," said Debbie, "that if E.STAT were TRUE before your last query, new statistics would have replaced the ones we'd been dealing with. They would have been generated from the three lines of query results."

"That's true," he replied. "The OUTPUT command would have given different answers for the #AVER elements. The first would have had no value because the first column contains strings and #AVER(2) would be the average of the three monthly salaries displayed."

QUERIES AND STATISTICS DURING TEXT PROCESSING

Ad hoc query and statistics capabilities are very useful for supporting data explorations during a decision-making process. They can also be very helpful during the preparation or editing of a piece of text, provided they are integrated with a text management capability. In this environment, the query and statistics capabilities can be blended with the text management capability. In effect, they extend the text management facility to accomplish processing that is not possible with conventional text management software.

"We have already seen" Jack recalled, "how to do calculations in the midst of text processing. We just preface the OUTPUT command with a backslash and its result will appear at the cursor's last position in the text. Well, the same approach can be used for SELECT and STAT commands.

"Suppose you're merrily typing along on a piece of text when, on the spur of the moment, you find that you'd like to have selected contents or statistics from some table appear right there in the text. Well, it's easy! You just escape to the status line, enter a backslash followed by the desired SELECT or STAT command. Its result appears in your text where you can edit it to your heart's content, just like any other part of the text!"

He left it to the managers to explore this for themselves in the break that immediately followed. They found that the first line of query or statistics results is inserted into the text at the cursor's last position (as indicated on the left side of the status line). Each successive line is inserted to begin a new line in the text. Any preexisting text beyond the cursor's prior position is pushed down accordingly.

AFTER-HOURS EXPLORATIONS

As dusk descended, the managers were reinforcing what they had learned, using their computers to explore reps, products, and sales performances on their own. At the same time, Joy was about to explore a very different kind of performance with Jack, one that she had not experienced before but was destined to enjoy. When they met at his hotel, he could not help but notice that her expression was as calm and peaceful as the autumn night. Somehow it had a very soothing effect on him after the rigors of the day.

She wore a black skirt, white shirt, and well-tailored jacket of gray and black tones. His French-cut gray suit with black pinstripes made a nice match. His tie was maroon while her adornments were, as always, golden. As they started on their way, Jack thanked her for her help that day. She smiled one of her refreshing smiles as he went on to say, "I have a few private queries for you, Joy. Of all the people I know you are uniquely qualified to handle them. They are matters that are best not discussed around the others. They've enough to absorb for the moment."

"Fine," she replied, "and maybe later you could field a few 'what if' queries that I have for you."

Intrigued at that prospect, he began to query her as she drove. "Last night you said that the SELECT command was related to the relational calculus. Could you elaborate on that?"

"Sure," she nodded. "It's actually the heart of the relational calculus. You should bear in mind that SELECT evolved over the years. The one that you know and love has some differences from the ANSI standard."

Joy explained that she was referring to the American National Standards Institute proposals for SQL (Structured Query Language), an Englishized rendition of relational calculus [1].

"The term *SQL*," she opined, "is something of a misnomer, since that language actually lets you do more than ask queries. In some implementations of SQL, the focus is on its query ability as embodied in the SELECT command. This is the approach you're acquainted with. In other implementations, additional SQL commands that really have nothing to do with queries are provided. They're often intended for use by programmers and they fall into two categories."

She went on to explain that those SQL categories are called DDL (Data Description Language) and DML (Data Manipulation Language) [1]. The former includes data management commands that a programmer would use to define, delete, and structurally alter tables. It also allows "views" to be defined, where a view can be thought of as a virtual table whose "content" is defined in terms of a query. The SQL DML includes commands for manipulating (i.e., creating, modifying, deleting, listing) records in a table. It also includes a "cursor" mechanism that has nothing to do with the usual notion of a cursor on a console screen. In SQL terminology, a "cursor" is an ordered collection of records in a table or view. It gives a limited way of accessing records on a one at a time basis (à la the NEXT variation of the Chapter 6 OBTAIN command).

"Enough of that," Jack sighed. "What about the SELECT command for making queries? How different is the SELECT command that I know from the SELECT that has emerged from ANSI?"

"Basically, they're the same, but there are some differences," she answered [4]. "If you know one, it doesn't take much effort to get the knack of the other. Each has some features that the other doesn't. For instance, take the first clause of a SELECT command where you list the fields and expressions that will become columns in the result. ANSI SELECT does not allow string or logical expressions and its numeric expressions cannot involve any of the many built-in functions you are accustomed to. Macros are not allowed by ANSI. Nor can you use pictures to control the presentation of data values in query results.

"For a single table query, the ANSI SELECT's second clause is just like the one you know. It begins with FROM and is followed by a table name. But for multitable queries, the two differ somewhat. With the ANSI SELECT, the FROM appears only once followed by a list of the table names in no particular order."

"So all the mating of fields to indicate interrelations will happen in a single condition," Jack speculated. "There's probably no notion of having a condition to go along with each table."

"Exactly," she confirmed. "As for the WHERE clause in an ANSI SELECT command, most everything you're familiar with is supported with the exceptions of string expressions, functions, and macros. There are also a couple of relational operators that you've not seen before. For instance, the BETWEEN operator gives an easier way of specifying MOSAL between 2200 and 2500, than saying MOSAL greater than 2200 and MOSAL less than 2500. Also there's a LIKE operator that's used for wild card matching rather than the IN operator to which you are accustomed.

"The ANSI SELECT's ORDER BY clause is like the one you know, except the direction follows rather than precedes the field name. ASC is used to indicate ASCENDING and DESC indicates a descending direction. Ordering can be based only on fields, not on the full-blown expressions that some of your examples today used.

"Perhaps the biggest difference between the two SELECTs lies in the GROUP BY clause. If you use such a clause with the ANSI SELECT it can involve fields only—no calculations. Furthermore, such a query can include only those fields in its first clause, or any of five built-in statistical functions such as average, sum, or count. The query then outputs only one line for an entire group instead of every line in the group followed by a break and statistical summary. For instance, SELECT PID SUM(Q1) FROM PERF GROUP BY PID ORDER BY PID would produce nine lines—one for each product ID. Each line would show a PID value and the sum of the Q1 values for that product ID."

"I see," he mused. "That is a different approach to grouping and statistics. Because your columns can't be fields that aren't in the GROUP BY clause or statistical functions that operate on the group as a whole, every line in such a group would be identical anyway. So you really only get to see group summaries—one per line—rather than the detailed values that make up a group. What about the UNIQUE qualifier?"

"Well, in an ANSI SELECT you would use the word DISTINCT rather than UNIQUE," Joy replied, "but the effect is the same. Of course, you can let DISTINCT be a macro for UNIQUE if you like the ANSI terminology."

"No," he replied, "UNIQUE is just fine with me. What about environment and utility variables?"

"ANSI SQL has no concept of such things," she said. "You must remember it doesn't attempt to provide a knowledge management environment. Naturally that means you can't blend ANSI queries with text management or spreadsheet usage. By the way, there is one kind of query that ANSI allows that isn't in your repertoire."

"Oh, and what's that?" he asked curiously, as they pulled into the parking garage.

"It's the ability to put one query within the condition of another query," Joy replied. "This lets you condition a query based on the results of another query. It's called query nesting. As you might suspect there are quite a few restrictions on what the query nested in the condition can look like and the overall query can become quite long and complex." Table 8–1 summarizes the results of Jack's ad hoc query explorations.

Glancing at his watch, Jack's face registered concern. "I don't want to cut you off, but we'll probably need to hurry to make it on time. We don't want to miss the first movement."

Jack and Joy emerged onto the sidewalk at a brisk pace. She moved gracefully in high heels as they hurried along. Their eyes met and then locked for a magical moment. A spirited smile danced on her lips and he suddenly felt as if he had discovered a missing part of himself.

TABLE 8–1 Environment SELECT versus ANSI SELECT

	ANSI SELECT	*Environment SELECT*
Column selection can include:	Fields	Fields
	Expressions (numeric)	Expressions (numeric, string, logical)
	—	Working variables, utility variables
	—	Array elements
	—	Spreadsheet cells
	—	Macros
	Functions (5 statistical)	Functions (numerous)
	DISTINCT qualifier	UNIQUE qualifier
	—	Pictures
Table designation:	Single table in FROM clause	Single table in FROM clause
	Multiple tables in FROM clause	Multiple FROM clauses
	Tables listed in any sequence	Tables listed in many-to-one sequence
Condition specification:	One condition per query	One condition per designated table
	Simple or compound condition	Simple or compound condition
	AND, OR, NOT operators	AND, OR, XOR, NOT operators
	Relational operators (>, <, >=, <=, <>, =, IN, LIKE, BETWEEN, NULL)	Relational operators (<, >, >=, <=, <>, =, IN)
	Wild card string match (LIKE operator with % symbol)	Wild card string match (IN operator with * symbol)
	Relational operands (fields, 5 statistical functions, numeric expressions)	Relational operands (fields, numerous functions, macros, array elements, working and utility variables, spreadsheet cells, numeric expressions, string expressions)
	Can contain nested queries	—
Ordering of results:	Any mix of ASC/DESC directions	Any mix of AZ/ZA directions
	Based on fields	Based on fields or computed expressions
Grouping:	Generates one line per group	Generates all lines in group plus statistical summary
	Allows condition to be specified on a group basis	—
	Only "group by" fields or statistical function can be a display column	Any normal columns can be displayed
Statistics:	Only via grouping	With or without grouping
	—	Statistics preserved in statistical utility arrays
	—	Independent STAT command

They moved in silence for a while before descending back to the world of words. "Joy," he hesitated, "sometime I'd like to talk some more about nesting with you."

"All in good time, Jack," she cooed as they reached the concert hall door. She had never before seen a live concert hall performance by a fine symphony orchestra, whereas Jack was a classical music devotee whose favorites included Rachmaninoff and Mahler. He had been fortunate in having procured a pair of second row seats to the right of center. They settled into the full house with barely a minute to spare. The program coupled early Mozart with Bruckner's last symphony. Mozart was nice but she really enjoyed the romantic strains of Bruckner and looked forward to exploring more music with Jack. As the final applause faded away and they left the concert hall, Joy slipped her hand into his and they melted into the night.

BASIC IDEAS

The capacity to receive quick answers to ad hoc queries is extremely important to effective decision making. Thus *a versatile ad hoc query capability is crucial in supporting the exploratory aspects of a decision process. These explorations may aid at picking out relevant facts from large volumes of data. Alternatively, they may also involve "what if" analyses. In addition, statistical analyses can be helpful.*

The environment's SELECT command, patterned along SQL lines, is an extremely potent and flexible realization of the ad hoc inquiry technique of knowledge management. Its results are displayed in a columnwise format. A column can contain field values or values calculated from some expression involving fields, array elements, working variables, functions, and so on. The fields whose values are retrieved may come from one or more tables. In the case of multiple tables, each must be identified and conditions indicating the basis of relating one table's records to those of another table are specified. Other relational expressions can be included in a condition.

Considerable control over the presentation of a query's results can be exercised. Beyond environment variables for governing such presentation traits as colors and column spacing, pictures can be directly specified in the query for determining the appearance of a column's contents. Alternate column headings as well as an overall title for a query's results can be specified. Readability of results can be aided by the UNIQUE qualifier.

Dynamic sorting can be requested in a query, causing the resultant lines to be arranged in a desired order. Another aid to detecting data patterns is the ability to group a query's results, with desired statistics displayed at each control break. Generated statistics are automatically preserved in statistical utility arrays for later reference. The STAT command is a variant of SELECT. It allows statistical results to be generated without a display of all the raw data observations on which those statistics are based. Both SELECT and STAT can be invoked on an ad hoc basis in the midst of text processing, with results being incorporated directly into the text.

References

1. *American National Standard Database Language SQL* (draft). Washington, D.C.: ANSI Technical Committee X3H2, 1985.
2. Chamberlin, D. D.; M. M. Astrahan; K. P. Eswaran; P. P. Griffiths; R. A. Lorie; J. W. Miehl; P. Reisner; and B. W. Wade. "SEQUEL 2: A Unified Approach to Data Definition, Manipulation and Control." *IBM Journal of Research and Development*, November 1976.
3. Chamberlin, D. D., and R. F. Boyce. "SEQUEL: A Structured English Query Language." *Proceedings of ACM SIGFIDET Workshop*, Ann Arbor, May 1974.
4. Holsapple, C. W. "SQL on the IBM PC." *PC Tech Journal* 1, no. 3 (1983).

Part IV

MANAGING PRESENTATION KNOWLEDGE

That forms a revealing way of looking at it.

Chapter Nine

Forms Management

To this juncture, Jack had concentrated primarily on the management of descriptive knowledge via techniques such as text management, data base management, and ad hoc inquiry. From time to time he had touched on the treatment of other kinds of knowledge. The managers had seen that macros and function keys involved linguistic knowledge. Pictures embody assimilative knowledge about what characters the environment should be willing to absorb as a new data value is being entered. Pictures can also serve as presentation knowledge governing the appearance of values when displayed. Format control codes in a piece of text are another kind of presentation knowledge that can be stored in the environment's knowledge system. There are also numerous environment variables (e.g., E.SPAC, E.DECI, E.BACG, E.FORG, E.LEGH) whose values influence the nature of presentations. Even these modest presentation conveniences can be valuable to a knowledge worker.

Now Jack was about to launch into much larger scale approaches of coping with presentation knowledge. These involve the widely used techniques of forms management, report generation, and graphics. As with other knowledge management techniques, each of these is concerned with the dual issues of representation and processing. Forms management deals with the representation of presentation knowledge as a form and with the processing of such forms [1], [5], [8]. Chapter 10 describes the representation of presentation knowledge as a report template and the processing of templates to generate customized reports. Chapter 11 examines the representation of presentation knowledge as graphical data sources and the processing that can generate graphs from them. The present chapter deals with Jack's presentation of forms management.

"Virtually every day," Jack began, "each of us processes various forms. We look at forms that others have filled in, such as the product progress forms and monthly expense account forms that our reps fill in and send to us. We also fill in forms and send them to others, such as the form we complete when reviewing a rep's annual performance and then send on to the personnel department here at headquarters. And then there are the infamous forms we all fill in by April 15 of each year.

"If you stop to think of it, a form is a way of presenting data. It imposes a certain visual organization on some data values with the intent of making it easy to convey or grasp the story that those values have to tell. Of course, the same collection of data could be presented through alternative forms that visually arrange the same values in different ways to suit different purposes or tastes. But most forms have certain basic traits in common. Think for a moment about what they are."

Tracey was the first to volunteer a thought. "A form normally has some preprinted strings of text arranged on the page. There's usually a title, perhaps some instructions to whoever is going to fill out or read the form, and then some description that accompanies each place where data are to be filled in. These elements of the form are literally always presented, no matter whether anything has been filled in yet or not."

"So really," Dan observed, "there are two kinds of elements in a form. The literal or preprinted portions are constant and unchanging. But then there are also the nonliteral slots in a form, where various things can be filled in as needed. Just think of a tax form."

"Depending on the purpose of the form," Debbie commented, "these two kinds of elements can be laid out in various ways. I mean, any element—be it literal text or a nonliteral slot—has a certain physical location in the form. Many times there'll be lines separating adjacent elements or bunches of elements might be grouped into a block because they are related in some way."

"Those are all very good points," rejoined Jack [4], [6], [7]. "Now the forms you're accustomed to dealing with in everyday life are on paper. It turns out that all of the traits you identified for paper forms are also traits of electronic forms that can be presented on the console screen. If you like, you can get paper printouts of these electronic forms. Between now and our next break, we'll see that you can invent your own electronic forms—in living color, no less. Once you have these forms in the environment's knowledge system you'll see that they can be processed in various ways."

As Jack was speaking, Joy settled in front of their demonstration computer, entered the environment in her usual way, and put the three tables into use. She was wearing a snug, form-fitting beige dress half a shade lighter than her well-tanned skin. It had a woven knit texture.

PHOTO 13   A blank form for a sales representative

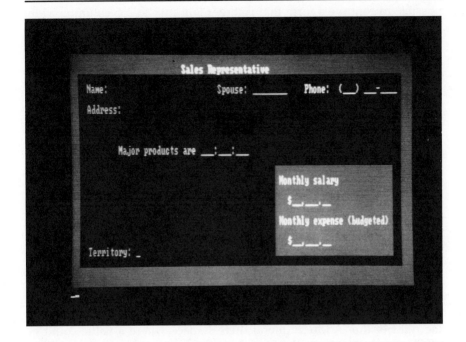

She interrupted, "Jack, let's show them what one of these electronic forms looks like."

As he agreed, she entered a command that brought the form shown in Photo 13 into view. There was a murmur of surprise among the sales managers. They were not accustomed to such colorful forms.[1] As Joy explained that they would soon be able to electronically paint their own elements and blocks of color on the screen, Jack's reaction was less overt than the sales managers' excitement. In silence, he stepped back and simply admired the exquisite form she presented.

ELECTRONIC FORMS

An *electronic form* is a rectangular area on the console screen. This area may be smaller than a console screen's usual 25 row by 80 column

---

[1] Although most of the forms discussed in this chapter actually have many colors on the console screen, those colors appear only as different shades in the black-and-white photos and cannot be seen in the figures. Photos 14, 17, and 18 in the color insert show examples of forms in their full glory.

(i.e., character) dimensions. On the other hand, a form can be designed to occupy the entire console screen. In this environment, it is even possible to contrive a form that is larger (e.g., up to 255 columns wide) than the physical dimensions of the console screen. However, such forms are used primarily for producing form printouts on wide paper. Jack did not plan to discuss such oversized forms.

In addition to its size, a form can have a *default location* on the console screen. This is the place (i.e., row-column coordinate) where its upper left corner will normally appear on the screen. Form management software should allow this default location to be overriden whenever desired. A paper form may have some customary position on a desktop, but it can be placed in other positions. The same should be allowed for an electronic form on a console screen. Because multiple electronic forms can simultaneously exist in a processing context or even on the same screen, each form is given a unique name. This allows a form-processing command to easily identify which of the forms is to be processed at any given moment.

Gazing at Joy's form, Jack commented, "Notice that this form has both literal and nonliteral elements. The *literal elements* are in plain sight, whereas the *nonliteral elements* are not. But you can see hints where the nonliteral elements are located. For instance, beneath the literal 'Monthly salary' there is a place where a value could be filled in, to the right of the 'Address' literal there's space where a value could be filled in, and so forth. Such places and spaces are for the form's nonliteral elements. They correspond to the blank spots that could be filled in on a paper form."

"I can see that," Brad remarked, "but how do the slots in an electronic form become filled in? A blank form is all well and good, but I'd like to see the data values for a sales rep."

Filling in a Form

Joy had been waiting for someone to make such a request. In response to the underscore prompt near the bottom of the screen, she executed the command

```
tally rform
```

explaining that once a blank form has been put on the screen, the TALLY command can be used to tally up values for its nonliteral elements. The cursor zipped through the nonliterals, depositing a value for each on the screen. The result is shown in Photo 14 of the color insert. In this command, RFORM is simply the name of the form Joy was processing.

"That's sure a lot faster than manually completing a blank form," Brad said. He was impressed. "I guess the environment got data at the top from the #DATE variable and got the rest of the values from the REP table's current record. But how did it know which field value to fill in for which nonliteral element? The layout of nonliteral elements in the form is clearly different than the sequence of fields in REP's structure."

"You're right," Jack replied. "When a form is invented, each nonliteral element is specified not only in terms of its location; it is also designated as being a place where the environment will either *put* a value for display to a user, *get* a value from the user, or *both*. If we want the environment to be able to put out a value for some nonliteral, then we have to specify where that value is to come from. We can specify a utility variable such as #DATE, a field such as REP.NAME, or a more elaborate expression whose calculated value will be put into the form. Working variables and other things we've not yet talked about, like spreadsheet cells, can also be specified for a nonliteral's expression.

"When Joy tallied the form, the environment evaluated the expression specified for each nonliteral and displayed its value in the form. For the first nonliteral element, it saw that #DATE's value was October 4 and displayed that value in the element's location. For the next nonliteral element, it evaluated the virtual field REP.NAME for the current REP record and displayed Kevin R. Andrews at that element's location, and so forth.

"I presume," observed Debbie, "that the environment gets a value in the opposite way that it puts a value. If we designate that a nonliteral element is for getting values from us rather than putting values out to us, then what we type into a nonliteral's slot becomes the new value for its associated variable or field."

Ready-Made Forms

"Correct," responded Jack. "Later, you'll see that we can easily enter new knowledge into the environment through forms. In fact, if you stop to think about it, each of you has already done both data entry and data viewing through forms."

There was a silence of puzzlement, for none of them had previously seen the likes of Photos 13 and 14. Jack gave a hint, reminding them of the BROWSE and CREATE commands (recall Figures 6–21 and 6–8).

"Oh, I get it," remarked Stan. "When browsing through or creating records, the environment furnished us with *ready-made forms*. They just weren't very fancy compared to what we're seeing now. The field names appeared as a stack of literals in those forms and each was followed by a nonliteral element where the environment could put or get a value."

"That's the idea," nodded Jack. "In the case of CREATE, each of the actual fields has a corresponding nonliteral element, designated as the place where the environment can get its value from you. In the case of a BROWSE form, every field has a corresponding nonliteral element, designated as a place where the environment can put its value for your viewing. Also, the elements for actual—as opposed to virtual—fields are designated as places where the environment can get values as well, thereby allowing you to do editing to field values."

"Right," chimed Joy, "you already know a lot about electronic forms though you didn't realize it before. What we're going to do now is extend your knowledge in that direction. We'll see that you can custom design your own forms to have exactly the contents, colors, and layout you desire. You'll simply use the PAINT command to sketch out your customized forms directly on the screen. It handles all aspects of form representation from painting, moving, recoloring, shrinking, and expanding color blocks to specifying a nonliteral element's Get or Put designation, corresponding variable or expression, and various special effects like a picture, blinking appearance, and reverse video display. After you see how to paint a form, Jack will demonstrate various possibilities for processing it."

PAINTING A FORM

Forms management software normally supports one of two distinct approaches to producing a form. Both are supported in Jack's environment. One approach is to make a *form declaration*, consisting of statements that describe the desired characteristics of RFORM. The exact syntax of such statements can differ from one forms management package to another. A sample showing part of this environment's declaration for the form of Photos 13 and 14 appears in Figure 9–1.

Together, the statements in Figure 9–1 are part of the environment's FORM command that (when executed) declares the existence of a form. They indicate the screen row-column coordinates where each element begins. There is an indication of whether the element's value can be put out to users or gotten from users. Notice that both kinds of processing are allowed for some elements. For literal elements, text strings are indicated. For nonliteral elements, variables (e.g., working variables, utility variables, fields) are specified. In the case of a nonliteral that is

FIGURE 9–1   Part of a form declaration

```
FORM RFORM
        AT 1, 60 PUT #DATE   USING "rrrrrr19rr"
        AT 2, 27 PUT "Sales Representative"
        AT 4, 5 PUT "Name:"
        AT 4, 11 PUT REP.NAME
        AT 4, 35 PUT "Spouse:"
        AT 4, 43 GET REP.SPOUSE   STR
        AT 4, 43 PUT REP.SPOUSE
        AT 4, 55 PUT "Phone:"
        AT 4, 63 GET REP.PHONE   STR
        AT 4, 63 PUT REP.PHONE
        AT 6, 5 PUT "Address:"
        AT 6, 14 PUT REP.ADDR
        AT 10, 12 PUT "Major products are"
        AT 10, 31 GET REP.MAJORP   STR
        AT 10, 31 PUT REP.MAJORP
        AT 13, 49 PUT "Monthly salary"
        AT 15, 51 GET REP.MOSAL   NUM USING "$ff,fff.dd"
        AT 15, 51 PUT REP.MOSAL   USING "$ff,fff.dd"
        AT 17, 49 PUT "Monthly expense (budgeted)"
        AT 19, 51 GET REP.MOEXP   NUM USING "$ff,fff.dd"
        AT 19, 51 PUT REP.MOEXP   USING "$ff,fff.dd"
        AT 20, 5 PUT "Territory:"
        AT 20, 16 GET REP.TID   STR
        AT 20, 16 PUT REP.TID
```

only being put, an expression involving calculations can be specified. Jack did not intend to dwell on the FORM command's declarative approach to producing a form [2]. Instead he concentrated on the other approach: interactive *form painting,* which gives immediate visual feedback of what the form looks like as it is being invented [3].

A New Form

"When you want to paint a new form," Jack declared, "execute the PAINT command. The screen will clear except for a two-line *status area* at the bottom. It will always show the current row-column coordinates of the cursor. It will also display painting instructions, usually in the guise of a menu of options you can pick from. Let me show you. Our present context already has one form in it: the RFORM that Joy showed you. Suppose we want to add a new form for presenting product line data."

He proceeded to execute the command

```
paint prodform
```

FIGURE 9–2   Status area with main menu for painting a new form

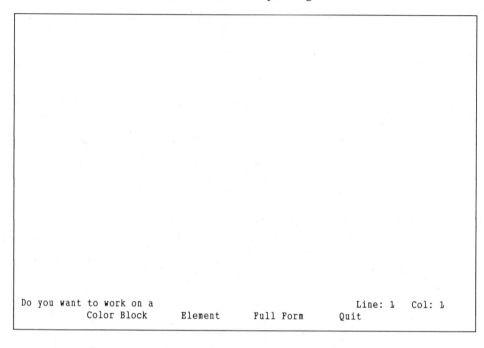

```
Do you want to work on a                          Line: 1    Col: 1
        Color Block       Element       Full Form   Quit
```

resulting in the Figure 9–2 screen appearance. He explained that any of the four options in this main Painting menu could be chosen in the usual way, by moving the cursor to it and pressing the Enter key. Alternatively, the key corresponding to the desired key's first letter could be pressed.

Jack remarked, "The form itself will materialize above the status area, in response to your menu selections. As you can see, the menu is very straightforward. It allows you to work on color blocks, elements, or the form as a whole. Each of these three options leads to a submenu with options of its own. The QUIT option causes your PAINT command to terminate and results in the usual underscore prompt for a new command.

"When painting a new form, you can work on color blocks first and then elements. Or, you could specify some elements first, and then paint in the color. You can also switch back and forth, working on some elements, then color blocks, some more elements, and so forth. Let's begin by working on some elements for PRODFORM."

FIGURE 9–3   **Starting an element in column 6 of line 5**

```
                                                          Line: 5   Col: 6
Move cursor to start of element.   Press FENTER.
```

The Painting Flow: Elements

With that he pressed the E key to select the Element option. The status area's menu was instantly replaced with a message asking him to move the cursor to the place where he wanted the element to start. Jack complied by moving it down and to the right, explaining that the cursor is moved the same way when painting a form as it is when entering text. He reminded them about the "diamond" key pattern (recall Figure 5–5) involving ˆE (up), ˆS (left), ˆX (down), and ˆD (right). As shown in Figure 9–3, the status area now showed that the cursor was located at line (i.e., row) 5 and column 6.

Jack pressed the Enter key as requested by the status area message,[2] causing a new menu to appear as shown in Figure 9–4. This is called the Element menu.

---

[2] Recall (Chapter 5) that FENTER is just the environment's general purpose way of referring to the functionality achieved by pressing the Enter key within the PC-DOS host.

FIGURE 9–4   The Element menu

```
┌──────────────────────────────────────────────────────────────────────┐
│                                                                        │
│                                                                        │
│                                                                        │
│                                                                        │
│                                                                        │
│                                                                        │
│                                                                        │
│                                                                        │
│                                                                        │
│                                                                        │
│                                                                        │
│                                                                        │
│                                                                        │
│                                                                        │
│                                                                        │
│                                                                        │
│                                                                        │
│                                                                        │
│                                                                        │
│ You have indicated an element.  Do you want to          Line: 5   Col: 6 │
│ Alter/Create It    Move It   Copy It   Delete It   Go To Another Element   Quit │
└──────────────────────────────────────────────────────────────────────┘
```

"Before you go on," interrupted Dan, "is there any particular reason why you wanted the first element to begin at that spot?"

"No," shrugged Jack with a noncomittal tone. "It just seemed like a decent place to begin an element denoting a product identifier. Later if we want to move it we can by just picking the Move option from the Element menu." He motioned to the second option in the Figure 9–4 screen.

"But before we can move an element, we must of course create it," continued Jack as he pressed the A key to pick the Alter/Create option. This changed the status area, giving the dual choice menu shown in Figure 9–5. He picked the Literal option because he wanted the words "Product ID:" to appear literally in the form. A message appeared in the status area, telling him to enter the literal element directly on the screen. With the cursor already poised at line 5 column 6, he proceeded to type

Product ID:

resulting in the screen appearance depicted in Figure 9–6. On pressing the Enter key, a special effects menu appeared in the status area as shown in Figure 9–7.

FIGURE 9–5   The literal versus nonliteral choice

```
                                                                    
                                                                    
                                                                    
                                                                    
                                                                    
                                                                    
                                                                    
                                                                    
                                                                    
                                                                    
 Do you want to create a                        Line: 5    Col: 6
                     Literal                   Nonliteral
```

FIGURE 9–6   Entering a literal element in a form

```
                                                                    
    Product ID:                                                     
                                                                    
                                                                    
                                                                    
                                                                    
                                                                    
                                                                    
                                                  Line: 5    Col: 17
 Enter or revise literal element.    Press FENTER.
```

FIGURE 9–7   Special effects menu for an element

```
Product ID:




Do you want to alter/initialize                    Line: 5   Col: 17
    Picture     Blink     Reverse Video     Intensity     Sound     Quit
```

"When you work on an element," Jack noted, "you get a chance to give it various *special effects*. You can make it blink, put it in reverse video, change the intensity of its display, or cause a bell to sound whenever the cursor touches it. You can also give it a picture if you like, provided the element is a nonliteral."

Jack pressed the B key and the entire "Product ID:" string began to blink. To make it appear in reverse video as well, he pressed the R key. Instead of white letters blinking against a black background, there were now black letters blinking against a white background.

"How can you make it stop blinking?" asked Tracey.

"I just choose the Blink option again and it stops," he replied, pressing the B key. "To revert to normal video, I just press R again. This makes it easy to switch back and forth among various special effects. When you have an element the way you want it, you just press Q to quit your creation of the element."

"What if I later wanted to alter this element's special effects in some way?" Don asked.

"Remember that we picked the Alter/Create option from the Element menu," Jack recalled. "If you pick that same option for an already existing element, you'll be guided through the same processing sequence

FIGURE 9–8 Element menu after creating an element

```
Product ID:









You have indicated an element.  Do you want to            Line: 5   Col: 17
Alter/Create It     Move It    Copy It    Delete It    Go To Another Element    Quit
```

that we've just experienced, with a chance to alter any aspect of the element's specification." He pressed the Q key to leave the Special Effects menu. The Element menu reappeared as shown in Figure 9–8.

"At this stage," he continued, "you could not only pick the first option to alter the present element, you could also choose to move the element, make a copy of it somewhere else in the form, or delete it. But for now let's go to another element. I want to create a nonliteral element following the literal element we just created. It will be a slot associated with the PID field in PROD."

Jack pressed the G key. As before, a message appeared in the status area asking him to move the cursor to the start of an element. He held down ^D until the cursor had moved to the right of the previous element's colon. It was now in column 18 of line 5. Pressing the Enter key brought the usual Element menu into view and he chose the Alter/ Create option as he had done before to create the "Product ID" element. As before (recall Figure 9–5), he was asked to indicate whether this was to be a literal or nonliteral element. This time he pressed N to select the Nonliteral option. Rather than being asked to type in a literal element, the Figure 9–9 menu appeared.

"Now here we're being asked whether we want to allow the environ-

FIGURE 9–9   Designating a nonliteral element as Put, Get, or Both

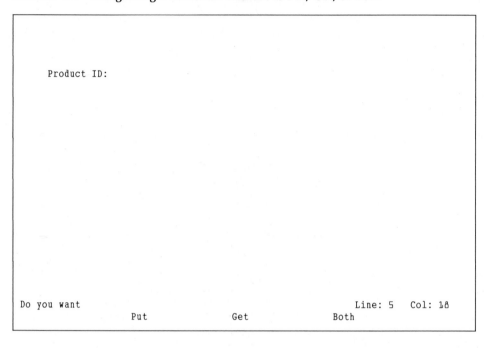

ment to put values into this element for our viewing, get values from us through this element, or both. When an element corresponds to an actual field or a working variable whose value you want to be able to change when the form is displayed, pick the Both option. If it is to be associated with a virtual field or expression involving calculations, pick the Put option."

Accordingly, Jack pressed the B key. In the status area he was prompted to enter the table name for the element's field. He typed

prod

and, on pressing the Enter key, was prompted to enter the field name. Jack typed

pid

yielding the screen appearance depicted in Figure 9–10. He explained that if they intended to specify a nonfield variable for the element, no table would need to be specified. It should be noted that fields from different tables can be assigned to elements in the same form.

FIGURE 9–10   Specifying a field for the new nonliteral element

```
    Product ID:
```
```
Enter variable's table name (or press FFENTER for nonfield  variable):prod
Enter variable name: pid
```

On pressing the Enter key, a new menu appeared in the status area as shown in Figure 9–11. Jack picked the Don't Care option, which caused the environment to use PID's type as the element's type. Equivalently, he could have chosen the String option. The Special Effects menu then came into view. If Jack were to choose its Picture option, he would be allowed to enter a picture at the element location in the form. For form-processing purposes this would override PID's native picture. He pressed the Q key without making a special picture for the element.

"And that's all there is to it," Jack declared. "You now can create as many literal or nonliteral elements as you like in any form. The PAINT command guides you each step of the way and you get visual feedback about the elements as you work on them."

"That's all very apparent," said Dan, "but what about putting some color into the form?"

"I'll get to that in a moment," Jack answered. "You'll see that it's very easy, taking only a few keystrokes. But first let me create some more literals."

He did so, using exactly the same painting flow as before. Four additional literal elements were created, each ending with a colon. A nonliteral element was created to the right of each of these and an

FIGURE 9–11   Picking an element's type

```
   Product ID:


















Do you want                                      Line: 5   Col: 18
          String Type      Number Type     Logic Type    Don't Care
```

appropriate field was specified for each. It took him a couple minutes to create these eight new elements, leaving the screen appearance as shown in Figure 9–12. Notice that Jack specified a picture for the non-literal element following the "Target:" element. When a picture is not specified for a nonliteral element, its associated field's picture will be used and any nonplaceholder symbols (e.g., decimal points) in such pictures will appear in the form.

The Painting Flow: Color Blocks

"Now let's add a little color to our form," Jack said. He pressed the C key to choose the Color Block option from the main Painting menu shown in the status area of Figure 9–12. A status area message appeared, telling him to move the cursor to the northwest corner of the color block he wanted to work on (i.e., create). He complied by moving the cursor to the fourth column in the fourth line so it was blinking just above and to the left of the "Product ID:" element. The screen now appeared as shown in Figure 9–13.

Jack pressed the Enter key and an asterisk appeared on the screen to mark what would be the new color block's northwest corner. A

FIGURE 9–12 Elements in a product form

```
Product ID:                    Product name:

    Target: $fff,fff

        Commission rate:   .

            Gross margin rate:   .
```

```
Do you want to work on a                         Line: 5    Col: 41
            Color Block     Element      Full Form    Quit
```

FIGURE 9–13 Designating the northwest corner of a color block

```
Product ID:                    Product name:

    Target: $fff,fff

        Commission rate:   .

            Gross margin rate:   .
```

```
                                                 Line: 4    Col: 4
Move cursor to northwest corner of desired color block.  Press FENTER.
```

FIGURE 9–14   Designating the opposite corner of a color block

```
 *
   Product ID:                        Product name:

      Target: $fff,fff

         Commission rate:   .

            Gross margin rate:   .




                                                    Line: 12   Col: 77
Move cursor to southeast corner of new color block.   Press FENTER.
```

message appeared in the status area asking him to move the cursor to the desired southeast corner of the new color block. Because he wanted the color block to encompass all of the form's elements, he moved it down and to the right, letting it come to rest in column 77 of row 12. Figure 9–14 portrays the resultant screen appearance. When he pressed the Enter key, an asterisk appeared there too and the Color Block menu showed up in the status area. This is depicted in Figure 9–15.

"We now have a colorless color block whose boundaries are designated by asterisks," Jack observed. "I'm going to pick the first option to assign it some colors. Once a color block has some colors, you could again pick this same option to assign some different colors to it. Notice that we can also pick options allowing us to move the block to a different location, enlarge or shrink its size, or completely delete it. Any of these takes only a few keystrokes. I'd encourage you to experiment with them when you practice forms management during the next break. I'll just demonstrate color assignment for now."

Jack selected the Assign Colors option. As Figure 9–16 shows, a Background Color menu appeared. Each option in this menu was in color (i.e., the word "Red" was actually red). He pressed the U key to choose blue as the block's background color. A similar foreground color

FIGURE 9–15   The Color Block menu

```
   *
     Product ID:                    Product name:

        Target: $fff,fff

           Commission rate:  .

              Gross margin rate:  .
                                                      *




You have indicated a color block.  Do you want to       Line: 12  Col: ??
Assign Colors   Move It    Change Size    Delete It   Go To Another Block    Quit
```

FIGURE 9–16   Choosing a block's background color

```
   *
     Product ID:                    Product name:

        Target: $fff,fff

           Commission rate:  .

              Gross margin rate:  .
                                                      *




Do you want a background color of                       Line: 12  Col: ??
  Black(a)     Blue(u)     Green    Cyan     Red    Magenta   Brown(o)    White
```

FIGURE 9–17   Choosing a block's foreground color

```
 *
   Product ID:                    Product name:

      Target: $fff,fff

         Commission rate:  .

            Gross margin rate:  .
                                                              *




Do you want a foreground color of                 Line: 12  Col: 77
 Black(a)    Blue(u)    Green    Cyan    Red    Magenta    Brown(o)    White
```

menu appeared as portrayed in Figure 9–17. Jack pressed the O key
to choose brown as the foreground color for any characters appearing
in the block. He explained that on this console screen, "brown" actually
appeared as more of a yellow color. The block markers disappeared as
soon as he pressed the O key. The area that they had designated was
now entirely blue, except for the displayed elements, which were colored
yellow. Photo 15 shows the result (with colors appearing as different
shades).

"As I recall, Joy's RFORM had a different color boundary around
a color block," Stan said. "How could we get, say, a yellow casing
around the blue block?"

"Easy," Jack replied. "We just make a yellow block that's slightly
larger than the blue block. The blue one starts in column 4 of line 4.
So we let the yellow one start in, say, column 2 of line 3. As the status
area shows, the blue block ends at column 77 of line 12. So our new
yellow block might extend to column 79 of line 13. Watch how this
works."

Because he was done with the blue block, Jack selected the Go To
Another Block option from the Color Block menu of Photo 15. As before
he was asked to move the cursor to the northwest corner of a block.

PHOTO 15   Blue color block in a form

```
    Product ID:                     Product name:
        Target: $ffff,fff
            Commission rate:  .
                Gross margin rate:  .




    You have indicated a color block.  Do you want to        Line: 12  Col: 77
    Assign Colors   Move It   Change Size   Delete It   Go To Another Block   Quit
```

He moved it to column 2 of line 3 and it was marked by an asterisk when he pressed the Enter key. When asked to indicate the new block's southeast corner, he positioned it at column 79 of line 13. Jack proceeded to give this block a brown (i.e., yellow) background color and black foreground color. As soon as he had done so, this new block appeared with the blue block lying on top of it. Because he was done with color blocks, Jack chose the Quit option from the Color Block menu, resulting in Photo 16 (with colors appearing as different shades).

"I see," Stan nodded. "We can have multiple color blocks in a form and they can overlap if we like."

"Right," chimed Joy. "One block can be entirely within another as shown here. Or, if you wanted, you could move the blue block so that it covers one or two of the yellow blocks' boundaries. You could even move the blue block so it doesn't overlap at all with the yellow block. And keep in mind that you can make a block as small or as large as you like. A color block could be as little as one column wide and one row high or it might occupy the entire screen. A block can be long and thin or short and thick, whatever you like."

PHOTO 16   Blue color block on yellow color block

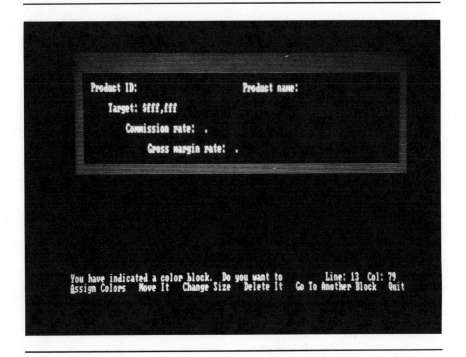

Full Form Options

"I believe we all understand color blocks and elements," Debbie commented, evoking several nods from the others. "But what can we do with the main menu's Full Form option? I presume it allows us to do things to the form as a whole."

"Right," affirmed Jack, as he pressed the F key to pick that option. This brought the Full Form menu into the status area, presenting them with the options

```
Save Form    View Form    Move Form    Release Form    Quit
```

Jack pressed the S key to pick the Save Form option and was presented with the prompt

```
Enter context file name:
```

in the status area. He responded by typing

```
a:prodform
```

to have the present rendition of the form stored in a file named PROD-FORM.ICF on the diskette in drive A. The Full Form menu reappeared.

"Like working variables, environment variable settings, and macros, a form is part of your context," Jack explained. "Remember, when you leave the environment, all aspects of the processing context vanish. Normally, you'll want to save the forms you've painted. One way to save a form is with the SAVE FORM option as I've just shown you. Because this form now exists in a context file on disk, we could leave the environment, later reenter it, and use the LOAD command to make that form part of the new processing context."

Jack was referring to the same LOAD command they had all used earlier (recall Chapter 4). In this case, the command

```
load "a:prodform"
```

would make the PRODFORM form available for processing. He went on to explain that the SAVE command (recall Chapter 4), as opposed to PAINT's Save Form option, would be another way to save a new form. However, unlike the Save Form option, it saves everything about a context, not just forms.

"When we used the SAVE command before," recalled Tracey, "we could specify codes, such as M for macros, with it to restrict which aspects of a context are actually saved. Could we do the same for forms?"

"Sure," answered Jack. "You would use F as the SAVE code and *all* forms in the context would be saved in the context file you indicate. You could later invoke the LOAD command with that file name to have all of those forms loaded into the context of a subsequent session." For instance, the command

```
save to "a:myforms" with "f"
```

would save all forms existing in the present context in a context file named MYFORMS.ICF on the drive A diskette.

"Personally," Jack continued, "I tend to save an individual form in an individual context file via PAINT's Save Form option. I can then load them individually on an as-needed basis. If you were dealing with large numbers of related forms, preserving them all in a single context file with the SAVE command might be preferable. It's up to you. The main point to remember is that after altering or creating a form you should save it if you intend to use it in the future."

Because a form is part of the processing context, it consumes space

FIGURE 9–18 **Viewing the declaration of PRODFORM**

```
FORM PRODFORM
        AT 5, 6 PUT "Product ID:"
        AT 5, 18 GET PROD.PID   STR
        AT 5, 18 PUT PROD.PID
        AT 5, 41 PUT "Product name:"
        AT 5, 55 GET PROD.PNAME   STR
        AT 5, 55 PUT PROD.PNAME
        AT 7, 10 PUT "Target:"
        AT 7, 18 GET PROD.TARGET   NUM USING "$fff,fff"
        AT 7, 18 PUT PROD.TARGET   USING "$fff,fff"
        AT 9, 14 PUT "Commission rate:"
        AT 9, 31 GET PROD.CRATE   NUM
        AT 9, 31 PUT PROD.CRATE
        AT 11, 19 PUT "Gross margin rate:"
        AT 11, 38 GET PROD.GMR   NUM
        AT 11, 38 PUT PROD.GMR
        AT 3, 2 TO 13, 79 PUT "FABO"
        AT 4, 4 TO 12, 77 PUT "FOBU"
ENDFORM
```

in the environment's main memory work area. "This," explained Jack, "is why you might want to pick the Release Form option when you no longer want to process a form in the present session. The RELEASE command could also be used to free up the space consumed by a form. In any case, remember to save a form before you release it if you want to process it again later. As for the Move Form option, it does what you'd expect. It lets you move all the form's contents as a whole."

Jack pressed the V key to choose the View Form option. The screen cleared momentarily and then the form declaration shown in Figure 9–18 appeared. It let them view the FORM command that could have been executed instead of the painting process, to make PRODFORM part of the present processing context. Jack pressed the space bar to get back to the Full Form menu, the Q key to get back to the main menu, and then pressed Q again to quit the painting process. He was now faced with the usual underscore prompt.

"At this point, PRODFORM is part of our context and we could begin processing with it right away. Or we may change our minds about some trait of the form. We might want to touch it up or massage it in some way."

Revising an Existing Form

Jack proceeded to explain that the PAINT command can be invoked to revise the presentation knowledge embodied in any form presently existing in the context. For example, to modify PRODFORM, the command

```
paint prodform
```

would be executed. The same main Painting menu would appear in the status area (recall Figure 9–2). Only this time the screen above it would not be blank. It would be filled with the visualization of PROD-FORM.

Any characteristics of the form could be revised as desired. Each change is reflected immediately in the form's image on the screen, as well as in the definition of that form existing in the present context (i.e., in the environment's work area in main memory). However, the PRODFORM.ICF file is unaffected. When all desired changes have been made to a form, the Save Form option can be picked to commit them all at once to the PRODFORM.ICF file.

"As a variation," observed Jack, "we might want to keep PROD-FORM as it is, but make a new form that employs a copy of PRODFORM as our starting point. We then edit that copy and save it in its own context file. Such a feature is very useful when you want to have several new forms that are variations of one existing form."

He proceeded to give a hypothetical example, using the command

```
paint splash from prodform
```

which would make a new form named SPLASH. Except for its name, this new form would be identical to PRODFORM. It could then be altered in any way desired and saved in the environment's knowledge system (e.g., in SPLASH.ICF).

FORM PROCESSING

Each of the possible forms in a knowledge system represents some presentation knowledge. Clearly, a form embodies much more than a sequence of OUTPUT statements. A form is processed as a whole, not as a series of line-at-a-time outputs. Commands that process forms are said to do form-at-a-time processing. Software that does not support such commands is not forms management software. Jack now turned his attention to form-processing commands available in the knowledge management environment.

Browsing and Creating Records with Forms

"So, how do we make use of a form once we've painted it?" Jack asked rhetorically. "Well, one way is to browse or create records with our own customized form rather than the default forms we'd seen earlier. For instance, PRODFORM has a nonliteral element for every field in the PROD table and each was specified to be a place where the environment could both put and get data values. This makes PRODFORM ideally suited for use with either the BROWSE or CREATE command."

He proceeded to demonstrate by executing the command

```
browse prod with prodform
```

making PROD's first record immediately visible through PRODFORM, as can be seen in Photo 17 of the color insert. Notice the screen's first line is the same as it is when browsing without a customized form. Had E.SUPH been switched from its default FALSE value to TRUE, this heading would have been suppressed. Jack went on to demonstrate that they could browse through the records exactly as they had done before, editing any value as desired. The only difference was that the values were presented through PRODFORM.

When browsing via a form, all elements whose values can be put onto the screen (recall the PUTs in Figure 9–18) will be displayed. These include nonliteral elements designated as either Put or Both during the painting process, as well as literal elements. Of course, color blocks are also put on the screen. Any element designated as either Get or Both during painting can have its value edited during browsing, with the alteration being immediately reflected in the associated field. When painting PRODFORM, Jack picked the Both option for the PID, PNAME, TARGET, CRATE, and GMR elements because he wanted the environment to be able to both put and get values for them.

Jack demonstrated that new PROD records could also be created with PRODFORM by executing the command

```
create records for prod with prodform
```

As with BROWSE, this CREATE command behaved in exactly the same way as the managers were accustomed. The only difference was that PRODFORM appeared on the screen instead of the default record creation form. Naturally, the environment is able to get new data values for any field that has been designated as either a "Get" or "Both" element.

"It's clear to me," observed Stan, "that forms can help us browse and create more quickly, because we can arrange the visual layout and special effects highlighting to suit our needs. But I'm wondering if we couldn't also have some automatic calculations done as we're browsing or creating so that not only the record's values appear but calculation results based on those values show up in the same form. I guess what I'm asking is whether a form can behave like a miniature spreadsheet as I'm browsing through a table's records."

"It just so happens," said Jack with a wink, "that I have just such a form, because I've found that kind of form processing to be helpful. As I browse through performance records, I like to see not only the raw quota and sales figures. I also like to see the excess, if any, of sales over corresponding quotas for each record. To do this I've painted a form that I call PERFFORM."

He executed the command

```
load "a:perfform"
```

to load PERFFORM from its context file into main memory. To show which forms presently existed in the processing context he executed the command

```
show form
```

to which the environment responded by listing the names of three forms presently available for processing. These were Joy's RFORM, the PRODFORM Jack had earlier painted before their very eyes, and now PERFFORM as well.

As an aside he explained that the RELEASE command could be used to release any of these forms from memory. To illustrate this, he released Joy's form with the command

```
release rform
```

and issued another SHOW command to confirm that it was now missing from the present processing context. Not wanting to be without this form for long, Jack loaded RFORM from its context file. He also loaded a form named SCALC from its context file, explaining that he intended to discuss it later. The SHOW command now showed that there were four forms available for immediate processing.

Returning to Stan's question, Jack typed the command

```
browse perf where pid="rom" with perfform
```

to process the PERF table and PERFFORM form in a single operation. He pointed out that conditional browsing is permitted with customized

FIGURE 9–19   Basic form manipulations

```
_load "a:perfform"
_show form
PERFFORM
PRODFORM
RFORM
_release rform
_show form
PERFFORM
PRODFORM
_load "a:rform"
_load "a:scalc"
_show form
PERFFORM
PRODFORM
RFORM
SCALC
_browse perf where pid="rom" with perfform
```

forms. The screen appeared as shown in Figure 9–19. When Jack pressed the Enter key to execute the BROWSE command, it was instantly transformed to the appearance shown in Photo 18 in the color insert. Here they saw not only the data values for the first romance record in PERF, but also the results of five calculations involving those values.

"First of all," offered Jack, "I'd like you to notice the gridlike arrangement of elements. Remember, you're free to lay out the elements in whatever way you find to be visually appealing or exciting. As you can see Stan, this is comparable to what you'd expect in a spreadsheet display."

"Except," interrupted Stan, "it's a lot more colorful."

Jack continued, "The word 'Sales' is, of course, a literal element, but the other five elements in that row are nonliteral elements. As you would probably surmise, their specified fields are S1, S2, S3, S4, and SYTD. The first four of these are designated for both putting and getting data. The fifth is naturally for putting only, since it's associated with a virtual field. The form's quota row is constructed similarly for the fields Q1 through Q4 and QYR. Obviously, this form lets us examine performance data in a very different way from the default browsing form.

"In my opinion, this form makes it much easier to grasp the data being presented. And as a further aid, I've included another line that displays the extra amount by which sales exceeds quota in each time period. As you know these values don't exist in the PERF table, not even virtually. Instead, I built calculations for them directly into the form. So when I painted the first nonliteral into the extra line, I designated it as a place where the environment should put values and the expression I specified for it is PERF.S1−PERF.Q1."

"What you've done then is to blend data management, forms management, and calculations into a single operation," observed Stan. "That's pretty slick and the calculated information can really help you to more quickly get a feel for the performance record. Could you show me the declaration for this form?"

Nodding, Jack switched E.OPRN to TRUE and executed the command

```
show perfform
```

to produce the printout appearing in Figure 9–20. As he handed it to Stan, he commented that the SHOW command could be used to get a form's declaration without having to use PAINT's Full Form menu. To remind them what that menu looked like, Jack executed the command

```
paint perfform
```

and chose the Full Form option. The resultant screen (minus the displayed color blocks) appeared as shown in Figure 9–21. Notice that he had defined pictures for all of the numeric nonliterals.

Basic Form-Processing Commands

"We can also do calculations via forms entirely independent of BROWSE and CREATE," Jack claimed. "This is accomplished with commands such as PUTFORM, TALLY, and GETFORM. I'll go over their usage with the SCALC form. It's a little form I painted for testing out the effects of potential salary adjustments. The idea of this salary calculation form is that the environment puts up a blank form displaying literals only. All the form's nonliterals are then tallied to display a particular rep name, territory ID, and monthly salary. Next, I type in the proposed salary increase. The effect of this increase is then displayed in the form."

"So it's a form for doing a little 'what if' analysis," said Debbie.

Agreeing with her assessment, Jack executed the command

```
show scalc
```

FIGURE 9–20 Form declaration for PERFFORM

```
FORM PERFFORM
AT 3, 23 PUT "Performance Record"
AT 3, 2 TO 17, 74 PUT "FABM"
AT 4, 1 TO 18, 72 PUT "FWBU"
AT 7, 1 TO 15, 69 PUT "FMBA"
AT 8, 8 TO 15, 19 PUT "FCBU"
AT 8, 21 TO 15, 32 PUT "FCBU"
AT 8, 34 TO 15, 45 PUT "FCBU"
AT 8, 47 TO 15, 58 PUT "FCBU"
AT 17, 8 TO 19, 58 PUT "FUBC"
AT 18, 21 TO 18, 45 PUT "FCBA"
AT 5, 2 PUT "Product ID:"
AT 5, 14 PUT PERF.PID USING "uuuu"
AT 5, 29 PUT "Sales rep:"
AT 5, 40 PUT PERF.FNAME
AT 5, 54 PUT "Territory:"
AT 5, 65 PUT PERF.TID
AT 7, 9 PUT "Quarter 1"
AT 7, 22 PUT "Quarter 2"
AT 7, 35 PUT "Quarter 3"
AT 7, 48 PUT "Quarter 4"
AT 7, 63 PUT "Total"
AT 9, 2 PUT "Sales"
AT 9, 12 GET PERF.S1   NUM USING "ff,fff"
AT 9, 12 PUT PERF.S1   USING "ff,fff"
AT 9, 25 GET PERF.S2   NUM USING "ff,fff"
AT 9, 25 PUT PERF.S2   USING "ff,fff"
AT 9, 38 GET PERF.S3   NUM USING "ff,fff"
AT 9, 38 PUT PERF.S3   USING "ff,fff"
AT 9, 51 GET PERF.S4   NUM USING "ff,fff"
AT 9, 51 PUT PERF.S4   USING "ff,fff"
AT 9, 62 PUT PERF.SYTD USING "fff,fff"
AT 11, 2 PUT "Quota"
AT 11, 12 GET PERF.Q1   NUM USING "ff,fff"
AT 11, 12 PUT PERF.Q1   USING "ff,fff"
AT 11, 25 GET PERF.Q2   NUM USING "ff,fff"
AT 11, 25 PUT PERF.Q2   USING "ff,fff"
AT 11, 38 GET PERF.Q3   NUM USING "ff,fff"
AT 11, 38 PUT PERF.Q3   USING "ff,fff"
AT 11, 51 GET PERF.Q4   NUM USING "ff,fff"
AT 11, 51 PUT PERF.Q4   USING "ff,fff"
AT 11, 62 PUT PERF.QYR  USING "fff,fff"
AT 14, 2 PUT "Extra"
AT 14, 11 PUT PERF.S1 - PERF.Q1   USING "fff,fff"
AT 14, 24 PUT PERF.S2 - PERF.Q2   USING "fff,fff"
AT 14, 37 PUT PERF.S3 - PERF.Q3   USING "fff,fff"
AT 14, 50 PUT PERF.S4 - PERF.Q4   USING "fff,fff"
AT 14, 60 PUT PERF.SYTD - PERF.QYR  USING "f,fff,fff"
AT 18, 22 PUT "(Extra = Sales - Quota)"
ENDFORM
```

FIGURE 9–21   Painting PERFFORM

```
                    Performance Record

Product ID: uuu              Sales rep:              Territory:

        Quarter 1    Quarter 2    Quarter 3   Quarter 4      Total

Sales     ff,fff       ff,fff       ff,fff      ff,fff      fff,fff

Quota     ff,fff       ff,fff       ff,fff      ff,fff      fff,fff


Extra    fff,fff      fff,fff      fff,fff     fff,fff     f,fff,fff


                (Extra = Sales - Quota)



Do you want to                                      Line: 2  Col: 2
        Save Form      View Form      Move Form    Release Form    Quit
```

to show them the SCALC form's declaration as portrayed in Figure
9–22. Observe that there are five nonliteral elements. One is a trimmed
version of TID, which will be pictured in parentheses. There are the
NAME and MOSAL fields from the REP table. The INCR is not a field
and therefore will be treated as a working variable. Notice that it was
painted to be both a place to put and get values. Fifth, there is the
numeric expression that specifies how to calculate a new salary from
INCR and MOSAL.

"Whatever REP record we want to do salary calculations for should
be made REP's current record," Jack explained. "Suppose it's Kim that
we want. Since I really don't want to see her entire record, I'll suppress
its display by switching E.SUPD to TRUE before invoking OBTAIN.
Then I'll execute the PUTFORM command to put the salary calculation
form on the screen."

Suiting his actions to his words, he executed the three commands

```
e.supd=true
obtain from rep where fname="Kim"
putform scalc
```

FIGURE 9–22   The salary calculation form's declaration

```
_show scalc
FORM SCALC
        AT 5, 19 PUT "Sales Representative"
        AT 5, 40 PUT TRIM(REP.TID)  USING "(r)"
        AT 7, 7 PUT "Name:"
        AT 7, 13 PUT REP.NAME
        AT 8, 7 PUT "Monthly salary:"
        AT 8, 23 PUT REP.MOSAL  USING "$f,fff.dd"
        AT 8, 50 PUT "Increase:"
        AT 8, 60 GET INCR  NUM USING "f.ddd"
        AT 8, 60 PUT INCR  USING "f.ddd"
        AT 10, 25 PUT "New salary:"
        AT 10, 37 PUT (1.00 + INCR) * REP.MOSAL  USING "fff.dd"
ENDFORM

_
```

causing the SCALC literal elements to be put on the screen as depicted in Figure 9–23. An underscore prompt appeared beneath the blank SCALC form, awaiting his next command.

"Now," he said briskly, "let's tally up the form's nonliteral elements, so that a value is showing for each. For that we issue a TALLY command. Remember, you've already seen Joy tally a form. Here, we're doing the same thing but with a different form."

Jack executed the command

```
tally scalc
```

resulting in the screen appearance shown in Figure 9–24. He pointed out that the increase was zero because he had yet to assign any value to the INCR variable. Thus the new salary was tallied to be the same as the present salary.

"So how," asked Jack, "could we check out the effect of a 6.2 percent increase?"

"You could," someone replied, "execute a LET command to give INCR a value of .062. But there ought to be a better way."

"There is," rejoined Jack. "We'll issue a GETFORM command. This

FIGURE 9–23 The PUTFORM command

```
_e.supd=true
_obtain from rep where fname="Kim"
_putform scalc

                  Sales Representative

     Name:
     Monthly salary:                        Increase: _.___

                    New salary:
```

FIGURE 9–24 The TALLY command

```
_e.supd=true
_obtain from rep where fname="Kim"
_putform scalc

                  Sales Representative (0)

     Name: Kim G. Anders
     Monthly salary: $2,600.00              Increase: 0.000

                    New salary: $2,600.00
_tally scalc
```

FIGURE 9–25 The GETFORM command

```
_e.supd=true
_obtain from rep where fname="Kim"
_putform scalc

                    Sales Representative (0)

      Name: Kim G. Anders
      Monthly salary: $2,600.00                    Increase:   .062

                        New salary: $2,600.00
_getform scalc
```

command causes the cursor to visit every nonliteral that has been designated as a place where the environment can get values from us. In
the SCALC case, there's only one such nonliteral, the one for the INCR
variable."

Executing he command

getform scalc

caused the cursor to jump to the nonliteral element following the "Increase:" element. There, Jack typed in

.062

and pressed the Enter key. Because there were no other elements designated for getting data, the GETFORM command terminated, leaving
the screen as shown in Figure 9–25. The INCR now had a .062 value.
To tally the new salary, Jack again issued the TALLY command, yielding
the Figure 9–26 result.

"It would be nice if we didn't have to do that extra TALLY at the

FIGURE 9–26 Tallying a new salary

```
_e.supd=true
_obtain from rep where fname="Kim"
_putform scalc

                    Sales Representative (0)

        Name: Kim G. Anders
        Monthly salary: $2,600.00                   Increase: 0.062

                        New salary: $2,761.20
_tally scalc
```

end," opined Dan. "Can't GETFORM go ahead and immediately compute the new salary as we enter the increase?"

"Good question," Jack responded, "and the answer is yes. If E.ICOM is switched from its FALSE default to TRUE, the immediate computation you want will occur. In effect, it causes our automatic TALLY to happen during GETFORM. Try it for yourselves during the break. By the way, this environment setting will also cause immediate computation of virtual field values as you make new entries while creating a record or editing its values when browsing."

Brad frowned, "All this seems like a lot of work to check out a salary adjustment. I'd like to activate the whole process with just a single keystroke rather than a series of three or four commands."

Jack smiled, "I was wondering when someone would point that out. Obviously, you wouldn't go to the effort of making and using the SCALC form if this were a once in a lifetime analysis. But if it's frequent, SCALC can be useful and we can cut the entire process down to a single keystroke, say B for Brad."

"With a macro, right?" asked Dan.

"Correct," replied Jack as he executed the command

FIGURE 9–27   Executing the B macro

```
                    Sales Representative (D)

      Name: Kim G. Anders
      Monthly salary: $2,b00.00              Increase: 0.000

                    New salary: $2,b00.00
```

```
macro b clear;incr=0;putform scalc;tally scalc;getform scalc;wait;clear
```

to define Brad's macro. Notice that this macro assumes E.ICOM is TRUE. Jack demonstrated by pressing the B key and then pressing Enter. The screen cleared for an instant before SCALC was put there and tallied as shown in Figure 9–27. The cursor was blinking at the INCR element, ready to get a value. As before, Jack entered

```
.0b2
```

and pressed the Enter key. The new salary appeared instantaneously as depicted in Figure 9–28. The macro's WAIT command caused processing to wait until the space bar was pressed before clearing the screen.

"Let's say I want to get a printout of the SCALC form," asked Tracey. "What would I do?"

Jack explained that the PRINT command gives an easy way to print a form. He demonstrated by executing the command

```
print scalc
```

FIGURE 9–28   Result of the B macro

```
                    Sales Representative (0)

        Name: Kim G. Anders
        Monthly salary: $2,600.00              Increase: 0.062

                      New salary: $2,761.20
```

yielding a printout of SCALC. It consisted of a printed rendition of a combination PUTFORM and TALLY. The setting of E.OPRN is irrelevant for the PRINT command.

Integrating Forms into Text

"I can imagine situations where I'd like to incorporate forms into a piece of text," Tracey continued. "It would be a shame if we couldn't take advantage of our forms in the midst of text processing."

"It sure would," Jack agreed. "Fortunately, you can do just that. Suppose you are working on a sales rep document called REPDOC and you decide you'd like to have RFORM appear right in your text. You just escape to the status line, type a blackslash, and then the PRINT command."

He demonstrated by executing the command

```
text "a:repdoc.txt"
```

to bring up the text screen. After escaping to the status line he issued the command

```
\print rform
```

PHOTO 19   Integrating a form into text

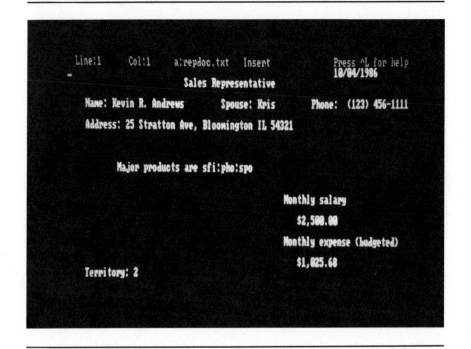

Line:1   Col:1   a:repdoc.txt   Insert   Press ^L for help
                                                              10/04/1986
                              Sales Representative
      Name: Kevin R. Andrews   Spouse: Kris   Phone: (123) 456-1111
      Address: 25 Stratton Ave, Bloomington IL 54321

          Major products are sfi:pho:spo

                                           Monthly salary
                                           $2,500.00
                                           Monthly expense (budgeted)
                                           $1,025.68
          Territory: 2

which immediately filled in the text area as shown in Photo 19. It was
subject to editing, just like any other text. Observe that PRINT behaves
just as it did before, except the form is "printed" into the text rather
than on paper.

"If I wanted the form printed in the text for some other rep, then
I'd first obtain that rep's record before invoking the PRINT command?"
Tracey said in a questioning tone.

"That's right," Jack confirmed, "and remember E.SUPD can be used
to suppress the display of OBTAIN results, keeping them out of the
text itself when you invoke \OBTAIN on the status line."

"So," Joy summarized, "you can paint your forms to contain passages of text or you can devise your text to contain tallied forms."

BASIC IDEAS

A form is one way to represent a chunk of presentation knowledge. A form
can be either declared (with the FORM command) or interactively painted
on the console screen (PAINT). In addition to blocks of color, a form

usually has elements. An element can be either literal or nonliteral. If it is a nonliteral, there is a choice of whether the environment can put data values on display through the element, get data values through the element, or both. In the latter two cases, a variable (e.g., working variable, field) is specified for the element. The value an environment gets through the element is assigned to the variable. In the former case, either a variable or a more complex expression is specified for the element. Its value is calculated whenever the form is tallied.

Basic form-processing commands allow a blank form to be put on the screen (PUTFORM), its expressions to be evaluated and displayed (TALLY), its "Get" elements to accept data entry (GETFORM), its declaration to be shown (SHOW), and a tallied version to be printed (PRINT). Forms can be processed by data management commands (CREATE, BROWSE) and in the midst of text processing.

By the time they broke for hands-on practice, the managers had formed a favorable opinion of this new knowledge management technique and the ways in which it fit with earlier techniques they had learned. After the practice began, Joy took Jack aside and complimented his efforts, saying, "You were certainly in fine form this morning."

"You were pretty good yourself," he replied with a wink. Referring to her RFORM and his own PERFFORM, he added, "I very much liked the attractive form you presented, but I'd put my form up against yours any time."

She smiled one of her scintillating smiles. "You sure have a way with words."

Jack chuckled, "And with forms too, I hope you'll agree."

References

1.　Kaiser, J. B. *Forms Design and Control*. New York: American Management Association, 1968.

2.　*KnowledgeMan Reference Manual*, version 2. Lafayette, Ind.: MDBS, Inc., 1985.

3.　*K-Paint Supplement*, version 2. Lafayette, Ind.: MDBS, Inc., 1985.

4.　Mathies, L. H., and G. Myers. "Good Forms Design Is Vital to Management." *The Office*, September 1981.

5.　Myers, G. "Forms Management." *Journal of Systems Management*, October 1976.

6.　Seager, D. "The Ten Commandments of Forms Design." *Canadian Datasystems*, October 1977.

7.　Stubbs, J. "Forms Are Main User Connection." *Data Management*, June 1977.

8.　Tsichritzis, D. "Form Management." *Communications of ACM* 25, no. 7 (July 1982).

Now that's what I call a first-hand report!

Chapter Ten

Report Generation

Following the managers' hands-on excursions into forms management, and then lunch, the session resumed with a perceptive comment from Debbie. "Before you begin with new material, Jack, I noticed something I'd like to do with forms but wasn't able to. Basically, we are able to process one record at a time with a form. I'd like to go a step further and, in a single operation, process many records with the same form. For instance, it would be great if we had a command similar to SELECT, except that instead of displaying lines it would display the results in forms. Is there some way to do this?"

"There is," answered Jack, "but you don't use forms. Instead you make use of a template to generate a customized report containing data from many records in one or more tables. As with forms, the reported data could also come from other sources such as utility variables, working variables, and calculations. As a matter of fact, customized report generation is exactly what I'd planned to present this afternoon."

Remember from Chapter 8 that the results of a SELECT command can be thought of as a tabular report consisting of lines of data. Some degree of control over the presentation of these lines is furnished, including pictures, column headings, and intercolumn spacing. Nevertheless, this falls far short of the free-form layouts provided by forms and necessary for elaborate reports. *Report generation* is a technique of knowledge management that gives extensive control over the presentation of report contents [2], [3], [4], [6].

Like ad hoc inquiry, report generation software can present results on a line-by-line basis. Each such line is called a *report detail.* However, unlike query results, a report detail can be spread over several lines if desired. The arrangement of data values of each report detail is determined by a form. This detail form has nonliteral elements where the data values are to appear, and can also have literal elements. Figure

FIGURE 10–1   Report with two-line report details

```
Name: Kevin R. Andrews        Addr: 25 Stratton Ave, Bloomington IL 54321
      (123) 456-1111 Sal: $2,500  Exp: $1,025.68    sfi:pho:spo 08/30/1981   Kris

Name: Kim G. Anders           Addr: 8242 Wabash, Chicago IL 68909
      (312) 553-6754 Sal: $2,600  Exp:    $896.74   ref:bus:spo 04/06/1979

Name: Kris H. Raber           Addr: 314 Miami, Dayton OH 46783
      (513) 333-9989 Sal: $2,400  Exp: $1,132.61    rom:psy:bio 04/08/1982  Kevin

Name: Tina F. Lee             Addr: 7892 Meridian, Indianapolis IN 46662
      (317) 299-8393 Sal: $2,800  Exp:    $988.20   bus:com:rom 12/13/1981   Ben

Name: Toby C. Terry           Addr: 2028 Prescott, Fort Wayne IN 45567
      (345) 123-4567 Sal: $2,000  Exp: $1,080.53    rom:psy:bus 02/25/1985

Name: Kerry H. Jones          Addr: 128 Spiceland, Grand Rapids MI 35988
      (632) 098-7654 Sal: $2,250  Exp: $1,229.64    pho:ref:psy 06/10/1983  Kendra

Name: Karen V. Bruckner       Addr: 44 Tan Ave., Madison WI 66667
      (433) 442-8201 Sal: $2,800  Exp: $1,335.00    com:bus:rom 05/14/1982

Name: Kathy F. Smith          Addr: 85 Griese Ln, Milwaukee WI 65543
      (415) 567-8901 Sal: $2,100  Exp:    $882.74   pho:ref:sfi 07/03/1984   Tom

Name: Jackie V. Smith         Addr: 32 New Jersey, Columbus OH 33464
      (322) 861-6543 Sal: $2,400  Exp: $1,006.45    spo:ref:bio 04/12/1980  David

Name: Carol O. Lynn           Addr: 58 Cater Dr., Midland MI 40098
      (412) 832-5643 Sal: $2,750  Exp: $1,229.73    com:rom:bus 11/01/1979
```

10–1 shows a report consisting of 10 details, each occupying two lines. Notice that each detail has the same pattern of literal and nonliteral elements. Only the values of nonliterals differ from one detail to the next.

In addition, report generation software allows a report to have header and footer forms. A *header* form appears before report details, while a *footer* appears after report details. Normally, three kinds of headers and footers are supported. First, there is a *report header and footer* pair that encases all details in the report. In Figure 10–2 the report header consists of a title, date, and underlined column headings. The report footer consists of the manager line near the bottom of the printout's page.

Second, there is a *page header and footer* pair that surrounds all details on each page of a report. Examples of page headers and footers appear in Figure 10–3. Third, a *group header and footer* pair denotes the beginning and end of each group of report details, where the group is defined according to some control break criterion. In Figure 10–4, territory ID is the control break criterion. The group of details for each territory has a header showing the ID, rep name, and underlined column headings. Each group footer consists of column totals for the group's details.

FIGURE 10–2   Report with report header and footer

```
                        Sales Rep List                    10/04/1986

Rep Name  (territory)   Address                            Spouse
=====================   ====================================  ========

Kim G. Anders (0)       8242 Wabash, Chicago IL 68909
                        Phone: (312) 553-6754

Kris H. Raber (1)       314 Miami, Dayton OH 46783          Kevin
                        Phone: (513) 333-9989

Kevin R. Andrews (2)    25 Stratton Ave, Bloomington IL 54321  Kris
                        Phone: (123) 456-1111

Tina F. Lee (3)         7892 Meridian, Indianapolis IN 46662  Ben
                        Phone: (317) 299-8393

Toby C. Terry (4)       2028 Prescott, Fort Wayne IN 45567
                        Phone: (345) 123-4567

Kerry H. Jones (5)      128 Spiceland, Grand Rapids MI 35988  Kendra
                        Phone: (632) 098-7654

Karen V. Bruckner (6)   44 Tan Ave., Madison WI 66667
                        Phone: (433) 442-8201

Kathy F. Smith (7)      85 Griese Ln., Milwaukee WI 65543    Tom
                        Phone: (415) 567-8901

Jackie V. Smith (8)     32 New Jersey, Columbus OH 33464     David
                        Phone: (322) 861-6543

Carol O. Lynn (9)       58 Cater Dr., Midland MI 40098
                        Phone: (412) 832-5643




                                                 Manager: Jack Vander
```

FIGURE 10–3 Report with page headers and footers

```
Performance Report                                              Page 2

Product   Rep         Year-to-date sales      Annual quota
=======   =========   ==================      ============

          Carol            $16,945                 $22,525

          Tina             $13,619                 $17,889

   sfi    Kevin            $27,794                 $35,739

          Kathy            $11,990                 $17,423

   spo    Kevin            $22,742                 $28,531

          Kim              $20,267                 $27,929

          Jackie           $16,945                 $22,525
```

```
Performance Report                                             Page 1

Product   Rep         Year-to-date sales      Annual quota
=======   =========   ==================      ============

   bio    Kris             $22,858                 $28,895

          Jackie           $11,990                 $17,423

   bus    Karen            $32,534                 $38,082

          Tina             $24,307                 $32,742

          Kim              $21,882                 $30,273

          Toby             $14,909                 $19,130

          Carol            $13,439                 $17,108

          Kevin            $13,330                 $13,575

   com    Karen            $34,786                 $43,630

          Carol            $24,830                 $27,272

          Tina             $23,874                 $25,667

   pho    Kerry            $32,534                 $38,082

          Kevin            $22,858                 $29,794

          Kathy            $22,023                 $28,553

   psy    Kris             $23,499                 $29,654

          Kerry            $14,909                 $19,130

          Toby             $14,496                 $21,913

          Tina             $10,125                 $14,927

   ref    Kim              $22,846                 $31,595

          Kerry            $16,790                 $19,899

          Jackie           $13,996                 $19,692

          Kathy            $13,432                 $19,047

          Kevin            $10,125                 $14,927

   rom    Kris             $30,535                 $38,912

          Karen            $18,894                 $23,281

          Toby             $18,043                 $25,836


                            ***CONFIDENTIAL***
```

FIGURE 10–4 Report with group headers and footers

```
Territory 0          Name: Kim G. Anders

        Product           Sales            Quota         Sales  -  Quota
        =======        =========        ========        ==============

          bus           $21,882          $30,273             $-8,391
          ref           $22,846          $31,595             $-8,749
          spo           $20,267          $27,929             $-7,662

        Totals:         $64,995          $89,797            $-24,802


Territory 1          Name: Kris H. Raber

        Product           Sales            Quota         Sales  -  Quota
        =======        =========        ========        ==============

          bio           $22,858          $28,895             $-6,037
          psy           $23,499          $29,654             $-6,155
          rom           $30,535          $38,912             $-8,377

        Totals:         $76,892          $97,461            $-20,569


Territory 2          Name: Kevin R. Andrews

        Product           Sales            Quota         Sales  -  Quota
        =======        =========        ========        ==============

          bus           $13,330          $13,575              $-245
          pho           $22,858          $29,794             $-6,936
          ref           $10,125          $14,927             $-4,802
          sfi           $27,794          $35,739             $-7,945
          spo           $22,742          $28,531             $-5,789

        Totals:         $96,849         $122,566            $-25,717


Territory 3          Name: Tina F. Lee

        Product           Sales            Quota         Sales  -  Quota
        =======        =========        ========        ==============

          bus           $24,307          $32,742             $-8,435
          com           $23,874          $25,667             $-1,793
          psy           $10,125          $14,927             $-4,802
          rom           $13,619          $17,889             $-4,270

        Totals:         $71,925          $91,225            $-19,300
```

Collectively, the visual patterns of a report detail form, header forms, and footer forms are called a *template*. A template consists of the presentation knowledge that dictates the structure and appearance of a report. In an environment, templates exist alongside tables, forms, contexts, and so on as objects in the knowledge system. Once designed, a template can be used repeatedly to generate reports adhering to the structure and appearance it prescribes. As Jack was about to describe, his environment allowed templates to be designed interactively with the DESIGN command and reports to be generated from them with the REPORT command [4].

Jack also planned to demonstrate a variation of the PRINT TEXT command discussed in Chapter 5. This variation allows each report detail to appear not as values in a displayed detail form, but as values embedded in a piece of text [5]. In other words, it generates multiple copies of a piece of text, each of which contains the values of a report detail located at an appropriate location in the text. This is sometimes referred to as *mail merge* processing, since it can be used to generate customized versions of a form letter to be mailed to various destinations. Word processing software often has a mail merge ability in which a letter's basic text in one file can be merged with data values in a second text file. An integrated environment's mail merge ability has no need for a second text file. Merged data can come directly from a table's records.

TEMPLATE DESIGN

"If you can paint a form, you can design a template," Jack asserted. "I think of a template as being a collection of one or more miniature forms, each specifying the pattern that should be used for generating some part of a report. Actually a pattern in a template doesn't have to be tiny, but for most reports I do, the patterns are pretty simple."

Joy added, "Because an entire template could be very large, templates are not part of a context as forms are. Instead, each template is stored in a *template file* in the environment's knowledge system. By convention, such files are tagged with a TPL extension. When you want to design a template or generate a report with it, you'll need to refer to the name of that template's file."

Addressing Jack, Dan commented, "You said that there could be various 'parts' to a report. What exactly do you mean?"

"Good question," acknowledged Jack. "Think about the result displayed for a SELECT command. You get lines consisting of one value for each column specified in the SELECT command. Each of these corresponds to what's called a report detail. When we generate a report, details will have the same basic form. That form is determined by the detail pattern we design into a template. Aside from details there may be two other parts to reports: headers and footers."

"They're what comes before and after a report's details," interjected Dan as he began to get the idea.

"Right," confirmed Jack. "Of course, they are optional parts for a report. If you want a report to have a header or footer, you merely design the desired header pattern or footer pattern into your template. When a report is generated from a template, its headers and footers conform to those patterns."

"Are you implying that there can be multiple headers or footers in the same report?" asked Tracey.

"Yep," he replied briskly. "Actually there are three basic kinds of headers and three corresponding kinds of footers. You can have a header for all the details in a report, for each page of details, or for groups of details. The same goes for footers. Each can be very useful for certain types of reports. By stepping through a few report examples, the uses of different kinds of headers and footers will become clear. For each example, we'll first design a template and then generate reports with it. Let's begin with the simplest type of report: one with no headers or footers, but details only."

REPORT DETAILS

"Remember from the SELECT command," he continued, "that when too many columns are selected, all their values for a record won't fit on the same line. So lines that are too long wrap around to the next line. This makes for a fairly unattractive display, certainly one that we wouldn't want to send into headquarters as a formal report. Well, the report generation technique gives us a way to present all the data from each lengthy REP record without the wraparound behavior. First, we design a template that specifies the arrangement of data for each report detail. Then we can generate reports with that template."

Design

Wanting to design a template for rep reports, he proceeded to execute the command

```
design "a:reprep"
```

allowing the design of a template to begin. The screen cleared momentarily before taking on the appearance shown in Figure 10–5. If a file

FIGURE 10–5   **Main template Design menu**

```
                                                                          I
                                                                          I
                                                                          I
                                                                          I
                                                                          I
                                                                          I
                                                                          I
                                                                          I
                                                                          I
                                                                          I
                                                                          I
                                                                          I
                                                                          I
                                                                          I
                                                                          I
                                                                          I
                                                                          I
                                                                          I
                                                                          I
                                                                          I
                                                                          I
 Do you want to work on a                              Line: 1    Col: 1
    Detail Pattern    Header Pattern    Footer Pattern    Whole Template    Quit
```

named REPREP.TPL had already existed on the drive A diskette, its template would have appeared on the screen where it could be modified. However, in this case Jack was designing a rep report template from scratch, to be held in the new REPREP.TPL file.

As Figure 10–5 suggests, the DESIGN command works in a way that is comparable to the PAINT command. There is a two-line status area at the bottom of the screen. In addition to showing the cursor's present line and column, this area can display menus and prompts that guide a user through the design process. Initially, DESIGN's main menu gives the choice of working on the template's detail pattern, a header pattern, a footer pattern, or the template as a whole. Options are chosen in the usual way.

All eyes were on the right side of the screen, as Stan asked, "What does that column of Is mean?"

With a chuckle, Jack replied, "At this stage, I only have Is for you. But, if you bear with me, I'll give you much more." He stole a glance in Joy's direction. As their blue eyes touched, she understood what he meant. It was clear to her that he had certain designs in mind.

For the benefit of the managers Jack elaborated, "When designing a template, the right edge of the screen is reserved to indicate the

FIGURE 10–6   **The Detail menu**

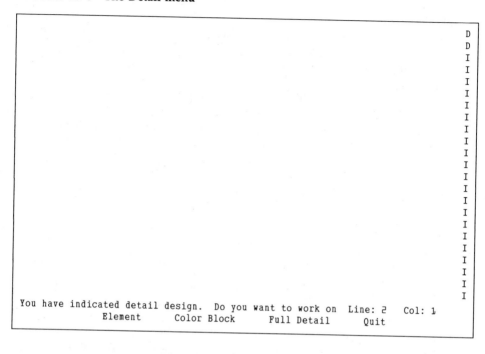

```
                                                                        D
                                                                        D
                                                                        I
                                                                        I
                                                                        I
                                                                        I
                                                                        I
                                                                        I
                                                                        I
                                                                        I
                                                                        I
                                                                        I
                                                                        I
                                                                        I
                                                                        I
                                                                        I
                                                                        I
                                                                        I
                                                                        I
                                                                        I
                                                                        I
You have indicated detail design.  Do you want to work on  Line: 2   Col: 1
            Element        Color Block      Full Detail      Quit
```

nature of each template line. Initially each line is marked with an I, indicating that it will be ignored for report generation purposes. As we design a template some of the lines will be marked with other letters—like D for detail—to indicate what kind of pattern they belong to."

"So the markers won't actually appear in generated reports," added Joy. "They just appear during the design phase as a convenient way for keeping track of where each pattern in a template begins and ends."

Jack demonstrated by pressing the D key to pick the Detail Pattern option from DESIGN's main menu. In the status area he was now told to move the cursor to the top line of the detail pattern. He left the cursor on the top line and pressed the Enter key, explaining that he wanted the detail pattern to begin on the first line and extend through the second template line. In the status area, he was now told to move the cursor to the bottom line desired for the detail pattern. He moved the cursor down to the second line and pressed the Enter key, resulting in the screen appearance shown in Figure 10–6.

"Notice," Jack said, "that the first two lines have D marks. This means that whatever pattern we design there will determine the appearance of details in reports generated with this template."

Referring to the status area (Figure 10–6), Tracey commented, "It looks almost identical to the main Painting menu we've used in forms management."

"Correct," Jack responded, and added with a wink, "you might say it differs only in a couple of details. Now you can see why I said that if you can paint a form you can design a template. In effect, designing the detail pattern in D lines is like painting a little form."

"So elements and color blocks mean the same thing here as they did when painting a form," Tracey continued. "And the menus we get while designing one of a template's patterns are like those we've already seen when painting a form."

"That's right," Jack replied and paused, "almost. There are a few differences, but you won't find them surprising. When you're making a nonliteral element in a template, you won't be asked to designate it as 'Put,' 'Get,' or 'Both.' "

"Of course," nodded Tracey, "I should have thought of that before. Because the environment only puts data out through a report, we only need to provide the expressions for nonliterals, along with any special effects we might want."

Confirming that she was on the right track, Jack picked the Element option from the Detail Pattern menu in Figure 10–6. First, he defined the literal element "Name:" as part of the detail pattern. He decided to go to another element and was told to move the cursor to its starting point. He moved it to directly follow the literal (line 1, column 7), which is where he wanted a value of REP.NAME to appear in each generated report detail. As when painting a form, a menu appeared asking him to choose between the Literal and Nonliteral options. Because he chose the latter, he was prompted to provide the expression whose value would appear for this element in each generated report detail. Jack typed

```
rep.name
```

resulting in the screen appearance shown in Figure 10–7. On pressing the Enter key, the status area changed as shown in Figure 10–8. Jack picked the All Values option. As he would later show in another template, the Unique option causes the expression's value to be suppressed in a generated report detail if that value is the same as for the prior detail. In spirit, it is comparable to using the SELECT command's UNIQUE qualifier for a column of query results.

He went on to specify three more literal elements ("Addr:", "Sal:", "Exp:") in the template's detail pattern. A nonliteral element was specified to follow each of these (with expressions of REP.ADDR, REP.MOSAL, and REP.EXP, respectively). In addition, Jack made a non-

FIGURE 10–7   Entering a nonliteral element's expression

```
Name:                                                                    D
                                                                         D
                                                                         I
                                                                         I
                                                                         I
                                                                         I
                                                                         I
                                                                         I
                                                                         I
                                                                         I
                                                                         I
                                                                         I
                                                                         I
                                                                         I
                                                                         I
                                                                         I
                                                                         I
                                                                         I
                                                                         I
                                                                         I
                                                                         I
                                                                         I
                                                       Line: 1   Col: 7
Enter expression: rep.name
```

FIGURE 10–8   UNIQUE qualifier for a nonliteral element

```
Name:                                                                    D
                                                                         D
                                                                         I
                                                                         I
                                                                         I
                                                                         I
                                                                         I
                                                                         I
                                                                         I
                                                                         I
                                                                         I
                                                                         I
                                                                         I
                                                                         I
                                                                         I
                                                                         I
                                                                         I
                                                                         I
                                                                         I
                                                                         I
For this expression, do you want to allow display of     Line: 1   Col: 7
                  All values          Unique Values Only
```

FIGURE 10–9   The Full Detail menu

```
                                                                        D
 Name:                         Addr                                     D
                    Sal:    $f,fff  Exp: $f,fff.dd                       I
                                                                        I
                                                                        I
                                                                        I
                                                                        I
                                                                        I
                                                                        I
                                                                        I
                                                                        I
                                                                        I
                                                                        I
                                                                        I
                                                                        I
                                                                        I
                                                                        I
                                                                        I
                                                                        I
                                                                        I
                                                                        I
                                                                        I
                                                                        I
 ─────────────────────────────────────────────────────────────────────
 For this detail pattern, do you want to            Line: 1    Col: 1
      Change Top/Bottom    Assign Spacing    Delete It  Force Break   Quit
```

literal element for REP.PHONE near the start of the second line and non-literal elements for REP.MAJORP, REP.HDATE, and REP.SPOUSE at the end of that line. Because he did not give them any special pictures, the four additional elements were not visible in the displayed detail pattern.

Having completed his work with elements, Jack got back to the Detail Pattern menu (recall the status area of Figure 10–6). "Now as report details are generated according to this pattern we've designed, I'd like them to be separated by a blank line. To do this, I'll pick the Full Detail option in the Detail Pattern menu."

As he chose that option, the screen assumed the appearance depicted in Figure 10–9. The status area contained a menu for operating on the full detail pattern as a whole. Jack explained that one way to get a blank line after each generated detail's elements would be to choose the first option. This would allow the lower boundary of the detail pattern to be moved downward by a line, in effect leaving a blank line in each generated detail. Instead he chose the more obvious Assign Spacing option.

In the status area, Jack was asked how many blank lines should appear after each report detail generated from this template. He typed

FIGURE 10-10   Specifying interdetail spacing

```
Name:                        Addr:                                            D
                   Sal: $f,fff  Exp: $f,fff.dd                                D
                                                                             D
                                                                             I
                                                                             I
                                                                             I
                                                                             I
                                                                             I
                                                                             I
                                                                             I
                                                                             I
                                                                             I
                                                                             I
                                                                             I
                                                                             I
                                                                             I
                                                                             I
                                                                             I
                                                                             I
                                                                             I
                                                                             I
                                                                             I

How many blank lines after each report detail? 1
```

1

producing the screen appearance shown in Figure 10–10. When he pressed the Enter key the screen reverted to the Figure 10–9 appearance. He pointed out that there was an option for deleting the entire detail pattern from a template and a Force Break option. The latter lets a designer specify the maximum number of generated details that can appear on each page of a report generated from the template. Jack quit the Full Detail menu. As the Detail Pattern menu reappeared, he picked its Quit option too, reverting back to DESIGN's main menu (recall the status area of Figure 10–5).

Jack chose the main menu's Quit option because he did not want to design any header or footer patterns for this template. The environment responded with the screen portrayed in Figure 10–11. Jack picked the Yes option in the status area to preserve the newly designed template in REPREP.TPL on the drive A diskette. This terminated the DESIGN command and the underscore prompt appeared, awaiting the next command. Had he picked the No option, the environment would have prompted him to provide a different file name for preserving the template. Such a feature is handy when making a variant of an existing

FIGURE 10–11   Preserving a template

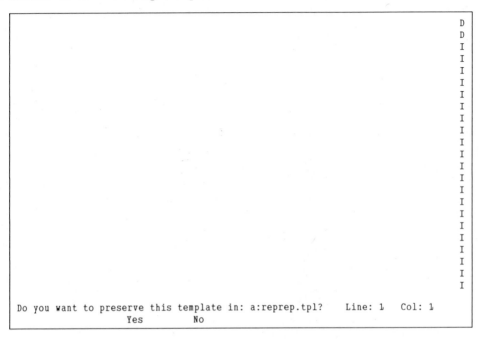

```
                                                                   D
                                                                   D
                                                                   I
                                                                   I
                                                                   I
                                                                   I
                                                                   I
                                                                   I
                                                                   I
                                                                   I
                                                                   I
                                                                   I
                                                                   I
                                                                   I
                                                                   I
                                                                   I
                                                                   I
                                                                   I
                                                                   I
                                                                   I
                                                                   I
                                                                   I
Do you want to preserve this template in: a:reprep.tpl?   Line: 1   Col: 1
                   Yes        No
```

template. The variant is preserved in a different file without affecting the original template file.

Generation

Having saved the template in REPREP.TPL, Jack exclaimed, "Now for the payoff! Let's generate a report with this template."

Without further ado, he executed the commands

```
e.oprn=true
report "a:reprep" from rep
```

As usual, the first readied the printer for receiving the report. The REPORT command then applied the template to present one report detail for every record in the REP table. The resultant printout appears in Figure 10–1. Observe that for each of the 10 report details, the REPORT command extracted data from a REP record and presented it according to the template's detail pattern. As specified in the template, one blank line follows each detail in the generated report. The printer automatically ejected to the top of a new page.

"It sure would be nice if the report's contents could be ordered differently," offered Don, "by descending salary for instance."

"Oh," Jack said nonchalantly, "that's easy. You all know how to do that already."

Without a pause, he pressed ^Z and tacked an ordering clause onto the prior command. He executed the resultant command

```
report "a:reprep" from rep order by za mosal
```

producing the same result as shown in Figure 10–1, except the details were now ordered by descending salaries. Jack explained that any ORDER BY clause that could be used for ad hoc queries could also be used for formal report generation.

"That's slick," remarked Stan, "but I'll bet you can't do conditional reports."

"Why not?" Jack asked rhetorically. "In fact you already know how to do that too!"

As an example, he pressed ^Z and edited the prior command, yielding

```
report "a:reprep" from rep where mosal-2000>moexp order by za mosal
```

which he executed. Only those details for which salary exceeded expenses by more than 2,000 appeared in the resultant report printout.

"What you're saying," observed Debbie, "is that the REPORT command really isn't all that different from the SELECT command."

"Exactly!" he replied. "If you can issue an ad hoc query, you can generate a report. Its details can be in whatever order you like and you can restrict it with whatever conditions you like. The main difference is that with SELECT, you list the columns you want right there in the ad hoc query, but with REPORT you give the name of a template file instead. Each can get at the same data, but REPORT gives you far more control over the presentation of that data. Obviously, the price that you pay for fancier presentation is the effort that goes into designing a template."

"So REPORT isn't meant for handling ad hoc information needs," Debbie continued. "But once we have a template, we can use it over and over again to get at data for different conditions and in different orders—just as quickly as we could get at the same data with an ad hoc query."

"True," Jack confirmed. "Basically, that's all there is to report generation. But to get even fancier, you might want to design headers and footers for some of your templates. They're easy too. If you can design a detail pattern then you can also design header and footer patterns."

REPORT HEADERS AND FOOTERS

As explained earlier, a report header appears before all details in a report and a report footer appears after all details. A report will have a header if its template has a report header pattern. Similarly, if a template has a report footer pattern, every report generated with that template will have a report footer. Like a template's detail pattern, report header and footer patterns can contain both literal and nonliteral elements arranged in any desired form. When a report is generated, the header's nonliterals are evaluated immediately and their values appear in the header. After all details have been produced, the footer's nonliteral elements are evaluated and their values appear in the report footer.

Design

"To show you how report headers and footers can be valuable," Jack declared, "I'm going to design a different template for getting at sales rep data. Because reports generated with it will present rep data in a listlike fashion, I'll call the template file REPLIST.TPL."

Jack switched E.OPRN to FALSE. To begin designing this new template, he executed the command

```
design "a:replist"
```

causing the screen depicted in Figure 10–5 to appear, with the same set of Is they had seen before staring at them once more. This time Jack pressed the H key (instead of D) to begin working on a header first. He was immediately confronted with the choices shown in Figure 10–12. Jack pressed R since it was a report header that he wanted to design.

Messages in the status area told him to move the cursor to indicate the top and bottom lines of the report header pattern. He did so, letting the header occupy the first six template lines. The resultant screen appeared as depicted in Figure 10–13. The letters RH marked those lines participating in the report header pattern and the status area contained the header design menu.

"Déjà vu!" Jack remarked. "You already know how to deal with this kind of menu."

He proceeded to create four elements in the report header pattern. On its second line he typed in the literal element "Sales Rep List"

FIGURE 10–12   Choosing the type of header

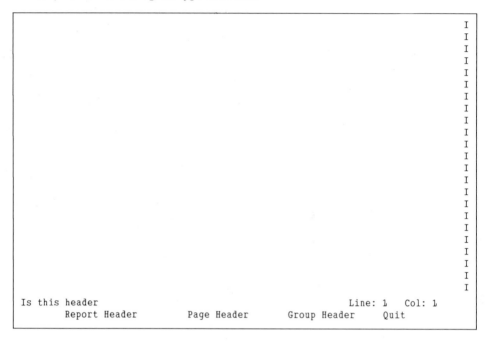

```
                                                                          I
                                                                          I
                                                                          I
                                                                          I
                                                                          I
                                                                          I
                                                                          I
                                                                          I
                                                                          I
                                                                          I
                                                                          I
                                                                          I
                                                                          I
                                                                          I
                                                                          I
                                                                          I
                                                                          I
                                                                          I
                                                                          I
                                                                          I
                                                                          I
Is this header                                      Line: 1   Col: 1
        Report Header          Page Header       Group Header    Quit
```

and specified a nonliteral element for #DATE, giving it a picture of rrrrrr19rr. On the fifth line he made a very long literal element consisting of several words that stretched across the entire length of the line. Similarly, the sixth line was spanned by a literal element composed of three groups of = symbols. Having specified the desired elements, he chose the Full Header option from the Header Design menu (recall the status area of Figure 10–13). This resulted in the screen appearing in Figure 10–14.

Explaining that he wanted one blank line to follow the report header and precede the details in reports generated with this template, Jack pressed the A key. As Figure 10–15 illustrates, he was asked to enter the number of blank lines desired and he did so. The Full Header menu of Figure 10–14 reappeared. Jack reminded them that its options were the same as those seen earlier (recall Figure 10–9) in the Full Detail menu. He noted that the Force Break option could be used to force the report to break to a new page as soon as the report header had been printed. In other words, a report header can be forced to appear as a report's cover page if desired.

Having finished with the report header pattern, Jack went on to design the template's detail pattern. He picked the Quit option until

FIGURE 10–13 The Header Design menu

```
                                                                        RH
                                                                        RH
                                                                        RH
                                                                        RH
                                                                        RH
                                                                        RH
                                                                         I
                                                                         I
                                                                         I
                                                                         I
                                                                         I
                                                                         I
                                                                         I
                                                                         I
                                                                         I
                                                                         I
                                                                         I
                                                                         I
                                                                         I
                                                                         I
                                                                         I
                                                                         I
                                                                         I
 You have indicated a header design.  Do you want to work onLine: 6   Col: 1
              Element        Color Block       Full Header      Quit
```

FIGURE 10–14 The Full Header menu

```
                                                                        RH
                         Sales Rep List                 rrrrrr1⁹rr     RH
                                                                        RH
                                                                        RH
 Rep Name  (territory)   Address                         Spouse        RH
 ====================    =================================   ========   RH
                                                                         I
                                                                         I
                                                                         I
                                                                         I
                                                                         I
                                                                         I
                                                                         I
                                                                         I
                                                                         I
                                                                         I
                                                                         I
                                                                         I
                                                                         I
                                                                         I
                                                                         I
 For this header pattern, do you want to          Line: 1   Col: 1
    Change Top/Bottom    Assign Spacing    Delete It    Force Break    Quit
```

FIGURE 10–15   Specifying spacing between header and details

```
                                                                        RH
                        Sales Rep List                    rrrrrrl⁹rr   RH
                                                                        RH
                                                                        RH
Rep Name  (territory)   Address                           Spouse        RH
====================    ====================================  ========  RH
                                                                        I
                                                                        I
                                                                        I
                                                                        I
                                                                        I
                                                                        I
                                                                        I
                                                                        I
                                                                        I
                                                                        I
                                                                        I
                                                                        I
                                                                        I
                                                                        I
                                                                        I
                                                                        I

How many blank lines after this header? 1
```

he was back at DESIGN's main menu. Once there, he chose the Detail
option and proceeded to designate the template's 10th and 11th lines
as the scope of the detail pattern. Thus those two lines were automatically
marked with the letter D at the right edge of the screen. Jack positioned
the first element in the detail beneath the report header's first column
heading.

"What I have in mind," he explained, "is that rep names will be
aligned under this column heading. Furthermore, I want each name
that appears in generated reports to be followed by the rep's territory
ID in parentheses. I can do all of that in a single expression for this
nonliteral element."

When the environment prompted him to enter an expression for
the nonliteral element, he typed

```
trim(rep.name)+" ("+trim(rep.tid+")"
```

as shown in Figure 10–16. He proceeded to specify a picture of

```
rrrrrrrrrrrrrrrrrrrrrr
```

FIGURE 10–16   Entering an expression for a detail element

```
                                                                        RH
                           Sales Rep List                  rrrrrrl9rr   RH
                                                                        RH
                                                                        RH
Rep Name  (territory)   Address                            Spouse       RH
====================    =====================================  ========  RH
                                                                         I
                                                                         I
                                                                         I
                                                                         D
                                                                         D
                                                                         I
                                                                         I
                                                                         I
                                                                         I
                                                                         I
                                                                         I
                                                                         I
                                                                         I
                                                                         I
                                                                         I
                                                                         I
                                                                         I
                                                             Line: 10  Col: 2
Enter expression: trim(rep.name)+" ("+trim(rep.tid)+")"
```

for this element. If he had not specified a picture, E.LSTR would (as usual) control how many characters of the calculated value would be displayed (i.e., default of 15). Jack defined two more nonliteral elements on line 10 in the usual way. An element for REP.ADDR was defined beneath the "Address" heading and an element for REP.SPOUSE was defined beneath the "Spouse" heading.

On the second line of the detail pattern, he made the literal element "Phone:" and positioned it directly under the REP.ADDR element. A nonliteral element for REP.PHONE was then specified directly to the right of the "Phone:" element. He assigned an interdetail spacing of one line. That completed the detail pattern's design, so Jack returned to DESIGN's main menu (recall the status area of Figure 10–5) and pressed the F key to begin work on a pattern for the report footer. As shown in Figure 10–17, he was asked to indicate the type of footer.

"That's very similar to the way you began designing the report header pattern," remarked Tracey, remembering the screen of Figure 10–12. "Is it fair to say that designing a footer pattern is like designing a header pattern?"

"Yes," answered Jack. "If you can design a header pattern then

FIGURE 10–17   Selecting the type of footer

```
                                                                        RH
                        Sales Rep List                    rrrrrr1ᑫrr    RH
                                                                        RH
                                                                        RH
Rep Name  (territory)   Address                           Spouse        RH
====================    ====================================    ====    RH
                                                                        I
                                                                        I
                                                                        I
rrrrrrrrrrrrrrrrrrrrr                                                   D
                        Phone:                                          D
                                                                        I
                                                                        I
                                                                        I
                                                                        I
                                                                        I
                                                                        I
                                                                        I
                                                                        I
                                                                        I
                                                                        I
                                                                        I
Is this footer                                  Line: 10  Col: 1
        Report Footer          Page Footer      Group Footer    Quit
```

you already know how to do a footer pattern. Only remember that in the reports we generate a footer follows details while a header precedes them. That's the main difference."

He pressed the R key to begin work on the template's report footer pattern. Line 14 was designed as its top boundary and line 16 as its bottom boundary. The encompassed lines were automatically marked with RF at the right edge of the screen. As shown in Figure 10–18, Jack created one literal element ("Manager: Jack Vander") in the REPLIST footer pattern. He then quit the design activity, saving the template in REPLIST.TPL on the drive A diskette.

Generation

"Now," sighed Jack, "we can generate all the reports we want from this template. We just use the REPORT command exactly as we've seen before, but specify the REPLIST template instead of REPREP."

With E.OPRN switched to TRUE, Jack executed the command

```
report "a:replist" from rep order by tid
```

FIGURE 10–18   Entering a literal element in a report footer pattern

```
                                                                   RH
                        Sales Rep List                rrrrrrₗªrr   RH
                                                                   RH
                                                                   RH
Rep Name   (territory)   Address                       Spouse      RH
====================     ====================================   ========   RH
                                                                   I
                                                                   I
                                                                   I
rrrrrrrrrrrrrrrrrrrrr                                              D
                   Phone:                                          D
                                                                   I
                                                                   I
                                       Manager: Jack Vander        RF
                                                                   RF
                                                                   RF
                                                                   I
                                                                   I
                                                                   I
                                                                   I
                                                                   I
                                                                   I
                                                                   I
                                             Line: 14    Col: 73
Enter or revise literal element.    Press FENTER.
```

producing the printout in Figure 10–2. Notice that the report details are indeed ordered by territory ID and that the current date appears in the report header. To restrict the report to only certain reps, a condition could have been included in the REPORT command.

"For frequently used templates, I tend to define macros," Jack reported. "For instance, if I frequently generated reports with the REPLIST.TPL template, I'd probably define a macro called, say, RL. It would save me quite a few keystrokes."

He demonstrated by executing the command

```
macro rl "a:replist"
```

to define RL and then executed the command

```
report rl from rep order by tid
```

to show that it generated the same report printout as Figure 10–2.

"Will the REPORT command still work if E.OPRN is not TRUE?" asked Brad.

"Sure," answered Jack, "only you won't get a printout. The report will just flash by on the screen. Actually, that can be helpful if you want to *preview* a report before committing it to paper. But I'd suggest you switch E.PAUS to TRUE before your preview so it won't go by too fast for you. In any event, your preview may show that you should adjust your REPORT command, modifying its condition for instance. Or, you may see that you need to revise your template design, moving an element, for example."

PAGE HEADERS AND FOOTERS

"Now that you understand report headers and footers," Jack asserted, "I think you'll find page headers and footers to be very easy. The main difference is that a page header appears at the top of every page. So it can appear multiple times in a generated report, compared to a report header, which appears only once at the very start. Similarly, a page footer appears at the bottom of every report page, rather than just at the very end of the report."

"So if we have only one page in a report," Stan speculated, "a page header and report header produce the same effect."

"Right," affirmed Jack, "but keep in mind the fact that a report can have both an overall report header and page headers as well. The example I'm going to present now involves page headers and footers only. I've already made a template with a page header pattern and a page footer pattern. Because the flow of designing these page patterns is like that of report header and footer patterns, I won't bother to design a new template from scratch. You already know how to do that. Obviously, when you're asked to indicate the type of your header or footer, you would pick the Page rather than Report option." Recall the status areas of Figures 10–12 and 10–17.

Design

To help the managers envision the template he had already designed, Jack executed the command

```
design "a:perfrep"
```

producing the screen appearance depicted in Figure 10–19. Notice that there are lines marked with PH (page header) and a line marked with PF (page footer), as well as a single-line detail pattern.

"Obviously," Jack commented, "this is a template for a performance report. As you might guess by looking at the header, the detail pattern has four nonliteral elements. Left to right, they are for PERF.PID,

FIGURE 10–19 A template with page header and footer patterns

```
Performance Report                                                     PH
                                                                       PH
Product  Rep         Year-to-date sales      Annual quota              PH
=======  =========   ==================      =============            PH
                                                                       PH
                                                                       I
   rrr                   $fff,fff                 $fff,fff             D
                                                                       I
                     ***CONFIDENTIAL***                               PF
                                                                       I
                                                                       I
                                                                       I
                                                                       I
                                                                       I
                                                                       I
                                                                       I
                                                                       I
                                                                       I
                                                                       I
                                                                       I
                                                                       I
                                                                       I
Do you want to work on a                         Line: 9   Col: 1
   Detail Pattern   Header Pattern   Footer Pattern   Whole Template   Quit
```

PERF.FNAME, PERF.SYTD, and PERF.QYR. As you can see, I've given each of them a picture, with the exception of the element for PERF.FNAME. For the moment, both the page header and page footer patterns consist solely of literal elements. But I'd like to make a couple of changes to this template before we generate a report with it."

He proceeded to work on the page footer pattern's lone element, simply moving it rightward, just as an element can be moved when painting a form. For the page header pattern, he added a new literal element ("Page") in the upper right corner.

"What I'd like," Jack said, "is to have every page in the report consecutively numbered. It turns out to be easy to get this effect if you know about a special kind of nonliteral element. If you specify a percent sign for a nonliteral's expression, automatic pagination will occur."

He positioned a new nonliteral element following the Page element. When asked to enter its corresponding expression, Jack simply typed

%

FIGURE 10–20   Entering an expression for automatic page numbering

```
Performance Report                                          Page          PH
                                                                          PH
Product  Rep        Year-to-date sales        Annual quota               PH
=======  =========  ==================        ============               PH
                                                                          PH
                                                                          I
  rrr                    $fff,fff                  $fff,fff               D
                                                                          I
                                           ***CONFIDENTIAL***             PF
                                                                          I
                                                                          I
                                                                          I
                                                                          I
                                                                          I
                                                                          I
                                                                          I
                                                                          I
                                                                          I
                                                                          I
                                                                          I
                                                                          I
                                               Line: 1    Col: 69
Enter expression: %
```

yielding the screen appearance portrayed in Figure 10–20. Jack proceeded to terminate the DESIGN command in the usual way. He preserved the changes just made by responding positively to the status area question shown in Figure 10–21. The original version of the template no longer existed in the knowledge system.

Generation

To generate a report with the just preserved template, Jack executed the command

```
report "a:perfrep" from perf order by pid za qyr
```

producing the two printed pages shown in Figure 10–3. The report's details are ordered as requested in the REPORT command. Observe that actual page numbers replace the page header's % element. The same basic header and footer appeared on both pages.

"Your template must have assigned one blank line to follow each

FIGURE 10–21 Preserving the modified template

```
Performance Report                                          Page         PH
                                                                         PH
Product  Rep        Year-to-date sales      Annual quota                 PH
=======  =========  ==================      =============                PH
                                                                         PH
                                                                         I
  rrr                   $fff,fff                $fff,fff                  D
                                                                         I
                                          ***CONFIDENTIAL***             PF
                                                                         I
                                                                         I
                                                                         I
                                                                         I
                                                                         I
                                                                         I
                                                                         I
                                                                         I
                                                                         I
                                                                         I
                                                                         I
                                                                         I
                                                                         I
Do you want to preserve this template in: a:perfrep.tpl?    Line: 1   Col: 1
                     Yes          No
```

detail," remarked Dan. "That's clear. But what caused the product IDs
to be suppressed?"

"I know," Debbie volunteered, thinking back to how nonliteral elements are specified (recall the status area of Figure 10–8). "When you
defined the PERF.PID element in the template's detail pattern, you
must have indicated that only unique values were desired."

"Exactly," confirmed Jack. "In effect, I built a unique qualifier for
PID right into the template. So whenever the template is employed,
successive repeated values for that element are suppressed."

"In a report like this," contended Brad, "I'd like to see grand totals
and maybe averages for the sales and quota columns. Could I do that
by amending the template to have a report footer?"

"That's right," Jack answered. "You'd have two kinds of footer
patterns in the template. What nonliteral elements would you specify?"

Brad thought a moment. "Well, couldn't we specify elements from
the statistical utility arrays such as #SUM?"

"That's the idea!" said Jack in a congratulatory tone. "As a matter
of fact, we'll make use of #SUM for some of the elements in the next
template we look at."

GROUP HEADERS AND FOOTERS

"We've seen that the REPORT command is like SELECT, in terms of conditions and ordering," said Jack. "Now we'll see that you can have a GROUP BY clause in a REPORT command just as you could in a SELECT command. Remember that in the case of SELECT, breaks occur between groups in the displayed results and we can even get a statistical summary for each group."

Recalling the query results in Figure 8–29, Tracey interrupted, "So the group's statistics are sort of like a group footer."

"Right," nodded Jack, "except they're produced on an ad hoc basis. As you'll see, we can design our own customized footers for groups— and headers too."

The knowledge management environment's report generation capability allows up to 26 group header patterns and 26 group footer patterns per template. This allows up to 26 levels of grouping per report. When designing a template each level is denoted by one of the letters of the alphabet, from a (highest level group header and footer) to z (lowest level group header and footer). The first grouping criterion (e.g, field) mentioned in a REPORT command's GROUP BY clause activates the template's highest level header and footer pattern. Whenever that criterion's value changes, a new group begins. Each high-level group of details is encased in the high-level header and footer. The same principle is followed for succeeding grouping criteria and their corresponding levels. To keep his presentation simple, Jack had decided to deal with only one level of grouping. This would satisfy most of the managers' needs until they became more experienced.

Design

Jack described what he intended to do. "I want to design a template for a report that will group performance data by territory. For each desired territory, I want a generated report to show not only the territory's ID but also the *full* name of its rep. This will be in the header for each territory group. Each of a group's details should show the product ID, year-to-date sales, annual quota, and the difference between sales and quota. So there will be a numeric computation for each detail. Also, I want each generated group to have a footer that shows the sum total of the group's sales, quotas, and sales-quota difference.

"Now all this may sound ambitious, but it's actually quite straightforward. Fortunately, there is very little that is different when designing group headers and footers."

Jack executed the command

FIGURE 10–22   Choosing a group level

```
                                                                        I
                                                                        I
                                                                        I
                                                                        I
                                                                        I
                                                                        I
                                                                        I
                                                                        I
                                                                        I
                                                                        I
                                                                        I
                                                                        I
                                                                        I
                                                                        I
                                                                        I
                                                                        I
                                                                        I
                                                                        I
                                                                        I
                                                                        I

In Use:                        Available: abcdefghijklmnopqrstuvwxyz
Enter group level:a
```

```
design "a:terrep"
```

to begin designing his territory report template. The screen appeared as portrayed in Figure 10–5. After picking the main menu's Header option, the Figure 10–12 screen was in view. He pressed the G key to begin working on a group header. In the status area, he was asked to enter a level for the group header. He pressed the A key to give the group header the highest level. The screen appeared as shown in Figure 10–22. On pressing the Enter key, Jack was asked to indicate the top and bottom boundaries of the header pattern. He designated the template's top seven lines, which were automatically marked with aH (level a header).

Jack proceeded to define elements within the group header. The literal elements are visible in Figure 10–23. In addition, there were two nonliteral elements: PERF.TID and REP.NAME positioned after the "Territory" and "Name:" elements, respectively. Jack emphasized the fact that these came from different tables. He then set out to design a one-line detail pattern consisting of four nonliteral elements: one for each underlined term shown in the header pattern. The expressions specified

FIGURE 10–23   A group header pattern

```
Territory        Name:                                             aH
                                                                   aH
                                                                   aH
   Product        Sales        Quota      Sales - Quota            aH
   =======      ========     ========     ==============           aH
                                                                   aH
                                                                   aH
                                                                    I
                                                                    I
                                                                    I
                                                                    I
                                                                    I
                                                                    I
                                                                    I
                                                                    I
                                                                    I
                                                                    I
                                                                    I
                                                                    I
                                                                    I
                                                                    I
                                                                    I
Do you want to work on a                         Line: 1    Col: 1
   Detail Pattern    Header Pattern    Footer Pattern   Whole Template   Quit
```

for the first three of these were simply the fields: PERF.PID, PERF.SYTD, and PERF.QYR. He gave pictures of $fff,fff to the latter two elements.

Figure 10–24 shows the expression Jack specified for the detail pattern's fourth nonliteral element. As with a nonliteral element in a form, the expression for a nonliteral element in a template can be a calculation. It can involve variables other than fields, including array elements, working variables, utility variables, and spreadsheet cells (to be discussed in Chapter 12). Jack gave a picture of $fff,fff to the calculated element.

Turning his attention to the group footer, Jack picked the Footer option from DESIGN's main menu. As he had done with the header, he indicated that it was to be a group footer for level a. It was designed as a two-line pattern (lines 12 and 13) with an aF marker at the right edge of each line.

"I'll leave the first footer line blank," he explained, "since I want one blank line to separate each group of generated details from its footer. Remember, I've not assigned any interdetail spacing. So the details in each group will be single spaced."

Toward the left end of the pattern's second line, Jack defined a literal "Totals:" element. On that same line he positioned a nonliteral

FIGURE 10–24   Specifying a calculation for a detail element

```
Territory          Name:                                                  aH
                                                                          aH
                                                                          aH
     Product        Sales        Quota        Sales - Quota               aH
     =======        =======      =======      =============               aH
                                                                          aH
                                                                          aH
                                                                          I
                    $fff,fff     $fff,fff                                 D
                                                                          I
                                                                          I
                                                                          I
                                                                          I
                                                                          I
                                                                          I
                                                                          I
                                                                          I
                                                                          i
                                                                          I
                                                                          I
                                                                          I
                                                                          I
                                                  Line: 9    Col: 54
  Enter expression: perf.sytd-perf.qyr
```

element beneath the Sales heading (line 13, column 17) and was prompted to enter its expression.

"What do we want here?" he asked.

"The sum of the group's second column of detail values," Debbie answered quickly, "the sum of the group's sales values."

"Exactly!" Jack confirmed. "And just as we saw in our discussion of statistics, we can reference that value as #SUM(2)."

As shown in Figure 10–25, he typed

#sum(2)

in response to the prompt to enter an expression. He then gave this element a picture of $f,fff,fff. Similarly, Jack defined two more nonliteral elements in the same line, corresponding to the third and fourth elements in the detail pattern. Their expressions were specified as #SUM(3) and #SUM(4), respectively and they were given the same picture of $f,fff,fff. His last action for the group footer pattern was to assign a spacing of three blank lines to follow every group footer in a generated report. This is depicted in Figure 10–26.

"I get the idea of how to design elements into a template's various

FIGURE 10–25   A statistical element in a group footer pattern

```
Territory          Name:                                            aH
                                                                    aH
                                                                    aH
      Product          Sales         Quota      Sales - Quota       aH
      =======       ========      ========      =============       aH
                                                                    aH
                                                                    aH
                    $fff,fff      $fff,fff         $fff,fff          I
                                                                     D
                                                                     I
                                                                     I
                                                                    aF
                                                                    aF
                                                                     I
                                                                     I
                                                                     I
                                                                     I
                                                                     I
                                                                     I
                                                                     I
                                                                     I
                                                                     I
                                                                     I
                                              Line: 13   Col: 17
Enter expression: #sum(2)
```

FIGURE 10–26   Assigning spacing to follow a group footer

```
Territory          Name:                                            aH
                                                                    aH
                                                                    aH
      Product          Sales         Quota      Sales - Quota       aH
      =======       ========      ========      =============       aH
                                                                    aH
                                                                    aH
                    $fff,fff      $fff,fff         $fff,fff          I
                                                                     D
                                                                     I
                                                                     I
                                                                    aF
      Totals:   $f,fff,fff    $f,fff,fff       $f,fff,fff          aF
                                                                     I
                                                                     I
                                                                     I
                                                                     I
                                                                     I
                                                                     I
                                                                     I
                                                                     I
                                                                     I
How many blank lines after this footer? 3
```

PHOTO 20   Colored report template with group header and footer pattern

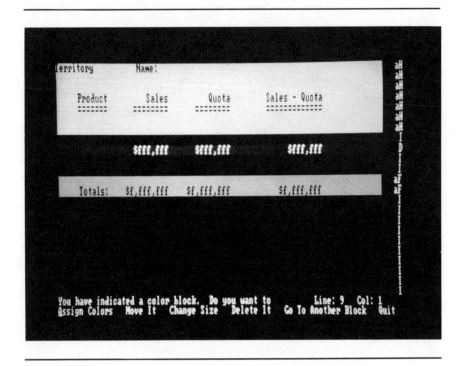

patterns. But I've been wondering," said Pete, rubbing his chin, "why you haven't used any color blocks. I've seen them in several of the status area menus."

"Mainly because I get printouts of generated reports and the printer does things in black and white," answered Jack. "But you're free to design color blocks into your template if you like."

For Pete's sake, he colored in blocks of the template as Joy added, "Color blocks can be useful when working on large and intricate patterns, helping to visually separate or color code portions of the template. Also, when you preview a generated report on the console screen the foreground colors of all elements show up." The console now projected the appearance shown in Photo 20 (with colors indicated by differing shades). Jack terminated the DESIGN command, preserving the template in file TERREP.TPL on the drive A diskette.

Generation

To demonstrate how grouping worked with the new template, Jack executed the command:

```
report "a:terrep" from perf from rep where pid=rep.pid & tid<"4"
group by tid order by tid, pid
```

generating the report printout in Figure 10–4. As with a SELECT command, when data is being extracted from two tables, both are specified and the condition contains a term equating their matching fields. Observe that the report is ordered by territory ID and, within each group, by product ID. Each group header has related data values drawn from two different tables. Each detail in a group contains a calculated value. Each group footer has the appropriate sums of data values from the group's details.

"Of course," Jack concluded, "this template could be used in generating many different reports, involving different territories or various subsets of the products. But each report will have the same structural appearance."

BLENDING REPORTS AND TEXT

The foregoing examples illustrate that calculations, text strings (i.e., literal elements), data base contents, formlike patterns, and parts of queries can all be used in generating a report. It also happens that the report generation capabilty can be used when working with pieces of text. Debbie perceived one way of doing this, remarking, "I presume we can execute the REPORT command right in the midst of text processing and its results will be inserted into the text we're working on."

"Correct," Jack confirmed, "just preface it with a backslash, as you've done earlier with OUTPUT and SELECT. Suppose we want to prepare a memo about sales reps. We might generate a report within the text area, then edit it, and elaborate as desired."

To demonstrate, Jack executed the command

```
text "a:repmemo.txt"
```

to bring a fresh text screen into view. He escaped to the status line and issued the command

```
\report "a:replist from rep"
```

FIGURE 10–27   Immediate incorporation of a report into text

```
 Line:1     Col:1     a:repmemo.txt  Insert            Press ^L for help

                            Sales Rep List              10/04/1986


 Rep Name  (territory)   Address                               Spouse
 =====================   ====================================   ========

 Kevin R. Andrews (2)    25 Stratton Ave, Bloomington IL 54321  Kris
                         Phone: (123) 456-1111

 Kim G. Anders (0)       8242 Wabash, Chicago IL 68909
                         Phone: (312) 553-6754

 Kris H. Raber (1)       314 Miami, Dayton OH 46783             Kevin
                         Phone: (513) 333-9989

 Tina F. Lee (3)         7892 Meridian, Indianapolis IN 46662   Ben
                         Phone: (317) 299-8393

 Toby C. Terry (4)       2028 Prescott, Fort Wayne IN 45567
                         Phone: (345) 123-4567

 Kerry H. Jones (5)      128 Spiceland, Grand Rapids MI 35988   Kendra
                         Phone: (632) 098-7654
```

resulting in the Figure 10–27 screen appearance. Instead of being pre-
viewed or printed, the report was incorporated directly into the rep
memo. It could now be processed just like any other text. Jack moved
the cursor downward, eventually causing the new text to scroll upward
and showing that the entire report did indeed exist as part of the text.
He then used ^T to eliminate all of the lines from REPMEMO.TXT.

Delayed Incorporation

"So far," he declared, "you've seen how to incorporate things into a
piece of text on the fly. And that's extremely valuable. But sometimes
I find that I'd rather not incoporate data from other sources immediately.
Instead, I'd like it incorporated on a delayed basis, as the text is actually
being printed. Suppose I want a list of the sales reps in this memo
and I need to print the memo at the end of each month. Obviously, it
takes only a single command to get the current sales rep data into the
memo. I can then edit it and print it. No problem. But what happens
when I need to print it next month?"

"You might have a problem there," Tracey noted. "If any of the
data in the REP table changed since you incorporated it into the memo,

FIGURE 10–28   Embedding a command in text for delayed evaluation

```
 Line:10     Col:52    a:repmemo.txt  Insert                 Press ^L for help
   The following is a list of sales representatives who are in my region:

.nf
.ev select name,addr,phone from rep order by lname tid



                          Sincerely,


                          Jack Vander
```

then the memo would be out-of-date. You'd have to remember what had changed in the table and then make the corresponding changes to the memo before again printing it."

"Or," offered Dan, "you could delete the rep data from the current memo text, reissue your SELECT or REPORT command to incorporate the most up-to-date REP data into the text, edit it in whatever way you did the month before, and then print it."

"Either way," complained Brad, "having to do that every month sounds like a lot of work to me! What if we had to do it every week or every day?"

"That's definitely something you want to avoid, and you can," Jack reassured them. "All you do is embed the SELECT command *directly* in the text itself. As the text is printed, the command is executed. Its results become part of the printed text. So we always have an up-to-date memo without having to touch the text in any way whatsoever!"

"That sounds amazing," Tracey said, recalling her own past efforts at updating repeatedly used text to conform with changes in the world.

Jack typed a few lines into the now blank rep memo to show them how it is done. The screen appeared as shown in Figure 10–28. There was first an ordinary line of text, followed by a blank line. The .nf format control code meant that succeeding lines were not to be filled, but rather printed verbatim (recall Chapter 5, e.g., Figure 5–24).

Explaining the fourth line, Jack said, "When you embed a command within the text, put it on a line that begins with the dot ev printing control code. When PRINT TEXT is executed, it will evaluate the command and insert the command's output beginning at that position in the text. That's all there is to it. Instead of immediately incorporating a command's results into text as you're working on it, you now have a way to delay the incorporation until print time. And it's automatic, so you're sure that the most up-to-date data is used. Let me show you."

He escaped to the status area and issued the WRITE command (recall Chapter 5, e.g., Figure 5–14) to write the text into REPMEMO.TXT. Terminating the TEXT command (i.e., by BYE), Jack was now faced with the underscore prompt. He executed the commands

```
e.suph=true;e.spgn=true
e.pdep=66
e.oprn=true
```

to set up the environment for printing text. By switching E.SUPH and E.SPGN to TRUE, column headings and page numbering would not appear in SELECT's results as they are printed in the memo. Jack executed the command

```
print text "a:repmemo.txt" from rep
```

yielding the printout in Figure 10–29.

"So what you're driving at is that a piece of text can serve as a sort of template in its own right," Debbie said perceptively. "And, used in this way, PRINT TEXT is a kind of report generation command. The lines that begin with dot control codes are akin to a template's nonliterals. Only some of them, like nf, control the layout of the textual report, whereas others, like ev, control its content."

Jack and Joy beamed at her insight. Joy reinforced Debbie's point, "You're exactly right! Both a template and a piece of text can present data from other sources. In a way, embedding a command in text is even more powerful than a template's nonliteral elements. Each element involves only the evaluation of an expression, yielding one value. A single command can, of course, yield many, many values."

Having been previously acquainted with a stand-alone word processing package, Tracey was perceptibly excited by the new prospects of integrated text management. "Can I embed any commands I like in

FIGURE 10–29   Printout of text with delayed execution of SELECT

```
    The following is a list of sales representatives who are in my region:


Kim G. Anders          8242 Wabash, Chicago IL 68909            (312) 553-6754
Kevin R. Andrews       25 Stratton Ave, Bloomington IL 54321    (123) 456-1111
Karen V. Bruckner      44 Tan Ave., Madison WI 66667            (433) 442-8201
Kerry H. Jones         128 Spiceland, Grand Rapids MI 35988     (632) 098-7654
Tina F. Lee            7892 Meridian, Indianapolis IN 46662     (317) 299-8393
Carol O. Lynn          58 Cater Dr., Midland MI 40098           (412) 832-5643
Kris H. Raber          314 Miami, Dayton OH 46783               (513) 333-9989
Kathy F. Smith         85 Griese Ln, Milwaukee WI 65543         (415) 567-8901
Jackie V. Smith        32 New Jersey, Columbus OH 33464         (322) 861-6543
Toby C. Terry          2028 Prescott, Fort Wayne IN 45567       (345) 123-4567


                       Sincerely,


                       Jack Vander
```

any piece of text? The REPORT command? The SELECT command? Calculations?"

"Sure," Jack smiled. "Whatever the command is, the results that it would normally send to your console screen end up in the printed text. This includes commands for generating graphs, which we'll examine tomorrow, and commands for displaying spreadsheet cells, which we'll see the next day."

Mail Merge

"Can we carry the correspondence between templates and text a bit further?" Debbie asked. "In the case of report generation from a template, each report detail conforms to the template's detail pattern and with a single REPORT command we can generate lots of details. I think it would be useful if each report detail could be exploded into a piece of text. Rather than conforming to a template's detail pattern, it would conform to the pattern of words inherent in a piece of text. So a single command could generate multiple printed copies of the same piece of text. Each copy would play the role of a textual report detail, having different data values than the other copies."

"That's an explosive question," said Jack to the amusement of the group. "It just so happens that I have a ready-made example of what you're talking about. Instead of having each detail's values printed according to a template's detail pattern, you want to see them printed in a copy of a text pattern.

"The example I'll show you is for a letter that I wanted to send to

FIGURE 10–30   A form letter set up for automatic customization

```
   Line:1      Col:1     a:letter.txt   Insert          Press ^L for help
.nf
.ev ?rep.name
.ev ?rep.street
.ev ?trim(city)+" "+state+" "+zip using "%23r"

.ev ?#date using "%45 rrrrrr19rr"


.fi
.ad
Dear
.ev ?trim(fname)+":"

     It is very important that we meet our annual quota for the
business product line.  This means that during the fourth quarter
your sales should be at least
.ev e.supd=true
.ev obtain record from perf for perf.pid="bus"&perf.tid=rep.tid
.ev ?perf.qyr-perf.sytd using "$ff,fff"
for business books.  This compares to your fourth quarter business
quota of
.ev ?perf.q4 using "$ff,fff."
Please let me know if I can be of any assistance in meeting this
goal.
```

each of my reps. Each copy of the letter said the same basic things
and had the same basic structure. But each was customized to an individual rep's particular circumstances. I generated all 10 letters with a single
PRINT TEXT command."

To view the letter's text, he executed the command

```
text "a:letter.txt"
```

resulting in the Figure 10–30 screen appearance. Notice that the first
three commands embedded in the text are OUTPUT commands. Because
the "no fill" (nf) format is requested, their outputs will make up three
distinct lines in the printed text. The first will be a rep name, the second
will be that rep's street address, and the third will be the remainder
of the rep's address. Following a blank line, each printed letter will
then contain the current date, garnered from #DATE. The date's picture
will cause 45 spaces to precede the appearance of the date in the date
line.

"Now I want the body of the printed letters to have nice filled
lines, adjusted to have an aligned right margin. So I've used the dot fi
and dot ad format control codes. Remember, this means that any succeed-

ing line not beginning with a blank will be filled into the prior line until the right margin is hit. The rest of it becomes the start of the next printed line. So the trimmed first name from the REP table will be filled in after the word 'Dear.' A blank line follows and then the first sentence will begin a new line. Because it begins with a blank, it is not filled into the prior line. The rest of the letter is constructed in a similar way."

Observe that the next two embedded commands do not produce any outputs, so they will not directly affect the appearance of printed letters. The first of these switches E.SUPD to TRUE to suppress the display of results for ensuing OBTAIN commands. The second obtains the present rep's business performance record from the PERF table, making it the current PERF record. The present sales shortfall is then calculated from that record's data and output into the letter. The final embedded command outputs the corresponding fourth quarter quota into the letter. Jack scrolled downward in the text to show that it also contained a customary sign-off.

"Now let's print it!" exclaimed Jack. "As you'll see, a single PRINT TEXT command will generate one letter of this kind for each rep in the REP table, obtaining related data from the PERF table as it goes along. I'll put a condition on the PRINT TEXT command to restrict the letters to those reps having business books as a major product line, plus Kevin, who doesn't have business as a major product but to whom I want to send a letter anyway."

To demonstrate Jack left the TEXT command and then executed the commands

```
e.pmar=5;e.pwid=75
```

to adjust the page margin and page width the way he wanted. He then executed the command

```
print text "a:letter.txt" from rep where majorp in ["*bus*"] or fname="Kevin"
```

producing several letters on the printer. An automatic page eject occurred at the end of each letter, allowing the succeeding letter to begin at the top of the next page. Three of the customized letters that were printed are shown in Figure 10–31. Notice that each presented the proper data for a rep as extracted and calculated from the REP and PERF tables. Each also had the current date from the #DATE utility variable.

"It seems that the PRINT TEXT command is similar to the REPORT command," observed Stan. "You just specify a text file instead of a template file. You specify what table it's supposed to generate copies

```
        Tina F. Lee
        7892 Meridian
        Indianapolis IN 46662

                                         10/04/1986

        Dear Tina:

                It is very important that we  meet  our  annual  quota  for  the
        business  product line. This means that during the fourth quarter your
        sales should be at least $8,435 for business books. This  compares  to
        your  fourth quarter business quota of $9,311. Please let me know if I
        can be of any assistance in meeting this goal.



                                         Sincerely,


                                         Jack Vander
```

```
     Kim G. Anders
     8242 Wabash
     Chicago IL 68909

                                      10/04/1986

     Dear Kim:

             It is very important that we  meet  our  annual  quota  for  the
     business  product line. This means that during the fourth quarter your
     sales should be at least $8,391 for business books. This  compares  to
     your  fourth quarter business quota of $8,503. Please let me know if I
     can be of any assistance in meeting this goal.



                                      Sincerely,


                                      Jack Vander
```

```
     Kevin R. Andrews
     25 Stratton Ave
     Bloomington IL 54321

                                      10/04/1986

     Dear Kevin:

             It is very important that we  meet  our  annual  quota  for  the
     business  product line. This means that during the fourth quarter your
     sales should be at least $245 for business  books.  This  compares  to
     your  fourth quarter business quota of $3,456. Please let me know if I
     can be of any assistance in meeting this goal.



                                      Sincerely,


                                      Jack Vander
```

of the text for and what conditions should apply to the data presented in each copy."

"That's a good way of putting it, Stan," said Joy with a complimentary tone. "Let me add that what you've just witnessed is a very flexible rendition of what's often called a 'mail merge' facility in the jargon of word processing software packages. Of course, since they're not environments those packages don't get the merged data directly from fields, utility variables, working variables, spreadsheet cells, calculation results, and so forth. Nor do they normally allow you to embed full-fledged commands of the kind we've seen. Instead, they merge in data from a separately constructed, specially formatted file of data [1]."

BASIC IDEAS

As hands-on practice began, Jack and Joy felt confident that the managers grasped the basic ideas of report generation. So they quietly slipped away for a break of their own. Together, they touched on some advanced aspects of embedded commands and merging during the course of the evening.

As with the other knowledge management techniques, they had not presented a complete coverage of all that is possible with the environment's report generation capability. But they had provided enough of the basics to allow the managers to accomplish a great deal of useful processing.

At this stage, each manager understood that *a template is a valuable way of representing presentation knowledge*. Each was able to use the DESIGN command to design any of a variety of patterns into a template. These included detail, header, and footer patterns. When the REPORT command was executed to generate a report with a template, the template's patterns controlled both the structure and content of the report. The report's content could also be restricted and ordered by including a condition and ordering clause in the REPORT command. As with ad hoc queries, a report could involve the simultaneous retrieval of related data from multiple tables.

Customized reports can assume several distinct styles, depending on the nature of headers and footers. If no header or footer pattern is designed in a template, a report will consist only of details each conforming to the same pattern. A report header and footer pair embraces all report details. A page header and footer pair appears on each page of a report and embraces only those details that are on a page. A group header and footer pair embraces each group of details, where the desired grouping criterion is specified in the REPORT command just as it can be specified in a SELECT command. Typically a group footer will show some statistics or calculations pertaining to its group.

A piece of text can also serve as the basis for generating reports that have a textual, rather than structured template, orientation. On the one hand, there is always the ability to immediately incorporate results of commands like SELECT and REPORT into a piece of text as it is being edited. The result can serve as a report. On the other hand, it can be beneficial to delay the incorporation of data into text until the text is actually printed. Such an effect is achieved by embedding nontext commands directly into the text itself. This strategy can be used to generate a single copy of the text or multiple copies of the text (each copy being analogous to a report detail) via the PRINT TEXT command.

References

1. Ashley, R.; J. N. Fernandez; and R. Sansom. *WordStar without Tears: A Self-Teaching Guide.* New York: John Wiley & Sons, 1985.
2. Bernard, S. *System/360 RPG.* Englewood Cliffs, N.J.: Prentice-Hall, 1970.
3. Curtice, R. M. "Some Tools for Data Base Development." *Datamation* 20, no. 7 (1974).
4. *K-Report Supplement,* version 2. Lafayette, Ind.: MDBS, Inc., 1985.
5. *K-Text Supplement,* version 2. Lafayette, Ind.: MDBS, Inc., 1985.
6. *Mark IV Systems, Technical System Description.* Canoga Park, Calif.: Informatics, Inc., 1974.

Mmm . . . This plot tells an interesting story.

Chapter Eleven

Business Graphics

It was nearly 8 A.M., Monday, October 6. Jack turned to look at Joy. Her expression was serene as the autumn dawn. It gave him a deep sense of both strength and contentment that would last through the day. But the softness of the moment was soon broken by a beeping alarm. Dan's wristwatch reminded them that it was time to get started. Jack plunged right in to the new knowledge management topic, explaining to the assembled managers that they would spend the day getting acquainted with business graphics [1],[2],[9].

"There are many kinds of graphics software packages available for today's desktop computers," Joy said. "Some let you treat the computer like an electronic Etch-A-Sketch® machine. They allow you to draw diagrams on the console screen by rolling a mouse around on the desktop [5]. Many of these don't stop with line drawings, but let you sketch out scenes and color in various parts of the landscape. Some even permit you to produce an animation effect on the console screen, by arranging for the rapid-fire or slow-motion display of a sequence of scenes.

"Then there is graphics software used by engineers in the course of designing and manufacturing products. You've all probably seen television ads for cars in which a graphical image of a car's design is shown on a console screen where it can be rotated, magnified, and modifed. Such software is known as CAD and CAM: computer-assisted design and computer-assisted manufacturing [4],[7],[8].

"While these and other kinds of graphics software are valuable for certain classes of users, we'll be focusing on bread-and-butter business graphics: pie charts, bar graphs, line plots, scattergrams, and so on. As you'd expect, we'll be examining business graphics within the environment. You don't have to learn how to use a separate graphics software package."

Taking the lead, Jack elaborated, "We've seen that data can be

427

presented via forms of both the standardized and customized varieties. We've also seen that data can be presented via reports. These too may be pretty much standardized as in the case of SELECT results, or highly customized as in the case of REPORT. We even saw that data could be presented by incorporating it into a piece of text on either an immediate or delayed basis.

"Now in each of these presentation approaches, the data values were presented as numbers or strings. And that's fine, except it can often be useful to see those values presented graphically. I find that plotting graphs can help to quickly spot patterns, trends, and proportions that exist in a collection of data values. By seeing a plot I can get the full story that the data have to tell."

"But," objected Brad, "doesn't it take a lot of effort to plot a graph? I mean when you think about drawing a graph that corresponds to a bunch of data values, it seems that a lot of effort would be involved, even if you can draw the graph electronically."

"You're right," Jack replied. "It would take a lot of effort if *you* had to draw the graph and it would also be error prone. So we'll just let the *environment* do it for us, quickly and precisely [6]. In fact, we don't even have to look at the data that provides the source for generating a graph. It's all done automatically for us when we execute a PLOT command. In a PLOT command we simply tell the environment what kind of graph we want and what data source to use in generating the plot. That's all there is to it!"

Before entering the environment, Jack issued the command

GRAPHICS

in response to the operating system prompt [3]. He explained that the environment made use of the operating system's ability to display graphics characters, which have an oversized appearance (recall Photo 8). By executing the operating system's GRAPHICS command, they would be able to make printouts of plotted graphs.

GRAPHIC DATA SOURCES

A graph is generated from a *data source* that serves as a kind of presentation knowledge. This presentation knowledge controls the sizes, heights, and locations of a graph's contents. When generating a bar chart, the data source controls how many bars will be in the chart, how they will be clustered in the graph, and how high the individual bars will be. When generating a pie graph, the data source determines the relative sizes of slices in the pie and the labeling of those slices. In general, it may be possible to plot different kinds of graphs from a single data source, or the same kind of graph using different portions of that data source.

"Simply put," said Jack, "a data source is a place where the environment looks to get the data values for plotting the graph you want."

"In this environment," chimed Joy, "a data source exists in your present processing context. Because it is held in the environment's main memory work area, graphs can be plotted more quickly than if the data source were on disk."

"As you'd expect," Jack continued, "you can simultaneously have many data sources present in your processing context, just as you can have many forms, macros, and working variables. As you'll see, the SAVE command can be used to save a data source in a context file and the LOAD command lets you load it back into the present processing context."

Structure of a Data Source

"I understand that you can't plot a graph if you don't have any data to plot it from," Dan announced. "Obviously, there has to be some data source. But exactly what is a data source?"

"Traditionally," Joy responded, "an array structure is used as a data source. In this environment the values of an array's elements can provide the data for generating graphs. It turns out that an array offers a particularly convenient and versatile approach to representing the presentation knowledge from which graphs are generated. I should mention though that some graphs can be plotted from working variables and tomorrow Jack will show that a spreadsheet can also serve as a data source."

"But for now," Jack declared, "let's just think of a data source as being an array. You've already used some special built-in arrays such as #SUM and we can easily plot the data values held in such arrays. But beyond this, we're free to invent our own arrays by invoking the DIM command. When you're dimensioning an array to serve as a data source, you'll usually let it be two dimensional."

Turning to the whiteboard, Jack sketched out a sample array to show what he meant. This two-dimensional array is portrayed in Figure 11–1. The statistical arrays they had dealt with earlier were one dimensional. Each could be thought of as being a column of *array elements*. As Jack's example suggests, a two-dimensional array is made up of multiple columns as well as multiple rows of elements. He explained that to declare an array named, say, DS (i.e., data source) capable of holding 12 values, the command

FIGURE 11–1   Data values in a two-dimensional arry

4	2800	4000
5	2950	3014
6	2500	2820
7	3005	2400

```
dim ds(4,3)
```

would be executed. This would give the DS array the capacity to hold four rows of three values each.

"Each element in this four-row by three-column array can have a particular data value," said Jack. "Each element is referenced by indicating its row and column. For instance, DS(2,3) has the value 3014. It's the value of the array element in the second row's third column. In general, you can reference individual array elements in any command where you can reference a working variable. But when we're generating graphs we'll usually refer to an entire chunk of an array as a whole."

"So," Dan observed, "an array is just a grid of storage compartments or elements. We're free to put any value we want in any compartment and we can tell the environment to plot a graph based on whatever values happen to be there."

"That's the right idea!" confirmed Jack.

"But," frowned Brad, "what kind of graph could you generate from the DS array?"

"Actually, there are many kinds of graphs we can plot from this single data source," Jack responded. "We could do pies, lines, bars, areas, and more. Be patient. I'll show you how it all works as we go through the day. But first, I want you to see how to go about filling in an array's values once you've declared its dimensions."

Filling in an Array

"OK," Brad agreed, "but wouldn't we just use the LET command to assign values to individual array elements?"

"Well, that's certainly one way," Jack replied. "But suppose the data you want to graph is already in a table. You sure don't want to have to retrieve it and then retype it in a lot of LET commands."

"Right," said Brad, "it would be nice if we could just issue a single command that would fill in an array with selected data from a table."

"That's exactly what we can do," Jack announced. "And you're already familiar with the command that can do it."

He reminded them of the CONVERT command (recall Chapter 6) that they had previously used to convert data from one table to another. Instead of converting the data to a table, they would now convert it to an array. Instead of producing new records in a specified table, they would now produce new values in the rows of a specified array. To demonstrate how this worked, Jack executed the command

```
dim sales(10,4)
```

to declare the existence of a 10-row by 4-column array named SALES. Initially, the 40 elements of SALES have no values. Explaining that he wanted to graphically analyze quotas for the romance product line, Jack executed the command

```
convert trim(tid) s1 s2 s3 from perf where pid="rom" to array sales(1,1)
```

to fill sales data into the SALES array, beginning with its first row and first column.

"You can see," Jack commented, "why I chose to have four columns for SALES. The first is for trimmed TID values, the second for S1 values, and so forth."

"But why did you declare 10 rows for SALES?" asked Tracey. "Are there 10 performance records for romance in the PERF table?"

"I'm pretty sure there aren't that many," he replied. "But offhand I don't remember exactly how many records there are for romance, so I picked a number that was certain to be large enough. If I had dimensioned SALES with too few rows, not all of the romance records' values could have been converted into it. There are a couple of utility variables, #ROW and #COL, that we can check to see how much of the QUOTA array was actually filled in."

To check the values of these two environmental sensors, Jack executed the commands

```
?#col
```

```
?#row
```

As expected, a value of 4 was output for #COL, indicating that all of the SALES columns now had data in them. The value of 5 for #ROW meant that the first five rows of the SALES array had been filled in by the CONVERT command.

"I have a couple of questions about using the CONVERT command in this way," said Stan. "First, can we convert related data from multiple tables into an array with a single CONVERT command? Second, can we have an ORDER BY clause in a CONVERT command so that data are filled into the array's rows in a particular order?"

"Yes on both counts," Jack answered briskly. "It's just like the CONVERT commands you've used before, only the converted data goes into an array instead of a table. And remember, CONVERT is a lot like SELECT. For instance, I could issue a SELECT command that would simply display the data on the screen instead of converting it into the SALES array." He did so, by executing the command

```
select trim(tid) s1 s2 s3 from perf for pid="rom"
```

resulting in five lines of data, as expected.

"What about E.CF?" asked Don, remembering that it needed to be set to 4 when converting into a table.

"Don't worry about it here," Jack replied. "Its value is irrelevant when converting into an array."

"I presume," speculated Debbie, "that we could cause the conversion to begin with any element in the array by just identifying that element in the CONVERT command."

"Correct," he responded. "I find that I normally begin with an array's first element such as SALES(1,1). But sometimes, I'll want the results of multiple CONVERTs to go into the same array. The first CONVERT would still specify the first element, but the second would specify the element where the first left off. For instance, it would be row 6 and column 1 if the first CONVERT had filled the first five rows. By the way, let's take a look at what has been converted into the SALES array."

As shown in Figure 11–2, he executed the OUTPUT commands.

```
?sales(1,1),sales(1,2),sales(1,3),sales(1,4)
?sales(2,1),sales(2,2),sales(2,3),sales(2,4)
?sales(5,1),sales(5,2),sales(5,3),sales(5,4)
```

to display the first, second, and last of the rows converted into SALES. Notice that they match the corresponding lines of SELECT results. Jack also executed the command

```
?sales(#row,#col)
```

yielding the same value as SALES(5,4). Because #ROW equals 5 and #COL equals 4, SALES(5,4) and SALES(#ROW,#COL) are simply equivalent ways of referring to the same array element.

FIGURE 11–2 Dimensioning and filling in the SALES array

```
_e.deci=0
_dim sales(10,4)
_convert trim(tid) s1 s2 s3 from perf for pid="rom" to array sales(1,1)
_?#col
            4
_?#row
          5
_?select trim(tid) s1 s2 s3 from perf for pid="rom"
        TO1          S1      S2     S3

1                  10050   12453   8032
6                   6090    5900   6904
4                   5009    3997   9037
9                   5345    5400   6200
3                   4590    3997   5032
_?sales(1,1),sales(1,2),sales(1,3),sales(1,4)
1         10050           12453          8032
_?sales(2,1),sales(2,2),sales(2,3),sales(2,4)
6          6090            5900          6904
_?sales(5,1),sales(5,2),sales(5,3),sales(5,4)
3          4590            3997          5032
_?sales(#row,#col)
          5032

_
```

Saving an Array

To complete his discussion of arrays, Jack added, "Once you have filled
in some arrays, you may want to save them in a context file. This will
allow you to reload them in some later session. The SAVE and LOAD
commands automatically save and load arrays, unless you've designated
that only certain aspects of a context are to be saved or loaded."

He explained that the commands

```
save "a:dsource.icf" with "a"
load "a:dsource.icf" with "a"
```

respectively save all of the present context's arrays in DSOURCE.ICF
on the drive A diskette and load that file's arrays into the present context.
Furthermore, any array can be released from the present context via
the RELEASE command. For instance, the command

```
release sales
```

would release the main memory occupied by SALES for other uses.

GENERATING GRAPHS

Any business graphics software package requires the construction of a data source before graphs can be generated. Many depend on the construction being accomplished by some external piece of software that produces a file of the data to be graphed. The data must be formatted in the file in such a way that it can be processed by the graphics package. As previously noted, all data sources in this environment exist as part of the present processing context rather than as external files on disk. They can take several guises other than user-defined arrays (e.g., statistical arrays, working variables, spreadsheets). Files in the environment's knowledge system can be used for long-term storage of a context's graphical data sources.

"You now know how to use the DIM command to define a data source," Jack said. "You also know how to fill in the array elements, either one at a time with the LET command or en masse with a single CONVERT command. In so doing, you are representing presentation knowledge and now the question is how to process that knowledge. As you'll see, there are many ways to process a data source, each producing a particular graph on the console screen."

"One way of looking at it," added Joy, "is that there are all sorts of graphical treasures buried in an array such as SALES. Believe it or not, there are many bar graphs, pie plots, and area graphs in the SALES array. They're not visible to the naked eye, but can be instantly revealed on the console screen if you know the right commands. As Jack goes through these commands with you, you'll become clearer about the relationship between a data source's contents and the kinds of graphs that can be generated from those contents."

Bar Graphs

As Joy spoke, Jack typed

```
plot bar from sales(1,1) to sales(5,4)
```

to show just how easy it is to dig a graph out of an array. If Jack had tried to plot elements from beyond the fifth SALES row, an error message (e.g., "undefined name") would have resulted. In general, an attempt to plot from elements that have no values results in such a message rather than a graph.

He interpreted, "Here, I'm giving a command to plot a *bar graph* from the data held in elements 1,1 through 5,4 of the SALES array. We've already seen that there is no data beyond the fifth row of

PHOTO 21   A bar graph of romance sales

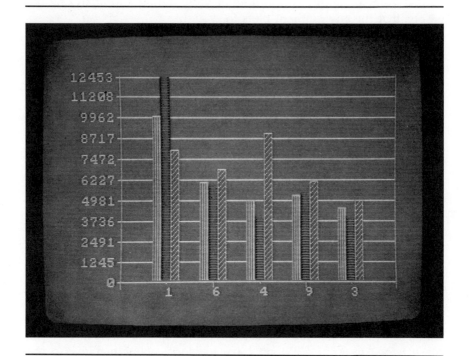

SALES, so it wouldn't make any sense to try to graph from those beyond row 5.

Now when I press the Enter key to execute this PLOT command, you'll see a bar graph on the screen. And it will contain one cluster of bars for each of the five SALES rows; that is, for each of the five territories having romance sales we'll get some bars showing its quarterly sales levels."

He pressed the Enter key. The screen cleared immediately and then the bar graph of Photo 21 appeared. As Jack had predicted, it contained a cluster of bars for each of the five territories. Each cluster had three bars whose heights depicted the levels of romance sales in the three quarters.

"There are several things to notice about this graph," Jack stressed. "First, it has an X axis that is aligned horizontally and a Y axis that is aligned vertically."

"Just like the graphs you used to draw yourselves in junior high math classes," Joy chimed. Much earlier in her career, she had taught such classes after majoring in mathematics at an eastern university.

"The main difference is that now you don't have to do any plotting of points. You can simply concentrate on interpreting and analyzing the graphs that the environment plots for you."

Continuing, Jack said, "Notice that values for the X axis come from the first column of the array. There are five of them: 1, 6, 4, 9, and 3. For each of these values there is a cluster of three bars that correspond to the three additional values in a row."

"I see," Tracey nodded. "Each row in the array generated a cluster of bars. The first value in a row is used to designate the cluster along the X aixs. The other values in a row determine how high the bars will be. So really, in each row we have three Y values to go along with the X value. The first bar in each cluster shows the first quarter romance sales. The second bar shows the second quarter sales in the territory. And the third bar is for the third quarter."

"You mean," asked Brad, "that if we were plotting from five columns instead of four, then each cluster would have four bars instead of three? And if we were plotting from three rows instead of five, we'd get a graph with three clusters instead of five?"

"Exactly right!" answered Jack. He paused, pointed to the left edge of the graph, and then added, "Another thing to notice are the numbers along the Y axis. The environment generates these automatically for us. It takes the highest Y value from the data source as the top Y value, 0 as the lowest, and calculates 10 evenly spaced intervals between these two extremes. We don't have to worry about making up our own range of Y-axis numbers, though I'll later show how to do so if you like."

Sorted Bar Graphs

"Why," Pete inquired, "aren't the IDs along the X axis in sorted order? Is there some way to have them sorted?"

"Remember," Jack explained, "that territory ID values are strings and not numbers. When the values for your X axis are strings, they'll be arranged in the same order in which they exist in the array. If we had wanted, we could have included an ORDER BY TID clause in the CONVERT command. Then the SALES rows would have been filled in sorted order. But it's too late for that now, so I'll show you another way."

He pressed the space bar to clear the graph from the screen. When the underscore prompt reappeared, he pressed ^Z and proceeded to edit the previous PLOT command by inserting the word SORTED immediately after PLOT. Jack then executed the command

```
plot sorted bar from sales(1,1) to sales(5,4)
```

to generate a graph almost identical to the one in Photo 21. The only difference was that the clusters were rearranged so that territory 3 followed 1, 4 followed 3, 6 followed 4, and the bar cluster for 9 was now on the right side of the graph.

"Before I show you some of the other sorts of bar graphs," Jack announced, "let's spruce up the graph a bit by giving it a title and some axis labels. Also, since we'll be generating lots of graphs from the first five rows of SALES, I'm going to make a macro to save some typing effort. Let's call it RS for romance sales."

Graph Title and Labels

To define the RS macro, Jack executed the command

```
macro rs sales(1,1) to sales(5,4)
```

and proceeded to execute the command

```
#title="QUARTERLY ROMANCE SALES BY TERRITORY"
```

to specify a title for the graph. He explained there were two utility variables, #XLABEL and #YLABEL, whose values determined what labels would appear alongside a graph's X axis and Y axis. Initially, these built-in variables have no values. He executed the commands

```
#xlabel="TERRITORY ID"
#ylabel="SALES"
```

to specify labels for each axis. When Jack had typed in

```
plot bar from rs
```

the screen appeared as portrayed in Figure 11–3. He pressed the Enter key to generate Photo 22. Notice that its content is the same as that of Photo 21, except for the title and labels. He mentioned that he would be using the RS macro for specifying a data source in many of the subsequent PLOT commands.

"Now it's worth pausing for a moment," Jack said thoughtfully, "to consider the graph itself. Recall why we would want to generate a graph anyway: to quickly spot patterns and trends. In this case, you can readily see many things. For instance, territory 9 is the only one

FIGURE 11–3   Macros, titles, and labels for graph generation

```
_macro rs sales(1,1) to sales(5,4)
_#title="QUARTERLY ROMANCE SALES BY TERRITORY"
_#xlabel="TERRITORY ID"
_#ylabel="SALES"
_plot bar from rs
```

where sales have improved in each quarter; territory 1 had blockbuster results in the first two quarters and territory 4 was tops in the third quarter; territory 3 seems to be a consistent laggard when it comes to romance. It's important to keep in mind why you're generating a graph."

There was a murmur of agreement, topped by Debbie's observation. "Once you have a data source, which only takes a command or two, you're ready to really go to town in terms of analyzing and evaluating data in a graphic way."

3-D Bar Graphs

"Speaking of going to town," Jack said with bemusement, "let's go to Chicago with our next graph."

The group's puzzlement was dispelled when he executed the command

```
plot solid bar from rs
```

PHOTO 22   A titled and labeled bar graph

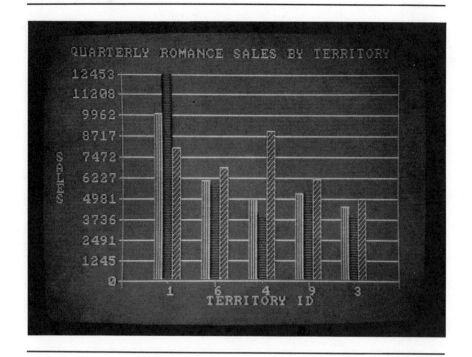

generating Photo 23. Instead of a flat bar chart, they could now view a 3-D (i.e., "solid") rendition of the same bars. This skyscraper appearance was caused by inclusion of the word SOLID before BAR.

"I do believe I see the Sears tower on the left," joked Don. "But seriously, I'd like to see a bar graph that shows each territory's sales in percentage terms. For instance, what percentage of romance sales in territory 4 occurred in the third quarter?"

Percentage Bar Graphs

"Good question," Jack replied quickly, "and I have a good answer for you. If you know how to plot a bar graph, then it's trivial to plot a percentage bar graph. By that I mean you'll see percentages rather than absolute numbers along the Y axis. Suppose we want to see the percentages to two decimal places."

PHOTO 23   A 3-D bar graph

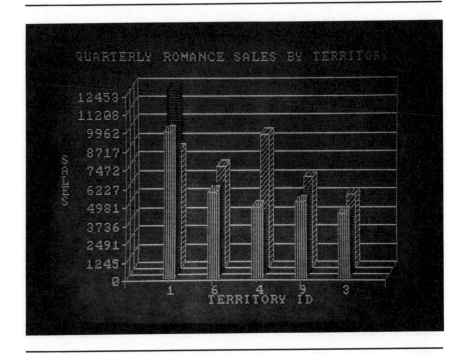

To switch E.DECI from its present value of 0 and establish an appropriate Y-axis label, he executed the commands

```
e.deci=2
#ylabel="SALES % IN TERRITORY"
```

and then

```
plot percent bar from rs
```

to generate Photo 24. This plot tells a very different story than the ones in Photos 22 and 23. Don could immediately see that the answer to his question was 50.09 percent.

"But," Don said, "the second bar for territory 4 seems to be missing."

"At first glance that's true," Jack agreed. "However, if you look at the Y axis, you'll see that it doesn't start with 0, but 22.15 instead. That's the minimum of all the percentages and it corresponds to the apparently missing bar for territory 4."

PHOTO 24   A percentage bar graph

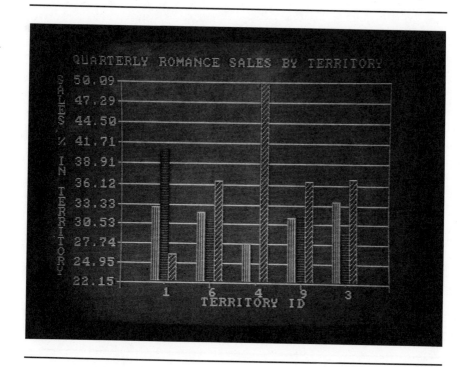

"I get it," Don said, "and as you said earlier there is a way we can cause a different range of values, say 0 to 100, to appear along the Y axis. Of course, a percentage bar chart doesn't give any clue as to who has generated the most sales. From your regular bar chart it was clear that territory 1 was in the lead and territory 3 brought up the rear. But it was tough to tell where the other three territories fell in terms of year-to-date sales. Is there another kind of bar chart for making that clearer? Maybe you could stack the bars to see their cumulative effect?"

Stacked Bar Graphs

"You're right. Things that are nicely stacked can be very appealing," replied Jack, switching E.DECI back to 0 and letting #YLABEL have "CUMULATIVE SALES" as its value. He then executed the command

```
plot stacked bar from rs
```

PHOTO 25   **A stacked bar graph**

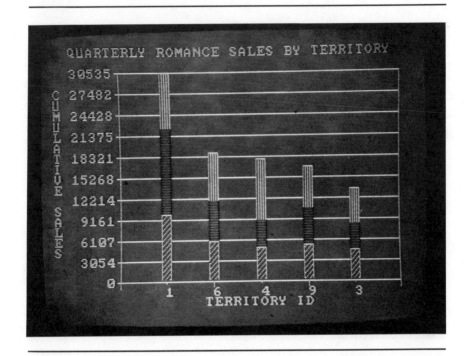

generating Photo 25. Such a graph makes the cumulative sales for each territory obvious, while still depicting the relative contributions of each quarter.

"Now let's say I want to concentrate on only the second and third quarter results," Stan said hypothetically. "Do I need to make a new data source that's like SALES only without its second column of S1 data? Or can I have the PLOT command skip over the second SALES column when it generates a graph?"

"Excellent question," answered Jack in a congratulatory tone. "When you only want to use a subset of a data source's columns, you just specify which columns to use right in the PLOT command."

To demonstrate, he executed the command

```
plot stacked bar from rs using 1,3,4
```

generating Photo 26. As the graph shows, the first column of the data source furnished the X-axis values and there were only two bars per stack. Their heights were based on data values in the third and fourth

PHOTO 26   **A graph using selected data source columns**

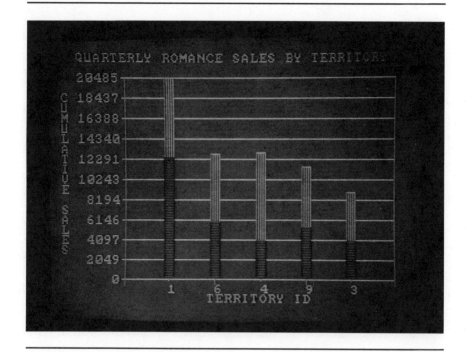

columns of SALES. The second SALES column (first quarter sales) was ignored. In general, any data source columns can be excluded from a graph in this manner and the chosen columns can be designated in any sequence.

Area Graphs

"Now that you've passed the bar, so to speak, let's look at a different kind of graph," Jack declared. "It's what's known as an *area graph*. Once you understand stacked bar graphs, area graphs are easy. Let me show you what I mean."

He executed the command

```
plot area from rs
```

generating Photo 27. Compare it with the stacked bar graph in Photo 25. Their X and Y axes are identical. The area graph has three distinct areas. The bottom area corresponds to first quarter sales and is produced

PHOTO 27   An area graph

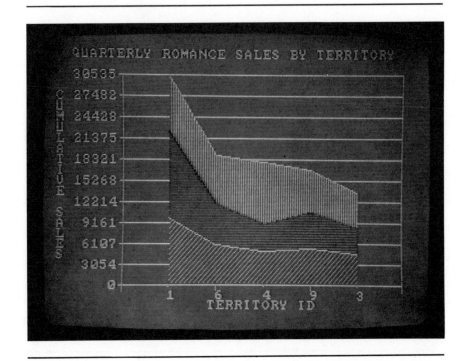

from the second column of SALES. For each territory, its upper border shows the level of first quarter romance sales. Similarly, the middle area is for second quarter sales. Its upper border shows the cumulative sales through the first two quarters. Finally, the top area is derived from third quarter sales. Its upper bound above a territory ID shows the year-to-date level of sales for that territory.

"It seems to me," commented Dan, "that this kind of graph is good not only for visualizing the cumulative sales for each territory, but also for getting a feel about one time period versus another. For instance, the fact that the top area is much larger than the other two clearly shows that the region had heavier romance sales in the third quarter than it did in either of the other two. Is there some way to see this in percentage terms?"

Percentage Area Graphs

After changing the #YLABEL value and switching E.DECI back to 2, Jack answered Dan's question by executing the command

PHOTO 28   A percentage area graph

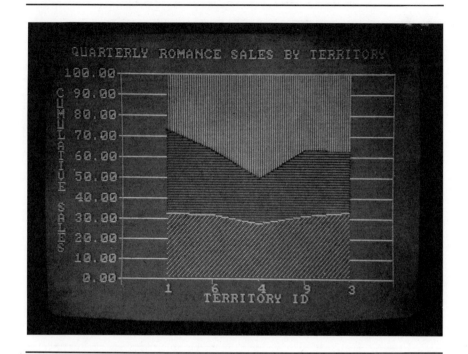

```
plot percent area from rs
```

yielding Photo 28. For each territory, this graph shows the cumulative quarterly romance sales. In looking at the graph, it is clear that territory 4 had achieved only about 50 percent of its total romance sales by the end of the second quarter and that this is a lower level than any other territory.

As with bar graphs, the X-axis values of an area graph can be sorted by including the word SORTED after PLOT. Jack also mentioned that they were free to designate which data source columns were to be used and in what order they were to be used. For instance, the command

```
plot sorted percent area from rs using 1,4,3,2
```

would yield a percentage area graph in which territories are arranged from 1 through 9 on the X axis and in which third quarter sales make up the bottom area while first quarter sales make up the top area. Figure 11–4 is a printout of such a graph.

FIGURE 11–4　**Reversed areas and a sorted X axis**

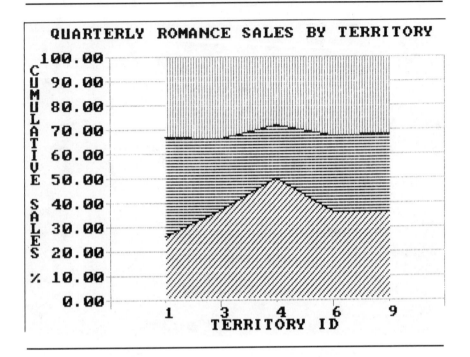

Pie Graphs

"You've shown that we can use bar and area graphs to see proportions of quarterly sales within each territory. That's all well and good," remarked Brad. "But I'd like to get a better feel for proportions of, say, third quarter romance sales that each territory contributes to the regional total."

"It's easy as pie," was Jack's cheery reply. To demonstrate, he executed the commands

```
#title="TERRITORIAL ROMANCE SALES IN QTR 3"
plot labeled pie from rs using 1,4
```

which generated Photo 29. Notice that the first column used for generating a *pie graph* furnishes the labels for the slices. The second data source column that is used (i.e., column 4 in this example) determines the slice sizes. The number of slices is, of course, determined by the number of rows in the data source.

PHOTO 29   A labeled pie graph

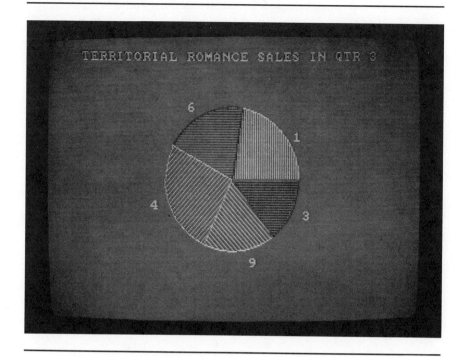

"As you can see," interpreted Jack, "territories 1 and 4 appear to have made the greatest contributions to third quarter romance sales."

"If you ask me," Brad said crustily, "your pie is only half baked. I can't tell for sure whether slice 1 is bigger or smaller than slice 4. I can tell that slice 3 is smaller than slice 4. But by how much?"

"So my pie isn't firm enough for your taste," laughed Jack. "I guess you'd like to have some actual percentages to sink your teeth into."

"Right," Brad responded. "And now that you've whetted my appetite, I'd also like to see rep names rather than territory IDs alongside the slices."

Brad thought he had finally found something Jack couldn't do and was therefore surprised at the reply. "That's a good idea. But as you might surmise, I'll have to begin with different ingredients. As it stands, the SALES array doesn't hold any names, so we'll need to expand it so it does. While I'm at it, I'll also fill year-to-date sales data into the array."

To concoct the array's new filling, Jack executed the two commands

FIGURE 11–5   Enlarging a data source

```
_dim sales(10,6)
_convert fname trim(tid) s1 s2 s3 sytd from perf where pid="rom" to array sales
(1,1)
_release rs
_macro rs sales(1,1) to sales(5,6)
_plot labeled percent pie from rs using 1,5
```

```
dim sales(10,6)
convert fname trim(tid)s1 s2 s3 sytd from perf where pid="rom" to array sales(1,1)
```

The first of these extended the SALES dimensions to allow six columns instead of just four. The CONVERT command then filled in all six columns. The new SALES array had all the same data as before, plus FNAME values as its first column and SYTD values for its last column. Because the array was now larger, Jack released the RS macro and respecified it to extend through the SALES(5,6) element.

"Now we're cooking!" Jack exclaimed as he typed the command

```
plot labeled percent pie from rs using 1,5
```

producing the screen appearance portrayed in Figure 11–5. This is just like the previous PLOT PIE command, except that percentages are being requested and the data source's fifth column is to be used. Because the first column of SALES now contained names, they would be used as slice labels. Because the fifth column was filled with S3 data, the pie's slices would be identical to those in Photo 29. He pressed the Enter key to generate the graph shown in Photo 30 in the color insert.

Having satisfied Brad's intellectual hunger, Jack declared, "There are other variations of pie graphs that I'll leave for you to sample on your own. The reference manual tells how they work. But now I want to give you all the flavor of another kind of graph."

Line Graphs

Like bar and area graphs, *line graphs* have X and Y axes. As usual the first data source column that is used furnishes the X-axis values. These can be string values or numeric values. Each remaining column that is used results in a line in the graph. For instance, the array of Figure 11–1 could be used to generate two lines in a graph. A line connects certain points in the graph. A point is determined by an X value and a Y value. Referring again to the Figure 11–1 array, one line would connect the four points: (4,2800), (5,2950), (6,2500), and (7,3005). A second line would connect the XY coordinates of (4,4000), (5,3014), (6,2820), and (7,2400). Thus, each line has one point for every row of data.

"Let's plot a line graph that compares first and third quarter romance sales across the territories," suggested Jack. "That is, the graph will have one line for the first quarter and another line for the third quarter. We'll use the SALES array as our data source."

As Figure 11–6 shows, he assigned relevant values to #TITLE, #YLABEL, and #XLABEL. Mentioning that he wanted a different background color for the graph, Jack output the present value of E.BACG. He pointed out that the second color code in this value controls the background color of graphics screens. He changed it from its blue (i.e., U) default to black (i.e., A) and proceeded to type in

```
plot sorted line from rs using 2,3,5
```

explaining that the second SALES column would furnish X-axis values. The third and fifth columns, containing first and third quarter sales, furnished the corresponding Y coordinates for points in the two desired lines.

Pressing the Enter key executed the PLOT command, generating Photo 31. Jack explained that if the word SCATTER had been used in place of SORTED LINE, only the points would have been marked in the graph. There would be no lines connecting them. Such a graph is typically called a *scattergram*. Notice that the lines in Photo 31 are styled and colored differently.[1] One is a dashed line while the other is not.

---

[1] In black-and-white photos, colors appear as different shades.

FIGURE 11–6   Plotting a line graph

```
_#title="First Qtr Vs Third Qtr Romance"
_#ylabel="Sales"
_#xlabel="Territories"
_?e.bacg
UUUUA
_e.bacg="UAUUA"
_plot sorted line from rs using 2,3,5
```

With a troubled look, Brad asked, "Which is which? Is the dashed line for first or third quarter sales?"

Graph Legends

"Good question," Jack responded briskly. "Let's find out by plotting a legend in this graph. Let's put the legend in that empty area in the upper right portion of the grid, at about the fourth line down and about three fourths of the way across the screen.

Jack pressed the space bar to get the underscore prompt. As shown in Figure 11–7, he dimensioned the #LEGEND array to have two elements and gave a value to each. Jack then typed

```
plot legend for line at 4,30
```

explaining that a graphics screen was only 40, rather than 80, characters wide. This is because each displayed graphics character is twice as wide as the normal characters. Thus, by specifying 4,30, Jack would cause the legend to begin three fourths of the way across the fourth line of the graphics screen.

PHOTO 31   A multiline graph

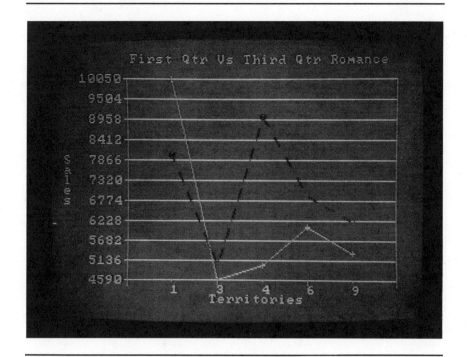

He pressed the Enter key, causing the line legend to appear as shown in Photo 32. The line type corresponding to the first Y column (i.e., column 3) appears alongside #LEGEND(1)'s value. Similarly, the dashed line, connecting the points derived from the second Y column (i.e., column 5) accompanies #LEGEND(2)'s value. In this way, the environment automatically associates a line style with each #LEGEND value.

Superimposing Text on a Graph

"Alternatively," Jack explained, "we could have superimposed a text string such as 'Qtr 1' right next to the solid line and 'Qtr 3' next to the dashed line. But I prefer a legend myself."

The commands

```
plot ontop text "Qtr 1" at 20,36
plot ontop text "Qtr 3" at 16,36
```

FIGURE 11–7   Plotting a legend

```
_dim #legend(2)
_#legend(1)="Qtr 1"
_#legend(2)="Qtr 3"
_plot legend for line at 4,30
```

would superimpose the two text strings on the graph. The "Qtr 1" label would appear at the right end of the solid line (i.e., screen coordinates of line 20, column 36). The other would appear above it, at the right end of the dashed line (i.e., line 16, column 36). In general, PLOT ONTOP TEXT can be invoked to insert any desired text at any place in a graphics screen. It is a useful feature for calling attention to certain aspects of a graph, as well as for documenting the graph's contents.

The environment can generate another kind of graph that resembles a line graph, but that does not make use of any explicit data source. Instead, the environment is directed to plot the line implied by a mathematical function. Such a graph is called a *function plot*. For instance, the command

```
plot function=2*X+3 from 0 to 10 by 10
```

would produce a straight line, intercepting the Y axis at 3 and extending to the point (10,23). For function plots, the environment calculates its own data source from the numeric expression within the specified range (e.g., 0 to 10) and based on the indicated increment (e.g., by increments

PHOTO 32   **Graph with a line legend**

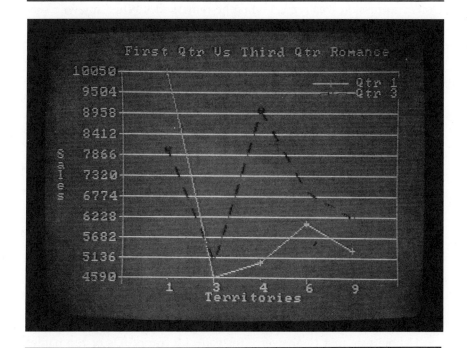

of 10). In general, the numeric expression can involve any of the environment's built-in functions such as SQRT, LOG, and LN.

ADDITIONAL GRAPHICS PROCESSING

At this juncture, the managers were familiar with the basics of representing and processing presentation knowledge via the business graphics technique. They saw how this technique could be of value in presenting data during their own decision-making deliberations, as well as in presenting data to others (e.g., to substantiate their decisions). There are other kinds of graphs that the environment can generate, such as high-low-close graphs and free-form figures [6], but Jack did not deem them particularly important for the sales management application. However, there were several additional aspects of graphics processing that he had found to be especially valuable. These would be covered after the present break for hands-on practice, for then the managers could better appreciate their value.

As the practice break progressed, Jack and Joy sensed a growing enthusiasm. The vortex was strong and the atmosphere contagious as the managers realized just how simple it was to produce polished graphs. Don's impression was typical when he remarked, "When my wife sees the graphs I can do in just seconds, she'll think I'm a real computer whiz! And maybe I am, in a way. Yet it all seems so straightforward."

When the session resumed that afternoon, the group was brimming with questions. Can the colors in a graph be altered? Can the patterns used for filling areas and drawing lines be controlled? Can a graph be kept in main memory for instant recall, without having to reissue a PLOT command? How can a printout of a graphics screen be produced? Can a graph be preserved on disk for use at a later time? Exactly how can the numeric ranges displayed along an axis be controlled? If text can be superimposed on top of an existing graphics screen, is it also possible to superimpose one graph on top of an existing graphics screen? Can a graph be restricted to a certain portion of the screen?

More Elaborate Data Sources

"To begin to answer your questions," responded Jack, "let's make another data source. Whereas the SALES array deals with territorial sales for a particular product line, let's take a look at an individual rep's sales versus quotas across several product lines. To do this, what data will we need to convert into the new array?"

Debbie was first to answer. "Instead of territory IDs or rep names in the first column we should convert product IDs. The remaining columns will hold not only sales figures, but there will also be columns of quota numbers."

"And," added Dan, "the CONVERT command will have a condition that restricts the conversion to only those products we're interested in for a particular rep."

"Correct!" Jack said enthusiastically. He was pleased to see the group's progress. At the start of the day's instruction, they would not have had the slightest idea of what his question meant, much less how to answer it correctly. "Just to make things interesting, I'll convert performance data for two reps, say, Karen and Carol, into the same array. Let's call the array SQ, since it will contain sales and quota data. Now if I tell you that I want SQ to have sales and quotas for business, romance, and computer books, how many rows should the array have?"

"Six," replied several of the managers simultaneously.

"Right," confirmed Jack, "to allow for up to three rows of data for each rep. Let's say we want sales and quotas for each of the completed quarters as well as the year-to-date sales and annual quota. How many columns does SQ need?"

"Nine," Stan answered quickly, "one for the product ID, six for the quarterly numbers, and two columns for the yearly numbers."

Taking the group's advice, Jack executed the commands

```
dim sq(6,9)
#title=" "
```

to give SQ dimensions of six rows by nine columns. The second command got rid of the title used for the last graph. It was no longer relevant. Jack then issued the query

```
select pid s1 q1 s2 q2 s3 q3 sytd qyr from perf for tid in ["6","9"] &
pid in ["bus", "rom", "com"] order by tid pid
```

producing a nine-column, six-line display of data on the console screen. See Figure 11–8.

"This," said Jack, pointing to the screen, "is what we want to fill in the SQ array. Because of the ORDER BY clause, we know that the first three lines are for Karen in territory 6 and the other three are for Carol in territory 9. When preparing a data source, it's not a bad idea to issue the corresponding query first. You can then easily preview what will go into the array. You can also easily edit the SELECT command to get the corresponding CONVERT command."

Jack pressed ^Z to bring the SELECT command back into view. With a few keystrokes, he edited it by inserting the array destination ahead of the ORDER BY clause and replacing the word SELECT with CONVERT. The resultant command

```
convert pid s1 q1 s2 q2 s3 q3 sytd qyr from perf for tid in ["6","9"] &
pid in ["bus","rom","com"] to array sq(1,1) order by tid pid
```

was then executed to fill in all six lines and nine columns of the SQ array.

"Now because I want to be able to look at Karen's performance in one graph and Carol's in another graph, I'll define the KAREN macro for the first three rows of SQ and the CAROL macro for the last three rows," Jack explained, suiting his actions to his words (see Figure 11–8). "This makes it easy to plot a graph from either Karen's data or Carol's data without having to explicitly specify SQ elements. Of course, we can still plot data from the entire SQ array if we want to see both reps' performances in the same graph."

"Alternatively," Joy declared, "you could have used two DIM commands and two CONVERT commands to make separate data sources for Karen and Carol. If you then wanted to include them both in a

FIGURE 11–8   A multi-rep data source

```
_dim sq(6,9)
_#title=""
_select pid s1 q1 s2 q2 s3 q3 sytd qyr from perf for tid in ["6","9"] & pid in [
"bus","rom","com"] order by tid pid
PID    S1      Q1      S2      Q2      S3      Q3      SYTD    QYR

bus    12222   10700   11980   11009   8332    8443    32534   38082
com    13121   12090   11590   11069   10075   10806   34786   43630
rom    6090    6040    5900    5020    6904    5555    18894   23281
bus    4005    3997    4436    4378    4998    4832    13439   17108
com    8488    6903    9321    5882    7021    6031    24830   27272
rom    5345    5004    5400    4468    6200    5830    16945   22525
_convert pid s1 q1 s2 q2 s3 q3 sytd qyr from perf for tid in ["6","9"] & pid in
["bus","rom","com"] to array sq(1,1) order by tid pid
_macro karen sq(1,1) to sq(3,9)
_macro carol sq(4,1) to sq(6,9)
_#xlabel="PRODUCTS"
_#ylabel="SALES & QUOTAS"
_plot bar from karen
```

single PLOT command, you could do so. For the present, we won't be concerned about how to simultaneously plot from multiple data sources. If you're interested, you can issue the HELP command to find out more about it. We'll just focus on the ability to plot from row and column subsets of a single array."

Pattern Control

As shown in Figure 11–8, Jack proceeded to give labels to the X and Y axes, before typing

```
plot bar from karen
```

When he pressed the Enter key, Photo 33 in the color insert appeared. As expected, it has three clusters of bars (one for each of the first three rows) and eight bars per cluster (one for each of the eight Y columns in SQ). Observe that each bar in a cluster has a distinct colored *pattern* filling its area. The first has vertical stripes, the second has horizontal stripes, the seventh is solid, and the eighth is empty.

"I realize that the bars alternately denote sales and quotas," Brad

FIGURE 11–9   Controlling patterns

```
_pattern order for area 7,8
_#legend(1)="SALES"
_#legend(2)="QUOTA"
_plot bar from karen; plot legend for area at 1,30
```

remarked. "But, as it stands, the graph looks like a patchwork quilt. There are too many different patterns. I'd like to see all the sales bars have one pattern, say solid, and all the quota bars have a different pattern, say empty."

"Good suggestion," Jack said. "We can control the pattern filled into a bar's area, a slice's area, and an area's area with the PATTERN command. Each of the eight distinct patterns shown in this graph has a corresponding number in the range 1 through 8. With the PATTERN command we can specify which of these we want and what order they should be in. An example will give you the idea."

Jack executed the command

```
pattern order for area 7,8
```

to tell the environment to alternate between solid (7) and empty (8) patterns for bar, slice, and area areas in subsequent graphs. As Figure 11–9 shows, he also assigned corresponding values to the #LEGEND elements and typed in

```
plot bar from karen; plot legend for area at 1,30
```

PHOTO 34   Alternating graphics patterns

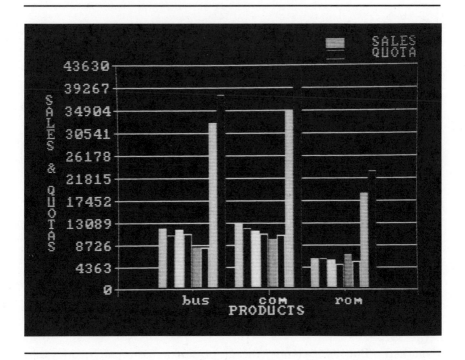

When he pressed the Enter key a bar graph appeared. It was the same as Photo 33, except the first bar was solid, the second bar was empty, the third was solid, the fourth empty, and so forth. He pressed the space bar and Enter, causing the legend for area patterns to appear in the upper right corner of the screen (see Photo 34).

"So," Stan remarked, "if I wanted sales to be horizontal stripes and quotas to be vertical stripes, I would have specified a pattern order of 2,1 instead of 7,8. Would this have been automatically reflected in the legend as well?"

Jack nodded, as Debbie added, "I presume we can use the PATTERN command in a similar manner to control the order of line patterns and mark patterns, such as those that appear in a line graph."

"That's true," Jack affirmed. "You'd just use the words LINE or MARK instead of AREA in the PATTERN command. You can experiment with those on your own if you like. Typing HELP PATTERN should get you a description of the permissible line and mark patterns, along with their corresponding numbers.

"You can also use the PATTERN command to control the order in which things are colored in a graph. The host machine and operating system we're using allow up to three distinct foreground colors on a graphics screen. It has a further restriction that red, green, and brown have to be used together; and white, cyan, and magenta have to be used together. Colors from the two groups can't be mixed within our hosts."

"Other host hardware and operating systems do not impose this restriction on the environment," Joy noted.

Graph Positioning

"Now that we have a nice graph for one rep," said Stan, "I think it would be very handy to show a comparable graph for the other rep. I realize it may be asking too much, but ideally I'd like to see them side by side on the same screen for easy comparison."

"No problem," Jack replied nonchalantly. "If you can plot a graph for the full screen, then you can plot a graph on just one half of a screen and another graph on the other half."

As a prelude, Jack executed the command

```
pattern order for color "MC"
```

to illustrate that PATTERN could indeed be used to control the order of colors in a graph. From this point onward, colors in generated graphs would alternate between magenta (M) and cyan (C). As Figure 11–10 shows, he also specified a title for the graph before typing

```
plot bar from karen at left
```

Notice that this PLOT command is identical to that of Figure 10–9, except for its indication that the bar graph should be positioned at the left side of the screen.

Jack pressed the Enter key to generate the graph of Photo 35. It contained alternating magenta and cyan bars.[2] Because of the smaller horizontal space available, the bars are naturally much thinner, so thin in fact that different area patterns are indistinguishable.

As the oohs and ahs subsided, Don asked, "If we wanted Karen's graph to be on the other side of the screen, could we have specified right instead of left?"

"Right," Jack smiled.

---

[2] Colors appear as various shades in black-and-white photos.

FIGURE 11–10   Positioning a graph at the left side

```
_pattern order for color "MC"
_#title="Karen"
_plot bar from karen at left
```

Superimposing Graphs

"OK then," Don continued, "I could now just do a PLOT BAR FROM CAROL AT RIGHT to have her graph appear next to Karen's."

"Not quite," Jack replied quickly. "That would produce a new graphics screen having Carol's graph at the right and the left half of the screen would be blank. Because I don't want to lose Karen, something else is required."

"I see," Don said, "what you want to do is superimpose Carol's graph on top of the existing graphics screen."

"Then it's the same idea that you mentioned earlier about superimposing text on top of an existing graphics screen," observed Tracey. "Only in this case, we need to superimpose a bar graph instead of some text."

"Exactly!" responded Jack. "And though it may seem like an imposing task, it's very easy to accomplish. Whenever you want to superimpose a plot on top of your current graphics screen, you just say PLOT ONTOP instead of PLOT. Watch how it works."

He pressed the space bar to remove the current graphics screen from view and get the underscore prompt. He executed the command

PHOTO 35   A left-half graph

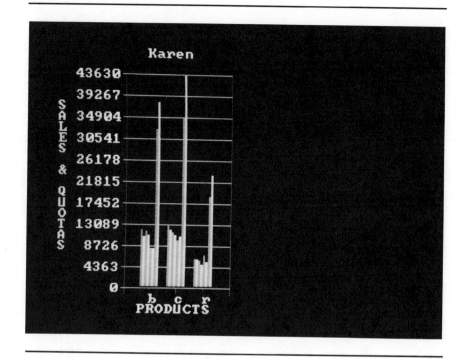

```
#title="Carol"
```

to set the upcoming graph's title. This was followed by

```
plot ontop bar from carol at right
```

to generate Photo 36. Carol's bar graph now appeared at the right side of the current graphics screen.

Ranges and Scales

"That's neat," said Brad, "but it would be easier to compare the two graphs if they had the same range of numbers along their Y axes. As it is, Carol's highest sales bar is visually higher than Karen's highest sales bar, even though Carol's is numerically about 15,000 less."

"Good point," Jack agreed. "What we'd like is for Carol's Y axis to range up from 0 to 43630, just like Karen's. We can do that with the RANGE command, but first let's clear out the right side of the

PHOTO 36   A second graph superimposed on the same screen

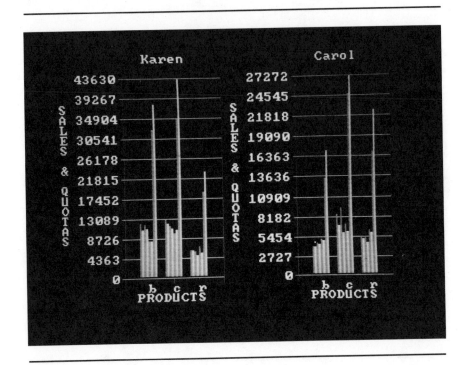

screen. We'll then specify the desired range and superimpose a revised graph for Carol at the right side."

He executed the command

```
clear right
```

to clear the right side of the screen. Carol's graph began to vanish from the top of the screen downward. It was as if a black shade was pulled down over the right half of the screen. Karen's perfection was left untouched so Photo 35 was once again the current screen. Jack pressed the space bar to remove the graphics screen from view and get the underscore prompt.

"The most recent graphics screen we've seen is called the *current screen*," he explained. "Because I want to use the now current screen again in a few minutes, I'll keep it before we go ahead and change it. Later, I'll demonstrate how you can make a kept screen current again."

Jack executed the command

```
keep graph1
```

causing the environment to keep the current screen's image (i.e., Photo 35) in its main memory work area. To the environment, the kept image was now known by the name GRAPH1. The KEEP command can be invoked at any juncture to keep a current graphics screen with whatever name the user specifies. Multiple graphs with different names can be kept simultaneously. As Jack would demonstrate later, any of them can again be made current with the SHOW command. For now, he proceeded to change the current screen by superimposing a different Carol plot on top of it.

The RANGE command can be used to override the automatic range determined for a numeric axis. In this case, Jack executed the command

```
range up from 0 to 43630
```

to cause the Y axis in all subsequent plots to range from 0 to 43630. The command

```
range reset up
```

would reinstitute the automatic determination of Y-axis ranges. He explained that for a numeric X axis, the range could be manually determined or reset in a similar manner by substituting the word ACROSS for UP.

Jack again executed the command

```
plot ontop bar from carol at right
```

producing Photo 37 in the color insert. The result was much more to Brad's liking. Though Jack did not demonstrate it, values appearing along the Y axis could be scaled by powers of 10. Such a facility is very useful when dealing with very large or very small numbers. Scaling of Y-axis values is determined by the E.YPOW environment variable. For instance, if E.YPOW were changed from its default of 0 to 4 and E.DECI were set to 2, the top Y-axis value in Photo 37 would appear as 4.36 (i.e., it is $4.36 * 10^4$), the next as 3.93 (i.e., $3.93 * 10^4$), and so on. Scaling of numeric X-axis values is similarly governed by E.XPOW.

To reinforce the concepts of pattern control, graph positioning, superimposed plots, and manual range setting, Jack presented another example. Instead of generating graphs for the left and right halves of the screen, he intended to generate them for the top and bottom halves. Also, he planned to restrict the graphs to quarterly sales and quotas. After pressing the space bar to remove the current graphics screen

FIGURE 11–11   Plotting a graph in the top half

```
_range up from 0 to 15000
_#title="Karen"
_#xlabel=""
_#ylabel=""
_pattern order for area 7
_pattern order for color "MW"
_plot bar from karen using 1,2,3,4,5,6,7 at top
```

from view, Jack entered a series of commands as shown in Figure 11–11.

Because yearly sales and quotas were not going to be included, he set the Y-axis range from 0 to 15,000. After establishing the title and blanking out the labels, he specified a single area pattern of 7. This would cause the area occupied by each bar to have the same solid pattern. Jack then established an alternating color pattern of magenta and white. When he executed it, the PLOT command in Figure 11–11 caused Karen's bar graph to appear at the top of the screen.

Jack pressed the space bar to get the underscore prompt. He executed the commands

```
#title="Carol"
plot ontop bar from carol using 1,2,3,4,5,6,7 at bottom
```

causing Carol's graph to be superimposed on the bottom. To polish off his work, Jack executed the command

```
plot legend for area at 12,30
```

producing Photo 38.

PHOTO 38   A top-bottom graph

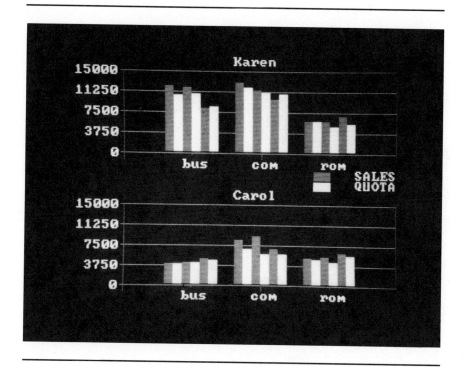

Graphics Printouts

"When we want to get a printout of the current graphics screen, the PRINT command should be invoked," noted Jack. "Of course, be sure the printer is online first."

To demonstrate, he executed the command

```
print current
```

resulting in the Figure 11–12 printout. Though it shows shades of black on white, it does not include colors. Like many graphics packages, the environment's graphics capability does allow color printouts to be produced on pen plotters and ink-jet printers [6].

KEEPING GRAPHICS SCREENS

"Remember that earlier I kept a graphics screen named GRAPH1," recalled Jack. "Now let's say we want to look at it again and perhaps superimpose some things on it. First, I'll keep our present screen so

FIGURE 11–12   Graphics printout

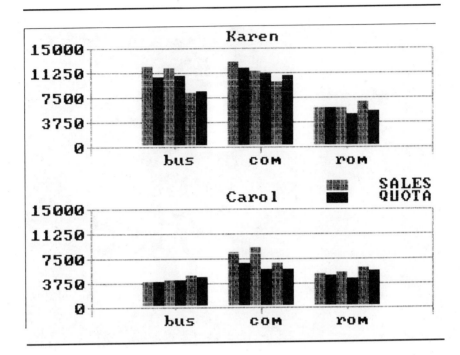

we'll be able to get it back later. If you don't keep a screen before making another one current, about the only way you'll be able to see it again is to generate it again with the PLOT command.''

He executed the command

```
keep graph2
```

to keep the image of Photo 38. Following this up with

```
show graph1
```

Jack caused GRAPH1 to appear as shown in Photo 35. It became the new current screen. He modified it with the commands

```
pattern order for area 1,2,3
#title="YTD Sales"
plot ontop percent labeled pie from karen using 1,8 at top right
```

FIGURE 11–13   Printout with pie in top-right quadrant

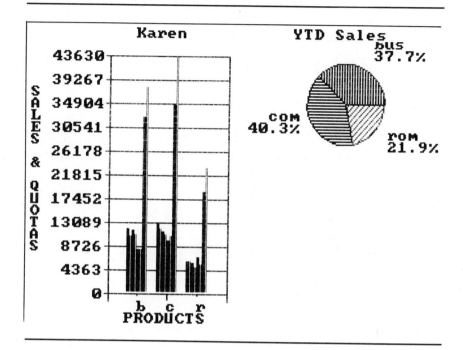

and then printed it as shown in Figure 11–13. Notice that a graph can be positioned in any of four quadrants: top right, top left, bottom right, or bottom left.

Jack's modifications to the current screen did not affect either GRAPH1 or GRAPH2. When he issued the command

```
show graph2
```

Photo 38 appeared as the newly current screen. Similarly, the command

```
show graph1
```

restored Photo 35 as the current screen. He further explained that the command

```
show plot
```

would result in a list of the names of kept screens.

"By the way," Jack remarked, "if you ever forget which graphics screen happens to be current, just type SHOW CURRENT and it will come into view. Also, when you no longer need a kept screen, it's a good idea to release it. A kept screen does consume a sizable amount of main memory."

To demonstrate, Jack executed the commands

```
print graph1
release graph1
```

to first print GRAPH1 and then release it from memory. In general, the PRINT command can be used to PRINT not only the current graphics screen, but any kept screen. On executing

```
show current
```

Photo 38 reappeared.

Jack explained that any kept screen can be incorporated into a piece of text as it is printed. For instance, if the line

```
.ev print graph2
```

were embedded in a piece of text, then a printed version of GRAPH2 would appear at that point in the text when PRINT TEXT is invoked.

Plotting to and from Disk

"Suppose," Dan speculated, "I want to preserve a graphics screen on a longer term basis. A graph is here today and I want it to be here tomorrow too. Obviously, a screen kept in main memory will not survive when I leave the environment and turn off the machine."

"True," Jack replied. "Keeping screens is very handy when you're working on several graphs at the same time. It can also be a good idea to keep a screen before you superimpose something on it. That way, if you superimpose the wrong thing on it, you can merely make the kept screen current again and try superimposing something else. You don't have to try to clear away the offending part of the screen or reexecute any of your earlier PLOT commands. But kept screens don't address the issue of long-term storage. Nevertheless there is a way to preserve a graphics screen in a disk file and then get it back at any later time."

The graphics screen to be preserved in a knowledge system *plot file* should be made current if it isn't already current. Jack executed the command

```
plot to "a:gs.plt"
```

to preserve the current graphics screen (Photo 38) in a file named GS.PLT on the drive A diskette. He explained that at any future time, the command

```
plot from "a:gs.plt"
```

would present the preserved graphics screen on the console. It would then again be the current graphics screen.

NATURAL LANGUAGE GRAPHICS

"Now that you're familiar with graphic commands," Jack said, "I think you might find it interesting to harken back to requests that are less explicit. Remember on our first day, we saw that a natural language request could result in a graph."

Recall the request in Figure 3–15 that produced Photo 8. After giving #TITLE a blank value, Jack executed the command

```
chat
```

to bring up the natural language interface. His first request

```
preview
```

would allow them to see the underlying commands devised by the environment as it attempted to understand subsequent natural language requests.

"What I want you to see," Jack commented, "are the commands that are produced in response to a natural language graphics request. They turn out to be practically the same that you would issue via the command interface."

For his first natural language graphics request, Jack typed

```
do a graph of s1 s2 s3 versus tid for rom
```

to ask for a graph of romance sales for the various territories. On pressing the Enter key, the screen appeared as depicted in Figure 11–14. He

FIGURE 11–14   Natural language graphics request

```
┌─────────────────────────────────────────────────────────────┐
│ ┌──────────────────────Kman Natural Language──────────────┐ │
│ └──────────────────────────────────────────────────────────┘ │
│ Your request? do a graph of s1 s2 s3 versus tid for rom      │
│                                                               │
│                                                               │
│ Kman Chat encountered unknown word: "versus"                 │
│                                                               │
│                     Unrecognized Word Menu                   │
│                                                               │
│                    ┌─────────────────────────┐               │
│                    │ Temporary correction    │               │
│                    │ Permanent definition    │               │
│                    │ Define a larger phrase   │               │
│                    │ Ignore the unknown      │               │
│                    │ Cancel the query        │               │
│                    └─────────────────────────┘               │
│                                                               │
│                                                               │
│                                                               │
└─────────────────────────────────────────────────────────────┘
```

pressed the I key to cause the unknown word to be ignored. This resulted in the screen appearance shown in Figure 11–15, asking him to indicate what type of graph was desired. As Jack pressed the B key to select a bar graph, he noted that this menu would not have appeared had he included the word "bar" in his original request.

Now that the environment understood his request, it displayed the underlying commands that it would execute to carry out the request. These are shown in Figure 11–16. He paused for a few seconds to let the group examine the four generated commands. Notice that the third command (CONVERT) extends across two lines.

"That's very interesting," Debbie observed. "It sets up the X-axis label, dimensions a data source array named CPLOT, converts the right data from PERF into CPLOT, and then issues the correct PLOT command. But what is E.CMAX?"

Joy replied, "It's just an environment variable that governs how many array rows will be available for holding converted data. Its default value is sufficiently large for our purposes."

"The impressive thing," Debbie continued, "is that the environment knows how to come up with a proper series of commands in response to your request."

FIGURE 11–15   Selecting a graph type

```
┌─────────────────────────────────────────────────────────────────────┐
│  ┌──────────────────Kman Natural Language──────────────────────────┐ │
│  └─────────────────────────────────────────────────────────────────┘ │
│ Your request? do a graph of s1 s2 s3 versus tid for rom              │
│                                                                       │
│                                                                       │
│                                                                       │
│                            Select Plot Type                           │
│                                                                       │
│                        ┌───────────────────┐                          │
│                        │ Area Plot         │                          │
│                        │ Bar Chart         │                          │
│                        │ HiLo Plot         │                          │
│                        │ Line Plot         │                          │
│                        │ Pie Chart         │                          │
│                        │ Scatter Plot      │                          │
│                        │ No Plot           │                          │
│                        │ Cancel Query      │                          │
│                        └───────────────────┘                          │
│                                                                       │
│                                                                       │
│                                                                       │
└─────────────────────────────────────────────────────────────────────┘
```

FIGURE 11–16   Underlying commands to execute graphics request

```
┌─────────────────────────────────────────────────────────────────────┐
│  ┌──────────────────Kman Natural Language──────────────────────────┐ │
│  └─────────────────────────────────────────────────────────────────┘ │
│ Your request? do a graph of s1 s2 s3 versus tid for rom              │
│                                                                       │
│                                                                       │
│                                                                       │
│                                                                       │
│ Generated Command: LET #XLABEL = "tid"                                │
│                    DIM CPLOT(E.CMAX, 4)                                │
│                    CONVERT tid s1 s2 s3 FROM perf WHERE pid EQ "rom" TO ARRAY C │
│                    PLOT(1, 1) TO CPLOT(E.CMAX, 4)                      │
│                    PLOT BAR FROM CPLOT(1, 1) TO CPLOT(#ROW, #COL)      │
│                                                                       │
│                                                                       │
│                                                                       │
│                                                                       │
│                                                                       │
│                                                                       │
│ Please press space bar to continue                                    │
└─────────────────────────────────────────────────────────────────────┘
```

FIGURE 11–17   Requesting a 3-D version of the graph

```
┌────────────────────────────────────────────────────────────────────────┐
│ ┌──────────────────────────Kman Natural Language────────────────────┐   │
│ └────────────────────────────────────────────────────────────────────┘  │
│ Your request? a 3d bar                                                   │
│                                                                          │
│                                                                          │
│                                                                          │
│ Generated Command: LET #XLABEL = "tid"                                   │
│                    PLOT SOLID BAR FROM CPLOT(1, 1) TO CPLOT(#ROW, #COL)   │
│                                                                          │
│                                                                          │
│                                                                          │
│                                                                          │
│                                                                          │
│                                                                          │
│                                                                          │
│ Please press space bar to continue                                       │
└────────────────────────────────────────────────────────────────────────┘
```

"It's a good example of a kind of artificial intelligence," chimed Joy.

"And," added Brad, "it takes less effort than keying them in yourself."

As requested at the bottom of the screen, Jack pressed the space bar to continue. The screen cleared and a graph appeared. With the exception of its colors, it was almost identical to Photo 21. It did have "tid" as an X-axis label and the territory IDs were not trimmed (i.e., they appeared slightly to the left of their X-axis hash marks). He pressed the space bar to again get the natural language prompt.

"Let's see it in three dimensions," demanded Brad.

Jack responded by issuing the request

a 3d bar

resulting in the screen portrayed in Figure 11–17. The group was quick to notice that the generated PLOT command correctly used SOLID as an adjective for BAR. Jack pressed the space bar and a graph like that

FIGURE 11–18   Requesting a stacked version of the graph

```
┌─────────────────────────────────────────────────────────────────┐
│ ┌─────────────────────────Kman   Natural   Language──────────────┐ │
│ └───────────────────────────────────────────────────────────────┘ │
│ Your request? stack them                                          │
│                                                                   │
│                                                                   │
│                                                                   │
│ Generated Command: LET #XLABEL = "tid"                            │
│                    PLOT STACKED BAR FROM CPLOT(1, 1) TO CPLOT(#ROW, #COL) │
│                                                                   │
│                                                                   │
│                                                                   │
│                                                                   │
│                                                                   │
│                                                                   │
│ Please press space bar to continue                                │
└─────────────────────────────────────────────────────────────────┘
```

of Photo 23 appeared. The only differences were again its colors, labels, title, and untrimmed IDs. Jack pressed the space bar to get back to the natural language prompt.

"That's pretty good," Brad remarked. "Can you now stack them?"

Nodding, Jack typed

```
stack them
```

and pressed the Enter key to produce the screen shown in Figure 11–18. Sure enough, the generated PLOT command was correct. When he pressed the space bar a graph like that of Photo 25 was produced. It had the same cosmetic variations they had previously seen.

"So you see," Jack concluded, "natural language graphics requests can be handy. On the other hand, many of the things you can do with graphics commands can't be duplicated with the natural language, or the menu-guided interface for that matter. I'd suggest that you use the preview facility when making natural language requests to check on how well it understood what you meant."

BASIC IDEAS

As had become their custom, Jack and Joy left together when the managers had settled into the day's final practice period. The graphic details of how they occupied themselves are not recounted here. Suffice it to say, they were becoming increasingly comfortable and appreciative. The managers now recognized that *business graphics is an important technique for managing presentation knowledge.* They were at ease with the environment's facilities for constructing data sources and generating graphs. They appreciated the potential value of these facilities for supporting their own decision-making activities.

Once an array has been dimensioned (DIM), data values can be filled into it. One approach is to use assignment commands (LET) to assign values to individual elements of the array. If the desired values already exist in one or more tables, they can be converted into the array with a single command (CONVERT). This command is comparable to the SELECT command except the data become values of array elements rather than being displayed on the screen. Environment sensors (#ROW and #COL) detect how many array rows and columns are actually filled by the conversion process.

Once an array has been filled in, any block of its values can be plotted (PLOT). There are several basic kinds of graphs that can be generated from a data source including bar charts (flat, solid, stacked, percent), area graphs (cumulative, percentage), pies, line graphs, and scattergrams. The order and selection of patterns for filling areas, drawing lines, making marks, and using colors in a graph can be controlled by the user (PATTERN). Where applicable, X- and Y-axis ranges are determined automatically from the data source. Numeric ranges can also be manually specified (RANGE) and scaled (E.XPOW, E.YPOW). The environment can be directed to position a graph in any half or quadrant of a graphics screen.

The most recently displayed graphics screen is referred to as the current screen. The current graphics screen is subject to various kinds of processing. It can be kept in main memory for later recall (KEEP), printed (PRINT), redisplayed (SHOW), stored in a disk file (PLOT TO), and enhanced to include a legend (PLOT LEGEND). It can also be modified by superimposing text or additional graphs on it. A kept screen can be made current (SHOW), printed (PRINT), released (RELEASE), or incorporated into printed text (PRINT TEXT). A graphics screen stored in one of the knowledge system's disk files can be brought into main memory for processing as the current graphics screen (PLOT FROM).

References

1. Brown, M. D. "Mainframe Business Graphics." *Datamation* 30, no. 6 (1984).
2. Cooper, M. S. "Micro-Based Business Graphics." *Datamation* 30, no. 6 (1984).
3. *Disk Operating System.* Boca Raton, Fla.: IBM, 1983.
4. Gabel, D. "CAD/CAM Software." *PC Week* 3, no. 33 (1986).
5. Greitzer, J. "Freehand-Graphics." *PC Week* 3, no. 33 (1986).
6. *K-Graph Supplement,* version 2. Lafayette, Ind.: MDBS, Inc., 1985.
7. McLeod, J. "Graphics." *Systems and Software* 3, no. 8 (1984).
8. Medland, A. J. *CAD/CAM in Practice: A Manager's Guide to Understanding and Using.* New York: John Wiley & Sons, 1986.
9. Whieldon, D. "Computer Graphics: Art Serves Business." *Computer Decisions* 16, no. 6 (1984).

Part V

MANAGING PROCEDURAL KNOWLEDGE

Each cell is ever ready for our next calculation.

Chapter Twelve

Spreadsheet Analysis

The knowledge management techniques examined thus far have been concerned primarily with the representation and processing of descriptive and presentation knowledge. The focus now shifts to procedural knowledge. A *procedure* is a series of steps that are to be followed in a regular definite order. These steps are followed in the interest of accomplishing some task. Essentially, procedural knowledge is knowledge about the series of steps required to accomplish some task. In the course of formal education and practical experience, a knowledge worker learns many procedures. When confronted with the need to accomplish some task, he or she carries out the steps in a relevant procedure.

For familiar, frequently used procedures, the person does not have to consciously think of each step along the way. Following such a procedure becomes almost second nature, with the steps being carried out in automatic, rapid-fire succession. On the other hand, less well-known procedures tend to necessitate a careful consideration or remembering of each step along the way to accomplishing some task. The knowledge worker may need to refer to a book, notes, or another person in order to get the steps right. The procedure's steps may even be spelled out in a text file to which the knowledge worker can refer.

For instance, a narrative specification of the steps involved in reviewing a rep's performance can exist in a text file. Such a text file holds procedural knowledge, rather than descriptive knowledge. But it is up to the knowledge worker to process and apply that knowledge. The text management technique itself has no processing facility for carrying out steps that may be specified in a text file. As another example, Figure 12–1 shows that a text file may hold a narrative explanation of how to compute a rep's monthly expense budget. But text management provides no processing commands capable of actually applying that knowledge to prepare an expense budget.

FIGURE 12–1   Procedural knowledge represented as narrative text

```
Line:1     Col:1     a:budget.txt    Insert          Press ^L for help


    Every rep has a monthly expense allocation. For each rep
this allocation is to be determined in the following way:

   1. Set a reasonable daily hotel rate and meal rate to be
      allowed for each day the rep is out of town for the
      night.

   2. Estimate the average number of nights out for the rep.

   3. Compute the total hotel allowance for the rep by
      multiplying the number of nights out by the allowed
      hotel rate.

   4. Based on the number of nights out and the territory
      size, estimate the number of full meal day equivalents.

   5. Compute the total meal allowance by multiplying the
      meal days times the allowed meal rate.

   6. Give the rep a phone allowance of $175.00.

   7. Compute the rep's entertainment allowance based on the
```

A narrative specification of a procedure can be held in a knowledge system, for viewing and updating like any other piece of text. But there are much more powerful and flexible techniques for managing procedural knowledge. One of these is called *spreadsheet analysis* and is examined in this chapter. Another technique, called *programming,* is covered in Chapter 13. Though these two techniques provide different approaches to representing procedural knowledge, both provide processing facilities that allow the computer itself to carry out the steps prescribed in a procedure.

As with other knowledge management techniques, there are many software packages designed exclusively for spreadsheet analysis. Some have command interfaces and many have menu-guided interfaces to appeal to first-time and casual computer users. Of all the knowledge management techniques available for desktop computers, spreadsheet analysis is probably the most widely used for do-it-yourself computing. This is due in large measure to the convenience with which spreadsheets can handle such ubiquitous tasks as budgeting and managing cash flow [4]. They can also be helpful for activities such as project planning and scheduling, network analysis, forecasting, decision tree analysis, and even optimization [3]. Today's widespread use of spreadsheets owes much to the popularity of two spreadsheet packages called Visi-Calc® and 1–2–3.

VisiCalc was the first significant software package for spreadsheet analysis and in many respects defined the basic traits of this knowledge management technique [1]. It appeared on the scene in the late 1970s at about the same time as the first usable microcomputers. In fact, VisiCalc made a major contribution to the usability of these machines by beginning to make their latent power accessible to large numbers of people who were not computer scientists and programmers. At the time VisiCalc appeared, there was no appreciable microcomputer software for word processing, data base management, SQL inquiry, forms management, report generation, or graphics.

In the early 1980s a new class of faster and higher capacity microcomputers became available. New spreadsheet packages geared to take advantage of these more potent machines were developed. Among these, one of the earliest was 1–2–3 [2]. Introduced by Lotus Development Corporation in 1983, this second-generation spreadsheet package is today the most widely used and recognized. It is the spreadsheet package with which Stan had become familiar.

A spreadsheet capability can also exist as part of a knowledge management environment [5]. Jack planned to spend the day acquainting the managers with the ins and outs of spreadsheet analysis within their environment [6]. For Stan, much of this would be review, though to the others it would all be new. Regardless of what spreadsheet software is being used, a spreadsheet is a spreadsheet. Aside from cosmetic differences, spreadsheets supported by one piece of software have the same fundamental structure and characteristics as spreadsheets supported by some other software. Moreover, most any spreadsheet software supports the same basic kinds of operations for spreadsheet processing.

But there can be differences too, and they can go beyond user interface variations. As the day progressed, Stan would discover a number of spreadsheet possibilities that he had not encountered with 1–2–3. Many of these result directly from the fact that spreadsheet analysis is only one of the environment's integral capabilities. As a result, a user is able not only to do traditional kinds of spreadsheet analysis, but also to blend spreadsheet and other knowledge management techniques to achieve effects that go beyond ordinary spreadsheet packages. Thus, Jack's coverage of the spreadsheet topic would include both traditional and more advanced aspects of spreadsheet analysis.

FIGURE 12–2   A blank spreadsheet

```
                                                20 , 15   > #A1

1-  :A        :B        :C        :D        :E        :F        :G        :H
   1: [         ]                                                                    :
   2:                                                                                :
   3:                                                                                :
   4:                                                                                :
   5:                                                                                :
   6:                                                                                :
   7:                                                                                :
   8:                                                                                :
   9:                                                                                :
  10:                                                                                :
  11:                                                                                :
  12:                                                                                :
  13:                                                                                :
  14:                                                                                :
  15:                                                                                :
  16:                                                                                :
  17:                                                                                :
  18:                                                                                :
  19:                                                                                :
```

SPREADSHEET STRUCTURE

"Today's topic," began Jack, "is spreadsheet analysis. Like all the other techniques you already know, it is an integral capability in the environment. At any moment, our present processing context can have a spreadsheet in it. We're free to put knowledge into that spreadsheet and process it in various ways. Let's begin by getting familiar with the basic structure of a spreadsheet."

With that, he executed the command

```
calc 20,15
```

yielding the screen portrayed in Figure 12–2. Like a text screen, the spreadsheet screen was colored with a white foreground against a blue background. However, the last line on the screen appeared in reverse video (a white background presently having nothing displayed on it). Also like text screens, the spreadsheet colors can be altered by changing the values of E.FORG and E.BACG. Specifically, the first color code for each of these environment variables controls the spreadsheet colors.

Recall that the third code controls text colors, the second controls graphics screen colors, and the fifth controls colors for most other processing.

"Structurally," Jack explained, "a spreadsheet is composed of rows and columns. At the left edge of the screen you can see the row numbers. Across the top, you can see that each column is designated by a letter. This spreadsheet has a capacity of 20 rows and 15 columns because that's what I requested in the CALC command. The capacity of any spreadsheet you're working with will always be displayed on the top line of the screen."

"Wait a minute!" Brad interrupted. "I see only 19 rows and 8 columns."

Viewing Window

"You should think of the screen as a *viewing window* for looking into the spreadsheet," Jack advised. "Because of the physical limitations of a screen, we can't see all the rows and columns at the same time. But, as I'll show you later, we can easily use the window for looking into any desired portion of the spreadsheet. In fact, we can even partition the screen into several smaller windows, each showing a different portion of the spreadsheet. For now, we'll just deal with one large window. By the way, the 1 followed by a dash at the upper left edge of the window is the window's number. When there are multiple windows on the screen, each will have a different identifying number."

"What about those three lines at the bottom of the screen, below row 19?" asked Tracey. "Why aren't they part of the viewing window? You'd then be able to see up to 22 rows through the window."

"Those lines," explained Jack, "are reserved to interact with the spreadsheet. The very bottom line, the one in reverse video, is a *message line*. As we're processing a spreadsheet, this is where the environment can display various messages to us. Above it is the *entry line*, where we type in entries that tell the environment what to do. The other line is a *utility line* that can serve various purposes, some of which we'll see later."

Every spreadsheet software package provides a viewing window comparable to the one in Figure 12–2. Some allow multiple windows along the lines Jack described. Most use the convention of designating rows by numbers and columns by letters. However, some use numbers for both rows and columns (e.g., R12 would refer to row 12 and C5 would refer to column 5). It is not uncommon for a spreadsheet package to position lines for user interaction above, rather than below, the viewing window.

As noted earlier, spreadsheet software (e.g., 1-2-3) may furnish a menuized approach to interaction rather than the command approach that Jack will discuss. In such cases, menus appear in the interaction area of the spreadsheet screen. In terms of basic functionality, the same operations can be achieved via either kind of interface. In terms of advanced functionality, there are operations that are at best difficult to achieve via menu interfaces. For instance, the environment's menu-guided interface for spreadsheet analysis handles the basics and may be suitable for pedestrian spreadsheet usage. But Jack chose not to discuss it, since it does not offer the power or versatility of the command interface.

Cells

"The most important thing to understand about spreadsheet structure," claimed Jack, "is the notion of a *cell*. A cell is the place where a row intersects a column. For instance, the place where column A and row 1 intersect is called cell A1, the place where column B and row 5 intersect is called cell B5, and so forth. Thus this spreadsheet consists of 300 cells, 152 of which are presently visible on the screen. Whenever you want to refer to a cell in a command, it should be prefaced by the crosshatch symbol. This tells the environment that you are referring to the place where a spreadsheet row intersects a column."

Jack gave a few examples on the whiteboard. Cell A1 is typed as #A1 and cell B5 is typed as #B5. The leading crosshatch for #A1 and #B5 lets the environment know that cells A1 and B5 are being referenced rather than working variables named A1 and B5. This is important because any command that can process a working variable can equivalently process a cell. Obviously, the environment needs to know which is being referenced. Because conventional spreadsheet packages do not support the notion of working variables, they often do not require a designator such as the # symbol.

"All the cells in this spreadsheet are now blank," said Jack. "But as you'll see momentarily, any cell can have a value. When a cell has a value, you'll see the value at that cell's position in the spreadsheet. It might be a string, numeric, or logical value. Once a cell has a value, you can reference that cell in lieu of a working variable in any of the commands you've already learned."

"Well then," asked Don, "what's the difference between a cell and an array element? Isn't a spreadsheet like an array?"

"In certain ways it is," agreed Jack. "You can think of it as a grid of storage compartments that are called cells instead of array elements. Each compartment can have a value that we can reference in many different commands such as OUTPUT and LET."

"As a matter of fact," chimed Joy, "you can think of a spreadsheet's cell values as forming an array whose name is #. When Jack executed the CALC command, he effectively specified the dimensions of # to be 20 by 15. And, if you like, you can refer to #A1 as #(1,1) and #B5 as #(5,2). Advanced users can take good advantage of this fact, but I'd suggest that you stick with names like #A1 and #B5 when referencing cells."

"Despite these similarities between a spreadsheet and an array, there are significant differences." Pointing to the screen, Jack continued, "Obviously, it's very easy to visualize a spreadsheet. It's right there on the screen. As we'll see, there is a wealth of commands that exist exclusively for processing spreadsheets. The environment has no counterparts to these for processing arrays. But most fundamental and crucial is the fact that cells have definitions specifying how to calculate their values. For an array element, all we can do is store a value there. For a cell, we can define how its value is to be determined. This has far-reaching implications."

DEFINING A CELL

As Jack had pointed out, each spreadsheet cell that has a value must also have a definition. Initially, the spreadsheet shown in Figure 12–2 is blank because none of its cells have definitions. When a cell has a definition, the environment knows how to determine that cell's value and displays that value at the cell's position. Thus there are always two essential characteristics of a cell: its definition and its value. As will be discussed later cells can optionally have other characteristics such as pictures and colors.

In conventional first- and second-generation spreadsheets, a definition can be either a constant (i.e., a string or number) or a more complex expression involving constants, functions, and cells, together with operators (e.g., +, *, −, /). In the former case, the cell's value is simply the defined constant. In the latter case, the cell's value is the result of calculating the expression's value. The environment's spreadsheet capability allows both of these traditional kinds of cell definitions. But it also allows an expression to include fields, working variables, array elements, and macros. In short, any expression whose value could be output by the OUTPUT command can serve as a cell definition.

It is noteworthy that the environment takes a major step beyond expressions as cell definitions by allowing a cell to be defined in terms of one or more commands. In principle, any command discussed in prior or subsequent chapters can be embedded in the definition of a cell. It should not be too long before a new generation of spreadsheet packages emerges, taking advantage of this versatile and powerful approach to cell definition.

Interactive Cell Definition

"One way to define a cell is to do so interactively," Jack declared. He pointed to cell A1 in the screen (Figure 12–2). "Do you see the square brackets in cell A1? They're called the *cell cursor*. You can move them to any cell with the numeric keypad's arrow keys. Well, whatever cell is highlighted by the cell cursor is called the current or *active cell*. Thus #A1 is now the active cell. In addition, the top line of the screen will always indicate which cell is presently the active one.

"When we want to define a cell, we move the cell cursor to that cell. If it already has a definition, that defintion will be shown in the message line at the bottom of the screen. The active cell is defined by simply typing in its definition on the entry line. The definition may be a constant or an expression whose value must be calculated."

"So," Debbie interjected, "defining a cell is similar in spirit to defining an element in a form. Just like a form element, it can be either literal or nonliteral. If it's literal then a constant value will appear at the cell's position. If it's nonliteral, then the value expression we provide is calculated for display."

"In a sense," added Joy, "you can think of a spreadsheet as a rigidly structured, gridlike form having 'Put' elements called cells. Any expression, be it literal or nonliteral, that you could specify for a form element can also be specified as a cell definition."

"But," Jack elaborated, "we can do even more when defining a cell. We can specify commands that will determine the cell's value. For instance, a cell's definition might consist of an OBTAIN command that obtains the cell's value from a table. We'll look at that more closely this afternoon."

To illustrate the mechanics of interactively defining a cell, Jack moved the cell cursor to #C1 by pressing the right arrow key twice. The top line now indicated that #C1 was the active cell and there was nothing in the message line, indicating that #C1 had no definition. To define the cell, Jack typed

```
"MONTHLY EXPENSES"
```

yielding the screen appearance portrayed in Figure 12–3. As he typed, each character appeared in the entry line. He mentioned that typing errors in the entry line could be corrected in the usual way (i.e., with

FIGURE 12–3 Entering a definition for the active cell

```
                                              20 , 15   > #C1

 1-  :A        :B        :C        :D       :E       :F       :G        :H
  1:                      [         ]                                            :
  2:                                                                             :
  3:                                                                             :
  4:                                                                             :
  5:                                                                             :
  6:                                                                             :
  7:                                                                             :
  8:                                                                             :
  9:                                                                             :
 10:                                                                             :
 11:                                                                             :
 12:                                                                             :
 13:                                                                             :
 14:                                                                             :
 15:                                                                             :
 16:                                                                             :
 17:                                                                             :
 18:                                                                             :
 19:                                                                             :

 "MONTHLY  EXPENSES" _____
```

^S, ^D, and the destructive Backspace key). On pressing the Enter key, the screen changed as shown in Figure 12–4.

Jack interpreted, "The message line now shows the active cell's definition and the corresponding value appears in cell C1. Notice that the value actually spills over into cell D1. That's OK as long as we don't plan to give #D1 a definition of its own. Also notice that what I just entered on the entry line is still there. It will go away as soon as I begin typing a new entry there. Let's define cell A3 as being another string constant."

He moved the cell cursor to #A3 and typed

```
"Hotel:"
```

on the entry line. As shown in Figure 12–5, this became the definition of #A3 when he pressed the Enter key.

"Now alongside the hotel cell I want to have the daily hotel allowance. Let's say it should be $38.75. How would I get it there?" asked Jack.

Tracey was first to answer, "Just make #B3 the active cell by moving the cursor there. Then, type 38.75 on the entry line."

FIGURE 12–4   A constant definition for #C1

```
                                                  20 , 15    >  #C1

1-  :A        :B        :C        :D       :E       :F       :G       :H
  1¦                    [MONTHLY]EXPENSES                                    ¦
  2¦                                                                         ¦
  3¦                                                                         ¦
  4¦                                                                         ¦
  5¦                                                                         ¦
  6¦                                                                         ¦
  7¦                                                                         ¦
  8¦                                                                         ¦
  9¦                                                                         ¦
 10¦                                                                         ¦
 11¦                                                                         ¦
 12¦                                                                         ¦
 13¦                                                                         ¦
 14¦                                                                         ¦
 15¦                                                                         ¦
 16¦                                                                         ¦
 17¦                                                                         ¦
 18¦                                                                         ¦
 19¦                                                                         ¦

"MONTHLY   EXPENSES"
"MONTHLY   EXPENSES"
```

FIGURE 12–5   A constant definition for #A3

```
                                                  20 , 15    <  #A3

1-  :A        :B        :C        :D       :E       :F       :G       :H
  1¦                    MONTHLY   EXPENSES                                   ¦
  2¦                                                                         ¦
  3¦[Hotel: ]                                                                ¦
  4¦                                                                         ¦
  5¦                                                                         ¦
  6¦                                                                         ¦
  7¦                                                                         ¦
  8¦                                                                         ¦
  9¦                                                                         ¦
 10¦                                                                         ¦
 11¦                                                                         ¦
 12¦                                                                         ¦
 13¦                                                                         ¦
 14¦                                                                         ¦
 15¦                                                                         ¦
 16¦                                                                         ¦
 17¦                                                                         ¦
 18¦                                                                         ¦
 19¦                                                                         ¦

"Hotel:"
"Hotel:"
```

FIGURE 12–6   A constant definition for #B3

```
                                              20 , 15   > #B3

1-  :A        :B        :C        :D       :E       :F       :G        :H
 1:                     MONTHLY   EXPENSES                                    :
 2:                                                                           :
 3:Hotel:     [38.7500]                                                       :
 4:                                                                           :
 5:                                                                           :
 6:                                                                           :
 7:                                                                           :
 8:                                                                           :
 9:                                                                           :
10:                                                                           :
11:                                                                           :
12:                                                                           :
13:                                                                           :
14:                                                                           :
15:                                                                           :
16:                                                                           :
17:                                                                           :
18:                                                                           :
19:                                                                           :


38.75
38.75
```

Jack followed her instructions, producing the screen depicted in Figure 12–6. The active cell was now #B3. As the message line shows, it had a numeric constant as its definition. The corresponding value appears in #B3, but it has extra decimal digits because of the E.DECI setting.

Jack frowned, "We really don't want those extra zeros. What we'd like is to switch E.DECI to 2."

"But isn't that hard to do?" asked Stan. "If you tried typing in the command E.DECI=2, it would be on the entry line and the environment would think it should be the new definition of the active cell. It seems you'd need to somehow get out of the spreadsheet screen and back to the underscore prompt, execute the command, and then return to the spreadsheet screen."

"Well, it's possible to do it that way," responded Jack, "but not at all necessary. It turns out that you can enter commands for immediate execution right on the entry line, as long as you first type a backslash. It's that easy! Whenever the environment sees an entry line that begins with a backslash, it knows that you were entering a command for immediate execution rather than entering a definition for the active cell. Let's switch E.DECI."

FIGURE 12–7   Entering a command on the entry line

```
                                              20 , 15   > #B3

1-  :A        :B        :C       :D       :E        :F        :G        :H
 1¦                    MONTHLY  EXPENSES                                      ¦
 2¦                                                                           ¦
 3¦Hotel:    [38.7500]                                                        ¦
 4¦                                                                           ¦
 5¦                                                                           ¦
 6¦                                                                           ¦
 7¦                                                                           ¦
 8¦                                                                           ¦
 9¦                                                                           ¦
10¦                                                                           ¦
11¦                                                                           ¦
12¦                                                                           ¦
13¦                                                                           ¦
14¦                                                                           ¦
15¦                                                                           ¦
16¦                                                                           ¦
17¦                                                                           ¦
18¦                                                                           ¦
19¦                                                                           ¦

\ e.deci=2 _____
38.75
```

Jack typed

`\e.deci=2`

and as he typed the command appeared on the entry line. Figure 12–7 shows the screen appearance before he pressed the Enter key to execute the command. After execution the value of #B3 was still displayed with the extra decimal digits, so Jack typed

and pressed the Enter key to have the spreadsheet redrawn on the screen according to the new environment setting. The resultant screen is portrayed in Figure 12–8.

"The backslash command," observed Jack, "can be used at any time to redraw the spreadsheet screen. This is especially handy after you enter and execute a command on the entry line, where that command's results overwrite part of the spreadsheet screen. For instance, the results of commands such as SELECT, STAT, and so on would overwrite part or all of the spreadsheet screen. So if ever you see some-

FIGURE 12–8 Redrawn screen

```
                                                    20 , 15   > #B3

1- :A        :B        :C        :D        :E        :F        :G        :H
  1¦                   MONTHLY   EXPENSES                                            ¦
  2¦                                                                                 ¦
  3¦Hotel:   [   38.75]                                                              ¦
  4¦                                                                                 ¦
  5¦                                                                                 ¦
  6¦                                                                                 ¦
  7¦                                                                                 ¦
  8¦                                                                                 ¦
  9¦                                                                                 ¦
 10¦                                                                                 ¦
 11¦                                                                                 ¦
 12¦                                                                                 ¦
 13¦                                                                                 ¦
 14¦                                                                                 ¦
 15¦                                                                                 ¦
 16¦                                                                                 ¦
 17¦                                                                                 ¦
 18¦                                                                                 ¦
 19¦                                                                                 ¦


 38.75
```

thing unwanted on a spreadsheet screen, pressing the backslash and
Enter key restores it to its usual appearance."

Batch Definition

Jack proceeded to define constant values in the same way for seven
more cells: #A4, #B4, #A7, #A8, #B6, #B7, and #B8. The definitions
that he entered were

```
"Meal:"
22
"Name"
"========"
" Monthly"
" Salary"
" ========"
```

respectively, leaving the screen as shown in Figure 12–9. He explained
that he next wanted the cells under #A8 to be defined to be the names
of his 10 reps and those under #B8 to be defined as the corresponding
monthly salaries.

FIGURE 12–9   Seven additional cells with constant definitions

```
                                                    20 , 15   V #B8

 1- :A         :B        :C       :D      :E      :F      :G      :H
    ;                    MONTHLY  EXPENSES                              ;
  2;                                                                    ;
  3;Hotel:      38.75                                                   ;
  4;Meal:       22.00                                                   ;
  5;                                                                    ;
  6;            Monthly                                                 ;
  7;Name        Salary                                                  ;
  8;========= [ ======]                                                 ;
  9;                                                                    ;
 10;                                                                    ;
 11;                                                                    ;
 12;                                                                    ;
 13;                                                                    ;
 14;                                                                    ;
 15;                                                                    ;
 16;                                                                    ;
 17;                                                                    ;
 18;                                                                    ;
 19;                                                                    ;

 "  ========"
 "  ========"
```

"I presume," offered Debbie, "that you have a quick way of converting data from the REP table into definitions for those cells. It would be a shame if you had to interactively define those 20 cells with data that's already in a table."

"It certainly would," agreed Jack. "Fortunately, I can issue a single CONVERT command that will define the entire batch of 20 cells. Just for good measure let's order them from lowest to highest monthly salary."

Because he was entering a command rather than a definition for the active cell, Jack first typed a backslash. The entire CONVERT command that he entered was

```
\convert fname mosal from rep to cell #a9 order by mosal
```

As soon as he pressed the Enter key to execute it, names and salaries appeared in the spreadsheet as shown in Figure 12–10. Each of the cells from #A9 through #A18 now had a string constant as its definition and #B9 through #B18 now had numeric constants as their definitions.

"That's practically identical to the way we used the CONVERT command to fill in an array," remarked Dan. "All we have to do is

FIGURE 12–10 Batch definition of cells by converting table data

```
                                                    20 , 15   V #B8

1-  :A        :B        :C       :D      :E      :F      :G       :H
 1:                     MONTHLY EXPENSES                                    ;
 2:                                                                         ;
 3:Hotel:        38.75                                                      ;
 4:Meal:         22.00                                                      ;
 5:                                                                         ;
 6:            Monthly                                                      ;
 7:Name        Salary                                                       ;
 8:========  [  ======]                                                     ;
 9:Toby         2000                                                        ;
10:Kathy        2100                                                        ;
11:Kerry        2250                                                        ;
12:Kris         2400  ·                                                     ;
13:Jackie       2400                                                        ;
14:Kevin        2500                                                        ;
15:Kim          2600                                                        ;
16:Carol        2750                                                        ;
17:Tina         2800                                                        ;
18:Karen        2800                                                        ;
19:                                                                         ;

\convert fname mosal from rep to cell #a9 order by mosal
" ========"
```

substitute the word CELL for ARRAY and specify the cell where we want definitions to begin?"

"Right," replied Jack. "As you'd expect, your CONVERT to a spreadsheet can have calculations, a condition, and multiple tables specified in it. You really don't have to learn anything new."

Nonconstant Definitions

As shown in Figure 12–11, Jack interactively defined #C7 through #C18 with string and numeric constants. He explained that these were estimates of how many nights per month each rep would be away from home.

With a tone of mild impatience, Brad said, "I think I understand the mechanics of defining cells interactively or in a batch. But what's the point of defining all these cells?"

"I'm getting to that," Jack replied. "You're right that a spreadsheet isn't a particularly convenient place to store data, especially if large amounts of data are involved. The real payoff comes when we begin to define some cells that are not constants. Suppose, for instance, that

FIGURE 12–11 **Defining 12 more C column cells**

```
                                          20 , 15   V  #C18

1-  :A       :B       :C       :D      :E      :F      :G      :H
  1:                MONTHLY  EXPENSES                                  :
  2:                                                                   :
  3:Hotel:    38.75                                                    :
  4:Meal:     22.00                                                    :
  5:                                                                   :
  6:         Monthly                                                   :
  7:Name     Salary   Nights                                          :
  8:======== ======== ========                                        :
  9:Toby       2000     4.00                                          :
 10:Kathy      2100     3.00                                          :
 11:Kerry      2250     2.40                                          :
 12:Kris       2400     6.10                                          :
 13:Jackie     2400     4.80                                          :
 14:Kevin      2500     2.75                                          :
 15:Kim        2600     3.30                                          :
 16:Carol      2750     4.00                                          :
 17:Tina       2800     5.25                                          :
 18:Karen      2800[    7.00]                                         :
 19:                                                                  :


 ?
 ?
```

we want #D9's value to be Toby's hotel total. Notice that it can be calculated from the values of two other cells in the spreadsheet. Do you see which cells?"

Brad looked at the spreadsheet for a few seconds before replying, "It would be computed by multiplying the #B3 value times the #C9 value. Right?"

"Exactly," answered Jack, "so let's define #D9 in that way."

After defining a hotel total heading, he moved the cell cursor to #D9 and entered Brad's recommendation of

#b3*#c9

on the entry line. As soon as he pressed the Enter key, the environment computed the value for #D9 according to this definition. As Figure 12–12 shows, the calculated value is displayed in #D9. Jack pointed out that any cell could have an arbitrarily complex expression as its definition.

FIGURE 12–12 A nonconstant cell definition

```
                                                20 , 15    V  #D9

1-  :A       :B       :C       :D       :E       :F       :G       :H
 1¦                   MONTHLY  EXPENSES                                    ¦
 2¦                                                                        ¦
 3¦Hotel:    38.75                                                         ¦
 4¦Meal:     22.00                                                         ¦
 5¦                                                                        ¦
 6¦          Monthly           Hotel                                       ¦
 7¦Name      Salary   Nights   Total                                       ¦
 8¦========  ========  ========  ========                                  ¦
 9¦Toby       2000     4.00¦ 155.00¦                                       ¦
10¦Kathy      2100     3.00                                                ¦
11¦Kerry      2250     2.40                                                ¦
12¦Kris       2400     6.10                                                ¦
13¦Jackie     2400     4.80                                                ¦
14¦Kevin      2500     2.75                                                ¦
15¦Kim        2600     3.30                                                ¦
16¦Carol      2750     4.00                                                ¦
17¦Tina       2800     5.25                                                ¦
18¦Karen      2800    ,7.00                                                ¦
19¦                                                                        ¦

#b3*#c9
#b3*#c9
```

Copying a Definition

"Now I'd like to have similar definitions for the D cells corresponding to the other nine reps," he continued. "Fortunately, I don't have to define them one by one. Instead, I'll execute a new command, named COPY, to copy the definition of #D9 so that it becomes the definition of the cells beneath #D9 as well."

"But," objected Brad, "we don't want those cells to have exactly the same definitions as #D9. For instance, #D10 should be defined as #B3 times #C10, not as #B3*#C9. So we don't really want a verbatim copy."

"That's true," agreed Jack. "As you'll see, COPY can automatically adjust any part of a copied definition so it is correct relative to the cell's location. But first, I want to set E.ICOM to TRUE. Remember when we were processing forms? Setting this environment variable to TRUE caused an immediate computation of all expressions in a form each time a new value was entered into one of the form's elements. It works in a similar fashion here. Each time a cell's definition is changed,

FIGURE 12–13 Copying a cell's definition

```
                                                    20 , 15   v #D9

1-   :A        :B        :C        :D        :E        :F        :G        :H
 1:                      MONTHLY  EXPENSES                                    :
 2:                                                                          :
 3:Hotel:      38.75                                                         :
 4:Meal:       22.00                                                         :
 5:                                                                          :
 6:            Monthly            Hotel                                      :
 7:Name        Salary   Nights   Total                                       :
 8:========   ========  ========  ========                                   :
 9:Toby        2000      4.00[ 155.00]                                       :
10:Kathy       2100      3.00                                                :
11:Kerry       2250      2.40                                                :
12:Kris        2400      6.10                                                :
13:Jackie      2400      4.80                                                :
14:Kevin       2500      2.75                                                :
15:Kim         2600      3.30                                                :
16:Carol       2750      4.00                                                :
17:Tina        2800      5.25                                                :
18:Karen       2800      7.00                                                :
19:                                                                          :

\ copy #d9, #d10 to #d18 _____
#b3*#c9
```

the environment will immediately compute and display values for all the cells."

Jack executed the command

`\e.icom=true`

on the entry line. The spreadsheet's appearance was unaltered. He proceeded directly to the COPY command, typing

`\copy #d9, #d10 to #d18`

on the entry line as shown in Figure 12–13. This command tells the environment to define #D10 to #D18 (inclusive) in terms of a copy of #D9's definition. But Jack will be given a chance to indicate which parts of #D9's definition should be adjusted in the copying process. When he pressed the Enter key to execute the COPY, all three lines beneath the spreadsheet window changed as shown in Figure 12–14. The entry line now contained the definition to be copied. The utility line contained a "v" marker pointing to the first cell referenced in the

FIGURE 12–14   A chance to have #B3 adjusted in copied definitions

```
                                                  20 , 15   V #D9

1-  :A        :B        :C        :D        :E        :F        :G        :H
  1!                    MONTHLY   EXPENSES                                    !
  2!                                                                         !
  3!Hotel:    38.75                                                          !
  4!Meal:     22.00                                                          !
  5!                                                                         !
  6!          Monthly             Hotel                                      !
  7!Name      Salary    Nights    Total                                      !
  8!========  ========  ========  =======                                    !
  9!Toby      2000      4.00[ 155.00]                                        !
 10!Kathy     2100      3.00                                                 !
 11!Kerry     2250      2.40                                                 !
 12!Kris      2400      6.10                                                 !
 13!Jackie    2400      4.80                                                 !
 14!Kevin     2500      2.75                                                 !
 15!Kim       2600      3.30                                                 !
 16!Carol     2750      4.00                                                 !
 17!Tina      2800      5.25                                                 !
 18!Karen     2800      7.00                                                 !
 19!                                                                         !
 V
#b3*#c9
#b3*#c9                            Adjust (y/n)?
```

definition and the message line asked whether that cell should be adjusted in the copying process.

"We don't want this part of the definition to be adjusted as copies are made," Jack said. "Every one of the copied definitions should contain #B3 times something. So I just press the N key for no adjustment."

This resulted in the Figure 12–15 screen. Here, Jack was given a chance to have #C9 adjusted as the definition was copied. He pressed the Y key and the copying commenced. As it concluded, the environment did an immediate compute to display the new values for #D10 to #D18 based on their new definitions. Jack moved the cell cursor through these cells, allowing the managers to see their new definitions in the message line. Figure 12–16 shows what the screen looked like when the cell cursor was at #D12. Notice that the entry line still shows the original definition used as a basis for copying. The message line shows the new definition of #D12 with the second term properly adjusted to be #C12 instead of the original #C9.

Jack explained that the COPY command copied not only definitions, but values as well. If E.ICOM had been FALSE, a value of 155 would have appeared in all of the cells from #D10 to #D18. That is, their values would have been copies of the #D9 value. To have their new

FIGURE 12–15   A chance to have #C9 adjusted in copied definitions

```
                                                    20 , 15   V #D9

1- :A         :B        :C        :D       :E       :F      :G       :H
  1¦                   MONTHLY   EXPENSES                                    ¦
  2¦                                                                         ¦
  3¦Hotel:     38.75                                                         ¦
  4¦Meal:      22.00                                                         ¦
  5¦                                                                         ¦
  6¦           Monthly            Hotel                                      ¦
  7¦Name       Salary   Nights    Total                                      ¦
  8¦========   ======== ========  ========                                   ¦
  9¦Toby        2000     4.00   [ 155.00]                                    ¦
 10¦Kathy       2100     3.00                                                ¦
 11¦Kerry       2250     2.40                                                ¦
 12¦Kris        2400     6.10                                                ¦
 13¦Jackie      2400     4.80                                                ¦
 14¦Kevin       2500     2.75                                                ¦
 15¦Kim         2600     3.30                                                ¦
 16¦Carol       2750     4.00                                                ¦
 17¦Tina        2800     5.25                                                ¦
 18¦Karen       2800     7.00                                                ¦
 19¦                                                                         ¦
        V
 #b3*#c9
 #b3*#c9                         Adjust (y/n)?
```

FIGURE 12–16   New definitions and their computed values after a COPY command

```
                                                    20 , 15   V #D12

1- :A         :B        :C        :D       :E       :F      :G       :H
  1¦                   MONTHLY   EXPENSES                                    ¦
  2¦                                                                         ¦
  3¦Hotel:     38.75                                                         ¦
  4¦Meal:      22.00                                                         ¦
  5¦                                                                         ¦
  6¦           Monthly            Hotel                                      ¦
  7¦Name       Salary   Nights    Total                                      ¦
  8¦========   ======== ========  ========                                   ¦
  9¦Toby        2000     4.00    155.00                                      ¦
 10¦Kathy       2100     3.00    116.25                                      ¦
 11¦Kerry       2250     2.40     93.00                                      ¦
 12¦Kris        2400     6.10  [ 236.37]                                     ¦
 13¦Jackie      2400     4.80    186.00                                      ¦
 14¦Kevin       2500     2.75    106.56                                      ¦
 15¦Kim         2600     3.30    127.87                                      ¦
 16¦Carol       2750     4.00    155.00                                      ¦
 17¦Tina        2800     5.25    203.44                                      ¦
 18¦Karen       2800     7.00    271.25                                      ¦
 19¦                                                                         ¦

 #b3*#c9
 #b3*#C12
```

values computed, based on their new definitions, he would have executed the COMPUTE command

```
\compute
```

on the entry line. As it was, the environment did an automatic COMPUTE after the COPY because the definition of a cell had changed.

There are other variations of the COPY command. Like Jack's example, each identifies the source cell definition before the comma and the target cells to get new definitions after the comma. For instance, it is permissible to specify a single target cell if desired. At the other extreme the COPY target can be a range or block of cells that span multiple columns and rows (e.g., #F3 to #H12, encompassing all intervening cells). It is also permissible for the source to be a range of cells rather than a single cell. For example, the command

```
\copy #b9 to #d18, #f3 to #h12
```

would copy all of the definitions for cells in the source range of #B9 to #D18 into the corresponding target range of #F3 to #H12.

CHANGING AN EXISTING DEFINITION

Brad was still somewhat troubled. "It's nice that we can define cells in terms of calculations. But why not just redefine REP to have a couple of extra fields called NIGHTS and HOTEL? NIGHTS would be a numeric actual field, whereas HOTEL would be a virtual field. Its definition would be something like NIGHTS*HRATE, where HRATE is a working variable whose value we could set to 38.75 or whatever other value we might choose to use. It would sure take less effort than defining all these cells, plus we could then subject the NIGHTS and HOTEL values to all the data management ad hoc query, statistics, and report generation commands we want."

Jack pondered for a few seconds before responding. "What you say is certainly true. But in defining cell values we can be even more flexible than what you've seen so far. For instance, suppose I know that hotel rates in Kris's territory tend to be 12 percent above the normal rate. I could not easily represent that fact with the virtual field you suggested."

"Right," agreed Brad. "Virtual fields can't handle exceptions to the calculation being defined."

"But it's easy to do with a spreadsheet," Jack claimed. "Let's change

FIGURE 12–17   Command to edit the active cell's definition

```
                                                    20 , 15   V #D12

1-  :A        :B       :C       :D       :E       :F       :G       :H
  1:                   MONTHLY  EXPENSES                                    :
  2:                                                                        :
  3:Hotel:    38.75                                                         :
  4:Meal:     22.00                                                         :
  5:                                                                        :
  6:          Monthly           Hotel                                       :
  7:Name      Salary   Nights   Total                                       :
  8:========  =======  =======  =======                                    :
  9:Toby       2000     4.00    155.00                                      :
 10:Kathy      2100     3.00    116.25                                      :
 11:Kerry      2250     2.40     93.00                                      :
 12:Kris       2400     6.10 [ 236.37]                                      :
 13:Jackie     2400     4.80    186.00                                      :
 14:Kevin      2500     2.75    106.56                                      :
 15:Kim        2600     3.30    127.87                                      :
 16:Carol      2750     4.00    155.00                                      :
 17:Tina       2800     5.25    203.44                                      :
 18:Karen      2800     7.00    271.25                                      :
 19:                                                                        :

\edit_____
#b3*#C12
```

the definition for #D12. What we want to do is edit the existing definition so that it is multiplied by 1.12."

As Figure 12–17 shows, Jack typed

\edit

to tell the environment that he wanted to edit the active cell's definition. When he pressed the Enter key to execute the EDIT command, #D12's definition appeared on the entry line. Jack used ^D to move the entry cursor to the space after the 2 and typed

*1.12

yielding the screen appearance shown in Figure 12–18. When he pressed the Enter key, the edited definition became #D12's new definition. The environment computed and displayed a new value for #D12 based on this definition. Figure 12–19 shows the result.

Of course, definitions for other cells could be similarly changed. In general, any cell can be defined in terms of any other cell. Definitions of two cells in the same row or same column can be very different.

FIGURE 12–18   Editing the active cell's definition

```
                                          20 , 15   V #D12

 1-  :A        :B       :C       :D      :E      :F      :G       :H
  1:                  MONTHLY  EXPENSES                                   :
  2:                                                                      :
  3:Hotel:     38.75                                                      :
  4:Meal:      22.00                                                      :
  5:                                                                      :
  6:           Monthly          Hotel                                     :
  7:Name       Salary  Nights   Total                                     :
  8:========   ======= =======  =======                                  :
  9:Toby        2000    4.00    155.00                                    :
 10:Kathy       2100    3.00    116.25                                    :
 11:Kerry       2250    2.40     93.00                                    :
 12:Kris        2400    6.10 [ 236.37]                                    :
 13:Jackie      2400    4.80    186.00                                    :
 14:Kevin       2500    2.75    106.56                                    :
 15:Kim         2600    3.30    127.87                                    :
 16:Carol       2750    4.00    155.00                                    :
 17:Tina        2800    5.25    203.44                                    :
 18:Karen       2800    7.00    271.25                                    :
 19:                                                                      :

 #b3*#C12*1.12_____
 #b3*#C12
```

FIGURE 12–19   Value and definition for the hotel exception cell

```
                                          20 , 15   V #D12

 1-  :A        :B       :C       :D      :E      :F      :G       :H
  1:                  MONTHLY  EXPENSES                                   :
  2:                                                                      :
  3:Hotel:     38.75                                                      :
  4:Meal:      22.00                                                      :
  5:                                                                      :
  6:           Monthly          Hotel                                     :
  7:Name       Salary  Nights   Total                                     :
  8:========   ======= =======  =======                                  :
  9:Toby        2000    4.00    155.00                                    :
 10:Kathy       2100    3.00    116.25                                    :
 11:Kerry       2250    2.40     93.00                                    :
 12:Kris        2400    6.10 [ 264.74]                                    :
 13:Jackie      2400    4.80    186.00                                    :
 14:Kevin       2500    2.75    106.56                                    :
 15:Kim         2600    3.30    127.87                                    :
 16:Carol       2750    4.00    155.00                                    :
 17:Tina        2800    5.25    203.44                                    :
 18:Karen       2800    7.00    271.25                                    :
 19:                                                                      :

 #b3*#C12*1.12
 #b3*#C12*1.12
```

One factor to keep in mind is that the environment computes cell values on a row-by-row basis: #A1, #B1, . . . , #A2, #B2, . . . and so forth. This means that a cell is normally defined in terms of cells that are in higher rows or that precede it to the left in the same row. If E.COMP is switched from its TRUE default to FALSE, spreadsheet computation will occur column by column instead of rowwise.

"There is," Jack declared, "another way to change the definition of a cell. Rather than invoking the EDIT command to edit the active cell's definition, you can simply type in a new definition. It replaces whatever the active cell's former definition happened to be. If a definition is fairly short or requires radical revision, I tend to just replace the existing definition rather than edit it."

To demonstrate the replacement approach, Jack typed

```
#b3*#c9
```

on the entry line. When he pressed the Enter key, the screen reverted to the way it looked in Figure 12–16. Brad was mollified, at least for the time being. Jack also mentioned that a cell's definition could be entirely eliminated with the UNDEFINE command. For instance the command

```
\undefine #a1 to #h1
```

would eliminate the definitions of all cells in the range #A1 to #H1. Naturally, cells without definitions would no longer have values to display on the spreadsheet screen.

CELL APPEARANCES

"I want to take a few minutes," Jack announced, "to introduce a couple of commands for altering the appearance of a cell. They are the USING and WIDTH commands. USING allows us to specify a picture for a cell or block of cells. WIDTH allows us to alter the width of a cell."

To demonstrate the USING command, he typed

```
\using "$f,fff" #b9 to #b18
```

on the entry line. After pressing the Enter key to execute it, the screen looked like Figure 12–20. All cell values for the range #B9 to #B18 were instantly displayed with the indicated picture. In general, any of the pictures that could be used anywhere else in the environment could also be used for cells. As usual, a single cell could be specified in a

FIGURE 12–20   Giving pictures to cells

```
                                              20 , 15   V #D12

1-  :A        :B        :C       :D       :E       :F       :G       :H
 1:                   MONTHLY  EXPENSES                                    :
 2:                                                                        :
 3:Hotel:       38.75                                                      :
 4:Meal:        22.00                                                      :
 5:                                                                        :
 6:           Monthly           Hotel                                      :
 7:Name       Salary   Nights   Total                                      :
 8:========   ======== ======== ========                                   :
 9:Toby        $2,000    4.00   155.00                                     :
10:Kathy       $2,100    3.00   116.25                                     :
11:Kerry       $2,250    2.40    93.00                                     :
12:Kris        $2,400    6.10 [ 236.37]                                    :
13:Jackie      $2,400    4.80   186.00                                     :
14:Kevin       $2,500    2.75   106.56                                     :
15:Kim         $2,600    3.30   127.87                                     :
16:Carol       $2,750    4.00   155.00                                     :
17:Tina        $2,800    5.25   203.44                                     :
18:Karen       $2,800    7.00   271.25                                     :
19:                                                                        :


\using "$f,fff" #b9 to #b18
#b3*#C12
```

USING command. Alternatively, a range involving multiple rows and columns could be specified.

"Another way to change the appearance of cells is to make them wider or narrower," continued Jack. "Each cell is initially wide enough to hold nine characters. Suppose you want the full name of each rep in the spreadsheet. Nine characters are enough to accommodate first names, but not enough for full names. A full name would try to spill over into column B and interfere with the values there. What we need is a way to make the cells in column A wide enough to hold about 20 characters instead of 9. The WIDTH command makes this easy."

As shown in Figure 12–21, Jack executed the command

```
\width #a20
```

on the entry line. Here, the #A20 is not referring to a cell, but says to make cells in column A 20 characters wide. Notice that the other columns were automatically pushed to the right to make room for the wider cells in column A. Their cell definitions and values were unaffected. Jack proceeded to execute the command

FIGURE 12–21 Expanding the width of column A cells

```
                                                      20 , 15   V #D12

1-  :A                :B      :C      :D      :E      :F      :G
  1!                          MONTHLY  EXPENSES                        !
  2!                                                                   !
  3!Hotel:            38.75                                            !
  4!Meal:             22.00                                            !
  5!                                                                   !
  6!                  Monthly          Hotel                           !
  7!Name              Salary  Nights   Total                           !
  8!========          ======== ======== ========                      !
  9!Toby              $2,000   4.00     155.00                         !
 10!Kathy             $2,100   3.00     116.25                         !
 11!Kerry             $2,250   2.40      93.00                         !
 12!Kris              $2,400   6.10 [ 236.37]                          !
 13!Jackie            $2,400   4.80     186.00                         !
 14!Kevin             $2,500   2.75     106.56                         !
 15!Kim               $2,600   3.30     127.87                         !
 16!Carol             $2,750   4.00     155.00                         !
 17!Tina              $2,800   5.25     203.44                         !
 18!Karen             $2,800   7.00     271.25                         !
 19!                                                                   !

\width #a20
#b3*#C12
```

```
\convert name from rep to cell #a9 order by mosal
```

with the results depicted in Figure 12–22. Existing definitions for #A9 through #A18 were replaced by new string constants embodying full names.

Jack demonstrated that the process could be reversed. He pressed ^Z, which allowed him to edit the previous CONVERT command. He inserted an "f" in front of "name" and pressed the Enter key to execute

```
\convert fname from rep to cell #a9 order by mosal
```

causing the viewing window to appear as it did in Figure 12–21. Next, he executed the command

```
\width #a9
```

producing the same window view seen earlier in Figure 12–20.

"Let's say I want all columns to be 12 characters wide," commented Stan. "Would I have to execute 15 WIDTH commands, 1 for each column?"

FIGURE 12–22   Converting full names into column A

```
                                              20 , 15   V #D12

1-  :A              :B      :C      :D      :E      :F      :G
  1:                        MONTHLY EXPENSES                      :
  2:                                                              :
  3:Hotel:              38.75                                     :
  4:Meal:               22.00                                     :
  5:                                                              :
  6:                 Monthly           Hotel                      :
  7:Name             Salary   Nights   Total                      :
  8:========         ======== ======== ========                  :
  9:Toby C. Terry      $2,000    4.00   155.00                    :
 10:Kathy F. Smith     $2,100    3.00   116.25                    :
 11:Kerry H. Jones     $2,250    2.40    93.00                    :
 12:Kris H. Raber      $2,400    6.10 [ 236.37]                   :
 13:Jackie V. Smith    $2,400    4.80   186.00                    :
 14:Kevin R. Andrews   $2,500    2.75   106.56                    :
 15:Kim G. Anders      $2,600    3.30   127.87                    :
 16:Carol O. Lynn      $2,750    4.00   155.00                    :
 17:Tina F. Lee        $2,800    5.25   203.44                    :
 18:Karen V. Bruckner  $2,800    7.00   271.25                    :
 19:                                                              :


\ convert name from rep to cell #a9 order by mosal
#b3*#C12
```

Jack shook his head and said that it could all be accomplished with a single WIDTH command. Executing

```
\width all 12
```

would make all columns 12 characters wide.

WHAT IF?

Earlier chapters have illustrated that "what if" processing can be accomplished via ad hoc queries, forms, templates, and even text. In each instance, this was made possible by the ability to specify complex expressions whose values are calculated by the environment and displayed in query results, forms, reports, or printed text. Because cells can also be defined in terms of complex expressions whose values can be calculated, spreadsheets can also be used for "what if" purposes during decision-making processes.

Cell definitions can be much more highly interdependent than calculated columns specified for a query. A value calculated by a query can depend only on other values in the same line of results and on values of individual variables assigned prior to executing the query. It cannot depend on values in other lines of the result. In contrast, a value calculated for a cell can depend on the value of any cell that precedes it in the flow of spreadsheet computation (i.e., a row-by-row flow in Jack's environment).

This same degree of flexibility can be achieved with a form such as SCALC (recall Chapter 9). However, unlike a form, a spreadsheet does not need to be painted from scratch. In effect, it can be thought of as a specially structured, ready-made form whose cells behave like a form's "Put" elements. All that is necessary is to provide the literal (i.e., constant) or nonliteral definitions for cells. A spreadsheet has no counterpart to a form's "Get" elements, nor does it provide the same layout flexibility. However, as Jack would show later, a spreadsheet can have blocks of color.

Looking in Brad's direction, Jack asserted, "The main value of a spreadsheet is, in my opinion, its ability to do 'what if' analyses. By changing the definition of one cell, not only will its value be affected, but the values of many other cells may also change as the spreadsheet is recomputed either automatically—if E.ICOM is TRUE—or by a COMPUTE command.

"For example, what if the hotel rate is increased to $42.13? What will be the effects of this on the reps' budgeted hotel totals? Well, the effects are very easy to see. All we need to do is change the definition of #B3."

He made #B3 the active cell and typed

```
42.13
```

on the entry line. When Jack pressed the Enter key, this became the new definition of #B3 and the environment did an immediate computation of all the spreadsheet cell values. As Figure 12–23 indicates, all the hotel totals were revised to reflect the higher rate. Again, if E.ICOM had been FALSE, the new definition would have changed only the value of #B3. The command

```
\compute
```

would have recomputed the values of all cells, yielding the same values shown in Figure 12–23. In either case, the effect of changing the hotel rate is plainly evident.

"I see how changing #B3's definition affected the values of cells such as #D9 and #D10, whose own definitions refer to #B3," commented Dan. "What if there were other cells whose definitions didn't

FIGURE 12–23 What if the hotel rate is 42.13?

```
                                                    20 , 15  < #B3

1-  :A        :B        :C       :D       :E      :F      :G       :H
 1¦                   MONTHLY  EXPENSES                                   ¦
 2¦                                                                       ¦
 3¦Hotel:    [  42.13]                                                    ¦
 4¦Meal:        22.00                                                     ¦
 5¦                                                                       ¦
 6¦           Monthly           Hotel                                     ¦
 7¦Name       Salary   Nights   Total                                     ¦
 8¦========  ========  ======== ========                                  ¦
 9¦Toby       $2,000    4.00    168.52                                    ¦
10¦Kathy      $2,100    3.00    126.39                                    ¦
11¦Kerry      $2,250    2.40    101.11                                    ¦
12¦Kris       $2,400    6.10    256.99                                    ¦
13¦Jackie     $2,400    4.80    202.22                                    ¦
14¦Kevin      $2,500    2.75    115.86                                    ¦
15¦Kim        $2,600    3.30    139.03                                    ¦
16¦Carol      $2,750    4.00    168.52                                    ¦
17¦Tina       $2,800    5.25    221.18                                    ¦
18¦Karen      $2,800    7.00    294.91                                    ¦
19¦                                                                       ¦

42.13
42.13
```

refer directly to #B3; but referred instead to cells like #D9 and #D10, which in turn depend on #B3? Would the values of these other cells that depend indirectly on #B3 also be revised during the computation?"

"Yes," Jack answered. "When a spreadsheet's cell values are computed there's a ripple effect that propagates throughout the entire spreadsheet. Let's take an example. Suppose we want the total of all 10 hotel allowances to appear in #D19. We'll define #D19 to be the sum of the values of #D9 through #D18. Though this definition doesn't directly refer to #B3, #D19's value will indirectly depend on #B3."

While he was at it, Jack defined four cells: #A19, #B19, #C19, and #D19. The definitions he entered were

```
" TOTALS:"
sum(#b9,#b18)
sum(#c9,#c18)
sum(#d9,#d18)
```

respectively. He also gave a picture of "$ff,fff" to #B19. Jack explained that SUM is a built-in function whose two arguments identify a range of cells. The value of the function is always the sum of the cell values in the range. Thus, #B19's value will always be the sum of the #B9

FIGURE 12–24   The SUM function

```
                                                      20 , 15    > #D19

1-  :A        :B        :C        :D        :E      :F      :G        :H
  1:                    MONTHLY   EXPENSES                                  ┊
  2:                                                                        ┊
  3:Hotel:     42.13                                                        ┊
  4:Meal:      22.00                                                        ┊
  5:                                                                        ┊
  6:          Monthly            Hotel                                      ┊
  7:Name      Salary   Nights    Total                                      ┊
  8:========  ======== ========  ========                                  ┊
  9:Toby       $2,000    4.00     168.52                                    ┊
 10:Kathy      $2,100    3.00     126.39                                    ┊
 11:Kerry      $2,250    2.40     101.11                                    ┊
 12:Kris       $2,400    6.10     256.99                                    ┊
 13:Jackie     $2,400    4.80     202.22                                    ┊
 14:Kevin      $2,500    2.75     115.86                                    ┊
 15:Kim        $2,600    3.30     139.03                                    ┊
 16:Carol      $2,750    4.00     168.52                                    ┊
 17:Tina       $2,800    5.25     221.18                                    ┊
 18:Karen      $2,800    7.00     294.91                                    ┊
 19: TOTALS:  $24,600   42.60  [1794.74]                                    ┊

sum(#d9,#d18)
sum(#d9,#d18)
```

through #B18 values (i.e., the total of all monthly salaries). Similarly, the sum of the #D9 through #D18 values is the value of #D19. As Figure 12–24 shows, the proper values were computed and displayed for these newly defined cells.

It is worthwhile at this juncture to pause and contemplate the essential nature of a spreadsheet. A spreadsheet is a repository of procedural knowledge that specifies what to do at each step in a computational process. This procedural knowledge controls what values appear when the spreadsheet is computed. The first step is to calculate and display a value of #A1 based on its definition (if any). The second step is to calculate and display a value for #B1 based on its definition. The steps continue in this fashion, row by row, until all cells have been processed.

Each cell represents a step in a procedure. Each definition tells the environment what to do at that step in the procedure. The user's activity of defining cells is therefore a way to capture procedural knowledge in a spreadsheet. The environment's activity of computing a spreadsheet (i.e., via COMPUTE or implicitly via a TRUE E.ICOM) is an exercise in actually carrying out a procedure, of following the steps prescribed by a user.

"If you think about it," Joy concluded, "this spreadsheet's cell definitions form a definite sequence of calculations. Because there are 300 cells, there could be up to 300 calculations defined for a spreadsheet of this size. If you didn't have a spreadsheet capability, you could carry out exactly the same sequence of calculations, one at a time, with repeated use of the LET command. That would require up to 300 executions of LET to assign a value to each of up to 300 variables. Obviously, this would be extremely cumbersome compared to computing a spreadsheet and then you'd also need to use OUTPUT commands to display the values assigned to the variables. So you can begin to see why people find spreadsheets to be so handy."

INSERTING AND DELETING ROWS AND COLUMNS

"Now that we're convinced of the value of spreadsheets for 'what if' procedures, I have a different 'what if' question for you," Brad chuckled. "What if we now wanted to add a new column, say for territory IDs, between the monthly salary and nights columns. Do we have to copy column D into E and column C into D to make room for TIDs in column C? That strikes me as pretty laborious."

"It is," nodded Jack. "To make room in a column for new definitions, you just move the cell cursor to that column and execute the +COLUMN command. Everything defined for that column and the columns to the right is moved rightward by a column to make room for your new definitions."

To demonstrate, Jack positioned the cell cursor in column C and typed

`\+column`

on the entry line leaving the screen as shown in Figure 12–25. When he pressed the Enter key to execute this command the definitions and values of columns C and D shifted into columns D and E. Column C was blank and ready to receive new definitions.

Since they all understood how to enter new definitions, Jack did not bother to define any of the column C cells. Instead, he typed

`\-column`

on the entry line as shown in Figure 12–26. He explained that the −COLUMN command is the converse of +COLUMN. It deletes all

FIGURE 12–25   Command to push column C and D definitions to the right

```
                                                20 , 15  < #C19

1-  :A        :B       :C        :D       :E       :F       :G        :H
 1:                  MONTHLY  EXPENSES                                      :
 2:                                                                        :
 3:Hotel:     42.13                                                        :
 4:Meal:      22.00                                                        :
 5:                                                                        :
 6:          Monthly           Hotel                                       :
 7:Name      Salary   Nights   Total                                       :
 8:========  ======== ======== ========                                    :
 9:Toby      $2,000   4.00     168.52                                      :
10:Kathy     $2,100   3.00     126.39                                      :
11:Kerry     $2,250   2.40     101.11                                      :
12:Kris      $2,400   6.10     256.99                                      :
13:Jackie    $2,400   4.80     202.22                                      :
14:Kevin     $2,500   2.75     115.86                                      :
15:Kim       $2,600   3.30     139.03                                      :
16:Carol     $2,750   4.00     168.52                                      :
17:Tina      $2,800   5.25     221.18                                      :
18:Karen     $2,800   7.00     294.91                                      :
19: TOTALS:  $24,600[ 42.60]   1794.74                                     :


\+column _____
sum(#C9,#C18)
```

FIGURE 12–26   Command to push columns D and E definitions to the left

```
                                                20 , 16  < #C19

1-  :A        :B       :C        :D       :E       :F       :G        :H
 1:                           MONTHLY  EXPENSES                             :
 2:                                                                        :
 3:Hotel:     42.13                                                        :
 4:Meal:      22.00                                                        :
 5:                                                                        :
 6:          Monthly                    Hotel                              :
 7:Name      Salary            Nights   Total                              :
 8:========  ========          ======== ========                          :
 9:Toby      $2,000            4.00     168.52                             :
10:Kathy     $2,100            3.00     126.39                             :
11:Kerry     $2,250            2.40     101.11                             :
12:Kris      $2,400            6.10     256.99                             :
13:Jackie    $2,400            4.80     202.22                             :
14:Kevin     $2,500            2.75     115.86                             :
15:Kim       $2,600            3.30     139.03                             :
16:Carol     $2,750            4.00     168.52                             :
17:Tina      $2,800            5.25     221.18                             :
18:Karen     $2,800            7.00     294.91                             :
19: TOTALS:  $24,600[          ] 42.60  1794.74                            :


\-column _____
```

definitions from the column holding the cell cursor.[1] It moves definitions and values of columns on the right leftward to fill in the empty space. After he pressed the Enter key, the viewing window again appeared as it had earlier (i.e., in Figure 12–25).

When column insertion or deletion causes a shifting of definitions, cell references in those definitions are automatically adjusted to reflect the new location. For example, Toby's hotel allowance (#D9 in Figure 12–25) was originally defined as #B3*#C9. But when the blank column was inserted for C, his hotel allowance (#E9 in Figure 12–26) was automatically adjusted to have #B3*#D9 as its definition. This is because the value that was formerly in #C9 had shifted to #D9. As a result, Toby's hotel allowance is the same (168.52) in both Figures 12–25 and 12–26.

When working with a spreadsheet, it is sometimes desirable to insert or delete space for multiple columns. The desired number is specified in the +COLUMN or −COLUMN command. For example, the command

```
\+column 3
```

would make space for three new columns of definitions and the command

```
\-column 3
```

would restore the spreadsheet to its former appearance.

Jack explained that row insertion and deletion worked in an analogous manner to columns, only the applicable commands are +ROW and −ROW. The +ROW command inserts a blank row prior to the row holding the cell cursor. Definitions and values of existing rows are shifted downward as needed, with definitions being automatically adjusted. The −ROW command deletes definitions of the row holding the cell cursor. Definitions and values of lower rows are shifted up, with automatic definition adjustments.

SPREADSHEET PRINTOUTS

"Occasionally," Jack said, "you'll want to get a printout of a spreadsheet or some block of its cells. This is accomplished by switching E.OPRN to TRUE and then executing the DISPLAY command."

---

[1] In general, caution should be exercised during such a deletion because other definitions may depend on values produced by definitions being deleted. In this case, no such dependencies exist.

FIGURE 12–27   Command to display a block of cells

```
                                        20 , 15   > #D19

1-  :A        :B        :C        :D        :E       :F       :G       :H
 1:                     MONTHLY  EXPENSES                                    :
 2:                                                                          :
 3:Hotel:       42.13                                                        :
 4:Meal:        22.00                                                        :
 5:                                                                          :
 6:           Monthly             Hotel                                      :
 7:Name       Salary   Nights    Total                                       :
 8:========  ========  ========  ========                                    :
 9:Toby       $2,000     4.00    168.52                                      :
10:Kathy      $2,100     3.00    126.39                                      :
11:Kerry      $2,250     2.40    101.11                                      :
12:Kris       $2,400     6.10    256.99                                      :
13:Jackie     $2,400     4.80    202.22                                      :
14:Kevin      $2,500     2.75    115.86                                      :
15:Kim        $2,600     3.30    139.03                                      :
16:Carol      $2,750     4.00    168.52                                      :
17:Tina       $2,800     5.25    221.18                                      :
18:Karen      $2,800     7.00    294.91                                      :
19: TOTALS:  $24,600    42.60 (1794.74)                                      :

\display #a6 to #d19_____
sum(#d9,#d18)
```

To demonstrate, he executed the command

```
\e.oprn=true
```

on the entry line. Next he typed

```
\display #a6 to #d19
```

producing the screen appearance of Figure 12–27. When he pressed the Enter key to execute this command, values of the cells ranging from #A6 to #D19 were displayed on both a printed page and the console screen. As Figure 12–28 shows the printed display comes complete with the row and column borders for the designated block of cells. He redrew the screen by pressing backslash and then the Enter key.

"What if I want the printout without the row and column borders?" asked Tracey.

"There is a BORDER command that, among other things, can be invoked to turn the spreadsheet's borders off and on," Jack responded.

FIGURE 12–28   Printout displaying a block of cells

```
    : A          : B        : C          : D
  6 :           Monthly                Hotel      :
  7 : Name      Salary      Nights      Total      :
  8 : ========  ========   ========   ========:
  9 : Toby       $2,000      4.00        168.52:
 10 : Kathy      $2,100      3.00        126.39:
 11 : Kerry      $2,250      2.40        101.11:
 12 : Kris       $2,400      6.10        256.99:
 13 : Jackie     $2,400      4.80        202.22:
 14 : Kevin      $2,500      2.75        115.86:
 15 : Kim        $2,600      3.30        139.03:
 16 : Carol      $2,750      4.00        168.52:
 17 : Tina       $2,800      5.25        221.18:
 18 : Karen      $2,800      7.00        294.91:
 19 :  TOTALS:   $24,600    42.60       1794.74:
```

"If the borders are not visible when you execute the DISPLAY command, they won't appear in the printout either."

The command

```
\border
```

was executed to illustrate. The row indicators, column indicators, and vertical lines framing the viewing window instantly disappeared. The line at the top of the screen, with the name of the current cell, also vanished. To bring the border back onto the screen, he again executed the same BORDER command.

A printed page is sufficiently wide to handle Jack's example. However, spreadsheets often are too wide to have all of their columns displayed side by side on a single printed page. Some spreadsheet software solves this problem by printing spreadsheets sideways across consecutive pieces of paper. Where such a feature is not available, multiple DISPLAY commands would be used, each designating a block of cells. The resultant pages can be laid side by side and attached. For instance, the commands

```
\display #a1 to #h64
\display #i1 to #p64
```

would produce two pages that, when attached, would show cell values from the first 16 columns and 64 rows of a spreadsheet.

SAVING AND LOADING A SPREADSHEET

"Usually," asserted Jack, "you'll want to keep a spreadsheet around for future analysis once you've defined its cells. Because the spreadsheet we've been working on is part of our present processing context, we can save it along with macros, working variables, and all the rest in a context file. Just use the SAVE command. However, I'm inclined to save a spreadsheet in its own context file without all the other aspects of a context."

To demonstrate this, Jack typed

```
\save "a:hotelexp.icf" with "c"
```

on the entry line as Figure 12–29 shows. He explained that the "c" caused the context's cells to be saved in the HOTELEXP.ICF file on the drive A diskette. Executing this command produced a new file of procedural knowledge in the environment's knowledge system. It did not affect the present processing context. As expected, the command

```
\load "a:hotelexp.icf" with "c"
```

would load the spreadsheet into any future processing context.

"Keep in mind," Joy cautioned, "the fact that there is only one spreadsheet at a time in your present processing context. You may have saved many spreadsheets in context files, but you can't process any of them until you've loaded it with the LOAD command. If you happen to be using one spreadsheet when you load another one, the newly loaded one replaces the existing one in your processing context. So, before loading another spreadsheet, you should be sure to save your present spreadsheet if it has any changes that you want to preserve."

PROCESSING A SPREADSHEET THAT IS NOT VISIBLE

With a conventional spreadsheet package, a window into the spreadsheet currently being processed is nearly always visible on the screen. One exception is found in those packages (e.g., 1–2–3) that allow a graph to be generated from cell values. While the graph is displayed, cell values may not be visible. But when graph viewing is finished, the spreadsheet is again in sight. When spreadsheet analysis is but one of many knowledge management capabilities available in an environment, the current spreadsheet need not be visible on the screen at all times. Nevertheless, it is still susceptible to processing at all times.

FIGURE 12–29 Saving spreadsheet cells in a context file

```
                                              20 , 15   > #D19

1-  :A      :B      :C      :D      :E      :F      :G      :H
 1:                 MONTHLY  EXPENSES                              :
 2:                                                               :
 3:Hotel:          42.13                                          :
 4:Meal:           22.00                                          :
 5:                                                               :
 6:          Monthly         Hotel                                :
 7:Name      Salary  Nights  Total                                :
 8:========  ======= ======= =======                             :
 9:Toby      $2,000   4.00   168.52                               :
10:Kathy     $2,100   3.00   126.39                               :
11:Kerry     $2,250   2.40   101.11                               :
12:Kris      $2,400   6.10   256.99                               :
13:Jackie    $2,400   4.80   202.22                               :
14:Kevin     $2,500   2.75   115.86                               :
15:Kim       $2,600   3.30   139.03                               :
16:Carol     $2,750   4.00   168.52                               :
17:Tina      $2,800   5.25   221.18                               :
18:Karen     $2,800   7.00   294.91                               :
19: TOTALS:  $24,600  42.60 (1794.74)                             :

\save "a:hotelexp.icf" with "c" _____
sum(#d9,#d18)
```

"When using a spreadsheet to help analyze the impacts of various alternatives," Jack remarked, "I sometimes find that I'd like to temporarily do some other kind of processing before continuing the spreadsheet analysis. As a basis for conceiving or identifying what alternative to try next, I might want to browse through a table, do a calculation, ask a query, process a form, or generate a graph. Or, I might want the most recently computed spreadsheet results to be incorporated into text, presented in a customized report, stored in a table, included in a query's condition, and so forth. While doing such things I, of course, want the screen to be used for something other than showing cell values. As with the text screen, you are no longer constrained to the spreadsheet screen when you invoke the BYE command."

On the spreadsheet's entry line Jack typed

```
\bye
```

producing the screen appearance depicted in Figure 12–30. When he pressed the Enter key, the entire spreadsheet screen scrolled up a line and the underscore prompt appeared at the bottom. Jack could now enter any of the many commands described in earlier chapters. However,

FIGURE 12–30   Exiting from the spreadsheet screen

```
                                                    20 , 15   > #D19

1-  :A        :B       :C       :D       :E      :F       :G        :H      ¦
  1¦                  MONTHLY  EXPENSES                                     ¦
  2¦                                                                        ¦
  3¦Hotel:     42.13                                                        ¦
  4¦Meal:      22.00                                                        ¦
  5¦                                                                        ¦
  6¦          Monthly          Hotel                                        ¦
  7¦Name      Salary   Nights  Total                                        ¦
  8¦========  =======  ======= =======                                      ¦
  9¦Toby      $2,000    4.00   168.52                                       ¦
 10¦Kathy     $2,100    3.00   126.39                                       ¦
 11¦Kerry     $2,250    2.40   101.11                                       ¦
 12¦Kris      $2,400    6.10   256.99                                       ¦
 13¦Jackie    $2,400    4.80   202.22                                       ¦
 14¦Kevin     $2,500    2.75   115.86                                       ¦
 15¦Kim       $2,600    3.30   139.03                                       ¦
 16¦Carol     $2,750    4.00   168.52                                       ¦
 17¦Tina      $2,800    5.25   221.18                                       ¦
 18¦Karen     $2,800    7.00   294.91                                       ¦
 19¦ TOTALS:  $24,600  42.60  [1794.74]                                     ¦

\bye _____
sum(#d9,#d18)
```

he wanted to show that all of the cells' values were still accessible
even though they may not be visible, just as a working variable or
array element value is always available without regard to whether it
can presently be seen on the screen.

After switching E.OPRN to FALSE, Jack executed the OUTPUT
command

```
?#d18/#b18
```

to see the ratio of Karen's hotel allowance to her monthly salary. The
environment made the calculation and output the result just as it would
do for working variables, fields, or array elements. After switching
E.STAT to FALSE, he executed the query

```
select moexp-#d18, #d18/moexp from rep where fname="Karen"
```

to assess the relationship between this rep's present budgeted monthly
allowance and the spreadsheet's current hotel allowance. The query
was processed just like all the queries they had used before. The only

difference was that this query accesses the result of a spreadsheet computation as well as tabular data.

Although the other managers seemed to take this kind of spreadsheet processing in stride, Stan was somewhat amazed. "What you're telling us is we can refer to cells in any command we want, whenever we want, without even having the spreadsheet on the screen?"

"That's right," Joy answered. "In the environment there are really no arbitrary dividing lines between spreadsheet analysis and the other knowledge management techniques. So in a way, the SELECT command becomes more than a standard ad hoc query. It can also be viewed as a spreadsheet command as well. You can think of a cell as being a special kind of variable whose value is determined by a spreadsheet computation. Any command that can involve a working variable could involve a cell in place of the variable. This includes painting forms and designing templates that have cells in the expressions of their non-literal elements."

"Not only that," continued Jack, "we can also execute spreadsheet-specific commands even when the spreadsheet is not visible. Commands such as COMPUTE, BORDER, WIDTH, and DISPLAY are examples of commands specific to spreadsheets. They have no meaning with respect to other things. But we can still execute any of them right now! For instance, let's get a display of #A6 to #D19."

To accomplish this, he executed the command

```
calc display #a6 to #d19
```

with the results shown in Figure 12–31. Notice that this is practically the same command he had previously executed from the spreadsheet screen's entry line (recall Figure 12–27). The backslash preface used there was replaced with the word CALC. In general, when executing a spreadsheet-specific command outside of a spreadsheet's entry line, just preface it with the word CALC.

"I presume," Debbie said, "we could have the DISPLAY results deposited in a piece of text."

Jack hesitated. "I suppose so, though I've not tried it before. Let's find out."

He executed the command

```
text "a:expmemo.txt"
```

to bring a text screen into view. Jack escaped to the status line where he issued the command

```
\calc display #a6 to #d19
```

FIGURE 12–31   Spreadsheet processing without a visible spreadsheet

```
_e.oprn=false
_?#d18/#b18
        0.11
_e.stat=false
_select moexp-#d18, #d18/moexp from rep where fname="Karen"
        TO1             TO2

     1040.09              0.22
_calc display #a6 to #d19
    :A        :B       :C        :D
  6!                Monthly         Hotel   !
  7!Name        Salary   Nights   Total   !
  8!========  ========  ========  ========!
  9!Toby        $2,000    4.00   168.52!
 10!Kathy       $2,100    3.00   126.39!
 11!Kerry       $2,250    2.40   101.11!
 12!Kris        $2,400    6.10   256.99!
 13!Jackie      $2,400    4.80   202.22!
 14!Kevin       $2,500    2.75   115.86!
 15!Kim         $2,600    3.30   139.03!
 16!Carol       $2,750    4.00   168.52!
 17!Tina        $2,800    5.25   221.18!
 18!Karen       $2,800    7.00   294.91!
 19! TOTALS:   $24,600   42.60  1794.74!

 —
```

resulting in the text screen portrayed in Figure 12–32. Again escaping to the status line he issued the command

```
bye
```

to leave the text screen.

The CALC command can be used to bring the spreadsheet screen back into view. When Jack executed the command

```
calc
```

the viewing window of Figure 12–30 reappeared.

Glancing at his watch, he called for a break so they could practice what they had learned about the spreadsheet technique. When they resumed later in the afternoon, Jack intended to acquaint them with a larger spreadsheet that he had already constructed. He would also cover a variety of additional spreadsheet topics including cell protection, stylized cells, multiple viewing windows, cell values as a graphical data source, and command definitions for cells.

FIGURE 12–32   Incorporating a display of cell values into text

```
 Line:1        Col:1       a:expmemo.txt  Insert              Press ^L for help
   :A          :B      :C        :D
   6!                Monthly           Hotel   !
   7!Name            Salary   Nights   Total   !
   8!========        ======== ======== ========!
   9!Toby            $2,000     4.00    168.52!
  10!Kathy           $2,100     3.00    126.39!
  11!Kerry           $2,250     2.40    101.11!
  12!Kris            $2,400     6.10    256.99!
  13!Jackie          $2,400     4.80    202.22!
  14!Kevin           $2,500     2.75    115.86!
  15!Kim             $2,600     3.30    139.03!
  16!Carol           $2,750     4.00    168.52!
  17!Tina            $2,800     5.25    221.18!
  18!Karen           $2,800     7.00    294.91!
  19! TOTALS:       $24,600    42.60   1794.74!
```

LARGER SPREADSHEETS

As the session resumed, Jack and Joy were satisfied with the managers'
practical grasp of basic spreadsheet mechanics. They had freely mingled
as the managers were working on the spreadsheet exercises Jack had
provided. Like Jack's earlier example, these exercises had involved
spreadsheets small enough to fit all values into a single viewing window.
It was now time to examine a spreadsheet with too many cell values
to simultaneously be visible through a viewing window. To load such
a spreadsheet, Jack executed the command

```
load "a:expss.icf" with "c"
```

in response to the underscore prompt. The resultant screen appearance
is shown in Figure 12–33.

He moved the cell cursor rightward to column H at the right edge
of the viewing window. Explaining that there were still other columns
in the spreadsheet, Jack again pressed the right arrow key. Column A
disappeared from view and column I appeared at the right edge of
the window as shown in Figure 12–34. The simple act of moving the

FIGURE 12–33   Loading a larger spreadsheet

```
                                                    30 , 30    /\ #A1

1-  :A        :B        :C        :D       :E       :F       :G        :H
  1:|[      ]        MONTHLY EXPENSE ALLOCATION        Jack Vander           :
  2:                                                                         :
  3:Hotel:      39.10                                                        :
  4:Meal:       22.75                                                        :
  5:                                                                         :
  6:          Monthly             Hotel               Meal    Enter-         :
  7:Name      Salary   Nights     Total    Meals      Total  tainment  Phone :
  8:                                                                         :
  9:Kevin     2500.00    4.00    156.40    12.50     284.37    71.09  155.00:
 10:Kim       2600.00    3.00    117.30    12.00     273.00    68.25  155.00:
 11:Kris      2400.00    4.00    156.40    12.50     284.37    71.09  155.00:
 12:Tina      2800.00    6.00    234.60    13.50     307.12    76.78  155.00:
 13:Toby      2000.00    4.80    187.68    12.90     293.48    73.37  155.00:
 14:Kerry     2250.00    3.00    117.30    12.00     273.00    68.25  155.00:
 15:Karen     2800.00    3.00    117.30    12.00     273.00    68.25  155.00:
 16:Kathy     2100.00    3.50    136.85    12.25     278.69    69.67  155.00:
 17:Jackie    2400.00    6.00    234.60    13.50     307.12    76.78  155.00:
 18:Carol     2750.00    4.00    156.40    12.50     284.37    71.09  155.00:
 19: TOTALS: 24600.00   41.30   1614.83   125.65    2858.54   714.63 1550.00:
```

FIGURE 12–34   Scrolling through a spreadsheet's columns

```
                                                    30 , 30    > #I1

1-  :B        :C        :D       :E       :F       :G        :H       :I
  1:         MONTHLY EXPENSE ALLOCATION        Jack Vander       [       ] :
  2:                                                                       :
  3:    39.10                                                              :
  4:    22.75                                                              :
  5:                                                                       :
  6: Monthly             Hotel               Meal    Enter-                :
  7: Salary   Nights     Total    Meals      Total  tainment  Phone  Postage:
  8:                                                                       :
  9: 2500.00    4.00    156.40    12.50     284.37    71.09   155.00  118.00:
 10: 2600.00    3.00    117.30    12.00     273.00    68.25   155.00  118.00:
 11: 2400.00    4.00    156.40    12.50     284.37    71.09   155.00  118.00:
 12: 2800.00    6.00    234.60    13.50     307.12    76.78   155.00  118.00:
 13: 2000.00    4.80    187.68    12.90     293.48    73.37   155.00  118.00:
 14: 2250.00    3.00    117.30    12.00     273.00    68.25   155.00  118.00:
 15: 2800.00    3.00    117.30    12.00     273.00    68.25   155.00  118.00:
 16: 2100.00    3.50    136.85    12.25     278.69    69.67   155.00  118.00:
 17: 2400.00    6.00    234.60    13.50     307.12    76.78   155.00  118.00:
 18: 2750.00    4.00    156.40    12.50     284.37    71.09   155.00  118.00:
 19:24600.00   41.30   1614.83   125.65    2858.54   714.63  1550.00 1180.00:
```

FIGURE 12–35   Rightmost cells in the expense budgeting spreadsheet

```
                                                  30 , 30   > #L1

1-  :E        :F         :G      :H       :I       :J       :K        :L
 1¦LOCATION            Jack Vander                                   [        ]¦
 2¦                                                                           ¦
 3¦                                          Per Mile:                        ¦
 4¦                                             0.22                          ¦
 5¦                                          Mile/day:    Rate:               ¦
 6¦                      Meal    Enter-        110.00     0.03                ¦
 7¦         Meals        Total tainment  Phone    Postage  Mileage  Misc.  Totals ¦
 8¦                                                                           ¦
 9¦         12.50       284.37   71.09  155.00   118.00   580.80   80.00  1445.67¦
10¦         12.00       273.00   68.25  155.00   118.00   562.65   83.20  1377.40¦
11¦         12.50       284.37   71.09  155.00   118.00   580.80   76.80  1442.47¦
12¦         13.50       307.12   76.78  155.00   118.00   617.10   89.60  1598.21¦
13¦         12.90       293.48   73.37  155.00   118.00   595.32   64.00  1486.84¦
14¦         12.00       273.00   68.25  155.00   118.00   562.65   72.00  1366.20¦
15¦         12.00       273.00   68.25  155.00   118.00   562.65   89.60  1383.80¦
16¦         12.25       278.69   69.67  155.00   118.00   571.72   67.20  1397.13¦
17¦         13.50       307.12   76.78  155.00   118.00   617.10   76.80  1585.41¦
18¦        ·12.50       284.37   71.09  155.00   118.00   580.80   88.00  1453.67¦
19¦        125.65      2858.54  714.63 1550.00  1180.00  5831.60  787.20 14536.80¦
```

cell cursor when it is already at a window boundary causes previously unseen portions of a spreadsheet to come into view.

Jack pressed on until the cell cursor had brought column L into the window. The resultant screen appears in Figure 12–35. Notice that column L consisted of row totals, just as row 19 consisted of column totals. Jack moved the cell cursor to #L9 and its definition of

#d9 + sum(#f9,#k9)

appeared on the message line. Moving the cursor left to #K9 brought a definition of

#k5*#b9

to the message line. Jack explained that he was allowing miscellaneous expenses to be a certain percentage of a rep's monthly salary. At the moment this was 3 percent (i.e., the value of #K5). He moved the cell cursor left to #J9, bringing its fairly complex definition of

FIGURE 12–36   Making column A part of the spreadsheet's left border

```
                                               30 , 30   < #J9

 1─  :A         :F        :G        :H      :I        :J       :K        :L
   1!                          Jack Vander                                          !
   2!                                          Per Mile:                            !
   3!Hotel:                                        0.22                             !
   4!Meal:                                     Mile/day:      Rate:                 !
   5!                                            110.00       0.03                  !
   6!              Meal    Enter-                                                   !
   7!Name          Total  tainment  Phone    Postage  Mileage   Misc.   Totals  !
   8!                                                                                !
   9!Kevin        284.37    71.09  155.00   118.00( 580.80)   80.00  1445.67!
  10!Kim          273.00    68.25  155.00   118.00   562.65   83.20  1377.40!
  11!Kris         284.37    71.09  155.00   118.00   580.80   89.60  1442.47!
  12!Tina         307.12    76.78  155.00   118.00   617.10   64.00  1598.21!
  13!Toby         293.48    73.37  155.00   118.00   595.32   64.00  1486.84!
  14!Kerry        273.00    68.25  155.00   118.00   562.65   72.00  1366.20!
  15!Karen        273.00    68.25  155.00   118.00   562.65   89.60  1383.80!
  16!Kathy        278.69    69.67  155.00   118.00   571.72   67.20  1397.13!
  17!Jackie       307.12    76.78  155.00   118.00   617.10   76.80  1585.41!
  18!Carol        284.37    71.09  155.00   118.00   580.80   88.00  1453.67!
  19! TOTALS:    2858.54   714.63 1550.00  1180.00  5831.60  787.20 14536.80!


\border left 1
#J3*(#J5*21+#c9*#J5*.75)
```

#j3*(#j5*21+#c9*#j5*.75)

to the message line.

"But," asked Tracey, "how do we know which rep goes with which row?"

"You don't," answered Jack, "unless you have a better memory than mine. But we can *lock* column A in as part of the spreadsheet's left border, so no matter how far to the right we go, the rep names will always be visible through a window. This is done with the BORDER command."

To illustrate, he executed the command

\border left 1

on the entry line. Column E shown in Figure 12–35 was immediately replaced by Column A as shown in Figure 12–36. If he had specified 3 instead of 1 in the BORDER command, columns A through C would have become part of the left border. Once a column becomes part of the border, the cell cursor cannot be moved into it and its definitions cannot be changed until it is no longer part of the border. The command

```
\border left 0
```

causes no columns to any longer be part of the left border.

"Can we do something similar for the topmost rows in the spread-sheet?" asked Stan. "You'd probably want to do that when working with a deep spreadsheet, one having more than 19 rows."

"Right," confirmed Jack. "The command is the same except you use the word ONTOP instead of LEFT. Then you simply indicate how many of the upper rows you want to be locked into the spreadsheet's top border. Once you've made a row part of the top border, it will always appear in the window and you won't be able to alter definitions in that row."

PROTECTING A CELL'S DEFINITION

"That reminds me," commented Stan, "the spreadsheet package I've been using lets me specify that the definitions of certain cells are to be protected from change. How would I do that with the environment's spreadsheet capability?"

"Why would you want to do that?" Brad interjected.

"To avoid making an inadvertant change to a definition that I'm satisfied with," replied Stan.

"For instance," added Jack, "suppose you want to execute a command on the entry line, but you forget to preface it with a backslash. The environment will take your command and make it the new definition for the active cell. To correct your error you'd then have to remember and reenter the cell's former definition. Any cell's definition can be protected from inadvertant change via the PROTECT command."

To demonstrate, Jack executed the command

```
\protect #B1 to #L1
```

on the entry line. From this point onward it would be impossible to enter a new definition for any cell in the range #B1 to #L1. If it so happens that a protected cell's definition needs to be changed, the UNPROTECT command can be invoked. For example, the command

```
\unprotect #B1 to #L1
```

returns all cells in the indicated range to their former unprotected status. In general, either command can operate on an individual cell, as well as an entire cell block.

Though Jack did not demonstrate them, there are a couple of companion commands: CONCEAL and REVEAL. They deal with concealing and revealing a cell's definition. For example, the command

`\conceal #j9 to #j18`

would prevent definitions of the indicated cells from being revealed in the message line. Conversely, the command

`\reveal #j9 to #j18`

would allow their definitions to again be revealed (as normal) in the message line.

Conventional spreadsheet packages allow any user to unprotect any protected cell and to see any cell's definition. The environment's spreadsheet capability goes a step further by controlling exactly which users can unprotect or reveal which of the protected or concealed cells [6]. When PROTECT is invoked, security codes can be specified that will prohibit users without sufficient access privileges from unprotecting the specified cells. Similarly, security codes can be specified with CONCEAL to govern which users will be able to execute REVEAL for the specified cells. Such security features prevent users from tampering with or viewing proprietary procedural knowledge. This is of particular interest to developers of spreadsheet applications and in settings where a spreadsheet is shared by multiple users with different security clearances. However, as with data base management, spreadsheet security issues were of no immediate concern to the sales managers.

CUSTOMIZING THE VIEW

To this point they had been dealing with a standard, one-window view of spreadsheets. Beyond E.FORG, E.BACG, pictures, customized borders, and border suppression, there are other ways to usefully affect the spreadsheet screen. Jack was about to discuss the basics of two of them: stylized cell presentation and multiwindow viewing. In this environment, any cell or range of cells can be given a presentation style involving certain colors and special effects, allowing various cells to be visually highlighted in various ways. Also, the spreadsheet screen can be broken into multiple viewing windows, allowing the simultaneous viewing of physically distant cells. Second-generation spreadsheet packages usually support multiwindow viewing, but stylized cell presentation is rare.

Viewing in Style

"Let's add a little color and excitement to this spreadsheet," Jack suggested brightly. "You already know how to change the foreground and background colors. Now, I'll show you how to alter the colors of individual cells. Not only can this make the spreadsheet more visually appealing, but it lets you color code certain cells. For instance, we might want the regional totals to be yellow against the same blue background and the rep totals to be red against a black background."

To specify these color schemes, Jack successively executed the commands

```
\style color "fobu" #b19 to #k19
\style color "frba" #L9 to #L19
```

on the entry line. The first says that all cells from #B19 to #K19 are to be styled with colors of brown (O) on blue (U). Similarly, the color style for #L9 to #L19 is a foreground of red (R) on a background of black (A). Notice that these are the same color codes used throughout the environment. What Jack had done with the STYLE commands was to specify presentation knowledge that would be stored as part of the spreadsheet.

"So where are the colors?" asked Stan, for the cells remained unaffected by the two commands. They were all still white on blue.

Jack answered with a smile, "A cell's presentation style will show up on the screen once we activate it. We can activate or deactivate any cell whenever we want."

He moved the cell cursor to #L1 to bring column L into the viewing window. After executing the command

```
\activate #A9 to #L19
```

Photo 39 in the color insert resulted. All styles of all cells in the range #A9 to #L19 were now visually evident. To demonstrate how the DEACTIVATE command worked, he executed

```
\deactivate #h19 to #i19
```

on the entry line. These two cells reverted to their normal appearance of white on blue. In general, the STYLE, ACTIVATE, or DEACTIVATE command can refer to either a range of cells or an individual cell.

"I'm looking forward to trying out this spreadsheet coloring on my own," Stan volunteered as he absorbed what was, for him, a new phenomenon. "Earlier you drew an analogy between a cell and a form element. We've seen that form elements can not only be colored but can have various special effects such as blinking and reverse video. It sure would be nice if cells could also have special effects. I can just imagine a spreadsheet where the cells of greatest interest are blinking."

"That's a good idea," responded Jack. "Actually you can include special effects in a cell's style, either in addition to or instead of colors."

As an example, he executed the command

```
\style color "fobm" with "bs" #h1¹ to #i1¹
```

on the entry line. This altered the two cells' styles to have a foreground of brown (i.e., yellow) on a magenta background and to involve two special effects: blinking (B) and sound (S). He activated the two cells via the

```
\activate #h1¹ to #i1¹
```

command. Both began blinking in their new colors and whenever Jack moved the cell cursor into either of them a bell sounded.

"That's pretty gaudy," laughed Joy as she shielded her eyes.

Wanting to please her, Jack restyled the two cells to brown on blue without special effects. Addressing the managers, he commented, "It's up to you to make things as gaudy or as classy as you like. You're free to experiment to find the styles that fit your needs and tastes."

Multiple Windows

"Not only does the environment cater to your stylistic tastes, it does windows too," chuckled Jack. "Sometimes you may want to see two parts of a spreadsheet that are so far apart they can't fit into the same window and neither of them is locked into a customized border. This can be accomplished by breaking the existing window into two windows. Each of these can, in turn, be broken into two more windows and so forth. You just move the cell cursor to the place where you want the break to occur and issue a WINDOW BREAK command."

To illustrate this processing, he moved the cell cursor to #H1 and typed

```
\window break up
```

on the entry line. Figure 12–37 shows the spreadsheet screen just prior to breaking the window. By specifying UP, the break would be vertical.

FIGURE 12–37   Cell cursor positioned at vertical breaking point

```
                                                   30 , 30   < #H1

1-  :A        :F       :G      :H      :I       :J       :K       :L
  1¦                 Jack Vand[er      ]                                ¦
  2¦                                                                    ¦
                                              Per Mile:
  3¦Hotel:                                       0.22                   ¦
  4¦Meal:                                     Mile/Day:   Rate:         ¦
  5¦                                           110.00     0.03          ¦
  6¦                 Meal    Enter-                                     ¦
  7¦Name            Total tainment  Phone    Postage  Mileage   Misc.  Totals ¦
  8¦                                                                    ¦
  9¦Kevin          284.37   71.09  155.00   118.00   580.80   80.00  1445.67¦
 10¦Kim            273.00   68.25  155.00   118.00   562.65   83.20  1377.40¦
 11¦Kris           284.37   71.09  155.00   118.00   580.80   76.80  1442.47¦
 12¦Tina           307.12   76.78  155.00   118.00   617.10   89.60  1598.21¦
 13¦Toby           293.48   73.37  155.00   118.00   595.32   64.00  1486.84¦
 14¦Kerry          273.00   68.25  155.00   118.00   562.65   72.00  1366.20¦
 15¦Karen          273.00   68.25  155.00   118.00   562.65   89.60  1383.80¦
 16¦Kathy          278.69   69.67  155.00   118.00   571.72   67.20  1397.13¦
 17¦Jackie         307.12   76.78  155.00   118.00   617.10   76.80  1585.41¦
 18¦Carol          284.37   71.09  155.00   118.00   580.80   88.00  1453.67¦
 19¦ TOTALS:      2858.54  714.63 1550.00  1180.00  5831.60  787.20 14536.80¦

\ window break up _____
```

The cursor's present physical position on the screen would become the breaking point, with the new window's left edge being aligned with that position.

When Jack pressed the Enter key to execute the command, the spreadsheet screen was redrawn as shown in Figure 12–38. Each window had an identifying number at the upper left corner of its border and column A was locked into the left border of each. Notice the cell cursor in window 1. Whichever window holds the cell cursor is called the *current window* and the arrow keys can be used to position the cursor in that window. They can also be used to scroll other cells into the window. To demonstrate, Jack pressed the left arrow key until column B appeared alongside column A in the current window.

He then made window 2 the current window by executing the command

```
\current window 2
```

with the result shown in Figure 12–39. The cell cursor had jumped into window 2. Any portion of the spreadsheet could now be viewed through this window. Whatever window is current can be broken again

FIGURE 12–38 Two windows for spreadsheet viewing

```
                                                      30 , 30    > #F1

 1-  :A        :F              2-  :A        :I      :J        :K
   1¦        [      ]¦           1¦                                       ¦
   2¦                ¦           2¦                  Per Mile:            ¦
   3¦Hotel:          ¦           3¦Hotel:              0.22              ¦
   4¦Meal:           ¦           4¦Meal:              Mile/day:  Rate:¦
   5¦                ¦           5¦                    110.00     0.03¦
   6¦          Meal¦             6¦                                     ¦
   7¦Name     Total¦             7¦Name     Postage  Mileage   Misc.¦
   8¦                ¦           8¦                                     ¦
   9¦Kevin    284.37¦            9¦Kevin    118.00   580.80    80.00¦
  10¦Kim      273.00¦           10¦Kim      118.00   562.65    83.20¦
  11¦Kris     284.37¦           11¦Kris     118.00   580.80    76.80¦
  12¦Tina     307.12¦           12¦Tina     118.00   617.10    89.60¦
  13¦Toby     293.48¦           13¦Toby     118.00   595.32    64.00¦
  14¦Kerry    273.00¦           14¦Kerry    118.00   562.65    72.00¦
  15¦Karen    273.00¦           15¦Karen    118.00   562.65    89.60¦
  16¦Kathy    278.69¦           16¦Kathy    118.00   571.72    67.20¦
  17¦Jackie   307.12¦           17¦Jackie   118.00   617.10    76.80¦
  18¦Carol    284.37¦           18¦Carol    118.00   580.80    88.00¦
  19¦ TOTALS: 2858.54¦          19¦ TOTALS: 1180.00  5831.60   787.20¦

 \ window break up
```

FIGURE 12–39 Making window 2 current

```
                                                      30 , 30    > #I1

 1-  :A        :B              2-  :A        :I      :J        :K
   1¦                ¦           1¦          [      ]                     ¦
   2¦                ¦           2¦                  Per Mile:            ¦
   3¦Hotel:    39.10¦            3¦Hotel:              0.22              ¦
   4¦Meal:     22.75¦            4¦Meal:              Mile/Day:  Rate:¦
   5¦                ¦           5¦                    110.00     0.03¦
   6¦          Monthly¦          6¦                                     ¦
   7¦Name      Salary ¦          7¦Name     Postage  Mileage   Misc:¦
   8¦                ¦           8¦                                     ¦
   9¦Kevin    2500.00¦           9¦Kevin    118.00   580.80    80.00¦
  10¦Kim      2600.00¦          10¦Kim      118.00   562.65    83.20¦
  11¦Kris     2400.00¦          11¦Kris     118.00   580.80    76.80¦
  12¦Tina     2800.00¦          12¦Tina     118.00   617.10    89.60¦
  13¦Toby     2000.00¦          13¦Toby     118.00   595.32    64.00¦
  14¦Kerry    2250.00¦          14¦Kerry    118.00   562.65    72.00¦
  15¦Karen    2800.00¦          15¦Karen    118.00   562.65    89.60¦
  16¦Kathy    2100.00¦          16¦Kathy    118.00   571.72    67.20¦
  17¦Jackie   2400.00¦          17¦Jackie   118.00   617.10    76.80¦
  18¦Carol    2750.00¦          18¦Carol    118.00   580.80    88.00¦
  19¦ TOTALS: 24600.00¦         19¦ TOTALS: 1180.00  5831.60   787.20¦

 \ current window 2
```

and can have its borders altered in any of the usual ways. All of the same commands for processing the underlying spreadsheet have their usual effects, regardless of which window happens to be current.

"As you can see," commented Jack, "breaking up is not so hard to do. You just push the cell cursor to the breaking point and issue the command. Similarly, you can break a window horizontally by using the word ACROSS instead of UP. The top of the new window will be where the cell cursor's row was."

For instance, if the cell cursor were moved down to row 8 of window 2, the command

```
\window break across
```

would break off window 2 at that screen position. A new window (numbered 3) would appear beneath window 2. There are other ways to break windows (e.g., at specific screen coordinates), but Jack did not go into them. Nor did he discuss the command for stylizing a window as a whole by giving it its own colors and special effects. [6]

Instead he executed the command

```
\-window all
```

to eliminate both windows from the spreadsheet screen. A normal large window like the one in Figure 12–40 reappeared. Jack explained that the −WINDOW command could also delete an individual window by specifying the window number instead of ALL. The space it had occupied would become blank and available for other activities such as forms processing.

CELLS AS A DATA SOURCE

Earlier it was noted that cells could be defined so that their values appeared in an arraylike fashion on the spreadsheet screen. They can even be referenced as elements of the special # array (e.g., #(9,1) to #(18,11)). The values of #A9 to #K18 are an example. For this reason, a block of spreadsheet cells can serve as an alternative data source for generating graphs. During the course of spreadsheet analysis, it can be helpful to see a graphic portrayal of "what if" results.

"Let's look at a graph of how entertainment stacks up against proposed hotel and meal allowances," suggested Jack. "To do this we'll want to plot from the cell values in columns A, D, F, and G. Fortunately, the values don't have to be put in an ordinary array first. We can plot them directly from the spreadsheet."

FIGURE 12–40   Plotting a graph from a spreadsheet data source

```
                                                    30 , 30   ∧ #B1

1-  :A        :B        :C       :D       :E       :F       :G        :H
  1:          [         ]MONTHLY EXPENSE ALLOCATION          Jack Vander        :
  2:                                                                            :
  3:Hotel:       39.10                                                          :
  4:Meal:        22.75                                                          :
  5:                                                                            :
  6:          Monthly             Hotel              Meal    Enter-             :
  7:Name      Salary    Nights    Total    Meals     Total   tainment  Phone    :
  8:                                                                            :
  9:Kevin     2500.00    4.00     156.40   12.50    284.37    71.09   155.00:
 10:Kim       2600.00    3.00     117.30   12.00    273.00    68.25   155.00:
 11:Kris      2400.00    4.00     156.40   12.50    284.37    71.09   155.00:
 12:Tina      2800.00    6.00     234.60   13.50    307.12    76.78   155.00:
 13:Toby      2000.00    4.80     187.68   12.90    293.48    73.37   155.00:
 14:Kerry     2250.00    3.00     117.30   12.00    273.00    68.25   155.00:
 15:Karen     2800.00    3.00     117.30   12.00    273.00    68.25   155.00:
 16:Kathy     2100.00    3.50     136.85   12.25    278.69    69.67   155.00:
 17:Jackie    2400.00    6.00     234.60   13.50    307.12    76.78   155.00:
 18:Carol     2750.00    4.00     156.40   12.50    284.37    71.09   155.00:
 19: TOTALS:  24600.00  41.30    1614.83  125.65   2858.54   714.63  1550.00:

\plot bar from #a9 to #g13 using 1,4,6,7 at top ----------------------------
```

He began by setting the graph's title by executing the command

`\#title= "HOTEL, MEAL, ENTERTAINMENT ALLOWANCES"`

on the entry line. Jack proceeded to type in

`\plot bar from #a9 to #g13 using 1,4,6,7 at top`

as shown in Figure 12–40. This was just like the PLOT commands they had executed before, except a range of cells was specified instead of a usual range of array elements. Of course, if this were a frequently referenced range of cells, Jack most likely would have defined a macro for it. The macro could be referenced in PLOT commands and any of the spreadsheet-specific commands involving that same cell block.

Pressing the Enter key to execute the PLOT command caused a graphics screen to appear with the specified bar graph at the top. There was one cluster of bars for each of the five designated spreadsheet rows and each cluster had the three desired bars. Jack pressed the space bar and the spreadsheet screen reappeared. After setting #TITLE back to its original blank value, he executed the command

FIGURE 12–41   Printing the current graphics screen

```
                                                    30 , 30   ∧ #B1
 1─  :A      :B      :C       :D       :E      :F      :G        :H
  1¦          [         ¦MONTHLY EXPENSE ALLOCATION          Jack Vander        ¦
  2¦                                                                            ¦
  3¦Hotel:    39.10                                                            ¦
  4¦Meal:     22.75                                                            ¦
  5¦                                                                            ¦
  6¦          Monthly          Hotel                Meal   Enter-              ¦
  7¦Name      Salary   Nights  Total     Meals     Total  tainment  Phone      ¦
  8¦                                                                            ¦
  9¦Kevin     2500.00   4.00   156.40    12.50    284.37   71.09    155.00¦
 10¦Kim       2600.00   3.00   117.30    12.00    273.00   68.25    155.00¦
 11¦Kris      2400.00   4.00   156.40    12.50    284.37   71.09    155.00¦
 12¦Tina      2800.00   6.00   234.60    13.50    307.12   76.78    155.00¦
 13¦Toby      2000.00   4.80   187.68    12.90    293.48   73.37    155.00¦
 14¦Kerry     2250.00   3.00   117.30    12.00    273.00   68.25    155.00¦
 15¦Karen     2800.00   3.00   117.30    12.00    273.00   68.25    155.00¦
 16¦Kathy     2100.00   3.50   136.85    12.25    278.69   69.67    155.00¦
 17¦Jackie    2400.00   6.00   234.60    13.50    307.12   76.78    155.00¦
 18¦Carol     2750.00   4.00   156.40    12.50    284.37   71.09    155.00¦
 19¦ TOTALS:  24600.00 41.30  1614.83   125.65   2858.54  714.63   1550.00¦

\ print current _____
```

\plot ontop bar from #a14 to #g18 using 1,4,6,7 at bottom

on the entry line. The graphics screen again appeared and a bar graph
for the five remaining reps was superimposed on the bottom half.

Jack pressed the space bar. The spreadsheet screen reappeared and
he typed

\print current

as shown in Figure 12–41. The resultant printout of the current graphics
screen is depicted in Figure 12–42. He pressed the space bar and issued
the

command to redraw the spreadsheet screen.

"It seems to me," Dan said thoughtfully, "that we could use a
spreadsheet solely as a graphics data source, without regard to its computational and 'what if' facilities. Instead of converting data to an array,
we could just convert it into a fresh spreadsheet and issue all our PLOT

FIGURE 12–42   Printout of graph generated from spreadsheet

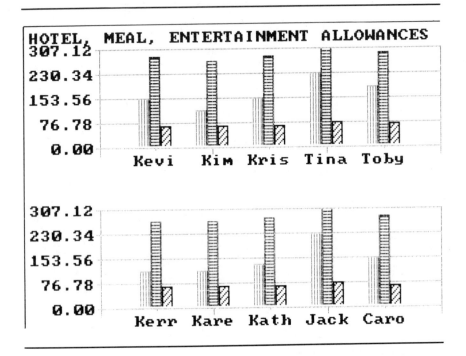

commands on the spreadsheet screen's entry line. That way we'd always be able to see the data source's values as we are typing in a PLOT command."

"That's a good idea," Jack replied. "It's a handy approach I've sometimes used myself. And you may even want to use multiple CON-VERT commands to deposit multiple data sources in the same spread-sheet. In effect, you would not be using a spreadsheet to hold procedural knowledge, but strictly presentation knowledge. Obviously, the COM-PUTE command would have no effect on such spreadsheets, since all their cell definitions are constants."

"But you should keep in mind," cautioned Joy, "that, as a data source, a spreadsheet is not nearly as efficient as an array. Each cell consumes much more of the environment's main memory work area than an array element. That's because cells are designed to be so much more than just storage compartments for data values.

"Also, it's worth mentioning that you are free to plot from a spread-sheet even when the spreadsheet screen is not visible. The PLOT com-mands would be the same as those Jack has shown you, only there would be no leading backslash since you'd be executing the command in response to the underscore prompt."

MINIMIZING KEYSTROKES

"I appreciate the flexibility of the environment's spreadsheet capability," said Stan, "but I do have a reservation. In the spreadsheet package I've been using most operations take only one or a few keystrokes to initiate. It's a menu rather than command interface and an option can be chosen by pressing a single key."

"If you like," responded Jack, "you can interact with a spreadsheet through the environment's menu-guided interface. There, an option is selectable by keying in its first letter. For instance, right now if I changed the value of E.GUID from its FALSE default to TRUE we'd immediately be confronted by the menu-guided interface. I'll leave that for you to experiment with on your own if you like.

"But, staying with the command interface, there are ways to drastically reduce the number of keystrokes required without sacrificing flexibility. I often use macros and function keys for this purpose. For instance, there's no need to type in \COMPUTE when you can just type C instead."

Macros

To show what he had in mind, Jack executed the commands

```
\macro c \compute
\macro pb \plot bar from
\macro hotel #d9 to #d18
\macro kim #a10 to #k10
\macro s \style
\macro a \activate
\macro gonr \color "fgbr"
```

on the entry line. They defined seven macros C, PB, HOTEL, KIM, S, A, and GONR. As a result, the commands

```
\compute
\style color "fgbr" #d9 to #d18
\activate #d9 to #d18
\plot bar from #a10 to #k10
```

could now be more briefly expressed by the equivalent commands

```
c
s gonr hotel
a hotel
pb kim
```

on the spreadsheet entry line. The macros could, of course, have been defined outside of the spreadsheet screen in response to underscore prompts.

Function Keys

"Alternatively," suggested Jack, "you may want to assign your most heavily used spreadsheet commands to function keys. One thing I tend to do is let F10 be the crosshatch symbol. Whenever I press F10 I get a crosshatch without having to use the Shift key and reach for the # key at the top of the keyboard."

He gave several examples by way of executing the following REDEFINE FUNCTION commands on the entry line

```
\redefine function 10 "#"
\redefine function 2 "\\compute\13"
\redefine function 3 "\\activate "
```

Recall from Chapter 4 that \13 will cause the Enter keystroke to be the last key produced by pressing F2. Also, to have a backslash keystroke produced, a double backslash is used in a function key's definition.

Jack demonstrated that pressing F10 now caused the crosshatch symbol to appear on the entry line. Pressing F2 caused

```
\compute
```

to not only appear on the entry line, but be executed immediately. Pressing F3 and typing h o t e l caused

```
\activate hotel
```

to appear on the entry line for execution or editing (e.g., inserting "de" after the backslash).

COMMANDS IN CELL DEFINITIONS

"So far," noted Jack, "whenever we've typed a command on the entry line we prefaced it with a backslash, causing it to be executed right away. But we can leave the backslash off. If we do, the command is not executed, but becomes the definition of the active cell. The command becomes embedded in the spreadsheet and is executed whenever the spreadsheet is computed. Though I've by no means tried to use every possible command in this way, you should be able to embed any command into a spreadsheet in the same manner. The one exception is

CONVERT, which according to the documentation cannot be embedded."

"So it's sort of like the delayed execution of commands embedded in text," Tracey observed. "The mechanics of embedding are obviously different, but the effects are basically the same. When text is printed, embedded commands are executed as they are encountered. When a spreadsheet's cell values are computed, embedded commands are executed as they are encountered."

"That's the idea," Joy declared. "It's a very simple, yet enormously powerful, concept. It means that each step in a spreadsheet's procedure is no longer restricted to calculating an expression's value for display at that cell's position. Instead, you can have the spreadsheet execute any command or commands that you want at each step of the procedure. It can be something as simple as switching an environment variable or as exotic as plotting a graph and then doing a GETFORM to gather user impressions of the graph as a basis for the remainder of the spreadsheet computation."

"There's no way we have time to cover all the possibilities," Jack asserted. "All I'll attempt to do is show you a few of the ways I've used this concept of embedding commands in spreadsheets. The first three examples involve commands you already know about: LET, OBTAIN, and ACTIVATE. Then I'll introduce you to a new command, named IF, that we'll see more of tomorrow."

An Embedded Command with No Cell Value

Because he intended to make some changes to cells in column A, Jack executed the command

```
\border left 0
```

to take that column out of the left border. He moved the cell cursor to make #A1 the active cell and typed the command

```
e.deci=2
```

on the entry line. Notice that he did not preface it with a backslash. After he pressed the Enter key to signal the end of his entry, the screen appeared as portrayed in Figure 12–43. The message line showed that Jack's entry was now the definition of #A1. Whenever the environment computes this spreadsheet, it will first carry out the step prescribed by #A1's definition, which is simply a command letting E.DECI have

FIGURE 12–43   **A cell definition yielding no cell value**

```
                                              30 , 30   < #A1

1- :A        :B        :C       :D       :E       :F       :G        :H
 1![        ]          MONTHLY EXPENSE ALLOCATION      Jack Vander          !
 2!                                                                         !
 3!Hotel:    39.10                                                          !
 4!Meal:     22.75                                                          !
 5!                                                                         !
 6!          Monthly            Hotel                 Meal    Enter-        !
 7!Name      Salary   Nights    Total    Meals        Total   tainment Phone!
 8!                                                                         !
 9!Kevin     2500.00   4.00     156.40   12.50  284.37    71.09   155.00!
10!Kim       2600.00   3.00     117.30   12.00  273.00    68.25   155.00!
11!Kris      2400.00   4.00     156.40   12.50  284.37    71.09   155.00!
12!Tina      2800.00   6.00     234.60   13.50  307.12    76.78   155.00!
13!Toby      2000.00   4.80     187.68   12.90  293.48    73.37   155.00!
14!Kerry     2250.00   3.00     117.30   12.00  273.00    68.25   155.00!
15!Karen     2800.00   3.00     117.30   12.00  273.00    68.25   155.00!
16!Kathy     2100.00   3.50     136.85   12.25  278.69    69.67   155.00!
17!Jackie    2400.00   6.00     234.60   13.50  307.12    76.78   155.00!
17!Carol     2750.00   4.00     156.40   12.50  284.37    71.09   155.00!
19! TOTALS:  24600.00  41.30   1614.83  125.65 2858.54   714.63  1550.00!

e.deci=2
e.deci=2
```

a value of 2. As Figure 12–43 shows, this definition does not produce any value for #A1.

"I oftentimes use a cell at the start of a spreadsheet to be sure E.DECI is set to a value consistent with the numeric displays I want for the cells," remarked Jack. "That way, I don't have to worry about setting it to the desired value every time I use the spreadsheet. It's done automatically at the start of each spreadsheet computation. Other commands setting environment variables can be similarly embedded in a spreadsheet."

Embedded Commands with Cell Values

Earlier Jack had established the definitions for #A9 through #B18 with a CONVERT command. They therefore had constant definitions. He was now going to explain how #A9 through #A18 could be defined as OBTAIN commands, to yield the desired values for #A9 through #B18. But he first wanted the managers to see why such an approach might be desirable.

"What," he asked, "would happen if I changed one or more of the rep's salaries in the REP table?"

Aside from a few inaudible whispers and blank looks, there was no response to his question.

"You're absolutely right!" Jack exclaimed. "Nothing would happen. The spreadsheet would be entirely unaffected."

"But that's no good," said Don with a frown. "The spreadsheet would not be consistent with the table. It would be out-of-date."

"You'd have to do a new CONVERT command to bring the spreadsheet up to date," offered Tracey.

"Yes, but when?" demanded Brad. "If I'm in the midst of doing data base updates, the last thing I want to think about is which spreadsheets happen to have definitions that have just become outdated. Even if I could remember which ones they are, I'd find it bothersome to have to interrupt my data base processing to go off and do spreadsheet processing that I really don't care about at the moment!"

"I see what you mean," Tracey agreed. "It would be especially bad if there were many spreadsheets depending on different parts of the same changed data. The other possibility would be to update the cell definitions when we actually go to use a spreadsheet. But if we wait until then, we're likely to have forgotten whether the cells need to be updated or not. Or, we may not remember which cells need their definitions updated. So to be on the safe side, we'd need to remember which definitions came from tables and update them accordingly. That's not a happy prospect!"

Unable to resist any longer, Joy stepped in to calm the discussion. "You're all correct in realizing the importance of maintaining the consistency of definitions across spreadsheets and with a data base. You've also identified the importance of working with up-to-date definitions. Without consistent and up-to-date definitions, a spreadsheet is not of much value in supporting your decisions. Worst of all is the situation of basing your decisions on spreadsheets that you believe to be OK, but that are actually inconsistent or outdated. But don't despair, Jack has a solution that guarantees consistent and up-to-date spreadsheets."

"Right," Jack affirmed. "The specter of inconsistent or outdated salaries in this spreadsheet is due to one simple fact. Their cell definitions are constants and constants don't change by themselves. The solution then is to replace the constant definitions by something that is not constant. What do we really want #B9 to always be?"

"The monthly salary from the first record in REP," someone answered.

"Correct!" Jack exclaimed. "And we want #A9 to be the first name from that same record. Similarly, #A10 and #B10 should always be the FNAME and MOSAL values from the second REP record, and so on. So as the environment is computing the spreadsheet what do we want it to do when it hits #A9's definition?"

"I get it!" Stan replied. "We want it to obtain the first record and use its FNAME value as the cell's value."

"Exactly!" confirmed Jack. "Instead of regurgitating a constant, the spreadsheet would execute an OBTAIN command to get the latest data from the REP table. And then, when it has carried out that step in the spreadsheet procedure, what's next?"

"Well," Stan continued, "it would then carry out the step specified by #B9's definition, which would just be to use the obtained record's MOSAL value."

To demonstrate Stan's solution, Jack moved the cell cursor to #A9 and typed

```
e.supd=true;obtain first record from rep;rep.fname
```

on the entry line. Again, notice that this becomes the definition of #A9 because there is no leading backslash indicating immediate execution. When he pressed the Enter key the screen appeared as depicted in Figure 12–44, showing #A9's new definition in the message line. When #A9 is encountered during spreadsheet computation, the definition's first command will set E.SUPD to TRUE to suppress the display of subsequent OBTAIN results. Jack didn't want them overwriting the spreadsheet screen. The definition's second command will obtain REP's first record, making it the current record of REP. The final part of the definition simply says that the value of REP.FNAME should be used as #A9's value.

Jack moved the cell cursor to #B9. Because the first REP record would already have been obtained by the time this step in the spreadsheet procedure was reached, there was no need to again obtain it. He merely entered the field name

```
rep.mosal
```

as #B9's new definition, leaving the screen as shown in Figure 12–45. Whenever #B9 is encountered during spreadsheet computation, the environment will use the MOSAL value from the current REP record as the value of #B9.

"Now," Jack continued, "we'll define #A10 to be like #A9, but with two exceptions. We don't need to keep switching E.SUPD to TRUE once it's already TRUE, so we'll omit that command from #A10's defini-

FIGURE 12–44 Defining a cell in terms of a data management command

```
                                            30 , 30   V #A9

1- :A       :B      :C       :D      :E      :F      :G       :H
  1:               MONTHLY EXPENSE ALLOCATION          Jack Vander        !
  2:                                                                      !
  3:Hotel:      39.10                                                     !
  4:Meal:       22.75                                                     !
  5:                                                                      !
  6:          Monthly          Hotel          Meal   Enter-              !
  7:Name      Salary   Nights  Total   Meals  Total  tainment  Phone     !
  8:                                                                      !
  9:[Kevin  ]  2500.00   4.00   156.40  12.50  284.37   71.09   155.00!
 10:Kim        2600.00   3.00   117.30  12.00  273.00   68.25   155.00!
 11:Kris       2400.00   4.00   156.40  12.50  284.37   71.09   155.00!
 12:Tina       2800.00   6.00   234.60  13.50  307.12   76.78   155.00!
 13:Toby       2000.00   4.80   187.68  12.90  293.48   73.37   155.00!
 14:Kerry      2250.00   3.00   117.30  12.00  273.00   68.25   155.00!
 15:Karen      2800.00   3.00   117.30  12.00  273.00   68.25   155.00!
 16:Kathy      2100.00   3.50   136.85  12.25  278.69   69.67   155.00!
 17:Jackie     2400.00   6.00   234.60  13.50  307.12   76.78   155.00!
 18:Carol      2750.00   4.00   156.40  12.50  284.37   71.09   155.00!
 19: TOTALS:  24600.00  41.30  1614.83 125.65 2858.54  714.63  1550.00!

 e.supd=true;obtain first record from rep;rep.fname
 e.supd=true;obtain first record from rep;rep.fname
```

FIGURE 12–45 Defining a cell in terms of a table's field

```
                                            30 , 30   > #B9

1- :A       :B      :C       :D      :E      :F      :G       :H
  1:               MONTHLY EXPENSE ALLOCATION          Jack Vander        !
  2:                                                                      !
  3:Hotel:      39.10                                                     !
  4:Meal:       22.75                                                     !
  5:                                                                      !
  6:          Monthly          Hotel          Meal   Enter-              !
  7:Name      Salary   Nights  Total   Meals  Total  tainment  Phone     !
  8:                                                                      !
  9:Kevin     [2500.00]  4.00   156.40  12.50  284.37   71.09   155.00!
 10:Kim        2600.00   3.00   117.30  12.00  273.00   68.25   155.00!
 11:Kris       2400.00   4.00   156.40  12.50  284.37   71.09   155.00!
 12:Tina       2800.00   6.00   234.60  13.50  307.12   76.78   155.00!
 13:Toby       2000.00   4.80   187.68  12.90  293.48   73.37   155.00!
 14:Kerry      2250.00   3.00   117.30  12.00  273.00   68.25   115.00!
 15:Karen      2800.00   3.00   117.30  12.00  273.00   68.25   155.00!
 16:Kathy      2100.00   3.50   136.85  12.25  278.69   69.67   155.00!
 17:Jackie     2400.00   6.00   234.60  13.50  307.12   76.78   155.00!
 18:Carol      2750.00   4.00   156.40  12.50  284.37   71.09   155.00!
 19: TOTALS:  24600.00  41.30  1614.83 125.65 2858.54  714.63 15550.00!

 rep.mosal
 rep.mosal
```

FIGURE 12–46　Copying a command definition

```
                                              30 , 30   < #A10

1-  :A        :B        :C        :D        :E        :F        :G        :H
  1!                    MONTHLY EXPENSE ALLOCATION              Jack Vander        !
  2!                                                                               !
  3!Hotel:        39.10                                                            !
  4!Meal:         22.75                                                            !
  5!                                                                               !
  6!              Monthly               Hotel                   Meal    Enter-     !
  7!Name          Salary    Nights      Total     Meals        Total  tainment  Phone !
  8!                                                                               !
  9!Kevin        2500.00      4.00      156.40     12.50      284.37     71.09   155.00!
 10![Kim     ]   2600.00      3.00      117.30     12.00      273.00     68.25   155.00!
 11!Kris         2400.00      4.00      156.40     12.50      284.37     71.09   155.00!
 12!Tina         2800.00      6.00      234.60     13.50      307.12     76.78   155.00!
 13!Toby         2000.00      4.80      187.68     12.90      293.48     73.37   155.00!
 14!Kerry        2250.00      3.00      117.30     12.00      273.00     68.25   155.00!
 15!Karen        2800.00      3.00      117.30     12.00      273.00     68.25   155.00!
 16!Kathy        2100.00      3.50      136.85     12.25      278.69     69.67   155.00!
 17!Jackie       2400.00      6.00      234.60     13.50      307.12     76.78   155.00!
 18!Carol        2750.00      4.00      156.40     12.50      284.37     71.09   155.00!
 19! TOTALS:    24600.00     41.30     1614.83    125.65     2858.54    714.63  1550.00!

\copy #a10, #a11 to #a18
obtain next record from rep;rep.fname
```

tion. Secondly, instead of obtaining the first record, we want the environment to obtain the next record when it hits this step in the spreadsheet procedure."

He moved the cell cursor to #A10 and proceeded to enter

```
obtain next record from rep;rep.fname
```

as the cell's new definition. After a spreadsheet computation this cell would always display the obtained record's FNAME value as its own value. Because the cells beneath #A10 depended on successive REP records, their definitions can be identical to that of #A10. Thus Jack executed the command

```
\copy #a10, #a11 to #a18
```

to copy #A10's definition as the new definition for each cell in the range #A11 to #A18. Figure 12–46 shows the resultant screen appearance. Similarly he executed the command

```
\copy #b9, #b10 to #b18
```

FIGURE 12–47   Result of spreadsheet computation involving execution of data management compounds

```
                                                30 , 30   < #A10

1-   :A        :B       :C       :D       :E       :F       :G        :H
  1:                  MONTHLY EXPENSE ALLOCATION           Jack Vander       :
  2:                                                                         :
  3:Hotel:        39.10                                                      :
  4:Meal:         22.75                                                      :
  5:                                                                         :
  6:           Monthly           Hotel            Meal    Enter-             :
  7:Name        Salary   Nights   Total   Meals   Total  tainment  Phone    :
  9:                                                                         :
  9:Kevin      2600.00    4.00   156.40   12.50   284.37   71.09  155.00:
 10:[Kim    ]  2700.00    3.00   117.30   12.00   273.00   68.25  155.00:
 11:Kris      2500.00    4.00   156.40   12.50   284.37   71.09  155.00:
 12:Tina      2900.00    6.00   234.60   13.50   307.12   76.78  155.00:
 13:Toby      2100.00    4.80   187.68   12.90   293.48   73.37  155.00:
 14:Kerry     2350.00    3.00   117.30   12.00   273.00   68.25  155.00:
 15:Karen     2900.00    3.00   117.30   12.00   273.00   68.25  155.00:
 16:Kathy     2200.00    3.50   136.85   12.25   278.69   69.67  155.00:
 17:Jackie    2500.00    6.00   234.60   13.50   307.12   76.78  155.00:
 18:Carol     2850.00    4.00   156.40   12.50   284.37   71.09  155.00:
 19: TOTALS:  25600.00  41.30  1614.83  125.65  2858.54  714.63  1550.00:

\compute
obtain next record from rep;rep.fname
```

to make REP.MOSAL the definition of each cell in the range #B10 to #B18.

"Now let's change the values of MOSAL in the REP table," said Jack. "Then we'll see what happens when we compute the spreadsheet."

On the entry line he typed and executed the command

```
\change mosal in rep to mosal+100
```

to increase each rep's MOSAL value by 100. Naturally, this had no effect on the spreadsheet's cell values since it did not alter any of the definitions. It affected only the REP table contents. However, by executing the command

```
\compute
```

the new MOSAL values were reflected in the spreadsheet, as Figure 12–47 shows. The spreadsheet computation involved 10 executions of OBTAIN commands, each determining a pair of cell values. Observe that each cell value in the range #B9 to #B18 is now 100 greater than it was in Figure 12–46. Also, the value of #B19 is correspondingly larger.

"No matter what values exist for a field in the REP table," Jack stressed, "this spreadsheet is poised to handle them. We are entirely free from worrying about updating definitions for #A9 through #B18. Because of the definitions we've made, the computed values of those cells are eternally and automatically consistent with the REP table. Let's restore the original salaries."

This time Jack did not execute CHANGE on the spreadsheet's entry line. For variety, he invoked \BYE there to leave the spreadsheet screen and get the underscore prompt. After executing

```
change mosal in rep to mosal-100
```

to change REP's MOSAL values back to their original numbers, he executed

```
calc
```

to bring up the spreadsheet screen. The spreadsheet's cell values were unchanged from what they were in Figure 12–47. When he executed the command

```
\compute
```

on the entry line the new values were computed, reverting to the levels shown in Figure 12–46.

"I can embed *any* command in the definition of a cell?" asked Stan incredulously. He was overwhelmed by the wealth of new spreadsheet processing possibilities presented by that prospect. The other managers seemed to accept embedded commands as a matter of course, perhaps because they were unfamiliar with conventional spreadsheet packages.

"Sure enough," Joy replied. "If it's a PLOT command, a graph will appear when the spreadsheet computation gets to the cell. It may be a graph based on cell values calculated earlier in the computation procedure. As usual the graph will remain on the screen until you press the space bar, at which point the spreadsheet computation will proceed.

"If the embedded command is REPORT, a report will be generated at that step in the spreadsheet procedure. You might want REPORT to have a condition based on previously calculated cells and elements in the template it uses may have been defined in terms of cells. Similarly, you could embed a PRINT TEXT command whose condition involves cells and whose text has embedded commands that themselves reference spreadsheet cells.

"You might want to embed commands that change the value of fields in some record, based on what has been computed so far. For instance, you might define #M9 as REP.MOEXP = #L9. This would cause the MOEXP field updated every time the spreadsheet is computed. The embedded commands could involve forms processing. For instance, when the environment gets to a certain point in the spreadsheet procedure, you may want it to interact with you through a customized form. The values it gets from you through the form could be the result of your judgments about what has happened so far in the spreadsheet computation and the remainder of the computation may depend on the values you provide."

Embedding Spreadsheet-Specific Commands in Cell Definitions

Joy paused to catch her breath and let her sampling of examples sink in, knowing that it would be a while before they would begin to fully comprehend the implications. Jack again took the lead, noting that all examples to this point had involved commands that were not specific to spreadsheet processing. It turns out that spreadsheet-specific commands can also be embedded in cell definitions. This is accomplished by prefacing the command with the word CALC, just as was done earlier when executing such commands in response to the underscore prompt. Recall the CALC DISPLAY command in Figure 12–31.

In preparation for his example, Jack executed the commands

```
\border left 1
\deactivate #A1 to #L19
```

to make column A part of the left border and deactivate the stylized presentations of cell values. He then moved the cell cursor to #M9.

"What I have in mind," he explained, "is the conditional activation of cells in column L. Whenever I do a spreadsheet computation for 'what if' purposes, I'd like each expense total that exceeds, say, 60 percent of the corresponding monthly salary to be highlighted automatically. To do this, I'm going to embed the ACTIVATE command in column M cell definitions."

On the entry line he typed the definition

```
calc activate #L9 for #L9>.6*#B9
```

and pressed the Enter key. As the message line in Figure 12–48 shows, this command was now the definition of #M9. The command's condition indicates that activation of #L9's presentation style will occur if #L9's

FIGURE 12–48   Defining a cell to conditionally activate another cell

```
                                              30 , 30   V #M9

1- :A       :G       :H       :I      :J      :K       :L        :M
  1¦         Jack Vander                                                      ¦
  2¦                                    Per Mile:                             ¦
  3¦Hotel:                                0.22                                ¦
  4¦Meal:                               Mile/Day:  Rate:                      ¦
  5¦                                      110.00    0.03                      ¦
  6¦           Enter-                                                         ¦
  7¦Name       tainment  Phone   Postage  Mileage   Misc:  Totals            ¦
  8¦                                                                          ¦
  9¦Kevin        71.09   155.00  118.00   580.80   80.00  1445.67[        ]¦¦
 10¦Kim          68.25   155.00  118.00   562.65   83.20  1377.40            ¦
 11¦Kris         71.09   155.00  118.00   580.80   76.80  1442.47            ¦
 12¦Tina         76.78   155.00  118.00   617.10   89.60  1598.21            ¦
 13¦Toby         73.37   155.00  118.00   595.32   64.00  1486.84            ¦
 14¦Kerry        68.25   155.00  118.00   562.65   72.00  1366.20            ¦
 15¦Karen        68.25   155.00  118.00   562.65   89.60  1383.80            ¦
 16¦Kathy        69.67   155.00  118.00   571.72   67.20  1397.13            ¦
 17¦Jackie       76.78   155.00  118.00   617.10   76.80  1585.41            ¦
 18¦Carol        71.09   155.00  118.00   580.80   88.00  1453.67            ¦
 19¦ TOTALS:    714.63  1555.00 1180.00  5831.60  787.20 14536.80            ¦

calc activate #L9 for #L9>.6*#B9
calc activate #L9 for #L9>.6*#B9
```

value exceeds 60 percent of #B9's value. Recall that the style for the total expense allowance cells is a red foreground and black background.

Jack copied #M9's definition to the cells below by executing the command

```
\copy #m9, #m10 to #m19
```

on the entry line. When asked, he responded that all three cell references in the definition being copied should be adjusted. Thus, the definition of #M10 became

```
calc activate #L10 for #L10>.6*#B10
```

and so forth for the other column M cells. He moved the cell cursor leftward to column F so that column L was now the last column visible in the window. To show the effects of the new cell definitions, he executed the command

```
\compute
```

by pressing the F2 key. This resulted in Photo 40 in the color insert. It shows that, under the spreadsheet's proposed budget, five reps would have expense allowances exceeding 60 percent of their respective salaries.

"What would happen if in a subsequent computation one of these five was reduced to less than 60 percent?" asked Jack.

"It would still be highlighted, wouldn't it?" asked Debbie, "unless you deactivated it before then."

"That's right," Jack acknowledged. "Once a cell's activated, it stays activated until we tell the environment to deactivate it. Thus, we could get some misleading signals if we don't deactivate the cells at the start of each computation."

"Couldn't you just define one of the early cells in the spreadsheet procedure to be a DEACTIVATE command?" Debbie asked.

"Yes, but remember to preface it with a CALC," answered Jack. "That way it's handled automatically every time we do a COMPUTE and we don't have to bother typing and executing it before each spreadsheet computation."

Conditional Cell Values

As his final example of embedding commands in cell definitions, Jack planned to introduce the IF command. As the next chapter will show, this is not a spreadsheet-specific command. Nevertheless, it can be handy in a cell definition. When embedded in a cell's definition, the IF command lets a cell's value depend on whether a condition is satisfied. The IF command specifies what the value will be when the condition is satisfied and what it will be when the condition is not satisfied.

"Presently, each of the entertainment cells is defined to be one fourth of the corresponding meal allowance," explained Jack, as he moved the cell cursor to #G9. "But what if we want to try a more sophisticated way of determining entertainment allowances? Let's say that if the sum of a rep's hotel and meal allowances is less than 500 then we want to put a cap of 50 on the entertainment allowance. Otherwise, we'll let entertainment be one fourth of the meal allowance. I can specify all this in a single IF command in #G9's definition. Watch."

On the entry line, Jack typed

```
if #d9+#f9<500 then x=50;else x=.25*#f9;endif;x
```

as the definition of #G9. The word IF can be followed by any condition. The word THEN can be followed by one or more commands, each terminated by a semicolon. Here, there is one LET command that will be executed if the condition is found to be TRUE. The word ELSE can

FIGURE 12–49   Definition for a conditional cell value

```
                                                  30 , 30   > #G9

1— :A      :F      :G       :H      :I      :J      :K       :L
  1¦               Jack Vander                                        ¦
  2¦                                        Per Mile:                 ¦
  3¦Hotel:                                    0.22                    ¦
  4¦Meal:                                   Mile/Day:  Rate:          ¦
  5¦                                         110.00    0.03           ¦
  6¦               Meal    Enter-                                     ¦
  7¦Name           Total  tainment Phone   Postage Mileage  Misc.  Totals ¦
  8¦                                                                 ¦
  9¦Kevin         284.37[  50.00] 155.00  118.00  580.80   80.00  1424.58¦
 10¦Kim           273.00   68.25  155.00  118.00  562.65   83.20  1377.40¦
 11¦Kris          284.37   71.09  155.00  118.00  580.80   76.80  1442.47¦
 12¦Tina          307.12   76.78  155.00  118.00  617.10   89.60  1598.21¦
 13¦Toby          293.48   73.37  155.00  118.00  595.32   64.00  1486.84¦
 14¦Kerry         273.00   68.25  155.00  118.00  562.65   72.00  1366.20¦
 15¦Karen         273.00   68.25  155.00  118.00  562.65   89.60  1383.80¦
 16¦Kathy         278.69   69.67  155.00  118.00  571.72   67.20  1397.13¦
 17¦Jackie        307.12   76.78  155.00  118.00  617.10   76.80  1585.41¦
 18¦Carol         284.37   71.09  155.00  118.00  580.80   88.00  1453.67¦
 19¦ TOTALS:     2858.54  693.54 1550.00 1180.00 5831.60  787.20 14515.70¦

if #d9+#f9<500 then x=50; else x=.25*#f9;endif;x
if #d9+#f9<500 then x=50; else x=.25*#f9;endif;x
```

also be followed by one or more commands, each terminated by a semicolon. Here, there is one LET command telling the environment what to execute if the condition evaluates to FALSE. The word ENDIF denotes the end of the IF command. The cell's value will be determined by the value of the working variable X after the IF command is executed.

As the message line in Figure 12–49 shows, the IF command became #G9's definition when Jack pressed the Enter key. Based on this new definition, the value of #G9 changed from 71.09 to 50.00. Because E.ICOM was TRUE, the spreadsheet was computed to yield new values for #G9, #L9, and #L19 as well. The COPY command could be used to give #G10 through #G18 adjusted versions of #G9's definition if desired.

"It seems," observed Debbie, "that what you've done with IF is to put commands within another command. There's the overall IF command that is ended by ENDIF and within it there are two other commands. One goes along with THEN and the other with ELSE."

"You're right," responded Jack. "In effect, we've established two alternative definitions for #G9. One tells the environment to let #G9 have a value of 50. The other says to let #G9's value be one fourth of #F9's value. By way of its condition, the IF command lets us tell the environment which of the alternatives should be used in any particular spreadsheet computation. As you'll see tomorrow, there's another command in addition to IF that lets us specify more than two alternatives."

"I take it," continued Debbie, "that there's no restriction on the IF command's condition. For instance, it could be like any of the conditions we've used in SQL queries."

"Right again," said Jack. "For instance, we could edit this IF command, replacing its condition by something like REP.TID IN ["3", "6","9"]. We'd then copy it with adjustments to cells #G10 through #G18. The entertainment cap of 50 would then result only for those territories 3, 6, and 9. Notice that this condition depends solely on data in the REP table's current record. A condition does not have to reference cells. Because the first step in each row of this spreadsheet procedure obtains a record and makes it current, everything is ready by the time a row's seventh step in column G is reached. The IF condition can be properly evaluated."

BASIC IDEAS

After the session adjourned for the day, the managers took some time to try out for themselves what Jack had shown them that afternoon. By now, many had become acclimated to using the HELP command to jog their memories and answer questions about available commands. Jack and Joy mingled with them for awhile to provide backup assistance. Though Jack had acquainted the group with most of the spreadsheet facilities he knew, he was well aware that the environment's spreadsheet capability went beyond what he had mastered. He was interested in learning more.

Taking Joy aside, Jack proposed, "I'd like to spend some time on spreadsheets with you, touching some of the areas I'm not yet familiar with."

"That's an interesting proposition." She touched his arm and smiled a knowing smile. "Let's do it this evening. You obviously already know a great deal, but maybe I can expose you to some of the finer points. Anyway, we'll cover whatever topics you want, including some of the more advanced embedded commands if you like."

As the evening wore on, they shared a variety of rewarding spreadsheet experiences. Jack and Joy were pleased with the progress the managers had made that day. They now understood both the purpose and mechanics of the spreadsheet approach to managing knowledge. *A spreadsheet represents procedural knowledge in a grid of cells.* Each cell can have a definition and a value. Its definition specifies what is to be done when that cell is encountered in the course of computing the spreadsheet. Collectively, all the cell definitions for a spreadsheet are sometimes called a spreadsheet template.

Spreadsheet computation consists of processing the cell definitions, step by step, to determine values for the cells. Cell values can be seen through a viewing window on the spreadsheet screen. By altering cell definitions and recomputing the spreadsheet, the effects of different assumptions can be readily seen on the screen. This kind of "what if" investigation lies at the heart of spreadsheet analysis. It is what makes spreadsheet analysis so valuable in supporting decision-making activities.

In conventional spreadsheet packages, a cell definition is an expression that either is a constant or involves a calculation based on other cells' values. A cell is defined by moving the cell cursor to make it the active cell and then typing in the definition. An existing definition can be altered by replacing it with a new definition, editing it (EDIT), or eliminating it (UNDEFINE). When columns and rows are inserted or deleted from a spreadsheet, existing cell definitions are altered as needed (COLUMN, ROW).

A cell can also be defined as a copy of an existing cell's definition (COPY). Any cell referenced in the copied definition can be selected for automatic adjustment with respect to relative cell locations. In the environment, a batch of cell definitions can be established with a single command that draws on tabular data (CONVERT). *In addition, the environment allows any cell to be defined in terms of one or more commands* (e.g., LET, OBTAIN, ACTIVATE, IF). Any definition can be safeguarded from alteration or viewing (PROTECT, UNPROTECT, CONCEAL, REVEAL).

Cell values are the result of a spreadsheet computation (COMPUTE or E.ICOM=TRUE). The computation consists of following the steps prescribed by successive cell definitions. The resultant values appear in the spreadsheet screen. Any block of cell values can also be displayed on a printout (DISPLAY with E.OPRN=TRUE). Cell values can also be referenced just like working variable or field values in a wide variety of commands. Cell references can be made not only on the spreadsheet screen's entry line, but also in response to the underscore prompt while the spreadsheet screen is not even visible.

There are several ways to customize the presentation of cell values. Pictures can be used with cells (USING). The widths of columns can be enlarged or reduced (WIDTH). Cells can be styled with desired colors and special audiovisual effects (STYLE). Cell presentation styles can be conditionally activated and deactivated when desired (ACTIVATE, DEACTIVATE). Cells along the top or left edges of a spreadsheet can be locked into the borders, so their values will always be visible on the spreadsheet screen. In addition, the spreadsheet screen can contain multiple windows for looking at distant cells simultaneously (WIN-DOW).

References

1. Allen, B. R. *VisiCalc—IBM PC: An Executive's Guide*. Reston, Va.: Reston, 1984.

2. Cain, N. W. *1-2-3 at Work*. Reston, Va.: Reston, 1984.

3. Carroll, T. O. *Decision Power with Supersheets*. Homewood, Ill.: Dow Jones-Irwin, 1986.

4. Glau, G. R. *Controlling Your Cash Flow with 1-2-3 or Symphony*. Homewood, Ill.: Dow Jones-Irwin, 1987.

5. Holsapple, C. W. "Synergistic Software Integration for Microcomputers." *Systems and Software* 3, no. 2 (1984).

6. *KnowledgeMan Reference Manual*, version 2. Lafayette, Ind.: MDBS, Inc., 1985.

There's Relhoks, still out of step. Someday, maybe he'll learn about the automatic steps!

Chapter Thirteen

Programming

It was shortly before the training session was to reconvene that Jack and Joy became engaged in a lively conversation with Don. He was uncharacteristically excited as he told them of a discovery he had made the prior evening. "There I was, embedding commands in a spreadsheet, when it suddenly dawned on me! Here was the solution to something that had been bothering me for several days."

"And what was that?" asked Joy curiously.

"Well," Don explained, "every time I went to enter the environment during a practice break, I started off by executing the same series of commands. They are mostly for setting the environment the way I like it, for putting tables in use, and redefining some of the function keys. For instance, I like a green background better than blue so I switch E.BACG; I usually switch E.DECI to 2; and I define F1 to be HELP. As I became increasingly familiar with what the environment could do, there were more and more initial things I wanted to do on each entry into the environment. In fact, I keep a list of the series of commands I want to execute at the start of each practice. Otherwise, I tend to forget some of them."

"So you find it bothersome to have to type in the list of commands every time you enter the environment," Joy speculated.

"Right," confirmed Don. "Gradually it has become clear to me that I'd like to automate this repetitious procedure of setting up the environment. What I'd like is a way to type in my list of commands one time and somehow save them in the knowledge system. Each time I enter the environment, I'd like a way to tell it to execute all the commands in the saved list."

"So, a spreadsheet gives you that ability?" asked Jack. He, as well as Joy, saw where Don was leading. It was encouraging to see one of their "children," as Joy privately called them, develop his own insights based on experiences they provided.

"It sure does!" Don exclaimed. "All I have to do is define #A1 to be the first command on my list, #B1 is the second, and so forth. The spreadsheet doesn't have any cells defined as constant or calculated expressions. They're all defined as commands. Once I had embedded all of my commands in the spreadsheet, I exited from the spreadsheet screen and used the SAVE command to preserve the spreadsheet in a context file."

"I see," mused Jack. "You captured a procedure of commands in a spreadsheet and did not intend to use them for 'what if' analysis."

"Then," Don continued, "I left the environment back to the operating system. When I reentered the environment, the first thing I did was load the context file. Interestingly, the spreadsheet screen did not reappear."

"That's because you didn't save the spreadsheet from the entry line, but in response to the underscore prompt instead," Jack explained.

"I figured as much," said Don. "I don't care about seeing the spreadsheet screen anyway. It's cells wouldn't have any values. Well, once it was loaded, all I had to do was execute the COMPUTE command by typing: CALC COMPUTE. Behind the scenes this went through the spreadsheet and executed each of the embedded commands! Pretty nifty, right?"

Jack and Joy smiled in unison and nodded in agreement, as Don went on, "Later, if I want to add a new command to the procedure or edit an existing one, I'll just use CALC to bring up the spreadsheet screen and make the change. It's easy!"

"Well then, I think you'll really like what we're going to discuss today, and you might find it even easier," said Jack, glancing at his watch. "In fact, it's time to get started."

BEYOND SPREADSHEETS

Spreadsheets are handy for presenting the results of a series of steps in a special matrix form. They are very workable when procedural knowledge can be naturally organized into a sequence of assignment statements, each assigning a value to a cell by evaluating the cell's definition. There is added flexibility when cell definitions can include commands. Valuable as they are, spreadsheets are no panacea when it comes to representing and processing procedural knowledge.

For some procedures, the mode of presentation embodied in a spreadsheet screen is inappropriate. As Don had discovered, it may be that no presentation of values is needed or desired as a procedure's steps are followed. Some procedures may be highly interactive. In such a procedure there can be many steps that involve getting inputs from the user, interspersed with other steps that do calculations, data management, graphics, and so forth. Customized user interfaces may be desired for this interaction. With ordinary spreadsheets, the following of a procedure is not at all interactive. Once the computation begins, it proceeds without user interaction until the last cell definition has been processed.

Aside from presentation limitations, the restriction of conventional spreadsheets to a sequence of calculations makes them inappropriate for many procedures. A more flexible way of representing procedural knowledge would be quite beneficial. The ability to embed commands in cell definitions is a dramatic step toward increased flexibility, as Don had discovered, but there is an alternative way to represent procedural knowledge. It offers the same degree of flexibility and is much more convenient for specifying many kinds of procedures.

Instead of embedding commands in a spreadsheet, they are simply typed into a text file. The first command is typed as the first line of text, the next command is typed as the second line, and so forth. Usually it is permissible for a large command to extend across multiple lines. Each command represents a step in a procedure. As a whole, the text file represents a procedure. A single command is all that is needed to perform such a procedure, causing each of its commands to be executed in sequence.

Because the procedure's commands are stored in a text file, all of the usual text management facilities are available for revising, inserting, and deleting individual commands as needed. Unlike Don's solution, this makes it possible to see the entire flow of commands in a glance, rather than looking at them one at a time on a spreadsheet's message line. A procedure represented and processed in the foregoing manner is commonly called a *program*. The activity of specifying the commands that make up a program is commonly called *programming* [6], [7].

NONINTERACTIVE PROGRAMS

"Don has pointed out a problem that I suspect all of you have encountered," said Jack. "There is a sequence of commands that you tend to repeatedly type in and execute. Every time you enter the environment, you know that there are certain steps you want to take to get set for the processing that will follow. Taken as a whole, these steps form a chunk of procedural knowledge that you've stored in your own memory. Whenever you enter the environment, you perform the steps. That is, you type in and execute a series of commands."

"Yeah, that is a bit of a drag," remarked Brad, as the others nodded in agreement.

"You'll be glad to hear that after today you'll never have to do that again if you don't want to," Jack announced. "I'm going to show you that the procedural knowledge in your memory can be stored in the environment's memory. Once it's there, you can command the environment to perform all of its steps automatically. For instance, when you enter the environment all you need do is execute a single PERFORM command and the environment will carry out all the setup steps automatically!"

Typing Commands as Lines of Text

The managers were especially attentive as Jack elaborated. "All we need to do is enter the desired sequence of commands as text. We'll execute the text command to start a new file called SETUP.IPF on the drive A diskette. Because the file will contain a procedure consisting of commands, we'll give it an IPF extension. In this environment, it's common practice to use an IPF rather than TXT extension for *procedure files*. That makes it easy to tell them apart from files holding narrative text."

"Does text management work any differently when you're creating an IPF file than what we're accustomed to with TXT files?" asked Tracey.

"I'm glad you raised that question," Jack replied. "There is one small, but beneficial difference. Remember that we get automatic word wrap when entering lines in a TXT file. That doesn't happen when working on an IPF file. What we do is type in a command on one line and press the Enter key to signal that we're finished with it, the cursor jumps to the start of the next line where we begin the next command, and so on. As you know, some commands can be lengthy, while others are short. We don't want a long command wrapping to the next line. Instead we can just keep on typing a command on a single line until we've completed it."

"But what if the command is too long to fit on one line of the text screen?" asked Brad.

"Just keep on typing," Jack answered, "even if it's more than 80 characters long. The text will automatically scroll horizontally in the text area."

"Ah," said Brad, "like the spreadsheet scrolls to the left within the viewing window when the cell cursor is already at the right edge of the window and we press the right arrow key."

"Right," Jack confirmed. "It's the same idea with text. In fact, you can think of the screen's text area as being a viewing window into a big piece of text that can have hundreds or thousands of lines, each of which can be up to 255 characters long."

"OK. But what if a command is more than 255 characters long?" persisted Brad.

"Then you'll need to continue it on the next line," Jack answered. "Whenever you want to continue a command on the next line, just type a backslash before pressing the Enter key. When the environment performs the procedure, it will then understand that you want it to interpret the next line as a continuation of the command.

An Example

To demonstrate what he had been describing, Jack executed the command

```
text "a:setup.ipf"
```

as soon as he entered the environment. The usual blue text screen appeared. Because SETUP.IPF had not previously existed, the text area was blank. He immediately began to type commands into the text area, one command per line. They were all examples of commands someone might want to execute at the outset of a processing session. When he had entered several lines, Jack escaped to the status line and typed

```
write
```

yielding the screen shown in Figure 13–1. When he pressed the Enter key, the text area's command sequence was written to the SETUP.IPF file on the drive A diskette.

The first three commands in Jack's procedure are obviously for switching some environment controls. Next is a REDEFINE command for making function key F1 equivalent to the HELP command. It is followed by commands to put the REP, PERF, and PROD tables in use. Then there is a line beginning with an exclamation mark. Jack explained that whenever an exclamation mark appears outside of quotes, the remainder of the line is considered to be a *comment* rather than part of a command. When the environment performs a procedure, all comments are ignored.

"The purpose of commands in this procedure are pretty obvious," Jack asserted. "So I really didn't have to include any comments. But as you develop larger or more complex procedures, you'll probably want to include comments. Weeks or months later when you go back to look at a procedure, the comments can help you remember just what it was you had in mind for a particular step. Comments can also make a procedure more readable, as can indentation. It's OK to indent commands. They don't all have to begin in the first column."

Jack's SETUP procedure also illustrates that multiple commands

FIGURE 13–1   Commands in a noninteractive program

```
   Line:21     Col:1      a:setup.ipf    Command: write
e.deci=2
e.lstr=25
e.bacg="ggggg"
redefine function 1 "help\\13"
use "a:rep.itb"
use "a:perf.itb" with "a:perftp.ind"
use "a:prod.itb"
! Display sum and average statistics only
   e.dvar=false
   e.dcnt=false
   e.dmin=false
   e.dmax=false
   e.dsdv=false
! Initially, suppress page numbering & don't calculate statistics for queries
   e.spgn=true;e.stat=false
! Declare some macros for commonly used pictures
macro f4dd using "$f,fff.dd"
macro f6 using "$fff,fff"
! Set up normal page depth
e.pdep=65
```

can be specified on a single line, provided they are separated by semi-colons. As an alternative to loading previously saved macros from a context file, MACRO commands can be included in a procedure file. When the file is performed, those commands will be executed, making the macros part of the present processing context.

After giving the managers sufficient time to be satisfied that he had done nothing more than type in ordinary commands as text, Jack escaped to the status line. He issued the command

```
bye
```

to get the underscore prompt. With special emphasis he declared, "We have just represented our procedural knowledge in an IPF file. But none of that knowledge has been used yet! Not one of the commands I just typed in has been executed. As you can see, the environment variables still have their original default values."

As he spoke, Jack executed the OUTPUT command

```
?e.deci,e.lstr,e.pdep
```

and the environment responded by outputting 5, 15, and 60. The screen background was its usual black, rather than the green requested in the SETUP procedure. He executed the commands

```
show
show macro
```

to prove that there were presently no tables in use and no macros in the present context.

"Now, with a single command," continued Jack, "I'm going to execute all the commands in SETUP. As I'd mentioned earlier, this is the PERFORM command. It can carry out all the steps in any procedure file we've stored in the knowledge system, and there can be many such files."

When Jack executed the command

```
perform "a:setup"
```

the disk drive light came on and a moment later a fresh underscore prompt appeared against a green background. The entire procedure had been performed. Notice that the IPF extension was not specified in the PERFORM command. When no extension is specified, IPF is assumed. To prove that the procedure's commands had indeed been executed, Jack executed a few additional commands as shown in Figure 13–2.

"You might be interested in knowing," chimed Joy, "that SETUP is a program! It is a little piece of software. It is composed of instructions that, when executed, cause the computer to behave in a certain way. When Jack performed the SETUP procedure, he was executing a program. The operating system, the environment, and SETUP are all examples of programs. Just as the operating system serves as the host for executing the environment, the environment serves as the host for executing SETUP or any other program you might construct from the environment's commands."

"So now you know how to write a program!" Jack exclaimed. "Right now, each of you could use the TEXT command to specify your own sequence of commands. And once you've preserved it in an IPF file, you can later perform it whenever you want. Neither you nor I are professional programmers like those in the company's MIS department, but we can still develop our own programs for carrying out procedures that we need to use over and over again. Capturing such procedural knowledge in a program makes life easier and can save a good deal of time and effort."

FIGURE 13–2   **Before and after performing the SETUP procedure**

```
_?e.deci,e.lstr,e.pdep
        5.00000        15.00000        60.00000
_show
No tables open
_show macro
_perform "a:setup"
_?e.deci,e.lstr,e.pdep
          2.00          25.00          65.00
_show
Tables Currently In Use:
Table name    File name
----------    ---------
  PROD        a:prod.itb
  PERF        a:perf.itb
  REP         a:rep.itb (default)
_show macro
F4DD
F6
_Select name phone mosal f4dd moexp f4dd from rep where mosal > 2700
         NAME                    PHONE        MOSAL      MOEXP

Tina F. Lee            (317) 299-8393     $2,800.00     $988.20
Karen V. Bruckner     (433) 442-8201     $2,800.00   $1,335.00
Carol O. Lynn         (412) 832-5643     $2,750.00   $1,229.73

 —
```

"But it all seems so simple," remarked Tracey with a trace of disbelief in her voice, "just typing a sequence of commands pretty much like we'd type in regular text. Can a program contain any of the commands we've learned?

"It *is* simple!" Jack affirmed enthusiastically. He executed the TEXT command to again bring the text area of Figure 13–1 into view. "The reason you find it simple is that you already understand all the individual commands. So it's just a matter of specifying them in the sequence you desire. Any command that you could execute directly, in response to the underscore prompt, can also be included in any program you develop [10]. If we know enough to type in and directly execute a sequence of commands one by one, then we know enough to specify a program composed of that same command sequence."

INTERACTIVE PROGRAMS

"It's clear," observed Dan, "that a program can be a big time saver for a procedure that we need to use repeatedly. But for my own usage, I don't think I'd want to perform the same setup every time I enter the environment. Depending on the kind of processing I intend to do,

I may want E.DECI to be 0 or 1 sometimes and I may want a larger E.LSTR. And if I'm not in a 'green' mood that day, I might want some other background color."

"Wouldn't you just write several variations of the setup procedure to different IPF files?" offered Stan. "That would give you numerous setup programs. When you enter the environment, you'd just perform the one that matches your needs and moods."

"That might be OK in principle," retorted Dan, "but I think it would be unwieldy in practice. I'd have to keep umpteen programs hanging around that vary just slightly from each other. I'd have to remember which one did what. And if I wanted to make a change that affected them all, such as adding a new macro, it would be pretty laborious to go in and do the same editing to each one of them. Surely, there's a better way."

Remembering her college programming days, Debbie suggested, "What you'd like is a program that asks you to enter values for the things that you want to vary in a setup procedure. So instead of blindly switching E.DECI to 2, you'd like the SETUP program to let you tell it what value you want for E.DECI."

Debbie had hit on the solution to Dan's problem: an *interactive program*. This is a program that, when executed, allows the user to interact with it. That is, the program has certain steps that solicit responses from whoever is executing it. One kind of command for getting input from a user is the INPUT command.

Input Prompting

"Let's see how we would revise the SETUP program along the lines of Debbie's suggestion," Jack declared. "As you all know, executing a GETFORM command allows us to enter values for the variables corresponding to a form's Get elements. If we wanted, we could include GETFORM as a step in our procedure. Of course, we'd have to paint a form first. I'm not going to get that fancy here. Instead, we'll use a new command named INPUT for several of the steps in our procedure."

He escaped to the status line and issued the command

```
number
```

which caused the text area to shift rightward by nine columns. Line numbers appeared on the left side of the screen. Numbers are not part of the text itself. Reissuing the NUMBER command would cause the text area to revert to its normal appearance. When explaining the

FIGURE 13–3   Commands in the interactive SETUP program

```
   Line:21     Col:2      a:setup.ipf    Insert              Press ^L for help
1       clear
2       e.deci=2
3       e.lstr=80
4       at 1,1 output "ENVIRONMENT  SETUP" using "%31*%18r%31*"
5       templstr=25
6       at 3,5 input e.deci using "n" with "How many decimal digits?"
7       at 5,5 input templstr using "nnn" with "Default length of strings?"
8       at 7,5 output "Color codes: A(black) O(brown) U(blue) W(white)"
9       at 8,18 output "C(cyan)  G(green) R(red)  M(magenta)"
10      at 9,10 output "What background color do you want for:"
11      at 10,15 input s using "a" with "spreadsheet?"
12      at 11,15 input g using "a" with "graphics?"
13      at 12,15 input t using "a" with "text?"
14      at 13,15 input o using "a" with "other screens?"
15      e.bacg=s+g+t+o+o
16      e.lstr=templstr
17      release variable
18      redefine function 1 "help\\13"
19      !use "a:rep.itb"
20      !use "a:perf.itb" with "a:perftp.ind"
21      !use "a:prod.itb"
22      ! Display sum and average statistics only
23          e.dvar=false
24          e.dcnt=false
```

workings of a program, line numbers can be useful for reference purposes.

Jack began editing the SETUP program to conform with the more elaborate and flexible procedure Debbie had suggested. After making a number of changes, the text screen appeared as shown in Figure 13–3. He explained each change as he proceeded.

By inserting the CLEAR command as the program's first step, Jack was specifying that he always wanted the screen to clear as soon as SETUP is performed. As the command was inserted the line numbers were automatically adjusted. He changed the initial value of E.LSTR to 80, explaining that for the interaction that would follow he wanted to be able to have some long (i.e., greater than 25) strings appear on the screen. The first of these would be produced by the new OUTPUT command in line 4.

When executed, line 5 would give an initial value of 25 to a new working variable named TEMPLSTR. This variable is where the program would keep the string length specified by the user until the very long E.LSTR value was no longer needed by SETUP for long strings in its own interaction with the user. Line 6 is the first example of an INPUT command. When executed, this command will input a value from the user and assign it to E.DECI. The picture indicates that exactly one numeral will be accepted as input. The INPUT command will reject any mistaken attempt to input any character other than a single numeral.

When this INPUT command is executed, the user will be presented with the prompt message of

How many decimal digits?

beginning at column 5 of line 3 on the screen. Because E.DECI will have a value of 2 when the INPUT command is executed, that value will appear immediately following the prompt. By pressing the Enter key alone, the user can stay with the value 2. If a numeral is typed before pressing the Enter key, it replaces the 2 on the screen and becomes E.DECI's new value.

The INPUT command on line 7 will input a value to the TEMPLSTR working variable. Its picture will let an entered value be up to three numerals. As with E.DECI, the TEMPLSTR variable will have a value when the INPUT command is executed. Thus the user will see 25 appear following the prompt message. That value can be edited or replaced as desired.

Lines 8 through 10 are ordinary OUTPUT commands. When executed, their results will appear at the specified screen coordinates. As lines 11 through 14 show, they will be followed by the execution of four more INPUT commands, each accepting a color code input from the user. The input values are assigned to the working variables S, G, T, and O. Because none of these has a value before its INPUT command is executed, the user will simply see an underscore following the prompt message. When a color code is typed, it will replace the underscore. When the Enter key is pressed, that code will become the variable's value as the INPUT command's processing terminates and the next command is executed.

When executed, the LET command on line 15 constructs a proper value for E.BACG by concatenating the variables' values in proper sequence. Remember, the first E.BACG code controls the spreadsheet background, the second controls graphics screen backgrounds, the third is for text screens, and the last is for ordinary command entry screens. At this stage in the procedure there are no further pictureless strings to be displayed. As a result, it is now reasonable to let E.LSTR be equal to the value input into TEMPLSTR.

Line 17's command will release all working variables (i.e., S, G, T, O, TEMPLSTR) from memory. They are no longer of any value once this step in the procedure is reached. If there is a possibility of other working variables existing when SETUP is performed, then the command

```
release s,g,t,o,templstr
```

should be used instead.

Program Comments

Next, Jack inserted exclamation marks in front of the three USE commands. "As you may have found out in your practices," he explained, "if you attempt to use a table that is already in use, the environment issues an error message on the screen. Because of our last SETUP performance, all three tables are now in use. To avoid getting error messages when we perform the new SETUP, I'm going to turn these commands into comments for the time being. The exclamation marks will cause them to be ignored when I do the next PERFORM."

"What Jack has just done," chimed Joy, "is a common practice when developing programs. It's called 'commenting out' a command. It lets you get rid of a step from a procedure without actually deleting it. Later, if you want the command to again participate in the program, you just delete the exclamation mark."

As Figure 13–4 shows, Jack made one last change to the program. He moved the cursor to the bottom of the text. The text area and line numbers scrolled accordingly. The new final command would simply output a message indicating that the SETUP program had finished its execution. He escaped to the status line and issued the command

```
write
```

to write the new rendition of the program to its disk file.

Performing an Interactive Program

After issuing the BYE command to leave the text screen, Jack executed the command

```
perform "a:setup"
```

to illustrate the effects of the changes just made. The screen cleared momentarily before taking on the appearance shown in Figure 13–5. A cursor was blinking on the numeral 2, awaiting user input. Rather than pressing the Enter key to accept 2 as the number of decimal digits,

FIGURE 13–4   Adding a new final command to the program

```
    Line:35      Col:60      a:setup.ipf    Insert            Press ^L for help
 12      at 11,15 input g using "a" with "graphics?"
 13      at 12,15 input t using "a" with "text?"
 14      at 13,15 input o using "a" with "other screens?"
 15      e.bacg=s+g+t+o+o
 16      e.lstr=templstr
 17      release variable
 18      redefine function 1 "help\\13"
 19      !use "a:rep.itb"
 20      !use "a:perf.itb" with "a:perftp.ind"
 21      !use "a:prod.itb"
 22      ! Display sum and average statistics only
 23         e.dvar=false
 24         e.dcnt=false
 25         e.dmin=false
 26         e.dmax=false
 27         e.dsdv=false
 28      ! Initially, suppress page numbering & don't calculate statistics for q
 29         e.spgn=true;e.stat=false
 30      ! Declare some macros for commonly used pictures
 31      macro f4dd using "$f,fff.dd"
 32      macro f6 using "$fff,fff"
 33      ! Set up normal page depth
 34      e.pdep=65
 35      at 15,1 ? "ENVIRONMENT SETUP COMPLETE" using "%27*%26r%27*"
```

FIGURE 13–5   Executing line 6 of the revised SETUP program

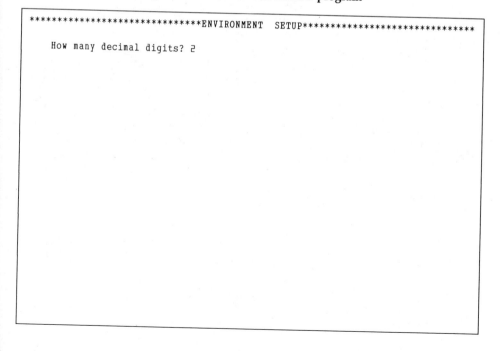

```
********************************ENVIRONMENT   SETUP********************************

    How many decimal digits? 2
```

FIGURE 13–6   Executing line 11 of the revised SETUP program

```
*******************************ENVIRONMENT  SETUP*********************************

    How many decimal digits?  0

    Default length of strings?  25

    Color codes: A(black)  O(brown)  U(blue)  W(white)
                 C(cyan)  G(green)  R(red)  M(magenta)
        What background color do you want for:
            spreadsheet?  _
```

he typed a zero. It replaced the 2 on the screen. When he now pressed the Enter key, the INPUT command in line 6 of SETUP concluded its execution by giving E.DECI a value of 0.

Execution proceeded to the next command, which was also an INPUT. This time Jack merely pressed the Enter key to accept the value of 25 that was already displayed on the screen. Execution of lines 8 through 10 caused the specified outputs to appear at the specified places on the screen. Execution of the INPUT command in line 11 caused processing to again pause, waiting for a user response as portrayed in Figure 13–6. Notice that no default value appeared. There was simply an underscore prompt where one of the color codes output above it could be entered.

When Jack typed

u

and pressed the Enter key, the next INPUT command began executing. He was instantly prompted to input a color code for graphics as shown in Figure 13–7. He typed

a

FIGURE 13-7   Executing line 12 of the revised SETUP program

```
*******************************ENVIRONMENT  SETUP********************************

    How many decimal digits? 0

    Default length of strings?  25

    Color codes: A(black) O(brown) U(blue) W(white)
                 C(cyan)  G(green) R(red)  M(magenta)
        What background color do you want for:
             spreadsheet? u
             graphics? _
```

to request a black graphics background. In a similar fashion, he responded with

```
u
r
```

to get blue and red backgrounds for text and other screens respectively. The remainder of the program's commands executed in sequence, until the PERFORM command had completed its processing of SETUP. As depicted in Figure 13–8, the underscore prompt appeared, against a red background.

Jack executed the commands

```
?e.deci,e.lstr,e.pdep
?e.bacg
```

to verify that the environment variables had the values Jack had specified during his interaction with the SETUP program. Figure 13–9 shows the results.

Dan liked the interaction program solution. "That's certainly better

FIGURE 13–8   Execution of SETUP via the PERFORM command completed

```
*******************************ENVIRONMENT  SETUP********************************

    How many decimal digits? 0

    Default length of strings?  25

    Color codes: A(black) O(brown) U(blue) W(white)
                 C(cyan)  G(green) R(red)  M(magenta)
         What background color do you want for:
              · spreadsheet? u
                graphics? a
                text? u
                other screens? r


***************************ENVIRONMENT SETUP COMPLETE***************************
```

FIGURE 13–9   Resultant values for the environment variables

```
*******************************ENVIRONMENT  SETUP********************************

    How many decimal digits? 0

    Default length of strings?  25

    Color codes: A(black) O(brown) U(blue) W(white)
                 C(cyan)  G(green) R(red)  M(magenta)
         What background color do you want for:
                spreadsheet? u
                graphics? a
                text? u
                other screens? r

***************************ENVIRONMENT SETUP COMPLETE***************************
_?e.deci,e.lstr,e.pdep
              0          25            65
_?e.bacg
uaurr
  _
```

than creating, storing, and maintaining many different variations of SETUP. I'm a bit concerned about the commented USE commands. I'd really rather not have to worry about going into the SETUP text before each performance of it and checking to see if their comment status matches what I need to do."

CONTROLLING THE FLOW OF EXECUTION

"You bring up a very good point," Jack said seriously. "What you want is a way to capture more elaborate procedural knowledge in a program. You know that if a table is not in use then it should be put in use, otherwise nothing need be done. The question then is how to represent that knowledge in the program."

"The examples you've seen thus far," chimed Joy, "have involved a brute force, relentless execution of one command after another. There were no exceptions. If a command is there, it is executed. What you want is a way to *conditionally execute* a USE command. That is, a USE command should be executed only if a certain condition is satisfied, namely that the table isn't already in use.

"In general, we need ways to control the flow of command executions in a program. The environment gives us several commands for controlling the execution of other commands. Once you know how to use these, you'll see that not all commands in a program need be executed. Some will be executed exactly one time in the procedure. Others may be executed many times as the procedure is performed."

Though Joy did not mention them by name, the environment's commands for controlling execution flow are IF, TEST, PERFORM, and WHILE. The managers had already seen (recall Chapter 12) that the IF command will execute one series of commands if a specified condition is satisfied and a different series if it is not. The TEST command gives a way of controlling which one (or more) of many command series will be executed as the procedure is performed. The PERFORM command had already been discussed as the way for a user to execute a program. It also gives a program a means for executing other programs. The WHILE command lets a series of commands be repeatedly executed while a specified condition is satisfied. As soon as it is not satisfied, execution proceeds to other commands.

If-Then

To address Dan's concern about the program's commented USE commands, Jack brought up the Figure 13–4 text screen by executing the TEXT command. He edited line 19 so that the command

```
if not inuse("rep") then use "a:rep.itb";endif
```

resided there. This is an example of the IF command with only one command in its THEN clause and without an ELSE clause. Jack explained that the INUSE function in its condition evaluates to TRUE if REP is in use and FALSE if REP is not in use.

"So," summarized Jack, "this command simply says that if REP is not in use then put it in use. Notice that we've embedded one command, USE, within another command, IF. As you saw yesterday, when we defined a cell as an IF command, it is possible to embed many commands within an IF command."

Referring to the new IF command on line 19, Dan asked, "What happens if REP is in use when this command is executed?"

"Well," replied Jack, "the INUSE function will evaluate to TRUE, which means that the overall condition is FALSE. That is, NOT TRUE is the same as FALSE. Because the condition is not satisfied, the USE command isn't executed. The program's execution proceeds to the next command following ENDIF. Speaking of the next command, we need to edit lines 20 and 21 in a similar way."

Jack edited those lines accordingly, embedding the USE command of each in the THEN clause of a new IF command. He escaped to the status line and typed

```
write
```

producing the screen appearance shown in Figure 13–10. On pressing the Enter key, the new version of SETUP replaced the former one on disk. When Jack then performed SETUP, it had the same apparent behavior as the first time it was performed. The environment generated no error messages about tables already being in use, because the program's USE commands were not executed.

As Jack was typing in color codes during the demonstration of the new SETUP program (recall Figure 13–7), Stan interrupted. "I realize that the permissible color codes are on the screen while you're responding to the prompts. But what if you make an inadvertent mistake and type B instead of U when you want blue. It seems that would cause problems, because the program would then make B one of the E.BACG color codes."

"You're right," confirmed Jack. "That would be a problem, for the environment wouldn't know what to make of B as a color code. So the program has a loophole in it and that's undesirable."

He finished his SETUP interaction and again brought up the Figure 13–10 text screen as Joy elaborated, "In general, a program should be

FIGURE 13–10   Embedding USE commands in IF commands

```
    Line:21      Col:49     a:setup.ipf     Command: write
12       at 11,15 input g using "a" with "graphics?"
13       at 12,15 input t using "a" with "text?"
14       at 13,15 input o using "a" with "other screens?"
15       e.bacg=s+g+t+o+o
16       e.lstr=templstr
17       release variable
18       redefine function 1 "help\\13"
19       if not inuse("rep") then use "a:rep.itb";endif
20       if not inuse("perf") then use "a:perf.itb" with "a:perftp.ind";endif
21       if not inuse("prod")then use "a:prod.itb";endif
22       ! Display sum and average statistics only
23          e.dvar=false
24          e.dcnt=false
25          e.dmin=false
26          e.dmax=false
27          e.dsdv=false
28       ! Initially, suppress page numbering & don't calculate statistics for q
29          e.spgn=true;e.stat=false
30       ! Declare some macros for commonly used pictures
31       macro f4dd using "$f,fff.dd"
32       macro f6 using "$fff,fff"
33       ! Set up normal page depth
34       e.pdep=65
35       at 15,1 ? "ENVIRONMENT SETUP COMPLETE" using "%27*%26r%27*"
```

airtight, crashproof. It should guard against possible errors that a user could make when interacting with it. Thus by the time line 15 is executed to set E.BACG's value, the program should have ensured that S, G, T, and O have valid color codes."

"I see," responded Stan, "our programs should be designed to protect us from ourselves! So the program should accept a user's input for one of those variables only if it is a valid code. For instance, if the input value for S is not a valid code, then the program should perhaps use the current code for spreadsheets."

"You said it very well," smiled Jack. "Let's put your 'if' statement into the program as an IF command. After each code is input we'll have the program check whether it is an improper color code and take corrective action if it is not proper."

He edited the program by inserting an IF command after each of the four color code INPUT commands. The result is shown in Figure 13–11. Notice that each new IF command extends across multiple lines for easy readability. For instance, the first extends from lines 13 through 16 where it is ended by the word ENDIF. Its condition of

```
not (s in ccodes)
```

FIGURE 13–11   IF commands to ensure valid color codes

```
Line:31      Col:11    a:setup.ipf    Insert              Press ^L for help
8        ! Set up the colors
9           at 7,5 output "Color codes: A(black) O(brown) U(blue) W(white)"
10          at 8,18 output "C(cyan)  G(green) R(red)  M(magenta)"
11          at 9,10 output "What background color do you want for:"
12          at 10,15 input s using "a" with "spreadsheet?"
13              if not (s in ccodes) then s=substr(e.bacg,1,1)
14                              at 10,35 ? "INVALID CODE"
15                              at 10,50 ? s using "u", " is still used"
16              endif
17          at 11,15 input g using "a" with "graphics?"
18              if not (g in ccodes) then g=substr(e.bacg,2,1)
19                              at 11,35 ? "INVALID CODE"
20                              at 11,50 ? g using "u", " is still used"
21              endif
22          at 12,15 input t using "a" with "text?"
23              if not (t in ccodes) then t=substr(e.bacg,3,1)
24                              at 12,35 ? "INVALID CODE"
25                              at 12,50 ? t using "u", " is still used"
26              endif
27          at 13,15 input o using "a" with "other screens?"
28              if not (o in ccodes) then o=substr(e.bacg,4,2)
29                              at 13,35 ? "INVALID CODE"
30                              at 13,50 ? o using "uu", " still used"
31              endif
```

refers to CCODES. Jack explained that this was a macro that he would define later to be the class of valid color codes. The condition will be satisfied if it is not true that the input S value is in the color code class. In that event three commands are executed.

The first assigns a valid color code to S. This code is determined by the SUBSTR function. In general this function has three arguments. Its value will be a substring of the first argument, beginning at the character position indicated by the second argument and having a length equal to the third argument. In this case, the first color code of E.BACG will be assigned to S. The second command alerts the user that an invalid code was entered. The third tells the user that the present spreadsheet color code (i.e., S's new value) will still be used.

The other new IF commands are similar. In each instance, the multiple commands embedded in the THEN clause appear on separate lines, rather than being strung out along the same line and separated by semicolons. The ENDIF is on a line by itself with a level of indentation matching that of IF. Jack explained that he often uses this layout to make it easy to quickly see where a long IF command begins and ends. Notice that when G is invalid, the second code of E.BACG will be assigned to it. When T is invalid, the third E.BACG code is assigned

FIGURE 13–12 **Defining a macro in a program**

```
 Line:9      Col:50    a:setup.ipf    Insert              Press ^L for help
8       ! Set up the colors
9         macro ccodes ["a","o","u","w","c","g","r","m"]
10        at 7,5 output "Color codes: A(black) O(brown) U(blue) W(white)"
1B        at 8,18 output "C(cyan)  G(green) R(red)  M(magenta)"
12        at 9,10 output "What background color do you want for:"
13        at 10,15 input s using "a" with "spreadsheet?"
14          if not (s in ccodes) then s=substr(e.bacg,1,1)
15                        at 10,35 ? "INVALID CODE"
16                        at 10,50 ? s using "u", " is still used"
17          endif
18        at 11,15 input g using "a" with "graphics?"
19          if not (g in ccodes) then g=substr(e.bacg,2,1)
20                        at 11,35 ? "INVALID CODE"
21                        at 11,50 ? g using "u", " is still used"
22          endif
23        at 12,15 input t using "a" with "text?"
24          if not (t in ccodes) then t=substr(e.bacg,3,1)
25                        at 12,35 ? "INVALID CODE"
26                        at 12,50 ? t using "u", " is still used"
27          endif
28        at 13,15 input o using "a" with "other screens?"
29          if not (o in ccodes) then o=substr(e.bacg,4,2)
30                        at 13,35 ? "INVALID CODE"
31                        at 13,50 ? o using "uu", " still used"
```

to it. In the case of O, the fourth and fifth E.BACG codes are assigned to it.

As Figure 13–12 shows, Jack next inserted a MACRO command following the comment in line 8. Had he not defined this CCODES macro, the entire bracketed class of valid codes would have to have been typed in place of CCODES on lines 14, 19, 24, and 29. Obviously, the macro must be defined in a procedural step that precedes the commands that make use of CCODES. Because he did not intend to reference CCODES after checking the color codes, Jack edited the program's RELEASE command. The result was

```
release templstr,s,g,t,o,ccodes
```

which would cause CCODES to be released along with the working variables.

To get a printout of the new rendition of SETUP, Jack escaped to the status line where he issued the PRINT command. Figure 13–13 shows the printout of the full 53-line program. After invoking WRITE to preserve the new version of SETUP, Jack left the text screen. He executed the command

FIGURE 13–13 Printout of the full SETUP program containing IF commands

```
1     clear
2     e.deci=2
3     e.lstr=80
4     at 1,1 output "ENVIRONMENT  SETUP" using "%31*%18r%31*"
5     templstr=25
6     at 3,5 input e.deci using "n" with "How many decimal digits?"
7     at 5,5 input templstr using "nnn" with "Default length of strings?"
8     ! Set up the colors
9         macro ccodes ["a","o","u","w","c","g","r","m"]
10        at 7,5 output "Color codes: A(black) O(brown) U(blue) W(white)"
11        at 8,18 output "C(cyan) G(green) R(red)  M(magenta)"
12        at 9,10 output "What background color do you want for:"
13        at 10,15 input s using "a" with "spreadsheet?"
14           if not (s in ccodes) then s=substr(e.bacg,1,1)
15                               at 10,35 ? "INVALID CODE"
16                               at 10,50 ? s using "u", " is still used"
17           endif
18        at 11,15 input g using "a" with "graphics?"
19           if not (g in ccodes) then g=substr(e.bacg,2,1)
20                               at 11,35 ? "INVALID CODE"
21                               at 11,50 ? g using "u", " is still used"
22           endif
23        at 12,15 input t using "a" with "text?"
24           if not (t in ccodes) then t=substr(e.bacg,3,1)
25                               at 12,35 ? "INVALID CODE"
26                               at 12,50 ? t using "u", " is still used"
27           endif
28        at 13,15 input o using "a" with "other screens?"
29           if not (o in ccodes) then o=substr(e.bacg,4,2)
30                               at 13,35 ? "INVALID CODE"
31                               at 13,50 ? o using "uu", " still used"
32           endif
33        e.bacg=s+g+t+o+o
34     e.lstr=templstr
35     release templstr,s,g,t,o,ccodes
36     redefine function 1 "help\\13"
37     if not inuse("rep") then use "a:rep.itb";endif
38     if not inuse("perf") then use "a:perf.itb" with "a:perftp.ind";endif
39     if not inuse("prod") then use "a:prod.itb";endif
40     ! Display sum and average statistics only
41        e.dvar=false
42        e.dcnt=false
43        e.dmin=false
44        e.dmax=false
45        e.dsdv=false
46     ! Initially, suppress page numbering & don't calculate statistics for queries
47        e.spgn=true;e.stat=false
48     ! Declare some macros for commonly used pictures
49     macro f4dd using "$f,fff.dd"
50     macro f6 using "$fff,fff"
51     ! Set up normal page depth
52     e.pdep=65
53     at 15,1 ? "ENVIRONMENT SETUP COMPLETE" using "%27*%26r%27*"
```

```
perform "a:setup"
```

to test out his modifications. Joy explained that the way to check whether a program behaves as expected is to perform it and test its reactions.

"Once you've written a program," Joy advised [4], "you should always test it thoroughly to be sure that it behaves the way you expect. If it does not, then there is a *bug* in it. That's computer jargon for saying that there's an error in the program. The activity of finding the error and fixing it is called *debugging*. To debug a program, mentally step through its commands, thinking out the effect of each step. It can sometimes be helpful to put extra OUTPUT commands in the program to output the effects of individual commands, allowing you to focus in on where things begin to go astray. The most common kinds of bugs are due to improper command syntax, omitted commands, and illogical sequencing of commands."

When the program prompted him for the spreadsheet color, Jack typed

```
x
```

knowing that this was an invalid code. Figure 13–14 depicts the resultant screen. When he pressed the Enter key, the screen immediately took on the appearance shown in Figure 13–15. As expected, the "INVALID CODE" message was displayed along with an indication that the present spreadsheet color code of U (recall Figure 13–8) would still be used.

After entering valid codes of G and U for the graphics and text prompts, he made an invalid entry of

```
b
```

for the other screens prompt. Again the program gave the correct response. It recognized that B is not a valid color code and indicated that the present codes for other screens (i.e., R and R) would be used. After the SETUP program completed execution, Jack executed the command

```
?e.bacg
```

to verify that it now had the expected value. As Figure 13–16 indicates, it did. Observe that even though O (with a two-character value) was concatenated twice in assigning the new E.BACG value (see line 33 in Figure 13–13), the environment only keeps the first five characters for E.BACG's value.

FIGURE 13–14   Entering an invalid color code

```
********************************ENVIRONMENT  SETUP********************************

    How many decimal digits? 2

    Default length of strings?  25

    Color codes: A(black) O(brown) U(blue) W(white)
                 C(cyan)  G(green) R(red)  M(magenta)
       What background color do you want for:
           spreadsheet? x
```

FIGURE 13–15   Result of an invalid code entry

```
********************************ENVIRONMENT  SETUP********************************

    How many decimal digits? 2

    Default length of strings:  25

    Color codes: A(black) O(brown) U(blue) W(white)
                 C(cyan)  G(green) R(red)  M(magenta)
       What background color do you want for:
           spreadsheet? x      INVALID CODE  U is still used
           graphics? _
```

FIGURE 13–16   Verifying the resultant E.BACG value

```
*******************************ENVIRONMENT  SETUP*********************************

    How many decimal digits? 2

    Default length of strings?  25

    Color codes: A(black) O(brown) U(blue) W(white)
                 C(cyan)  g(green) R(red)  M(magenta)
        What background color do you want for:
                 spreadsheet? x     INVALID CODE   U is still used
                 graphics? g
                 text? u
                 other screens? b   INVALID CODE   RR still used

*****************************ENVIRONMENT SETUP COMPLETE***************************

_?e.bacg
ugurr
_
```

If-Then-Else

"Programs can be developed for many other tasks aside from setting up the environment," Jack stressed. "In fact, if you think back to Saturday when we first worked with forms, you may remember that we represented some procedural knowledge in the text of a macro."

"I remember," said Brad. (Recall Figures 9–27 and 9–28.) "That was my B macro. It was defined to be a series of forms management commands for processing the SCALC form. All we had to do was use the B key to have the environment carry out an entire sequence of commands. So even though I didn't realize it at the time, we were using a macro to represent and automate the processing of procedural knowledge."

"Exactly!" agreed Jack. "Macros can be useful for fairly short or simple command sequences. But you probably wouldn't want to try defining a macro in place of the entire SETUP program."

"However, you might want to define a macro for performing SETUP," added Joy, "especially if you frequently need to perform it." She had a command like

```
macro setup perform "a:setup"
```

in mind. This would enable a user to simply type

```
setup
```

whenever the setup program needed to be performed.

"Anyway," Jack continued, "we can go a lot farther in automating our processing of the salary calculation form if we use a program instead of a macro. We can do everything that the B macro did and a good deal more. Let me show you."

Recall from Chapter 9 that the command

```
macro b clear;incr=0;putform scalc;tally scalc;getform scalc;wait;clear
```

was used to define the B macro as a procedure consisting of seven commands. Before carrying out the procedure, the SCALC form had to be in the present processing context, E.ICOM had to be TRUE, E.SUPD was switched to TRUE and a desired REP record had to be obtained. Jack planned to automate all of these steps in a new program named SCALC.

To begin, he executed the command

```
text "a:scalc.ipf"
```

bringing up a fresh text screen. Figure 13–17 shows what he typed into the text area. Notice that it has more profuse comments than the SETUP program. The first four lines document the overall purpose of the SCALC program. At a more detailed level, each subsequent comment describes the role of the commands that directly follow it.

"In my opinion," offered Jack, "it's a good idea to document the steps in a program with plenty of comments. Even though the purpose of all steps may seem clear as you are developing your program, when you take a look at it a month or year later it may not be so clear if you don't use any comments.

"I didn't put comments in the first few programs I wrote. I thought it would be a waste of time. I just entered the commands I wanted, tested the procedure, and was done with it. Or so I thought. But it wasn't long before I discovered I was wrong. After using a program for a while, I'd hit on ways that I wanted to expand it, to make it more powerful and flexible than my original conception. So I'd bring it up in the text screen. But without comments, I found that it took a good deal of effort to get sufficiently reacquainted with it to be able to make the changes correctly. Believe me, putting in a little more effort up front is worth it in the long run!"

FIGURE 13–17   Beginning of the SCALC program for data base retrieval and forms processing

```
 Line:24      Col:62    a:scalc.ipf    Insert              Press ^L for help
1          ! This program is intended to make salary calculations via the SCALC
2          ! form stored in A:SCALC.ICF. It lets the user identify which rep is
3          ! of interest and make the calculation for that rep by entering the
4          ! desired percentage increase in the form.
5             clear
6
7          ! Make sure the REP table is in use and the SCALC form is loaded
8             if not inuse ("rep") then use "a:rep.itb"; endif
9             load "a:scalc.icf" with "f"
10
11         ! Save current environment settings before switching them
12            esupd=e.supd; e.supd=true; elstr=e.lstr; e.lstr=80
13            eicom=e.icom; e.icom=true; esuph=e.suph; e.suph=true
14
15         ! Find out what rep the user wants and then obtain that record
16            input who using "%8r" \
17               with "For which rep do you want to make a salary calculation?"
18            obtain from rep where fname=who
19            if #found then clear
20                        incr=0
21                        putform scalc
22                        tally scalc
23                        getform scalc
24                        at 25,1 ? "PROCESSING COMPLETE";wait; clear
```

"Jack makes an excellent point," Joy confirmed. "Good documentation in a program is essential to maintaining that program over time. Not only that, documenting things as you go along can help you avoid oversights in your program logic. Ideally, a professional programmer documents a program before actually typing in its commands."

Referring to lines 12 and 13, Tracey asked, "Why do you bother to save the environment settings before changing them?"

"There's no telling when we might want to perform the SCALC program," Jack replied. "Those environment variables may have different values than what SCALC will switch them to. But when SCALC is done executing, we'd like the environment settings to be the same as they were before it began. Otherwise, we'd have to go to the trouble of switching them back ourselves after each performance of SCALC."

"I get it," acknowledged Tracey. "Near the end of the program you'll include commands that reset the environment variables to the values these steps saved in the working variables."

Jack nodded. He went on to point out that the INPUT command beginning in line 16 ended with a backslash. This meant that the command continues on the next line. He indented the continuation for readability. The INPUT command prompts for the name of the rep whose salary adjustment is to be calculated. That name becomes the value of the WHO working variable and the subsequent OBTAIN command tries to find the REP record whose FNAME value matches WHO's value.

"As you know," Jack said, "one of two things can happen when the OBTAIN command is executed. Either the desired record will be found or it won't be found. There's a built-in utility variable, #FOUND, that senses whether the last attempt to find a record succeeded or failed. When a record is found, #FOUND automatically becomes TRUE. When no record is found, the environment gives #FOUND a FALSE value. Obviously, if OBTAIN succeeds, we want to carry out the same sequence of steps we earlier defined for the B macro."

Lines 19 through 24 accomplish just that. Jack did add one embellishment: an OUTPUT command to indicate when processing of the salary calculation form is complete.

"What should we have the program do when OBTAIN doesn't find a record?" asked Jack. "For instance, you might have misspelled the rep's name."

"It should tell that what we've typed in is not an existent rep and give us another chance to enter a correct name," volunteered Don.

"And it would be nice," added Debbie, "if it displayed a list of the correct rep spellings so we don't get it wrong again."

Accordingly, Jack completed the IF command as shown in lines 25 through 39 of Figure 13–18. Line 25 began the ELSE portion of the IF command. Its commands would be executed if the IF command's condition is not TRUE (i.e., if #FOUND is FALSE). When executed, the ELSE clause's first command alerts the user that the entered name is invalid. The second and third commands produce a list of existing rep names. Because E.SUPH was switched to TRUE (line 13), the SELECT command's results will be presented without a column heading.

Notice that lines 28 through 36 basically repeat lines 16 through 24. As Don suggested, the user is given another chance to carry out the same processing that would have resulted had a correct name been entered the first time. This causes a new IF command (beginning on line 30) to be *nested* within the IF command that began earlier (line 19). The ELSE clause of the nested IF presents a "PROCESSING HALTED" message in the event of a user's second failure to identify an existing rep. The nested IF ends with the matching ENDIF on line 38 and the outer IF command ends with the matching ENDIF on line 39.

Jack completed the program with commands that would restore the environment variables to their original settings and a command to

FIGURE 13–18 Nesting one IF command within another

```
  Line:41     Col:58     a:scalc.ipf     Insert                Press ^L for help
18           obtain from rep where fname=who
19           if #found then clear
20                           incr=0
21                           putform scalc
22                           tally scalc
23                           getform scalc
24                           at 25,1 ? "PROCESSING COMPLETE";wait; clear
25                      else output trim(who), " is not a valid rep name"
26                           output "Enter one of the following names:"
27                           select fname using "%35 %8r" from rep
28                           input who using "%8r" with "Enter desired name:"
29                           obtain from rep where fname=who
30                           if #found then clear
31                                           incr=0
32                                           putform scalc
33                                           tally scalc
34                                           getform scalc
35                                           at 25,1 ? "PROCESSING COMPLETE"
36                                           wait; clear
37                                      else ? "INVALID NAME: PROCESSING HALTED"
38                           endif
39           endif
40       ! Cleanup by restoring the environment variables and releasing SCALC
41           e.supd=esupd; e.suph=esuph; e.icom=eicom; e.lstr=elstr
```

release SCALC from working memory. A printout of the full SCALC program is provided in Figure 13–19. Jack wrote the program to disk and left the text screen to test his handiwork. As soon as he executed the command

```
perform "a:scalc"
```

the screen cleared and the initial INPUT command's prompt message appeared. He responded by typing

```
Kim
```

as Figure 13–20 shows. On pressing the Enter key the screen cleared as expected.

The SCALC form with Kim's data was put on the screen instantly. The screen now appeared as it had earlier in Figure 9–27. Jack typed

```
.062
```

in response to the form's "Increase:" prompt. When he pressed the Enter key, the new salary was calculated and the "PROCESSING COM-

FIGURE 13–19   Printout of the full SCALC program

```
1     ! This program is intended to make salary calculations via the SCALC
2     ! form stored in A:SCALC.ICF. It lets the user identify which rep is
3     ! of interest and make the calculation for that rep by entering the
4     ! desired percentage increase in the form.
5        clear
6
7     ! Make sure the REP table is in use and the SCALC form is loaded
8        if not inuse("rep") then use "a:rep.itb"; endif
9        load "a:scalc.icf" with "f"
10
11    ! Save current environment settings before switching them
12       esupd=e.supd; e.supd=true; elstr=e.lstr; e.lstr=80
13       eicom=e.icom; e.icom=true; esuph=e.suph; e.suph=true
14
15    ! Find out what rep the user wants and then obtain that record
16       input who using "%8r" \
17          with "For which rep do you want to make a salary calculation?"
18       obtain from rep where fname=who
19       if #found then clear
20                       incr=0
21                       putform scalc
22                       tally scalc
23                       getform scalc
24                       at 25,1 ? "PROCESSING COMPLETE";wait; clear
25                  else output trim(who), " is not a valid rep name"
26                       output "Enter one of the following names:"
27                       select fname using "%35 %8r" from rep
28                       input who using "%8r" with "Enter desired name:"
29                       obtain from rep where fname=who
30                       if #found then clear
31                               incr=0
32                               putform scalc
33                               tally scalc
34                               getform scalc
35                               at 25,1 ? "PROCESSING COMPLETE"
36                               wait; clear
37                          else ? "INVALID NAME: PROCESSING HALTED"
38                       endif
39       endif
40    ! Cleanup by restoring the environment variables and releasing SCALC
41       e.supd=esupd; e.suph=esuph; e.icom=eicom; e.lstr=elstr
42       release scalc,incr,who
```

FIGURE 13–20 Entering a valid rep name to the SCALC program

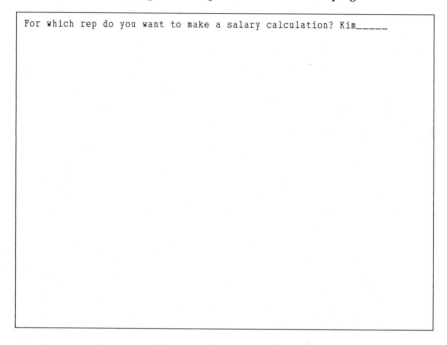

```
For which rep do you want to make a salary calculation? Kim_____
```

PLETE" message was displayed at the bottom of the screen as shown in Figure 13–21. On pressing the space bar the screen cleared and the underscore prompt appeared.

"Now," Jack declared, "let's check out what happens when we enter an invalid name. SCALC should inform us of that fact, provide a list of valid names, and give us a second chance to enter a correct name. If it doesn't, then something is wrong in the program and we'll need to fix it. Let's see."

He executed the command

```
perform "a:scalc"
```

and was prompted to enter a rep name. Jack typed

```
Tobby
```

to see if SCALC would detect his error. When he pressed the Enter key, SCALC immediately responded that Tobby is not a valid rep name. In the blink of an eye, the expected list of rep names appeared and he was prompted to enter the desired name. As Figure 13–22 shows, his

FIGURE 13–21   Result of SCALC program for a valid rep

```
                    Sales Representative (0)

        Name: Kim G. Anders
        Monthly salary: $2,600.00              Increase: 0.062

                        New salary: $2,761.20
```

PROCESSING COMPLETE

FIGURE 13–22   Response of SCALC program for an invalid rep entry

```
For which rep do you want to make a salary calculation? Tobby
Tobby is not a valid rep name
Enter one of the following names:
                                    Kevin
                                    Kim
                                    Kris
                                    Tina
                                    Toby
                                    Kerry
                                    Karen
                                    Kathy
                                    Jackie
                                    Carol
Enter desired name: Tobby___
```

FIGURE 13–23   Result of SCALC program for two invalid rep entries

```
For which rep do you want to make a salary calculation? Cathey
Cathey is not a valid rep name
Enter one of the following names:
                            Kevin
                            Kim
                            Kris
                            Tina
                            Toby
                            Kerry
                            Karen
                            Kathy
                            Jackie
                            Carol
Enter desired name: Kathey
INVALID NAME: PROCESSING HALTED
```

previous incorrect entry appeared after the prompt so he could edit it as he pleased. As soon as Jack corrected the spelling, the screen cleared and the SCALC form with Toby's data appeared.

After processing Toby in the usual fashion, Jack again executed the command

```
perform "a:scalc"
```

this time to test a third possibility. When prompted for a rep name, he entered

```
Cathey
```

which SCALC rejected as invalid. For his second chance, he edited this entry by replacing the C with a K. As expected, SCALC rejected this name as well and the underscore prompt reappeared. Figure 13–23 displays the resultant screen.

With these three tests, Jack had checked the three branches of processing that can occur when performing the SCALC program: entering a valid rep, entering an invalid rep followed by a valid rep, and entering two invalid reps. The THEN and ELSE clauses allow the flow of execution to branch in one of two directions, depending on whether the condition is satisfied. For this reason, a programming language's IF command behavior is often called *conditional branching*. By nesting a second IF command in the ELSE clause, SCALC branches in three possible directions. That is, the outer IF's ELSE clause has two subbranches. When developing a program's behavior, the flow of execution in each possible branch should be tested to ensure the program works as expected in every situation.

Nested Programs

Much as an IF command can be nested within another IF command, a PERFORM command can be nested within a program that is executed by another PERFORM command. This is valuable when there is some sequence of steps that needs to be used repeatedly within one or more programs. Rather than repeat the full sequence of steps every place it is needed, those steps become a separate procedure in their own right. They are represented and maintained in their own IPF file. Wherever another program needs to use these steps, it simply has a PERFORM command that will cause them to be performed.

"On the printout you passed around, I notice that the two THEN clauses in your SCALC program have exactly the same commands," observed Brad (see Figure 13–19). "It seems a waste of time and space to keep the same sequence of steps in more than one place. If you ever want to change something in those steps, then you have to remember to change it everywhere they're repeated!"

"You're right," agreed Jack, "so let's get rid of the repetition in SCALC. The repeated sequence of steps can be thought of as a miniature procedure that we want to carry out when a rep has been found. So let's make a separate program called REPFOUND out of those steps. In SCALC itself, each THEN clause will consist of a single command to PERFORM the REPFOUND program."

Jack edited the SCALC program to include the command

```
perform "a:repfound"
```

in each of the two THEN clauses. All of the former commands in those clauses were commented out. He escaped to the status line and typed

```
write
```

as shown in Figure 13–24. He pressed the Enter key to preserve this new rendition of the program in SCALC.IPF on the drive A diskette.

FIGURE 3–24 Nested PERFORM commands

```
 Line:36      Col:35      a:scalc.ipf      Command: write
18           obtain from rep where fname=who
19           if #found then perform "a:repfound" !clear
20                           !incr=0
21                           !putform scalc
22                           !tally scalc
23                           !getform scalc
24                           !at 25,1 ? "PROCESSING COMPLETE";wait; clear
25                else output trim(who), " is not a valid rep name"
26                     output "Enter one of the following names:"
27                     select fname using "%35 %8r" from rep
28                     input who using "%8r" with "Enter desired name:"
29                     obtain from rep where fname=who
30                     if #found then perform "a:repfound" !clear
31                                     !incr=0
32                                     !putform scalc
33                                     !tally scalc
34                                     !getform scalc
35                                     !at 25,1 ? "PROCESSING COMPLETE"
36                                     !wait; clear
37                               else ? "INVALID NAME: PROCESSING HALTED"
38                     endif
39           endif
40    ! Cleanup by restoring the environment variables and releasing scalc
41         e.supd=esupd; e.suph=esuph; e.icom=eicom; e.lstr=elstr
```

Announcing that he would now construct the REPFOUND program, Jack used ˆT to delete all lines from the text area other than those in the second THEN clause. He removed the exclamation marks and deleted the words preceding the CLEAR command on its line. The resultant seven lines provided the basis of REPFOUND. As depicted in Figure 13–25, Jack inserted some comment lines for documenting the program. He eliminated the OUTPUT command in favor of the new lines 10 through 13. These would give the user a chance to have the salary calculation form printed once the calculation finishes. Whenever the RETURN command (e.g., line 16) is executed, the flow of execution returns to the command following the PERFORM command that initiated the program (e.g., REPFOUND) processing.

Jack escaped to the status line and issued the command

```
write "a:repfound.ipf"
```

to preserve the present text in a new file named REPFOUND.IPF on the drive A diskette. It was time to test the effects of his changes. Leaving the text screen, he executed the command

```
perform "a:scalc"
```

FIGURE 13–25 The REPFOUND program to be performed within the SCALC program

```
   Line:16      Col:8      a:scalc.ipf     Command: write "a:repfound.ipf"
1        !This program processes the SCALC form once a particular REP
2        !record has been found. The SCALC form must be loaded into the
3        !present processing context prior to performing this program.
4
5        clear
6        incr=0
7        putform scalc
8        tally scalc
9        getform scalc
10       at 20,1 ? "SALARY CALCULATION COMPLETE"
11       at 22,1 input yn using "a" with "Do you want a printout of it?(y/n) "
12       if yn in ["Y","y"] then eject; print scalc; endif
13       at 24,1 ? "Press the space bar when finished viewing the form"
14       wait; clear
15       release yn
16       return
```

FIGURE 13–26 Result of SCALC performing REPFOUND

```
                    Sales Representative (0)

        Name: Kim G. Anders
        Monthly salary: $2,600.00                Increase: 0.062

                       New salary: $2,761.20




SALARY CALCULATION COMPLETE

Do you want a printout of it?(y/n) n

Press the space bar when finished viewing the form
```

which began in the usual way by prompting him for a rep name. He responded with Kim, which caused the SCALC form with Kim's data to appear. After entering a 6.2 percent increase, he was asked whether a printout was desired. After a response of

n

the screen appeared as shown in Figure 13–26. Jack checked the program's other branches of command execution (including a positive response to the printout question) to verify that they too worked as expected. Satisfied with the new SCALC, he edited it to eliminate the commented commands. Figure 13–27 is a printout of the result. Notice how much more compact it is than the Figure 13–19 printout.

The just completed example is a small illustration of what is known as *modular programming*. Procedural knowledge is organized into separate program modules. Each module is designed to represent a unit of procedural knowledge that may need to be performed many times. One module such as SCALC can perform other modules such as REPFOUND. A module at a lower level in the flow of execution is often referred to as a *subprogram* or subroutine with respect to the higher level module. For instance, REPFOUND is a subprogram with respect to SCALC.

In general, there can be many levels of modules. In addition to being performed directly by a user, SCALC could also be performed by a higher level module. At the other end of the spectrum, REPFOUND could be revised to include PERFORM commands that carry out the commands of still lower level modules. When it is possible to identify a chunk of procedural knowledge that may need to be used in multiple places within the flows of higher level procedures, it is best to develop it as a distinct program module. This greatly facilitates the use and maintenance of that procedural knowledge [6], [7].

Modular programming can also be helpful even when a chunk of procedural knowledge is needed in only one place in only one larger procedure. It can help structure the program design process and break a large problem into smaller, more easily managed modules. For instance, the SETUP program of Figure 13–13 could have originally been designed to consist of the following seven commands

```
clear
at 1,1 output "ENVIRONMENT  SETUP" using "%31*%18r%31*"
perform "a:setenv"
perform "a:settable"
perform "a:setkey"
perform "a:setmacro"
at 15,1 ? "ENVIRONMENT SETUP COMPLETE" using "%27*%26r%27*"
```

FIGURE 13–27   Printout of SCALC with nested PERFORM commands

```
1        ! This program is intended to make salary calculations via the SCALC
2        ! form stored in A:SCALC.ICF. It lets the user identify which rep is
3        ! of interest and make the calculation for that rep by entering the
4        ! desired percentage increase in the form.
5          clear
6
7        ! Make sure the REP table is in use and the SCALC form is loaded
8          if not inuse("rep") then use "a:rep.itb"; endif
9          load "a:scalc.icf" with "f"
10
11       ! Save current environment settings before switching them
12         esupd=e.supd; e.supd=true; elstr=e.lstr; e.lstr=80
13         eicom=e.icom; e.icom=true; esuph=e.suph; e.suph=true
14
15       ! Find out what rep the user wants and then obtain that record
16         input who using "%8r" \
17             with "For which rep do you want to make a salary calculation?"
18         obtain from rep where fname=who
19         if #found then perform "a:repfound"
20                 else output trim(who), " is not a valid rep name"
21                      output "Enter one of the following names:"
22                      select fname using "%35 %8r" from rep
23                      input who using "%8r" with "Enter desired name:"
24                      obtain from rep where fname=who
25                      if #found then perform "a:repfound"
26                              else ? "INVALID NAME: PROCESSING HALTED"
27                      endif
28         endif
29       ! Cleanup by restoring the environment variables and releasing SCALC
30         e.supd=esupd; e.suph=esuph; e.icom=eicom; e.lstr=elstr
31         release scalc,incr,who
```

Then, the next level of program modules would have been developed. The SETENV program would have the commands that pertain to setting up the environment variables. One of these might be

```
perform "a:setcolor"
```

where the SETCOLOR program is later designed to consist of the commands on lines 8 through 33 of Figure 13–13. Similarly, the SETTABLE, SETKEY, and SETMACRO program modules would have commands for using tables, redefining function keys, and establishing macros, respectively. The approach of first developing the top-level module and then developing lower level modules is often referred to as *top-down design* and is commonly employed by professional programmers [5], [6], [7].

As the session adjourned for a midday practice break, Jack put the technique of programming into proper perspective. "Keep in mind the fact that each of you can accomplish a great deal without knowing the first thing about programming. But if you are able to write your own programs, you'll be able to accomplish even more. Almost every command you've learned before today can be incorporated in a program, including SELECT, STAT, REPORT, PLOT, TEXT, and all the data base, spreadsheet, and forms management commands. The environment's programming capability gives you a way of automating the use of any mix of the other knowledge management techniques. I think you can see that the possibilities are mind-boggling. But don't let that deter you. Just remember, you can use as little or as much of the capabilities as you desire and you can grow into them at your own pace."

Conditional Iteration

The session resumed that afternoon with a question from Pete. He had been experimenting with some changes to the SCALC program. There was a change he wanted to make, but was unable to handle in a satisfactory manner. "Is there some way to have a sequence of commands in a program executed repeatedly? As it stands, SCALC does a one-shot calculation. To do another calculation I have to perform it again. When doing salary calculations, what I'd really like is the ability to try out several different increases for the same rep without having to reperform SCALC and type in the same rep's name each time. Better yet, I'd like to switch among reps without ever leaving the SCALC execution!"

Jack brought up the text screen with the SCALC program in view. Referring to lines 16 through 28 (Figure 13–27), he responded, "So what you want is a way to have the execution of this sequence of commands repeated indefinitely, until you tell the program that you don't want to do any more calculations. What we'll do is embed that entire command sequence in another command that will continue executing it as long as a certain condition is satisfied. This new command for controlling the flow of execution is the WHILE command. While a certain condition is satisfied, the commands embedded in the WHILE command are iteratively executed."

To demonstrate this *conditional iteration*, Jack edited the SCALC pro-

FIGURE 13–28   Modifying SCALC to allow conditional iteration

```
   Line:37      Col:12    a:scalc.ipf    Insert            Press ^L for help
14
15       ! The program will allow repeated calculations with SCALC as long
16       ! as the variable MORE has "y" as its value. While MORE has this
17       ! value, the calculation process will iterate.
18          more="y"
19          while more in ["y","Y"] do
20
21          ! Find out what rep the user wants and then obtain that record
22             input who using "%8r" \
23                with "For which rep do you want to make a salary calculation?"
24             obtain from rep where fname=who
25             if #found then perform "a:repfound"
26                   else output trim(who), " is not a valid rep name"
27                        output "Enter one of the following names:"
28                        select fname using "%35 %8r" from rep
29                        input who using "%8r" with "Enter desired name:"
30                        obtain from rep where fname=who
31                        if #found then perform "a:repfound"
32                              else ? "INVALID NAME: PROCESSING HALTED"
33                        endif
34             endif
35             input more using "a" with "Do you want more calculations?(y/n) "
36             if more in ["Y","y"] then clear; endif
37          endwhile
```

gram as shown in Figure 13–28. Line 14 was still blank, but he inserted
six new lines after it. The first three were comment lines explaining
the role of a new working variable named MORE. When SCALC is
executed, MORE would initially be set to a "y" value. The WHILE
command begins in line 19 and extends to the matching ENDWHILE
in line 37. Like an IF command, a WHILE command has a condition.
In this case, the condition involves the value of MORE.

When the WHILE command is executed, the condition is evaluated.
If it is TRUE, all the commands between DO and ENDWHILE are executed. The condition is then reevaluated. If it is still TRUE, all the
embedded commands are again executed. After this second iteration,
the condition is again evaluated. A third iteration through the commands
occurs if it is again TRUE. Processing continues in this fashion while
the condition remains TRUE. As soon as the condition is evaluated to
be FALSE, execution of the WHILE command ends. The command
following ENDWHILE is then processed.

When executed, the Figure 13–28 WHILE command will do exactly
the same commands as those on lines 16 through 28 of the previous
version of SCALC. In addition there are two other commands. On line

FIGURE 13–29   Getting a chance to do more salary calculations

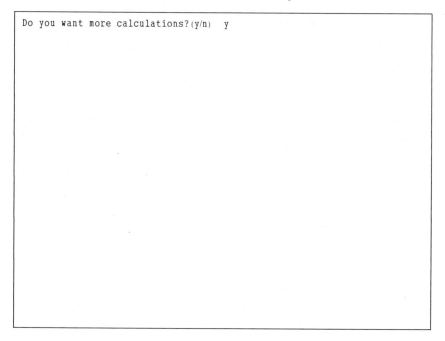

```
Do you want more calculations?(y/n)   y
```

35 is a command that asks whether more calculations are desired. The user's response becomes the new value of MORE. If more calculations are desired, the command in line 36 clears the screen and the WHILE condition will be satisfied resulting in another iteration. If no more calculations are desired the WHILE condition will not be satisfied and no further iterations will occur.

Jack wrote the new version of SCALC to disk and proceeded to test it just as he had done in Figures 13–20 and 13–21. When he pressed the space bar to clear the form from the screen, the new prompt asking about more calculations appeared as expected. Jack responded by typing

y

yielding the screen depicted in Figure 13–29. When he pressed the Enter key the screen cleared and he was prompted to enter the desired rep name. As Figure 13–20 shows, the previous rep name appeared automatically following the prompt message. By pressing the Enter key he was able to do another calculation for that rep. Of course, he could have typed in any other rep name if desired. Jack ran through several

FIGURE 13–30   Nested iteration

```
  Line:35      Col:1     a:scalc.ipf    Insert              Press ^L for help
  15      ! The program will allow repeated calculations with SCALC as long
  16      ! as the variable MORE has "y" as its value. While MORE has this
  17      ! value, the calculation process will iterate.
  18          more="y"
  19          while more in ["y","Y"] do
  20
  21          ! Find out what rep the user wants and then obtain that record
  22              input who using "%8r" \
  23                with "For which rep do you want to make a salary calculation?"
  24              obtain from rep where fname=who
  25              if #found then perform "a:repfound"
  26                      else output trim(who), " is not a valid rep name"
  27                           output "Enter one of the following names:"
  28                           select fname using "%35 %8r" from rep
  29                           #found=false !SELECT finds records, but not WHO
  30                           while not #found do
  31                               input who using "%8r" with "Enter desired name:"
  32                               obtain from rep where fname=who
  33                           endwhile
  34                           perform "a:repfound"
  35          endif
  36          input more using "a" with "Do you want more calculations?(y/n) "
  37          if more in ["Y","y"] then clear; endif
  38          endwhile
```

other tests to ensure that the program worked as expected. As the
final test, he responded to the prompt about more calculations by typing

n

and pressing the Enter key. As expected, execution of SCALC ceased
and the underscore prompt appeared.

Nested Iteration

"Are we allowed to nest one WHILE command in the DO list of another
WHILE command?" asked Debbie. "I'm thinking we could improve
SCALC by giving a user more than just two chances to enter a valid
rep name."

"Sure, that's possible," Jack replied, rubbing his chin. "We'd put
a WHILE command after the SELECT and get rid of the IF command
that's there. Let's see what it would look like."

He edited the commands following the SELECT command until
SCALC appeared as shown in Figure 13–30. He explained that as long
as #FOUND remains FALSE, execution will continue to iterate through

the commands on lines 31 and 32. When a valid name is input for WHO, the following OBTAIN command will find a record. The next time the WHILE condition is evaluated it will not be satisfied (i.e., NOT #FOUND will be FALSE) and execution will proceed to the PER-FORM command following ENDWHILE. Notice that #FOUND is set to FALSE before the WHILE command. This is necessary because it will be TRUE after SELECT is executed. SELECT finds records, but will not have found one matching the invalid rep name.

The printout in Figure 13–31 shows the full revised SCALC program. Notice that there are IF commands (lines 25–35 and 37) nested within a WHILE command. Moreover, there are a WHILE command (lines 30–33) and a PERFORM command (line 34) nested within one of those IF commands. Jack wrote the new SCALC to disk and then performed SCALC to check the accuracy of his programming logic. As Figure 13–32 shows, he intentionally made two consecutive errors when asked for a rep name, as he had in Figure 13–23. This time, SCALC gave him another chance. He edited the name to make it valid. On pressing the Enter key, the SCALC form appeared and he proceeded to process it in the normal way.

Automatic Menu Processing

"Giving multiple chances to get the name right is nice," Stan remarked. "But I think it would be even better if we had a foolproof way of getting a valid name the first time. Is there a way we could program SCALC to present a menu of valid rep names? The names would be options in the menu, so when the user picks one, the program doesn't have to worry about the possibility of an invalid name."

"I agree it would be better," Debbie added, "provided it's not too complex to program. In COBOL, the programming language I used in school, it would be quite cumbersome and complex to program menu-oriented input instead of the line-oriented input like SCALC now uses."

"You're right about that," confirmed Joy [11]. "But in this environment the entire activity of presenting a menu to the user and getting the user's response is handled by a single built-in function named MENU. Go ahead and show them, Jack."

"Alright," he consented. "Before using the MENU function we need to fill an array with the options to be presented in the menu. Because we'll no longer need to input a name into the WHO variable, I'll just call the array WHO. It will need to be dimensioned to have the same number of elements as the REP table has records. Because we'll want the menu's options to be rep names, we'll have SCALC convert the names into the WHO array."

FIGURE 13–31   Revised SCALC with nested PERFORM, WHILE, and IF commands

```
1       ! This program is intended to make salary calculations via the SCALC
2       ! form stored in A:SCALC.ICF. It lets the user identify which rep is
3       ! of interest and make the calculation for that rep by entering the
4 .     ! desired percentage increase in the form.
5          clear
6
7       ! Make sure the REP table is in use and the SCALC form is loaded
8          if not inuse("rep") then use "a:rep.itb"; endif
9          load "a:scalc.icf" with "f"
10
11      ! Save current environment settings before switching them
12         esupd=e.supd; e.supd=true; elstr=e.lstr; e.lstr=80
13         eicom=e.icom; e.icom=true; esuph=e.suph; e.suph=true
14
15      ! The program will allow repeated calculations with SCALC as long
16      ! as the variable MORE has "y" as its value. While MORE has this
17      ! value, the calculation process will iterate.
18         more="y"
19         while more in ["y","Y"] do
20
21          ! Find out what rep the user wants and then obtain that record
22             input who using "%8r" \
23                with "For which rep do you want to make a salary calculation?"
24             obtain from rep where fname=who
25             if #found then perform "a:repfound"
26                     else output trim(who), " is not a valid rep name"
27                          output "Enter one of the following names:"
28                          select fname using "%35 %8r" from rep
29                          #found=false !SELECT finds records, but not WHO
30                          while not #found do
31                             input who using "%8r" with "Enter desired name:"
32                             obtain from rep where fname=who
33                          endwhile
34                          perform "a:repfound"
35             endif
36             input more using "a" with "Do you want more calculations?(y/n) "
37             if more in ["Y","y"] then clear; endif
38         endwhile
39
40      ! Cleanup by restoring the environment variables and releasing SCALC
41         e.supd=esupd; e.suph=esuph; e.icom=eicom; e.lstr=elstr
42         release scalc,incr,who
```

FIGURE 13–32 Getting more than two chances to enter a name correctly

```
For which rep do you want to make a salary calculation? Cathey
Cathey is not a valid rep name
Enter one of the following names:
                              Kevin
                              Kim
                              Kris
                              Tina
                              Toby
                              Kerry
                              Karen
                              Kathy
                              Jackie
                              Carol
Enter desired name: Kathey
Enter desired name: Kathy___
```

As shown in lines 15 through 18 of Figure 13–33, Jack inserted three commands to handle what he had just described. The first of these involves a built-in function named LASTREC. Its value is always the number of the last record in an indicated table. In this case, the number of records in the REP table will be assigned to the OPTIONS working variable. OPTIONS will then be used to dimension the WHO array. Line 18 will, when executed, convert the rep first names into WHO.

Jack then inserted two more commands, explaining that he wanted the menu options to be presented in black on a red background. When executed, these two commands (in lines 21 and 22 of Figure 13–33) would alter the fourth color codes of E.BACG and E.FORG to be R and A, respectively. Thus the group had now seen the role played by each of these environment variables' five color codes.

He proceeded to delete the first line of SCALC's first INPUT command and replace the WITH at the start of the second line with OUTPUT. Compare line 31 of Figure 13–33 with lines 22 and 23 of Figure 13–31. The prompt message to identify a rep would now simply be output with no place for a name to be input. Instead, evaluation of the MENU function in line 33 would cause a menu to appear on the screen. The

FIGURE 13–33 Revising SCALC to provide a menu interface

```
  Line:23      Col:1      a:scalc.ipf      Insert           Press ^L for help
15       ! Set up the WHO array of rep options to present in a menu
16           options=lastrec(rep)
17           dim who(options)
18           convert trim(fname) from rep to array who(1) order by fname
19
20       ! Set up the rep menu's option colors: black on red
21           e.bacg=substr(e.bacg,1,3)+"r"+substr(e.bacg,5,1)
22           e.forg=substr(e.forg,1,3)+"a"+substr(e.forg,5,1)
23
24       ! The program will allow repeated calculations with SCALC as long
25       ! as the variable MORE has "y" as its value. While MORE has this
26       ! value, the calculation process will iterate.
27           more="y"
28           while more in ["y","Y"] do
29
30           ! Find out what rep the user wants and then obtain that record
31               output "For which rep do you want to make a salary calculation?"
32               !Menu begins in row 3/col 6; row spacing 2; col width 12; 5 cols
33                 Choice=menu(who,1,options,3,6,2,12,5)
34               obtain from rep where fname=who(choice)
35               perform "a:repfound"
36               input more using "a" with "Do you want more calculations?(y/n) "
37               if more in ["Y","y"] then clear; endif
38           endwhile
```

value assigned to the CHOICE working variable would be the number of the option chosen by a user.

The MENU function has more arguments than the other built-in functions [9]. Jack explained that they offer considerable control over the presentation of the menu on the screen. The meanings of these arguments can be summarized as follows:

First:	Name of the array holding the menu's options.
Second:	Number of the default option where cursor will initially rest.
Third:	Number of options to display from the array in the menu.
Fourth:	Screen row where menu's options will begin to be displayed.
Fifth:	Screen column where menu's options will begin to be displayed.
Sixth:	Number of blank lines to leave between rows of options.
Seventh:	Total width (in characters) of each column of options.
Eighth:	Number of option columns desired in the menu.

When line 33 is executed a menu will be presented having an option for each element in the array. A reverse video cursor will rest on the option taken from WHO's first element. This option will begin at the sixth column of the third row of the screen. There will be two blank lines between successive rows of options in the menu. Each option can be up to 12 characters wide and the options will be organized into five columns.

Jack altered the OBTAIN command slightly, equating FNAME to the WHO option chosen in the preceding step. Because the menu made it impossible to indicate an invalid rep, there was no longer any need to check #FOUND. Thus, the IF command extending from line 25 through line 35 in Figure 13–31 was eliminated in favor of the PERFORM command on line 35 in Figure 13–33. As the printout of the edited SCALC in Figure 13–34 shows, Jack also edited the final RELEASE command to include WHO, OPTIONS, and CHOICE.

After writing the revised SCALC to disk, Jack performed it to demonstrate the new menu-guided interface. The screen cleared and then took on the appearance portrayed in Figure 13–35. As expected, the menu had 10 options arranged into five columns. A reverse video (red on black) cursor highlighted the Carol option. The options were black on red. Using the arrow keys, Jack showed that the cursor could be moved to any of the 10 options. With the menu cursor highlighting the Kim option, he pressed the Enter key to make his choice. The screen cleared momentarily before the SCALC form appeared with Kim's data. He entered 6.2 percent as shown in Figure 13–21 and proceeded with the remainder of SCALC processing as usual.

Parameterized Procedures

"Could we go back to nested procedures for a minute?" Stan asked. "I noticed that the SETUP program contains four little command sequences that are very much alike. They're the ones that get the colors for the various kinds of screens. Because they're so similar, I tried to find a way to replace each by a PERFORM command that, when executed, would perform the same procedure. But I couldn't see how to do it, because the procedure would need to be a little different for each."

Jack brought up a text screen with SETUP (Figure 13–12) to take a look. "I see what you mean. You'd like a single program that can get a color code. You could then just perform it four times in place of lines 13 through 32. It turns out that we can make a single GETCOLOR program, which can be performed four times in SETUP to accomplish the same processing that is now done by the four INPUT and IF commands."

To demonstrate, Jack edited the SETUP program by deleting lines 13 through 32. He replaced them with the five new commands shown

FIGURE 13–34   SCALC program with a menu-guided interface

```
1     ! This program is intended to make salary calculations via the SCALC
2     ! form stored in A:SCALC.ICF. It lets the user identify which rep is
3     ! of interest and make the calculation for that rep by entering the
4     ! desired percentage increase in the form.
5        clear
6
7     ! Make sure the REP table is in use and the SCALC form is loaded
8        if not inuse("rep") then use "a:rep.itb"; endif
9        load "a:scalc.icf" with "f"
10
11    ! Save current environment settings before switching them
12       esupd=e.supd; e.supd=true; elstr=e.lstr; e.lstr=80
13       eicom=e.icom; e.icom=true; esuph=e.suph; e.suph=true
14
15    ! Set up the WHO array of rep options to present in a menu
16       options=lastrec(rep)
17       dim who(options)
18       convert trim(fname) from rep to array who(1) order by fname
19
20    ! Set up the rep menu's option colors: black on red
21       e.bacg=substr(e.bacg,1,3)+"r"+substr(e.bacg,5,1)
22       e.forg=substr(e.forg,1,3)+"a"+substr(e.forg,5,1)
23
24    ! The program will allow repeated calculations with SCALC as long
25    ! as the variable MORE has "y" as its value. While MORE has this
26    ! value, the calculation process will iterate.
27       more="y"
28       while more in ["y","Y"] do
29
30          ! Find out what rep the user wants and then obtain that record
31          output "For which rep do you want to make a salary calculation?"
32             !Menu begins in row 3/col 6; row spacing 2; col width 12; 5 cols
33             choice=menu(who,1,options,3,6,2,12,5)
34          obtain from rep where fname=who(choice)
35          perform "a:repfound"
36          input more using "a" with "Do you want more calculations?(y/n) "
37          if more in ["Y","y"] then clear; endif
38       endwhile
39
40    ! Cleanup by restoring the environment variables and releasing SCALC
41       e.supd=esupd; e.suph=esuph; e.icom=eicom; e.lstr=elstr
42       release scalc,incr,who,options,choice
```

FIGURE 13–35 Menu generated by the MENU Function

```
For which rep do you want to make a salary calculation?

      Carol      Karen      Kerry      Kim        Tina

      Jackie     Kathy      Kevin      Kris       Toby
```

in lines 14 through 18 of Figure 13–36. Each of the four PERFORM commands had a USING clause. Jack explained that when the first one is executed the values 10 and "ss" would be passed along to GET-COLOR. As GETCOLOR is performed, these values would influence its behavior, causing it to handle the spreadsheet color code. Similarly, when the second PERFORM is executed the values 11 and "gr" will be passed to the same GETCOLOR program. They will influence the GETCOLOR behavior in a different way to handle the graphics color code. The other two PERFORMs pass yet other values to the GETCOLOR program, tailoring its behavior in still other ways.

After writing the new rendition of SETUP to disk, Jack developed the GETCOLOR program as shown in Figure 13–37. As the initial comment lines explain, this program contains two *parameters:* #A and #B. These correspond to the two values passed to GETCOLOR whenever it is performed. The mechanics of passing values are straightforward. The value of the first argument used with a PERFORM command automatically replaces every instance of the first parameter, #A, in the program that is being performed. Similarly, the second value replaces every instance of #B in the program being performed.

Jack elaborated, "Think about what will happen when the first PER-

FIGURE 13–36   Passing values when performing a program

```
    Line:21    Col:32    a:setup.ipf   Command: write
1       ! This program performs A:GETCOLOR while setting up the environment
2         clear
3         e.deci=2
4         e.lstr=80                          \
5         at 1,1 output "ENVIRONMENT  SETUP" using "%31*%18r%31*"
6         templstr=25
7         at 3,5 input e.deci using "n" with "How many decimal digits?"
8         at 5,5 input templstr using "nnn" with "Default length of strings?"
9       ! Set up the colors
10        macro ccodes ["a","o","u","w","c","g","r","m"]
11        at 7,5 output "Color codes: A(black) O(brown) U(blue) W(white)"
12        at 8,18 output "C(cyan) G(green) R(red)  M(magenta)"
13        at 9,10 output "What background color do you want for:"
14            promline=10
15            perform "a:getcolor" using promline,"ss"
16            perform "a:getcolor" using promline+1,"gr"
17            perform "a:getcolor" using promline+2,"te"
18            perform "a:getcolor" using promline+3,"ot"
19        e.bacg=s+g+t+o+o
20      e.lstr=templstr
21      release templstr,s,g,t,o,ccodes
22      redefine function 1 "help\\13"
23      if not inuse("rep") then use "a:rep.itb";endif
24      if not inuse("perf") then use "a:perf.itb" with "a:perftp.ind";endif
```

FIGURE 13–37   Using parameters in a program

```
    Line:24    Col:31    a:getcolor.ipf Command: write
1       ! This program prompts the user for a color code. The CCODES macro
2       ! must be in the present processing context before this program is
3       ! performed. It is the class of all valid color codes. If an invalid
4       ! code is entered, the user is notified and appropriate action is
5       ! taken. The program's parameters are:
6       !              #A   the line position for the input prompt
7       !              #B   variable designating screen type (SS,GR,TE,OT)
8
9       ! Give matching values to the variables designating screen types
10          ss="ss"; gr="gr"; te="te"; ot="ot"
11      ! Identify proper prompt message, code position, code length, variable
12          local prompt, codepos, codelen, var
13          codelen=1; var="o"
14          if #b=ss then prompt="spreadsheet?";codepos=1;var="s";endif
15          if #b=gr then prompt="graphics?";codepos=2;var="g";endif
16          if #b=te then prompt="text?";codepos=3;var="t";endif
17          if #b=ot then prompt="other screens?";codepos=4;codelen=2;endif
18          at #a,15 input `var using "a" with prompt
19      ! If the user's input is invalid, give the variable a valid code
20          if not (`var in ccodes) then `var=substr(e.bacg,codepos,codelen)
21                      at #a,35 ? "INVALID CODE"
22                      at #a,50 ? `var using "u", " is still used"
23          endif
24          release ss,gr,te,ot; return
```

FIGURE 13–38   Getting acquainted with the substitution indicator

```
_var="s"
_?var
s
_s="g"
_?s
g
_?^var
g
_^var="r"
_?^var
r
_?s
r
_
```

FORM in SETUP is executed. The steps in GETCOLOR will be carried out. When line 14 is reached, the IF command's condition is interpreted as being SS=SS, which is TRUE. The next condition is interpreted as being SS=GR, which is FALSE, and so on for the other IF commands. Similarly, in line 18 the #A,15 will be interpreted as 10,15."

"I get it," said Stan. "But what is that hat symbol doing in front of VAR?"

"Whenever a variable is prefaced with a hat symbol, the command is executed as if the variable's value were substituted in place of the variable itself," answered Jack. "For that reason it's called the *substitution indicator*. Let me run through a little interactive example to give you the idea of how this works."

He left the text screen and executed several commands as portrayed in Figure 13–38. Jack gave the variables VAR and S the string values "s" and "g" respectively. Notice that the commands

```
?s
?^var
```

gave the same result. This was because ^VAR was interpreted as being identical to VAR's value, which was S. That is, ^VAR was another way of referring to the variable S, because VAR's value was the "s" string. When Jack executed the command

```
˙var="r"
```

he was assigning the "r" string value to the variable S.

Returning to the GETCOLOR program, Jack explained, "The IF commands use the value passed through #B to determine which variable should be set by the present GETCOLOR performance. That variable's name becomes the VAR value. Later in the INPUT command we want the user's entry to become the value of that variable, so the substitution indicator is used there in front of VAR. We don't want the user's entry to become the value of VAR, which is what would happen if the indicator were omitted. I've used ˙VAR for the same reason in lines 20 and 22."

Jack brought up one other point about the GETCOLOR program. Line 12 contains the LOCAL command. When LOCAL is executed in a program, all of the variables specified in this command are considered to be *local* to the program. When the program ceases execution local variables and their values disappear. Variables that are not local are called *global*. They exist and keep their values without regard to the programs that reference them.

After writing the GETCOLOR program on disk, Jack left the text screen and performed the new SETUP program. He ran several tests to show that, from a user's point of view, it exhibited the same behavior as the earlier version of SETUP. Sensing that some of the managers had not fully grasped all the aspects of Jack's answer to Stan's question, Joy offered a few words of comfort. "The features that Jack has just covered in this new version of SETUP are fairly advanced. So if you don't understand all the details, don't worry about it. With what we've covered earlier, you still know a good amount about the practicalities of developing programs that work."

Case Processing

"While I'm at it," Jack continued, "there is one last command for controlling the flow of command execution in a program. I'll just give a brief example of it for those of you who are pretty keen about programming. Those who aren't shouldn't be concerned about it. The command is called TEST and is really just a generalization of the IF command, because it allows control to branch in more than two directions."

Returning to the text screen of Figure 13–37, he continued, "Look at the IF commands on lines 14 through 17. What we're really interested in is having the program test #B to see whether it equals the value of

FIGURE 13–39   Case processing in a program

```
   Line:20     Col:14     a:getcolor.ipf Command: write
4       ! code is entered, the user is notified and appropriate action is
5       ! taken. The program's parameters are:
6       !                    #A    the line position for the input prompt
7       !                    #B    variable designating screen type (SS,GR,TE,OT)
8
9       ! Give matching values to the variables designating screen types
10          ss="ss"; gr="gr"; te="te"; ot="ot"
11      ! Identify proper prompt message, code position, code length, variable
12          local prompt, codepos, codelen, var
13          codelen=1; var="o"
14              test #b
15                  case ss: prompt="spreadsheet?";codepos=1;var="s";break
16                  case gr: prompt="graphics?";codepos=2;var="g";break
17                  case te: prompt="text?";codepos=3;var="t";break
18                  case ot: prompt="other screens?";codepos=4;codelen=2;break
19                  otherwise: at #a,1 ? "ERROR IN 2ND PERFORM ARGUMENT";return
20              endtest
21          at #a,15 input 'var using "a" with prompt
22      ! If the user's input is invalid, give the variable a valid code
23          if not ('var in ccodes) then 'var=substr(e.bacg,codepos,codelen)
24                          at #a,35 ? "INVALID CODE"
25                          at #a,50 ? 'var using "u", " is still used"
26          endif
27          release ss,gr,te,ot; return
```

SS, GR, TE, or OT. Then, depending on which of these four *cases* is detected, the program will execute an appropriate sequence of commands to get ready for processing in line 18 and onward. Let me show you how the four IF commands can be replaced by a single equivalent TEST command."

Jack edited the GETCOLOR program to make the replacement. As he was about to write the new version of GETCOLOR to disk, the screen appeared as shown in Figure 13–39. The TEST command extended from line 14 through line 20. When this command is executed, the value of whatever variable replaces #B (i.e., either SS, GR, TE, or OT) is compared to the value of the first case's expression (i.e., the value of SS). If they are equal, the commands following the colon for that case are executed. If they are not equal the case's commands are not executed and a comparison is made with the value of the second case's expression (i.e., the value of GR), and so forth.

If no case is satisfied, then the commands following the OTHERWISE are executed. Because this would be an indication that a PERFORM command in SETUP had an incorrect second argument, Jack wanted GETCOLOR to output a message to that effect and immediately return to SETUP. When it finished executing he could then debug it by changing the incorrect PERFORM command. In general, the OTHERWISE case in a TEST command is optional.

Jack explained that the BREAK command embedded in each of the first four cases would cause the flow of execution to immediately break away to the command following ENDTEST. In this example, there was no need to have other cases processed once the matching case's commands had been executed. Jack went on to test the new program by invoking

```
perform "a:setup"
```

and demonstrated that its behavior was the same as it had previously been.

In general, the value of any expression can be tested by the TEST command. Each case can involve any expression of the same type as the expression being tested. For instance, the command

```
if not inuse("rep") then use "a:rep.itb";endif
```

could be restated as

```
test not inuse("rep")
  case true: use "a:rep.itb"
endtest
```

where the tested expression has a logical rather than string value.

PROFESSIONAL PROGRAMMING

Having covered the major commands for controlling a program's flow of execution, Jack adjourned the meeting for individual practice. It was unlikely that any of the managers, including Jack himself, would ever become professional programmers. Nevertheless, they all now grasped enough of this knowledge management technique to be able to devise their own programs. To a pro, their programs may seem modest and may perhaps lack optimal efficiency. But the important point is that the programs would work to save the managers both time and effort when it comes to carrying out routine, repetitive procedures.

With their knowledge of programming, the managers were now able to build their own customized user interfaces (recall Chapter 3) to the environment. Programs such as those in Figures 13–13, 13–31, and 13–34 not only automate procedures, they provide new ways of allowing a user to interface with the environment, ways that are customized to address specific user needs. This interface customization can involve line-oriented INPUT and OUTPUT commands, form-processing commands, and menu generation.

With their present knowledge of programming, the managers could begin to appreciate what the application developers in KC's MIS department do. Some of the developers are *systems analysts* who determine or discover the requirements of how prospective application software should behave [1], [5], [12]. Because this is normally accomplished by understanding the needs and problems of potential users of the software, effective interpersonal skills and a good background in the functional areas of management are important for successful systems analysis. Other developers are *systems designers* who take specifications of what an application system is required to do and create plans of how those requirements can be met [1], [6], [7], [12]. Still other developers are the programmers who actually *implement* full-scale application systems by writing programs corresponding to the designs [6], [12]. The resultant application software (i.e., programs) gives its users customized interfaces for dealing with various record-keeping and decision support activities. Once a user executes such a program (e.g., via an operating system command or an environment command such as PERFORM), the interaction begins and follows the flow dictated by the program's commands.

Unlike professional application software developers, the managers are users of what they themselves develop. Each manager who writes a program also does preliminary analysis and design for that program. Wearing an analyst hat, the manager thinks out what it is that he or she needs the program to do. Wearing a designer hat, the manager then plans a flow of steps that will meet the analyzed needs. Wearing a programmer hat, the manager formally specifies and tests the commands corresponding to the plan. Then, the manager actually uses the developed program. It should be emphasized that the activities of analysis and design are not peculiar to using the programming technique of knowledge management. As the preceding chapters have shown, effective use of any knowledge management technique depends on analyzing what the needs are (i.e., understanding what problem is being faced) and designing a plan for meeting those needs (e.g., selecting suitable knowledge management capabilities).

Compiled Languages

A professional programmer may use the environment's programming language to write programs. This lets a user operate entire application systems within the environment, as well as directly execute any of the environment's own innate commands. Alternatively, professional programmers can write programs with independent languages. Some of the most widely used of these languages include COBOL, FORTRAN, C, BASIC, and Pascal [3], [8], [11], [13], [16]. Though each has its own unique commands and syntax, all of these languages support the control flow mechanisms of conditional branching, conditional iteration, and nested procedure execution.

Because of their stand-alone nature, these languages do not support the wealth of commands that can be used in the environment's programming language. For instance, commands such as SELECT, TEXT, STAT, OBTAIN, CONVERT, PLOT, COMPUTE, and REPORT have no counterparts in the above-mentioned programming languages. However, all of them do provide commands for assigning the results of calculations to variables, line-oriented input and output for variables, and the preservation (and recall) of variable values in disk files.

With the exception of BASIC, programs written in these languages must be *compiled* before they can be executed. The programmer uses separate text management software to prepare a text file containing commands allowed by the programming language. This is called the *source program* and it is saved in a disk file. The source program is then processed by a special program called a *compiler*. For instance, COBOL programs are processed by a COBOL compiler, programs written in the FORTRAN language are processed by a FORTRAN compiler, and so forth. A compiler examines the source program for errors. If any are detected they are reported to the programmer, who then debugs the program and again tries to process it with the compiler.

When the compiler detects no errors in a source program, it generates a new version of the program in a different language whose commands can be more directly and rapidly executed by the computer hardware. This new version of the program is saved on a file and is called the *object program* or an *executable program*. When intended for use within the PC-DOS operating system the files holding such programs are normally given EXE extensions. Simply specifying the name of an object program's file in response to the operating system's command prompt (e.g., C>) causes the program to be executed.

Once an object program is acquired from the compiler, a programmer can execute it to begin testing its behavior and logic. If bugs are found, the source program needs to be edited and again submitted to the compiler for generating a new object program. The new object program is then tested. As Figure 13–40 suggests, the debugging process of editing the source program, compiling, and testing the object program continues until the programmer is satisfied with the program's behavior. Program-

FIGURE 13–40   Program creation with a compiled language

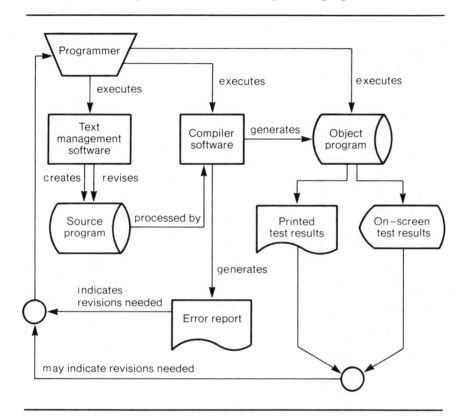

ming languages such as the one the managers have learned do not require the use of a compiler. They are called *interpretive languages.*

Generally, the execution speed of a program written with a compiled language is faster than a comparable program written with an interpretive language. This is because much of the work of translating a programmer's commands into commands that the hardware can process is done prior to execution rather than during the execution of the program. For large, extensive, or complex programs the difference in execution times can be significant. For most do-it-yourself programming efforts the difference will not be significant. The added convenience of avoiding the compilation step and having a wealth of commands that normally do not exist in compiled languages is the positive trade-off that results from an interpretive language.

FIGURE 13–41 Flowchart for SCALC program in Figure 13–31

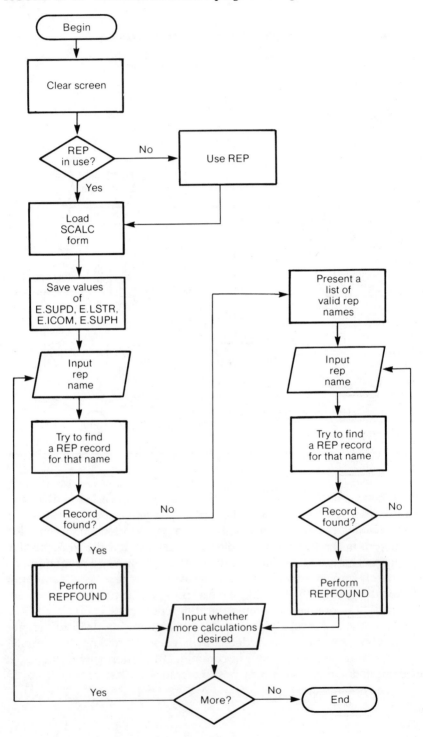

Flowcharting

Regardless of the programming language adopted, professional developers typically work on much larger and more complex programs than the sales managers would attempt. For large projects, it is important to first understand what the potential users' requirements are. This is the job of the systems analyst. Second, it is important to think out the flow of a program's logic in advance of actually creating the program. Professional systems designers do this preliminary design work by sketching diagrams called flowcharts [3]. A *flowchart* shows the procedural flow of steps that should be followed when a program executes. It provides a highly visual guideline for the programmer who specifies and tests a program's commands.

Figure 13–41 shows a flowchart that a designer might have designed prior to creating the SCALC program of Figure 13–31. By convention, the various geometric shapes in the diagram represent different kinds of steps in a procedure. The meanings of some commonly used flowcharting shapes are explained in Figure 13–42. Though Jack did not design explicit flowcharts for the small programs he developed, flowcharts become increasingly beneficial as the size of a programming task grows. Even for a small program like SCALC, a flowchart can be beneficial. For instance, it is immediately obvious in Figure 13–41 that there is a duplicate series of steps. Seeing this, Jack might want to revamp his program design to eliminate the duplication and produce a more efficient program.

BASIC IDEAS

Programming is a much more versatile and general-purpose technique for managing procedural knowledge than what can be achieved with conventional spreadsheets. In simplest terms, a program is a sequence of commands existing in a disk file. When a program is performed (i.e., executed), the commands are executed in sequence. There are certain commands that can divert the flow of command execution in various ways via conditional branching (IF, TEST), conditional iteration (WHILE), and nested program execution (PERFORM).

The environment's programming language allows a command that can be directly executed in response to an underscore to be incorporated into a program. These commands can be placed between or within the commands that control the program's flow of execution. This means that a program can do calculations, initiate text management, carry out data base management, execute queries, gather statistics, process forms, generate formal reports, produce graphics, create or alter spread-

FIGURE 13–42   Some common flowcharting conventions

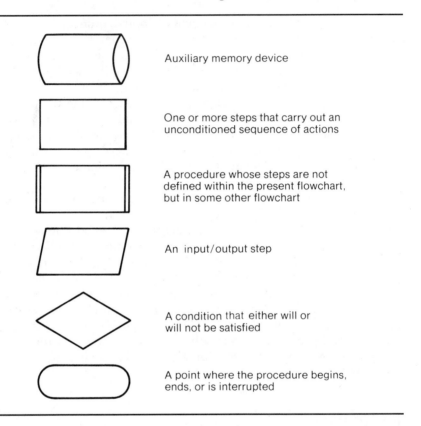

Auxiliary memory device

One or more steps that carry out an unconditioned sequence of actions

A procedure whose steps are not defined within the present flowchart, but in some other flowchart

An input/output step

A condition that either will or will not be satisfied

A point where the procedure begins, ends, or is interrupted

sheet templates, carry out operations on cells or the spreadsheet as a whole, and so forth. This degree of versatility is unavailable with conventional, compiled programming languages.

Because a spreadsheet cell can be defined in terms of commands, a PERFORM command can be included in a cell's definition. Whenever the spreadsheet is computed, that cell's value will be established by automatically performing an entire program. Such a program can be used and maintained independently of the spreadsheets that perform it. Conventional spreadsheet packages do not support such a feature.

Programming gives both do-it-yourself computer users and professional application developers a valuable way of automating procedural knowledge. It is stored in the environment's knowledge system along with other kinds of knowledge. Once it is there, the environment will perform it instead of the user having to enter and carry out the steps one by one. This chapter's treatment of programming in general, or even programming in an environment, is by no means exhaustive. In fact, that very evening Jack and Joy worked out some customized interfacing techniques that neither had previously used. More examples of programming in an environment can be found in other books [2], [14], [15]. Many of those are more advanced than what Jack covered and are of special interest to professional developers of application software.

References

1. Awad, E. M. *Systems Analysis and Design*. Homewood, Ill.: Richard D. Irwin, 1985.
2. Baker, J. *Mastering KnowledgeMan/2*. Lafayette, Ind.: J. Baker, 1987.
3. Bohl, M. *Information Processing with BASIC*. Chicago: SRA, 1984.
4. Cougar, J. D. *The Art of Software Testing*. New York: John Wiley & Sons, 1979.
5. Demarco, T. *Structured Analysis and System Specification*. New York: Yourdon, 1978.
6. Higgins, D. A. *Program Design and Construction*. Englewood Cliffs, N.J.: Prentice-Hall, 1979.
7. Jackson, M. A. *Principles of Program Design*. New York: Academic Press, 1979.
8. Kiebwitz, R.B. *Structured Programming and Problem-Solving with Pascal*. Englewood Cliffs, N.J.: Prentice-Hall, 1978.
9. *K-Mouse Supplement*, version 2. Lafayette, Ind.: MDBS, Inc., 1985.
10. *KnowledgeMan Reference Manual*, version 2. Lafayette, Ind.: MDBS, Inc., 1985.
11. Murach, M. *Business Data Processing with COBOL*. Chicago: SRA, 1977.
12. Pressman, R. S. *Software Engineering: A Practitioner's Approach*. New York: McGraw-Hill, 1987.
13. Purdum, J. *C Programming Guide*. Indianapolis: Que, 1985.
14. Roeder, G. *The Book of KnowledgeMan*, vol. 1. Chelmsford, Mass.: All-Hands-On Press, 1984.
15. _____. *The Book of KnowledgeMan*, vol. 2. Chelmsford, Mass.: All-Hands-On Press, 1985.
16. Schriber, T. J. *FORTRAN Case Studies for Business Applications*. New York: John Wiley & Sons, 1969.

Part VI

BEYOND THE LIMITS

It's only reasonable that we can also get expert advice from it.

Chapter Fourteen

Rule Management

Jack rolled onto his side and adjusted the pillow. Through half-opened eyes he looked at Joy and smiled a smile of quiet contentment. Glancing at the clock on the nightstand he saw that it was nearly 6 P.M. There was still more than an hour before the evening's "graduation" banquet was to begin. Wanting to be as fresh as possible, he decided to extend his brief nap for a few more winks. From the clock, his eyes returned to the photo Joy had given him, propped against the base of the lamp. The short white outfit she wore highlighted her deep tan.

Closing his eyes, he saw her eyes and thought of all they had accomplished. The training session's eight days seemed to have passed very quickly. Although it was unexpected, Jack had in his own way learned as much as the other managers. Joy had shown him not only some of the more advanced aspects of techniques he already knew, but had introduced him to an altogether new technique. This happened when he visited her home on the prior Sunday afternoon. She had touched only on certain basics, but it was enough that Jack became intrigued by the possibilities Joy presented.

Sunday was a day off for the managers, so Joy invited Jack to the house for some of her home cooking. Naturally, he accepted. The brick exterior gave way to a tasteful brass and glass decor. He could tell that her favorite color was blue. After the lasagna, she offered him some food for thought.

"You know," she said, "there is a relatively new and very interesting knowledge management technique that we're working with here at headquarters. It involves representing knowledge in terms of rules. A user interface is provided that allows users to ask for advice about various problems they face. Whenever advice is requested, the rule-processing software uses a set of rules and interacts with the user in order to generate and present some advice about a specific problem.

The user can then have the software explain the line of reasoning it followed in producing the advice. Together, a set of rules, the user interface, and the processing software are commonly called an *expert system.*"

EXPERT SYSTEMS

"Ah, yes," said Jack with an air of recognition. "I remember reading about expert systems in *The Wall Street Journal* and other publications. From what I could discern, the main purpose of an expert system is to serve as the computerized counterpart to a human expert. When someone needs some expert advice about a problem, a human expert may not be available. Instead of waiting to consult a human expert, the person could immediately consult an expert system to get comparable advice."

"That's the basic idea," confirmed Joy. "Expert system technology is a branch of artificial intelligence that tries to make computers capable of emulating human reasoning behavior. An expert system can be consulted in much the same spirit as advice is sought from a human expert. Via a user interface such as a command language, a user poses a specific problem to the expert system. Like its human counterpart, it will probably ask the user for further information to help clarify or more fully describe the exact nature of the problem. Like a human expert, its objective is to offer some advice, recommendation, or solution to the user. To meet this objective, the software portion of an expert system draws on reasoning expertise."

"I see," acknowledged Jack. "A human expert's reasoning knowledge must somehow be captured in an expert system. Otherwise, the computer couldn't possibly emulate the human."

"Right, that's the key!" Joy declared. "As a result of training and experience, a human expert acquires the reasoning knowledge that allows him or her to function as an expert in a particular problem domain. When a specific problem is posed, the expert draws on relevant fragments of that stored reasoning knowledge as needed in the course of deriving some advice. Similarly, in the case of an expert system, reasoning knowledge for a particular problem domain must be acquired and stored in the computer. Furthermore, there must be software that is able to actively process that knowledge to derive advice.

"Rule management is a valuable computer-based technique for representing and processing reasoning knowledge. Reasoning knowledge can be represented as rules that tell what conclusions can be drawn under various circumstances. With various commands we can tell the rule management software to process a set of rules. The processing result could be some advice or an explanation of the rationale behind that advice."

Reasoning knowledge is decidedly different than descriptive, linguistic, presentation, assimilative, and procedural knowledge. The techniques for managing these other kinds of knowledge are not particularly conducive to handling reasoning knowledge. For instance, fragments of reasoning knowledge could be expressed as narrative text. But text management software has no way of deriving and explaining advice from a piece of narrative text. The rule management technique has evolved to specifically address the representation and processing of reasoning knowledge in a straightforward manner [1], [7], [8].

Development Tools

"But," interjected Jack with some concern, "isn't this artificial intelligence stuff beyond me? Those articles I read implied that developing an expert system requires a college degree in artificial intelligence, a knowledge of complex programming languages, worker-years of effort, or expensive special-purpose machines."

She soothed him with a smile and explained, "Once upon a time that may have been true, but no longer. In fact, I'd say you already know about 80 percent of what you need for developing your own useful expert systems! And you don't need to deal with exotic languages or go back to college to learn the rest."

"So," surmised Jack, "there must be some recent advances that facilitate the development of expert systems."

"Right," she nodded [4]. "Back in the 70s and early 80s an expert system was typically developed by writing a large-scale program. When executed, the program was able to infer advice from stored expertise about a particular problem domain. Such programs came to be known as *inference engines*. They were developed with complex programming languages such as LISP. Even today, there are people who claim that you have to know LISP or some other such language in order to develop nontrivial expert systems. Thus far, our experience at KC is exactly the opposite of that claim.

"We are developing bona fide expert systems without doing any programming whatsoever! In fact, much of what we're developing would be extremely difficult, time-consuming, and expensive—if even possible—with something like LISP. In the early 80s a nonprogramming approach to developing expert systems began to be commercially available. It involves the use of what's known as an *expert system shell*.

"A shell usually consists of two pieces of software. One lets you type, store, scan, analyze, and edit a set of rules. It is often called a rule set manager. The second piece of software that you get with a shell is a ready-made inference engine. It is able to process any set of rules specified via the rule set manager that obey the shell's rule representation conventions."

"I can see where that is a big advance," Jack commented. "With a shell, the development process becomes one of specifying rules of reasoning, without bothering with programming. So a rule set is sort of like reusable fuel that a shell's inference engine draws on to generate advice about a problem. By using different rule sets, the same ready-made inference engine can generate advice in different problem domains."

"Exactly!" Joy affirmed. "One rule set might embody the reasoning knowledge necessary to give investment advice to the corporate treasurer. Another set of rules might represent the reasoning expertise needed to give advice about personnel evaluation. Yet another rule set might allow the inference engine to recommend shipping methods for various kinds of orders that require special handling.

"As you'd expect, the various shells that are commercially available vary widely in their facilities for representing and processing rules. Unfortunately, few of them seem to have been designed with an understanding of business problems in mind. This often makes it tough to represent the reasoning knowledge of an expert in some business problem domain. Another difficulty with many of the more powerful shells is their unavailability on common desktop computers. The special-purpose computers they require make them prohibitively expensive for many potential applications.

"But the biggest shortcoming we discovered for shells was that they stopped far short of the ideal. For us, the ideal is to fully emulate the reasoning behavior of a human expert in some problem domain. We interviewed various experts to gain insights into the rules they mentally applied when reasoning about problems. As we did so a very interesting pattern began to emerge. In the course of generating some advice about a problem, an expert does not merely reason but routinely does other things as well."

"Sure," nodded Jack [7]. "If a rep asks me for advice, the activity of reasoning out an answer may involve reading textual passages, making calculations, doing some ad hoc queries, looking at statistics, graphs, forms, or reports, analyzing spreadsheets, performing procedures, or even consulting other experts. It seems only natural that an expert system be able to do all this too. Reasoning doesn't happen in a vacuum."

"But the problem is that a shell doesn't have any innate concept of these other techniques of knowledge management that are so often exercised in a human's reasoning process. It is aware of rule management, period." Joy paused and touched his forearm as she continued,

"Imagine what it would be like if, when asked for advice, you couldn't use any of the ordinary knowledge management techniques in the course of your reasoning."

"I reckon I'd just be a shell of my present self," he joked.

"We certainly wouldn't want that," laughed Joy. "Well, last year a new kind of tool became available for expert system development. It's an *artificial intelligence environment*. It supports not only all the familiar knowledge management techniques, but rule management as well. Along with everything else you're accustomed to having in an environment's knowledge system, you can also have *rule sets.* When you ask the environment for advice about some problem, not only can it make inferences based on a rule set's rules, it can also exercise any of the other knowledge management techniques in the process."

"So," observed Jack, "instead of being in an isolated, stand-alone tool, the capabilities that once were available only in a shell are now available as innate capabilities of a full-fledged environment. That is, they are part of a much larger, integrated tool. Being able to build rule sets and do expert system processing along with everything else in an environment certainly is an alluring prospect. What's the name of this new expert system environment?"

"The first one to become commercially available is called Guru," she answered [3], [9]. "I've become quite familiar with it since it's the development tool used for all expert system projects in the company. The nice part is that every command and every feature you've taught the other managers is present in this environment too. So even though you've never worked with Guru, you already know how to use its capabilities for calculations, data management, text management, ad hoc queries, spreadsheets, and so on."

"Well then," Jack remarked, "it seems that all I need to learn is the technique of rule management. Maybe you'd be my guru and teach me?"

"I'd be happy to," she replied. "I'm sure you'll catch on to the basic ideas quickly. If you want to pursue it further, I'll see whether I can have the company provide you with the software."

Potential Benefits of Business Expert Systems

As Joy had explained, an expert system is able to provide timely advice when a human expert is unavailable. Unlike its human counterpart, an expert system can operate around the clock, seven days per week, every day of the year. An expert system does not get sick, take holidays, go on vacations, or resign. An expert system is not tied up in meetings, away on business, or otherwise inaccessible. Unlike the human experts that it emulates, an expert system can be readily replicated. The same expert system can simultaneously be used in many sites across the country or around the world. Once an expert system has been constructed, it is relatively inexpensive to distribute.

A good expert system functions as a clone of the human expert. In effect, it lets each user have an expert at his or her side to provide advice if and when it is desired. This does not threaten to put experts out of work. In some cases it will provide an expert advisory service not previously available. In other cases, a human expert may already be in place providing advice. The introduction of an expert system that can offer comparable advice should have a very positive impact on the human expert. It can reduce the demands on a human expert's time by insulating him or her from many kinds of consultation requests. The human expert is then able to focus on the most challenging problems and to concentrate on new creative activities. Human experts are normally a scarce resource for an organization. To the extent that their productivity can be increased by off-loading consultation activity to expert systems, the organization's human resources can be more effectively utilized.

Another benefit of an expert system is that it provides consistent, uniform advice. It is thorough and methodical. Unlike the human expert, an expert system does not have lapses that cause it to overlook important factors, skip steps, or forget. It is not politically motivated, temperamental, or biased (unless the developer designs it to be so). An expert system functions as a standardized problem solver that can be a substitute, supplement, or verifier for a human expert.

Like a human expert, an expert system is able to explain the line of reasoning it uses for each problem it solves. The flow of reasoning used for one problem may be quite different than that used for a different problem. This explanation ability enables the expert's advice to be critiqued. A user can study the rationale on which the advice is based and is free to accept it or reject it. It is important to understand that expert systems do not make decisions; they simply offer advice. Users are free to factor that advice into their decisions in whatever way they please. Thus an expert system can be viewed as a kind of decision support system [2].

Expert systems built with a shell or environment are able to evolve in a straightforward manner. Because the reasoning knowledge is represented as rules in a rule set, new expertise can be added by simply adding new rules or modifying existing rules. This modularity of rules means that there is no issue of programming or reprogramming. The developer of an expert system need not be a programmer. A developer can start out with a simple rule set that is initially useful, yet easily capable of many kinds of elaboration. Over time, the reasoning knowledge embodied in the rule set can be tailored, revised, and expanded—allowing the expert system's expertise to gradually evolve just as human expertise evolves.

A somewhat subtle, yet quite significant, benefit of expert systems is their effect of formalizing an organization's reasoning knowledge. The activity of converting an expert's reasoning knowledge into explicit rules can lead to a better understanding of the nature of an application problem area, as well as clearer insight about how the application's problems are solved. This introspection may well result in better decision making. In the very least, an expert system's formalization of reasoning knowledge provides a way of preserving that knowledge long after its human progenitor has left the scene. It can also provide a valuable basis for training new human experts.

Sample Applications

Applying expert systems technology to business problems can have significant strategic implications for an organization [6]. Traditionally, the reasoning knowledge embodied in an organization's employees has provided an important basis for achieving, improving, and maintaining its competitive position. All else being equal, organizations without comparable expertise are at a disadvantage. With business expert systems, there is an opportunity to amplify the competitive advantage derived from superior know-how. There is also the challenge of keeping pace with competitors that have embraced this new technology. Top management at KC has identified three ways in which business expert systems can contribute to the company's competitiveness, by:

Enhancing internal productivity.

Providing enhanced services.

Providing new services.

The company is also looking to business expert systems as part of a strategy aimed at spawning a completely new industry.

An example of an expert system that enhances productivity within the company is the one developed for the shipping department. There are a few simple rules that clerks use to determine how regular shipments are to be sent. But rush orders are not unusual and they require much greater expertise to handle effectively. The carrier selected for such a shipment depends on factors such as the time of day, day of the week, holiday proximity, destination, and shipment size. To enhance the productivity of the clerks and their supervisors alike, an expert system was developed to offer customized shipping advice for the exceptional cases.

Several expert systems under development at KC were not intended to improve internal productivity. Instead, they were part of a strategy aimed at providing kinds of customer services that no other publisher provided. One of these was an expert system for offering advice to bookstore patrons. When entering a bookstore, many people do not have a particular book in mind, but rather notions of the kinds of books in which they may be interested. There is thus the hurdle of identifying particular books before purchases are made. Traditionally, a customer will browse in search of books that meet his or her needs. This can result in many lost sales. Suitable books may be overlooked in the browsing process due to factors such as shelf positioning, cover design, temporary stockouts, or insufficient browsing time.

Bookstore clerks can be helpful in offering advice about book selection, but they are seldom experts in all subject areas and are frequently busy. Of course, KC's marketing group is the premier source of expertise when it comes to recommending a reading list that will satisfy a customer's need. For this reason, the company has undertaken a pilot project of placing an expert system in selected bookstores. The expert system is being developed to interact with a customer, eliciting factors such as the subject area, customer characteristics (e.g., age, education level), acceptable price range, books already read in the area, and so forth. These factors are to be elicited only on an as-needed basis as the system reasons out a solution for the customer.

There is some debate in the marketing group as to whether books from other publishers should be included in the customized reading lists that are generated. This issue will be studied in the pilot project. In some cases, a reading list may consist of a single book while other lists may be lengthy. When a list is presented to a customer each book is accompanied by an indication of the degree of its applicability to the customer's needs. There is also an indication of where in the store the book can be found. If response to the expert system is favorable KC plans to extend it to remember the characteristics of individual customers, track customer requests (as a basis for market research and direct mail advertising), provide a synopsis of any book on a recommended list, and allow certain kinds of ad hoc queries against the expert system's data base of descriptive knowledge about books.

At the time of Jack's visit, KC was involved in exploring an even more ambitious application of expert systems. Top management was convinced that new industries had been made possible by the advent of powerful and flexible tools for expert system development. Participation in such industries could produce a diversification that could help the company's long-range growth prospects. One such new industry is concerned with the publication and use of computerized expertise. This would nicely complement KC's present business of publishing expertise in the form of books.

There are two traditional ways of delivering advice. One is by means of books, articles, and lectures. For the recipient, it often requires considerable effort to ferret out the pertinent recommendation. Sometimes the advice is not explicit, but must be inferred by using reasoning expertise that is presented in books, articles, and lectures. The second major delivery method involves consulting firms and professional services offered by lawyers, accountants, and physicians. Here the generation of advice is more specialized to individual client needs. It requires less effort by the client than reading books or attending lectures. However, the availability of this delivery method is relatively limited and costly.

Mr. Rickert and others in top management recognized that expert system technology offers a striking alternative, supplement, and complement to traditional ways of delivering advice. Seeing this as an opportunity, he had formed a team to explore a new business concerned with producing and distributing chunks of reasoning knowledge. Each chunk would address one of a wide variety of problem areas, ranging from vehicle maintenance to financial management. Each chunk would be capable of being "plugged in" to a standard, generalized inference engine that could draw on that knowledge to generate advice. The team came up with the idea of "expert-of-the-month" offerings akin to the idea of book-of-the-month selections. There would also be subscription services for providing new and updated expertise. In summary, the new business would involve widespread distribution of expertise that, when plugged in to an inference engine, results in responsive consultations at relatively low prices.

At the same time, KC's management was considering entering another new business. It was clear that within a few short years masses of knowledge on optical compact disks would soon be commonplace. For instance, present hardware technology allows over 500 million characters to be stored on a single small compact disk (CD). Many kinds of knowledge can reside on a CD: descriptive, procedural, presentation, and so on. In the face of such massive knowledge storehouses, effective usage is a paramount issue. The availability of expert systems that can help users dig out and apply the immediately relevant subset of knowledge is akin to having the assistance of a combination librarian/teacher. KC's management expects an entire industry can develop around the automated, intelligent delivery and application of all types of knowledge on CDs.

REPRESENTING RULES

All of the expert systems developed by KC depend on the ability to represent rules of reasoning in a way that the environment can understand. The expert systems Jack was destined to develop depended on the same rule representation capability [7]. The power and flexibility of a software tool for building expert systems is highly dependent on what it allows a developer to express in a rule. A tool that permits only primitive rules will not be able to support expert systems comparable to tools that allow more versatility in representing rules [7].

Premise and Conclusion

Joy began her explanation of the environment's rule management capability by describing the fundamentals of rules. "A rule is a fragment of reasoning knowledge that tells the environment's inference engine what to do if a certain situation exists. In technical jargon, a rule has a *premise* and a *conclusion*. If it can be established that the premise is true, then the rule's conclusion can be regarded as valid. A premise is simply a condition and a conclusion consists of one or more actions."

"Can the premise be any kind of condition?" asked Jack.

"Sure," she nodded. "Any kind of condition you're familiar with can serve as a rule's premise. It can be a single logical expression or a compound condition formed from multiple logical expressions. It can involve constants, working variables, array elements, cells, fields, functions, macros, and any of the usual operators. So you're already an expert when it comes to stating a rule's premise."

"Beautiful," he murmured, looking deeply into her eyes. "But what about the conclusion of a rule? What kinds of actions can it have?"

"There again," Joy answered, "you're already an expert! Any command that you know can serve as an action in a rule. It could be a mere LET command for assigning a value to a variable, perhaps involving a calculation. It might be an INPUT, OUTPUT, or form-processing command. If your rule's conclusion pertains to a data base, then it would involve data management or SQL query commands. The conclusion might be to plot a graph, generate a customized report, process text, perform a program, interact via the MENU function, redefine function keys, analyze a spreadsheet, and so on. Any or all of these is fair game in the conclusion of a rule."

"Let's say," speculated Jack, "that I want to build an expert system to help set sales quotas for the reps. It should be able to give me advice about a specific product's quota for a particular rep in a certain quarter."

"Since you're an expert at setting quotas," offered Joy, "what you'd need to do is express your reasoning knowledge in terms of a set of rules. Each rule represents some fragment of knowledge that may be useful in coming up with a quota recommendation."

"You mean something like the fact that I base the new quota on past performance?" he asked. "If a rep's sales for a product exceeded the quota by more than 15 percent, then I combine the excess with that quota to determine a base amount."

"That's a good example of a rule!" Joy said as she saw that he was catching on quickly. "Formally, it would be expressed like this." On a piece of paper Joy wrote:

```
RULE:R1
   IF:SALES>1.15*QUOTA
   THEN:BASE=QUOTA+(SALES-1.15*QUOTA)
```

explaining that she arbitrarily named the rule R1. The rule's premise is a condition involving the variables SALES and QUOTA. When the environment's inference engine determines that the premise is TRUE, then it will take the single action specified in R1's conclusion—just as Jack would do in the course of reasoning about a quota.

Rule Sets

"So," Jack mused, "I just specify a set of rules that I'd use when reasoning. Another rule might state what conclusion I'd draw about BASE when sales did not exceed the quota by at least 15 percent. Still other rules would indicate the conditions under which I'd adjust the base amount by various factors such as local advertising, economic outlook, and product trends. What command would I use to actually build and edit a set of rules?"

"Either the TEXT or BUILD command," answer Joy [3]. "The TEXT command is the same as the one you already know and love. Just as you can use it to work on a file of narrative text or a program file, you can also use it to create or edit a file of rules. Such a file is typically identified with an extension of RSS. Alternatively, the BUILD command can be invoked to work on a rule set. It will step you through rule set creation or editing by means of various menus, prompts, and stylized screens."

Figure 14–1 shows what the text screen looks like after entering a couple of rules into a rule set named ADVISOR. The rule set is to be held in a knowledge system file having an RSS extension. Notice that a reason accompanies the rule's premise and conclusion. Such reasons allow the inference engine to explain the rationale of the advice that is

FIGURE 14–1   Entering rules via a text screen

```
   Line:13      Col:53     a:advisor.rss  Insert              Press ^L for help

 rule: r1

     if: sales > 1.15 * quota
     then: base = quota + (sales = 1.15 * quota)
     reason: In cases where the sales for this product exceeded
             the quota by more than 15%, the base amount for the
             new quota is set to the past quota plus the excess
             sales amount.


 rule: r2

     if: sales <= 1.15 * quota
     then: base = quota
     reason: The base amount for the new quota is the same as the
             past quota because this product's sales did not
             exceed the past quota by more than 15%.
```

FIGURE 14–2   Entering a rule via a BUILD screen

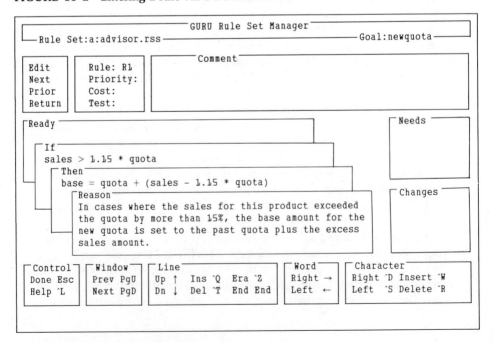

generated. Figure 14–2 shows the stylized BUILD screen that could be used to enter the same rule R1 into the same RSS file. As that screen suggests, there are many other characteristics that a rule can have beyond its name, premise, conclusion, and reason. A discussion of the role and value of such options can be found elsewhere [7].

With either the TEXT or BUILD command, Jack might create a rule set having the rules shown in Figure 14–3. A detailed discussion of these rules appears in [7]. Once a rule set is created, the developer *compiles* it to allow the inference engine to efficiently process the reasoning knowledge it holds. In this environment, compilation is accomplished by executing the COMPILE command. For instance, the command

```
compile "advisor.rss"
```

would analyze the ADVISOR rule set for correctness and produce a new file named ADVISOR.RSC. The inference engine can reason with a compiled version of a rule set much more rapidly than with a source version prepared by the developer. Figure 14–4 illustrates the role of the expert system developer as one of gathering reasoning expertise from experts and representing it as one or more rule sets in the knowledge system. When an environment is used as the development tool, many other kinds of knowledge can also exist in the knowledge system and an inference capability is one of many processing capabilities possessed by the environment software. A user can interact through various interfaces to request advice and respond to the environment's requests for clarification about the nature of the problem being posed. Notice the similarity between Figures 14–4 and 1–7. When an inference capability exists in the problem-processing system, a DSS is said to be artificially intelligent [5].

Joy went on to explain to Jack that a rule set can contain more than just rules. For instance, it may have what is called an *initialization sequence*, which is a series of commands that the inference engine will execute before actually beginning to reason with the rules. For instance, it may contain INPUT, GETFORM, LET, data management, spreadsheet, and other commands that establish initial values for variables referenced in the rules. Similarly, a rule set can have a *completion sequence*. This is a series of commands that tell the inference engine what to do when the reasoning with rules has been completed. These are typically commands for presenting (e.g., OUTPUT, PUTFORM, PLOT) or storing (e.g., LET, ATTACH, SAVE) the generated advice. Another optional part of a rule set is a *variable description section* in which variables referenced in the rules can be characterized in special ways. For instance, a variable description might tell the inference engine

FIGURE 14-3   Set of rules for giving quota advice

```
RULE: R1
    IF: SALES > 1.15 * QUOTA
    THEN: BASE = QUOTA + (SALES - 1.15 * QUOTA)
    REASON: In cases where the sales for this product exceeded the quota by more
            than 15%, the base amount for the new quota is set to the past quota
            plus the excess sales amount.

RULE: R2
    IF: SALES < = 1.15 * QUOTA
    THEN: BASE = QUOTA
    REASON: The base amount for the new quota is the same as the past quota
            because this product's sales did not exceed the past quota by more than
            15%.

RULE: R3
    IF: ECONOMY = "good" AND KNOWN ("GROWTH")
    THEN: EFACTOR = GROWTH
    REASON: When the local economic outlook is good, the economic factor is equal
            to the economy's anticipated growth rate.

RULE: R4
    IF: ECONOMY = "fair" AND KNOWN ("LOCALADS")
        AND KNOWN ("GROWTH")
    THEN: EFACTOR = GROWTH/3; LAFACTOR = LOCALADS/120000
    REASON: When the local economic outlook is fair, the economic factor is one
            third of the growth rate and the local advertising factor is 1/120,000th
            of the amount budgeted for local advertising.

RULE: R5
    IF: ECONOMY = "poor" AND KNOWN ("GROWTH")
        AND KNOWN ("UNEMPLOYMENT")
    THEN: EFACTOR = MIN (GROWTH, .085 - UNEMPLOYMENT)
    REASON: If the local economic outlook is poor, then the economic factor should
            be the lesser of the growth rate and the result of subtracting the
            unemployment rate from 8.5%.

RULE: R6
    IF: GROWTH > = .04 AND UNEMPLOYMENT < .076
    THEN: ECONOMY = "good"
    REASON: The economic outlook is good because the projected unemployment
            rate is below 7.6% and the anticipated growth rate is at least 4%.

RULE: R7
    IF: GROWTH > = .02 AND GROWTH < .04
        AND UNEMPLOYMENT < .055
    THEN: ECONOMY = "good"
    REASON: The economic outlook is good because projected unemployment is less
            than 5.5% and the anticipated growth rate is between 2% and 4%.

RULE: R8
    IF: GROWTH > = .02 AND GROWTH < .04
        AND UNEMPLOYMENT > = .055 AND UNEMPLOYMENT < .082
```

FIGURE 14–3   (continued)

```
THEN: ECONOMY = "fair"
REASON: The economic outlook is fair because of moderate growth and
        unemployment expectations.

RULE: R9
    IF: GROWTH < .02 OR UNEMPLOYMENT > = .082
    THEN: ECONOMY = "poor"
    REASON: The economic outlook is poor because either the anticipated growth
            rate is very low or projected unemployment is high or both.

RULE: R10
    IF: ECONOMY = "good" AND LOCALADS > 2000
    THEN: LAFACTOR = LOCALADS/100000
    REASON: When the economy is good and local advertising exceeds $2,000, the
            local advertising factor is 1% for every thousand dollar expenditure.

RULE: R11
    IF: ECONOMY = "poor" AND LOCALADS < 1500
    THEN: LAFACTOR = - .015
    REASON: When the economic outlook is poor and local advertising expenditures
            for the product are modest, then the local advertising factor is
            negative.

RULE: R12
    IF: (ECONOMY = "poor" AND LOCALADS > = 1500)
        OR (ECONOMY = "good" AND LOCALADS < = 2000)
    THEN: LAFACTOR = 0
    REASON: The local advertising factor is negligible because of low advertising in a
            good economy or a poor economy coupled with substantial local
            advertising for the product line.

RULE: R13
    IF: PROD IN ["computer", "romance", "scifi"]
    THEN: PFACTOR = (NEWTITLES + OLDTITLES)/OLDTITLES - 1
          STRONG = TRUE
          WEAK = FALSE
    REASON: This is a strong product line. the product factor is based on the growth
            in the number of titles in this line.

RULE: R14
    IF: PROD IN ["reference", "biography", "psychology", "sports"]
    THEN: PFACTOR = .75*((NEWTITLES + OLDTITLES)/ OLDTITLES - 1)
          STRONG = FALSE
          WEAK = FALSE
    REASON: This is neither a strong nor weak product line. the product factor is
            proportional to three fourths of the growth in the number of titles in
            this line.

RULE: R15
    IF: STRONG AND KNOWN ("BASE") AND KNOWN ("EFACTOR") AND
        KNOWN ("PFACTOR") AND KNOWN ("LAFACTOR")
```

FIGURE 14–3 (concluded)

```
THEN: INPUT RISE NUM\
      WITH "Enter estimate of percentage sales increase "\
      + "due to rising interest in " + PROD
      NEWQUOTA = BASE * (1 + EFACTOR + LAFACTOR + \
                PFACTOR + RISE/100)
REASON: This is a strong product line. The base amount, economic factor,
        product factor, and local advertising factor for calculating the new
        quota are all known. A subjective assessment of the expected sales
        increase due to general rising interest in the product is requested. The
        new quota is then calculated.

RULE: R16
    IF: WEAK AND KNOWN ("BASE") AND KNOWN ("EFACTOR") AND
        KNOWN ("PFACTOR") AND KNOWN ("LAFACTOR")
    THEN: INPUT FALL NUM\
          WITH "Enter estimate of percentage sales decrease "\
          + "due to falling interest in " + PROD
          NEWQUOTA = BASE * (1 + EFACTOR + LAFACTOR + \
                    PFACTOR - FALL/100)
    REASON: This is a weak product line. A subjective assessment of the expected
            sales decrease due to general declining interest in this product line is
            requested. The new quota can then be calculated.

RULE: R17
    IF: NOT (WEAK OR STRONG) AND KNOWN ("BASE")
        AND KNOWN ("EFACTOR") AND KNOWN ("PFACTOR")
        AND KNOWN ("LAFACTOR")
    THEN: NEWQUOTA = BASE*(1 + EFACTOR + LAFACTOR + PFACTOR)
    REASON: This is neither an especially strong nor weak product line. Its new
            quota is calculated from the base amount and factors for the economy,
            local advertising, and product line expansion.

RULE: R18
    IF: NOT (PROD IN ["computer", "romance", "scifi", "reference", "biography",
        "psychology", "sports"])
    THEN: WEAK = TRUE; STRONG = FALSE
          PFACTOR = .45*((NEWTITLES + OLDTITLES)/OLDTITLES - 1)
    REASON: This is a weak product line. The product factor is proportional to less
            than half of its growth in titles.
```

---

what actions to take if that variable's value happens to be unknown. A full discussion of these and other optional rule set sections can be found in [7].

Rule Sets versus Programs

"I notice," said Jack, "that a rule resembles an IF command like we can use in programs."

"In its simplest form, that's true," she confirmed. "But as you learn

FIGURE 14-4 Architecture of an artificially intelligent decision support environment

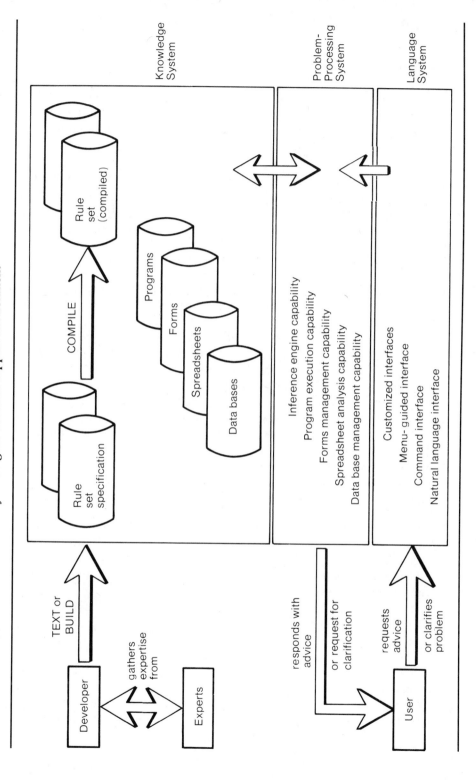

more about rules, you'll see that a rule can have many other useful parts beyond a premise and a conclusion. On the one hand, the similar syntax between rules and IF commands makes it easy for someone who knows programming to specify a rule. On the other hand, experienced programmers often have initial difficulty in understanding the basic philosophy of rule management."

"In what way?" he asked.

"Well," Joy explained, "programmers have been trained to specify procedural knowledge. They are very good at specifying a sequence of commands. But developing a rule set is an entirely different proposition. Although their conclusions contain commands, the rules themselves are not commands. The developer therefore does not specify them in any particular sequence. It is the inference engine that determines which rules will be used and when they will be used in the course of working on a particular problem. For the next problem, the inference engine may process a different subset of the rules in a different sequence.

"Even though you may occasionally hear the activity of expert system development referred to as 'rule-based programming,' that phrase is a misnomer. Unless you're using a tool like LISP, specifying a rule set has nothing whatsoever to do with programming. A rule set is not a sequence of commands that can be executed. Instead, it is a set of rules that can be used for reasoning about problems."

"I see," nodded Jack. "A set of rules is not a process for manufacturing advice. Instead, rules serve as raw materials. It's the inference engine that does the processing. When the inference engine is confronted with a problem, it manufactures advice by drawing on whatever rules it determines to be pertinent in whatever sequence it considers to be appropriate."

"Right, just as a human expert is free to do," she confirmed. "Extending your analogy, rules are not the only raw material available in an AI environment. In the course of manufacturing advice, the environment's inference engine can be exercised in tandem with other knowledge-processing capabilities."

"Which means that data bases, spreadsheets, programs, forms, and all the rest can also serve as raw materials for generating advice," interrupted Jack.

She smiled. "Exactly! Anything in the environment's knowledge system can be used during the reasoning process. Again, it's like a human expert who is free to use many kinds of knowledge in the course of manufacturing advice. You can think of each rule as telling the conditions under which and the way in which certain knowledge system contents can be processed. Because a rule is knowledge about the legitimate use of other knowledge, rules are sometimes called *metaknowledge.*"

PROCESSING RULES

Because rules can refer to other types of knowledge, an environment's inference engine capability must be blended with other knowledge management capabilities. That is, an environment's inference engine must be able to do calculations, data base management, statistics, queries, forms management, spreadsheet analysis, program execution, and other kinds of knowledge processing in the midst of generating advice. If it were unable to do so, it would be incapable of processing rules that refer to these other kinds of knowledge. It would be like the inference engine furnished with a shell, capable of processing only very rudimentary kinds of rules.

The activity of processing a set of rules to generate advice is called *inference.* Drawing on various rules, an inference engine *infers* a solution to a stated problem. Obviously, the power and flexibility that a tool offers for representing reasoning knowledge are primary determiners of what is possible during an inference process. Of equal importance are the inference abilities built into an inference engine. A rudimentary inference engine is able to process a given rule set in only one way. The technique it employs for reasoning (i.e., for operating on rules) is always the same, regardless of the rule set being processed.

At the opposite extreme, there are sophisticated inference engines. Such an inference engine is able to reason in many different ways. It can be set, tuned, or directed to process rules in a manner that most closely emulates a human expert. For a given rule set, different reasoning approaches can result in different advice for the same problem. Or, they may produce the same advice, but at differing speeds. Just as humans can reason in different ways at different times, so too can a flexible inference engine. The environment's inference capability is highly adaptable by means of environment variables that serve as reasoning controls [7].

"So tell me," Jack implored, "how does an inference engine actually reason with rules? It still seems pretty amazing that a computer can give advice comparable to a human expert, even if it does have all the rules the human uses."

"First," she cautioned, "you should understand that even the most sophisticated inference engine does have some limitations. In spite of some of the hype you may read about AI, an inference engine does not have a mind and there is no evidence to suggest that it thinks, in the same sense that a human thinks. It does not have creative imagination, intuition, or a decision-making capacity. It is able to reason with rules to infer advice that can support decisions. But the processes it can use to do this reasoning are not necessarily identical to the reasoning processes humans use. Nevertheless the advice that it generates is comparable to what a human would generate by reasoning with the same set of rules."

"Even without human faculties like creativity and imagination, just having a reasoning faculty is worthwhile," he observed. "And even if human and machine approaches to reasoning are different, the important point is that they can yield comparable advice. I guess you might say that artificial intelligence is better than no intelligence at all."

"Yes, I just might say that," she laughed.

Invoking an Inference Engine

Joy continued, "There's a second preliminary that I should tell you about before we look at the mechanics of an inference engine's reasoning ability. It's how you put the engine in gear. One way is to issue a CONSULT command along with the name of the rule set that should fuel the inference."

As Figure 14-4 suggests, the environment also allows any of the other three interface methods to be used when initiating a request for advice. In the case of the command interface, entering

```
consult advisor to seek newquota
```

would cause the inference engine to process the rules in a compiled rule set named ADVISOR [3]. The inference process would attempt to establish a value for a variable named NEWQUOTA. When such a value has been inferred from the available rules it would be presented as advice to the user.

The CONSULT command can be invoked interactively, in response to the underscore prompt. Alternatively, it could be executed as part of a macro, as a command within a program, or during a spreadsheet computation (i.e., embedded in a cell definition). In any event, once a consultation is under way, the inference engine (like a human expert) may discover that it needs more information from the user. In such cases, it simply requests the desired information. For instance, it may prompt the user for the rep, product, and quarter about which new quota advice is desired. Detailed examples may be found elsewhere [7].

Before answering a request from the inference engine, the user may want to know why such a request is being made. On demand, the inference engine can explain why. Provided sufficient, pertinent rules of reasoning are available to it, the inference engine uses them together with user responses to infer a solution for a specific problem. Once a solution is reported, the user may want to know what line of reasoning was constructed in the course of the inference. Like a human expert, an expert system is able to explain itself, stating why the inferred recommendation is justified in light of the specified problem and available expertise for reasoning about that problem. Such explanations can be requested with the environment's HOW and WHY commands [3].

The Unknown Variable

"When someone invokes the inference engine to request some advice from an expert system, it's a sign that something is unknown," explained Joy. "For instance, I might ask for quota advice because I don't know what the new quota should be."

"That makes sense," Jack agreed. "If we'd already decided what value to set for a certain new quota, there'd be no point in asking for advice about it."

"Well," Joy continued, "when we invoke an inference engine, there are things that it doesn't know either. For instance, it doesn't already know what new quota value to recommend, so it will try to reason out a solution using the ADVISOR rules."

"Ah," he noted, "you mean the environment can have variables whose values are unknown. That's very different from what I'm accustomed to."

"But," she added, "it's crucial for understanding how expert systems work. When we invoke an inference engine with a particular rule set, it's normally the case that one or more of the variables referenced in the rules have no known values. For instance, NEWQUOTA will have no initial value when ADVISOR is consulted.

"The inference engine will first execute any commands that exist in ADVISOR's initialization sequence. There you'd probably have commands to input a rep name, product name, and quarter. And you'd probably also have data management commands to retrieve past performance data. Thus, the values of some variables like SALES and QUOTA become known. Then rules are processed in an attempt to establish values for remaining *unknown variables*—NEWQUOTA in particular."

"I see," observed Jack. "There will be rules that tell the inference engine what conclusions can be drawn about NEWQUOTA's value under various conditions. So if it can identify which of these rules has a condition that is satisfied, the inference engine will know that it is OK to carry out the actions in the rule's conclusion. Thus NEWQUOTA's value will become known and can be presented to the user!"

"You're on the right track," Joy declared, "but there is a catch. What happens if none of the rules that have conclusions about NEWQUOTA have conditions that are satisfied?"

"That's a good question," he said thoughtfully. "If all their conditions are false, then it won't be possible to infer a valid value for NEWQUOTA. There's not enough expertise in the rule set to allow advice to be given."

"That's true," she agreed, "provided all the conditions turn out to be false. But just because a rule's condition isn't true doesn't necessarily mean that it is false."

Jack was momentarily puzzled. One of those Texas-sized smiles lit up Joy's face as she waited to see if he could discover the third possibility. Finally, he shrugged. "It must be good, but I can't seem to put my finger on it."

Taking his hand, she said with a reassuring tone, "Oh, I'm sure you can. All you need is a little guidance. Remember that a rule's condition is not constrained to be like the condition in a program's IF command."

That was the only hint he needed. "Of course! If a variable's value can be unknown, then it must be possible for an expression's value to be unknown. Because a condition is a logical expression, its value can be either TRUE or FALSE, or UNKNOWN. When the inference engine evaluates a rule's condition, the result may be unknown if some of the condition's variables' values are unknown."

"Now you have the feel of it," Joy said enthusiastically. "Of course, such conditions are unheard of in commands that control the flow of a program's execution. But they lie at the heart of an inference engine's reasoning ability. When an inference engine detects that a rule's condition is unknown, it can make use of other rules or interact with the user in an effort to make the condition's variables known. Then the condition can be determined to be either TRUE or FALSE."

Forward and Reverse Reasoning

There are two basic strategies inference engines follow when reasoning with rules: forward and reverse reasoning. In AI jargon they are commonly called *forward chaining* and *backward chaining*, respectively. Some inference engines are capable of only one of these two approaches to reasoning. Others, like that of the environment Joy was describing, can do either kind of reasoning and even a hybrid type of reasoning that mixes the two basic approaches. As noted earlier, the environment provides numerous environment variables that serve as reasoning controls. These controls can be set by experienced expert system developers to produce many variations of the basic forward and reverse approaches to reasoning [7].

"As its name suggests," said Joy, *"forward reasoning* is based on the idea of examining each rule in a forward direction, looking first at its premise. The inference engine ignores a rule's conclusion until it can determine that the premise is satisfied. When that happens the rule is *fired."*

"Fired?" he asked.

"Yes," she replied. "Firing a rule means that the inference engine takes whatever actions are specified in the rule's conclusion. If a rule's premise is not satisfied—the condition's value is either FALSE or UNKNOWN—then the rule is not fired. The inference engine goes on to consider another rule. Forward reasoning continues in this way until either a value has been established for a specified unknown variable such as NEWQUOTA or all of the rule set's rules have been considered.

"In the latter case, the inference engine makes a second pass through the rule set, reconsidering the unfired rules. As a result of firing some rules in the first pass, some previously unknown variables may have known values and some previously known variables may have different known values."

"So," interrupted Jack, "rules that previously had a false or unknown condition could have a true condition on the second pass. The inference engine would fire them and continue making passes."

"Right," confirmed Joy. "It continues reasoning and drawing conclusions in this way until either some user-specified variable attains a known value or no further rules can be fired. In either event, any of the variables whose values changed or became known during the reasoning process can have their values presented as advice to the user. Commands in the rule set's completion sequence can control the inference engine's presentation of these values."

Joy pointed out that her explanation did not cover all the details, subtleties, and variations of forward reasoning. Jack could pick those up gradually as he became more experienced with rule management [7]. She adopted the same attitude in her explanation of reverse reasoning, concentrating on the fundamentals.

"Reverse reasoning," she explained, "is based on the idea of considering rules in a reverse direction. The inference engine looks first at a rule's conclusion, rather than its premise."

"What is it looking for in a conclusion?" asked Jack.

"It's looking to see whether the conclusion contains an action that could change a certain unknown variable by giving that variable a value," she answered. "At any moment during the reverse reasoning process, the inference engine is focusing its efforts on trying to establish a value for a particular unknown variable. This is called the *current goal variable.* For instance, when the overall goal of a consultation is to generate a new quota, NEWQUOTA is the current goal variable at the outset of inference engine processing.

"By looking at the conclusions of rules in the rule set, the inference engine can detect which rules could possibly establish a value for the goal variable. These rules are candidates for further consideration. The inference engine selects one of these rules and examines its premise. If the premise is true, then the rule is fired to establish a value for the goal variable. Because remaining candidate rules may also affect the value of the goal variable, they too may then be considered in the same way. If the premise is false, then the rule is not fired and another of the candidate rules is selected for consideration. The other possibility is that a candidate rule's premise is unknown. When this occurs the inference engine attempts to make the premise known. It does this by trying to determine values for the unknown variables in the premise.

"There are two ways for the inference engine to make an unknown variable known during reverse reasoning. If the rule set contains a variable description for an unknown variable, the inference engine can carry out the actions specified there to determine a value. Otherwise, the unknown variable temporarily becomes the new current goal. The inference engine works on this goal in exactly the same way as the consultation's original overall goal."

"I get it," remarked Jack. "The inference engine detects which of the rule set's rules could possibly establish a value for this new current goal variable. These are treated as candidate rules for the new current goal. The inference engine selects one of these rules and examines its premise. If its premise is true, the rule is fired to establish a value for the current goal. If the premise is false, then the rule is not fired and another of the candidate rules for the current goal is selected for consideration. If the premise is unknown, then each of its unknown variables can in turn be subjected to the same reverse reasoning process."

"That's the idea," confirmed Joy. "I think you can see that reverse reasoning works by using rules to break the overall problem into subproblems. Each unknown variable in the premise of a candidate rule becomes a subproblem. Each subproblem may itself be broken into its own subproblems, and so on. By establishing values for the subproblems identified in a premise, the inference engine will be able to determine whether the premise is satisfied. If it is, then the rule can be fired to establish variable values according to the conclusion's actions."

"Whew!" sighed Jack. "There's no way I'd ever want to try to program that. Thank goodness, the inference engine does all of that reasoning for us, using the rules we give it."

Joy noted that both forward and reverse reasoning are valuable. Each is advantageous in certain situations. Forward reasoning is generally preferable in situations where all (or most) of a rule set's rules must be considered, where there are few unknown variables, or where there is no single goal. In the latter case, the consultation determines all the implications of a problem, rather than pursuing a specific goal. An example would be a consultation that aims to determine a broad financial plan rather than determining how much to invest in a specific stock. Reverse reasoning is generally preferable in situations where a substantial portion of rules may be irrelevant to the problem at hand, where there are relatively large numbers of unknown variables, or where there is a specific goal to be pursued.

Reasoning about Uncertain and Fuzzy Situations

"As you become more experienced with rule management," speculated Joy, "you may want to make use of certainty factors and perhaps some fuzzy variables as well."

"That sounds pretty hairy," he chuckled.

She smiled. "Actually, such features can be very useful once you get the knack of them. They allow an expert system to even more closely resemble the behavior of a human expert. It's a fact of life that we're not always certain about everything. When we pose a problem to an expert we may be somewhat uncertain about various aspects of the problem. We expect the expert to give us advice that takes those uncertainties into account."

Jack saw her point. "If someone asks me for quota advice, I'd probably counter by asking about things like the economic outlook for the territory. The person might reply that he or she is 70 percent certain that the outlook is good. I, as an expert, then need to factor that degree of certainty into the ultimate advice I give. I guess you could say that the certainty of any quota advice would be influenced by the certainty about a good economic outlook."

"A good inference engine similarly has the capacity to reason about uncertainties," Joy declared. "And when it offers advice, it indicates how certain it is about that advice. An inference engine does this by means of certainty factors. In this environment, a *certainty factor* is a number in the 0 to 100 range that can be assigned to the value of a variable. It is a measure of how certain or confident the inference engine is about the value for that variable. The lowest possible certainty is 0, while 100 is the highest."

"I see," Jack observed. "A user can respond to inference engine requests not only by providing a value for a variable, but by providing a certainty factor as well. Then, as the inference engine reasons, it combines all the various certainty factors of the variables' values to infer a certainty for the advice it generates."

"Right," nodded Joy. "The mathematics for combining certainty factors is called a *certainty algebra.* Among tools that handle certainty factors, most inference engines support only one certainty algebra, but that's quite limiting. In this environment there are many built-in algebras. By setting environment variables, a developer can pick the one that will most nearly match a particular human expert's approach to combining certainties."

"That makes sense," Jack said, "when you realize that different experts may combine certainties in different ways. Even the same expert may use different methods for different problem domains. Without the ability to choose from a healthy assortment of certainty algebras an inference engine will have difficulty in closely emulating diverse experts across diverse problem domains. But, tell me, where do fuzzy variables fit into all this?"

"A *fuzzy variable,*" answered Joy, "is a variable that has more than one value at a time. Each value of a fuzzy variable has its own certainty factor that may or may not be the same as certainties for other values of the same variable."

"Very interesting," mused Jack. "That means that the variable for economic outlook can simultaneously have values of good, fair, and poor. Each of the three values would have its own degree of certainty."

"When you have an inference engine that can process fuzzy variables," confirmed Joy, "each of your expert systems will be able to offer multiple simultaneous recommendations for a single problem. Thus fuzzy variables allow expert systems to more closely emulate human experts who routinely offer multiple alternative solutions to a problem. And each solution has its own level of certainty."

For fuzzy variable processing, an inference engine must have the capacity to simultaneously keep track of different values for the same variable. It must be able to deal with differing degrees of certainty about each value. It must be able to incorporate the multiple values and their respective certainty factors into subsequent reasoning activity. It must be able to react properly when it encounters a fuzzy variable in a rule's premise and when fuzzy variables are involved in the conclusion of a rule that is fired.

In the environment, certainty factors and fuzzy variables are not limited to rule management [3]. Any working variable's value can be given a certainty factor regardless of whether it is ever referenced in a rule. Similarly, any working variable can be fuzzy. Uncertain, fuzzy working variables can be referenced in all the traditional knowledge management techniques, including calculations, forms, spreadsheets, and programs. Extensive discussion of certainty factors and fuzzy variables can be found elsewhere [7].

BASIC IDEAS

In the years ahead, *rule management promises to be an increasingly important knowledge management technique. It is particularly valuable as a means for representing and processing reasoning knowledge.* Such knowledge is the cornerstone of artificially intelligent decision support systems. These may take the form of stand-alone expert systems or may be full-scale environments in which expert systems are but one contributor to decision support activities [5]. The former case results from the use of a tool known as an expert system shell. The latter results from using an environment that offers rule management as one of its many knowledge management techniques.

The objective of an expert system is to emulate the behavior of a human expert. Like a human expert, an expert system can accept requests for advice, ask the user to clarify the problem being posed, draw on stored reasoning expertise (e.g., rules) about the problem domain to infer a solution or recommendation, take uncertain and fuzzy situations into account during the reasoning process, present the generated advice to the user, and interact with the user to explain the line of reasoning that led to the advice. Expert systems have the potential for leveraging an organization's expertise by making advice readily available to workers, even when the human experts are unavailable. This technology has important and far-reaching strategic implications for modern organizations.

The opportunities that rule management presents for business expert systems are accompanied by challenges as well. If top management is to successfully exploit the opportunities, it must carefully address challenges that are managerial, economic, and technical in nature [6]. The central managerial challenge is to achieve a clear understanding of what expert systems are, what can and cannot be done with this emerging technology. Once this educational hurdle is cleared and a commitment is made to appropriate expert system projects, there remains the managerial challenge of gaining acceptance of business expert systems within the organization. It must be made clear that such systems threaten neither experts nor those seeking advice, but rather can enhance productivity.

As for the economic and technical challenges, they can be met by prudent tool selection and training. With a proper tool and modest training, both small and large business expert systems become practical. They become both economically and technically feasible. With modern tools for rule management, great expense, specialized machines, years of effort, advanced degrees in artificial intelligence, and knowledge of complex programming languages (like LISP [10]) are no longer prerequisites for the development of nontrivial, useful expert systems. There are significant differences among commercially available tools for expert system development [4].

Development of an expert system revolves around the specification of a set of rules that inference engine software can draw on in the course of generating advice. Each rule in a rule set minimally has a premise and a conclusion. It specifies dependencies that exist between variables in the premise and variables in the conclusion. The kinds of conclusions depend very much on the power and flexibility of the tool's inference engine. For instance, if an inference engine is incapable of data base management and spreadsheet processing, then it will be unable to process rules that reference fields and cells. In any event, an inference engine processes rules by using some variation of forward or reverse reasoning. Sophisticated inference engines support many such variations, as well as the processing of certainty factors and fuzzy variables.

In AI parlance, a rule set and the working variables it references are sometimes called a knowledge base, and an expert system is sometimes called a knowledge-based system. AI research is generally unconcerned with the many other types of knowledge that computers routinely represent and process. Such parochial use of the term *knowledge* should not be allowed to detract from the fact that there are many other valuable computerized knowledge management techniques used daily by millions of people around the world. The most widely used of these mainstream techniques have been introduced in Chapters 4–13. Rule management is just beginning to merge into the mainstream of knowledge management [7]. Data bases, spreadsheets, forms, text, programs, and all the rest are no less legitimate examples of knowledge than a rule set is. *The real payoff comes when a computer is able to manage all of the various kinds of knowledge in a highly integrated fashion.*

References

1. Barr, A., and E. A. Feigenbaum, eds. *The Handbook of Artificial Intelligence*, vols. 1–3. Los Altos, Calif.: William Kaufmann, 1982.

2. Bonczek, R. H.; C. W. Holsapple; and A. B. Whinston. *Foundations of Decision Support Systems*. New York: Academic Press, 1981.

3. *Guru Reference Manual.* Lafayette, Ind.: MDBS, Inc., 1985.

4. Holsapple, C. W., and M. D. Gagle. "Expert System Development Tools." *Hardcopy* 7, no. 2 (1987).

5. Holsapple, C. W., and A. B. Whinston. "Artificially Intelligent Decision Support Systems—Criteria for Tool Selection." In *Decision Support Systems: Theory and Application,* ed. C. Holsapple and A. Whinston. New York: Springer-Verlag, 1987.

6. ———. "Business Expert Systems—Gaining a Competitive Edge." Working paper, Krannert Graduate School of Management, Purdue University, West Lafayette, Indiana, 1986.

7. ———. *Manager's Guide to Expert Systems Using Guru.* Homewood, Ill.: Dow Jones-Irwin, 1986.

8. Shortliffe, E. H. *Computer-Based Medical Consultation: MYCIN.* New York: Elsevier, 1976.

9. Williamson, M. "In Guru, the Business World Finally Has Its First, True AI-Based Micro Package." *PC Week* 3, nos. 11–14 (1986).

10. Winston, P. H., and B. K. P. Horn. *LISP.* Reading, Mass.: Addison-Wesley, 1984.

It just goes to show you, the whole is greater than the sum of its parts. It's interesting how stand-alone software often blinds people to that fact.

Chapter Fifteen

The Architecture

A knock at the door roused Jack from his restful reverie. Joy had come for him. He opened the door for her and she glided in. Their eyes embraced softly and warmly. He felt that in some magical way her presence made him infinitely more than he could otherwise ever hope to be.

"I just need to tie the knot," said Jack, "and then I'll be with you." Turning to the closet he removed his favorite tie and quickly made a Windsor knot in it. He slipped on his suit coat and they were off. It was but a short drive to the club where the banquet was being held.

As they neared the destination, Jack reflected, "In a way, I'm glad the training session is over. Even with the day off last Sunday, it's been a long row to hoe. But in another way I'm sad about having to leave in the morning. I'll miss those times that we spent exploring various kinds of knowledge together. But most of all, I'll miss you."

"The feeling is mutual," she replied seriously.

The cocktail hour preceding dinner was just beginning as they arrived. As they mingled with the managers, they found that the training session was not quite over. They fielded a variety of questions, most of which related to the overall architecture of a knowledge management environment [11]. There was particular curiosity about how open the environment's architecture was. An open architecture lets a software tool make use of other independently developed software tools. It allows for an interchange of knowledge between them. The other architectural issue of primary concern revolved around alternative styles for integrating diverse knowledge management techniques into a single tool.

DATA IMPORT AND EXPORT

Stan approached Joy. "I'm wondering whether I can make use of my existing 1–2–3 spreadsheets in the environment. I could then apply all of the new techniques I've learned to the past work I've done."

"That's a good idea," responded Joy. "You can *import* all values from a 1–2–3 spreadsheet into the environment's knowledge system. Once they're there you can have your way with them. As I recall, the 1–2–3 package lets you save a range of cell values in a nonspreadsheet file."

"Right," Stan confirmed. "It lets me save the values as data in an ASCII text file or in what's called a DIF file. As I understand it, those are just two different ways for arranging data values in a file."

Joy nodded, "They're often called *file formats.* You don't have to worry about the details of ASCII or DIF formats. Because both 1–2–3 and the environment know how to interpret the contents of, say, a DIF file, it is possible to transfer data between the two packages."

"I think I get it," Stan said. "While within the 1–2–3 program I'd make a DIF file holding the desired cell values. Later, while working in the environment, I'd issue a command to incorporate the DIF file values into the knowledge system. But what command would do that?"

She answered his question with a question, "Remember the AT-TACH command? Earlier you saw how it could, in a single operation, attach data from a text file into a table. It can do the same thing with a DIF file. With ATTACH, every row of cell values that 1–2–3 exported into the DIF file is imported as values of a new record in a designated table. If the DIF format is being used to transport data into the environment, then E.CF should be switched to 1 before invoking the ATTACH command."

"Once the data is in a table," Stan observed, "I can subject it to many kinds of processing not possible when it's in a 1–2–3 spreadsheet: fancier graphics and report generation, forms processing, programming, text management, and more powerful spreadsheet operations."

"And it can even be used in rule processing," interrupted Jack.

"Sure enough," said Joy. "Now sometimes, Stan, you may want to transport data in a reverse direction, from one or more tables to a 1–2–3 spreadsheet where they become constant definitions for some range of cells. You're already accustomed to 1–2–3's menu-guided spreadsheet operations, so you might want to use them with data from a data base."

"Right," agreed Stan. "It would be nice to have a way to convert values from a data base into a file whose format 1–2–3 can accept."

"And you already know how to do it!" Joy declared. "Just execute the CONVERT command. There's only one difference. Instead of converting into an array or table or spreadsheet as you've done before, you'll convert into a separate file that is not part of the knowledge system. For instance, it could be a DIF file if you've switched E.CF to its DIF setting. The values that you *export* in this way can later be imported while using the 1–2–3 program. Each row of converted data should become a new row of constant definitions in your 1–2–3 spreadsheet."

A good software package is able to import and export data from and to other packages. The more formats a package is able to handle, the greater will be its compatibility with the universe of packages. A software package with a closed architecture is one that ignores the existence of other software. It is unable to process any knowledge that has not been represented in its own special ways. It is unable to format its knowledge in a way that can be used by other software packages.

RUNNING AN ALIEN PROGRAM

Beyond import and export facilities, there is another trait often found in a software package that has an open architecture. This is the ability to serve as a host (recall Chapter 2) for other software. Not only can such a tool carry out its own innate knowledge management tasks, it can also run other software, provided there is sufficient room in main memory.

"You all know how to write a program composed of the environment's commands," Joy declared. "You also know that the PERFORM command causes any such program to be executed while working within the environment. Well, you can also execute other programs while working in the environment, programs that are not composed of the environment's commands and whose programmers may have been entirely unaware of the environment.

"With a closed architecture, you'd have to leave the environment before executing an alien program. On seeing the operating system prompt, you could then execute the program. When it finishes executing, you'd then need to reenter the environment to resume processing."

"But," objected Tracey, "you'd have to use context files and other means to remember where you were in the environment so you could get back to that place when you reenter."

"Exactly!" Joy concurred. "That can be a big inconvenience. But with an open architecture, there's no problem. For instance, in our environment you could use the RUN command to run an alien program.

You don't need to leave the environment first. And when the program finishes executing, you're still in the environment—right where you left off before running the other program."

As an example, the PC-DOS operating system is provided with a number of utility programs [3]. One of these is named COPY. Typing

```
copy a:memo.txt c:letter.txt
```

and then using the Enter key in response to the operating system prompt would execute the COPY program. A copy of the MEMO.TXT file on the drive A diskette would be made in a file named LETTER.TXT on drive C. Entering the command

```
run "copy a:memo.txt c:letter.txt"
```

within the environment would have the same effect. In principle, any program that can be executed from the operating system can similarly be executed via the environment's RUN command.

REMOTE COMMUNICATIONS

Yet another aspect of an open architecture is the ability of a software package to communicate with other computers that are physically distant from it. There are many variants of this *remote communication* capability [13]. Perhaps the most common for today's desktop computers is known as asynchronous RS232 communications and commonly operates by sending transmissions across telephone lines. RS232 refers to a common standard for transmitting the bits that make up bytes in a *serial* fashion. This means the bits are transmitted one after another, in a series, rather than transmitting multiple bits simultaneously (i.e., in a parallel arrangement).

When one computer transmits characters (i.e., bytes) to another, the receiving computer must be synchronized with the sending computer. As bits arrive, it must have a way of knowing where each byte begins and ends. Otherwise, it will be unable to correctly interpret the transmissions that are received. *Synchronous transmission* means that the bits of one character immediately follow the bits of other characters in a continuous stream. The computers use a clock mechanism to keep track of beginnings and ends of transmitted bytes. A generally less costly, though also less efficient, method is *asynchronous transmission*. The transmitted bytes are separated by start and stop signals (e.g., bits) that make it clear to the receiving computer where each byte begins and ends.

FIGURE 15–1   Typical remote communications path

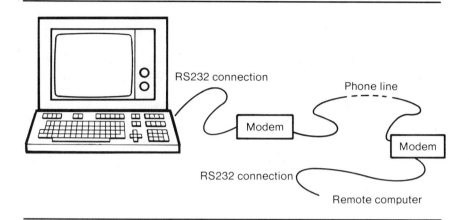

As the diagram in Figure 15–1 suggests, there is another piece of hardware often involved in remote communications. It is a small device called a *modem*. It is connected by a cable to a computer's system unit (e.g., with an RS232 standard connecting plug). The modem is also connected to an ordinary phone line. For direct-connect modems this connection is made by directly plugging a phone line into the modem instead of a telephone. A less expensive kind of modem uses an acoustic coupler. In this case, the phone line is connected to a telephone whose earpiece and mouthpiece are set into rubber cups of the modem's acoustic coupler.

Signals are transmitted over phone lines as continuous waves. However, ordinary computers deal with binary digits (i.e., bits) that take the form of pulses rather than waves. The activity of converting signals from a digital to a wave pattern is called *modulation*. Conversely, demodulation is the conversion of signals from waves to digital patterns. A modem is a device that performs the modulation and demodulation of signals during remote communications. The term *modem* is itself an acronym for *mo*dulator-*dem*odulator. In addition to the typical approach shown in Figure 15–1, there are other kinds of communications paths that can be established to a remote computer [1], [12], [13].

Regardless of the technology of communications paths, there are, from a user's perspective, two primary modes for communicating with a remote computer. One is known as *terminal emulation*, in which the user's local computer behaves like a terminal for interacting with software executing on the remote computer. The other common communication mode is known as *file transfer*. This involves sending files to and receiving files from a remote computer. A third mode involves carrying on split-screen dialogues with the user of a remote computer. A fourth mode for communicating involves the raw transmission of characters. It is of interest to professional developers of application systems. Though all of these communication modes are supported in the environment, the focus here is on the two primary modes [7].

Terminal Emulation

"With all the practice I've had," Dan said, "I know that I can now handle many kinds of knowledge management needs. One thing I noticed was that we seemed to learn from each other's experiences during the practice periods. On several occasions, one of us would come up with a new and nifty use of some feature in the environment and share it with the others. As we become more experienced in the weeks and months ahead, I'm sure each of us will discover new things that the others could benefit from knowing about. It would sure be nice if we could easily share our new findings even though we won't be sitting in the same room."

"That's a good observation," Joy responded. She gave him the names of newsletters that regularly share new ways of using the environment's features [8], [9]. She also suggested that he may want to join a *user's group* in his locale. Such groups are composed of people from many walks of life who all use the same software package. They meet regularly to share ideas and experiences. Joy had yet another solution. "As a matter of fact, the information center is now in the process of devising an *electronic bulletin board* for your use."

"What's that?" Dan asked quickly.

"Well," she explained, "you can think of it as a place where you can leave messages for others to read and where you can read messages that others have left. But it's all electronic, in the sense that a computer here at headquarters will be your bulletin board."

"But," he objected, "we won't be here at headquarters to leave and read messages on your bulletin board computer!"

"And you don't have to be," Joy said reassuringly. "That's because the environment you're working in has an open architecture that lets you communicate with the outside world. It lets you use your computer to get at the processing power and the knowledge held in other computers around the country. These could be micro, mini, or mainframe computers."

"You mean," asked Dan in disbelief, "I can sit in my Tempe office and use the environment to operate other computers that I may have never seen?"

"Sure," smiled Joy, "as long as you know the computer's phone number. For instance, once you've entered the environment, you can use its COMM DIAL command to dial up our bulletin board computer. You just type in the phone number that will be provided you. When you get an answer, you'll want your computer to behave as if it were a terminal connected to the remote computer. You just use the COMM TERMINAL command. In other words, you'll be using your computer's keyboard and console screen to directly interact with software executing on the remote computer!"

"So," interjected Jack, "prompts, menus, messages, data, and anything else we see on our screen is actually the result of the software executing on the other computer. And, when we type in something, it's transmitted to the other computer, whose software will process it. The bulletin board computer's software will let us leave messages about what we've discovered and questions we might have. It will also let us look at messages others have left."

"Exactly," she confirmed. "It's a kind of remote communications known as terminal emulation. You can use terminal emulation not only to get at a bulletin board, but for many other purposes as well. For instance, there are companies in the business of providing current data about a wide variety of topics via remote communications. By paying a fee, you can call one of their computers and its software will let you scan through the data held in its auxiliary memory."

An example of what Joy had alluded to is Dow Jones Information Services, which provides information (i.e., descriptive knowledge) to over 200,000 subscribers via remote communications [18]. From the knowledge management environment, a user can dial up a Dow Jones computer to read *The Wall Street Journal,* to view business, economic, and financial data, or to see general news of the day. In general, the remote computer's software is an application program that gives a user varying ways of retrieving data held in text files, data files, or data bases.

File Transfer

Jack had not previously worked with the environment's remote communications capability. Like the others listening to Joy, he was beginning to see that it could be useful. Looking at her, he declared, "How enticing! I'll have to explore this some more. But tell me, is there some way that I could communicate with, say, Dan's computer to send him a file from my environment's knowledge system. I wouldn't want to be directly interacting with software that is executing on his computer. I might just want to send him some text, or a program, or a template that he could then use as part of his environment's knowledge system."

Joy nodded, "That's entirely possible, as long as Dan knows you want to send him something. He'd be in his environment and would have his phone line connected to his modem, and would have issued the COMM RECEIVER command. You would issue the COMM DIAL command to call his computer. You would then issue the COMM SENDER command and specify the names of the files you want to send. That's all there is to it."

"Copies of Jack's files would then be on my disk?" asked Dan.

"Right," she answered. "And you could transfer files to Jack's computer using the same approach. Just about any kind of file is fair game for the file transfer mode of remote communications: text, program, table, spreadsheet, graphics, form, template, and even rule set files."

Communications Setup

Before dialing a remote computer to begin using any communication mode, the communications software must be used to establish *communication settings* that are consistent with those of the remote computer. In the environment, these settings are simply the values of environment variables and can be switched just like any other environment variables [7]. Whoever oversees the remote computer (e.g., Dow Jones, KC, Dan) will furnish the proper settings along with the phone number.

The environment supports a large number of settings, most of which are technical in nature. It is not necessary to understand the technicalities of communication settings in order to do remote communications. It is only necessary to set them to the same values as the remote computer is using. The settings that are most likely to need adjustment from their defaults are:

Baud rate (E.BAUD).

Bits per character (E.BITS).

Stop bits (E.STOP).

Parity type (E.PARI).

Handshaking status (E.XOFF).

Others, that are of primary interest to advanced users and developers, are discussed elsewhere [7], [13].

Baud rate is a measure of the speed with which transmissions occur.

Feasible baud rates depend on the nature of the physical communication path connecting the computers. Certain modems are capable of handling only certain transmission speeds. In general, the environment allows baud rates of as low as 50 or as high as 38400. Baud rates of 300, 1200, and 2400 are commonly used.

The *bits per character* setting indicates how many bits will be used to represent a transmitted character (i.e., byte). This is typically 6, 7, or 8. The *stop bits* setting indicates how many bits are used to denote the end of a transmitted byte during asynchronous transmission. In most cases, it will need to be set to either 1 or 2. The *parity* setting indicates what kind of error (i.e., parity) checking will be done during the transmission. The most common parity settings are odd, even, and none. A remote computer either will or will not expect *handshaking* to occur during communications. This is a technical issue related to the buffering of characters as they are received by a computer.

There are a couple of alternatives to directly using the LET command to establish different communications settings. The information center will provide a program consisting of LET commands that make the proper switches conform to the bulletin board computer. A manager simply performs that program prior to using the bulletin board. A second alternative is to invoke the command COMM SETUP. This produces the screen appearance shown in Figure 15–2. The present value of each setting is highlighted in reverse video and the user is free to change any of the settings as required by the remote computer. For instance, a menu of permissible settings is provided for the baud rate. The cursor can be moved to any option and the Enter key pressed to switch the baud rate. Additional screens exist for other communications settings and can be brought into view via the ^N key.

Line Access

When the environment's communications settings have been properly set, the remote computer can be accessed over a phone line. Before dialing a phone number, the command

```
comm open
```

is invoked to open the computer's *communications port*. This will allow transmissions to flow through the place (i.e., "port") where the RS232 connector plug has been plugged in. Then, the command

```
comm dial "000-000-0001"
```

FIGURE 15–2 A screen for communications settings

```
                          K-COMM Setup Menu #1
                       Communications Hardware Setup

Port (#PORT):  1

Baud rate (E.BAUD):     50     75    110   134   150   300   600  1200  1800
                      2000   2400   3600  4800  7200  9600 19200 38400


Parity (E.PARI): odd    even   none   mark  space
                                             Buffering Control
Data bits (E.BITS): 5   6   7   8            Rcv buffer size (E.RBUF):  256
                                             Trx buffer size (E.TBUF):    0
Stop bits (E.STOP): 1   2                    Rcv upper thld (E.UTHD):   240
                                             Rcv lower thld (E.LTHD):    16
                                             Xon/Xoff (E.XOFF): enabled  disabled

      Timeout Control
Ticks/tock (E.TICK):       18
Rcv tocks (E.RTOC):        10
Trx tocks (E.TTOC):        10




       MENUS          VARIABLES          OPTIONS            EXIT
     ^N Next        ^X/ENTER Next       ^D/^F Next      ESC S Save/Reset
     ^U Prior       ^E Prior            ^S/^A Prior     ESC Q Quit
```

could be executed to dial the number 000–000–0001. If the line is busy or the specified number is out of service, a "No carrier" message will appear. Otherwise, the remote computer's modem answers the call and the communication path is ready for use.

As Joy had explained, the COMM TERMINAL command could be invoked for the terminal emulation mode of communicating or the COMM SENDER command could be invoked to send files to the remote machine. If both computers have users working with the environment, both could execute the COMM TALKER command. Each user would see his or her screen split in half horizontally. Anything a user types appears in the lower half of the local computer's screen and the upper half of the remote computer's screen, enabling the two users to carry on a split-screen electronic dialogue.

When a user is finished communicating with the remote computer, he or she exits from the remote computer's executing program (for terminal emulation) or sees the familiar underscore prompt (for file transfer or talking modes). At this stage the command

```
comm hangup
```

can be used to terminate the call to the remote computer. If no further calls to or from other computers are anticipated, the command

```
comm close
```

is used to close the local computer's communications port.

Like LET commands for the communications setup, the commands for line access and communications mode selection could be included in a program. If desired, the communications commands can be embedded in cell definitions or they can serve as actions in an expert system's rule set [4]. The remote communications capability can be exercised via the environment's menu interface by choosing the Gateway option in the main menu. Recall Photo 2.

LOCAL AREA NETWORKS

Although KC's regional managers could not use them, workers at headquarters made use of local area networks. A *local area network* (LAN) is a communications network that links multiple computers in a particular locale [14], [15]. The locale may be a room, a building, or several buildings in close proximity to each other. The LAN that connects multiple computers consists of both hardware and software. For instance, the hardware involves cables that link the computers and circuitry that is added to each of the computers. The LAN software gives each computer's user a way to request and receive transmissions (i.e., communicate) through the connecting hardware.

Two of the most prominent approaches for organizing local area networks are known as the *bus* and *token ring* methods. An example of each is depicted in Figure 15–3. Several major computer companies have jointly devised ETHERNET as a standard for the bus method [15]. The computers are linked by coaxial cable. When one computer transmits a message out along the network, it is broadcast to every other device through the connecting cable. However, it is acted on only by the device (e.g., computer, printer) to which the message is addressed. In contrast, the token ring method involves an electronic token that circulates through a ring of connecting wire or cable. When a computer's user initiates a transmission, the computer waits until the token reaches it. It removes the token from the network, makes the transmission, and then returns the token to the network. Each method of LAN organization has certain advantages and disadvantages [15].

Because all computers on a LAN are using the LAN's transmission standards, there is no notion of communications setup involving such

FIGURE 15–3   LAN organizations

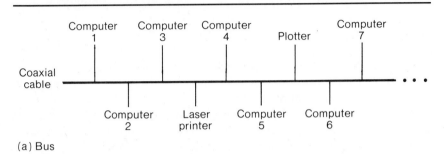

(a) Bus

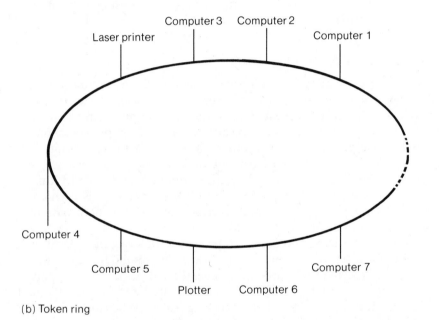

(b) Token ring

issues as baud rates and parity types. Nor are there line access issues such as dialing up another computer. The user of a computer on a LAN can transmit messages and files to other selected computers on the LAN. As Figure 15–3 suggests, other equipment such as printers, plotters, and high-capacity disk storage units can be connected to a LAN in such a way that the connected users can share these devices. For instance, all users could transmit files whose contents are to be printed by the same, relatively expensive, high-speed laser printer.

At any moment in time, the various computers connected via a LAN may be executing different software packages for carrying out the knowledge management tasks needed by their respective users. Occasionally, they may directly use the LAN software to make a transmission. An increasing number of software packages (both tools and application systems) are being designed to take advantage of local area networks, while insulating users from direct interaction with LAN software. An example is what is known as *electronic mail* software, which lets a user prepare and send memos and letters through a LAN. Each can be sent to all or certain designated users. The electronic mail software keeps track of everything that is sent. It will alert a user about what messages have been received for his or her viewing. Replies, in the guise of amendments to a received memo or as new memos, can be routed to the senders.

The environment is an example of software that has been specially adapted for use in a local area network [10]. For instance, multiple computers on a LAN can simultaneously be executing their own copies of the environment in such a way that all or some of them are processing the same data base. It could be either a relational or postrelational data base [5]. This is known as *multiuser processing*. Software that permits a single knowledge resource (e.g., a table or an entire data base) to be shared simultaneously by multiple users must provide mechanisms to safeguard the knowledge from undesirable situations [2]. These include cases where two users try to change the same record at the same time or where one user tries to view a record as another user is altering it.

INTEGRATED ARCHITECTURES

A definite trend in the 1980s has been the rise of software tools that integrate two or more knowledge management capabilities traditionally furnished by separate software tools. This trend is a reflection of the fact that people often find it handy to use multiple knowledge-handling techniques to support a decision process or to develop an application system. The trend toward integrated software is likely to accelerate. Environments like the one KC's regional managers now know are among the most ambitious realizations of software integration. However, there are other distinctive styles of integration that are quite different than the environment's architecture [6], [17].

Formally, *software integration* refers to the unification of multiple knowledge management techniques into a systemic whole. The style of integration is concerned with the nature of this unification. It deals with the way in which techniques are related to each other, interact with each other, and mutually cooperate within the system. Aside from the style of integration, two other key issues should be considered when assessing integrated software. They are the assortment of knowledge management techniques supported and the extent of each technique's functionality [6].

Stan brought up the topic of software integration. "I'm curious about something. The 1–2–3 package I've been using is often called an integrated software tool. The environment we've been using is substantially different, but still couldn't it be fairly called an integrated software tool too?"

"Certainly," Joy replied. "And what would you say are the major differences?"

After pondering for a moment, Stan replied, "Well, 1–2–3 provides a menu interface, but none of the other kinds of interfaces we've used. Basically, 1–2–3 integrates two knowledge management techniques: a nice spreadsheet capability and a modest business graphics capability."

"Sometimes," added Joy, "it's also purported to have a data base management capability."

"Yeah, I've heard that," Stan retorted. "But now that I know what data base management really is, calling a block of cell values a 'data base' now strikes me as a bit peculiar. Let's face it, a spreadsheet is a spreadsheet. Calling it a data base won't give me all the data base management abilities I've learned in the past week."

"Well put!" exclaimed Joy. "Spreadsheets are passable for managing small amounts of descriptive knowledge, but they are no data bases. Their real strength lies in the realm of procedural knowledge. It's worth mentioning that many people now use the term *data base* very loosely to refer to any collection of data, regardless of whether it is represented and processed according to one of the standard data models."

"So," piped Debbie, "the term has lost its meaning."

"I'm afraid that's true among a large segment of do-it-yourself computer users," nodded Joy. "It seems that the term began to be debased back in the early 80s when novices started equating the terms *file* and *data base*. Of course, many computer professionals understand what data base management really is and that it was invented to overcome difficulties inherent in the old file-oriented techniques for managing data. Unfortunately, many people who believe they know what data base management is about are oblivious to the real power and flexibility of this important technique."

With a furrowed brow, Stan remarked, "Even if 1–2–3 had a data base management capability and all the other capabilities we've learned about, it would still be different than the environment. Or, looking at it from the reverse angle, if all of the environment's capabilities other than spreadsheet analysis and graphics generation were eliminated there would still be a fundamental difference."

"That's because the environment is based on a fundamentally different style of integration than tools like 1–2–3," suggested Joy. "Regardless of what techniques are integrated into a tool, the style of integration is an extremely important consideration. Today, there are three prominent styles of integration known as the nested, confederation, and synergistic approaches. Tell me, Stan, how would you characterize the way in which techniques are integrated in 1–2–3?"

Nested Integration

"Well," Stan replied, "spreadsheet analysis is clearly the dominant capability. I mean this in two senses. First, it has much more extensive features than the graphics component. Second, if you want to do anything at all with the package, you have to know how to use its spreadsheet capability. You can't do graphics without knowing about and using a spreadsheet."

"What you've just described," declared Joy, "is symptomatic of the *nested style of software integration*. One technique serves as the dominant component. One or more additional techniques serve as secondary components. They can be exercised only within the confines of the dominant capability. These nested, secondary capabilities are usually not as strong as the dominant one."

"What's the point of not putting all the capabilities on an even footing?" asked Dan. "Why should I have to think of the world in spreadsheet terms?"

"Very good questions," acknowledged Joy, "but frankly I don't have very good answers for you. In a certain sense, such packages do go a useful step beyond stand-alone packages that consist solely of a dominant capability and offer no secondary capabilities. Perhaps if most of your processing needs could be handled by spreadsheet analysis and you only occasionally needed limited features of other techniques, the nested approach could be suitable."

"Maybe I'm spoiled," volunteered Jack, "but no thanks. I rather like being able to get at any of many techniques on an equal basis, where none gets in the way of or interferes with the functionality of any of the others. I shouldn't have to use a spreadsheet in order to do graphics, yet I'd like to have that ability for situations where it turns out to be convenient. Are there many tools that follow the nested integration approach?"

"Quite a few," Joy answered. "Some, such as the Ashton-Tate Framework and Lotus Symphony packages, offer a broader assortment of capabilities. Although most seem to have spreadsheets as their dominant component, a few do put other knowledge management techniques in the dominant position."

Confederation of Software Tools

After pausing to snack on some hors d'oeuvres, Joy continued. "Critics of the nested integration style raise the same objections you all have just done. They often advocate a different approach to meeting a person's need for diverse knowledge management techniques. Their solution is to purchase one stand-alone tool that specializes in each of the needed techniques. When you need to do spreadsheet analysis, you'd execute the spreadsheet tool. When you need to do graphics, you'd execute the graphics program, and so forth. This is the *confederation style*."

"I can see where that puts the use of each knowledge management technique on an even footing," observed Dan. "And for each technique, I could get a package whose features are as extensive as I want."

"That solves the problem of being able to use different techniques independently of each other," Jack offered. "But it loses the capacity of being able to use them together."

"Right," agreed Stan. "I wouldn't be able to plot a graph in the midst of spreadsheet processing like I can with 1–2–3. Having to switch among separate tools hardly seems integrated and could be downright inconvenient. If I had computed some spreadsheet cells, how would I make those values available to the graphics tool?"

"Assuming the tools have sufficiently open architectures," she suggested, "you would export the values from the spreadsheet tool to a file, exit from the spreadsheet program, execute the graphics program, import values from the file into a data source the graphics tool can use, and then generate the graph. To make this importing and exporting somewhat less cumbersome, some software vendors such as Software Publishing and Innovative Software have designed confederations of compatible tools. The tools within a confederation are compatible in the sense that all use a common file format."

"But you still have to switch back and forth among separate tools?" Stan asked.

"True," confirmed Joy. "You're not allowed to use multiple knowledge management techniques in a single operation. There is another way for transferring data between compatible programs. It involves the use of a special kind of host software that is more obtrusive than an ordinary operating system: a windowing shell. Microsoft's Windows is an example [16], [17].

"Within such a host, you can break the screen into windows. When a program is executed, you interact with it through a window. By switching to a different window, you can interact with a different program. The host software lets you transfer data between programs by what's known as a 'cut and paste' process. You indicate what data you want to cut out (or copy) from one program. It is temporarily held in what's known as a 'clipboard.' Later, data can be pasted from the clipboard into a different program's working memory."

Synergistic Integration

"Obviously," commented Dan, "a confederation has certain advantages over nested integration and nested integration has certain advantages over a confederation of separate tools."

"It seems to me," said Stan. "that the environment gives us the best of both worlds, without their respective disadvantages."

"It lets us use whatever techniques we like to suit our needs, either independently or interdependently," added Jack. "We're not constrained by a dominant component, we don't have to switch back and forth among separate programs, we need not bother with intermediate files or cut-and-paste operations. And if one of the integral capabilities can't meet our needs, we can always use the environment's open architecture to get at specialized external software and its processing results."

"That pretty much sums up the third major style of integration," explained Joy. "Environments use what is known as *synergistic integration*. All knowledge management techniques are provided by a single program, a single tool. No technique is dominated or constrained by any other. As you've seen, you can use any technique without worrying about or even knowing about the others. You've also seen many examples of synergy."

"Synergy," repeated Jack. "Doesn't that mean that the whole is greater than the sum of its parts?"

"Right," Joy confirmed. "In the environment, the total effect of the integrated techniques is much greater than the sum of their individual effects. You might say that synergistic integration destroys the conventional barriers among techniques by blending them together in such a way that it becomes unclear where one leaves off and the next one begins. For instance, cells can be defined in terms of data base management operations and data base processing commands can refer to cells. Where does one technique end and another begin? What you have is a fusion of multiple techniques in which each blends into the others. You're free to exercise as much or as little of each as you like and you can take advantage of as much or as little of the blending as you like."

Figure 15–4 visually contrasts the three integration styles. Hybrids of these styles are, of course, possible. Table 15–1 provides many examples of pairwise synergy that can exist between two knowledge management techniques. Notice that there are always two aspects to synergy that can be realized for any pair of techniques. That is, each can make

FIGURE 15–4   Styles of software integration

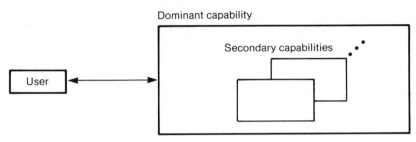

(a) Nesting of capabilities

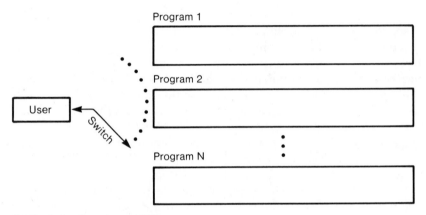

(b) Confederation of capabilities

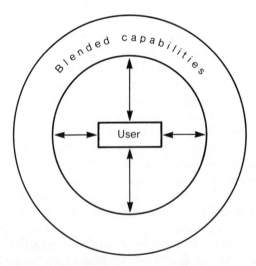

(c) Synergistic integration of capabilities

use of the other. For instance, the spreadsheet analysis row in Table 15–1 gives examples of ways that the spreadsheet technique can be used in the scopes of other knowledge management techniques. Conversely, the spreadsheet analysis column gives examples of ways in which the other techniques can be exercised within the scope of spreadsheet analysis. There are, of course, other examples of pairwise synergy and a multitude of examples that involve the joint use of three or more techniques to achieve effects not possible with other integration styles.

BASIC IDEAS

After dinner, H. J. Rickert addressed the group. He thanked Jack and Joy for their efforts and congratulated the managers on their new-found skills. Mr. Rickert stressed that the net effect of increased knowledge management proficiency would be better service to KC's customers. He was quite aware that the enhanced productivity of the managers could well translate into a competitive edge for the company. To the extent that competitors were instituting comparable training sessions for their regional managers, KC would at least be keeping pace. Until the time when the banquet broke up, the managers kept Joy and Jack busy with a variety of questions and discussions dealing with the architecture of computer-based systems for knowledge management.

All now had an appreciation of the value of an open architecture. Without such a design, a software package can be used only in isolation from other software packages. There are various aspects and degrees of openness. At a very basic level there are the abilities to import (AT-TACH) and export (CONVERT) descriptive knowledge from and to external packages. A tool's import and export versatility depends on the variety of common file formats (e.g., ASCII text, DIF) it can accept and generate. Another aspect of an open architecture is a tool's ability to serve as a host for executing alien programs. In the environment, this is accomplished with the RUN command.

Some software packages are capable of communicating with software executing on other computers that are at physically remote sites. This aspect of an open architecture is known as remote communications. Two major modes of remote communications are terminal emulation and file transfer. In the former case, a user's computer behaves as a terminal for interacting with application software executing on the remote computer. Common uses of terminal emulation are for communicating with electronic bulletin boards and for accessing information such as that kept by the Dow Jones Information Services computers. File transfer involves sending and receiving various kinds of files to and from remote computers. Establishing the communications settings (e.g., baud rate, parity

TABLE 15–1 Examples of pairwise synergy

In \ Using	Calculator	Text management	Relational data base management	Ad hoc inquiry	Forms management
Calculation	Include calculations within calculations	Direct incorporation of calculation result in text (immediate or delayed)	Embed calculation in any data base operation or treat as virtual field	Embed calculations in queries for conditional retrieval and "what if" analysis	Specify calculations for nonliteral form elements
Text management	String calculation based on text contents*	Incorporate one piece of text into another	Data base operation or virtual field drawing on text contents*	Query drawing on text contents*	Form drawing on text contents*
Relational data base management	Calculations based on field values	Direct incorporation of field values in text (immediate or delayed)	Incorporate one table into another	Multiple tables accessed in single query	Specify fields for nonliteral form elements
Ad hoc inquiry	Calculation based on array of query results	Direct incorporation of query results in text (immediate or delayed)	Table creation via query results	Query based on results of query	Specify nonliteral form elements as a query*
Forms management	Calculation based on parameters input via form	Direct incorporation of form in text (immediate or delayed)	Create, modify, view data via interactive forms	Query based on parameters input via form	Present one form within another
Report generation	Calculation based on data presented in report	Direct incorporation of report in text (immediate or delayed)	Create, modify, view data presented in report	Query based on data presented in report	Specify form as a template pattern*

Graphics	Calculation based on graphics data source	Direct incorporation of graphs into text (immediate* or delayed)	Incorporate graphics data source into table	Query based on data presented in graph	Specify graphs in forms
Spreadsheet analysis	Calculation based on cell values	Direct incorporation of cell values in text (immediate or delayed)	Embed cell references in data base operations and virtual field definitions	Embed cell references in queries	Specify cells for nonliteral form elements
Programming	Calculation based on program variables	Direct incorporation of program results in text (immediate or delayed)	Embed program variables in any data base operation	Embed program variables in queries	Specify program variables for nonliteral form elements
Rule management	Calculation based on inferred variables	Direct incorporation of inference results in text (immediate or delayed)	Embed inferred variable in any data base operation	Embed inferred variables in queries	Specify inferred variables for nonliteral form elements

*Not supported in KnowledgeMan (Version 2.01) or Guru (Version 1.0) environments.

TABLE 15–1 (concluded)

In / Using	Report generation	Graphics	Spreadsheet analysis	Programming	Rule management
Calculation	Specify calculations for nonliteral template elements	Request graph of a calculation's functional curve	Define cells in terms of any calculations	Embed calculations in programs	Specify calculations in rule premises and conclusions
Text management	Report incorporating text contents*	Graphics screen with textual display*	Define cells in terms of text contents*	Enable program to manipulate text contents;* textual specification of program	Enable rules to manipulate text contents;* textual specification of rule set
Relational data base management	Specify fields for nonliteral template elements	Generate graphs using fields as data source	Define cell as a field or data base operation	Fields used as program variables; embed data base operations in program	Rules reference fields; embed data base operations in rule conclusions
Ad hoc inquiry	Control report content with query conditions, sorting, grouping	Generate graphs using query results as data source	Define cells as query result	Embed queries in program	Specify queries in rule conclusions
Forms management	Specify forms for template header, footer, detail patterns*	Graphics screen with form display*	Define cell in terms of form input for interactive computation	Embed forms management operations in program	Specify forms management operations in rule conclusions
Report generation	Present one report within another*	Generate graph based on data presented in report	Define cell as report generation request	Embed report generation requests in program	Specify report generation requests in rule conclusions

Graphics	Specify graphs in templates*	Superimpose one graph on another graph	Define cell as graphics generation request	Embed graphics operations in program	Specify graphics operations in rule conclusions
Spreadsheet analysis	Specify cells for non-literal template elements	Generate graph using cells as data source	Define cell as a spreadsheet operation	Cells used as program variables; embed spreadsheet operations in program	Rules reference cells; embed spreadsheet operations in rule conclusions
Programming	Specify program variables for non-literal template elements	Generate graph using program variables as data source	Define cell as the execution of a program	Embed commands to perform programs within another program	Rules reference program variables; specify program executions in rule conclusions
Rule management	Specify inferred variable for non-literal template elements	Generate graph using inferred variables as data source	Define cell as the consultation of a rule set	Embed consultation requests in program	Embed consultation requests in rule conclusions

* Not supported in KnowledgeMan (Version 2.01) or Guru (Version 1.0) environments.

type) required by the remote computer is a necessary prelude to dialing up the remote computer and beginning to communicate.

Another kind of communication occurs in a local area network (LAN). The hardware and software of a LAN can connect many computers within a local area. The connections could be organized in the bus fashion of ETHERNET or in a token ring. In either case, computers on the network can send messages to each other and can share peripheral devices such as a laser printer. A data base can also be shared, provided the data base management software has facilities for protecting the data's validity when multiple users try to access it (e.g., change it) simultaneously.

There is a trend toward the integrated use of multiple knowledge management techniques. Aside from the assortment and extensiveness of techniques, the architecture or style with which they are integrated is significant. There are three basic styles of software integration: nesting, confederation, and synergy. The nested style yields a single software tool that treats one knowledge management technique as being dominant and the others as being secondary. The secondary techniques can be exercised within the confines of the dominant technique, but cannot be used independently. The confederation style involves multiple compatible software tools, normally one for each knowledge management technique. These are "integrated" by data import and export or by cut-and-paste operations. By switching back and forth among the separate programs, knowledge management techniques can be exercised independently, but they cannot be used together in a single operation.

Environments like those used for illustrative purposes in the preceding chapters are examples of the synergistic style of integration. Like the nested style, multiple techniques are integrated into a single software tool. However, all are on an equal footing without any dominant component. Like a confederation, any technique can be exercised independently of the others. However, techniques can also be used together without switching among programs, importing and exporting, or cutting and pasting. As a result the total effect that can be achieved is much greater than the sum of the individual techniques' effects and no technique interferes with the capacity or capability of another technique. The techniques are blended and fused into a unified whole such that there are no barriers separating them and each is an equal to the other.

Jack and Joy had come to understand the principle of synergy on a very personal level. In effect, each had become a part of the other, independent yet interdependent. A tremendous growth path of potential, discovery, and creativity awaited them.

There was little time left before his Thursday morning flight would depart. They sat together in a conveniently empty waiting area across the way from the departure gate. He gently caressed the back of her right hand with his left hand as they looked out on the runways. Curiously, her hand seemed cold. Perhaps she felt apprehensive about their impending separation.

They chatted about taking a warm vacation together around Christmastime. To Jack, it seemed so far away. Already, he was beginning to feel the emptiness that her absence would bring, an emptiness that he would try to fill with hope for the future and memories of their times together. In a quiet, serious voice he said, "I think we owe it to ourselves to pursue things. Together, we seem to be so much more than we could ever be separately. You're so very good for me and I'd like to think that I'm good for you too."

"I thought you knew that," she replied softly.

He felt better instantly. "I just need reassurance, lots of reassurance. Sometimes, this synergy seems almost too good to be true. Who knows what story the hand of time will write for us?"

"Let's make it a good, rich, rewarding story," she answered with a resolute smile that he mirrored. "In the very least, I'm sure we can find other kinds of knowledge to explore together."

They rose as the final boarding call was given. Their eyes exchanged a soulful message and Jack's heart leaped with joy as he melted into her encircling arms. "You're an armful of heaven," he whispered, "and this is where I belong," immediately recognizing this moment as one of life's rare unforgettable experiences.

Reluctantly they let go. Jack hurried to the departure gate. He paused, turned for a last lingering look, and called out, "When I get back, I'll give you a ring."

She sent him a big smile, waved, and called back, "I'll be counting on it!" As he disappeared, she could not help but wonder what kind of ring he had in mind.

References

1. Bartee, T. C., ed. *Data Communications, Networks, and Systems.* Indianapolis: Sams, 1985.
2. Bonczek, R. H.; C. W. Holsapple; and A. B. Whinston. *Micro Database Management—Practical Techniques for Application Development.* New York: Academic Press, 1984.
3. *Disk Operating System.* Boca Raton, Fla.: IBM, 1983.
4. *Guru Reference Manual.* Lafayette, Ind.: MDBS, Inc., 1985.

5. Holsapple, C. W. "Uniting Relational and Postrelational Database Management Tools." *Systems and Software* 3, no. 11 (1984).

6. Holsapple, C. W., and A. B. Whinston. "Aspects of Integrated Software." *Proceedings of the National Computer Conference,* Las Vegas, July 1984.

7. *K-Comm Supplement,* version 2. Lafayette, Ind.: MDBS, Inc., 1985.

8. *KMUG,* vols. 1–2. KnowledgeMan User Groups, International Association, Denver, 1985–1986.

9. *KnowledgeMatters,* vols. 1–2. Walnut Creek, Calif.: KnowledgeMatters Publishing Company, 1985–1986.

10. *KnowledgeMan LAN Reference Manual.* Lafayette, Ind.: MDBS, Inc., 1985.

11. *KnowledgeMan Reference Manual,* version 2. Lafayette, Ind.: MDBS, Inc., 1985.

12. Lane, M. G. *Data Communications Software Design.* Boston: Boyd & Frazier, 1985.

13. Misra, J., and B. Belitsos. *Business Telecommunications.* Homewood, Ill.: Richard D. Irwin, 1987.

14. Stallings, W. "Local Networks." *Computing Surveys* 16, no. 1 (1984).

15. ————. *Local Networks.* New York: Macmillan, 1987.

16. Sullivan, K. B. "Windows Is Edging Out TopView as a Standard." *PC Week* 3, no. 16 (1986).

17. Watabe, K.; C. W. Holsapple; and A. B. Whinston. "Solving Complex Problems via Software Integration." Working paper, Krannert Graduate School of Management, Purdue University, West Lafayette, Ind., 1987.

18. Woodwell, D. R. *Using and Applying the Dow Jones Information Services.* Homewood, Ill.: Dow Jones-Irwin, 1986.

Data Models[1]

A crucial factor in understanding the nature, value, and potential of data base management systems is a clear appreciation of the different data models on which they can be based. The commonalities and the differences that exist among the five major data models (hierarchical, shallow-network, CODASYL-network, relational, and postrelational) are examined here. As will be seen, these data models have certain traits in common. They also have differences that give them various advantages and disadvantages relative to each other.

A data base is a collection of records of many different types integrated together according to a single logical structure in such a way that data redundancy is eliminated, or at least substantially controlled. The logical structure, which defines the types of records that can exist and the natures of their interrelationships, is called the data base *schema*. A data base management system (DBMS) is the software tool that allows an application developer to define the data base schema for an application system and then manipulate (create, modify, retrieve) data organized according to that schema. It should be noted that this classical meaning of the term *data base* is considerably more rigorous than the loose usage that has become so commonplace over the past few years.

THE NATURE OF A DATA MODEL

A data base describes the current state of the world for some application system. A *data model* gives a developer facilities for *structuring* and *manipulating* descriptions of application worlds. That is, a data model

---

[1] Adapted from C. W. Holsapple, "A Perspective on Data Models," originally published in *PC Tech Journal* 2, no. 1 (1984).

provides formal conventions for specifying a data structure that models the nature of an application world. Data models differ in terms of the conventions they provide for representing the structure of an application world. They also differ in terms of the languages provided for manipulating the data organized according to a structure.

The nature of an application world can be understood in terms of *entities, attributes,* and *relationships.* The world is populated with various types of entities. Some of these entity types may be physical, such as customers, employees, or products. Other types of entities may be more abstract, such as accounts, jobs, or orders. In either case, each type of entity can be characterized in terms of one or more attributes. An employee has attributes such as a name, address, and salary. A job's attributes might include a job code and a job description.

Relationships can exist among the types of entities. For instance, jobs can be filled by employees. This is an example of a one-to-many relationship: one job can be filled by many employees, but no employee fills more than one job. Employees can possess skills. This "possess" relationship between the employee and skill entity types is many-to-many in nature: an employee can possess many skills and a skill can be possessed by many employees. Suppose that history is an abstract entity type whose attributes include birth date, description of the most recent job, and descriptions of educational background. Then there is a one-to-one biographical relationship between employee and history: each employee can have one history and a history belongs to no more than one employee.

One-to-many, many-to-many, and one-to-one are the three fundamental types of direct relationships that can exist in the real world between two types of entities. There are many types of indirect relationships that can exist. This involves two entity types being indirectly related by virtue of the fact that they are both related in some way to a third entity type. For instance, there is an indirect relationship between job and history because both are related to the employee entity type.

In the real world, not all relationships are binary in nature. That is, they do not always involve exactly two entities. For instance, employees can be related to each other by means of a "manage" relationship. This is an example of a *recursive* one-to-many relationship involving a single entity type: one employee can manage many other employees, but no employee is managed by more than one employee.

Sometimes a single relationship exists among three or more types of entities. This is called a *forked* relationship. Consider the three distinct types of entities: hourly employee, salaried employee, and department. Each has a different set of attributes. Because a department can contain both hourly and salaried employees, "contains" is a single relationship involving all three types of entities. Specifically, it is a one-to-many forked relationship: one department contains many hourly and/or salaried employees, but no hourly or salaried employee is contained in more than one department.

As an initial step in building a particular application system, a developer must reach at least an implicit understanding of the entities, attributes, and relationships existing in that application's world. These are then formally represented in terms of the data structuring conventions provided by a chosen data model. Ideally, a data model's structuring conventions should allow the developer to represent the application world in a natural, straightforward, self-documenting way. The result of this representation process is a data base schema for the application system. This schema captures all important aspects about the application's entity types, their respective attributes, and their interrelationships. It provides the DBMS with a blueprint for organizing the application system's data.

As noted earlier, a data model consists not only of data-structuring conventions, but also of a language for data access or manipulation. The language is oriented towards the data model's structuring conventions. Within an application system, all developer requests for data manipulation are stated in terms of the application system's schema. Clearly, the nature of a data model's access language(s) is strongly influenced by the kinds of schemas that the data model permits.

THE COMMON BASIS OF THE FIVE DATA MODELS

All five data models take the same basic approach to representing entity types and their attributes. The existence of entities of a particular type is represented in a schema by declaring a record type and giving it a descriptive name. For instance, the existence of employees in the application world might be represented by a record type named EMPLOYEE. A record type is an aggregate of fields that correspond to attributes. There is one field for each type of attribute that an employee can have. These fields are given descriptive names such as ENAME, EADDRESS, and so forth.

For each record type in a schema, the data base can contain many records of that type. The record type defines the logical structure of each of its records. A data base can have many records of the EMPLOYEE type, each of which has a data value for each of EMPLOYEE's fields. In this way, a real-world employee is described in terms of an EMPLOYEE record in the data base.

Though all data models use the principle of record types and their related fields to model the existence entity types and their related attributes, the terminology can vary from one model to another. In the hierarchical model, record types are called *segment types* and records are called *segments*. In the relational data model, a record type is a *relation structure* or *table structure*, a field is sometimes called an *attribute*, and a record is formally called a *tuple*. A table is the collection of all records of a particular type. In other data models, fields are sometimes referred to as *data items* and records are called *record occurrences*. For uniformity of presentation, the terms *record type, field,* and *record* are used for all data models discussed here.

It is important to bear in mind that record types and their fields exist in a schema, whereas records and their data values exist in the data base itself. The schema is a *logical* view of how data is organized. The issue of physically implementing a logical view is important, but is usually not considered to be a data model topic. The logical structuring conventions of a particular data model can be (and have been) implemented in a variety of ways. However, an extensive discussion of these is beyond the present scope.

VARIATIONS AMONG THE FIVE DATA MODELS

While the five data models use the same principle for entity/attribute representation, they differ significantly in their approaches to representing real-world relationships. Each model's conventions for representing relationships are examined below, beginning with the relational model and progressing to the postrelational model. For each, the implications for its data access languages are noted.

Relational

The relational model was introduced in a 1970 publication by Dr. E. F. Codd of the IBM Research Labs. In this model, relationships are represented by field redundancy in the schema. In Figure A–1, the fact that employees are related to departments is represented by the appearance of the DEPID field in the EMPLOYEE record type, as well as in the DEPARTMENT record type. The repetition of JOBID in both JOB and EMPLOYEE record types shows that there is a relationship between jobs and employees.

The relational model requires the designer to choose (and in some cases, invent) one or more fields in each record type to serve as that record type's *key*. These are underlined in the schema of Figure A–1. A relational record type's key is unique in the sense that the key value for each record uniquely identifies that record. It is the key of one

FIGURE A–1   A sample relational schema of seven record types

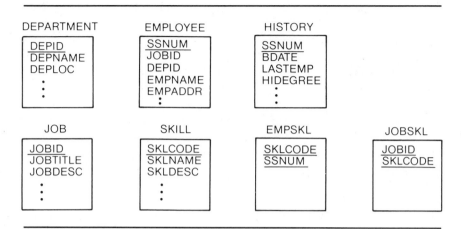

record type that is repeated in another record type, in order to represent a relationship.

The schema shown in Figure A–1 adheres to what is called a third normal form (3NF) design. Other normal forms have been identified by relational theorists. It is commonly recommended that developers using a relational schema should design their schemas so that they are at least in third normal form. Doing so eliminates a certain class of data integrity problems that can otherwise arise during data manipulation. The topic of normal forms is a complex one that is covered in great length in numerous DBMS textbooks that have appeared since the mid-1970s. Here, it suffices to examine how one-to-one, one-to-many, and many-to-many relationships between record types can be detected in a 3NF schema.

A one-to-one relationship is implied when two record types have the same key. In other words, when the key of one record type is repeated in another record type where it also serves as the key, then this explicit relationship between the two record types has a one-to-one nature. An example is the explicit relationship that exists between EMPLOYEE and HISTORY due to the repetition of the key field SSNUM in both.

A one-to-many relationship is implied when the key for one record type is repeated in a second record type where it is not the key. One record of the first record type can be related to many occurrences of the second record type. However, no record occurrence of the second type can be related to more than one record of the first type. An example is the relationship existing between DEPARTMENT and EMPLOYEE due to the repetition of DEPID. This field is the key for DEPARTMENT, but not for EMPLOYEE. As a result, a particular department id can exist in only one DEPARTMENT record, but can exist in many EMPLOYEE records. The relationship between JOB and EMPLOYEE due to the repetition of JOBID is also one-to-many because JOBID is the key of JOB and is not the key of EMPLOYEE.

In a 3NF relational schema, representation of a direct many-to-many relationship between two entities involves the invention of an extra record type. Because this record type does not correspond to any real-world entity, it is sometimes called an artificial record type. Its key consists of the keys of the two record types for which the many-to-many relationship exists. It has no fields apart from its key. An example is the EMPSKL record type shown in Figure A–1. Its key consists of a repetition of the key fields existing in EMPLOYEE and SKILL. It has no other fields. Any processing that attempts to discover the many employees related to a particular skill or the many skills related to a particular employee must utilize EMPSKL records. Thus EMPSKL provides an indirect way of representing the direct many-to-many relationship between employees and skills. Similarly, the many-to-many relationship between jobs and skills is represented by the extra intermediate record type named JOBSKL.

Languages for accessing a relational data base fall into two broad categories: relational algebra and relational calculus. The user of either kind of language states commands in terms of a relational schema such as the one shown in Figure A–1. The record occurrences of each record type are often thought of as constituting a table of data. Thus the user can think of a DEPARTMENT table composed of all DEPARTMENT records, a JOB table composed of all JOB records, and so forth. These tables make up the data base. Relational algebra provides a group of relatively low-level commands for operating on tables in order to produce new tables. The relational calculus is a high-level, nonprocedural language that allows a user to issue a single command to produce a desired listing from data held in multiple tables. There is no need to devise an appropriate series of low-level algebraic commands, nor is there a proliferation of new tables in the course of retrieving data.

Hierarchical

Hierarchical DBMSs began appearing in the late 1960s. The hierarchical data model allows each one-to-many relationship to be represented by designating one record type as the "parent" of the relationship and another record type as the "child" of the relationship. Pictorially, this

FIGURE A–2   A sample hierarchical schema of three hierarchies

is portrayed in a hierarchical schema by an arrow from the parent to the child. For instance, in Figure A–2 the one-to-many relationship between departments and their respective employees is represented by the arrow from the parent DEPARTMENT to the child EMPLOYEE. The designation of a parent-child pair eliminates the need for field redundancy in representing a one-to-many relationship.

The hierarchical data model has no special provisions for representing a one-to-one relationship between two entities. It is represented by a parent-child designation and it is up to the developer/user to remember which of the schema's parent-child couplings refer to strictly one-to-one relationships. Many-to-many relationships cannot be directly represented in a purely hierarchical schema. This is because the overall schematic structure of parent-child couplings is restricted to hierarchies. Within a hierarchy, a child of one relationship can be the parent in another relationship. However, the child in one relationship cannot also be the child in another relationship within the same hierarchy. Notice that the schema of Figure A–2 obeys this restriction.

The hierarchy stemming from DEPARTMENT shows that a department can have many employees. In turn each EMPLOYEE record can be related to a HISTORY record and to many EMPSKL records. The hierarchy headed by SKILL represents the facts that a particular skill can be needed in many jobs (via the SKLJOB child) and can be possessed by many employees (via the SKLEMP child). Similarly the third hierarchy specifies that a JOB record can be related to many JOBEMP records (all employees who fill that job) and to many JOBSKL records (all skills needed for that job).

Notice that it is only through multiple hierarchies and field redundancies that a many-to-many relationship can be represented in a hierarchical schema. For instance, EMPLOYEE and its EMPSKL child capture half of the many-to-many relationship that exists between employees and skills. The other half is captured by SKILL and its SKLEMP child. As in a relational 3NF schema, some record types in the hierarchical schema do not represent entities, but have instead been added to help represent the real-world relationships that exist among entities.

Languages for processing a hierarchical data base's data vary from one implementation to another, but do have several traits in common. Typically, an individual command operates on data within a single hierarchy at a time. The data access can begin at the head of the hierarchy or it can begin lower in the hierarchy. In any event, processing is generally restricted to working downward in the hierarchy from parent to child. This means that if we begin by accessing a particular EMPLOYEE record, we cannot then access the DEPARTMENT record to which it is related. However, we can access the HISTORY and EMPSKL records related to that EMPLOYEE record.

Shallow-Network

The shallow-network approach to data base organization and processing emerged in the late 1960s. Sometimes one sees shallow-network and CODASYL-network broadly grouped under the heading "network." However, the very substantial differences between the shallow-network and CODASYL-network models are every bit as great as those between the hierarchical and CODASYL-network models. Like the hierarchical model, a shallow-network schema can directly represent one-to-many relationships and these are traditionally portrayed with arrows. The hierarchical parent-child terminology is, however, replaced by the terms *master* and *detail* in the shallow-network. The one-to-many relationship from a master record type to a detail record type is called a "linkage path."

Recall that in the hierarchical model there is the restriction that no

FIGURE A–3   A sample shallow-network schema

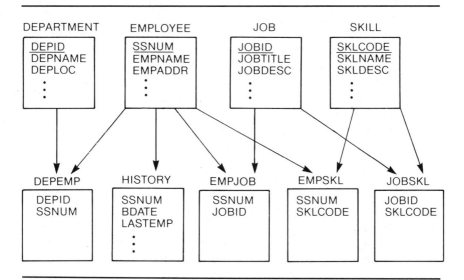

record type can be the child of more than one parent. This restriction does not exist in shallow-network systems. A record type can serve as the detail for multiple linkage paths. However, as the structure of Figure A–3 suggests, there is a restriction on the configuration of linkage paths in a shallow-network schema. A record type that is the detail for a linkage path cannot also be the master for a linkage path. The result is a schema that has only two levels and is therefore called shallow. Interestingly, this restriction does not exist in a hierarchical schema where the child of one relationship can be the parent of another.

Every master record type in a shallow-network schema must have a field(s) that serves as a unique identifier. Keys of the four master record types in Figure A–3 are underlined. Furthermore, the shallow-network model requires that a master record type's key be repeated in every detail record type linked to that master. For instance, the SSNUM key of EMPLOYEE is repeated in each of its four detail record types. As was the case with the hierarchical model, structural restrictions force the developer to invent extra record types when designing a shallow-network schema. These extra record types correspond to no entities of the application world, but exist solely to help represent certain kinds of relationships. For instance, the EMPSKL detail record type together with its two linkage paths exists solely to capture the fact of a many-to-many relationship between employees and skills. Through one of these linkage paths, a given EMPLOYEE record can be related to many EMPSKL records, each of which is related to a particular SKILL record through the other linkage path. Conversely, a given SKILL record can be related to many EMPSKL records, each of which is related to one EMPLOYEE record. In this way, the direct many-to-many relationship between skills and employees can indirectly be represented in a shallow-network schema.

The data access language of the shallow-network model is able to process in both directions along an access path. Processing begins by accessing a desired record of any of the master record types. From this master record processing can continue along any of its linkage paths to access any of the detail records related to the previously found master record. Once a detail record has been accessed, commands are available to find any master record that is related to it. Thus to find the names of all skills possessed by a particular employee, the desired EMPLOYEE record is accessed by providing that employee's ss-number. Then each EMPSKL record related to the EMPLOYEE record is accessed. As each is accessed, a further access is made to its SKILL master record and then SKLNAME data of that record is read.

CODASYL-Network

In 1971 the CODASYL Data Base Task Group published a report specifying the data structuring and data manipulation facilities of the CODASYL-network model. Like the earlier shallow-network and hierarchical data models, it allows one-to-many relationships to be represented without resorting to field redundancy. However, it does not restrict the overall configuration of a schema to either a hierarchical or a shallow-network pattern. The results of this added structuring flexibility are simpler schemas and less cumbersome processing.

With the CODASYL-network approach, an application developer does not have to devise ways of representing the nonhierarchical world in terms of hierarchies. Nor is the developer forced to try to represent multilevel worlds in terms of shallow-networks. The CODASYL-network model allows any record type to be both the owner and the member of multiple sets. The CODASYL notion of owner is like the hierarchical notion of parent and the shallow-network concept of master. Similarly, a member record type is akin to a child or detail record type. The CODASYL term *set* refers to a one-to-many relationship existing between two record types, one of which is called the set's owner and the other of which is called the set's member record type. A set, therefore, corresponds to a linkage path and to a parent-child relationship.

FIGURE A–4   A sample CODASYL-network schema

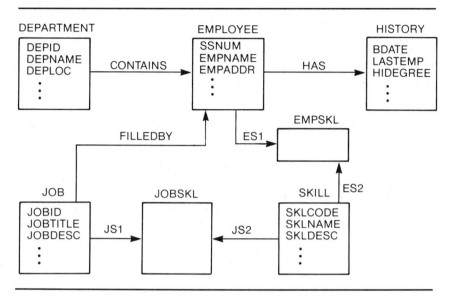

Each set in a CODASYL schema is represented by the traditional arrow pointing from the set's owner to the set's member record type. Each set is given a unique name. For instance, the CONTAINS set in Figure A–4 represents the one-to-many relationship between departments and employees. DEPARTMENT is the owner of CONTAINS and EMPLOYEE is the member. Like the earlier data models, the CODASYL-network approach makes no special allowance for one-to-one relationships. These are represented in the same way as one-to-many relationships, with the result that a single construct is used to depict two very different situations. It is up to the developer (or user) to remember which sets are actually intended to represent one-to-one rather than one-to-many relationships. Unlike the earlier models, multiple sets are allowed between two record types in a CODASYL schema.

To represent the existence of a direct many-to-many relationship between entities, the CODASYL approach makes use of an extra record type and two sets. In Figure A–4, for example, the many-to-many relationship between employees and skills is represented by the artificial record type EMPSKL and the two sets (ES1 and ES2) of which it is the member. This record type has no fields and does not correspond to any real-world entity. Its records have no data values, but they are vital in relating EMPLOYEE records to SKILL records. Through the ES1 set, each EMPLOYEE record can be related to many EMPSKL records. Each of these dataless records is, in turn, related to a particular SKILL record by the ES2 set. Thus, all skills of an employee can be found. Conversely, the ES2 set can relate each SKILL record to many EMPSKL records, each of which is related to a particular EMPLOYEE record. Thus, all employees having a particular skill can be found.

It is instructive to compare the schemas of Figures A–1 and A–4. Conversion from one to the other is a simple matter. Each schema has an identical number of record types. Although a CODASYL-network does not require a unique key for every record type, we can designate a key for each record type that owns a set (e.g., JOBID for JOB). If each set in Figure A–4 is eliminated and the key of its owning record type is repeated in its member record type, then the relational schema of Figure A–1 results. The reverse transformation is achieved by eliminating repeated keys in favor of labeled arrows. Notice that both schemas require the use of record types to represent many-to-many relationships.

Structurally, the relational and CODASYL-network models are much closer to each other than either is to the older hierarchical and shallow-network models. Perhaps the most significant difference between the relational and CODASYL schemas is the CODASYL ability to more clearly show the semantics of one-to-many relationships. Each set can be labeled with a descriptive name indicating the meaning of the relationship. Furthermore, the existence of each relationship can be immediately seen without hunting for duplicate key fields. For small schemas, such as the example used here or the examples commonly found in DBMS text books, these distinctions may not be important. However, for larger schemas encountered in practice (e.g., dozens of record types and dozens of relationships), the visually clear representation of relationships and their respective meanings is valuable.

The CODASYL model's data manipulation language has a record-at-a-time processing orientation. Processing can start with an occurrence of any record type. Commands are available to then find a related record of some other type via a set. This may be the owner record for a particular member or one of the member records related to the previously found owner record. At any stage in a processing procedure, only the most recently found record can be acted on (modified, viewed, deleted). The DBTG Report did not propose a higher level nonprocedural language for data access. However, some DBMS implementations based on the CODASYL model have added various higher level languages to their systems.

Postrelational

Just as the relational and CODASYL-network models overcame certain limitations of the earlier hierarchical and shallow-network approaches, there is a more recent data model that endeavors to improve on the relational and CODASYL-network approaches. This new model has been variously called postrelational, extended-network, and multiarchical. All of these labels are suggestive of its retention of the respective strengths of earlier models, while relaxing the restrictions they place on an application system developer. The term *postrelational* is used here.

Appearing in the late 1970s and early 1980s, the postrelational approach emphasizes straightforward, natural representation of the many types of relationships that exist in the real world. As such, it introduces fundamentally new constructs for specifying a data base's logical structure. Some of these are illustrated in the postrelational schema of Figure A–5.

One-to-many relationships (CONTAINS and FILLEDBY) are represented just as they are in the CODASYL-network model. These are

FIGURE A–5   A sample postrelational schema

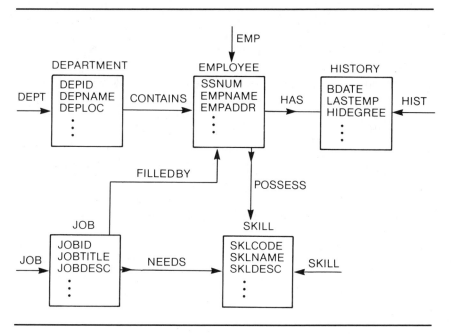

called 1:N sets and there is no structural restriction on the use of these 1:N sets in a schema. One-to-one relationships are directly represented by 1:1 sets. Pictorially, a 1:1 set is denoted by an arrow in the middle of a shank. An example is HAS in Figure A–5. The existence of this new construct means that the integrity of one-to-one relationships is automatically guaranteed. This guarantee does not exist in earlier models, where one-to-one relationships are represented in the same way as one-to-many relationships.

Another new construct is the N:M set, which allows direct many-to-many relationships to be immediately represented without redundancy and without contriving extra or artificial record types. This is why Figure A–5 has two fewer record types than either Figure A–1 or Figure A–4. Each N:M set is indicated by double arrows pointing from an owning record type to a member record type. The many-to-many relationship existing between employees and skills in the real world is simply represented by the POSSESS N:M set. Similarly, the NEEDS N:M set directly represents the real-world relationship between employees and skills.

The postrelational model places no restrictions on the overall configuration of 1:N sets, 1:1 sets, and N:M sets in a schema. Any of these types of sets can be used recursively in a schema to mirror a recursive relationship in the application world. Two common examples are shown in Figure A–6. By adding a TRAINING record type with the PASSED N:M set for EMPLOYEE, we can keep track of which subjects each employee has passed and which employees have passed any particular subject. One example of recursion is MANAGE. This is a 1:N set having the EMPLOYEE record type as both owner and member. It is a simple way of representing the one-to-many relationship that exists among employees: an employee can manage many other employees and an employee is managed by at most one other employee. The second example of recursion is PREREQ. This is a N:M set with TRAINING as both

FIGURE A–6   Examples of recursion in a postrelational schema

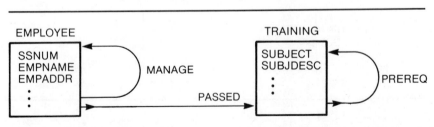

FIGURE A–7   Example of a forked relationship in a postrelational schema

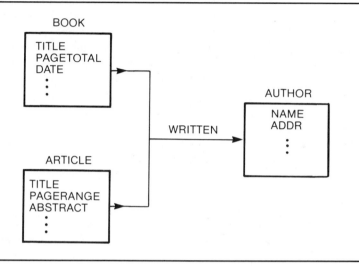

the owner and member record type. It compactly represents the fact that any subject can have many prerequisite subjects and can, at the same time, be a prerequisite for many other subjects. The older data models can represent the recursive relationships of the real world, but only by means of redundancy and/or invention of extraneous record types.

Yet another kind of real-world relationship that is naturally represented in the postrelational model is a forked relationship involving more than two entities. The postrelational model allows any 1:1 set, 1:N set, or N:M set to have multiple owning and/or member record types. A common example is shown in Figure A–7. In the real world authors can write books and/or articles; a book or article could have been written by one or more authors. This single "writing" relationship therefore involves three distinct entities: books, articles, authors. It is a many-to-many relationship between books/articles on one hand and authors on the other. This entire situation is represented by a single forked N:M set (WRITTEN) in a postrelational schema. Even the direct representation of recursive forked relationships is supported by the postrelational model. With the exception of one special case handled by CODASYL-networks, the representation of forked relationships is highly problematic with earlier data models.

It should be clear that the postrelational data structuring methods closely mirror the nature of the real world. One implication of this flexibility is that a developer need not perform various design tricks and contortions to directly represent real-world relationships. Instead they are concisely represented in such a way that the semantics of each relationship is readily apparent from the schema.

Like the relational model, the postrelational has a low-level access language and a high-level access language. The low-level language is procedural in orientation. It furnishes commands for record-at-a-time processing and other commands that operate on entire groups of records (of the same or different types) within the scope of a single command. The record-oriented commands somewhat resemble the CODASYL data manipulation language in spirit, though they are different in form and yield a considerably more streamlined processing logic. The nearest counterpart to the group-oriented commands is the relational algebra.

The high-level access language supports retrieval commands that are functionally equivalent and syntactically very similar to the SQL retrieval of relational calculus. However, the postrelational query tends to be less complex than its SQL counterpart. This is because in a postrelational query the user does not need to state all record types (i.e., tables) that are to be used, nor does the user state relationships that are to be used in terms of equating the redundant fields. Instead the user states the names of the relationships that are to be used for the retrieval.

Appendix B

Synopsis of Some Environment Commands

This appendix provides an alphabetic summary of some commonly used commands in the environment. It does not show all commands or all options for every command. Following a brief description the syntax of a command is shown. Keywords appear in uppercase and optional clauses are enclosed in square brackets.

AT: place cursor at indicated row, column coordinates

```
AT row, col
```

ATTACH: attach the number of blank records indicated by a numeric expression to end of table
attach records from external (e.g., text) file to end of table
attach cell values as records to end of table

```
ATTACH n TO table
ATTACH FROM "file" TO table [WITH fields]
ATTACH FROM CELL cellblock TO table [WITH fields]
```

BREAK: break out of the TEST or WHILE command

```
BREAK
```

BROWSE: browse through a table's records, editing the displayed values if desired
browse through the records with a customized form

```
BROWSE table [FOR conditions] [WITH fields]
BROWSE table [FOR conditions] WITH form
```

687

BYE: exit from the environment to the operating system

```
BYE
```

CALC: bring current spreadsheet into view for interactive calculations

```
CALC [rows,cols]
```

\ACTIVATE: activate a cell's presentation style
                activate presentation styles for all cells in a block

```
\ACTIVATE cell [FOR conditions]
\ACTIVATE cellblock [FOR conditions]
```

\BORDER: toggle the display of spreadsheet borders
                make the top n rows of cells behave like part of top border
                make the leftmost n cell columns behave like part of left border

```
\BORDER
\BORDER ONTOP n
\BORDER LEFT n
```

\BYE: eliminate current spreadsheet from view

```
\BYE
```

\COLUMN: insert or remove n columns

```
\+COLUMN n
\-COLUMN n
```

\COMBINE: copy source cell definition from context file into target cell in
                current spreadsheet
                copy definitions of source block of cells from context file
                into cells beginning with target in current spreadsheet

```
\COMBINE FROM "file.icf" scell,tcell
\COMBINE FROM "file.icf" scellblock,tcell
```

\COMPUTE: compute values for all cells or a block of cells

```
\COMPUTE [cellblock]
```

\COPY: copy definition of indicated source cell to indicated target cell
                copy definitions of source cell block into cells beginning with target
                copy definition of source cell to all cells in target block

```
\COPY scell,tcell
\COPY scellblock,tcell
\COPY scell,tcellblock
```

\CURRENT: make window n the current window
    make indicated cell the currently active cell

```
\CURRENT WINDOW n
\CURRENT CELL cell
```

\DEACTIVATE: deactivate a cell's presentation style
     deactivate presentation styles for all cells in a block

```
\DEACTIVATE cell [FOR conditions]
\DEACTIVATE cellblock [FOR conditions]
```

\DISPLAY: display values for cell block

```
\DISPLAY cellblock
```

\DUMP: dump out all characteristics about cells in a block

```
\DUMP cellblock
```

\EDIT: edit the currently active cell's definition

```
\EDIT
```

\ROW: insert or remove n rows

```
\+ROW n
\-ROW n
```

\STYLE: declare the presentation style for a cell
    declare the presentation style for all cells in a block

```
\STYLE [INVISIBLE] [COLOR "FfBb"] [WITH "speffects"] cell
\STYLE [INVISIBLE] [COLOR "FfBb"] [WITH "speffects"] cellblock
```

\UNDEFINE: eliminate definitions for a cell
     eliminate definitions for a block of cells

```
\UNDEFINE cell
\UNDEFINE cellblock
```

\USING: specify picture for a cell's value
    specify picture for values in a block of cells

```
\USING "pic" cell
\USING "pic" cellblock
```

\WIDTH: set the width of a column
    set the width of all columns to n characters each

```
\WIDTH cell
\WIDTH ALL n
```

\WINDOW: create window n at indicated position (e.g., TOP, LEFT)

```
\WINDOW n AT position [USING cell]
```

\WINDOW BREAK: break current window in UP or ACROSS direction

```
\WINDOW BREAK direction [USING cell]
```

\WINDOW RENAME: rename window from the number n to m

```
\WINDOW RENAME n to m
```

\−WINDOW: eliminate window n

```
\-WINDOW n
```

\=: bring an indicated cell into view in current window

```
\= cell
```

\: redraw spreadsheet screen

```
\
```

CHANGE: change a field's values in table's record based on an expression

```
CHANGE field IN table TO exp [WHERE conditions]
```

CHAT: begin natural language interaction (with specified dictionary)

```
CHAT ["file.dic"]
```

CLEAR: clear the console screen or a part (e.g., TOP, LEFT, BOTTOM, RIGHT)
        of it
    clear a form from the screen

```
CLEAR [part]
CLEAR form
```

COMPRESS: eliminate marked records from table

```
COMPRESS table
```

COMM: begin communicating with remote machine in one of several modes
        (terminal, sender, receiver, talker)

```
COMM AS mode
```

COMM CLOSE: close communications port

```
COMM CLOSE
```

COMM DIAL: dial the phone number of a remote machine

```
COMM DIAL phnum
```

COMM OPEN: open communications port

```
COMM OPEN
```

COMM SETUP: establish desired communications settings

```
COMM SETUP
```

CONTINUE: immediately proceed to next iteration in WHILE command

```
CONTINUE
```

CONVERT: convert selected data from table(s) to formatted (based on E.CF) file
convert selected data from table(s) into values for block of array elements
convert selected data from table(s) into definition for block of cells
convert selected data from table(s) to be new records in target table

```
CONVERT expressions FROM table [...] [FOR conditions] TO "file" [ORDER BY ord]
CONVERT expressions FROM table [...] [FOR conditions] TO CELL cellblock [ORDER BY ord]
CONVERT expressions FROM table [...] [FOR conditions] TO ARRAY arrblock [ORDER by ord]
CONVERT expressions FROM table [...] [FOR conditions] TO table
```

CREATE: interactively create new records for indicated table
interactively create new records for table with a customized form

```
CREATE FOR table [WITH fields]
CREATE FOR table WITH form
```

DEFAULT: make a desired table the present default table

```
DEFAULT IS table
```

DEFINE: interactively define structure of new table

```
DEFINE table
```

DESIGN: design template held in indicated file

```
DESIGN "file.tpl" [FROM "file.tpl"]
```

DESTROY: destroy a table physically existing on an indicated file

```
DESTROY table WITH "file.itb"
```

DIM: indicate dimension of array by specifying its last element

```
DIM elem
```

DIR: view directory for portion of auxillary memory indicated by value of string expression s

```
DIR s
```

EJECT: cause printer to eject to next page

```
EJECT
```

FINISH: finish the use of indicated table
finish the use of all tables

```
FINISH table
FINISH ALL
```

FORM: describe structure of form having indicated name

```
FORM name description ENDFORM
```

GETFORM: get data from user through indicated form

```
GETFORM form
```

HELP: request help about some aspect of environment
request help for specific command
request help screen number n

```
HELP
HELP command
HELP = n
```

IF: branch to other commands depending on whether or not conditions are satisfied

```
IF conditions THEN commands; ELSE commands; ENDIF
```

IMPRESS: define new table whose structure is identical to existing table's structure

```
IMPRESS etable TO ntable [WITH "file.itb"]
```

INDEX: generate an index file for a table based on an index key

```
INDEX "file.ind" FOR table BY key
```

INPUT: display a prompt string and assign user response to indicated variable

```
[AT row,col] INPUT var [USING "pic"] [WITH pstring [USING "pic"]]
```

LET: assign value of an expression to indicated variable
let value of expression become definition of indicated cell

```
[LET] var = expression
[LET] CELL cell = expression
```

LIST: synonym for SELECT

LOAD: load contents of context file into work area of main memory

```
LOAD "file.icf" [WITH "options"]
```

MACRO: declare existence of a macro and its meaning

```
MACRO macro meaning
```

MARK: mark records in table

```
MARK IN table [FOR conditions]
```

OBTAIN: obtain record at indicated position (e.g., FIRST, NEXT) from table

```
OBTAIN position RECORD FROM table [FOR conditions]
```

OUTPUT or ?: output values of indicated expressions

```
OUTPUT expression [USING "pic"][,expression [USING "pic"], ...]
```

PAINT: paint a form

```
PAINT form [FROM oldform] [TO "file.icf"]
```

PATTERN: set sequence for type (AREA, LINE, MARK) of graphics pattern
based on pattern numbers
set color sequence for graphs based on color codes

```
PATTERN FOR type pnumbers
PATTERN FOR COLOR "codes"
```

PERFORM: perform the commands in a procedure file

```
PERFORM "file.ipf" [USING expressions]
```

PLOT AREA: plot area graph from array block or cell block at location
(e.g., TOP)

```
PLOT [ONTOP] [SORTED] [%] AREA FROM block [USING columns] [AT loc]
```

PLOT BAR: plot bar graph from array block or cell block at location
(e.g., BOTTOM)

```
PLOT [ONTOP] [SORTED] [%] bartype BAR FROM block [USING columns] [AT loc]
```

PLOT FROM: plot graphics screen from indicated file

```
PLOT FROM "file.plt"
```

PLOT FUNCTION: plot function of X defined by numeric expression

```
PLOT [ONTOP] FUNCTION = nexpression [FROM n TO m] [BY i] [AT loc]
```

PLOT LEGEND: superimpose legend for indicated pattern type on current
graphics screen

```
PLOT LEGEND FOR type AT row,col
```

PLOT LINE: plot line graph from array block or cell block at location
(e.g., LEFT)

```
PLOT [ONTOP] [SORTED] LINE FROM block [USING columns] [AT loc]
```

PLOT PIE: plot pie graph from data source at location (e.g., RIGHT)

```
PLOT [ONTOP] [LABELED] [%] PIE FROM dsource [EXPLODING slices] [AT loc]
```

PLOT SCATTER: plot scattergram from block at location

```
PLOT [ONTOP] SCATTER FROM block [USING columns] [AT loc]
```

PLOT TEXT: plot string of text on graphics screen

```
PLOT [ONTOP] TEXT string [AT loc]
```

PLOT TO: plot current graphics screen to indicated file

```
PLOT TO "file.plt"
```

PLUCK: pluck record from table based on index key value

```
PLUCK keyval FROM table [USING "file.ind"]
```

PRINT: print indicated form

```
PRINT form [WITH GET]
```

PRINT TEXT: print formatted text file with embedded expression evaluation

```
PRINT TEXT "file.txt" [FROM table [...] [FOR conditions] [ORDER BY ord]]
```

PUTFORM: put indicated form's literal elements in view

```
PUTFORM form
```

RANGE: set graph range UP or ACROSS from n to m (with increments of i)
      reset graph range to automatic determination

```
RANGE direction FROM n [TO m] [BY i]
RANGE RESET direction
```

REDEFINE: interactively redefine structure of existing table
      redefine behavior of function key n to value of string expression

```
REDEFINE table
REDEFINE FUNCTION n string
```

RELEASE: release some object (e.g., macro, variable, form) from main memory
      work area

```
RELEASE object
```

RENAME: rename existing table

```
RENAME table TO name
```

REPORT: generate report using template

```
REPORT "file.tpl" [FROM table [...] [FOR conditions] [ORDER BY ord]]
```

RESET: reset the nonliteral elements in a form

```
RESET form
```

RETURN: return from procedure presently being performed

```
RETURN
```

SAVE: save present context in context file

```
SAVE TO "file.icf" [WITH "options"]
```

SELECT: select data from table

```
SELECT expressions FROM table [...] [FOR conditions]
   [GROUP BY brk] [ORDER BY ord]
```

SHOW: show indicated object (e.g., variable, macro, plot, table)

```
SHOW [object]
```

SORT: sort table's records into indicated order

```
SORT table [TO "file.itb"] BY ord
```

STAT: calculate statistics for data in table(s)

```
STAT expressions FROM table [...] [FOR condition]
```

STOP: stop processing of all procedures

```
STOP
```

TALLY: evaluate and display values for all nonliteral elements in a form

```
TALLY form
```

TEST: test expression and execute commands beginning in matching case

```
TEST expression
   CASE matchexp: commands
   .
   .
   .
   [OTHERWISE: commands]
ENDTEST
```

TEXT: process text stored in text file
      process commands in procedure file

```
TEXT "file.txt"
TEXT "file.ipf"
```

UNMARK: unmark records in table

```
UNMARK IN table [FOR conditions]
```

USE: put table held in file into use

```
USE "file.itb" [WITH "file.ind" ...]
```

WAIT: suspend processing until key is pressed

```
WAIT
```

WHILE: iterate through commands as long as conditions satisfied

```
WHILE conditions DO commands; ENDWHILE
```

Summary of Predefined Variables

Alphabetic summary of commonly used environment variables:

Name	Default value	Description
E.AUTO	false	Advance automatically when form element or cell definition completed.
E.BACG	UUUUA	Five color codes that control background screen color during spreadsheet, graphics, text, menu, and command processing, respectively (R: red, O: brown, U: blue, A: black, G: green, C: cyan, M: magenta).
E.CF	0	Conversion format for CONVERT target file (0: ASCII, 1: DIF, 2: BASIC, 3: unquoted ASCII, 4: table). If value is 1, ATTACH source file should be DIF.
E.COMP	true	Spreadsheet cells computed row by row (rather than column by column).
E.DAVE	true	Display average statistic.
E.DCNT	true	Display count statistic.
E.DDT	false	Graph transposed version of data in data source.
E.DECI	5	Number of decimal digits displayed when no picture specified.
E.DMAX	true	Display maximum statistic.
E.DMIN	true	Display minimum statistic.
E.DSDV	true	Display standard deviation statistic.

Name	Default value	Description
E.DSUM	true	Display sum statistic.
E.DTYP	M	Date format used by TOJUL and TODATE functions (M: month/day/year, Y: year/month/day, D: day/month/year).
E.DVAR	true	Display variance statistic.
E.ECHO	false	Echo input to printer (if E.OPRN = true) and #DSKOUT file (if E.ODSK = true).
E.ECOL	54	Column where error message displayed for spreadsheet and form processing.
E.EROW	25	Row where error message displayed for spreadsheet and form processing.
E.FORG	WWWWW	Five color codes that control foreground color during spreadsheet, graphics, text, menu, and command processing, respectively (R: red, O: brown, U: blue, A: black, G: green, C: cyan, M: magenta).
E.GRID	true	Background grid displayed for graphs.
E.ICAS	true	Ignore upper- versus lowercase differences in string values.
E.ICOM	false	Immediately recompute spreadsheet cells and form elements when a change is made.
E.IMAC	false	Ignore meanings of macros.
E.IMRK	false	Ignore marked records, unless using UNMARK, INDEX, COMPRESS, or SORT command.
E.INUP	true	Indexes updated automatically unless using REDEFINE, SORT, or COMPRESS command.
E.LEGH	false	Column headings for SELECT and STAT are taken from #LEGEND values.
E.LMOD	true	Create each new record by modifying replica of last record.
E.LSTR	15	Maximum length of string value displayed in absence of a picture.
E.M1	$	Character used for wild card symbol matching.
E.MS	*	Character used for wild card string matching.
E.OCON	true	Output displayed on console screen.
E.ODSK	false	Output stored on disk file indicated by #DSKOUT value.
E.OPRN	false	Output routed to computer's printer.
E.PAUS	false	Output pauses when screen fills until a key is pressed.

Name	Default value	Description
E.PDEP	60	Printed page depth (in lines).
E.PMAR	0	Printed page left margin size.
E.PWID	120	Printed page width.
E.SECB	false	Suppress ejection of pages at control breaks.
E.SERR	false	Suppress error message displays.
E.SKIP	false	Double space output from SELECT command.
E.SPAC	2	Spaces between output columns from SELECT and STAT.
E.SPGN	false	Suppress automatic page numbering from SELECT and STAT.
E.STAT	true	Statistics automatically computed for SELECT command.
E.SUPD	false	Suppress display from OBTAIN and PLUCK commands.
E.SUPH	false	Suppress headings for SELECT, STAT, CREATE, and BROWSE.
E.XPOW	0	Power for scaling labels on horizontal graph axis.
E.YPOW	0	Power for scaling labels on vertical graph axis.

Alphabetic summary of commonly used utility variables:

Name	Default value	Description
#AVER	none	Array holding average statistics from previous SELECT or STAT command.
#CNT	none	Array holding count statistics from previous SELECT or STAT command.
#DATE	06/01/82	Holds present date determined from computer clock if possible.
#DSKOUT	dskout.txt	Name of file that receives output when E.ODSK is true.
#FOUND	false	Becomes true when a retrieval command finds a record; otherwise the value becomes false.
#LEGEND	none	Array whose values are used by PLOT LEGEND and by both SELECT and STAT when E.LEGH is true.
#MAX	none	Array holding maximum statistics from previous SELECT or STAT command.
#MIN	none	Array holding minimum statistics from previous SELECT or STAT command.

Name	Default value	Description
#STDV	none	Array holding standard deviation statistics from previous SELECT or STAT command.
#SUM	none	Array holding sum statistics from previous SELECT or STAT command.
#TITLE	blank	Title to be used by SELECT, STAT, and PLOT commands.
#VAR	none	Array holding variance statistics from previous SELECT or STAT commands.
#XLABEL	blank	Label to be displayed along horizontal graph axis.
#YLABEL	blank	Label to be displayed along vertical graph axis.

Glossary

Access Code. A security mechanism that controls which users have access to what knowledge.

Active Cell. The cell highlighted by the cell cursor.

AI. Same as *artificial intelligence.*

AI Environment. A piece of software that integrates traditional (e.g., business) computing capabilities with AI technology such as natural language processing and inference. Within this environment, natural language conversation can be used to exercise many of the traditional capabilities (e.g., business graphics, statistics generation), expert systems that employ those capabilities (e.g., spreadsheet analysis, data base management) can be built, and the traditional capabilities (e.g., procedural models, spreadsheets) can themselves carry out expert system consultations. Thus, in a single piece of software, the capabilities of an inference engine, rule set manager, and natural language processor are blended with traditional capabilities.

ANSI. American National Standards Institue.

Application Developer. Someone who develops (i.e., conceives, designs, implements, tests, delivers) application software.

Application Software. Program that manages knowledge pertaining to a specific application area (e.g., payroll, order entry, market analysis).

Application System. The combination of application software, the knowledge managed by that software, and the interface that allows a user to interact with the software.

Argument. An input to a function.

Array. A named collection of elements arranged into columns and rows, where each element behaves and can be processed like a variable.

Artificial Intelligence (AI). A field of study and application concerned with identifying and using tools and techniques that allow machines to exhibit behavior that would be considered intelligent if it were observed in humans.

ASCII. American Standard Code for Information Interchange; commonly used for representing textual characters.

Assignment. The act of assigning a new value to a variable.

Assimilative Knowledge.   Knowledge that controls what knowledge is acceptable for assimilation into a knowledge system.

Asynchronous Transmission.   A method of transmission in which the sending and receiving machines are synchronized by signals indicating the start and end of each transmitted character.

Auxiliary Memory.   Memory used for temporary, intermediate, or long-term storage of knowledge, usually in the form of various kinds of files.

Backup.   Additional copy of some knowledge that can be used in the event of the loss of or damage to the original.

Backward Chaining.   An approach to rule-based reasoning in which the inference engine endeavors to find a value for an overall goal by recursively finding values for subgoals. At any point in the recursion, the effort of finding a value for the immediate goal involves examining rule conclusions to identify those rules that could possibly establish a value for that goal. An unknown variable in the premise of one of these candidate rules becomes a new subgoal for recursion purposes.

BASIC.   Beginners' All-purpose Symbolic Instruction Code. A programming language commonly used on microcomputers.

Baud Rate.   Communications transmission speed.

Bit.   A binary digit (i.e., either a 0 or 1) used to represent "on" and "off" states in a computer or on auxiliary memory media.

Block.
1. A contiguous series of characters or lines in a piece of text.
2. An adjacent group of array elements.
3. A "rectangle" of spreadsheet cells.
4. A rectangle of color in a form or template.

Booting.   The activity of initiating the execution of a computer's operating system.

B-Tree.   A multilevel approach to implementing indexes.

Buffer.   Portion of a work area that serves as a loading and unloading zone during the transferral of knowledge to or from a CPU.

Bug.   An error in a program that causes undesired results when the program is executed.

Bus.   A connection allowing transmissions between computer components.

Byte.   A contiguous series of bits (e.g., often eight) representing a single character or digits in a number.

C.   A programming language used by professional programmers to develop efficient host, tool, and application system software.

Calculation.   A knowledge management technique in which expressions serve as the representation method and evaluation as the processing method.

Candidate Rules.   A group of rules that the inference engine has determined to be of immediate relevance at the present juncture in a reasoning process. These rules will be considered according to a particular selection order and subject to a prescribed degree of rigor.

Cell. The smallest constituent of a spreadsheet. Visually, a spreadsheet's cells are arranged into rows and columns. Each cell is referenced by the row and column in which it exists. A cell can have a definition that indicates how to compute the value of that cell. Advanced spreadsheets allow cells to be defined in terms of commands in addition to traditional expressions.

Central Memory. Same as *main memory.*

Central Processing Unit. A computer's electronic circuitry that carries out software instructions. Main memory is often considered to be a part of the central processing unit.

Certainty Algebra. The mathematical conventions that are used to combine two or more certainty factors to yield a single certainty factor.

Certainty Factor. A numeric measure of the degree of certainty about the *goodness, correctness, likelihood,* and so forth of a variable value, an expression value (e.g., a premise), or an assignment action.

Clipboard. A "place" where data "cut" or copied from one program's work area may be deposited for subsequent "pasting" into another program's work area.

COBOL. Common Business Oriented Language. A programming language designed for developing business application software.

CODASYL-network. Conference On DAta SYstems Languages. The leading example of the network data model.

Command. An imperative statement telling a computer to carry out some task.

Command Language. A language consisting of all commands that a piece of software can understand.

Comment. A portion of a program (or rule) consisting of internal documentation about that program (or rule).

Communications Path. The interconnection of two (or more) devices that allows the transmission of knowledge and requests between them.

Compile. The act of producing an object program (or rule set) from a source language version of the program (or rule set).

Completion Sequence. A portion of a rule set composed of actions that the inference engine will carry out after all reasoning with the rule set's rules has been completed.

Conclusion. A portion of a rule composed of series of one or more actions that the inference engine can legitimately carry out if a rule's premise can be established to be true.

Condition. A logical expression composed of a logical variable, of a logical function, or of two expressions connected by a relational operator such as >, =, <=, IN, and so on. The two participating expressions must be of the same type (e.g., both numeric). In the case of the IN operator, the second expression is typically a collection of expressions.

Conditional Branching. A programming method that causes the flow of command execution to branch in a certain direction depending on whether a specified condition is satisfied.

Conditional Iteration. A programming method that causes the flow of execution to iterate through a sequence of commands for as long as a specified condition is satisfied.

Console Screen. A device that allows a computer user to view requests he or she makes of the computer and the computer's responses to those requests.

Constant. A known value that never changes.

Consultation. The activity of acquiring or producing expert advice or solutions to a problem.

Context. The environment settings and main memory contents (e.g., working variables, arrays, forms, macros, cells).

Control Break. A means for separating presented knowledge into groups, where each member of a group has some value in common.

Control Key. Involves pressing the Ctrl key and another key at the same time.

CPU. Same as *central processing unit*.

Current Record. The most recently accessed record of a particular record type.

Cursor. An indicator of the current position on a console screen.

Customized Interface. A user interface that has been custom-built to suit the needs and tastes of a particular user.

Customized Software. Software designed to meet the specific needs and tastes of a particular user.

Cut and Paste. An approach to transferring data from one executing program to another, usually by means of a *clipboard*.

Data. Same as *descriptive knowledge*.

Data Area. Same as *work area*.

Data Base. A collection of records of many different types organized according to a single, unified logical structure that allows data redundancy to be controlled. The logical structure must conform to the structuring conventions of one of the five major data models. A file is not a data base.

Data Base Management System. The software that supports one of the data models. It allows the logical structure of a data base to be defined and allows data to be accessed on the basis of that structure.

Data Management System. A data base management system or a file management system.

Data Model. Consists of a well-defined set of logical data structuring constructs and conventions, plus one or more access languages capable of manipulating data organized according to its logical structure mechanisms. Five major data models are hierarchical, shallow-network, relational, CODASYL-network, and postrelational.

Debugging. The activity of identifying and eliminating bugs from a program.

Decision Support System. A computer-based system composed of a language system, knowledge system, and problem-processing system whose purpose it is to support decision-making activities.

Default Table. Table that is used if no other table is explicitly specified.

Default Value. A value that exists unless explicitly changed by a user or program.

Descriptive Knowledge. Knowledge about past, present, and hypothetical states of an organization and its environment.

Desktop Publishing. The use of desktop computers for producing high-quality page layouts.

Dictionary. Linguistic knowledge consisting of vocabulary of words available for natural language interaction.

DIF. Data Interchange Format. A type of file format sometimes used for data import and export.

Disk. A common auxiliary memory medium that stores data magnetically.

Disk Drive. A common auxiliary memory device that is able to directly store and retrieve knowledge on a disk.

Diskette. A floppy (i.e., flexible) disk.

Do-It-Yourself Computing. The use of software tools by people who are not computer professionals.

DSS. Same as *decision support system.*

Emulation. An activity in which one entity (e.g., a computer) offers the same observable behavior as another (e.g., a human or a computer).

End User.
1. The user of application software.
2. One who is not a computer professional, yet directly uses software tools to meet some of his or her own knowledge management needs.

Environment. A type of software tool in which multiple knowledge management techniques are blended together in a balanced way for use by end users and application software developers.

Environment Knowledge. Same as *descriptive knowledge.*

Environment Variable. A variable whose value controls the behavior of some aspect of an environment.

Execution. The activity of performing a program's commands.

Expert System. A computer-based system composed of a user interface, an inference engine, and stored expertise (i.e., a rule set or an entire knowledge system). Its purpose is to offer advice or solutions for problems in a particular problem area. The advice is comparable to that which would be offered by a human expert in that problem area.

Expert System Development Tool. Software used to facilitate the development of expert systems. The three types of tools are programming languages (and their respective interpreter or compiler software), shells, and AI environments.

Expert System Environment. A knowledge management environment supporting the technique of rule management.

Expert System Shell. Same as *shell.*

Export. The act of outputting some knowledge system contents into a file whose format is acceptable to another program.

Expression. A constant, variable, or function, or a series of constants, variables, and/or functions connected by meaningful operators.

Field. A named category of data. Fields are used in defining the structure of a data base.

File.
1. A collection of knowledge that is treated as a whole by the operating system.
2. A collection of data records of some type that can be processed by file management (as opposed to data base management) operations.

File Management System. A type of data management system that organizes data into files without adhering to any of the major data models.

File Transfer. A kind of remote communications in which files are sent and received by connected computers.

Find Actions. Those actions stated in a variable description that an inference engine can use (e.g., as an alternative to backward chaining) to find the value of that variable when it is unknown.

Firing a Rule. The activity of carrying out the actions in a rule's conclusion, once it has been established that the rule's premise is true.

Flowchart. A diagram showing the flow of steps for accomplishing some procedure.

Footer. A portion of a customized report that appears at the end of the report, at the end of a page, or at the end of each group of report details.

Form. A piece of presentation knowledge that indicates the visual layout of display slots, the source of the value that can appear in each slot, and special attributes for the slot (e.g., reverse video, blinking).

Format.
1. Same as *picture.*
2. The way in which a file's contents are arranged.
3. The layout of a form, template, or menu.

Format Code. A code embedded in a piece of text to control some aspect of the way the text will be formatted as it is printed.

Form Management. The ability to define forms and to subsequently process an entire form at a time with any one of several commands.

FORTRAN. FORmula TRANslator. A programming language oriented toward mathematical calculations.

Forward Chaining. An approach to rule-based reasoning in which the inference engine determines the effect of currently known variable values on unknown variables by firing all rules whose premises can be established as being true.

Forward Reasoning. Same as *forward chaining.*

Function. A named object whose value is determined by performing a particular kind of operation. The function name (e.g., SQRT) indicates the nature of the operation (e.g., finding a square root). A function typically has one or more arguments whose values are operated on in order to determine the function's value. Each argument is an expression.

Function Keys. Special keys (labeled F1, F2, etc.) which, when pressed, cause the executing software to take prescribed actions.

Fuzzy Variable. A variable that simultaneously has two or more values. The certainty factor of one value may differ from that of another value.

Global. A variable, form, macro, and so on that continues to exist outside the scope of a single program's execution.

Graphical Data Source. Data values that can be used to generate a graphical presentation.

Graphics. A knowledge management technique concerned with the generation of figures and geometric shapes.

Hard Copy. A copy of computer output, usually on paper.

Hardware. Physical devices that employ electrical, magnetic, and mechanical technology.

Header. A portion of a customized report that appears at the start of the report, at the start of a page, or at the start of a group of report details.

Help Text. A textual description that appears on the console screen to help a computer's user.

Hierarchical. An early type of data model that allows limited (i.e., treelike) direct representation and processing of one-to-many relationships.

Host. A type of software in which other software executes (e.g., operating system, windowing shell).

Import. The act of assimilating the output of another program into the knowledge system being used by the present software.

Index. A file that contains index key values and indications of where to find the records having those values, as a basis for fast record access.

Index Key. A collection of one or more fields whose collective value for some record serves as a basis for quickly accessing that record.

Inference Engine. A piece of software that is able to accept a problem statement from the user, use reasoning knowledge about the problem area in attempting to derive a solution, gather needed problem-specific information (e.g., from the user) in the course of reasoning, explain why it needs this added information, present the solution to the user, and explain the line of reasoning used in reaching the solution.

Information Center.   A component of an organization that helps facilitate do-it-yourself computing.

Information System.   Same as *application system*.

Initialization Sequence.   A portion of a rule set composed of actions that the inference engine will carry out before considering the rule set's rules.

Input Device.   Hardware that allows a user to make requests of or enter knowledge into a computer.

Insert Mode.   Pressing a key causes a character to be inserted at the cursor position.

Integrated Software.   Software that allows multiple knowledge management techniques to be coordinated in some way (i.e., confederation, nesting, or synergy).

Interactive Computing.   A mode of computer usage permitting frequent interchanges between a user and the computer in the course of program execution.

Interface.   Same as *user interface*.

Interpretive Software.   A program that processes user requests one at a time, immediately processing each.

Iteration.   The repeated execution of a series of commands.

K.   Denotes the value 1024.

Key.
1.   One or more fields whose collective value for a record is used as a basis for identifying that record.
2.   One or more fields designated as the basis for forming an index (see index key).
3.   One or more fields designated as the basis for sorting a collection of records (see sort key).
4.   A pressable key on a keyboard.

KME.   Same as *environment*.

Knowledge.   An organizational resource consisting of the sum of what is known.

Knowledge-Based System.   An AI term that is typically taken to be synonomous with the notion of an expert system. Of course, management information systems and conventional decision support systems are also "knowledge-based" (i.e., concerned with the representation and processing of knowledge).

Knowledge Engineer.   A person (or group) that elicits reasoning knowledge from a human expert in the course of building an expert system. From the broader DSS viewpoint, anyone who is concerned with building any kind of knowledge into a knowledge system can be considered to be a knowledge engineer.

Knowledge Management.   The activity of representing and processing knowledge.

Knowledge Management Environment.   Same as *environment*.

Knowledge System. That subsystem of a decision support system in which all application-specific knowledge is represented for use by the problem-processing system. This includes knowledge of any or all types (e.g., descriptive, procedural, reasoning) represented in a variety of ways (e.g., as data bases, spreadsheets, procedural models, rule sets, text, graphs, forms, templates).

Knowledge Worker. A person who manages various kinds of knowledge in the course of filling some role in an organization.

LAN. Same as *local area network.*

Language System. That subsystem of a decision support system that consists of (or characterizes) the class of all acceptable problem statements.

Legend. An explanatory guide for output such as a graph or a query's result.

Linguistic Knowledge. Knowledge about languages used for communication purposes.

Literal Element. A constant in a form or template.

Local. A variable, form, macro, and so on whose existence is local to the program in which it is declared.

Local Area Network. A communications system designed to allow transmissions among two or more devices (e.g., computers) within a small geographic area.

Logical Constant. True or false.

Logical Data Structuring. The knowledge representation (as opposed to processing) aspect of a data model.

Logical Expression. An expression whose value (if it is known) is either true or false.

Logical Function. A function whose value is true or false.

Logical Variable. A variable whose value is presently either true or false.

Loop. A series of commands that can be executed repeatedly during the execution of a program; usually the commands involved in conditional iteration.

Macro. A name that is given to a sequence of keystrokes such that the name can be used instead of the keystroke sequence when interacting with computer software.

Mail Merge. The merging of different data values into repeated copies of the same basic text in order to produce customized versions of the text.

Mainframe. A large-scale computer, generally having greater capacity and processing power than a microcomputer.

Main Memory. The portion of a CPU whose contents (i.e., data, programs, rules, forms, graphs, etc.) can be immediately processed by the CPU's arithmetic, logic, and control circuitry.

Management Information System. An application system for keeping current records about some aspect of an organization or its environment.

Manager.
1. One who uses available resources to achieve some objective.
2. A decision maker.

Many-to-Many Relationship. A relationship in which each instance of either object can be related to many instances of the other object.

Many-to-One Relationship. A relationship in which many instances of one object are related to at most one instance of another object.

Menu. A collection of options available for user selection.

Metaknowledge. Knowledge about knowledge.

Microcomputer. A small (desktop or laptop) computer consisting of a system unit, keyboard, auxiliary memory device, console screen, and perhaps a printer.

Minicomputer. A medium-sized computer whose capacity, processing power, and cost generally fall between those of microcomputers and mainframes.

MIS. Same as *management information system*.

Modeling Knowledge. Same as *procedural knowledge*.

Modem. MOdulator-DEModulator. A device that connects a computer to a communications line, handling the conversion between digital and analog signals.

Module. A program that can be performed by other programs.

Natural Language. A kind of user interface that allows the user to carry on a conversation with a computer-based system in much the same way as he or she would converse with another human. The system is able to learn new terms, understand new requests in the context of prior requests, overlook grammatical errors, and carry out actions implied by the conversation.

Nested Integration. The approach to software integration in which all secondary components are constrained to being used within the confines of a single dominant component.

Network.
1. A collection of devices connected in such a way that they can communicate with each other via transmission of requests and/or knowledge.
2. A type of data model that is less restrictive than the hierarchical in allowing direct representation and processing of one-to-many relationships.

Nonliteral Element. A position in a form where a value of a nonconstant expression can be presented or where a value can be accepted for assignment to a variable (e.g., working variable, field, cell).

Nonprocedural. Indicates that a procedure (i.e., a definite *sequence* of steps) is not specified. That is, there is no explanation of how to accomplish a task. There is no programming. Reasoning knowledge captured in the guise of a rule set's rules is nonprocedural. Queries are nonprocedural.

Numeric Constant.   A number composed of digits, an optional decimal point, and an optional leading sign (+ or −). An integer constant is a special case of a numeric constant because it contains no decimal point.

Numeric Expression.   An expression whose value (if it is known) is a number. The expression can involve numeric constants, numeric variables, and/or numeric functions connected by numeric operators such as +,−,*,/,**, and MOD (modulus).

Numeric Function.   A function that yields a numeric value with respect to its argument(s).

Numeric Variable.   A variable whose value is presently a number. An integer variable is a special case of a numeric variable in that its value is an integer.

Object Program.   A program whose commands are in a language that can be immediately understood (i.e., carried out) by a particular computer.

Offline.   Situation in which a device is not actively connected to, under the direct control of, or in direct communication with a computer's CPU.

Off-the-Shelf Software.   Generic software designed for a class of users rather than for the customized needs of a specific user.

One-to-Many Relationship.   A relationship in which each instance of one object can be related to many instances of a second object, but no occurrence of the second object is related to more than one occurrence of the first object (i.e., a reverse way of viewing a many-to-one relationship).

One-to-One Relationship.   A relationship in which each instance of either object is related to no more than one instance of the other object.

Online.   Situation in which a device is actively connected to, under the direct control of, or in direct communication with a computer's CPU.

Open Architecture.   An approach to software design in which the software can make use of the output from other software (imports), furnish inputs that can be used by other software (exports), run other software (as a host), and/or communicate with other computers.

Operating System.   A common type of host software that controls the operation of a computer in such a way that other programs can be executed.

Option.   One of the user-selectable processing alternatives presented in a menu.

Output Device.   Hardware that displays a computer's requests or knowledge to a user.

Package.   A program, usually with accompanying documentation, written by a software vendor and typically offered for sale.

Parameter.   A term whose value, when a program is executed, influences the behavior of the program.

Parity Bits.   Extra bits that accompany bytes for the purpose of checking the validity of the byte during communications or transfer from auxiliary memory to main memory.

Pascal.   A programming language popular among computer scientists.

Password. A sequence of characters that must be entered in order to gain access to the processing capabilities of a program or to some stored knowledge resource.

Peripheral Device. A device (e.g., printer, auxiliary memory) that complements a computer's CPU.

Personal Computer. Same as *microcomputer*.

Picture. A sequence of placeholders and possibly some literal symbols that control the appearance of a value as it is being displayed.

Plotter. A device that uses pens (or electrostatic techniques) to draw graphical output on paper.

Pointer. An internal indicator telling where a record is located within a table or on disk.

Postrelational Data Base. A data base whose records are not restricted to tabular, hierarchical, or network organization and processing. All types of real-world relationships (e.g., one-to-one, one-to-many, many-to-many, recursive, forked) can be directly represented in a semantically lucid manner and can be processed with various postrelational access languages. This kind of data base is sometimes called a multiarchical or extended-network data base.

Premise. A portion of a rule composed of one or more conditions connected by Boolean operators such as AND, OR, XOR (exclusive OR), and NOT. If a rule's premise can be established as being true, then the rule's conclusion is valid. A premise is an example of a logical expression.

Presentation Knowledge. Knowledge that controls the way in which presentations are made.

Primary Memory. Same as *main memory*.

Printer. Device for producing printouts of characters on paper (or other media).

Problem-Processing System. That subsystem of a decision support system that accepts problems stated in terms of the language system and draws on the knowledge system in an effort to produce solutions.

Problem Processor. Same as *problem-processing system*.

Procedural. Indicates that a procedure (i.e., an explicit *sequence* of steps) has been specified. A program has been devised stating, in detail, how to accomplish a task.

Procedural Knowledge. Knowledge about how to produce a desired result by carrying out a prescribed series of processing steps.

Procedural Model. A program that represents a piece of procedural knowledge about how to analyze some set of input data. When a procedural model (e.g., for regression analysis) is executed it carries out a prescribed algorithm and reports the results.

Program. A sequence of commands that a computer can execute.

Programmer. One who captures procedural knowledge as a program.

Programming Language. A formal language for representing procedural knowledge as a program.

Prompt. A program's way of alerting the user that it is awaiting either a request or some additional knowledge before continuing its processing activities.

Query Language. A nonprocedural language for exploring and analyzing (e.g., "what if" processing) descriptive knowledge.

RAM. Random Access Memory. A kind of main memory whose contents can be altered by the CPU.

Read/Write Head. An electromagnetic part of a disk drive that "reads" the contents of a disk and "writes" new contents onto a disk.

Reasoning Knowledge. Knowledge about what circumstances allow particular conclusions to be considered to be valid.

Record. A group of data values consisting of one value for each of a prescribed set of related fields; an occurrence of a record type.

Record-Keeping. The activity of keeping records about some subject matter as a basis for subsequent retrieval and calculation.

Record Type. An aggregate of conceptually related fields that represents the attributes of some real-world object (concept or entity).

Redundancy.
1. The repetition of the same field in multiple record types (e.g., as the means for representing relationships in a relational data base).
2. The repetition of the same data value in multiple records.

Relation. Same as *table*.

Relational Algebra. The low-level access language whose commands produce new intermediate tables by operating on one or two existing tables.

Relational Calculus. The high-level access language whose commands operate on multiple tables simultaneously without requiring any intermediate tables.

Relational Data Base. A data base whose records are organized into tables that can be processed by either the relational algebra or relational calculus. Relationships between tables are represented by field redundancy.

Relational Operator. The operator in a condition that relates one expression to another (e.g., $>$, $<$, $=$).

Remote Communications. The transmission of requests and knowledge between two computers that may be far apart geographically.

Replace Mode. Pressing a key causes that key's character to replace the character at the cursor position.

Report Details. The primary contents of a customized report in which each report detail adheres to the same form.

Report Generation. A technique of presenting descriptive and calculated (i.e., derived) knowledge in a customized manner without needing to write a program.

Reverse Reasoning. Same as *backward chaining*.

Rule. A named fragment of reasoning knowledge consisting of a premise and a conclusion. In addition, a rule may have other attributes such as a textual description and an internal comment.

Rule Base. The collection of all rule sets available to an inference engine.

Rule Management. A technique of knowledge management concerned with rule representation and processing.

Rule Set. A named collection of rules that represent reasoning knowledge about some problem area. A rule set is used by an inference engine to solve specific problems in that area. In addition to rules, a rule set may also contain an initialization sequence, a completion sequence, and variable descriptions.

Rule Set Developer. A person who uses a rule set development tool to capture an expert's reasoning knowledge in the guise of a rule set (see *knowledge engineer*).

Rule Set Manager. Software that is used to formally specify, modify, analyze, and compile a rule set.

Run. The activity of executing a program from within a host.

Schema. The logical data structure designed for a particular application, representing all types of relevant objects (in terms of record types) and their interrelationships.

Secondary Memory. Same as *auxiliary memory*.

Secondary Storage. Same as *auxiliary memory*.

Security. Deals with the protection of knowledge from unauthorized disclosure, modification, and usage.

Semantics. The meaning of a symbol, expression, or relationship.

Sensor. Hardware or software that records the occurrence of some event.

Shell.
1. A kind of expert system development tool consisting of two stand-alone pieces of software: a rule set manager and an inference engine capable of reasoning with rule sets built with the rule set manager.
2. A kind of host software for executing other software.

Software. Same as *program*.

Sort Key. One or more fields whose values in records are used as a basis for sorting those records.

Source Program. A program written in a language that a computer's hardware cannot directly execute. The source program is either compiled into an object program whose commands the machine can understand or its commands are interpreted one at a time by another piece of software.

Spreadsheet. A collection of cells whose values can be displayed on the console screen. By changing cell definitions and having all cell values reevaluated, a user can readily observe the effects of those changes.

SQL. Structured Query Language.
1. A query language designed for processing descriptive knowledge represented as relational data tables.
2. A collection of commands that, in addition to the query capability, gives application developers data management capabilities for creating and manipulating tables of data.

Stand-Alone Tool. A software tool that supports one knowledge management technique in isolation from other techniques.

String Constant. A string of text composed of alphabetic characters, digits, punctuation, and/or other recognizable symbols.

String Expression. An expression whose value (if it is known) is a string of text. The expression can involve string constants, string variables, and/or string functions connected by the string concatenation (+) operator.

String Function. A function that yields a text string value with respect to its arguments.

String Variable. A variable whose value is presently a string of text composed of alphabetic characters, digits, punctuation, and/or other recognizable symbols.

Subprogram. Same as *module.*

Substitution Indicator. An indicator that, when prefacing a variable, causes the value of the variable to be substituted for the variable in a command.

Switch. Same as *environment variable.*

Synergistic Integration. The approach to software integration in which each component can be used independently or multiple components can be used in tandem to produce an overall effect that is greater than the sum of the individual component effects. There are no clear dividing lines between component capabilities and no component limits the use of any other.

System. An organized collection of components, designed and coordinated for the purpose of filling some defined role.

System Analysis. The activity of studying a phenomenon or a need in order to more fully understand it and to determine ways to improve or address it.

System Design. The activity of formulating a plan to guide the implementation of a system that will meet the requirements identified by a systems analyst.

System Unit. Piece of hardware housing a computer's CPU and frequently some auxiliary memory as well.

Table. A named collection of records of some record type. Each record is composed of one data value for each of the record type's fields. A table is not a file, but may exist in one or more operating system files.

Telecommunications. Same as *remote communications.*

Template.
 1. A piece of presentation knowledge that indicates the visual layout of a report's contents and the sources of values that can appear in particular locations.
 2. A piece of procedural knowledge consisting of spreadsheet cell definitions.

Terminal. A device for interacting with a computer by entering requests, entering knowledge, and viewing knowledge (e.g., console screen with keyboard).

Terminal Emulation.   A kind of remote communications in which one computer behaves as a terminal of another computer.

Text Editing.   A minimal variety of text management, of primary interest to programmers who are not concerned with narrative text.

Text Management.   A technique of knowledge management in which knowledge is represented and processed as pieces of text.

Text Processing.   The activity of manipulating (creating, altering, viewing) passages of text. The formatting capabilities of a text processor are not as extensive as those of a word processor.

Toggle.   A means for switching back and forth between two alternatives.

Tool.   A class of software that operates within a host but is not oriented toward any particular application. A software tool is used by computer professionals to build application systems and by nonprofessionals for do-it-yourself computing.

Top-Down Design.   An approach to designing a system in which the major characteristics are specified first. The process is then repeated with respect to each of these, and so forth, until all details are fully specified.

Unknown Expression.   An expression whose value is not known because the value of at least one of the expression's variables is unknown.

Unknown Variable.   A variable whose value is presently unknown.

User.   The person (or machine) that uses a program executing on some computer hardware. The user may be a computer professional or an end user.

User Interface.   The means by which a user is able to interact with an executing program.

Variable.   A named object whose value can change. A variable's present value is referenced via the variable name.

Variable Descriptions.   That portion of a rule set consisting of descriptions of the natures of variables used in the rule set's rules. Each variable can be described in terms of such characteristics as its find actions and the timing of those actions.

Virtual Field.   A field whose values are calculated as needed rather than actually being stored in a data base.

"What If" Processing.   A kind of analysis in which a user examines the impacts of certain potential changes without actually making changes in the knowledge system's basic contents.

Wild Card Symbol.   A symbol that, when encountered in a text string, is considered to match with any other symbol(s).

Window.
1.   A portion of a console screen for viewing a desired part of a spreadsheet, piece of text, table, and so on.
2.   A portion of a console screen through which a user interacts with an executing program.

Windowing Shell.   A type of host software that allows a user to interact with separate programs through separate windows.

Word Processing.   The most elaborate and extensive variety of text management, of primary interest for heavy-duty document preparation.

Word Wrap.   The ability of text management software to automatically move the cursor to the next line and place a partially completed word at the beginning of that new line when the right margin is reached.

Work Area.   A portion of main memory devoted to holding knowledge being processed by an executing software package.

Index

ABS function, 129
Access code
  defined, 65
  for fields, 207
  read and write, 207
Accounting information systems, 17
Acoustic couplers, 649
ACTIVATE command, 525–26
ad (adjust) format code, 189
Ad hoc inquiry, 250; *see also* ''What
    if'' processing
  with automatic statistics, 327–29
  commands for, 293–94
  conditional, 309–26
  defined, 19, 292–93
  effect on indexes, 321
  environmental variables in, 293–94
  expression selection in, 297–303
  field selection in, 295–97
  grouping of results, 324–26
  macros in, 314–15
  from multiple tables, 313–17
  in natural language, 315
  pictures in, 303–4
  presentation of results, 303–9, 322,
    324
  versus report generation, 309
  sorting by, 317–23
  with statistics, 333
  in text processing, 334
  unconditional, 293–309
  unique qualifier in, 322–23

AI; *see* Artificial intelligence
Application developer, 605
Application software, 53
Application system, 53, 605
Area graphs
  defined, 443–44
  percentage, 444–45
  sorted percent, 445
  uses for, 444
Arguments
  defined, 125–26
  HELP screen for, 128
  keying of, 125–26
  types of, 126
Array
  converting from a table, 431
  defined, 306
  elements in, 306, 429–30
  as graphics data source, 429–33
Arrow keys, 163
Artificial intelligence (AI); *see also* Ex-
    pert systems
  for decision support, 627, 631
  defined, 26
  research in, 26
  trends in, 16, 26
Artificial intelligence environments;
    see also Expert system environ-
    ment
  defined, 619
  features of, 632